STO

ACPL ITEM
DISCARDED

331. H19 1997

Handbook of U.S. labor
statistics

SO-BWU-779

Handbook of U.S. Labor Statistics

Handbook of U.S. Labor Statistics

Employment, Earnings, Prices, Productivity, and Other Labor Data

First Edition

Eva E. Jacobs, Editor

Bernan Press
Lanham, Maryland USA

Allen County Public Library
900 Webster Street
PO Box 2270
Fort Wayne, IN 46801-2270

© 1997 by Bernan Press, an imprint of Bernan Associates

All rights reserved. No part of this work covered by the copyrights hereon may be reproduced or used in any form or by any means, whether graphic, electronic, or mechanical—including photocopying, recording, taping, or information storage and retrieval systems—without written permission of the publisher.

Published 1997
Printed in the United States of America

98 97   4 3 2 1

Bernan Press
4611-F Assembly Drive
Lanham, MD 20706-4391
(800) 274-4447
e-mail: info@bernan.com

ISBN: 0-89059-062-1

Table of Contents

Handbook of
U.S. Labor
Statistics:
Employment,
Earnings, Prices,
Productivity, and
Other Labor Data
First Edition

Eva E. Jacobs, Editor

CONTENTS

CONTENTS

Preface

Welcome to the first edition of the *Handbook of U.S. Labor Statistics: Employment, Earnings, Prices, Productivity, and Other Labor Data*. This publication serves as an essential reference tool for those interested in historical data on labor market trends. It is, in large part, an updated version of the popular *Handbook of Labor Statistics* which was published by the Bureau of Labor Statistics (BLS) until 1989.

The *Handbook of U.S. Labor Statistics: Employment, Earnings, Prices, Productivity, and Other Labor Data* consists of comprehensive tables which are organized by subject matter. Each section is preceded by a concise description of the data. A few tables from the *Handbook of Labor Statistics* have been restructured to conform to the current publication format used by the Bureau of Labor Statistics, while several more have been excluded for lack of data.

BLS data are carefully collected from various surveys, but occasionally these surveys are modified to fit into the current structure of economic institutions. When these surveys are modified, or when improved survey techniques are implemented, the comparability of data can be affected. Additionally, current data are revised as a result of the availability of other data sources. These qualifications are noted and contain references to more comprehensive reports and bulletins specific to that subject.

Methodology descriptions, including sampling and estimation for all BLS programs are contained in *The Bureau of Labor Statistics Handbook of Methods*, last published in 1992 as *Bulletin 2414*. A revised version of the *Handbook of Methods* is scheduled for publication in early 1997. Other sources of current data and analytical articles include the *Monthly Labor Review* and *The Report of the American Workforce*. Information on these publications can be found via the internet on the BLS home page located at URL http://stats.bls.gov/.

The *Handbook of U.S. Labor Statistics: Employment, Earnings, Prices, Productivity, and Other Labor Data* was edited by Eva E. Jacobs. Ms. Jacobs is the former Chief of the Division of Consumer Expenditure Surveys of the Bureau of Labor Statistics. Major contributions were made by Michael S. Lee and Hongwei Zhang who produced the tables, and Cornelia Strawser who contributed to the text and reviewed tables. Deidre Gaquin compiled the data for the "Special Labor Force" data tables. The editor also wishes to thank Rebecca Zahn and Joyce Goodwine of Bernan Press for proofreading this work.

Special thanks go to BLS staff members too numerous to mention by name, who patiently answered questions and provided material.

Using the Handbook of U.S. Labor Statistics

How rapidly have prices risen for food? Housing? Medical care? What percentage of all women work? Which occupations offer the best job opportunities in the years ahead?

Answers to these questions and others that are crucial to understanding the economy and to making public and private decisions, are found in the *Handbook of U.S. Labor Statistics*. Bernan Associates is pleased to introduce this first edition of the *Handbook*—a compilation of important data from the U.S. Bureau of Labor Statistics (BLS).

The predecessor to this volume, the periodic *Handbook of Labor Statistics* published by the Bureau of Labor Statistics, was replete with statistical information on labor market conditions, prices, and productivity. The BLS ceased publication of this reference work, making way for the first edition of the *Handbook of U.S. Labor Statistics*. This comprehensive publication maintains and updates valuable labor information while adding new data and useful features.

The data tables are grouped in chapters according to their subject matter, as shown in the Table of Contents. Some key elements of this *Handbook* deserve special mention:

Historical coverage. The United States is fortunate to have a long history of relatively reliable economic statistics. The *Handbook* draws together basic BLS historical series into a single convenient source. Data for consumer and producer prices begin with 1913 and those for total payroll employment start with 1919. Data for many more series, including civilian labor force, employment, and unemployment; worker hours and earnings; and productivity begin with the late 1940s.

Special tabulations. Once each year, the Current Population Survey—the source of our monthly employment and unemployment estimates—gathers additional data on the income, education, family characteristics, and year-long work experience of the population. For this volume, we have used the basic data records from this survey to generate tables no longer routinely available. The section of the book entitled "Special Labor Force Data," beginning on page 93, presents these tabulations. Examples of data in that section include information on the employment status of women with children of different ages and on unemployment rates of persons with varying degrees of educational attainment.

Projections. Part III, beginning on page 157, presents the BLS' most recent projections of future employment. Projected employment by industry and by occupation is compared to 1994 employment levels so that projected growth of job opportunities in different industries and occupations can be compared. An article in the front of the book describes the trends in economic growth that lie behind these projections.

Coverage. The content of the *Handbook* is by no means limited to employment and prices, important as they are. The *Handbook* also includes, for example, comprehensive data from the Consumer Expenditure Survey (beginning on page 267), which show how consumers of different incomes, ages, and family types spend their money; data on the extent of participation in various employee benefit programs (beginning on page 233); data on occupational injuries and illnesses (beginning on page 277); and data on work stoppages (beginning on page 283).

Geographic detail. National data for the United States is the primary focus of the *Handbook*, but state and city data also are included. Data by state for employment, hours, and earnings begin on page 142. Consumer price data for selected cities begin on page 259.

International comparisons. Part IX provides international comparisons of employment status (page 293), manufacturing productivity (page 296), and consumer prices (page 298).

Graphics. Each chapter begins with a Section Introduction which features an illustration and a brief description of some of the key trends shown by the data in the chapter.

Documentation. At the beginning of each chapter is a "NOTES" section which provides descriptions of the data series in that chapter, definitions, and additional sources of information.

The Handbook of U.S. Labor Statistics is one of many Bernan publications that provide the public with statistical information from official government sources. As with the *County and City Extra, Business Statistics of the United States*, and our forthcoming *Housing Statistics*, every effort has been made to provide a useful, accurate, and up-to-date selection of information. We welcome you to the world of government statistics and urge you to provide us with your suggestions on how we can make future editions even more useful.

Courtenay Slater,
Managing Editor
Slater Hall Group of Bernan Associates

Summary of BLS Projects to 2005

The following article, reprinted from the November 1995 issue of the U.S. Bureau of Labor Statistics publication Monthly Labor Review, *describes the Bureau's most recent projections of U.S. economic growth and employment to the year 2005. More detailed projections of employment by industry and occupation, consistent with this overall economic projection, are found in Part III of this* Handbook.

The Labor force of Blacks, Hispanics, and Asian and other groups will expand rapidly; the share of administrative support occupations is expected to decline, as are jobs in the goods-producing sector; the services industry will account for 12 million of the increase in jobs by 2005.

For several decades, the Bureau of Labor Statistics has prepared projections of the U.S. economy. Since 1983, the projections have been completed on a regular 2-year cycle. The projections use three alternative scenarios (high, low, and moderate) for the 1994-2005 period. The scenarios highlight some of the uncertainties concerning the future and a possible range of some of the more critical factors, particularly factors which may have a significant impact on the labor market. This article summarizes the moderate projection results.

The Labor Force

Since the very large baby-boom group completed their entry into the labor force in the late 1970's and early 1980's, the labor force has continued to grow, but at a markedly slower rate. The 1994-2005 labor force is projected to continue that pattern. The change over this period is expected to be slightly more than 12 percent, or a growth rate of 1.1 percent a year. (See Table 1.) This change is compared with the 16-percent expansion, or a 1.4-percent growth rate per year over the 1982-93 period.

Two primary factors are important to labor force changes—population and participation in the labor force. Most of the change in the labor force growth results from population growth. However, the rapid entry of women into the labor force in the past indicated that labor force participation has also been an important contributing factor to labor force growth. Such changes are expected to be much less of a factor in

the future because the rate of increase in labor force participation is expected to slow for women and to decline somewhat faster for men. Participation is projected to increase for both men and women aged 55 and older. That increase results from a larger proportion of this age group being in the 55 to 64 age group with their higher participation. Chart 1 shows average annual rates of change of men and women in the labor force over the 1982-93 and 1994-2005 periods.

In the past, several other changes in the composition of the labor force have marked labor force growth. One change has been the relatively rapid growth of Blacks, Hispanics, and Asian and others[1] in the labor force. Over the 1982-93 period, the rate of labor force growth for these groups increased at rates consistently higher than those for whites; the difference is very pronounced for Hispanics and Asian and others. Over the project period, 1994-2005, the rate of labor force growth is projected to be faster for each of these

CHART 1. Average annual rates of change of men and women in the labor force

Change in	Total, 16 years and older	Men	Women
Labor force participation:			
1982-1993	0.31	-0.17	0.87
1994-2005	.07	-.26	.45
Population:			
1982-1993	1.06	1.17	.97
1994-2005	.98	1.01	.96
Labor force:			
1982-1993	1.37	.99	1.85
1994-2005	1.06	.75	1.41

TABLE 1. Civilian labor force by sex, age, race, and Hispanic origin, 1982, 1993, and 1994, and moderate growth projection to 2005
(Numbers in thousands)

Group	Level				Change		Percent change	
	1982	1993	1994	2005, moderate scenario	1982-93	1994-2005	1982-93	1994-2005
Total, 16 years and older..	110,204	128,040	131,056	147,106	17,836	16,050	16.2	12.2
Men	62,450	69,633	70,817	76,842	7,183	6,025	11.5	8.5
Women	47,755	58,407	60,239	70,263	10,652	10,024	22.3	16.6
White	96,143	109,359	111,082	122,867	13,216	11,785	13.7	10.6
Black	11,331	13,943	14,502	16,619	2,116	2,116	23.1	14.6
Asian and other	2,729	4,742	5,474	7,632	2,013	2,158	73.8	39.4
Hispanic	6,734	10,377	11,975	16,330	3,643	4,355	54.1	36.4

Note: Data for 1994 are not directly comparable with data for 1993 and 1982 because of the redesign of the Current Population Survey questionnaire and collection methodology and the introduction in January 1994 of 1990 census-based population controls adjusted for the estimated undercount. The "Asian and other" group includes (1) Asians and Pacific Islanders and (2) American Indians and Alaska Natives. The historic data are derived by subtracting "black" from the "black and other" group; projections are made directly not by subtraction.

groups than for whites; thus an increase in their share of the labor force. Still, the rate of growth is expected to be slower for each of these demographic groups over the 1994-2005 period than over the 1982-93 period, reflecting a general slowing of labor force growth as new entrants are drawn from smaller birth cohorts.

Another widely discussed phenomenon of the past has been women's very rapid entry rate into the labor force. While the projected 1994-2005 labor force growth continues at a notably faster rate for women than for men, it is also much slower than the increases for women in earlier periods. This is true for a number of women's age groups, but is most noticeable for women in the 20-39 year age group. The projected slowdown reflects an expected continuation of the very noticeable slowing in the rate of increase of women's labor force participation, particularly younger women, since 1989. In part, the slower growth may reflect that their participation rate had already reached relatively high levels, and may also reflect other factors such as no longer postponing childbirth, longer school attendance, or job availability factors.

The rapid rate of increase of women and minority groups into the labor force has been widely discussed. But, another important change in labor force activity has continued for a very long period and has received much less attention: the long-term decline in labor force participation rates of virtually all age groups of men. The following tabulation shows the percentage point change in the labor force participation rates of men by age group over the 1973-93 period:

Age group	1973-83	1983-93
25 to 29	-1.0	-0.6
30 to 34	-2.0	-1.1
35 to 39	-1.1	-1.8
40 to 44	-0.9	-1.7
45 to 49	-1.0	-1.6
50 to 54	-2.6	-1.0

In the 1973-83 period, the decline was most pronounced among the older men, as they moved toward earlier retirement. In the 1983-93 period, the decline in men's labor force participation was no longer primarily among older groups.

Reasons behind this trend have not been fully explored, but a contributing factor includes the increase in the number of men who report in the household survey that they are unable to work. Also, the structural changes in the U.S. economy have clearly left many men ill-prepared for the direction job growth has taken during the last two decades, particularly men with the least education or training who worked in manufacturing or mining industries. Consequently, many men displaced by structural adjustments in the economy left the labor force permanently if they had insufficient education or training for the available jobs. Further, the latest projections show a continuation of the compositional changes in employment by industry and occupation, which implies continued difficulty for those with the least training or education to find a job.[2]

Major Economic Trends

The U.S. economy's real gross domestic product (GDP) is projected to increase at 2.3 percent per year over the 1994-2005 period, according to the moderate scenario. This is slower than the 2.9 percent annual growth rate of the previous 11-year period, 1983-94.[3] (See Table 2.) Several factors contribute to this slower growth. Over the 1983-94 period, economic growth was boosted by a lowering of the unemployment rate, from 9.6 percent in 1983 to 6.1 in 1994. In the projected period, the unemployment rate is projected to decline to only 5.7 percent in 2005, providing significantly less impetus to the overall economic growth rate. In addition, the labor force is expected to increase 1.1 percent per year in the projected period, compared with 1.4 percent per year over the 1983-94 period. The only factor, important to the overall economic growth rate, projected to be somewhat higher in the projected period (1.4 percent per year) than in the past (1.2 percent), is labor productivity.

TABLE 2. Gross domestic product, 1983-94, and projected 1994-2005

Population	Average	
	1983-94	1994-2005, moderate scenario
Population, aged 16 and older	1.0	1.0
Civilian labor force	1.5	1.1
Nonfarm labor productivity	1.2	1.4
Civilian employment, household basis	1.8	1.1
Nonfarm wage and salary jobs	2.1	1.3
Unemployment	2.6	0.4
Capital per employee, 1987 dollars	0.6	1.7
GDP per employee, 1987 dollars	1.0	1.2
GDP, 1987 dollars	2.9	2.3

Source: Data for 1983-94 are from the Bureau of the Census, Bureau of Economic Analysis and the Bureau of Labor Statistics; projected data (1994-2005) are from the Bureau of Labor Statistics.

When the composition of real GDP is examined, several changes can be noted. Over the 1983-94 period, the share of GDP was relatively constant for personal consumption expenditures, Federal nondefense, and State and local government purchases of goods and services. (See Table 3.) Changes were more pronounced for the other demand components of GDP: investment, exports, and imports all expanded significantly, while Federal defense declined appreciably. Over the projected period, the components of GDP with relatively constant shares are personal consumption expenditures and gross private domestic investment; the components of demand projected to increase their share are exports and imports, and the components projected to decrease modestly are Federal defense and nondefense and State and local government.

The consumption and investment components of demand GDP assumes that factors such as taxes and the savings rate will hold consumption and investment relatively constant. Foreign trade is expected to continue to play an increasing role in the U.S. economy. The share of U.S. produced goods and services exported will expand from slightly more than 7 percent in 1983 to nearly 18 percent in 2005, under these projections. An equally dramatic

TABLE 3. Gross domestic product by major demand category, 1993, 1994, and projected to 2005
(Billions of 1987 dollars)

Category	1983	1994	Project 2005, moderate scenario	Average annual rate of growth	
				1983-94	1994-2005, moderate scenario
Gross domestic product	3,906.6	5,343.1	6829.7	2.9	2.3
Share of gross domestic product (in percent):					
Personal consumption expenditures	67.1	67.0	66.7	2.9	2.2
Gross private domestic investment	15.3	17.8	18.0	4.3	2.4
Exports	7.3	12.3	17.9	7.9	5.8
Imports	8.8	14.4	18.1	7.6	4.4
National defense purchases	6.0	4.2	3.2	-0.3	-0.4
Federal nondefense purchases	2.2	2.1	1.7	2.3	0.6
State and local purchases	10.8	11.0	10.6	3.0	1.9

Source: Historical data, Bureau of Economic Analysis, U.S. Department of Commerce; project data, Bureau of Labor Statistics.

TABLE 4. Employment by major industry division, 1983, 1994, and projected to 2005
(Numbers in thousands)

Industry	Employment Level			Change	
	1983	1994	2005, moderate scenario	1983-94	1994-2005, moderate scenario
Nonfarm wage and salary[1]	89,734	113,340	130,185	23,605	16,846
Goods producing	23,328	23,914	22,930	587	-985
Mining	952	601	439	-351	-162
Construction	3,946	5,010	5,500	1,064	490
Manufacturing	18,430	18,304	16,991	-126	-1,313
Service producing	66,407	89,425	107,256	23,019	17,803
Transportation, communications, utilities	4,958	6,006	6,431	1,048	425
Wholesale Trade	5,283	6,140	6,559	857	419
Retail trade	15,587	20,438	23,094	4,850	2,657
Finance, insurance, and real estate	5,466	6,933	7,373	1,468	439
Services[1]	19,242	30,792	42,810	11,550	12,018
Government	15,870	19,117	20,990	3,247	1,873
Agriculture[2]	3,508	3,623	3,399	115	-224
Private household wage and salary	1,247	966	800	-281	-166
Nonagricultural self-employment and unpaid family workers[3]	7,914	9,085	10,324	1,171	1,239
Total[4]	102,404	127,014	144,708	26,610	17,694

Industry	Percent distribution of wage and salary employment			Annual rate of change	
	1983	1994	2005, moderate scenario	1983-94	1994-2005, moderate scenario
Nonfarm wage and salary[1]	100.0	100.0	100.0	2.1	1.3
Goods producing	26.0	21.1	17.6	0.2	-0.4
Mining	1.1	0.5	0.3	4.1	-2.8
Construction	4.4	4.4	4.2	2.2	0.9
Manufacturing	20.5	16.1	13.1	-0.1	-0.7
Service producing	74.0	78.9	82.5	2.7	1.7
Transportation, communications, utilities	5.5	5.3	4.9	1.8	0.6
Wholesale trade	5.9	5.4	5.0	1.4	0.6
Retail trade	17.4	18.0	17.7	2.5	1.1
Finance, insurance, and real estate	6.1	6.1	5.7	2.2	0.6
Services[1]	21.4	27.2	32.9	4.4	3.0
Government	17.7	16.9	16.1	1.7	0.9
Agriculture[2]	—	—	—	0.3	-0.6
Private households	—	—	—	-2.3	-1.7
Nonagricultural self-employed and unpaid family workers[3]	—	—	—	1.3	1.2
Total[4]	—	—	—	2.0	1.2

[1]Excludes SIC 074,5,8 (agricultural services) and 99 (nonclassifiable establishments), and is therefore not directly comparable with data published in the Bureau of Labor Statistics *Employment and Earnings*.
[2]Excludes government wage and salary workers, and includes private sector SIC 08, 09 (forestry and fisheries).
[3]Exculdes SIC 08, 09 (forestry and fisheries).
[4]Wage and salary data are from the BLS Current Employment Statistics (payroll) survey, which counts jobs, whereas self-employed, unpaid family workers, agricultural, and private household data are from the Current Population (household) Survey which counts workers.

increase has occurred in the share of GDP devoted to imports, and the increase is projected to continue. Government is projected to account for a somewhat small share of GDP, not only for nondefense purposes at the Federal and State and local levels, but also the share devoted to defense expenditures is projected to continue to decline.

Employment by Industry

Employment shows a slower growth rate per year over the 1994-2005 period than over the 1983-94 period. The slowdown reflects the factors noted earlier: slower labor force growth and less unemployment reduction in the projected period than in the historical period. However, employment is still projected to expand by 17.7 million by 2005, of which 16.8 million are nonfarm wage and salary jobs. (See Table 4.)

In the past, the sectoral composition of employment has undergone considerable shifts. The 1994-2005 projections continue many of those shifts as well as other shifts. For decades, employment in the goods-producing portion of the U.S. economy—while increasing in absolute terms—has been declining in relative terms. From 1983 to 1994, the goods-producing sector, in absolute terms, added just 0.6 million jobs, as increases in construction offset modest employment declines in manufacturing and mining. However, reviewing only 1983 and 1994 gives a somewhat false picture, because the long-run trend in manufacturing has been for more pronounced employment declines, with cyclical ups and downs, after peaking in 1979.

In the 1994-2005 projections, the goods-producing sector's share of nonfarm wage and salary jobs declines in absolute as well as in relative terms. The 0.5 million growth projected for construction jobs is not enough to offset a modest employment decline in mining, and a 1.3 million decline projected in manufacturing jobs—thus also a loss in share. The decline in

manufacturing jobs is particularly concentrated in durable goods manufacturing. Significant employment declines are projected for fabricated metal, industrial machinery and equipment, electronic and other electrical equipment, and transportation equipment. The declines result from a projected rate of productivity growth that more than offsets projected gains in real output.

A somewhat different or contrasting picture emerges in the service-producing sector. Over the 1983-94 period, all major service-producing sectors gained employment in absolute terms. However, the picture was somewhat mixed in relative terms. Transportaion, communications and utilities, wholesale trade, and government lost employment shares in the historical period. Retail trade gained shares, while the services industry group gained considerably. In the 1994-2005 projections, all service-producing sectors are expected to increase in absolute terms, but only the service industry division is projected to increase its share of employment. Thus, the services industry (primarily the medical, personal, professional, and business services) is extremely important in the job picture of the future. This broad grouping of services industries accounts for nearly 12.0 million of the job growth projected over the 1994-2005 period. Individual industries important to job growth in these sectors are business services, such as personnel supply and computer and data processing services. In the health services sector, physician offices, nursing and personal care facilities, and home health services are important to the economy's job growth.

Employment by Occupation

A review of the patterns of occupational change over the 1983-94 and projected change over the 1994-2005 periods reveals several noteworthy developments. Over the historical period, significantly faster growth and a resulting increase in the share of employment is noted for the executive,

administrative, and managerial occupations, professional specialty occupants, marketing and sales occupations, and service occupations. (See Table 5.) In contrast, several occupational categories increased very slowly and, as a consequence, their share of employment declined. Included were agriculture, forestry, fishing, and related occupations; precision production and craft occupations; and operators, fabricators, and laborers occupations.

Two groups—technicians and related support occupations and the administrative support occupations, including clerical—increased at a rate about equal to that of the overall economy; as a consequence, their share of employment increased only modestly. An important element of the composition of changes by major occupations over the historical period was the increase of occupations requiring post-secondary education or training, except for service occupations. Further, occupations requiring the least education and/or training had significant declines in their shares of overall employment.

One perspective on the projected 1994-2005 employment change by major occupational group is to review those groups whose changes mirror their 1983-94 pattern and those whose changes significantly depart from the pattern. When this is done, three groups show important changes from their most recent past. The group with the most significant change is administrative support occupations, including clerical; its employment shares increased very modestly over the 1983-94 period, but it is expected to decline 1.7 percentage points over the 1994-2005 period, despite a projected slight increase in employment. This important change reflects the expected impact of office automation on many clerical occupations. A modest departure from past trends is projected for the executive, administrative, and managerial occupations. While this group's employment share will increase in the 1994-2005 period, the increase is projected to be much smaller than that

EMPLOYMENT OUTLOOK: 1994-2005

TABLE 5. Employment by major occupational group, 1983, 1994, and projected 2005, moderate scenario
(Number of thousands)

Occupation	1983		1994		2005, moderate scenario		Employment change			
							1983-94		1994-2005	
	Number	Percent	Number	Percent	Number	Percent	Number	Percent	Number	Percent
Total, all occupations	102,404	100.0	127,014	100.0	144,708	100.0	24,610	24.0	17,694	13.9
Executive, administrative, and managerial occupations	9,591	9.4	12,903	10.2	15,071	10.4	3,312	34.5	2,168	16.8
Professional specialty occupations	12,639	12.3	17,314	13.6	22,387	15.5	4,675	37.0	5,073	29.3
Technicians and related support occupations	3,409	3.3	4,439	3.5	5,316	3.7	1,030	30.2	876	19.7
Marketing and sales occupations	10,497	10.3	13,990	11.0	16,502	11.4	16,502	11.4	2,512	18.0
Administrative support occupations, including clerical	18,874	18.4	23,178	18.2	24,172	16.7	4,304	22.8	994	4.3
Service occupations	15,577	15.4	20,239	15.9	24,832	17.2	4,662	29.9	4,593	22.7
Agriculture, forestry, fishing, and related occupations	3,712	3.6	3,762	3.0	3,650	2.5	50	1.3	-112	-3.0
Precision production, craft, and repair occupations	12,731	12.4	14,047	11.1	14,880	10.3	1,316	10.3	883	5.9
Operators, fabricators, and laborers	15,374	15.0	17,142	13.5	17,898	12.4	1,768	11.5	757	4.4

of 1983-94. This slowing reflects that an important segment of downsizing has been and is expected to continue to be directed at managerial occupations—offset in part by the shift in employment to services where smaller establishments require relatively more managers than do larger enterprises.

Another occupational group with a notable departure from its 1983-94 trend is the professional specialty group. This group gained employment shares over the 1983-94 period, but its projected growth over the 1994-2005 period is twice as fast as that in the overall economy; as a result, its shares

of employment will increase more rapidly than in the past. The growth reflects, in particular, expected employment increases in the teaching occupations and professional health care occupations, a result of expected increases in school age and in older populations that demand these services.

Projected changes in the other major occupational groups are expected to more closely mirror their 1983-94 pattern. Only one group—agriculture, forestry, fishing, and related occupations—is projected to decline absolutely, attributable to a very modest

decline among self-employed farmers. This affirms that the fastest growing occupational group (except for service occupations) are those requiring more education. Note also that the two occupational groups projected to have the largest absolute increases in employment are professional speciality and service occupations, groups at the opposite ends of the spectrum in terms of education requirements and earnings.

Endnotes

1. The "Asian and other" group includes Asians, Pacific Islanders, Native Americans, and Alaskan Natives.

2. This article is taken from the issue of the *Monthly Labor Review* which is the initial publication of the 1994-2005 set of projections. Two related publications are planned: the fall *Occupational Outlook Quarterly* will summarize the projection; and *Employment Outlook: 1994-2005, Job Quality and Other Aspects of Projected Employment Growth (Bulletin 2472)*. This *Bulletin* explores the implications of the projections in terms of their educational requirements and earnings, groups educational requirements of current jobs into categories and examines the changes in those requirements over the 1994-2005 period, analyzes occupational employment to determine if growth is concentrated in occupations with high, low, or average earnings, and looks at the implication of employment growth, occupational change, earnings, and education on the job market for women, Hispanics, and other groups in the labor force. Other planned publications based on the projections are the *Occupational Outlook Handbook, 1996-97 Edition*, and *Occupational Projections and Training Data*.

3. As these projections were being prepared, the Bureau of Economic Analysis (BEA) announced plans to revise the methods used in developing constant-dollar GDP. These projections and the historical comparison are consistent with the BEA method where base-weighted price indexes are used rather than the chain-weighted indexes, which BEA is planned to develop. This also affects the measurement of labor productivity, because BLS uses constant-dollar GDP as the output measure in its measures of productivity change in the non-farm economy and for major sectors. It is very likely a major element in what appears in these projections as an acceleration in projection of capital stock per employee is more than likely just part of the broad index-number problem.

Part One

Population, Labor Force, and Employment Status

Population, Labor Force, and Employment Status

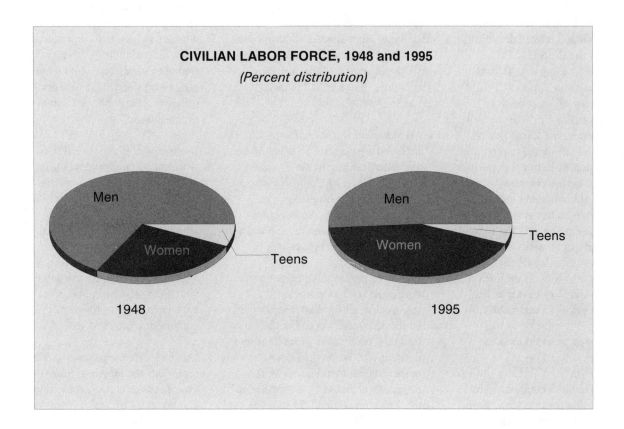

The Civilian Labor Force chart above illustrates that adult women (age 20 and over) made significant strides in joining the workforce after 1948, increasing their share of the total civilian labor force from 26 to 43 percent. At the same time, the share for men (age 20 and over) dropped to 51 percent from 67 percent. The number of men in the labor force rose by only 27 million while the number of women rose by 42 million. While the number of teens in the workforce increased from 1948, there was a decline from the peak of the late 1970s.

NOTES
Population, Labor Force, and Employment Status
(Current Population Survey of Households)

Collection and Coverage

Statistics on the employment status of the population and related data are compiled by the Bureau of Labor Statistics (BLS) using data from the Current Population Survey (CPS). This monthly survey of households is conducted for BLS by the Bureau of the Census through a scientifically selected sample designed to represent the civilian noninstitutional population. Respondents are interviewed to obtain information about the employment status of each member of the household 16 years of age and over. The inquiry relates to activity or status during the calendar week, Sunday through Saturday, which includes the 12th day of the month. This is known as the "reference week." Actual field interviewing is conducted in the following week, referred to as the "survey week."

Each month about 50,000 occupied units are eligible for interview. Some 3,200 of these households are contacted but interviews are not obtained because the occupants are not at home after repeated calls or are unavailable for other reasons. This represents a noninterview rate for the survey that ranges between six and seven percent. In addition to the 50,000 occupied units, there are about 9,000 sample units in an average month which are visited but found to be vacant or otherwise not eligible for enumeration. Part of the sample is changed each month. The rotation plan provides for three-fourths of the sample to be common from one month to the next, and one-half to be common with the same month a year earlier.

Concepts and Definitions

The concepts and definitions underlying labor force data have been modified, but not substantially altered, since the inception of the survey in 1940; those in use as of January 1994 are as follows:

- *Civilian noninstitutional population.* Included are persons 16 years of age and older residing in the 50 states and the District of Columbia who are not inmates of institutions (e.g., penal and mental facilities, homes for the aged), and who are not on active duty in the Armed Forces.

- *Employed persons.* All persons who, during the reference week, (a) did any work at all (at least one hour) as paid employees, worked in their own business, profession, or on their own farm, or who worked 15 hours or more as unpaid workers in an enterprise operated by a member of the family, and (b) all those who were not working but who had jobs or businesses from which they were temporarily absent because of vacation, illness, bad weather, child-care problems, maternity or paternity leave, labor management dispute, job training, or other family or personal reasons, whether or not they were paid for the time off or were seeking other jobs.

Each employed person is counted only once, even if he or she holds more than one job. For purposes of occupation and industry classification, multiple jobholders are counted in the job at which they worked the greatest number of hours during the reference week.

Included in the total are employed citizens of foreign countries who are temporarily in the United States but not living on the premises of an embassy. Excluded are persons whose only activity consisted of work around their own house (painting, repairing, or own home housework) or volunteer work for religious, charitable, and other organizations.

- *Unemployed persons.* All persons who had no employment during the reference week, were available for work, except for temporary illness, and had made specific efforts to find employment some time during the 4-week period ending with the reference week. Persons who were waiting to be recalled to a job from which they had been laid off need not have been looking for work to be classified as unemployed.

- *Duration of unemployment.* This represents the length of time (through the current reference week) that persons classified as unemployed had been looking for work. For persons on layoff, duration of unemployment represents the number of full weeks they had been on layoff. Mean duration is the arithmetic average computed from single weeks of unemployment; median duration is the midpoint of a distribution of weeks of unemployment.

- *Reason for unemployment.* Unemployment is also categorized according to the status of individuals at the time they began to look for work. The reasons for unemployment are divided into five major groups: (1) Job losers, comprised of (a) persons on temporary layoff who have been given a date to return to work or who expect to return within six months (persons on layoff need not be

4

looking for work to qualify as unemployed), and (b) permanent job losers, whose employment ended involuntarily and who began looking for work; (2) Job leavers, persons who quit or otherwise terminated their employment voluntarily and immediately began looking for work; (3) Persons who completed temporary jobs, who began looking for work after the jobs ended; (4) Reentrants, persons who previously worked but were out of the labor force prior to beginning their job search; and (5) New entrants, persons who never worked. Each of these categories of the unemployed can be expressed as a proportion of the entire civilian labor force; the sum of the rates thus equals the unemployment rate for all civilian workers. (For statistical presentation purposes, "job losers" and "persons who completed temporary jobs" are combined into a single category until seasonal adjustments can be developed for the separate categories.)

- *Labor force.* This group comprises all persons classified as employed or unemployed in accordance with the criteria described above.

- *Unemployment rate.* The unemployment rate represents the number unemployed as a percent of the labor force.

- *Participation rate.* This represents the proportion of the population that is in the labor force.

- *Employment-population ratio.* This represents the proportion of the population that is employed.

- *Not in the labor force.* Included in this group are all persons in the civilian noninstitutional population who are neither employed nor unemployed. Information is collected on their desire for and availability to take a job at the time of the CPS interview, job search activity in the prior year, and reason for not looking in the four week

period prior to the survey week. This group includes discouraged workers, defined as persons not in the labor force who want and are available for a job and who have looked for work sometime in the past 12 months (or since the end of their last job if they held one within the past 12 months), but are not currently looking, because they believe there are no jobs available or there are none for which they would qualify.

- *Occupation, industry and class of worker.* This information for the employed applies to the job held in the reference week. Persons with two or more jobs are classified in the job at which they worked the greatest number of hours. The unemployed are classified according to their last job. The occupational and industrial classification of CPS data is based on the coding systems used in the 1990 census.

The class-of-worker breakdown assigns workers to the following categories: Private and government wage and salary workers, self-employed workers, and unpaid family workers. Wage and salary workers receive wages, salary, commissions, tips, or pay in kind from a private employer or from a government unit. Self-employed persons are those who work for profit or fees in their own business, profession, trade, or farm. Only the unincorporated self-employed are included in the self-employed category in the class of worker typology. Self-employed persons who respond that their businesses are incorporated are included among wage and salary workers, because technically, they are paid employees of a corporation. Unpaid family workers are persons working without pay for 15 hours a week or more on a farm or in a business operated by a member of the household to whom they are related by birth or marriage.

- *Multiple jobholders.* These are employed persons who, during the reference week, had either two or

more jobs as a wage and salary worker, were self-employed and also held a wage and salary job, or worked as an unpaid family worker and also held a wage and salary job. A person employed only in private households (cleaner, gardener, babysitter, etc.) who worked for two or more employers during the reference week is not counted as a multiple jobholder, since working for several employers is considered an inherent characteristic of private household work. Also excluded are self-employed persons with multiple businesses and persons with multiple jobs as unpaid family workers.

- *At work part-time for economic reasons.* Sometimes referred to as involuntary part-time, this category refers to individuals who gave an economic reason for working 1 to 34 hours during the reference week. Economic reasons include slack work or unfavorable business conditions, inability to find full-time work, and seasonal declines in demand. Those who usually work part-time must also indicate that they want and are available to work full-time to be classified as on part-time for economic reasons.

- *At work part-time for noneconomic reasons.* This group includes those persons who usually work part-time and were at work 1 to 34 hours during the reference week for a noneconomic reason. Noneconomic reasons include, for example: illness or other medical limitations, child-care problems or other family or personal obligations, school or training, retirement or Social Security limits on earnings, and being in a job where full-time work is less than 35 hours. The group also includes those who gave an economic reason for usually working 1 to 34 hours but said they do not want to work full-time or were unavailable for such work.

- *Usual full- or part-time status.* Data on persons "at work" exclude persons who were temporarily absent from a job and therefore classified in the zero-hours-worked category, "with a job but not at work." These are persons who were absent from their jobs for the entire week for such reasons as bad weather, vacation, illness, or involvement in a labor dispute. In order to differentiate a person's normal schedule from their activity during the reference week, persons are also classified according to their usual full- or part-time status. In this context, full-time workers are those who usually worked 35 hours or more (at all jobs combined). This group will include some individuals who worked less than 35 hours in the reference week for either economic or noneconomic reasons and those who are temporarily absent from work. Similarly, part-time workers are those who usually work less than 35 hours per week (at all jobs), regardless of the number of hours worked in the reference week. This may include some individuals who actually worked more than 34 hours in the reference week, as well as those who are temporarily absent from work. The full-time labor force includes all employed persons who usually work full-time and unemployed persons who are either looking for full-time work or are on layoff from full-time jobs. The part-time labor force consists of employed persons who usually work part-time and unemployed persons who are seeking or are on layoff from part-time jobs. Unemployment rates for full- and part-time workers are calculated using the concepts of the full- and part-time labor force.

- *White, black, and other*. These are terms used to describe the race of persons. Included in the "other" group are Native Americans, Alaskan Natives, and Asians and Pacific Islanders. Because of the relatively small sample size, data for "other" races are not published. In the enumeration process, race is determined by the household respondent.

- *Hispanic origin*. This refers to persons who identified themselves in the enumeration process as Mexican, Puerto Rican, Cuban, Central or South American, or of other Hispanic origin or descent. Persons of Hispanic origin may be of any race; thus they are included in both the white and black population groups.

- *Single, never married; married, spouse present; and other marital status*. These are the terms used to define the marital status of individuals at the time of interview. Married, spouse present, applies to husband and wife if both were living in the same household, even though one may be temporarily absent on business, vacation, on a visit, in a hospital, etc. Other marital status applies to persons who are married, spouse absent; widowed; or divorced. Married, spouse absent relates to persons who are separated due to marital problems, as well as husbands and wives who are living apart because one or the other was employed elsewhere, on duty with the Armed Forces, or any other reasons.

- *Household*. A household consists of all persons—related family members and all unrelated persons—who occupy a housing unit and have no other usual address. A house, an apartment, a group of rooms, or a single room is regarded as a housing unit when occupied or intended for occupancy as separate living quarters. A householder is the person (or one of the persons) in whose name the housing unit is owned or rented. The term is never applied to either husbands or wives in married-couple families but relates only to persons in families maintained by either men or women without a spouse.

- *Family*. A family is defined as a group of two or more persons residing together who are related by birth, marriage, or adoption; all such persons are considered as members of one family. Families are classified

either as married-couple families or as families maintained by women or men without spouses. A family maintained by a woman or a man is one in which the householder is either single, widowed, divorced, or married, spouse absent.

In addition to the above concepts and definitions, the criteria below underlie the special labor force data collected annually in the March supplement to the monthly CPS.

- *Persons with work experience*. All civilians who worked at any time during the preceding calendar year at full- or part-time jobs for pay or profit (including paid vacations and sick leave) or worked without pay on a farm or in a business that was family operated. From 1989 forward, these supplementary tables also include members of the Armed Forces within the United States.

- *Year-round full-time workers*. Worked primarily at full-time jobs for 50 weeks or more during the preceding calendar year. Part-year workers worked either full- or part-time for 1 to 49 weeks.

- *Spell of unemployment*. A continuous period of unemployment of at least one week's duration. A spell is terminated by employment or withdrawal from the labor force.

- *Extent of unemployment*. The number and proportion of the labor force that was unemployed at some time during the year. The number of weeks unemployed is the total number of weeks accumulated during the entire year.

- *Children*. "Own" children of the husband, wife, or person maintaining the family, including sons and daughters, stepchildren, and adopted children. Excluded are other related children, such as grandchildren, nieces, nephews, and cousins, and unrelated children.

- *Earnings.* All money income of $1.00 or more from wages and salaries and net money income of $1.00 or more from farm and nonfarm self-employment.

- *Income.* Total amount of money received in the preceding calendar year from (1) money wages and salaries; (2) net income from self-employment; (3) Social Security; (4) dividends, interest (on savings and bonds), net rental income, and income from estates and trusts; (5) public assistance; (6) unemployment and workers' compensation, government employee pensions, and veterans payments; and (7) private pensions, annuities, alimony, regular contributions from persons not living in the same household, net royalties, and other periodic income. The amount received represents income before deductions of personal taxes, Social Security contributions, savings bonds purchases, union dues, health insurance, and the like. The total income of a family is the sum of the amounts received by all persons in the family.

- *Educational attainment.* Years of school completed in regular schools, which include graded public, private, and parochial elementary and high schools, whether day or night school; also college, university, or professional school.

- *School enrollment.* Based on replies to the inquiry as to whether the person was enrolled in day or night school in any type of public, parochial, or other private school in the regular school system, including elementary schools, junior or senior high schools, and colleges or universities. Persons enrolled in special schools not in the regular school system, such as trade schools or business colleges, are not included in enrollment. Persons enrolled in classes which do not require physical presence in school, such as correspondence courses or other courses of independent study, and training courses given directly on the job, are not reported as enrolled in school.

Historical Comparability

While current survey concepts and methods are very similar to those introduced at the inception of the survey in 1940, a number of changes have been made over the years to improve the accuracy and usefulness of the data. Some of the most important changes include:

- In 1953, the current 4-8-4 rotation system was adopted, whereby households are interviewed for four consecutive months, leave the sample for eight months, and then return to the sample for the same four months of the following year. Before this system was introduced, households were interviewed for six consecutive months and then replaced. The new system provided some year-to-year overlap in the sample, thereby improving measurement over time.

- In 1955, the survey reference week was changed to the calendar week including the 12th day of the month, for greater consistency with the reference period used for other labor-related statistics. Previously, the calendar week containing the 8th day of the month had been used as the reference week.

- In 1957, the employment definition was modified slightly as a result of a comprehensive interagency review of labor force concepts and methods. Two relatively small groups of persons classified as employed, under "with a job but not at work," were assigned to different classifications. Persons on layoff with definite instructions to return to work within 30 days of the layoff date, and persons volunteering that they were waiting to start a new wage and salary job within 30 days of interview, were, for the most part, reassigned to the unemployed classification. The only exception was the small subgroup in school during the reference week but waiting to start new jobs, which was transferred to "not in the labor force."

- In 1967, more substantive changes were made as a result of the recommendations of the President's Committee to Appraise Employment and Unemployment Statistics (the Gordon Committee). The principal improvements were as follows:

a) A 4-week job search period and specific questions on job-seeking activity were introduced. Previously, the questionnaire was ambiguous as to the time period for job-seeking and there were no specific questions concerning job-search methods.

b) An availability test was introduced whereby a person must be currently available for work in order to be classified as unemployed. Previously, there was no such requirement. This revision to the concept mainly affected students, who, for example, may begin to look for summer jobs in the spring although they will not be available until June or July. Such persons, until 1967, had been classified as unemployed but since have been assigned to the "not in the labor force" category.

c) Persons "with a job but not at work" because of strikes, bad weather, etc., who volunteered that they were looking for work, were shifted from unemployed status to employed.

d) The lower age limit for official statistics on employment, unemployment, and other labor force concepts was raised from 14 to 16 years. Historical data for most major series have been revised to provide consistent information based on the new minimum age limit.

e) New questions were added to obtain additional information on persons not in the labor force, including those referred to as "discouraged workers," defined as persons who indicate that they want a job but are not currently looking because they believe there are no jobs available or none for which they would qualify.

f) New "probing" questions were added to the questionnaire in order to increase the reliability of information on hours of work, duration of unemployment, and self-employment.

- In 1994, major changes to the CPS were introduced, which included a complete redesign of the questionnaire and the use of computer-assisted interviewing for the entire survey. In addition, there were revisions to some of the labor force concepts and definitions, including the implementation of some changes recommended in 1979 by the National Commission on Employment and Unemployment Statistics (NCEUS, also known as the Levitan Commission). Some of the major changes to the survey were:

a) The introduction of a redesigned and automated questionnaire. The CPS questionnaire was totally redesigned in order to obtain more accurate, comprehensive, and relevant information, and to take advantage of state-of-the-art computer interviewing techniques.

b) The addition of two more objective criteria to the definition of discouraged workers. Prior to 1994, to be classified as a discouraged worker, a person must have wanted a job and have been reported as not currently looking because of a belief that no jobs were available or that there were none for which he or she would qualify.

Beginning in 1994, persons classified as discouraged must also have looked for a job within the past year (or since their last job, if

they worked during the year), and must have been available for work during the reference week (a direct question on availability was added in 1994; prior to 1994, availability had been inferred from responses to other questions). These changes were made because the NCEUS and others felt that the previous definition of discouraged workers was too subjective, relying mainly on an individual's stated desire for a job and not on prior testing of the labor market.

c) Similarly, the identification of persons employed part-time for economic reasons (working less than 35 hours in the reference week because of poor business conditions or because of an inability to find full-time work) was tightened by adding two new criteria for persons who usually work part-time: they must want and be available for full-time work. Previously, such information was inferred. (Persons who usually work full-time but worked part-time for an economic reason during the reference week are assumed to meet these criteria.)

d) Specific questions were added about the expectation of recall for persons who indicate that they are on layoff. To be classified as "on temporary layoff," persons must expect to be recalled to their jobs. Previously, the questionnaire did not include explicit questions about the expectation of recall.

e) Persons volunteering that they were waiting to start a new job within 30 days must have looked for work in the four weeks prior to the survey in order to be classified as unemployed. Previously, such persons did not have to meet the job-search requirement in order to be included among the unemployed.

Noncomparability of Labor Force Levels

In addition to the refinements in concepts, definitions, and methods made over the years, other changes have also affected the comparability of the labor force data.

- Beginning in 1953, as a result of introducing data from the 1950 census into the estimating procedures, population levels were raised by about 600,000; labor force, total employment, and agricultural employment were increased by about 350,000, primarily affecting the figures for totals and men; other categories were relatively unaffected.

- Beginning in 1960, the inclusion of Alaska and Hawaii resulted in an increase of about 500,000 in the population and about 300,000 in the labor force. Four-fifths of this increase was in nonagricultural employment; other labor force categories were not appreciably affected.

- Beginning in 1962, the introduction of data from the 1960 census reduced the population by about 50,000 and labor force and employment by about 200,000; unemployment totals were virtually unchanged.

- Beginning in 1972, information from the 1970 census was introduced into the estimation procedures, increasing the population by about 800,000; labor force and employment totals were raised by a little more than 300,000; unemployment levels and rates were essentially unchanged.

- In March 1973, a subsequent population adjustment based on the 1970 census was introduced. This adjustment, which affected the white and black-and-other groups but had little effect on totals, resulted in the reduction of nearly 300,000 in the white population and an increase of the same magnitude in the black-and-other population. Civilian labor force and total employment figures were affected to a lesser degree; the white labor force was reduced by 150,000, and the black-and-other labor force rose by about 210,000. Unemployment levels and rates were not significantly affected.

• Beginning in January 1974, the method used to prepare independent estimates of the civilian noninstitutional population was modified to an "inflation-deflation" approach. This change in the derivation of the estimates had its greatest impact on estimates of 20- to 24-year-old men—particularly those of the black-and-other population—but had little effect on estimates of the total population 16 years and over.

• Effective in July 1975, as a result of the large inflow of Vietnamese refugees into the United States, the total and black-and-other independent population controls for persons 16 years and over were adjusted upward by 76,000 (30,000 men and 46,000 women). The addition of the refugees increased the black-and-other population by less than one percent in any age-sex group, with all of the changes being confined to the "other" component of the population.

• Beginning in January 1978, the introduction of an expansion in the sample and revisions in the estimation procedures resulted in an increase of about 250,000 in the civilian labor force and employment totals; unemployment levels and rates were essentially unchanged.

• Beginning in October 1978, the race of the individual was determined by the household respondent for the incoming rotation group households, rather than by the interviewer as before. The purpose of this change was to provide more accurate estimates of characteristics by race. Thus, in October 1978, one-eighth of the sample households had race determined by the household respondent and seven-eighths of the

sample households had race determined by interviewer observation. It was not until January 1980 that the entire sample had race determined by the household respondent. The new procedure had no significant effect on the estimates.

• Beginning in January 1982, the second-stage ratio adjustment method was changed. In addition, current population estimates used in the second-stage estimation procedure were derived from information obtained from the 1980 census, rather than the 1970 census. This change caused substantial increases in the total population and in the estimates of persons in all labor force categories. Rates for labor force characteristics, however, remained virtually unchanged. Some 30,000 labor force series were adjusted back to 1970 to avoid major breaks in series. The revisions did not, however, smooth out the breaks in series occurring between 1972 and 1979 (described above), and data users should consider them when comparing estimates from different periods.

• Beginning in January 1983, the first-stage ratio adjustment method was updated to incorporate data from the 1980 census. There were only slight differences between the old and new procedures in estimates of levels for the various labor force characteristics and virtually no differences in estimates of participation rates.

• Beginning in January 1985, most of the steps of the CPS estimation procedure were revised. Overall, the revisions had only a slight effect on most estimates. The greatest impact was on estimates of persons of Hispanic origin. Major estimates were revised back to January 1980.

• Beginning in January 1986, the population controls used in the second-stage ratio adjustment method were revised to reflect an explicit estimate of the number of undocumented immigrants (largely

Hispanic) since 1980 and an improved estimate of the number of emigrants among legal foreign-born residents for the same time period. As a result, the total civilian population and labor force estimates were raised by nearly 400,000; civilian employment was increased by about 350,000. The Hispanic-origin population and labor force estimates were raised by about 425,000 and 305,000, respectively, and Hispanic employment by 270,000. Overall and subgroup unemployment levels and rates were not significantly affected. Because of the magnitude of the adjustments for Hispanics, data were revised back to January 1980 to the extent possible.

• Beginning in January 1994, population estimates used in the second stage estimation procedure were based on information obtained from the 1990 census (adjusted for the undercount as measured by the Census Bureau's Post Enumeration Survey). To improve historical comparability, the population-control effects have been incorporated back to January 1990. This change resulted in substantial increases in total population and in all major labor force categories. Increases in levels were concentrated in younger age groups, races other than white or black, and persons of Hispanic origin. Data for older age groups generally decreased as a result of these revisions.

Over the four years subject to revision, the annual average estimates of the civilian noninstitutional population 16 years and over increased at a gradually increasing rate, beginning with an increase of about 1.1 million (0.6 percent) in 1990, and ending with an increase of about 1.3 million (0.7 percent) in 1993 and 1994. Because of the demographic distribution of the population increase, particularly with respect to age, the estimated levels of civilian labor force went up by almost as much as the population, resulting in average increases of 0.1 in overall labor force participation rates and employment-population ratios. Within the civilian labor force, the new controls caused average increases of 0.1 in the overall unemployment rate because demographic groups with relatively high unemployment rates, such as youth and persons of Hispanic origin, had relatively large upward population adjustments.

(In the case of data from the March supplement to the CPS, the 1990 controls were introduced in 1994 and have not been carried back to 1990.)

Changes in the Occupational and Industrial Classification System

Beginning in January 1983, the occupational and industrial classification systems used in the 1980 census were introduced into the CPS.

The 1980 census occupational classification system was so radically different in concepts and nomenclature from the 1970 system that comparisons of historical data are not possible without major adjustments.

The industrial classification system used in the 1980 census was based on the 1972 Standard Industrial Classification (SIC) system, as modified in 1977. The adoption of the new system had much less of an adverse effect on historical comparability than did the new occupational system.

Beginning in January 1992, the occupational and industrial classification systems used in the 1990 census were introduced into the CPS. There were a few breaks in comparability between the 1980 and 1990 census-based systems,

particularly within the "technical, sales, and administrative support" categories. The most notable changes in industry classification were the shift of several industries from "business services" to "professional services" and the splitting of some industries into smaller, more detailed categories.

Descriptions of sampling and estimation procedures and further information on the changes described above can be found in the Bureau of Labor Statistics, *Employment and Earnings*, February 1994 and March 1996 issues.

3 1833 03047 5351

Employment Status of the Civilian Noninstitutional Population, 1947-1995

(Thousands of persons)

Year	Civilian noninstitutional population	Civilian labor force								Not in labor force
		Total	Percent of population	Employed				Unemployed		
				Total	Percent of population	Agriculture	Non-agricultural industries	Number	Percent of labor force	
1947	101 827	59 350	58.3	57 038	56.0	7 890	49 148	2 311	3.9	42 477
1948	103 068	60 621	58.8	58 343	56.6	7 629	50 714	2 276	3.8	42 447
1949	103 994	61 286	58.9	57 651	55.4	7 658	49 993	3 637	5.9	42 708
1950	104 995	62 208	59.2	58 918	56.1	7 160	51 758	3 288	5.3	42 787
1951	104 621	62 017	59.2	59 961	57.3	6 726	53 235	2 055	3.3	42 604
1952	105 231	62 138	59.0	60 250	57.3	6 500	53 749	1 883	3.0	43 093
1953	107 056	63 015	58.9	61 179	57.1	6 260	54 919	1 834	2.9	44 041
1954	108 321	63 643	58.8	60 109	55.5	6 205	53 904	3 532	5.5	44 678
1955	109 683	65 023	59.3	62 170	56.7	6 450	55 722	2 852	4.4	44 660
1956	110 954	66 552	60.0	63 799	57.5	6 283	57 514	2 750	4.1	44 402
1957	112 265	66 929	59.6	64 071	57.1	5 947	58 123	2 859	4.3	45 336
1958	113 727	67 639	59.5	63 036	55.4	5 586	57 450	4 602	6.8	46 088
1959	115 329	68 369	59.3	64 630	56.0	5 565	59 065	3 740	5.5	46 960
1960	117 245	69 628	59.4	65 778	56.1	5 458	60 318	3 852	5.5	47 617
1961	118 771	70 459	59.3	65 746	55.4	5 200	60 546	4 714	6.7	48 312
1962	120 153	70 614	58.8	66 702	55.5	4 944	61 759	3 911	5.5	49 539
1963	122 416	71 833	58.7	67 762	55.4	4 687	63 076	4 070	5.7	50 583
1964	124 485	73 091	58.7	69 305	55.7	4 523	64 782	3 786	5.2	51 394
1965	126 513	74 455	58.9	71 088	56.2	4 361	66 726	3 366	4.5	52 058
1966	128 058	75 770	59.2	72 895	56.9	3 979	68 915	2 875	3.8	52 288
1967	129 874	77 347	59.6	74 372	57.3	3 844	70 527	2 975	3.8	52 527
1968	132 028	78 737	59.6	75 920	57.5	3 817	72 103	2 817	3.6	53 291
1969	134 335	80 734	60.1	77 902	58.0	3 606	74 296	2 832	3.5	53 602
1970	137 085	82 771	60.4	78 678	57.4	3 463	75 215	4 093	4.9	54 315
1971	140 216	84 382	60.2	79 367	56.6	3 394	75 972	5 016	5.9	55 834
1972	144 126	87 034	60.4	82 153	57.0	3 484	78 669	4 882	5.6	57 091
1973	147 096	89 429	60.8	85 064	57.8	3 470	81 594	4 365	4.9	57 667
1974	150 120	91 949	61.3	86 794	57.8	3 515	83 279	5 156	5.6	58 171
1975	153 153	93 775	61.2	85 846	56.1	3 408	82 438	7 929	8.5	59 377
1976	156 150	96 158	61.6	88 752	56.8	3 331	85 421	7 406	7.7	59 991
1977	159 033	99 009	62.3	92 017	57.9	3 283	88 734	6 991	7.1	60 025
1978	161 910	102 251	63.2	96 048	59.3	3 387	92 661	6 202	6.1	59 659
1979	164 863	104 962	63.7	98 824	59.9	3 347	95 477	6 137	5.8	59 900
1980	167 745	106 940	63.8	99 303	59.2	3 364	95 938	7 637	7.1	60 806
1981	170 130	108 670	63.9	100 397	59.0	3 368	97 030	8 273	7.6	61 460
1982	172 271	110 204	64.0	99 526	57.8	3 401	96 125	10 678	9.7	62 067
1983	174 215	111 550	64.0	100 834	57.9	3 383	97 450	10 717	9.6	62 665
1984	176 383	113 544	64.4	105 005	59.5	3 321	101 685	8 539	7.5	62 839
1985	178 206	115 461	64.8	107 150	60.1	3 179	103 971	8 312	7.2	62 744
1986	180 587	117 834	65.3	109 597	60.7	3 163	106 434	8 237	7.0	62 752
1987	182 753	119 865	65.6	112 440	61.5	3 208	109 232	7 425	6.2	62 888
1988	184 613	121 669	65.9	114 968	62.3	3 169	111 800	6 701	5.5	62 944
1989	186 393	123 869	66.5	117 342	63.0	3 199	114 142	6 528	5.3	62 523
1990	189 164	125 840	66.5	118 793	62.8	3 223	115 570	7 047	5.6	63 324
1991	190 925	126 346	66.2	117 718	61.7	3 269	114 449	8 628	6.8	64 578
1992	192 805	128 105	66.4	118 492	61.5	3 247	115 245	9 613	7.5	64 700
1993	194 838	129 200	66.3	120 259	61.7	3 115	117 144	8 940	6.9	65 638
1994	196 814	131 056	66.6	123 060	62.5	3 409	119 651	7 996	6.1	65 758
1995	198 584	132 304	66.6	124 900	62.9	3 440	121 460	7 404	5.6	66 280

NOTE: Data beginning in 1994 are not strictly comparable with data for 1993 and earlier years because of the introduction of a major redesign of the survey and collection methodology. Beginning in 1990, data are not strictly comparable with previous years because of the introduction of 1990 census-based population controls adjusted for the estimated undercount.

Employment Status of the Civilian Noninstitutional Population by Sex, 1963-1995

(Thousands of persons)

Year	Civilian noninstitutional population	Civilian labor force		Employed				Unemployed		Not in labor force
		Total	Percent of population	Total	Percent of population	Agriculture	Non-agricultural industries	Number	Percent of labor force	
MEN										
1963	57 921	47 129	81.4	44 657	77.1	3 809	40 849	2 472	5.2	10 792
1964	58 847	47 679	81.0	45 474	77.3	3 691	41 782	2 205	4.6	11 169
1965	59 782	48 255	80.7	46 340	77.5	3 547	42 792	1 914	4.0	11 527
1966	60 262	48 471	80.4	46 919	77.9	3 243	43 675	1 551	3.2	11 792
1967	60 905	48 987	80.4	47 479	78.0	3 164	44 315	1 508	3.1	11 919
1968	61 847	49 533	80.1	48 114	77.8	3 157	44 957	1 419	2.9	12 315
1969	62 898	50 221	79.8	48 818	77.6	2 963	45 855	1 403	2.8	12 677
1970	64 304	51 228	79.7	48 990	76.2	2 862	46 128	2 238	4.4	13 076
1971	65 942	52 180	79.1	49 390	74.9	2 795	46 595	2 789	5.3	13 762
1972	67 835	53 555	78.9	50 896	75.0	2 849	48 047	2 659	5.0	14 280
1973	69 292	54 624	78.8	52 349	75.5	2 847	49 502	2 275	4.2	14 667
1974	70 808	55 739	78.7	53 024	74.9	2 919	50 105	2 714	4.9	15 069
1975	72 291	56 299	77.9	51 857	71.7	2 824	49 032	4 442	7.9	15 993
1976	73 759	57 174	77.5	53 138	72.0	2 744	50 394	4 036	7.1	16 585
1977	75 193	58 396	77.7	54 728	72.8	2 671	52 057	3 667	6.3	16 797
1978	76 576	59 620	77.9	56 479	73.8	2 718	53 761	3 142	5.3	16 956
1979	78 020	60 726	77.8	57 607	73.8	2 686	54 921	3 120	5.1	17 293
1980	79 398	61 453	77.4	57 186	72.0	2 709	54 477	4 267	6.9	17 945
1981	80 511	61 974	77.0	57 397	71.3	2 700	54 697	4 577	7.4	18 537
1982	81 523	62 450	76.6	56 271	69.0	2 736	53 534	6 179	9.9	19 073
1983	82 531	63 047	76.4	56 787	68.8	2 704	54 083	6 260	9.9	19 484
1984	83 605	63 835	76.4	59 091	70.7	2 668	56 423	4 744	7.4	19 771
1985	84 469	64 411	76.3	59 891	70.9	2 535	57 356	4 521	7.0	20 058
1986	85 798	65 422	76.3	60 892	71.0	2 511	58 381	4 530	6.9	20 376
1987	86 899	66 207	76.2	62 107	71.5	2 543	59 564	4 101	6.2	20 692
1988	87 857	66 927	76.2	63 273	72.0	2 493	60 780	3 655	5.5	20 930
1989	88 762	67 840	76.4	64 315	72.5	2 513	61 802	3 525	5.2	20 923
1990	90 377	69 011	76.4	65 104	72.0	2 546	62 559	3 906	5.7	21 367
1991	91 278	69 168	75.8	64 223	70.4	2 589	61 634	4 946	7.2	22 110
1992	92 270	69 964	75.8	64 440	69.8	2 575	61 866	5 523	7.9	22 306
1993	93 332	70 404	75.4	65 349	70.0	2 478	62 871	5 055	7.2	22 927
1994	94 355	70 817	75.1	66 450	70.4	2 554	63 896	4 367	6.2	23 538
1995	95 178	71 360	75.0	67 377	70.8	2 559	64 818	3 983	5.6	23 818
WOMEN										
1963	64 494	24 704	38.3	23 105	35.8	878	22 227	1 598	6.5	39 791
1964	65 637	25 412	38.7	23 831	36.3	832	23 000	1 581	6.2	40 225
1965	66 731	26 200	39.3	24 748	37.1	814	23 934	1 452	5.5	40 531
1966	67 795	27 299	40.3	25 976	38.3	736	25 240	1 324	4.8	40 496
1967	68 968	28 360	41.1	26 893	39.0	680	26 212	1 468	5.2	40 608
1968	70 179	29 204	41.6	27 807	39.6	660	27 147	1 397	4.8	40 976
1969	71 436	30 513	42.7	29 084	40.7	643	28 441	1 429	4.7	40 924
1970	72 782	31 543	43.3	29 688	40.8	601	29 087	1 855	5.9	41 239
1971	74 274	32 202	43.4	29 976	40.4	599	29 377	2 227	6.9	42 072
1972	76 290	33 479	43.9	31 257	41.0	635	30 622	2 222	6.6	42 811
1973	77 804	34 804	44.7	32 715	42.0	622	32 093	2 089	6.0	43 000
1974	79 312	36 211	45.7	33 769	42.6	596	33 173	2 441	6.7	43 101
1975	80 860	37 475	46.3	33 989	42.0	584	33 404	3 486	9.3	43 386
1976	82 390	38 983	47.3	35 615	43.2	588	35 027	3 369	8.6	43 406
1977	83 840	40 613	48.4	37 289	44.5	612	36 677	3 324	8.2	43 227
1978	85 334	42 631	50.0	39 569	46.4	669	38 900	3 061	7.2	42 703
1979	86 843	44 235	50.9	41 217	47.5	661	40 556	3 018	6.8	42 608
1980	88 348	45 487	51.5	42 117	47.7	656	41 461	3 370	7.4	42 861
1981	89 618	46 696	52.1	43 000	48.0	667	42 333	3 696	7.9	42 922
1982	90 748	47 755	52.6	43 256	47.7	665	42 591	4 499	9.4	42 993
1983	91 684	48 503	52.9	44 047	48.0	680	43 367	4 457	9.2	43 181
1984	92 778	49 709	53.6	45 915	49.5	653	45 262	3 794	7.6	43 068
1985	93 736	51 050	54.5	47 259	50.4	644	46 615	3 791	7.4	42 686
1986	94 789	52 413	55.3	48 706	51.4	652	48 054	3 707	7.1	42 376
1987	95 853	53 658	56.0	50 334	52.5	666	49 668	3 324	6.2	42 195
1988	96 756	54 742	56.6	51 696	53.4	676	51 020	3 046	5.6	42 014
1989	97 630	56 030	57.4	53 027	54.3	687	52 341	3 003	5.4	41 601
1990	98 787	56 829	57.5	53 689	54.3	678	53 011	3 140	5.5	41 957
1991	99 646	57 178	57.4	53 496	53.7	680	52 815	3 683	6.4	42 468
1992	100 535	58 141	57.8	54 052	53.8	672	53 380	4 090	7.0	42 394
1993	101 506	58 795	57.9	54 910	54.1	637	54 273	3 885	6.6	42 711
1994	102 460	60 239	58.8	56 610	55.3	855	55 755	3 629	6.0	42 221
1995	103 406	60 944	58.9	57 523	55.6	881	56 642	3 421	5.6	42 462

NOTE: Data beginning in 1994 are not strictly comparable with data for 1993 and earlier years because of the introduction of a major redesign of the survey and collection methodology. Beginning in 1990, data are not strictly comparable with previous years because of the introduction of 1990 census-based population controls adjusted for the estimated undercount.

Employment Status of the Civilian Noninstitutional Population by Sex, Race, Hispanic Origin, and Age, 1980-1995

(Thousands of persons)

Employment status, sex, and age	1980	1981	1982	1983	1984	1985	1986	1987
TOTAL CIVILIAN NONINSTITUTIONAL POPULATION								
Population	167 745	170 130	172 271	174 215	176 383	178 206	180 587	182 753
Civilian labor force	106 940	108 670	110 204	111 550	113 544	115 461	117 834	119 865
Employed	99 303	100 397	99 526	100 834	105 005	107 150	109 597	112 440
Agriculture	3 364	3 368	3 401	3 383	3 321	3 179	3 163	3 208
Nonagriculture	95 938	97 030	96 125	97 450	101 685	103 971	106 434	109 232
Unemployed	7 637	8 273	10 678	10 717	8 539	8 312	8 237	7 425
Not in labor force	60 806	61 460	62 067	62 665	62 839	62 744	62 752	62 888
MEN, 16 YEARS AND OVER								
Population	79 398	80 511	81 523	82 531	83 605	84 469	85 798	86 899
Civilian labor force	61 453	61 974	62 450	63 047	63 835	64 411	65 422	66 207
Employed	57 186	57 397	56 271	56 787	59 091	59 891	60 892	62 107
Agriculture	2 709	2 700	2 736	2 704	2 668	2 535	2 511	2 543
Nonagriculture	54 477	54 697	53 534	54 083	56 423	57 356	58 381	59 564
Unemployed	4 267	4 577	6 179	6 260	4 744	4 521	4 530	4 101
Not in labor force	17 945	18 537	19 073	19 484	19 771	20 058	20 376	20 692
MEN, 20 YEARS AND OVER								
Population	71 138	72 419	73 644	74 872	76 219	77 195	78 523	79 565
Civilian labor force	56 455	57 197	57 980	58 744	59 701	60 277	61 320	62 095
Employed	53 101	53 582	52 891	53 487	55 769	56 562	57 569	58 726
Agriculture	2 396	2 384	2 422	2 429	2 418	2 278	2 292	2 329
Nonagriculture	50 706	51 199	50 469	51 058	53 351	54 284	55 277	56 397
Unemployed	3 353	3 615	5 089	5 257	3 932	3 715	3 751	3 369
Not in labor force	14 683	15 222	15 664	16 129	16 518	16 918	17 203	17 470
WOMEN, 16 YEARS AND OVER								
Population	88 348	89 618	90 748	91 684	92 778	93 736	94 789	95 853
Civilian labor force	45 487	46 696	47 755	48 503	49 709	51 050	52 413	53 658
Employed	42 117	43 000	43 256	44 047	45 915	47 259	48 706	50 334
Agriculture	656	667	665	680	653	644	652	666
Nonagriculture	41 461	42 333	42 591	43 367	45 262	46 615	48 054	49 668
Unemployed	3 370	3 696	4 499	4 457	3 794	3 791	3 707	3 324
Not in labor force	42 861	42 922	42 993	43 181	43 068	42 686	42 376	42 195
WOMEN, 20 YEARS AND OVER								
Population	80 065	81 497	82 864	84 069	85 429	86 506	87 567	88 583
Civilian labor force	41 106	42 485	43 699	44 636	45 900	47 283	48 589	49 783
Employed	38 492	39 590	40 086	41 004	42 793	44 154	45 556	47 074
Agriculture	584	604	601	620	595	596	614	622
Nonagriculture	37 907	38 986	39 485	40 384	42 198	43 558	44 943	46 453
Unemployed	2 615	2 895	3 613	3 632	3 107	3 129	3 032	2 709
Not in labor force	38 958	39 012	39 165	39 433	39 529	39 222	38 979	38 800
BOTH SEXES, 16-19 YEARS								
Population	16 543	16 214	15 763	15 274	14 735	14 506	14 496	14 606
Civilian labor force	9 378	8 988	8 526	8 171	7 943	7 901	7 926	7 988
Employed	7 710	7 225	6 549	6 342	6 444	6 434	6 472	6 640
Agriculture	385	380	378	334	309	305	258	258
Nonagriculture	7 325	6 845	6 171	6 008	6 135	6 129	6 215	6 382
Unemployed	1 669	1 763	1 977	1 829	1 499	1 468	1 454	1 347
Not in labor force	7 165	7 226	7 238	7 104	6 791	6 604	6 570	6 618

Employment Status of the Civilian Noninstitutional Population by Sex, Race, Hispanic Origin, and Age, 1980-1995—Continued

(Thousands of persons)

Employment status, sex, and age	1988	1989	1990	1991	1992	1993	1994	1995
TOTAL CIVILIAN NONINSTITUTIONAL POPULATION								
Population	184 613	186 393	189 164	190 925	192 805	194 838	196 814	198 584
Civilian labor force	121 669	123 869	125 840	126 346	128 105	129 200	131 056	132 304
Employed	114 968	117 342	118 793	117 718	118 492	120 259	123 060	124 900
Agriculture	3 169	3 199	3 223	3 269	3 247	3 115	3 409	3 440
Nonagriculture	111 800	114 142	115 570	114 449	115 245	117 144	119 651	121 460
Unemployed	6 701	6 528	7 047	8 628	9 613	8 940	7 996	7 404
Not in labor force	62 944	62 523	63 324	64 578	64 700	65 638	65 758	66 280
MEN, 16 YEARS AND OVER								
Population	87 857	88 762	90 377	91 278	92 270	93 332	94 355	95 178
Civilian labor force	66 927	67 840	69 011	69 168	69 964	70 404	70 817	71 360
Employed	63 273	64 315	65 104	64 223	64 440	65 349	66 450	67 377
Agriculture	2 493	2 513	2 546	2 589	2 575	2 478	2 554	2 559
Nonagriculture	60 780	61 802	62 559	61 634	61 866	62 871	63 896	64 818
Unemployed	3 655	3 525	3 906	4 946	5 523	5 055	4 367	3 983
Not in labor force	20 930	20 923	21 367	22 110	22 306	22 927	23 538	23 818
MEN, 20 YEARS AND OVER								
Population	80 553	81 619	83 030	84 144	85 247	86 256	87 151	87 811
Civilian labor force	62 768	63 704	64 916	65 374	66 213	66 642	66 921	67 324
Employed	59 781	60 837	61 678	61 178	61 496	62 355	63 294	64 085
Agriculture	2 271	2 307	2 329	2 383	2 385	2 293	2 351	2 335
Nonagriculture	57 510	58 530	59 349	58 795	59 111	60 063	60 943	61 750
Unemployed	2 987	2 867	3 239	4 195	4 717	4 287	3 627	3 239
Not in labor force	17 785	17 915	18 114	18 770	19 034	19 613	20 230	20 487
WOMEN, 16 YEARS AND OVER								
Population	96 756	97 630	98 787	99 646	100 535	101 506	102 460	103 406
Civilian labor force	54 742	56 030	56 829	57 178	58 141	58 795	60 239	60 944
Employed	51 696	53 027	53 689	53 496	54 052	54 910	56 610	57 523
Agriculture	676	687	678	680	672	637	855	881
Nonagriculture	51 020	52 341	53 011	52 815	53 380	54 273	55 755	56 642
Unemployed	3 046	3 003	3 140	3 683	4 090	3 885	3 629	3 421
Not in labor force	42 014	41 601	41 957	42 468	42 394	42 711	42 221	42 462
WOMEN, 20 YEARS AND OVER								
Population	89 532	90 550	91 614	92 708	93 718	94 647	95 467	96 262
Civilian labor force	50 870	52 212	53 131	53 708	54 796	55 388	56 655	57 215
Employed	48 383	49 745	50 535	50 634	51 328	52 099	53 606	54 396
Agriculture	625	642	631	639	625	598	809	830
Nonagriculture	47 757	49 103	49 904	49 995	50 702	51 501	52 796	53 566
Unemployed	2 487	2 467	2 596	3 074	3 469	3 288	3 049	2 819
Not in labor force	38 662	38 339	38 483	39 000	38 922	39 260	38 813	39 047
BOTH SEXES, 16-19 YEARS								
Population	14 527	14 223	14 520	14 073	13 840	13 935	14 196	14 511
Civilian labor force	8 031	7 954	7 792	7 265	7 096	7 170	7 481	7 765
Employed	6 805	6 759	6 581	5 906	5 669	5 805	6 161	6 419
Agriculture	273	250	264	247	237	224	249	275
Nonagriculture	6 532	6 510	6 317	5 659	5 432	5 580	5 912	6 144
Unemployed	1 226	1 194	1 212	1 359	1 427	1 365	1 320	1 346
Not in labor force	6 497	6 270	6 727	6 808	6 745	6 765	6 715	6 746

Employment Status of the Civilian Noninstitutional Population by Sex, Race, Hispanic Origin, and Age, 1980-1995—Continued

(Thousands of persons)

Employment status, sex, and age	1980	1981	1982	1983	1984	1985	1986	1987
TOTAL, WHITE								
Population	146 122	147 908	149 441	150 805	152 347	153 679	155 432	156 958
Civilian labor force	93 600	95 052	96 143	97 021	98 492	99 926	101 801	103 290
Employed	87 715	88 709	87 903	88 893	92 120	93 736	95 660	97 789
Agriculture	3 087	3 109	3 142	3 119	3 057	2 936	2 958	2 986
Nonagriculture	84 629	85 600	84 761	85 774	89 063	90 799	92 703	94 803
Unemployed	5 884	6 343	8 241	8 128	6 372	6 191	6 140	5 501
Not in labor force	52 523	52 856	53 298	53 784	53 855	53 753	53 631	53 669
MEN, 16 YEARS AND OVER								
Population	69 634	70 480	71 211	71 922	72 723	73 373	74 390	75 189
Civilian labor force	54 473	54 895	55 133	55 480	56 062	56 472	57 217	57 779
Employed	51 127	51 315	50 287	50 621	52 462	53 046	53 785	54 647
Agriculture	2 473	2 481	2 518	2 484	2 437	2 325	2 340	2 354
Nonagriculture	48 654	48 833	47 770	48 138	50 025	50 720	51 444	52 293
Unemployed	3 345	3 580	4 846	4 859	3 600	3 426	3 433	3 132
Not in labor force	15 161	15 585	16 078	16 441	16 661	16 901	17 173	17 410
MEN, 20 YEARS AND OVER								
Population	62 694	63 715	64 655	65 581	66 610	67 386	68 413	69 175
Civilian labor force	50 049	50 671	51 200	51 716	52 453	52 895	53 675	54 232
Employed	47 419	47 846	47 209	47 618	49 461	50 061	50 818	51 649
Agriculture	2 180	2 183	2 218	2 225	2 201	2 085	2 131	2 150
Nonagriculture	45 239	45 663	44 990	45 393	47 260	47 976	48 687	49 499
Unemployed	2 629	2 825	3 991	4 098	2 992	2 834	2 857	2 584
Not in labor force	12 645	13 044	13 455	13 865	14 157	14 490	14 738	14 942
WOMEN, 16 YEARS AND OVER								
Population	76 489	77 428	78 230	78 884	79 624	80 306	81 042	81 769
Civilian labor force	39 127	40 157	41 010	41 541	42 431	43 455	44 584	45 510
Employed	36 587	37 394	37 615	38 272	39 659	40 690	41 876	43 142
Agriculture	614	628	624	635	620	611	617	632
Nonagriculture	35 975	36 767	36 991	37 636	39 038	40 079	41 259	42 509
Unemployed	2 540	2 762	3 395	3 270	2 772	2 765	2 708	2 369
Not in labor force	37 361	37 272	37 220	37 342	37 193	36 852	36 458	36 258
WOMEN, 20 YEARS AND OVER								
Population	69 575	70 677	71 711	72 601	73 590	74 394	75 140	75 845
Civilian labor force	35 239	36 418	37 425	38 119	39 087	40 190	41 264	42 164
Employed	33 275	34 275	34 710	35 476	36 823	37 907	39 050	40 242
Agriculture	545	567	565	580	564	566	580	590
Nonagriculture	32 729	33 708	34 144	34 896	36 259	37 341	38 471	39 652
Unemployed	1 964	2 143	2 715	2 643	2 264	2 283	2 213	1 922
Not in labor force	34 336	34 258	34 286	34 482	34 503	34 204	33 876	33 681
BOTH SEXES, 16-19 YEARS								
Population	13 854	13 516	13 076	12 623	12 147	11 900	11 879	11 939
Civilian labor force	8 312	7 962	7 518	7 186	6 952	6 841	6 862	6 893
Employed	7 021	6 588	5 984	5 799	5 836	5 768	5 792	5 898
Agriculture	361	359	358	314	292	285	247	246
Nonagriculture	6 661	6 229	5 626	5 485	5 544	5 483	5 545	5 652
Unemployed	1 291	1 374	1 534	1 387	1 116	1 074	1 070	995
Not in labor force	5 542	5 554	5 557	5 436	5 195	5 058	5 017	5 045

Employment Status of the Civilian Noninstitutional Population by Sex, Race, Hispanic Origin, and Age, 1980-1995—Continued

(Thousands of persons)

Employment status, sex, and age	1988	1989	1990	1991	1992	1993	1994	1995
TOTAL, WHITE								
Population	158 194	159 338	160 625	161 759	162 972	164 289	165 555	166 914
Civilian labor force	104 756	106 355	107 447	107 743	108 837	109 700	111 082	111 950
Employed	99 812	101 584	102 261	101 182	101 669	103 045	105 190	106 490
Agriculture	2 965	2 996	2 998	3 026	3 018	2 895	3 162	3 194
Nonagriculture	96 846	98 588	99 263	98 157	98 650	100 150	102 027	103 296
Unemployed	4 944	4 770	5 186	6 560	7 169	6 655	5 892	5 459
Not in labor force	53 439	52 983	53 178	54 016	54 135	54 589	54 473	54 965
MEN, 16 YEARS AND OVER								
Population	75 855	76 468	77 369	77 977	78 651	79 371	80 059	80 733
Civilian labor force	58 317	58 988	59 638	59 656	60 168	60 484	60 727	61 146
Employed	55 550	56 352	56 703	55 797	55 959	56 656	57 452	58 146
Agriculture	2 318	2 345	2 353	2 384	2 378	2 286	2 347	2 347
Nonagriculture	53 232	54 007	54 350	53 413	53 580	54 370	55 104	55 800
Unemployed	2 766	2 636	2 935	3 859	4 209	3 828	3 275	2 999
Not in labor force	17 538	17 480	17 731	18 321	18 484	18 887	19 332	19 587
MEN, 20 YEARS AND OVER								
Population	69 887	70 654	71 457	72 274	73 040	73 721	74 311	74 879
Civilian labor force	54 734	55 441	56 116	56 387	56 976	57 284	57 411	57 719
Employed	52 466	53 292	53 685	53 103	53 357	54 021	54 676	55 254
Agriculture	2 104	2 149	2 148	2 192	2 197	2 114	2 151	2 132
Nonagriculture	50 362	51 143	51 537	50 912	51 160	51 907	52 525	53 122
Unemployed	2 268	2 149	2 431	3 284	3 620	3 263	2 735	2 465
Not in labor force	15 153	15 213	15 340	15 887	16 064	16 436	16 900	17 161
WOMEN, 16 YEARS AND OVER								
Population	82 340	82 871	83 256	83 781	84 321	84 918	85 496	86 181
Civilian labor force	46 439	47 367	47 809	48 087	48 669	49 216	50 356	50 804
Employed	44 262	45 232	45 558	45 385	45 710	46 390	47 738	48 344
Agriculture	648	651	645	641	640	609	815	847
Nonagriculture	43 614	44 581	44 913	44 744	45 070	45 780	46 923	47 497
Unemployed	2 177	2 135	2 251	2 701	2 959	2 827	2 617	2 460
Not in labor force	35 901	35 504	35 447	35 695	35 651	35 702	35 141	35 377
WOMEN, 20 YEARS AND OVER								
Population	76 470	77 154	77 539	78 285	78 928	79 490	79 980	80 567
Civilian labor force	43 081	44 105	44 648	45 111	45 839	46 311	47 314	47 686
Employed	41 316	42 346	42 796	42 862	43 327	43 910	45 116	45 643
Agriculture	599	608	598	601	594	572	772	799
Nonagriculture	40 717	41 738	42 198	42 261	42 733	43 339	44 344	44 844
Unemployed	1 766	1 758	1 852	2 248	2 512	2 400	2 197	2 042
Not in labor force	33 389	33 050	32 891	33 174	33 089	33 179	32 666	32 881
BOTH SEXES, 16-19 YEARS								
Population	11 838	11 530	11 630	11 200	11 004	11 078	11 264	11 468
Civilian labor force	6 940	6 809	6 683	6 245	6 022	6 105	6 357	6 545
Employed	6 030	5 946	5 779	5 216	4 985	5 113	5 398	5 593
Agriculture	263	239	252	233	228	209	239	262
Nonagriculture	5 767	5 707	5 528	4 984	4 757	4 904	5 158	5 331
Unemployed	910	863	903	1 029	1 037	992	960	952
Not in labor force	4 897	4 721	4 947	4 955	4 982	4 973	4 907	4 923

Employment Status of the Civilian Noninstitutional Population by Sex, Race, Hispanic Origin, and Age, 1980-1995—Continued

(Thousands of persons)

Employment status, sex, and age	1980	1981	1982	1983	1984	1985	1986	1987
TOTAL, BLACK								
Population	17 824	18 219	18 584	18 925	19 348	19 664	19 989	20 352
Civilian labor force	10 865	11 086	11 331	11 647	12 033	12 364	12 654	12 993
Employed	9 313	9 355	9 189	9 375	10 119	10 501	10 814	11 309
Agriculture	208	184	188	193	196	189	155	164
Nonagriculture	9 106	9 171	9 001	9 182	9 923	10 312	10 659	11 145
Unemployed	1 553	1 731	2 142	2 272	1 914	1 864	1 840	1 684
Not in labor force	6 959	7 134	7 254	7 278	7 315	7 299	7 335	7 359
MEN, 16 YEARS AND OVER								
Population	7 944	8 117	8 283	8 447	8 654	8 790	8 956	9 128
Civilian labor force	5 612	5 685	5 804	5 966	6 126	6 220	6 373	6 486
Employed	4 798	4 794	4 637	4 753	5 124	5 270	5 428	5 661
Agriculture	179	162	163	165	174	167	133	142
Nonagriculture	4 620	4 632	4 474	4 587	4 950	5 103	5 295	5 519
Unemployed	815	891	1 167	1 213	1 003	951	946	826
Not in labor force	2 333	2 433	2 481	2 482	2 528	2 570	2 583	2 642
MEN, 20 YEARS AND OVER								
Population	6 834	7 007	7 186	7 360	7 599	7 731	7 907	8 063
Civilian labor force	5 134	5 223	5 368	5 533	5 686	5 749	5 915	6 023
Employed	4 498	4 520	4 414	4 531	4 871	4 992	5 150	5 357
Agriculture	162	148	150	152	161	154	125	135
Nonagriculture	4 336	4 372	4 264	4 379	4 710	4 837	5 025	5 222
Unemployed	636	703	954	1 002	815	757	765	666
Not in labor force	1 701	1 785	1 819	1 828	1 913	1 982	1 991	2 040
WOMEN, 16 YEARS AND OVER								
Population	9 880	10 102	10 300	10 477	10 694	10 873	11 033	11 224
Civilian labor force	5 253	5 401	5 527	5 681	5 907	6 144	6 281	6 507
Employed	4 515	4 561	4 552	4 622	4 995	5 231	5 386	5 648
Agriculture	29	22	25	28	22	22	22	22
Nonagriculture	4 486	4 539	4 527	4 595	4 973	5 209	5 364	5 626
Unemployed	738	840	975	1 059	911	913	894	858
Not in labor force	4 627	4 701	4 773	4 796	4 787	4 729	4 752	4 717
WOMEN, 20 YEARS AND OVER								
Population	8 700	8 924	9 146	9 340	9 588	9 773	9 945	10 126
Civilian labor force	4 841	5 001	5 140	5 306	5 520	5 727	5 855	6 071
Employed	4 267	4 329	4 347	4 428	4 773	4 977	5 128	5 365
Agriculture	26	19	21	25	21	19	22	20
Nonagriculture	4 241	4 310	4 326	4 403	4 752	4 959	5 106	5 345
Unemployed	574	671	793	878	747	750	728	706
Not in labor force	3 859	3 923	4 006	4 034	4 069	4 046	4 090	4 054
BOTH SEXES, 16-19 YEARS								
Population	2 289	2 288	2 252	2 225	2 161	2 160	2 137	2 163
Civilian labor force	891	862	824	809	827	889	883	899
Employed	547	505	428	416	474	532	536	587
Agriculture	19	17	16	16	13	16	8	9
Nonagriculture	528	489	412	400	460	516	529	578
Unemployed	343	357	396	392	353	357	347	312
Not in labor force	1 400	1 426	1 429	1 416	1 334	1 271	1 254	1 264

Employment Status of the Civilian Noninstitutional Population by Sex, Race, Hispanic Origin, and Age, 1980-1995—Continued

(Thousands of persons)

Employment status, sex, and age	1988	1989	1990	1991	1992	1993	1994	1995
TOTAL, BLACK								
Population	20 692	21 021	21 477	21 799	22 147	22 521	22 879	23 246
Civilian labor force	13 205	13 497	13 740	13 797	14 162	14 225	14 502	14 817
Employed	11 658	11 953	12 175	12 074	12 151	12 382	12 835	13 279
Agriculture	153	150	142	160	153	143	136	101
Nonagriculture	11 505	11 803	12 034	11 914	11 997	12 239	12 699	13 178
Unemployed	1 547	1 544	1 565	1 723	2 011	1 844	1 666	1 538
Not in labor force	7 487	7 524	7 737	8 002	7 985	8 296	8 377	8 429
MEN, 16 YEARS AND OVER								
Population	9 289	9 439	9 573	9 725	9 896	10 083	10 258	10 411
Civilian labor force	6 596	6 701	6 802	6 851	6 997	7 019	7 089	7 183
Employed	5 824	5 928	5 995	5 961	5 930	6 047	6 241	6 422
Agriculture	133	127	124	139	138	128	118	93
Nonagriculture	5 691	5 802	5 872	5 822	5 791	5 919	6 122	6 329
Unemployed	771	773	806	890	1 067	971	848	762
Not in labor force	2 694	2 738	2 772	2 874	2 899	3 064	3 169	3 228
MEN, 20 YEARS AND OVER								
Population	8 215	8 364	8 479	8 652	8 840	9 008	9 171	9 280
Civilian labor force	6 127	6 221	6 357	6 451	6 568	6 594	6 646	6 730
Employed	5 509	5 602	5 692	5 706	5 681	5 793	5 964	6 137
Agriculture	129	119	117	131	131	120	115	89
Nonagriculture	5 381	5 483	5 576	5 575	5 550	5 673	5 849	6 048
Unemployed	617	619	664	745	886	801	682	593
Not in labor force	2 089	2 143	2 122	2 202	2 272	2 413	2 525	2 550
WOMEN, 16 YEARS AND OVER								
Population	11 402	11 582	11 904	12 074	12 251	12 438	12 621	12 835
Civilian labor force	6 609	6 796	6 938	6 946	7 166	7 206	7 413	7 634
Employed	5 834	6 025	6 180	6 113	6 221	6 334	6 595	6 857
Agriculture	20	24	18	21	15	15	18	8
Nonagriculture	5 814	6 001	6 162	6 092	6 206	6 320	6 577	6 849
Unemployed	776	772	758	833	944	872	818	777
Not in labor force	4 793	4 786	4 965	5 129	5 086	5 231	5 208	5 201
WOMEN, 20 YEARS AND OVER								
Population	10 298	10 482	10 760	10 959	11 152	11 332	11 496	11 682
Civilian labor force	6 190	6 352	6 517	6 572	6 778	6 824	7 004	7 175
Employed	5 548	5 727	5 884	5 874	5 978	6 095	6 320	6 556
Agriculture	18	23	18	20	15	14	17	7
Nonagriculture	5 530	5 703	5 867	5 853	5 963	6 081	6 303	6 548
Unemployed	642	625	633	698	800	729	685	620
Not in labor force	4 108	4 130	4 243	4 388	4 374	4 508	4 492	4 507
BOTH SEXES, 16-19 YEARS								
Population	2 179	2 176	2 238	2 187	2 155	2 181	2 211	2 284
Civilian labor force	889	925	866	774	816	807	852	911
Employed	601	625	598	494	492	494	552	586
Agriculture	7	8	7	8	7	9	1	5
Nonagriculture	594	617	591	486	485	485	547	581
Unemployed	288	300	268	280	324	313	300	325
Not in labor force	1 291	1 251	1 372	1 413	1 339	1 374	1 360	1 372

Employment Status of the Civilian Noninstitutional Population by Sex, Race, Hispanic Origin, and Age, 1980-1995—Continued

(Thousands of persons)

Employment status, sex, and age	1980	1981	1982	1983	1984	1985	1986	1987
TOTAL, HISPANIC								
Population	9 598	10 120	10 580	11 029	11 478	11 915	12 344	12 867
Civilian labor force	6 146	6 492	6 734	7 033	7 451	7 698	8 076	8 541
Employed	5 527	5 813	5 805	6 072	6 651	6 888	7 219	7 790
Agriculture	265	273	285	316	341	302	329	398
Nonagriculture	5 263	5 540	5 521	5 756	6 310	6 586	6 890	7 391
Unemployed	620	678	929	961	800	811	857	751
Not in labor force	3 451	3 628	3 846	3 997	4 027	4 217	4 268	4 327
MEN, 16 YEARS AND OVER								
Population	4 689	4 968	5 203	5 432	5 661	5 885	6 106	6 371
Civilian labor force	3 818	4 005	4 148	4 362	4 563	4 729	4 948	5 163
Employed	3 448	3 597	3 583	3 771	4 083	4 245	4 428	4 713
Agriculture	224	229	243	271	296	264	287	351
Nonagriculture	3 224	3 369	3 340	3 499	3 787	3 981	4 140	4 361
Unemployed	370	408	565	591	480	483	520	451
Not in labor force	871	963	1 055	1 070	1 098	1 157	1 158	1 208
MEN, 20 YEARS AND OVER								
Population	4 036	4 306	4 539	4 771	5 005	5 232	5 451	5 700
Civilian labor force	3 426	3 647	3 815	4 014	4 218	4 395	4 612	4 818
Employed	3 142	3 325	3 354	3 523	3 825	3 994	4 174	4 444
Agriculture	200	205	222	246	271	239	263	327
Nonagriculture	2 942	3 120	3 132	3 276	3 554	3 754	3 911	4 118
Unemployed	284	321	461	491	393	401	438	374
Not in labor force	610	659	724	758	787	837	839	882
WOMEN, 16 YEARS AND OVER								
Population	4 909	5 151	5 377	5 597	5 816	6 029	6 238	6 496
Civilian labor force	2 328	2 486	2 586	2 671	2 888	2 970	3 128	3 377
Employed	2 079	2 216	2 222	2 301	2 568	2 642	2 791	3 077
Agriculture	41	44	42	44	46	38	42	47
Nonagriculture	2 038	2 172	2 180	2 257	2 522	2 604	2 749	3 030
Unemployed	249	269	364	369	320	327	337	300
Not in labor force	2 580	2 665	2 792	2 927	2 929	3 059	3 110	3 119
WOMEN, 20 YEARS AND OVER								
Population	4 281	4 513	4 734	4 954	5 173	5 385	5 591	5 835
Civilian labor force	2 076	2 242	2 333	2 429	2 615	2 725	2 893	3 112
Employed	1 886	2 029	2 040	2 127	2 357	2 456	2 615	2 872
Agriculture	33	37	35	40	37	31	39	45
Nonagriculture	1 852	1 992	2 006	2 086	2 320	2 424	2 576	2 827
Unemployed	190	212	293	302	258	269	278	241
Not in labor force	2 205	2 271	2 401	2 525	2 558	2 660	2 698	2 723
BOTH SEXES, 16-19 YEARS								
Population	1 281	1 301	1 307	1 304	1 300	1 298	1 302	1 332
Civilian labor force	645	603	585	590	618	579	571	610
Employed	500	459	410	423	468	438	430	474
Agriculture	31	31	28	29	34	31	27	27
Nonagriculture	468	428	382	394	435	407	403	447
Unemployed	145	144	175	167	149	141	141	136
Not in labor force	636	697	722	714	682	719	730	722

Employment Status of the Civilian Noninstitutional Population by Sex, Race, Hispanic Origin, and Age, 1980-1995—Continued

(Thousands of persons)

Employment status, sex, and age	1988	1989	1990	1991	1992	1993	1994	1995
TOTAL, HISPANIC								
Population	13 325	13 791	15 904	16 425	16 961	17 532	18 117	18 629
Civilian labor force	8 982	9 323	10 720	10 920	11 338	11 610	11 975	12 267
Employed	8 250	8 573	9 845	9 828	10 027	10 361	10 788	11 127
Agriculture	407	440	517	512	524	523	560	604
Nonagriculture	7 843	8 133	9 328	9 315	9 503	9 838	10 227	10 524
Unemployed	732	750	876	1 092	1 311	1 248	1 187	1 140
Not in labor force	4 342	4 468	5 184	5 506	5 623	5 922	6 142	6 362
MEN, 16 YEARS AND OVER								
Population	6 604	6 825	8 041	8 296	8 553	8 824	9 104	9 329
Civilian labor force	5 409	5 595	6 546	6 664	6 900	7 076	7 210	7 376
Employed	4 972	5 172	6 021	5 979	6 093	6 328	6 530	6 725
Agriculture	356	393	449	453	468	469	494	527
Nonagriculture	4 616	4 779	5 572	5 526	5 625	5 860	6 036	6 198
Unemployed	437	423	524	685	807	747	680	651
Not in labor force	1 195	1 230	1 495	1 632	1 654	1 749	1 894	1 952
MEN, 20 YEARS AND OVER								
Population	5 921	6 114	7 126	7 392	7 655	7 930	8 178	8 375
Civilian labor force	5 031	5 195	6 034	6 198	6 432	6 621	6 747	6 898
Employed	4 680	4 853	5 609	5 623	5 757	5 992	6 189	6 367
Agriculture	327	366	415	419	437	441	466	501
Nonagriculture	4 353	4 487	5 195	5 204	5 320	5 551	5 722	5 866
Unemployed	351	342	425	575	675	629	558	530
Not in labor force	890	919	1 092	1 194	1 223	1 309	1 431	1 477
WOMEN, 16 YEARS AND OVER								
Population	6 721	6 965	7 863	8 130	8 408	8 708	9 014	9 300
Civilian labor force	3 573	3 728	4 174	4 256	4 439	4 534	4 765	4 891
Employed	3 278	3 401	3 823	3 848	3 934	4 033	4 258	4 403
Agriculture	51	48	68	59	57	55	66	76
Nonagriculture	3 227	3 353	3 755	3 789	3 877	3 978	4 191	4 326
Unemployed	296	327	351	407	504	501	508	488
Not in labor force	3 147	3 237	3 689	3 874	3 969	4 174	4 248	4 409
WOMEN, 20 YEARS AND OVER								
Population	6 050	6 278	7 041	7 301	7 569	7 846	8 122	8 382
Civilian labor force	3 281	3 448	3 857	3 941	4 110	4 218	4 421	4 520
Employed	3 047	3 172	3 567	3 603	3 693	3 800	3 989	4 116
Agriculture	49	44	62	53	51	49	61	72
Nonagriculture	2 998	3 128	3 505	3 549	3 642	3 751	3 928	4 044
Unemployed	234	276	289	339	418	418	431	404
Not in labor force	2 769	2 830	3 184	3 360	3 459	3 628	3 701	3 863
BOTH SEXES, 16-19 YEARS								
Population	1 354	1 399	1 737	1 732	1 737	1 756	1 818	1 872
Civilian labor force	671	680	829	781	796	771	807	850
Employed	523	548	668	602	577	570	609	645
Agriculture	32	31	40	41	36	33	32	31
Nonagriculture	492	517	628	562	541	537	577	614
Unemployed	148	132	161	179	219	201	198	205
Not in labor force	683	719	907	951	941	985	1 010	1 022

NOTE: Data beginning with March 1994 are not comparable with data for 1993 and earlier years because of the introduction of a major redesign of the survey and collection methodology. Beginning in 1990, data are not strictly comparable with previous years because of the introduction of 1990 census-based population controls adjusted for the estimated undercount.

Employment Status of the Civilian Noninstitutional Population by Marital Status, Sex, and Race, 1976-1995

(Thousands of persons)

TOTAL: SINGLE

Year	Men				Women			
	Civilian noninstitutional population	Civilian labor force			Civilian noninstitutional population	Civilian labor force		
		Total	Employed	Unemployed		Total	Employed	Unemployed
1976	18 694	13 007	11 063	1 943	15 878	9 689	8 517	1 171
1977	19 445	13 793	11 937	1 856	16 598	10 311	9 064	1 248
1978	20 238	14 619	12 915	1 703	17 364	11 067	9 861	1 206
1979	20 795	15 100	13 424	1 675	17 959	11 597	10 386	1 211
1980	21 541	15 636	13 515	2 120	18 434	11 865	10 567	1 298
1981	21 973	15 893	13 577	2 316	18 792	12 124	10 685	1 439
1982	22 410	16 157	13 304	2 853	19 135	12 460	10 765	1 694
1983	22 965	16 657	13 783	2 874	19 479	12 659	10 996	1 663
1984	23 233	16 997	14 699	2 298	19 628	12 867	11 444	1 423
1985	23 328	17 208	15 022	2 186	19 768	13 163	11 758	1 404
1986	23 662	17 553	15 407	2 146	20 113	13 512	12 071	1 442
1987	23 947	17 772	15 794	1 978	20 596	13 885	12 561	1 323
1988	24 572	18 345	16 521	1 824	20 961	14 194	12 979	1 215
1989	24 831	18 738	16 936	1 801	21 141	14 377	13 175	1 202
1990	25 870	19 357	17 405	1 952	21 901	14 612	13 336	1 276
1991	26 197	19 411	17 011	2 400	22 173	14 681	13 198	1 482
1992	26 436	19 709	17 098	2 611	22 475	14 872	13 263	1 609
1993	26 570	19 706	17 261	2 445	22 713	15 031	13 484	1 547
1994	26 786	19 786	17 604	2 181	23 000	15 333	13 847	1 486
1995	26 918	19 841	17 833	2 007	23 151	15 467	14 053	1 413

TOTAL: MARRIED, SPOUSE PRESENT

Year	Men				Women			
	Civilian noninstitutional population	Civilian labor force			Civilian noninstitutional population	Civilian labor force		
		Total	Employed	Unemployed		Total	Employed	Unemployed
1976	48 856	40 224	38 516	1 709	48 845	22 139	20 562	1 577
1977	49 206	40 367	38 905	1 462	49 109	22 776	21 291	1 485
1978	49 386	40 402	39 267	1 135	49 221	23 539	22 239	1 300
1979	50 116	40 874	39 740	1 134	49 712	24 378	23 126	1 253
1980	50 300	40 713	39 004	1 709	50 110	24 980	23 532	1 448
1981	50 516	40 648	38 882	1 766	50 345	25 428	23 915	1 513
1982	50 891	40 706	38 074	2 632	50 783	25 971	24 053	1 918
1983	51 118	40 601	37 967	2 634	51 084	26 468	24 603	1 865
1984	51 732	40 952	39 056	1 896	51 557	27 199	25 636	1 562
1985	52 128	41 014	39 248	1 767	51 832	27 894	26 336	1 558
1986	52 769	41 477	39 658	1 819	52 158	28 623	27 144	1 479
1987	53 223	41 889	40 265	1 625	52 532	29 381	28 107	1 273
1988	53 246	41 832	40 472	1 360	52 775	29 921	28 756	1 166
1989	53 530	42 036	40 760	1 276	52 885	30 548	29 404	1 145
1990	53 793	42 275	40 829	1 446	52 917	30 901	29 714	1 188
1991	54 158	42 303	40 429	1 875	53 169	31 112	29 698	1 415
1992	54 509	42 491	40 341	2 150	53 501	31 700	30 100	1 600
1993	55 178	42 834	40 935	1 899	53 838	31 980	30 499	1 482
1994	55 560	43 005	41 414	1 592	54 155	32 888	31 536	1 352
1995	56 100	43 472	42 048	1 424	54 716	33 359	32 063	1 296

TOTAL: WIDOWED, DIVORCED, OR SEPARATED

Year	Men				Women			
	Civilian noninstitutional population	Civilian labor force			Civilian noninstitutional population	Civilian labor force		
		Total	Employed	Unemployed		Total	Employed	Unemployed
1976	6 210	3 942	3 558	385	17 667	7 156	6 535	620
1977	6 542	4 236	3 885	349	18 132	7 526	6 936	591
1978	6 952	4 600	4 298	302	18 748	8 025	7 469	556
1979	7 108	4 753	4 443	310	19 173	8 260	7 705	554
1980	7 556	5 104	4 667	437	19 804	8 643	8 017	626
1981	8 023	5 433	4 938	495	20 480	9 144	8 400	744
1982	8 222	5 587	4 892	695	20 831	9 324	8 438	886
1983	8 448	5 788	5 036	752	21 121	9 376	8 447	929
1984	8 640	5 886	5 335	551	21 592	9 644	8 835	809
1985	9 013	6 190	5 621	568	22 136	9 993	9 165	828
1986	9 367	6 392	5 827	565	22 518	10 277	9 491	787
1987	9 729	6 546	6 048	498	22 726	10 393	9 665	727
1988	10 039	6 751	6 280	471	23 020	10 627	9 962	665
1989	10 401	7 066	6 618	448	23 604	11 104	10 448	656
1990	10 714	7 378	6 871	508	23 968	11 315	10 639	676
1991	10 924	7 454	6 783	671	24 304	11 385	10 600	786
1992	11 325	7 763	7 001	762	24 559	11 570	10 689	881
1993	11 584	7 864	7 153	711	24 955	11 784	10 927	856
1994	12 008	8 026	7 432	594	25 304	12 018	11 227	791
1995	12 160	8 047	7 496	551	25 539	12 118	11 407	712

POPULATION, LABOR FORCE, AND EMPLOYMENT STATUS

Employment Status of the Civilian Noninstitutional Population by Marital Status, Sex, and Race, 1976-1995—Continued

(Thousands of persons)

WHITE: SINGLE

Year	Men				Women			
	Civilian noninstitutional population	Civilian labor force			Civilian noninstitutional population	Civilian labor force		
		Total	Employed	Unemployed		Total	Employed	Unemployed
1976	15 783	11 281	9 762	1 518	12 998	8 255	7 400	856
1977	16 345	11 910	10 524	1 386	13 541	8 773	7 898	876
1978	16 968	12 582	11 337	1 246	14 036	9 284	8 466	818
1979	17 388	12 968	11 720	1 247	14 456	9 705	8 896	809
1980	17 911	13 340	11 757	1 582	14 768	9 924	9 055	870
1981	18 215	13 571	11 831	1 740	14 990	10 115	9 152	963
1982	18 521	13 723	11 609	2 114	15 189	10 334	9 201	1 134
1983	18 934	14 074	11 991	2 084	15 342	10 413	9 352	1 061
1984	19 034	14 281	12 677	1 605	15 365	10 528	9 622	906
1985	19 100	14 426	12 875	1 550	15 472	10 705	9 828	877
1986	19 316	14 672	13 162	1 510	15 686	10 965	10 060	906
1987	19 526	14 850	13 449	1 401	15 990	11 196	10 382	815
1988	19 966	15 279	13 982	1 297	16 218	11 428	10 674	754
1989	20 076	15 511	14 249	1 263	16 289	11 474	10 741	734
1990	20 746	15 993	14 617	1 376	16 555	11 522	10 729	794
1991	20 899	15 989	14 233	1 756	16 569	11 497	10 557	939
1992	21 025	16 129	14 285	1 844	16 684	11 502	10 526	976
1993	20 974	16 033	14 303	1 730	16 768	11 613	10 633	980
1994	21 071	16 074	14 539	1 535	16 936	11 805	10 885	920
1995	21 132	16 080	14 674	1 406	17 046	11 830	10 967	864

WHITE: MARRIED, SPOUSE PRESENT

Year	Men				Women			
	Civilian noninstitutional population	Civilian labor force			Civilian noninstitutional population	Civilian labor force		
		Total	Employed	Unemployed		Total	Employed	Unemployed
1976	44 360	36 579	35 123	1 456	44 496	19 746	18 398	1 348
1977	44 664	36 675	35 443	1 231	44 686	20 295	19 038	1 257
1978	44 847	36 668	35 718	951	44 809	20 976	19 899	1 077
1979	45 439	37 052	36 116	938	45 189	21 747	20 692	1 056
1980	45 604	36 950	35 504	1 445	45 476	22 260	21 035	1 226
1981	45 802	36 880	35 407	1 473	45 720	22 716	21 446	1 270
1982	46 019	36 809	34 600	2 209	45 982	23 140	21 532	1 609
1983	46 099	36 631	34 416	2 215	46 226	23 585	22 018	1 567
1984	46 616	36 905	35 318	1 588	46 599	24 196	22 888	1 308
1985	46 925	36 934	35 472	1 462	46 728	24 777	23 468	1 308
1986	47 399	37 230	35 727	1 503	46 892	25 368	24 141	1 226
1987	47 690	37 486	36 127	1 359	47 180	26 014	24 969	1 045
1988	47 685	37 429	36 304	1 125	47 364	26 499	25 540	959
1989	47 883	37 589	36 545	1 044	47 382	27 030	26 083	947
1990	47 841	37 515	36 338	1 177	47 240	27 271	26 285	986
1991	48 137	37 507	35 923	1 585	47 456	27 479	26 290	1 189
1992	48 416	37 671	35 886	1 785	47 705	27 951	26 623	1 329
1993	48 937	37 953	36 396	1 557	47 944	28 221	26 993	1 228
1994	49 169	38 008	36 719	1 288	48 120	29 017	27 888	1 129
1995	49 597	38 376	37 211	1 165	48 497	29 360	28 290	1 070

WHITE: DIVORCED, WIDOWED, OR SEPARATED

Year	Men				Women			
	Civilian noninstitutional population	Civilian labor force			Civilian noninstitutional population	Civilian labor force		
		Total	Employed	Unemployed		Total	Employed	Unemployed
1976	4 987	3 173	2 889	285	14 481	5 733	5 281	452
1977	5 292	3 448	3 181	266	14 852	6 039	5 614	427
1978	5 586	3 704	3 491	215	15 367	6 418	6 027	391
1979	5 720	3 835	3 616	220	15 702	6 616	6 221	395
1980	6 119	4 183	3 866	317	16 245	6 943	6 499	444
1981	6 463	4 444	4 077	367	16 718	7 325	6 796	529
1982	6 671	4 600	4 078	522	17 059	7 535	6 883	653
1983	6 889	4 775	4 214	560	17 316	7 543	6 902	642
1984	7 073	4 875	4 467	407	17 660	7 706	7 148	558
1985	7 348	5 112	4 698	414	18 106	7 973	7 393	580
1986	7 675	5 315	4 896	420	18 463	8 251	7 675	576
1987	7 974	5 443	5 070	373	18 599	8 300	7 791	509
1988	8 204	5 608	5 265	344	18 758	8 512	8 047	464
1989	8 509	5 887	5 558	329	19 200	8 863	8 409	454
1990	8 782	6 131	5 748	382	19 461	9 016	8 544	471
1991	8 941	6 159	5 641	518	19 757	9 111	8 538	573
1992	9 210	6 368	5 788	580	19 931	9 216	8 561	654
1993	9 459	6 498	5 957	541	20 206	9 382	8 764	618
1994	9 819	6 644	6 193	451	20 439	9 533	8 965	569
1995	10 005	6 689	6 261	428	20 638	9 613	9 087	526

Employment Status of the Civilian Noninstitutional Population by Marital Status, Sex, and Race, 1976-1995—Continued

(Thousands of persons)

BLACK AND OTHER: SINGLE

Year	Men				Women			
	Civilian noninstitutional population	Civilian labor force			Civilian noninstitutional population	Civilian labor force		
		Total	Employed	Unemployed		Total	Employed	Unemployed
1976	2 911	1 726	1 301	425	2 880	1 433	1 117	315
1977	3 100	1 883	1 413	470	3 057	1 538	1 166	372
1978	3 270	2 037	1 578	457	3 328	1 783	1 395	388
1979	3 407	2 132	1 704	428	3 503	1 892	1 490	402
1980	3 630	2 296	1 758	538	3 666	1 941	1 512	428
1981	3 758	2 322	1 746	576	3 802	2 009	1 533	476
1982	3 889	2 434	1 695	739	3 946	2 126	1 564	560
1983	4 031	2 583	1 792	790	4 137	2 246	1 644	602
1984	4 199	2 716	2 022	693	4 263	2 339	1 822	517
1985	4 228	2 782	2 147	636	4 296	2 458	1 930	527
1986	4 346	2 881	2 245	636	4 427	2 547	2 011	536
1987	4 421	2 922	2 345	577	4 606	2 689	2 179	508
1988	4 606	3 066	2 539	527	4 743	2 766	2 305	461
1989	4 755	3 227	2 687	538	4 852	2 903	2 434	468
1990	5 124	3 364	2 788	576	5 346	3 090	2 607	482
1991	5 298	3 422	2 778	644	5 604	3 184	2 641	543
1992	5 411	3 580	2 813	767	5 791	3 370	2 737	633
1993	5 596	3 673	2 958	715	5 945	3 418	2 851	567
1994	5 715	3 712	3 065	646	6 064	3 528	2 962	566
1995	5 786	3 761	3 159	601	6 105	3 637	3 086	549

BLACK AND OTHER: MARRIED, SPOUSE PRESENT

Year	Men				Women			
	Civilian noninstitutional population	Civilian labor force			Civilian noninstitutional population	Civilian labor force		
		Total	Employed	Unemployed		Total	Employed	Unemployed
1976	4 496	3 645	3 393	253	4 349	2 393	2 164	229
1977	4 542	3 692	3 462	231	4 423	2 481	2 253	228
1978	4 539	3 734	3 549	184	4 412	2 563	2 340	223
1979	4 677	3 822	3 624	196	4 523	2 631	2 434	197
1980	4 696	3 763	3 500	264	4 634	2 720	2 497	222
1981	4 714	3 768	3 475	293	4 625	2 712	2 469	243
1982	4 872	3 897	3 474	423	4 801	2 831	2 521	309
1983	5 019	3 970	3 551	419	4 858	2 883	2 585	298
1984	5 116	4 047	3 738	308	4 958	3 003	2 748	254
1985	5 203	4 080	3 776	305	5 104	3 117	2 868	250
1986	5 370	4 247	3 931	316	5 266	3 255	3 003	253
1987	5 533	4 403	4 138	266	5 352	3 367	3 138	228
1988	5 561	4 403	4 168	235	5 411	3 422	3 216	207
1989	5 647	4 447	4 215	232	5 503	3 518	3 321	198
1990	5 952	4 760	4 491	269	5 677	3 630	3 429	202
1991	6 021	4 796	4 506	290	5 713	3 633	3 408	226
1992	6 093	4 820	4 455	365	5 796	3 749	3 477	271
1993	6 241	4 881	4 539	342	5 894	3 759	3 506	254
1994	6 391	4 997	4 695	304	6 035	3 871	3 648	223
1995	6 503	5 096	4 837	259	6 219	3 999	3 773	226

BLACK AND OTHER: DIVORCED, WIDOWED, OR SEPARATED

Year	Men				Women			
	Civilian noninstitutional population	Civilian labor force			Civilian noninstitutional population	Civilian labor force		
		Total	Employed	Unemployed		Total	Employed	Unemployed
1976	1 223	769	669	100	3 186	1 423	1 254	168
1977	1 250	788	704	83	3 280	1 487	1 322	164
1978	1 366	896	807	87	3 381	1 607	1 442	165
1979	1 388	918	827	90	3 471	1 644	1 484	159
1980	1 437	921	801	120	3 559	1 700	1 518	182
1981	1 560	989	861	128	3 762	1 819	1 604	215
1982	1 551	987	814	173	3 772	1 789	1 555	233
1983	1 559	1 013	822	192	3 805	1 833	1 545	287
1984	1 567	1 011	868	144	3 932	1 938	1 687	251
1985	1 665	1 078	923	154	4 030	2 020	1 772	248
1986	1 692	1 077	931	145	4 055	2 026	1 816	211
1987	1 755	1 103	978	125	4 127	2 093	1 874	218
1988	1 835	1 143	1 015	127	4 262	2 115	1 915	201
1989	1 892	1 179	1 060	119	4 404	2 241	2 039	202
1990	1 932	1 247	1 123	126	4 507	2 299	2 095	205
1991	1 983	1 295	1 142	153	4 547	2 274	2 062	213
1992	2 115	1 395	1 213	182	4 628	2 354	2 128	227
1993	2 125	1 366	1 196	170	4 749	2 402	2 163	238
1994	2 189	4 568	1 239	143	4 865	2 485	2 262	222
1995	2 155	4 671	1 235	123	4 901	2 505	2 320	186

NOTE: Data beginning in 1994 are not strictly comparable with data for 1993 and earlier years because of the introduction of a major redesign of the survey and collection methodology. Beginning in 1990, data are not strictly comparable with previous years because of the introduction of 1990 census-based population controls adjusted for the estimated undercount.

POPULATION, LABOR FORCE, AND EMPLOYMENT STATUS

Civilian Noninstitutional Population by Sex, Race, Hispanic Origin, and Age, 1948-1995

(Thousands of persons)

Year, sex, race, and Hispanic origin	16 years and over	16 to 19 years			20 years and over						
		Total	16 to 17 years	18 to 19 years	Total	20 to 24 years	25 to 34 years	35 to 44 years	45 to 54 years	55 to 64 years	65 years and over
TOTAL											
1948	103 068	8 449	4 265	4 185	94 618	11 530	22 610	20 097	16 771	12 885	10 720
1949	103 994	8 215	4 139	4 079	95 778	11 312	22 822	20 401	17 002	13 201	11 035
1950	104 995	8 143	4 076	4 068	96 851	11 080	23 013	20 681	17 240	13 469	11 363
1951	104 621	7 865	4 096	3 771	96 755	10 167	22 843	20 863	17 464	13 692	11 724
1952	105 231	7 922	4 234	3 689	97 305	9 389	23 044	21 137	17 716	13 889	12 126
1953	107 056	8 014	4 241	3 773	99 041	8 960	23 266	21 922	17 991	13 830	13 075
1954	108 321	8 224	4 336	3 889	100 095	8 885	23 304	22 135	18 305	14 085	13 375
1955	109 683	8 364	4 440	3 925	101 318	9 036	23 249	22 348	18 643	14 309	13 728
1956	110 954	8 434	4 482	3 953	102 518	9 271	23 072	22 567	19 012	14 516	14 075
1957	112 265	8 612	4 587	4 026	103 653	9 486	22 849	22 786	19 424	14 727	14 376
1958	113 727	8 986	4 872	4 114	104 737	9 733	22 563	23 025	19 832	14 923	14 657
1959	115 329	9 618	5 337	4 282	105 711	9 975	22 201	23 207	20 203	15 134	14 985
1960	117 245	10 187	5 573	4 615	107 056	10 273	21 998	23 437	20 601	15 409	15 336
1961	118 771	10 513	5 462	5 052	108 255	10 583	21 829	23 585	20 893	15 675	15 685
1962	120 153	10 652	5 503	5 150	109 500	10 852	21 503	23 797	20 916	15 874	16 554
1963	122 416	11 370	6 301	5 070	111 045	11 464	21 400	23 948	21 144	16 138	16 945
1964	124 485	12 111	6 974	5 139	112 372	12 017	21 367	23 940	21 452	16 442	17 150
1965	126 513	12 930	6 936	5 995	113 582	12 442	21 417	23 832	21 728	16 727	17 432
1966	128 058	13 592	6 914	6 679	114 463	12 638	21 543	23 579	21 977	17 007	17 715
1967	129 874	13 480	7 003	6 480	116 391	13 421	22 057	23 313	22 256	17 310	18 029
1968	132 028	13 698	7 200	6 499	118 328	13 891	22 912	23 036	22 534	17 614	18 338
1969	134 335	14 095	7 422	6 673	120 238	14 488	23 645	22 709	22 806	17 930	18 657
1970	137 085	14 519	7 643	6 876	122 566	15 323	24 435	22 489	23 059	18 250	19 007
1971	140 216	15 022	7 849	7 173	125 193	16 345	25 337	22 274	23 244	18 581	19 406
1972	144 126	15 510	8 076	7 435	128 614	17 143	26 740	22 358	23 338	19 007	20 023
1973	147 096	15 840	8 227	7 613	131 253	17 692	28 172	22 287	23 431	19 281	20 389
1974	150 120	16 180	8 373	7 809	133 938	17 994	29 439	22 461	23 578	19 517	20 945
1975	153 153	16 418	8 419	7 999	136 733	18 595	30 710	22 526	23 535	19 844	21 525
1976	156 150	16 614	8 442	8 171	139 536	19 109	31 953	22 796	23 409	20 185	22 083
1977	159 033	16 688	8 482	8 206	142 345	19 582	33 117	23 296	23 197	20 557	22 597
1978	161 910	16 695	8 484	8 211	145 216	20 007	34 091	24 099	22 977	20 875	23 166
1979	164 863	16 657	8 389	8 268	148 205	20 353	35 261	24 861	22 752	21 210	23 767
1980	167 745	16 543	8 279	8 264	151 202	20 635	36 558	25 578	22 563	21 520	24 350
1981	170 130	16 214	8 068	8 145	153 916	20 820	37 777	26 291	22 422	21 756	24 850
1982	172 271	15 763	7 714	8 049	156 508	20 845	38 492	27 611	22 264	21 909	25 387
1983	174 215	15 274	7 385	7 889	158 941	20 799	39 147	28 932	22 167	22 003	25 892
1984	176 383	14 735	7 196	7 538	161 648	20 688	39 999	30 251	22 226	22 052	26 433
1985	178 206	14 506	7 232	7 274	163 700	20 097	40 670	31 379	22 418	22 140	26 997
1986	180 587	14 496	7 386	7 110	166 091	19 569	41 731	32 550	22 732	22 011	27 497
1987	182 753	14 606	7 501	7 104	168 147	18 970	42 297	33 755	23 183	21 835	28 108
1988	184 613	14 527	7 284	7 243	170 085	18 434	42 611	34 784	24 004	21 641	28 612
1989	186 393	14 223	6 886	7 338	172 169	18 025	42 845	35 977	24 744	21 406	29 173
1990	189 164	14 520	6 893	7 626	174 644	18 902	42 976	37 719	25 081	20 719	29 247
1991	190 925	14 073	6 901	7 173	176 852	18 963	42 688	39 116	25 709	20 675	29 700
1992	192 805	13 840	6 907	6 933	178 965	18 846	42 278	39 852	27 206	20 604	30 179
1993	194 838	13 935	7 010	6 925	180 903	18 642	41 771	40 733	28 549	20 574	30 634
1994	196 814	14 196	7 245	6 951	182 619	18 353	41 306	41 534	29 778	20 635	31 012
1995	198 584	14 511	7 407	7 104	184 073	17 864	40 798	42 254	30 974	20 735	31 448

Civilian Noninstitutional Population by Sex, Race, Hispanic Origin, and Age, 1948-1995—Continued

(Thousands of persons)

Year, sex, race, and Hispanic origin	16 years and over	16 to 19 years			20 years and over						
		Total	16 to 17 years	18 to 19 years	Total	20 to 24 years	25 to 34 years	35 to 44 years	45 to 54 years	55 to 64 years	65 years and over
MEN											
1948	49 996	4 078	2 128	1 951	45 918	5 527	10 767	9 798	8 290	6 441	5 093
1949	50 321	3 946	2 062	1 884	46 378	5 405	10 871	9 926	8 379	6 568	5 226
1950	50 725	3 962	2 043	1 920	46 763	5 270	10 963	10 034	8 472	6 664	5 357
1951	49 727	3 725	2 039	1 687	46 001	4 451	10 709	10 049	8 551	6 737	5 503
1952	49 700	3 767	2 121	1 647	45 932	3 788	10 855	10 164	8 655	6 798	5 670
1953	50 750	3 823	2 122	1 701	46 927	3 482	11 020	10 632	8 878	6 798	6 119
1954	51 395	3 953	2 174	1 780	47 441	3 509	11 067	10 718	9 018	6 885	6 241
1955	52 109	4 022	2 225	1 798	48 086	3 708	11 068	10 804	9 164	6 960	6 380
1956	52 723	4 020	2 238	1 783	48 704	3 970	10 983	10 889	9 322	7 032	6 505
1957	53 315	4 083	2 284	1 800	49 231	4 166	10 889	10 965	9 499	7 109	6 602
1958	54 033	4 293	2 435	1 858	49 740	4 339	10 787	11 076	9 675	7 179	6 683
1959	54 793	4 652	2 681	1 971	50 140	4 488	10 625	11 149	9 832	7 259	6 785
1960	55 662	4 963	2 805	2 159	50 698	4 679	10 514	11 230	10 000	7 373	6 901
1961	56 286	5 112	2 742	2 371	51 173	4 844	10 440	11 286	10 112	7 483	7 006
1962	56 831	5 150	2 764	2 386	51 681	4 925	10 207	11 389	10 162	7 610	7 386
1963	57 921	5 496	3 162	2 334	52 425	5 240	10 165	11 476	10 274	7 740	7 526
1964	58 847	5 866	3 503	2 364	52 981	5 520	10 144	11 466	10 402	7 873	7 574
1965	59 782	6 318	3 488	2 831	53 463	5 701	10 182	11 427	10 512	7 990	7 649
1966	60 262	6 658	3 478	3 180	53 603	5 663	10 224	11 294	10 598	8 099	7 723
1967	60 905	6 537	3 528	3 010	54 367	5 977	10 495	11 161	10 705	8 218	7 809
1968	61 847	6 683	3 634	3 049	55 165	6 127	10 944	11 040	10 819	8 336	7 897
1969	62 898	6 928	3 741	3 187	55 969	6 379	11 309	10 890	10 935	8 464	7 990
1970	64 304	7 145	3 848	3 299	57 157	6 861	11 750	10 810	11 052	8 590	8 093
1971	65 942	7 430	3 954	3 477	58 511	7 511	12 227	10 721	11 129	8 711	8 208
1972	67 835	7 705	4 081	3 624	60 130	8 061	12 911	10 762	11 167	8 895	8 330
1973	69 292	7 855	4 152	3 703	61 436	8 429	13 641	10 746	11 202	8 990	8 426
1974	70 808	8 012	4 231	3 781	62 796	8 600	14 262	10 834	11 315	9 140	8 641
1975	72 291	8 134	4 252	3 882	64 158	8 950	14 899	10 874	11 298	9 286	8 852
1976	73 759	8 244	4 266	3 978	65 515	9 237	15 528	11 010	11 243	9 444	9 053
1977	75 193	8 288	4 290	4 000	66 904	9 477	16 108	11 260	11 144	9 616	9 297
1978	76 576	8 309	4 295	4 014	68 268	9 693	16 598	11 665	11 045	9 758	9 509
1979	78 020	8 310	4 251	4 060	69 709	9 873	17 193	12 046	10 944	9 907	9 746
1980	79 398	8 260	4 195	4 064	71 138	10 023	17 833	12 400	10 861	10 042	9 979
1981	80 511	8 092	4 087	4 005	72 419	10 116	18 427	12 758	10 797	10 151	10 170
1982	81 523	7 879	3 911	3 968	73 644	10 136	18 787	13 410	10 726	10 215	10 371
1983	82 531	7 659	3 750	3 908	74 872	10 140	19 143	14 067	10 689	10 261	10 573
1984	83 605	7 386	3 655	3 731	76 219	10 108	19 596	14 719	10 724	10 285	10 788
1985	84 469	7 275	3 689	3 586	77 195	9 746	19 864	15 265	10 844	10 392	11 084
1986	85 798	7 275	3 768	3 507	78 523	9 498	20 498	15 858	10 986	10 336	11 347
1987	86 899	7 335	3 824	3 510	79 565	9 195	20 781	16 475	11 215	10 267	11 632
1988	87 857	7 304	3 715	3 588	80 553	8 931	20 937	17 008	11 625	10 193	11 859
1989	88 762	7 143	3 524	3 619	81 619	8 743	21 080	17 590	11 981	10 092	12 134
1990	90 377	7 347	3 534	3 813	83 030	9 320	21 117	18 529	12 238	9 778	12 049
1991	91 278	7 134	3 548	3 586	84 144	9 367	20 977	19 213	12 554	9 780	12 254
1992	92 270	7 023	3 542	3 481	85 247	9 326	20 792	19 585	13 271	9 776	12 496
1993	93 332	7 076	3 595	3 481	86 256	9 216	20 569	20 037	13 944	9 773	12 717
1994	94 355	7 203	3 718	3 486	87 151	9 074	20 361	20 443	14 545	9 810	12 918
1995	95 178	7 367	3 794	3 573	87 811	8 835	20 079	20 800	15 111	9 856	13 130

Civilian Noninstitutional Population by Sex, Race, Hispanic Origin, and Age, 1948-1995—Continued

(Thousands of persons)

Year, sex, race, and Hispanic origin	16 years and over	16 to 19 years			20 years and over						
		Total	16 to 17 years	18 to 19 years	Total	20 to 24 years	25 to 34 years	35 to 44 years	45 to 54 years	55 to 64 years	65 years and over
WOMEN											
1948	53 071	4 371	2 137	2 234	48 700	6 003	11 843	10 299	8 481	6 444	5 627
1949	53 670	4 269	2 077	2 195	49 400	5 907	11 951	10 475	8 623	6 633	5 809
1950	54 270	4 181	2 033	2 148	50 088	5 810	12 050	10 647	8 768	6 805	6 006
1951	54 895	4 140	2 057	2 084	50 754	5 716	12 134	10 814	8 913	6 955	6 221
1952	55 529	4 155	2 113	2 042	51 373	5 601	12 189	10 973	9 061	7 091	6 456
1953	56 305	4 191	2 119	2 072	52 114	5 478	12 246	11 290	9 113	7 032	6 956
1954	56 925	4 271	2 162	2 109	52 654	5 376	12 237	11 417	9 287	7 200	7 134
1955	57 574	4 342	2 215	2 127	53 232	5 328	12 181	11 544	9 479	7 349	7 348
1956	58 228	4 414	2 244	2 170	53 814	5 301	12 089	11 678	9 690	7 484	7 570
1957	58 951	4 529	2 303	2 226	54 421	5 320	11 960	11 821	9 925	7 618	7 774
1958	59 690	4 693	2 437	2 256	54 997	5 394	11 776	11 949	10 157	7 744	7 974
1959	60 534	4 966	2 656	2 311	55 570	5 487	11 576	12 058	10 371	7 875	8 200
1960	61 582	5 224	2 768	2 456	56 358	5 594	11 484	12 207	10 601	8 036	8 435
1961	62 484	5 401	2 720	2 681	57 082	5 739	11 389	12 299	10 781	8 192	8 679
1962	63 321	5 502	2 739	2 764	57 819	5 927	11 296	12 408	10 754	8 264	9 168
1963	64 494	5 874	3 139	2 736	58 620	6 224	11 235	12 472	10 870	8 398	9 419
1964	65 637	6 245	3 471	2 775	59 391	6 497	11 223	12 474	11 050	8 569	9 576
1965	66 731	6 612	3 448	3 164	60 119	6 741	11 235	12 405	11 216	8 737	9 783
1966	67 795	6 934	3 436	3 499	60 860	6 975	11 319	12 285	11 379	8 908	9 992
1967	68 968	6 943	3 475	3 470	62 026	7 445	11 562	12 152	11 551	9 092	10 220
1968	70 179	7 015	3 566	3 450	63 164	7 764	11 968	11 996	11 715	9 278	10 441
1969	71 436	7 167	3 681	3 486	64 269	8 109	12 336	11 819	11 871	9 466	10 667
1970	72 782	7 373	3 796	3 578	65 408	8 462	12 684	11 679	12 008	9 659	10 914
1971	74 274	7 591	3 895	3 697	66 682	8 834	13 110	11 553	12 115	9 870	11 198
1972	76 290	7 805	3 994	3 811	68 484	9 082	13 829	11 597	12 171	10 113	11 693
1973	77 804	7 985	4 076	3 909	69 819	9 263	14 531	11 541	12 229	10 290	11 963
1974	79 312	8 168	4 142	4 028	71 144	9 393	15 177	11 627	12 263	10 377	12 304
1975	80 860	8 285	4 168	4 117	72 576	9 645	15 811	11 652	12 237	10 558	12 673
1976	82 390	8 370	4 176	4 194	74 020	9 872	16 425	11 786	12 166	10 742	13 030
1977	83 840	8 400	4 193	4 206	75 441	10 103	17 008	12 036	12 053	10 940	13 300
1978	85 334	8 386	4 189	4 197	76 948	10 315	17 493	12 435	11 932	11 118	13 658
1979	86 843	8 347	4 139	4 208	78 496	10 480	18 070	12 815	11 808	11 303	14 021
1980	88 348	8 283	4 083	4 200	80 065	10 612	18 725	13 177	11 701	11 478	14 372
1981	89 618	8 121	3 981	4 140	81 497	10 705	19 350	13 533	11 625	11 605	14 680
1982	90 748	7 884	3 804	4 081	82 864	10 709	19 705	14 201	11 538	11 694	15 017
1983	91 684	7 616	3 635	3 981	84 069	10 660	20 004	14 865	11 478	11 742	15 319
1984	92 778	7 349	3 542	3 807	85 429	10 580	20 403	15 532	11 501	11 768	15 645
1985	93 736	7 231	3 543	3 688	86 506	10 351	20 805	16 114	11 574	11 748	15 913
1986	94 789	7 221	3 618	3 603	87 567	10 072	21 233	16 692	11 746	11 675	16 150
1987	95 853	7 271	3 677	3 594	88 583	9 776	21 516	17 279	11 968	11 567	16 476
1988	96 756	7 224	3 569	3 655	89 532	9 503	21 674	17 776	12 378	11 448	16 753
1989	97 630	7 080	3 361	3 719	90 550	9 282	21 765	18 387	12 763	11 314	17 039
1990	98 787	7 173	3 359	3 813	91 614	9 582	21 859	19 190	12 843	10 941	17 198
1991	99 646	6 939	3 353	3 586	92 708	9 597	21 711	19 903	13 155	10 895	17 446
1992	100 535	6 818	3 366	3 452	93 718	9 520	21 486	20 267	13 935	10 828	17 682
1993	101 506	6 859	3 415	3 444	94 647	9 426	21 202	20 696	14 605	10 801	17 917
1994	102 460	6 993	3 528	3 465	95 467	9 279	20 945	21 091	15 233	10 825	18 094
1995	103 406	7 144	3 613	3 531	96 262	9 029	20 719	21 454	15 862	10 879	18 318

Civilian Noninstitutional Population by Sex, Race, Hispanic Origin, and Age, 1948-1995—Continued

(Thousands of persons)

Year, sex, race, and Hispanic origin	16 years and over	16 to 19 years			20 years and over						
		Total	16 to 17 years	18 to 19 years	Total	20 to 24 years	25 to 34 years	35 to 44 years	45 to 54 years	55 to 64 years	65 years and over
WHITE											
1954	97 705	7 180	3 786	3 394	90 524	7 794	20 818	19 915	16 569	12 993	12 438
1955	98 880	7 292	3 874	3 419	91 586	7 912	20 742	20 110	16 869	13 169	12 785
1956	99 976	7 346	3 908	3 438	92 629	8 106	20 564	20 314	17 198	13 341	13 105
1957	101 119	7 505	4 007	3 498	93 612	8 293	20 342	20 514	17 562	13 518	13 383
1958	102 392	7 843	4 271	3 573	94 547	8 498	20 063	20 734	17 924	13 681	13 645
1959	103 803	8 430	4 707	3 725	95 370	8 697	19 715	20 893	18 257	13 858	13 951
1960	105 282	8 924	4 909	4 016	96 355	8 927	19 470	21 049	18 578	14 070	14 260
1961	106 604	9 211	4 785	4 427	97 390	9 203	19 289	21 169	18 845	14 304	14 581
1962	107 715	9 343	4 818	4 526	98 371	9 484	18 974	21 293	18 872	14 450	15 297
1963	109 705	9 978	5 549	4 430	99 725	10 069	18 867	21 398	19 082	14 681	15 629
1964	111 534	10 616	6 137	4 481	100 916	10 568	18 838	21 375	19 360	14 957	15 816
1965	113 284	11 319	6 049	5 271	101 963	10 935	18 882	21 258	19 604	15 215	16 070
1966	114 566	11 862	5 993	5 870	102 702	11 094	18 989	21 005	19 822	15 469	16 322
1967	116 100	11 682	6 051	5 632	104 417	11 797	19 464	20 745	20 067	15 745	16 602
1968	117 948	11 840	6 225	5 616	106 107	12 184	20 245	20 474	20 310	16 018	16 875
1969	119 913	12 179	6 418	5 761	107 733	12 677	20 892	20 156	20 546	16 305	17 156
1970	122 174	12 521	6 591	5 931	109 652	13 359	21 546	19 929	20 760	16 591	17 469
1971	124 758	12 937	6 750	6 189	111 821	14 208	22 295	19 694	20 907	16 884	17 833
1972	127 906	13 301	6 910	6 392	114 603	14 897	23 555	19 673	20 950	17 250	18 278
1973	130 097	13 533	7 021	6 512	116 563	15 264	24 685	19 532	20 991	17 484	18 607
1974	132 417	13 784	7 114	6 671	118 632	15 502	25 711	19 628	21 061	17 645	19 085
1975	134 790	13 941	7 132	6 808	120 849	15 980	26 746	19 641	20 981	17 918	19 587
1976	137 106	14 055	7 125	6 930	123 050	16 368	27 757	19 827	20 816	18 220	20 064
1977	139 380	14 095	7 150	6 944	125 285	16 728	28 703	20 231	20 575	18 540	20 508
1978	141 612	14 060	7 132	6 928	127 552	17 038	29 453	20 932	20 322	18 799	21 007
1979	143 894	13 994	7 029	6 964	129 900	17 284	30 371	21 579	20 058	19 071	21 538
1980	146 122	13 854	6 912	6 943	132 268	17 484	31 407	22 174	19 837	19 316	22 050
1981	147 908	13 516	6 704	6 813	134 392	17 609	32 367	22 778	19 666	19 485	22 487
1982	149 441	13 076	6 383	6 693	136 366	17 579	32 863	23 910	19 478	19 591	22 945
1983	150 805	12 623	6 089	6 534	138 183	17 492	33 286	25 027	19 349	19 625	23 403
1984	152 347	12 147	5 918	6 228	140 200	17 304	33 889	26 124	19 348	19 629	23 906
1985	153 679	11 900	5 922	5 978	141 780	16 853	34 450	27 100	19 405	19 620	24 352
1986	155 432	11 879	6 036	5 843	143 553	16 353	35 293	28 062	19 587	19 477	24 780
1987	156 958	11 939	6 110	5 829	145 020	15 808	35 667	29 036	19 965	19 242	25 301
1988	158 194	11 838	5 893	5 945	146 357	15 276	35 876	29 818	20 652	18 996	25 739
1989	159 338	11 530	5 506	6 023	147 809	14 879	35 951	30 774	21 287	18 743	26 175
1990	160 625	11 630	5 464	6 166	148 996	15 538	35 661	31 739	21 535	18 204	26 319
1991	161 759	11 200	5 451	5 749	150 558	15 516	35 342	32 854	22 052	18 074	26 721
1992	162 972	11 004	5 478	5 526	151 968	15 354	34 885	33 305	23 364	17 951	27 108
1993	164 289	11 078	5 562	5 516	153 210	15 087	34 365	33 919	24 456	17 892	27 493
1994	165 555	11 264	5 710	5 554	154 291	14 708	33 865	34 582	25 435	17 924	27 776
1995	166 914	11 468	5 822	5 646	155 446	14 313	33 355	35 222	26 418	17 986	28 153

POPULATION, LABOR FORCE, AND EMPLOYMENT STATUS

Civilian Noninstitutional Population by Sex, Race, Hispanic Origin, and Age, 1948-1995—Continued

(Thousands of persons)

Year, sex, race, and Hispanic origin	16 years and over	16 to 19 years			20 years and over						
		Total	16 to 17 years	18 to 19 years	Total	20 to 24 years	25 to 34 years	35 to 44 years	45 to 54 years	55 to 64 years	65 years and over
WHITE MEN											
1954	46 462	3 455	1 902	1 553	43 007	3 074	9 948	9 688	8 172	6 341	5 787
1955	47 076	3 507	1 945	1 563	43 569	3 241	9 936	9 768	8 303	6 398	5 923
1956	47 602	3 500	1 955	1 546	44 102	3 464	9 851	9 848	8 446	6 455	6 038
1957	48 119	3 556	2 000	1 557	44 563	3 638	9 758	9 917	8 605	6 518	6 127
1958	48 745	3 747	2 140	1 607	44 998	3 783	9 656	10 018	8 765	6 574	6 203
1959	49 408	4 079	2 370	1 710	45 329	3 903	9 499	10 081	8 909	6 639	6 298
1960	50 065	4 349	2 476	1 874	45 716	4 054	9 373	10 131	9 042	6 721	6 395
1961	50 608	4 479	2 407	2 073	46 129	4 204	9 290	10 178	9 148	6 819	6 490
1962	51 054	4 520	2 426	2 094	46 534	4 306	9 080	10 239	9 191	6 917	6 801
1963	52 031	4 827	2 792	2 036	47 204	4 610	9 039	10 309	9 297	7 031	6 919
1964	52 869	5 148	3 090	2 059	47 721	4 862	9 024	10 301	9 417	7 153	6 963
1965	53 681	5 541	3 050	2 492	48 140	5 017	9 056	10 262	9 516	7 261	7 028
1966	54 061	5 820	3 023	2 798	48 241	4 974	9 085	10 136	9 592	7 362	7 092
1967	54 608	5 671	3 058	2 613	48 937	5 257	9 339	10 013	9 688	7 474	7 167
1968	55 434	5 787	3 153	2 635	49 647	5 376	9 752	9 902	9 790	7 585	7 242
1969	56 348	6 005	3 246	2 759	50 343	5 589	10 074	9 760	9 895	7 705	7 320
1970	57 516	6 179	3 329	2 851	51 336	5 988	10 441	9 678	9 999	7 822	7 409
1971	58 900	6 420	3 412	3 008	52 481	6 546	10 841	9 578	10 066	7 933	7 517
1972	60 473	6 627	3 503	3 125	53 845	7 042	11 495	9 568	10 078	8 089	7 573
1973	61 577	6 737	3 555	3 182	54 842	7 312	12 075	9 514	10 099	8 178	7 664
1974	62 791	6 851	3 604	3 247	55 942	7 476	12 599	9 564	10 165	8 288	7 849
1975	63 981	6 929	3 609	3 320	57 052	7 766	13 131	9 578	10 134	8 413	8 031
1976	65 132	6 993	3 609	3 384	58 138	7 987	13 655	9 674	10 063	8 556	8 203
1977	66 301	7 024	3 625	3 399	59 278	8 175	14 139	9 880	9 957	8 708	8 420
1978	67 401	7 022	3 619	3 404	60 378	8 335	14 528	10 236	9 845	8 826	8 608
1979	68 547	7 007	3 568	3 439	61 540	8 470	15 008	10 563	9 730	8 949	8 820
1980	69 634	6 941	3 508	3 433	62 694	8 581	15 529	10 863	9 636	9 059	9 027
1981	70 480	6 764	3 401	3 363	63 715	8 644	16 005	11 171	9 560	9 139	9 195
1982	71 211	6 556	3 249	3 307	64 655	8 621	16 260	11 756	9 463	9 188	9 367
1983	71 922	6 340	3 098	3 242	65 581	8 597	16 499	12 314	9 408	9 208	9 556
1984	72 723	6 113	3 019	3 094	66 610	8 522	16 816	12 853	9 434	9 217	9 768
1985	73 373	5 987	3 026	2 961	67 386	8 246	17 042	13 337	9 488	9 262	10 010
1986	74 390	5 977	3 084	2 894	68 413	8 002	17 564	13 840	9 578	9 201	10 229
1987	75 189	6 015	3 125	2 890	69 175	7 729	17 754	14 338	9 771	9 101	10 481
1988	75 855	5 968	3 015	2 953	69 887	7 473	17 867	14 743	10 114	9 001	10 688
1989	76 468	5 813	2 817	2 996	70 654	7 279	17 908	15 237	10 434	8 900	10 897
1990	77 369	5 913	2 809	3 103	71 457	7 764	17 766	15 770	10 598	8 680	10 879
1991	77 977	5 704	2 805	2 899	72 274	7 748	17 615	16 340	10 856	8 640	11 074
1992	78 651	5 611	2 819	2 792	73 040	7 676	17 403	16 579	11 513	8 602	11 268
1993	79 371	5 650	2 862	2 788	73 721	7 545	17 158	16 900	12 058	8 590	11 470
1994	80 059	5 748	2 938	2 810	74 311	7 357	16 915	17 247	12 545	8 618	11 629
1995	80 733	5 854	2 995	2 859	74 879	7 163	16 653	17 567	13 028	8 653	11 815
WHITE WOMEN											
1954	51 242	3 725	1 884	1 841	47 517	4 720	10 870	10 227	8 397	6 652	6 651
1955	51 802	3 785	1 929	1 856	48 017	4 671	10 806	10 342	8 566	6 771	6 862
1956	52 373	3 846	1 953	1 892	48 527	4 642	10 713	10 466	8 752	6 886	7 067
1957	52 998	3 949	2 007	1 941	49 049	4 655	10 584	10 597	8 957	7 000	7 256
1958	53 645	4 096	2 131	1 966	49 549	4 715	10 407	10 716	9 159	7 107	7 442
1959	54 392	4 351	2 337	2 015	50 041	4 794	10 216	10 812	9 348	7 219	7 653
1960	55 214	4 575	2 433	2 142	50 639	4 873	10 097	10 918	9 536	7 349	7 865
1961	55 993	4 732	2 378	2 354	51 261	4 999	9 999	10 991	9 697	7 485	8 091
1962	56 660	4 823	2 392	2 432	51 837	5 178	9 894	11 054	9 681	7 533	8 496
1963	57 672	5 151	2 757	2 394	52 521	5 459	9 828	11 089	9 785	7 650	8 710
1964	58 663	5 468	3 047	2 422	53 195	5 706	9 814	11 074	9 943	7 804	8 853
1965	59 601	5 778	2 999	2 779	53 823	5 918	9 826	10 996	10 088	7 954	9 042
1966	60 503	6 042	2 970	3 072	54 461	6 120	9 904	10 869	10 230	8 107	9 230
1967	61 491	6 011	2 993	3 019	55 480	6 540	10 125	10 732	10 379	8 271	9 435
1968	62 512	6 053	3 072	2 981	56 460	6 809	10 493	10 572	10 520	8 433	9 633
1969	63 563	6 174	3 172	3 002	57 390	7 089	10 818	10 396	10 651	8 600	9 836
1970	64 656	6 342	3 262	3 080	58 315	7 370	11 105	10 251	10 761	8 769	10 060
1971	65 857	6 518	3 338	3 180	59 340	7 662	11 454	10 117	10 841	8 951	10 315
1972	67 431	6 673	3 407	3 267	60 758	7 855	12 060	10 105	10 872	9 161	10 705
1973	68 517	6 796	3 466	3 331	61 721	7 951	12 610	10 018	10 891	9 306	10 943
1974	69 623	6 933	3 510	3 424	62 690	8 026	13 112	10 064	10 896	9 356	11 236
1975	70 810	7 011	3 523	3 488	63 798	8 214	13 615	10 063	10 847	9 505	11 556
1976	71 974	7 062	3 516	3 546	64 912	8 381	14 102	10 153	10 752	9 664	11 860
1977	73 077	7 071	3 525	3 545	66 007	8 553	14 564	10 351	10 618	9 832	12 088
1978	74 213	7 038	3 513	3 524	67 174	8 704	14 926	10 696	10 476	9 974	12 399
1979	75 347	6 987	3 460	3 527	68 360	8 815	15 363	11 017	10 327	10 122	12 717
1980	76 489	6 914	3 403	3 511	69 575	8 904	15 878	11 313	10 201	10 256	13 022
1981	77 428	6 752	3 303	3 449	70 677	8 965	16 362	11 606	10 106	10 346	13 292
1982	78 230	6 519	3 134	3 385	71 711	8 959	16 603	12 154	10 015	10 402	13 579
1983	78 884	6 282	2 991	3 292	72 601	8 895	16 788	12 714	9 941	10 418	13 847
1984	79 624	6 034	2 899	3 135	73 590	8 782	17 073	13 271	9 914	10 412	14 138
1985	80 306	5 912	2 895	3 017	74 394	8 607	17 409	13 762	9 917	10 358	14 342
1986	81 042	5 902	2 953	2 949	75 140	8 351	17 728	14 223	10 009	10 277	14 551
1987	81 769	5 924	2 985	2 939	75 845	8 079	17 913	14 698	10 194	10 141	14 820
1988	82 340	5 869	2 878	2 991	76 470	7 804	18 009	15 074	10 537	9 994	15 052
1989	82 871	5 716	2 690	3 027	77 154	7 600	18 043	15 537	10 853	9 843	15 278
1990	83 256	5 717	2 654	3 063	77 539	7 774	17 895	15 969	10 937	9 524	15 440
1991	83 781	5 497	2 646	2 850	78 285	7 768	17 726	16 514	11 196	9 435	15 647
1992	84 321	5 393	2 659	2 734	78 928	7 678	17 482	16 727	11 851	9 350	15 841
1993	84 918	5 428	2 700	2 728	79 490	7 542	17 206	17 019	12 398	9 302	16 023
1994	85 496	5 516	2 772	2 744	79 980	7 351	16 950	17 335	12 890	9 306	16 148
1995	86 181	5 614	2 827	2 787	80 567	7 150	16 702	17 654	13 390	9 333	16 337

Civilian Noninstitutional Population by Sex, Race, Hispanic Origin, and Age, 1948-1995—Continued

(Thousands of persons)

Year, sex, race, and Hispanic origin	16 years and over	16 to 19 years			20 years and over						
		Total	16 to 17 years	18 to 19 years	Total	20 to 24 years	25 to 34 years	35 to 44 years	45 to 54 years	55 to 64 years	65 years and over
BLACK											
1972	14 526	2 018	1 061	956	12 508	2 027	2 809	2 329	2 139	1 601	1 605
1973	14 917	2 095	1 095	1 000	12 823	2 132	2 957	2 333	2 156	1 616	1 628
1974	15 329	2 137	1 122	1 014	13 192	2 137	3 103	2 382	2 202	1 679	1 689
1975	15 751	2 191	1 146	1 046	13 560	2 228	3 258	2 395	2 211	1 717	1 755
1976	16 196	2 264	1 165	1 098	13 932	2 303	3 412	2 435	2 220	1 736	1 826
1977	16 605	2 273	1 175	1 097	14 332	2 400	3 566	2 493	2 225	1 765	1 883
1978	16 970	2 270	1 169	1 101	14 701	2 483	3 717	2 547	2 226	1 794	1 932
1979	17 397	2 276	1 167	1 109	15 121	2 556	3 899	2 615	2 240	1 831	1 980
1980	17 824	2 289	1 171	1 119	15 535	2 606	4 095	2 687	2 249	1 870	2 030
1981	18 219	2 288	1 161	1 127	15 931	2 642	4 290	2 758	2 260	1 913	2 069
1982	18 584	2 252	1 119	1 134	16 332	2 697	4 438	2 887	2 263	1 935	2 113
1983	18 925	2 225	1 092	1 133	16 700	2 734	4 607	2 999	2 260	1 964	2 135
1984	19 348	2 161	1 056	1 105	17 187	2 783	4 789	3 167	2 288	1 977	2 183
1985	19 664	2 160	1 083	1 077	17 504	2 649	4 873	3 290	2 372	2 060	2 259
1986	19 989	2 137	1 090	1 048	17 852	2 625	5 026	3 410	2 413	2 079	2 298
1987	20 352	2 163	1 123	1 040	18 189	2 578	5 139	3 563	2 460	2 097	2 352
1988	20 692	2 179	1 130	1 049	18 513	2 527	5 234	3 716	2 524	2 110	2 402
1989	21 021	2 176	1 116	1 060	18 846	2 479	5 308	3 900	2 587	2 118	2 454
1990	21 477	2 238	1 101	1 138	19 239	2 554	5 407	4 328	2 618	1 970	2 362
1991	21 799	2 187	1 085	1 102	19 612	2 585	5 419	4 538	2 682	1 985	2 403
1992	22 147	2 155	1 086	1 069	19 992	2 615	5 404	4 722	2 809	1 996	2 446
1993	22 521	2 181	1 113	1 069	20 339	2 600	5 409	4 886	2 941	2 016	2 487
1994	22 879	2 211	1 168	1 044	20 668	2 616	5 362	5 038	3 084	2 045	2 524
1995	23 246	2 284	1 198	1 086	20 962	2 554	5 337	5 178	3 244	2 079	2 571
BLACK MEN											
1972	6 538	978	525	453	5 559	921	1 251	1 027	963	720	680
1973	6 704	1 007	539	468	5 697	979	1 326	1 027	962	718	684
1974	6 875	1 027	555	472	5 848	956	1 380	1 055	996	753	708
1975	7 060	1 051	565	486	6 009	1 002	1 452	1 061	998	769	730
1976	7 265	1 099	580	518	6 167	1 037	1 522	1 078	1 000	774	756
1977	7 431	1 102	585	516	6 329	1 080	1 588	1 103	997	786	775
1978	7 577	1 093	580	513	6 484	1 120	1 656	1 128	995	795	789
1979	7 761	1 100	581	520	6 661	1 151	1 739	1 160	998	809	804
1980	7 944	1 110	584	526	6 834	1 171	1 828	1 191	999	825	822
1981	8 117	1 110	577	534	7 007	1 189	1 914	1 224	1 003	844	835
1982	8 283	1 097	556	542	7 186	1 225	1 983	1 282	1 003	848	846
1983	8 447	1 087	542	545	7 360	1 254	2 068	1 333	1 000	857	847
1984	8 654	1 055	524	531	7 599	1 292	2 164	1 411	1 012	858	861
1985	8 790	1 059	543	517	7 731	1 202	2 180	1 462	1 060	924	902
1986	8 956	1 049	548	503	7 907	1 195	2 264	1 517	1 072	934	924
1987	9 128	1 065	566	499	8 063	1 173	2 320	1 587	1 092	944	947
1988	9 289	1 074	569	505	8 215	1 151	2 367	1 656	1 121	951	970
1989	9 439	1 075	575	501	8 364	1 128	2 403	1 741	1 146	956	990
1990	9 573	1 094	555	540	8 479	1 144	2 412	1 968	1 183	856	916
1991	9 725	1 072	546	526	8 652	1 168	2 416	2 060	1 211	864	933
1992	9 896	1 056	544	512	8 840	1 194	2 409	2 149	1 267	869	951
1993	10 083	1 075	559	517	9 008	1 181	2 426	2 227	1 330	874	969
1994	10 258	1 087	586	501	9 171	1 206	2 399	2 300	1 392	889	986
1995	10 411	1 131	601	530	9 280	1 162	2 389	2 362	1 462	901	1 006
BLACK WOMEN											
1972	7 988	1 040	536	503	6 948	1 106	1 558	1 302	1 176	881	925
1973	8 214	1 088	556	532	7 126	1 153	1 631	1 306	1 194	898	944
1974	8 454	1 110	567	542	7 344	1 181	1 723	1 327	1 206	926	981
1975	8 691	1 141	581	560	7 550	1 226	1 806	1 334	1 213	948	1 025
1976	8 931	1 165	585	580	7 765	1 266	1 890	1 357	1 220	962	1 070
1977	9 174	1 171	590	581	8 003	1 320	1 978	1 390	1 228	979	1 108
1978	9 394	1 177	589	588	8 217	1 363	2 061	1 419	1 231	999	1 143
1979	9 636	1 176	586	589	8 460	1 405	2 160	1 455	1 242	1 022	1 176
1980	9 880	1 180	587	593	8 700	1 435	2 267	1 496	1 250	1 045	1 208
1981	10 102	1 178	584	593	8 924	1 453	2 376	1 534	1 257	1 069	1 234
1982	10 300	1 155	563	592	9 146	1 472	2 455	1 605	1 260	1 087	1 267
1983	10 477	1 138	550	588	9 340	1 480	2 539	1 666	1 260	1 107	1 288
1984	10 694	1 106	532	574	9 588	1 491	2 625	1 756	1 276	1 119	1 322
1985	10 873	1 101	540	560	9 773	1 447	2 693	1 828	1 312	1 136	1 357
1986	11 033	1 088	542	545	9 945	1 430	2 762	1 893	1 341	1 145	1 374
1987	11 224	1 098	557	541	10 126	1 405	2 819	1 976	1 368	1 153	1 405
1988	11 402	1 105	561	544	10 298	1 376	2 867	2 060	1 403	1 159	1 432
1989	11 582	1 100	541	559	10 482	1 351	2 905	2 159	1 441	1 162	1 464
1990	11 904	1 144	546	598	10 760	1 410	2 995	2 360	1 435	1 114	1 446
1991	12 074	1 115	539	576	10 959	1 417	3 003	2 478	1 471	1 121	1 470
1992	12 251	1 099	542	557	11 152	1 421	2 995	2 573	1 542	1 127	1 495
1993	12 438	1 106	554	552	11 332	1 419	2 983	2 659	1 611	1 142	1 518
1994	12 621	1 125	582	543	11 496	1 410	2 963	2 738	1 692	1 156	1 538
1995	12 835	1 153	597	556	11 682	1 392	2 948	2 816	1 782	1 178	1 565

POPULATION, LABOR FORCE, AND EMPLOYMENT STATUS

Civilian Noninstitutional Population by Sex, Race, Hispanic Origin, and Age, 1948-1995—Continued

(Thousands of persons)

Year, sex, race, and Hispanic origin	16 years and over	16 to 19 years			20 years and over						
		Total	16 to 17 years	18 to 19 years	Total	20 to 24 years	25 to 34 years	35 to 44 years	45 to 54 years	55 to 64 years	65 years and over
HISPANIC											
1973	6 104	867	....	....	5 238	....	....	....	....	....	....
1974	6 564	926	....	....	5 645	....	....	....	....	....	....
1975	6 862	962	....	....	5 900	....	....	....	....	....	....
1976	6 910	953	494	480	6 075	1 053	1 775	1 261	936	570	479
1977	7 362	1 024	513	508	6 376	1 163	1 869	1 283	989	587	485
1978	7 912	1 076	561	515	6 836	1 265	2 004	1 378	1 033	627	529
1979	8 207	1 095	544	551	7 113	1 296	2 117	1 458	1 015	659	566
1980	9 598	1 281	638	643	8 317	1 564	2 508	1 575	1 190	782	698
1981	10 120	1 301	641	660	8 819	1 650	2 698	1 680	1 231	832	728
1982	10 580	1 307	639	668	9 273	1 724	2 871	1 779	1 264	880	755
1983	11 029	1 304	635	670	9 725	1 790	3 045	1 883	1 298	928	781
1984	11 478	1 300	633	667	10 178	1 839	3 224	1 996	1 336	973	810
1985	11 915	1 298	638	661	10 617	1 864	3 401	2 117	1 377	1 015	843
1986	12 344	1 302	658	644	11 042	1 899	3 510	2 239	1 496	1 023	875
1987	12 867	1 332	651	681	11 536	1 910	3 714	2 464	1 492	1 061	895
1988	13 325	1 354	662	692	11 970	1 948	3 807	2 565	1 571	1 159	920
1989	13 791	1 399	672	727	12 392	1 950	3 953	2 658	1 649	1 182	1 001
1990	15 904	1 737	821	915	14 167	2 428	4 589	3 001	1 817	1 247	1 084
1991	16 425	1 732	819	913	14 693	2 481	4 674	3 243	1 879	1 283	1 134
1992	16 961	1 737	836	901	15 224	2 444	4 806	3 458	1 980	1 321	1 216
1993	17 532	1 756	855	901	15 776	2 487	4 887	3 632	2 094	1 324	1 353
1994	18 117	1 818	902	916	16 300	2 518	5 000	3 756	2 223	1 401	1 401
1995	18 629	1 872	903	969	16 757	2 528	5 050	3 965	2 294	1 483	1 437
HISPANIC MEN											
1973	2 891	....	....	....	2 472	....	....	....	....	....	....
1974	3 130	....	....	....	2 680	....	....	....	....	....	....
1975	3 219	....	....	....	2 741	....	....	....	....	....	....
1976	3 241	485	251	234	2 764	494	824	579	444	260	211
1977	3 483	495	247	248	2 982	561	884	601	465	271	216
1978	3 750	525	287	238	3 228	621	934	655	484	293	240
1979	3 917	555	285	271	3 362	623	1 001	690	495	299	253
1980	4 689	653	326	327	4 036	792	1 245	760	570	367	301
1981	4 968	663	327	336	4 306	842	1 354	816	591	392	312
1982	5 203	664	324	340	4 539	882	1 450	865	607	414	321
1983	5 432	661	321	340	4 771	918	1 548	916	623	436	330
1984	5 661	656	319	337	5 005	944	1 649	973	641	457	341
1985	5 885	654	322	332	5 232	956	1 750	1 036	660	476	354
1986	6 106	655	330	325	5 451	1 006	1 787	1 088	735	466	368
1987	6 371	671	336	335	5 700	985	1 925	1 205	741	463	383
1988	6 604	683	319	364	5 921	1 003	1 963	1 268	775	516	397
1989	6 825	711	343	368	6 114	1 005	2 017	1 311	810	538	434
1990	8 041	915	431	484	7 126	1 319	2 369	1 512	890	573	463
1991	8 296	904	425	479	7 392	1 358	2 441	1 632	890	594	477
1992	8 553	899	436	463	7 655	1 306	2 547	1 728	972	603	499
1993	8 824	894	437	457	7 930	1 306	2 602	1 812	1 032	600	579
1994	9 104	....	....	....	8 178	....	....	....	....	....	....
1995	9 329	....	....	....	8 375	....	....	....	....	....	....
HISPANIC WOMEN											
1973	3 213	....	....	....	2 766	....	....	....	....	....	....
1974	3 434	....	....	....	2 959	....	....	....	....	....	....
1975	3 644	....	....	....	3 161	....	....	....	....	....	....
1976	3 669	490	244	246	3 263	559	952	682	493	310	268
1977	3 879	526	266	259	3 377	602	984	682	524	317	269
1978	4 159	551	274	277	3 608	642	1 069	723	548	335	289
1979	4 291	540	259	281	3 751	674	1 117	767	520	361	313
1980	4 909	628	312	316	4 281	771	1 263	815	619	415	398
1981	5 151	638	314	324	4 513	808	1 344	864	640	441	417
1982	5 377	643	314	329	4 734	842	1 421	914	657	466	434
1983	5 597	644	313	330	4 954	872	1 497	967	675	492	451
1984	5 816	644	313	330	5 173	895	1 575	1 022	695	516	469
1985	6 029	644	316	328	5 385	908	1 652	1 081	716	539	489
1986	6 238	647	328	319	5 591	893	1 723	1 151	760	557	507
1987	6 496	661	316	345	5 835	925	1 789	1 259	751	598	513
1988	6 721	671	343	328	6 050	945	1 844	1 297	796	643	524
1989	6 965	687	329	359	6 278	945	1 936	1 347	839	644	567
1990	7 863	822	391	431	7 041	1 109	2 220	1 489	927	675	621
1991	8 130	828	394	435	7 301	1 122	2 233	1 611	989	689	657
1992	8 408	839	400	439	7 569	1 138	2 259	1 729	1 008	718	716
1993	8 708	862	418	444	7 846	1 182	2 285	1 820	1 062	724	774
1994	9 014	....	....	....	8 122	....	....	....	....	....	....
1995	9 300	....	....	....	8 382	....	....	....	....	....	....

NOTE: Data beginning in 1994 are not strictly comparable with data for 1993 and earlier years because of the introduction of a major redesign of the survey and collection methodology. Beginning in 1990, data are not strictly comparable with previous years because of the introduction of 1990 census-based population controls adjusted for the estimated undercount.

Civilian Labor Force by Sex, Race, Hispanic Origin, and Age, 1948-1995

(Thousands of persons)

Year, sex, race, and Hispanic origin	16 years and over	16 to 19 years			20 years and over						
		Total	16 to 17 years	18 to 19 years	Total	20 to 24 years	25 to 34 years	35 to 44 years	45 to 54 years	55 to 64 years	65 years and over
TOTAL											
1948	60 621	4 435	1 780	2 654	56 187	7 392	14 258	13 397	10 914	7 329	2 897
1949	61 286	4 288	1 704	2 583	57 000	7 340	14 415	13 711	11 107	7 426	3 010
1950	62 208	4 216	1 659	2 557	57 994	7 307	14 619	13 954	11 444	7 633	3 036
1951	62 017	4 103	1 743	2 360	57 914	6 594	14 668	14 100	11 739	7 796	3 020
1952	62 138	4 064	1 806	2 257	58 075	5 840	14 904	14 383	11 961	7 980	3 005
1953	63 015	4 027	1 727	2 299	58 989	5 481	14 898	15 099	12 249	8 024	3 236
1954	63 643	3 976	1 643	2 300	59 666	5 475	14 983	15 221	12 524	8 269	3 192
1955	65 023	4 092	1 711	2 382	60 931	5 666	15 058	15 400	12 992	8 513	3 305
1956	66 552	4 296	1 878	2 418	62 257	5 940	14 961	15 694	13 407	8 830	3 423
1957	66 929	4 275	1 843	2 433	62 653	6 071	14 826	15 847	13 768	8 853	3 290
1958	67 639	4 260	1 818	2 442	63 377	6 272	14 668	16 028	14 179	9 031	3 199
1959	68 369	4 492	1 971	2 522	63 876	6 413	14 435	16 127	14 518	9 227	3 158
1960	69 628	4 841	2 095	2 747	64 788	6 702	14 382	16 269	14 852	9 385	3 195
1961	70 459	4 936	1 984	2 951	65 524	6 950	14 319	16 402	15 071	9 636	3 146
1962	70 614	4 916	1 919	2 997	65 699	7 082	14 023	16 589	15 096	9 757	3 154
1963	71 833	5 139	2 171	2 966	66 695	7 473	14 050	16 788	15 338	10 006	3 041
1964	73 091	5 388	2 449	2 940	67 702	7 963	14 056	16 771	15 637	10 182	3 090
1965	74 455	5 910	2 486	3 425	68 543	8 259	14 233	16 840	15 756	10 350	3 108
1966	75 770	6 558	2 664	3 893	69 219	8 410	14 458	16 738	15 984	10 575	3 053
1967	77 347	6 521	2 734	3 786	70 825	9 010	15 055	16 703	16 172	10 792	3 097
1968	78 737	6 619	2 817	3 803	72 118	9 305	15 708	16 591	16 397	10 964	3 153
1969	80 734	6 970	3 009	3 959	73 763	9 879	16 336	16 458	16 730	11 135	3 227
1970	82 771	7 249	3 135	4 115	75 521	10 597	17 036	16 437	16 949	11 283	3 222
1971	84 382	7 470	3 192	4 278	76 913	11 331	17 714	16 305	17 024	11 390	3 149
1972	87 034	8 054	3 420	4 636	78 980	12 130	18 960	16 398	16 967	11 412	3 114
1973	89 429	8 507	3 665	4 839	80 924	12 846	20 376	16 492	16 983	11 256	2 974
1974	91 949	8 871	3 810	5 059	83 080	13 314	21 654	16 763	17 131	11 284	2 934
1975	93 775	8 870	3 740	5 131	84 904	13 750	22 864	16 903	17 084	11 346	2 956
1976	96 158	9 056	3 767	5 288	87 103	14 284	24 203	17 317	16 982	11 422	2 895
1977	99 009	9 351	3 919	5 431	89 658	14 825	25 500	17 943	16 878	11 577	2 934
1978	102 251	9 652	4 127	5 526	92 598	15 370	26 703	18 821	16 891	11 744	3 070
1979	104 962	9 638	4 079	5 559	95 325	15 769	27 938	19 685	16 897	11 931	3 104
1980	106 940	9 378	3 883	5 496	97 561	15 922	29 227	20 463	16 910	11 985	3 054
1981	108 670	8 988	3 647	5 340	99 682	16 099	30 392	21 211	16 970	11 969	3 042
1982	110 204	8 526	3 336	5 189	101 679	16 082	31 186	22 431	16 889	12 062	3 030
1983	111 550	8 171	3 073	5 098	103 379	16 052	31 834	23 611	16 851	11 992	3 040
1984	113 544	7 943	3 050	4 894	105 601	16 046	32 723	24 933	17 006	11 961	2 933
1985	115 461	7 901	3 154	4 747	107 560	15 718	33 550	26 073	17 322	11 991	2 907
1986	117 834	7 926	3 287	4 639	109 908	15 441	34 591	27 232	17 739	11 894	3 010
1987	119 865	7 988	3 384	4 604	111 878	14 977	35 233	28 460	18 210	11 877	3 119
1988	121 669	8 031	3 286	4 745	113 638	14 505	35 503	29 435	19 104	11 808	3 284
1989	123 869	7 954	3 125	4 828	115 916	14 180	35 896	30 601	19 916	11 877	3 446
1990	125 840	7 792	2 937	4 856	118 047	14 700	35 929	32 145	20 248	11 575	3 451
1991	126 346	7 265	2 789	4 476	119 082	14 548	35 507	33 312	20 828	11 473	3 413
1992	128 105	7 096	2 769	4 327	121 009	14 521	35 369	33 899	22 160	11 587	3 473
1993	129 200	7 170	2 831	4 338	122 030	14 354	34 780	34 562	23 296	11 599	3 439
1994	131 056	7 481	3 134	4 347	123 576	14 131	34 353	35 226	24 318	11 713	3 834
1995	132 304	7 765	3 225	4 540	124 539	13 688	34 198	35 751	25 223	11 860	3 819

Civilian Labor Force by Sex, Race, Hispanic Origin, and Age, 1948-1995—Continued

(Thousands of persons)

Year, sex, race, and Hispanic origin	16 years and over	16 to 19 years			20 years and over						
		Total	16 to 17 years	18 to 19 years	Total	20 to 24 years	25 to 34 years	35 to 44 years	45 to 54 years	55 to 64 years	65 years and over
MEN											
1948	43 286	2 600	1 109	1 490	40 687	4 673	10 327	9 596	7 943	5 764	2 384
1949	43 498	2 477	1 056	1 420	41 022	4 682	10 418	9 722	8 008	5 748	2 454
1950	43 819	2 504	1 048	1 456	41 316	4 632	10 527	9 793	8 117	5 794	2 453
1951	43 001	2 347	1 081	1 266	40 655	3 935	10 375	9 799	8 205	5 873	2 469
1952	42 869	2 312	1 101	1 210	40 558	3 338	10 585	9 945	8 326	5 949	2 416
1953	43 633	2 320	1 070	1 249	41 315	3 053	10 736	10 437	8 570	5 975	2 543
1954	43 965	2 295	1 023	1 272	41 669	3 051	10 771	10 513	8 702	6 105	2 526
1955	44 475	2 369	1 070	1 299	42 106	3 221	10 806	10 595	8 838	6 122	2 526
1956	45 091	2 433	1 142	1 291	42 658	3 485	10 685	10 663	9 002	6 220	2 602
1957	45 197	2 415	1 127	1 289	42 780	3 629	10 571	10 731	9 153	6 222	2 477
1958	45 521	2 428	1 133	1 295	43 092	3 771	10 475	10 843	9 320	6 304	2 378
1959	45 886	2 596	1 206	1 390	43 289	3 940	10 346	10 899	9 438	6 345	2 322
1960	46 388	2 787	1 290	1 496	43 603	4 123	10 251	10 967	9 574	6 399	2 287
1961	46 653	2 794	1 210	1 583	43 860	4 253	10 176	11 012	9 668	6 530	2 220
1962	46 600	2 770	1 178	1 592	43 831	4 279	9 920	11 115	9 715	6 560	2 241
1963	47 129	2 907	1 321	1 586	44 222	4 514	9 876	11 187	9 836	6 675	2 135
1964	47 679	3 074	1 499	1 575	44 604	4 754	9 876	11 156	9 956	6 741	2 124
1965	48 255	3 397	1 532	1 866	44 857	4 894	9 903	11 120	10 045	6 763	2 132
1966	48 471	3 685	1 609	2 075	44 788	4 820	9 948	10 983	10 100	6 847	2 089
1967	48 987	3 634	1 658	1 976	45 354	5 043	10 207	10 859	10 189	6 937	2 118
1968	49 533	3 681	1 687	1 995	45 852	5 070	10 610	10 725	10 267	7 025	2 154
1969	50 221	3 870	1 770	2 100	46 351	5 282	10 941	10 556	10 344	7 058	2 170
1970	51 228	4 008	1 810	2 199	47 220	5 717	11 327	10 469	10 417	7 126	2 165
1971	52 180	4 172	1 856	2 315	48 009	6 233	11 731	10 347	10 451	7 155	2 090
1972	53 555	4 476	1 955	2 522	49 079	6 766	12 350	10 372	10 412	7 155	2 026
1973	54 624	4 693	2 073	2 618	49 932	7 183	13 056	10 338	10 416	7 028	1 913
1974	55 739	4 861	2 138	2 721	50 879	7 387	13 665	10 401	10 431	7 063	1 932
1975	56 299	4 805	2 065	2 740	51 494	7 565	14 192	10 398	10 401	7 023	1 914
1976	57 174	4 886	2 069	2 817	52 288	7 866	14 784	10 500	10 293	7 020	1 826
1977	58 396	5 048	2 155	2 893	53 348	8 109	15 353	10 771	10 158	7 100	1 857
1978	59 620	5 149	2 227	2 923	54 471	8 327	15 814	11 159	10 083	7 151	1 936
1979	60 726	5 111	2 192	2 919	55 615	8 535	16 387	11 531	10 008	7 212	1 943
1980	61 453	4 999	2 102	2 897	56 455	8 607	16 971	11 836	9 905	7 242	1 893
1981	61 974	4 777	1 957	2 820	57 197	8 648	17 479	12 166	9 868	7 170	1 866
1982	62 450	4 470	1 776	2 694	57 980	8 604	17 793	12 781	9 784	7 174	1 845
1983	63 047	4 303	1 621	2 682	58 744	8 601	18 038	13 398	9 746	7 119	1 842
1984	63 835	4 134	1 591	2 542	59 701	8 594	18 488	14 037	9 776	7 050	1 755
1985	64 411	4 134	1 663	2 471	60 277	8 283	18 808	14 506	9 870	7 060	1 750
1986	65 422	4 102	1 707	2 395	61 320	8 148	19 383	15 029	9 994	6 954	1 811
1987	66 207	4 112	1 745	2 367	62 095	7 837	19 656	15 587	10 176	6 940	1 899
1988	66 927	4 159	1 714	2 445	62 768	7 594	19 742	16 074	10 566	6 831	1 960
1989	67 840	4 136	1 630	2 505	63 704	7 458	19 905	16 622	10 919	6 783	2 017
1990	69 011	4 094	1 537	2 557	64 916	7 866	19 872	17 481	11 103	6 627	1 967
1991	69 168	3 795	1 452	2 343	65 374	7 820	19 641	18 077	11 362	6 550	1 924
1992	69 964	3 751	1 453	2 297	66 213	7 770	19 495	18 347	12 040	6 551	2 010
1993	70 404	3 762	1 497	2 265	66 642	7 671	19 214	18 713	12 562	6 502	1 980
1994	70 817	3 896	1 630	2 266	66 921	7 540	18 854	18 966	12 962	6 423	2 176
1995	71 360	4 036	1 668	2 368	67 324	7 338	18 670	19 189	13 421	6 504	2 201

Civilian Labor Force by Sex, Race, Hispanic Origin, and Age, 1948-1995—Continued

(Thousands of persons)

Year, sex, race, and Hispanic origin	16 years and over	16 to 19 years			20 years and over						
		Total	16 to 17 years	18 to 19 years	Total	20 to 24 years	25 to 34 years	35 to 44 years	45 to 54 years	55 to 64 years	65 years and over
WOMEN											
1948	17 335	1 835	671	1 164	15 500	2 719	3 931	3 801	2 971	1 565	513
1949	17 788	1 811	648	1 163	15 978	2 658	3 997	3 989	3 099	1 678	556
1950	18 389	1 712	611	1 101	16 678	2 675	4 092	4 161	3 327	1 839	583
1951	19 016	1 756	662	1 094	17 259	2 659	4 293	4 301	3 534	1 923	551
1952	19 269	1 752	705	1 047	17 517	2 502	4 319	4 438	3 635	2 031	589
1953	19 382	1 707	657	1 050	17 674	2 428	4 162	4 662	3 679	2 049	693
1954	19 678	1 681	620	1 028	17 997	2 424	4 212	4 708	3 822	2 164	666
1955	20 548	1 723	641	1 083	18 825	2 445	4 252	4 805	4 154	2 391	779
1956	21 461	1 863	736	1 127	19 599	2 455	4 276	5 031	4 405	2 610	821
1957	21 732	1 860	716	1 144	19 873	2 442	4 255	5 116	4 615	2 631	813
1958	22 118	1 832	685	1 147	20 285	2 501	4 193	5 185	4 859	2 727	821
1959	22 483	1 896	765	1 132	20 587	2 473	4 089	5 228	5 080	2 882	836
1960	23 240	2 054	805	1 251	21 185	2 579	4 131	5 302	5 278	2 986	908
1961	23 806	2 142	774	1 368	21 664	2 697	4 143	5 390	5 403	3 106	926
1962	24 014	2 146	741	1 405	21 868	2 803	4 103	5 474	5 381	3 197	913
1963	24 704	2 232	850	1 380	22 473	2 959	4 174	5 601	5 502	3 331	906
1964	25 412	2 314	950	1 365	23 098	3 209	4 180	5 615	5 681	3 441	966
1965	26 200	2 513	954	1 559	23 686	3 365	4 330	5 720	5 711	3 587	976
1966	27 299	2 873	1 055	1 818	24 431	3 590	4 510	5 755	5 884	3 728	964
1967	28 360	2 887	1 076	1 810	25 475	3 966	4 848	5 844	5 983	3 855	979
1968	29 204	2 938	1 130	1 808	26 266	4 235	5 098	5 866	6 130	3 939	999
1969	30 513	3 100	1 239	1 859	27 413	4 597	5 395	5 902	6 386	4 077	1 057
1970	31 543	3 241	1 325	1 916	28 301	4 880	5 708	5 968	6 532	4 157	1 056
1971	32 202	3 298	1 336	1 963	28 904	5 098	5 983	5 957	6 573	4 234	1 059
1972	33 479	3 578	1 464	2 114	29 901	5 364	6 610	6 027	6 555	4 257	1 089
1973	34 804	3 814	1 592	2 221	30 991	5 663	7 320	6 154	6 567	4 228	1 061
1974	36 211	4 010	1 672	2 338	32 201	5 926	7 989	6 362	6 699	4 221	1 002
1975	37 475	4 065	1 674	2 391	33 410	6 185	8 673	6 505	6 683	4 323	1 042
1976	38 983	4 170	1 698	2 470	34 814	6 418	9 419	6 817	6 689	4 402	1 069
1977	40 613	4 303	1 765	2 538	36 310	6 717	10 149	7 171	6 720	4 477	1 078
1978	42 631	4 503	1 900	2 603	38 128	7 043	10 888	7 662	6 807	4 593	1 134
1979	44 235	4 527	1 887	2 639	39 708	7 234	11 551	8 154	6 889	4 719	1 161
1980	45 487	4 381	1 781	2 599	41 106	7 315	12 257	8 627	7 004	4 742	1 161
1981	46 696	4 211	1 691	2 520	42 485	7 451	12 912	9 045	7 101	4 799	1 176
1982	47 755	4 056	1 561	2 495	43 699	7 477	13 393	9 651	7 105	4 888	1 185
1983	48 503	3 868	1 452	2 416	44 636	7 451	13 796	10 213	7 105	4 873	1 198
1984	49 709	3 810	1 458	2 351	45 900	7 451	14 234	10 896	7 230	4 911	1 177
1985	51 050	3 767	1 491	2 276	47 283	7 434	14 742	11 567	7 452	4 932	1 156
1986	52 413	3 824	1 580	2 244	48 589	7 293	15 208	12 204	7 746	4 940	1 199
1987	53 658	3 875	1 638	2 237	49 783	7 140	15 577	12 873	8 034	4 937	1 221
1988	54 742	3 872	1 572	2 300	50 870	6 910	15 761	13 361	8 537	4 977	1 324
1989	56 030	3 818	1 495	2 323	52 212	6 721	15 990	13 980	8 997	5 095	1 429
1990	56 829	3 698	1 400	2 298	53 131	6 834	16 058	14 663	9 145	4 948	1 483
1991	57 178	3 470	1 337	2 133	53 708	6 728	15 867	15 235	9 465	4 924	1 489
1992	58 141	3 345	1 316	2 030	54 796	6 750	15 875	15 552	10 120	5 035	1 464
1993	58 795	3 408	1 335	2 073	55 388	6 683	15 566	15 849	10 733	5 097	1 459
1994	60 239	3 585	1 504	2 081	56 655	6 592	15 499	16 259	11 357	5 289	1 658
1995	60 944	3 729	1 557	2 172	57 215	6 349	15 528	16 562	11 801	5 356	1 618

Civilian Labor Force by Sex, Race, Hispanic Origin, and Age, 1948-1995—Continued

(Thousands of persons)

Year, sex, race, and Hispanic origin	16 years and over	16 to 19 years			20 years and over						
		Total	16 to 17 years	18 to 19 years	Total	20 to 24 years	25 to 34 years	35 to 44 years	45 to 54 years	55 to 64 years	65 years and over
WHITE											
1954	56 816	3 501	1 448	2 054	53 315	4 752	13 226	13 540	11 258	7 591	2 946
1955	58 085	3 598	1 511	2 087	54 487	4 941	13 267	13 729	11 680	7 810	3 062
1956	59 428	3 771	1 656	2 113	55 657	5 194	13 154	14 000	12 061	8 080	3 166
1957	59 754	3 775	1 637	2 135	55 979	5 283	13 044	14 117	12 382	8 091	3 049
1958	60 293	3 757	1 615	2 144	56 536	5 449	12 884	14 257	12 727	8 254	2 964
1959	60 952	4 000	1 775	2 225	56 952	5 544	12 670	14 355	13 048	8 411	2 925
1960	61 915	4 275	1 871	2 405	57 640	5 787	12 594	14 450	13 322	8 522	2 964
1961	62 656	4 362	1 767	2 594	58 294	6 026	12 503	14 557	13 517	8 773	2 917
1962	62 750	4 354	1 709	2 645	58 396	6 164	12 218	14 695	13 551	8 856	2 912
1963	63 830	4 559	1 950	2 608	59 271	6 537	12 229	14 859	13 789	9 067	2 790
1964	64 921	4 784	2 211	2 572	60 137	6 952	12 235	14 852	14 043	9 239	2 817
1965	66 137	5 267	2 221	3 044	60 870	7 189	12 391	14 900	14 162	9 392	2 839
1966	67 276	5 827	2 367	3 460	61 449	7 324	12 591	14 785	14 370	9 583	2 793
1967	68 699	5 749	2 432	3 318	62 950	7 886	13 123	14 765	14 545	9 817	2 821
1968	69 976	5 839	2 519	3 320	64 137	8 109	13 740	14 683	14 756	9 968	2 884
1969	71 778	6 168	2 698	3 470	65 611	8 614	14 289	14 564	15 057	10 132	2 954
1970	73 556	6 442	2 824	3 617	67 113	9 238	14 896	14 525	15 269	10 255	2 930
1971	74 963	6 681	2 894	3 787	68 282	9 889	15 445	14 374	15 343	10 351	2 880
1972	77 275	7 193	3 096	4 098	70 082	10 605	16 584	14 399	15 283	10 402	2 809
1973	79 151	7 579	3 320	4 260	71 572	11 182	17 764	14 440	15 256	10 240	2 687
1974	81 281	7 899	3 441	4 459	73 381	11 600	18 862	14 644	15 375	10 241	2 656
1975	82 831	7 899	3 375	4 525	74 932	12 019	19 897	14 753	15 308	10 287	2 668
1976	84 767	8 088	3 410	4 679	76 678	12 444	20 990	15 088	15 187	10 371	2 599
1977	87 141	8 352	3 562	4 790	78 789	12 892	22 099	15 604	15 053	10 495	2 647
1978	89 634	8 555	3 715	4 839	81 079	13 309	23 067	16 353	15 004	10 602	2 745
1979	91 923	8 548	3 668	4 881	83 375	13 632	24 101	17 123	14 965	10 767	2 787
1980	93 600	8 312	3 485	4 827	85 286	13 769	25 181	17 811	14 956	10 812	2 759
1981	95 052	7 962	3 274	4 688	87 089	13 926	26 208	18 445	14 993	10 764	2 753
1982	96 143	7 518	3 001	4 518	88 625	13 866	26 814	19 491	14 879	10 832	2 742
1983	97 021	7 186	2 765	4 421	89 835	13 816	27 237	20 488	14 798	10 732	2 766
1984	98 492	6 952	2 720	4 232	91 540	13 733	27 958	21 588	14 899	10 701	2 660
1985	99 926	6 841	2 777	4 065	93 085	13 469	28 640	22 591	15 101	10 679	2 605
1986	101 801	6 862	2 895	3 967	94 939	13 176	29 497	23 571	15 379	10 583	2 732
1987	103 290	6 893	2 963	3 931	96 396	12 764	29 956	24 581	15 792	10 497	2 806
1988	104 756	6 940	2 861	4 079	97 815	12 311	30 167	25 358	16 573	10 462	2 943
1989	106 355	6 809	2 685	4 124	99 546	11 940	30 388	26 312	17 278	10 533	3 094
1990	107 447	6 683	2 543	4 140	100 764	12 397	30 174	27 265	17 515	10 290	3 123
1991	107 743	6 245	2 432	3 813	101 498	12 248	29 794	28 213	18 028	10 129	3 086
1992	108 837	6 022	2 388	3 633	102 815	12 187	29 518	28 580	19 200	10 196	3 135
1993	109 700	6 105	2 458	3 647	103 595	11 987	29 027	29 056	20 181	10 215	3 129
1994	111 082	6 357	2 681	3 677	104 725	11 688	28 580	29 626	21 026	10 319	3 486
1995	111 950	6 545	2 749	3 796	105 404	11 266	28 325	30 112	21 804	10 432	3 466

Civilian Labor Force by Sex, Race, Hispanic Origin, and Age, 1948-1995—Continued

(Thousands of persons)

Year, sex, race, and Hispanic origin	16 years and over	16 to 19 years			20 years and over						
		Total	16 to 17 years	18 to 19 years	Total	20 to 24 years	25 to 34 years	35 to 44 years	45 to 54 years	55 to 64 years	65 years and over
WHITE MEN											
1954	39 759	1 989	896	1 095	37 770	2 654	9 695	9 516	7 913	5 653	2 339
1955	40 197	2 056	935	1 121	38 141	2 803	9 721	9 597	8 025	5 654	2 343
1956	40 734	2 114	1 002	1 110	38 620	3 036	9 595	9 661	8 175	5 736	2 417
1957	40 826	2 108	992	1 114	38 718	3 152	9 483	9 719	8 317	5 735	2 307
1958	41 080	2 116	1 001	1 116	38 964	3 278	9 386	9 822	8 465	5 800	2 213
1959	41 397	2 279	1 077	1 202	39 118	3 409	9 261	9 876	8 581	5 833	2 158
1960	41 743	2 433	1 140	1 293	39 310	3 559	9 153	9 919	8 689	5 861	2 129
1961	41 986	2 439	1 067	1 372	39 547	3 681	9 072	9 961	8 776	5 988	2 068
1962	41 931	2 432	1 041	1 391	39 499	3 726	8 846	10 029	8 820	5 995	2 082
1963	42 404	2 563	1 183	1 380	39 841	3 955	8 805	10 079	8 944	6 090	1 967
1964	42 894	2 716	1 345	1 371	40 178	4 166	8 800	10 055	9 053	6 161	1 942
1965	43 400	2 999	1 359	1 639	40 401	4 279	8 824	10 023	9 130	6 188	1 959
1966	43 572	3 253	1 423	1 830	40 319	4 200	8 859	9 892	9 189	6 250	1 928
1967	44 041	3 191	1 464	1 727	40 851	4 416	9 102	9 785	9 260	6 348	1 944
1968	44 553	3 236	1 504	1 732	41 318	4 432	9 477	9 662	9 340	6 427	1 981
1969	45 185	3 413	1 583	1 830	41 772	4 615	9 773	9 509	9 413	6 467	1 996
1970	46 035	3 551	1 629	1 922	42 483	4 988	10 099	9 414	9 487	6 517	1 978
1971	46 904	3 719	1 681	2 039	43 185	5 448	10 444	9 294	9 528	6 550	1 922
1972	48 118	3 980	1 758	2 223	44 138	5 937	11 039	9 278	9 473	6 562	1 846
1973	48 920	4 174	1 875	2 300	44 747	6 274	11 621	9 212	9 445	6 452	1 740
1974	49 843	4 312	1 922	2 391	45 532	6 470	12 135	9 246	9 455	6 464	1 759
1975	50 324	4 290	1 871	2 418	46 034	6 642	12 579	9 231	9 415	6 425	1 742
1976	51 033	4 357	1 869	2 489	46 675	6 890	13 092	9 289	9 310	6 437	1 657
1977	52 033	4 496	1 949	2 548	47 537	7 097	13 575	9 509	9 175	6 492	1 688
1978	52 955	4 565	2 002	2 563	48 390	7 274	13 939	9 858	9 068	6 508	1 744
1979	53 856	4 537	1 974	2 563	49 320	7 421	14 415	10 183	8 968	6 571	1 761
1980	54 473	4 424	1 881	2 543	50 049	7 479	14 893	10 455	8 877	6 618	1 727
1981	54 895	4 224	1 751	2 473	50 671	7 521	15 340	10 740	8 836	6 530	1 704
1982	55 133	3 933	1 602	2 331	51 200	7 438	15 549	11 289	8 727	6 520	1 677
1983	55 480	3 764	1 452	2 312	51 716	7 406	15 707	11 817	8 649	6 446	1 691
1984	56 062	3 609	1 420	2 189	52 453	7 370	16 037	12 348	8 683	6 410	1 606
1985	56 472	3 576	1 467	2 109	52 895	7 122	16 306	12 767	8 730	6 376	1 595
1986	57 217	3 542	1 502	2 040	53 675	6 986	16 769	13 207	8 791	6 260	1 663
1987	57 779	3 547	1 524	2 023	54 232	6 717	16 963	13 674	8 945	6 200	1 733
1988	58 317	3 583	1 487	2 095	54 734	6 468	17 018	14 068	9 285	6 108	1 787
1989	58 988	3 546	1 401	2 146	55 441	6 316	17 077	14 516	9 615	6 082	1 835
1990	59 638	3 522	1 333	2 189	56 116	6 688	16 920	15 026	9 713	5 957	1 811
1991	59 656	3 269	1 266	2 003	56 387	6 619	16 709	15 523	9 926	5 847	1 763
1992	60 168	3 192	1 260	1 932	56 976	6 542	16 512	15 701	10 570	5 821	1 830
1993	60 484	3 200	1 292	1 908	57 284	6 449	16 244	15 971	11 010	5 784	1 825
1994	60 727	3 315	1 403	1 912	57 411	6 294	15 879	16 188	11 327	5 726	1 998
1995	61 146	3 427	1 429	1 998	57 719	6 096	15 669	16 414	11 730	5 809	2 000
WHITE WOMEN											
1954	17 057	1 512	552	959	15 545	2 098	3 531	4 024	3 345	1 938	607
1955	17 888	1 542	576	966	16 346	2 138	3 546	4 132	3 655	2 156	719
1956	18 694	1 657	654	1 003	17 037	2 158	3 559	4 339	3 886	2 344	749
1957	18 928	1 667	645	1 021	17 261	2 131	3 561	4 398	4 065	2 356	742
1958	19 213	1 641	614	1 028	17 572	2 171	3 498	4 435	4 262	2 454	751
1959	19 555	1 721	698	1 023	17 834	2 135	3 409	4 479	4 467	2 578	767
1960	20 172	1 842	731	1 112	18 330	2 228	3 441	4 531	4 633	2 661	835
1961	20 670	1 923	700	1 222	18 747	2 345	3 431	4 596	4 741	2 785	849
1962	20 819	1 922	668	1 254	18 897	2 438	3 372	4 666	4 731	2 861	830
1963	21 426	1 996	767	1 228	19 430	2 582	3 424	4 780	4 845	2 977	823
1964	22 027	2 068	866	1 201	19 959	2 786	3 435	4 797	4 990	3 078	875
1965	22 737	2 268	862	1 405	20 469	2 910	3 567	4 877	5 032	3 204	880
1966	23 704	2 574	944	1 630	21 130	3 124	3 732	4 893	5 181	3 333	865
1967	24 658	2 558	968	1 591	22 100	3 471	4 021	4 980	5 285	3 469	877
1968	25 423	2 603	1 015	1 588	22 821	3 677	4 263	5 021	5 416	3 541	903
1969	26 593	2 755	1 115	1 640	23 839	3 999	4 516	5 055	5 644	3 665	958
1970	27 521	2 891	1 195	1 695	24 630	4 250	4 797	5 111	5 781	3 738	952
1971	28 060	2 962	1 213	1 748	25 097	4 441	5 001	5 080	5 816	3 801	958
1972	29 157	3 213	1 338	1 875	25 945	4 668	5 544	5 121	5 810	3 839	963
1973	30 231	3 405	1 445	1 960	26 825	4 908	6 143	5 228	5 811	3 788	947
1974	31 437	3 588	1 520	2 068	27 850	5 131	6 727	5 399	5 920	3 777	897
1975	32 508	3 610	1 504	2 107	28 898	5 378	7 318	5 522	5 892	3 862	926
1976	33 735	3 731	1 541	2 189	30 004	5 554	7 898	5 799	5 877	3 935	940
1977	35 108	3 856	1 614	2 243	31 253	5 795	8 523	6 095	5 877	4 003	959
1978	36 679	3 990	1 713	2 276	32 689	6 035	9 128	6 495	5 936	4 094	1 001
1979	38 067	4 011	1 694	2 318	34 056	6 211	9 687	6 940	5 997	4 196	1 024
1980	39 127	3 888	1 605	2 284	35 239	6 290	10 289	7 356	6 079	4 194	1 032
1981	40 157	3 739	1 523	2 216	36 418	6 406	10 868	7 704	6 157	4 235	1 049
1982	41 010	3 585	1 399	2 186	37 425	6 428	11 264	8 202	6 152	4 313	1 065
1983	41 541	3 422	1 314	2 109	38 119	6 410	11 530	8 670	6 149	4 285	1 074
1984	42 431	3 343	1 300	2 043	39 087	6 363	11 922	9 240	6 217	4 292	1 054
1985	43 455	3 265	1 310	1 955	40 190	6 348	12 334	9 824	6 371	4 303	1 010
1986	44 584	3 320	1 393	1 927	41 264	6 191	12 729	10 364	6 588	4 323	1 069
1987	45 510	3 347	1 439	1 908	42 164	6 047	12 993	10 907	6 847	4 297	1 073
1988	46 439	3 358	1 374	1 984	43 081	5 844	13 149	11 291	7 288	4 354	1 156
1989	47 367	3 262	1 284	1 978	44 105	5 625	13 311	11 796	7 663	4 451	1 259
1990	47 809	3 161	1 210	1 951	44 648	5 709	13 254	12 239	7 802	4 333	1 312
1991	48 087	2 976	1 166	1 810	45 111	5 629	13 085	12 689	8 101	4 282	1 324
1992	48 669	2 830	1 128	1 702	45 839	5 645	13 006	12 879	8 630	4 375	1 305
1993	49 216	2 905	1 167	1 739	46 311	5 539	12 783	13 085	9 171	4 430	1 304
1994	50 356	3 042	1 278	1 764	47 314	5 394	12 702	13 439	9 699	4 593	1 487
1995	50 804	3 118	1 320	1 798	47 686	5 170	12 656	13 697	10 074	4 622	1 466

Civilian Labor Force by Sex, Race, Hispanic Origin, and Age, 1948-1995—Continued

(Thousands of persons)

Year, sex, race, and Hispanic origin	16 years and over	16 to 19 years			20 years and over						
		Total	16 to 17 years	18 to 19 years	Total	20 to 24 years	25 to 34 years	35 to 44 years	45 to 54 years	55 to 64 years	65 years and over
BLACK											
1972	8 707	788	293	496	7 919	1 393	2 107	1 735	1 496	909	281
1973	8 976	833	307	525	8 143	1 489	2 242	1 741	1 513	901	258
1974	9 167	851	317	534	8 317	1 492	2 358	1 777	1 517	917	253
1975	9 263	838	312	524	8 426	1 477	2 466	1 775	1 519	929	258
1976	9 561	837	304	532	8 724	1 544	2 646	1 824	1 518	925	268
1977	9 932	861	304	557	9 072	1 641	2 798	1 894	1 530	943	267
1978	10 432	930	341	589	9 501	1 739	2 961	1 975	1 560	978	289
1979	10 678	912	340	572	9 766	1 793	3 094	2 039	1 584	974	281
1980	10 865	891	326	565	9 975	1 802	3 259	2 081	1 596	978	257
1981	11 086	862	308	554	10 224	1 828	3 365	2 164	1 608	1 009	249
1982	11 331	824	268	556	10 507	1 849	3 492	2 303	1 610	1 012	243
1983	11 647	809	248	561	10 838	1 871	3 675	2 406	1 630	1 032	224
1984	12 033	827	268	558	11 206	1 926	3 800	2 565	1 671	1 020	224
1985	12 364	889	311	578	11 476	1 854	3 888	2 681	1 742	1 059	252
1986	12 654	883	322	562	11 770	1 881	4 028	2 793	1 793	1 051	224
1987	12 993	899	336	563	12 094	1 818	4 147	2 942	1 838	1 098	251
1988	13 205	889	344	545	12 316	1 782	4 226	3 069	1 894	1 069	276
1989	13 497	925	353	572	12 573	1 789	4 295	3 227	1 954	1 023	285
1990	13 740	866	306	560	12 874	1 758	4 307	3 566	2 003	977	262
1991	13 797	774	266	508	13 023	1 750	4 254	3 719	2 042	1 001	256
1992	14 162	816	285	532	13 346	1 763	4 309	3 843	2 142	1 029	259
1993	14 225	807	283	524	13 418	1 764	4 232	3 960	2 212	1 013	237
1994	14 502	852	351	501	13 650	1 800	4 199	4 068	2 308	1 007	267
1995	14 817	911	366	545	13 906	1 754	4 267	4 165	2 404	1 046	271
BLACK MEN											
1972	4 816	453	180	272	4 364	761	1 158	935	824	522	165
1973	4 924	460	175	286	4 464	819	1 217	935	842	499	153
1974	5 020	480	189	291	4 540	798	1 279	953	838	519	152
1975	5 016	447	168	279	4 569	790	1 328	948	833	520	150
1976	5 101	454	168	285	4 648	820	1 383	969	824	504	149
1977	5 263	476	178	299	4 787	856	1 441	1 003	818	515	154
1978	5 435	491	186	306	4 943	883	1 504	1 022	829	540	166
1979	5 559	480	179	301	5 079	928	1 577	1 049	844	524	156
1980	5 612	479	181	298	5 134	935	1 659	1 061	830	509	138
1981	5 685	462	169	293	5 223	940	1 702	1 093	829	524	134
1982	5 804	436	137	300	5 368	964	1 769	1 152	824	525	135
1983	5 966	433	134	300	5 533	997	1 840	1 196	845	536	119
1984	6 126	440	141	299	5 686	1 022	1 924	1 270	847	505	118
1985	6 220	471	162	310	5 749	950	1 937	1 313	879	544	125
1986	6 373	458	164	294	5 915	957	2 029	1 359	901	552	116
1987	6 486	463	179	284	6 023	914	2 074	1 406	915	586	130
1988	6 596	469	186	283	6 127	913	2 114	1 459	936	565	139
1989	6 701	480	190	291	6 221	904	2 157	1 544	945	530	141
1990	6 802	445	161	284	6 357	879	2 142	1 733	988	496	119
1991	6 851	400	140	260	6 451	896	2 111	1 806	1 010	507	122
1992	6 997	429	149	280	6 568	900	2 121	1 859	1 037	521	130
1993	7 019	425	154	270	6 594	875	2 118	1 918	1 065	506	112
1994	7 089	443	176	266	6 646	891	2 068	1 975	1 102	484	125
1995	7 183	453	184	269	6 730	866	2 089	1 987	1 148	490	150
BLACK WOMEN											
1972	3 890	335	113	224	3 555	632	949	800	672	387	116
1973	4 052	373	133	240	3 678	670	1 026	806	670	402	105
1974	4 148	371	128	243	3 777	694	1 079	824	679	398	100
1975	4 247	391	144	245	3 857	687	1 138	827	686	409	108
1976	4 460	384	136	247	4 076	723	1 264	855	694	421	119
1977	4 670	385	127	258	4 286	785	1 357	891	712	429	113
1978	4 997	439	155	283	4 558	856	1 456	953	731	439	124
1979	5 119	432	161	271	4 687	865	1 517	990	740	451	124
1980	5 253	412	144	267	4 841	867	1 600	1 020	767	469	119
1981	5 401	400	139	261	5 001	888	1 663	1 071	779	485	115
1982	5 527	387	131	256	5 140	885	1 723	1 151	786	487	108
1983	5 681	375	114	261	5 306	874	1 835	1 210	785	496	105
1984	5 907	387	127	260	5 520	904	1 876	1 294	823	515	106
1985	6 144	417	149	268	5 727	904	1 951	1 368	862	515	127
1986	6 281	425	157	268	5 855	924	1 999	1 434	892	499	107
1987	6 507	435	157	278	6 071	904	2 073	1 537	924	512	121
1988	6 609	419	158	262	6 190	869	2 112	1 610	958	504	137
1989	6 796	445	163	281	6 352	885	2 138	1 683	1 009	493	144
1990	6 938	421	145	276	6 517	879	2 165	1 833	1 015	481	143
1991	6 946	374	126	248	6 572	854	2 143	1 913	1 032	494	135
1992	7 166	387	135	252	6 778	863	2 188	1 985	1 105	508	129
1993	7 206	383	129	254	6 824	889	2 115	2 042	1 147	506	125
1994	7 413	409	174	235	7 004	909	2 131	2 093	1 206	523	142
1995	7 634	458	182	276	7 175	887	2 177	2 178	1 256	556	121

Civilian Labor Force by Sex, Race, Hispanic Origin, and Age, 1948-1995—Continued

(Thousands of persons)

Year, sex, race, and Hispanic origin	16 years and over	16 to 19 years			20 years and over						
		Total	16 to 17 years	18 to 19 years	Total	20 to 24 years	25 to 34 years	35 to 44 years	45 to 54 years	55 to 64 years	65 years and over
HISPANIC											
1976	4 205	447	176	285	3 820	729	1 248	875	625	294	48
1977	4 536	493	184	305	4 059	813	1 325	916	656	293	55
1978	4 979	533	221	312	4 446	901	1 446	1 008	701	323	67
1979	5 219	551	207	343	4 668	960	1 532	1 062	704	339	72
1980	6 146	645	241	404	5 502	1 136	1 843	1 163	860	414	85
1981	6 492	603	215	388	5 888	1 231	2 015	1 239	886	430	87
1982	6 734	585	192	393	6 148	1 251	2 163	1 313	891	444	85
1983	7 033	590	189	401	6 442	1 282	2 267	1 380	931	495	86
1984	7 451	618	209	409	6 833	1 325	2 436	1 509	954	524	84
1985	7 698	579	199	379	7 119	1 358	2 571	1 595	985	527	82
1986	8 076	571	203	368	7 505	1 414	2 685	1 713	1 097	511	84
1987	8 541	610	206	404	7 931	1 425	2 890	1 904	1 086	545	81
1988	8 982	671	234	437	8 311	1 486	2 957	1 996	1 147	621	103
1989	9 323	680	224	456	8 643	1 483	3 118	2 092	1 205	625	120
1990	10 720	829	276	554	9 891	1 839	3 590	2 386	1 320	647	110
1991	10 920	781	249	532	10 139	1 835	3 596	2 539	1 376	681	111
1992	11 338	796	263	533	10 542	1 815	3 740	2 735	1 442	687	122
1993	11 610	771	246	525	10 839	1 811	3 800	2 865	1 534	684	145
1994	11 975	807	285	522	11 168	1 863	3 865	2 965	1 626	698	151
1995	12 267	850	291	559	11 417	1 818	3 943	3 113	1 671	720	152
HISPANIC MEN											
1976	2 580	260	104	155	2 326	433	771	541	398	189	34
1977	2 817	285	105	179	2 530	485	828	567	416	197	42
1978	3 041	299	129	171	2 742	546	882	620	425	217	52
1979	3 184	315	121	194	2 869	562	941	648	445	216	56
1980	3 818	392	147	245	3 426	697	1 161	713	522	270	62
1981	4 005	359	130	229	3 647	747	1 269	756	535	278	61
1982	4 148	333	111	221	3 815	759	1 361	808	539	290	58
1983	4 362	348	109	239	4 014	789	1 447	852	557	311	58
1984	4 563	345	113	232	4 218	822	1 540	910	570	325	51
1985	4 729	334	116	218	4 395	835	1 629	957	591	331	53
1986	4 948	336	114	222	4 612	888	1 669	1 015	661	323	56
1987	5 163	345	112	233	4 818	865	1 801	1 121	652	325	55
1988	5 409	378	123	255	5 031	897	1 834	1 189	686	355	69
1989	5 595	400	129	271	5 195	909	1 899	1 221	719	375	71
1990	6 546	512	165	346	6 034	1 182	2 230	1 403	775	380	65
1991	6 664	466	141	325	6 198	1 202	2 260	1 487	780	401	67
1992	6 900	468	154	314	6 432	1 141	2 366	1 593	844	414	74
1993	7 076	455	145	310	6 621	1 147	2 417	1 675	900	394	88
1994	7 210	463	163	300	6 747	1 184	2 430	1 713	922	410	89
1995	7 376	479	168	311	6 898	1 153	2 469	1 795	965	417	98
HISPANIC WOMEN											
1976	1 625	201	71	130	1 454	295	479	334	227	105	13
1977	1 720	204	80	125	1 523	327	497	349	240	96	13
1978	1 938	233	93	142	1 704	354	564	388	275	106	16
1979	2 035	235	86	149	1 800	397	590	413	258	124	15
1980	2 328	252	93	159	2 076	439	682	450	337	144	22
1981	2 486	244	85	159	2 242	484	745	483	351	152	27
1982	2 586	252	81	172	2 333	492	802	504	352	155	28
1983	2 671	242	80	162	2 429	493	820	529	374	184	29
1984	2 888	273	96	177	2 615	503	896	599	384	199	34
1985	2 970	245	84	161	2 725	524	943	639	394	196	29
1986	3 128	236	89	147	2 893	526	1 016	698	436	189	28
1987	3 377	265	94	171	3 112	559	1 090	783	434	220	27
1988	3 573	293	111	182	3 281	589	1 123	806	461	267	34
1989	3 728	280	95	185	3 448	574	1 219	871	486	251	49
1990	4 174	318	110	207	3 857	657	1 360	983	545	268	45
1991	4 256	315	107	207	3 941	633	1 336	1 052	596	279	44
1992	4 439	328	110	219	4 110	674	1 374	1 142	599	273	48
1993	4 534	316	101	215	4 218	664	1 383	1 190	633	290	57
1994	4 765	345	122	222	4 421	679	1 435	1 252	704	288	62
1995	4 891	371	123	249	4 520	666	1 473	1 318	706	303	54

NOTE: Data beginning in 1994 are not strictly comparable with data for 1993 and earlier years because of the introduction of a major redesign of the survey and collection methodology. Beginning in 1990, data are not strictly comparable with previous years because of the introduction of 1990 census-based population controls adjusted for the estimated undercount.

Civilian Labor Force Participation Rates by Sex, Race, Hispanic Origin, and Age, 1948-1995

(Percent)

Year, sex, race, and Hispanic origin	16 years and over	16 to 19 years	20 years and over						
			Total	20 to 24 years	25 to 34 years	35 to 44 years	45 to 54 years	55 to 64 years	65 years and over
TOTAL									
1948	58.8	52.5	59.4	64.1	63.1	66.7	65.1	56.9	27.0
1949	58.9	52.2	59.5	64.9	63.2	67.2	65.3	56.2	27.3
1950	59.2	51.8	59.9	65.9	63.5	67.5	66.4	56.7	26.7
1951	59.2	52.2	59.8	64.8	64.2	67.6	67.2	56.9	25.8
1952	59.0	51.3	59.7	62.2	64.7	68.0	67.5	57.5	24.8
1953	58.9	50.2	59.6	61.2	64.0	68.9	68.1	58.0	24.8
1954	58.8	48.3	59.6	61.6	64.3	68.8	68.4	58.7	23.9
1955	59.3	48.9	60.1	62.7	64.8	68.9	69.7	59.5	24.1
1956	60.0	50.9	60.7	64.1	64.8	69.5	70.5	60.8	24.3
1957	59.6	49.6	60.4	64.0	64.9	69.5	70.9	60.1	22.9
1958	59.5	47.4	60.5	64.4	65.0	69.6	71.5	60.5	21.8
1959	59.3	46.7	60.4	64.3	65.0	69.5	71.9	61.0	21.1
1960	59.4	47.5	60.5	65.2	65.4	69.4	72.2	60.9	20.8
1961	59.3	46.9	60.5	65.7	65.6	69.5	72.1	61.5	20.1
1962	58.8	46.1	60.0	65.3	65.2	69.7	72.2	61.5	19.1
1963	58.7	45.2	60.1	65.1	65.6	70.1	72.5	62.0	17.9
1964	58.7	44.5	60.2	66.3	65.8	70.0	72.9	61.9	18.0
1965	58.9	45.7	60.3	66.4	66.4	70.7	72.5	61.9	17.8
1966	59.2	48.2	60.5	66.5	67.1	71.0	72.7	62.2	17.2
1967	59.6	48.4	60.9	67.1	68.2	71.6	72.7	62.3	17.2
1968	59.6	48.3	60.9	67.0	68.6	72.0	72.8	62.2	17.2
1969	60.1	49.4	61.3	68.2	69.1	72.5	73.4	62.1	17.3
1970	60.4	49.9	61.6	69.2	69.7	73.1	73.5	61.8	17.0
1971	60.2	49.7	61.4	69.3	69.9	73.2	73.2	61.3	16.2
1972	60.4	51.9	61.4	70.8	70.9	73.3	72.7	60.0	15.6
1973	60.8	53.7	61.7	72.6	72.3	74.0	72.5	58.4	14.6
1974	61.3	54.8	62.0	74.0	73.6	74.6	72.7	57.8	14.0
1975	61.2	54.0	62.1	73.9	74.4	75.0	72.6	57.2	13.7
1976	61.6	54.5	62.4	74.7	75.7	76.0	72.5	56.6	13.1
1977	62.3	56.0	63.0	75.7	77.0	77.0	72.8	56.3	13.0
1978	63.2	57.8	63.8	76.8	78.3	78.1	73.5	56.3	13.3
1979	63.7	57.9	64.3	77.5	79.2	79.2	74.3	56.2	13.1
1980	63.8	56.7	64.5	77.2	79.9	80.0	74.9	55.7	12.5
1981	63.9	55.4	64.8	77.3	80.5	80.7	75.7	55.0	12.2
1982	64.0	54.1	65.0	77.1	81.0	81.2	75.9	55.1	11.9
1983	64.0	53.5	65.0	77.2	81.3	81.6	76.0	54.5	11.7
1984	64.4	53.9	65.3	77.6	81.8	82.4	76.5	54.2	11.1
1985	64.8	54.5	65.7	78.2	82.5	83.1	77.3	54.2	10.8
1986	65.3	54.7	66.2	78.9	82.9	83.7	78.0	54.0	10.9
1987	65.6	54.7	66.5	78.9	83.3	84.3	78.6	54.4	11.1
1988	65.9	55.3	66.8	78.7	83.3	84.6	79.6	54.6	11.5
1989	66.5	55.9	67.3	78.7	83.8	85.1	80.5	55.5	11.8
1990	66.5	53.7	67.6	77.8	83.6	85.2	80.7	55.9	11.8
1991	66.2	51.6	67.3	76.7	83.2	85.2	81.0	55.5	11.5
1992	66.4	51.3	67.6	77.0	83.7	85.1	81.5	56.2	11.5
1993	66.3	51.5	67.5	77.0	83.3	84.9	81.6	56.4	11.2
1994	66.6	52.7	67.7	77.0	83.2	84.8	81.7	56.8	12.4
1995	66.6	53.5	67.7	76.6	83.8	84.6	81.4	57.2	12.1

Civilian Labor Force Participation Rates by Sex, Race, Hispanic Origin, and Age, 1948-1995—Continued

(Percent)

Year, sex, race, and Hispanic origin	16 years and over	16 to 19 years	20 years and over						
			Total	20 to 24 years	25 to 34 years	35 to 44 years	45 to 54 years	55 to 64 years	65 years and over
MEN									
1948	86.6	63.7	88.6	84.6	95.9	97.9	95.8	89.5	46.8
1949	86.4	62.8	88.5	86.6	95.8	97.9	95.6	87.5	47.0
1950	86.4	63.2	88.4	87.9	96.0	97.6	95.8	86.9	45.8
1951	86.3	63.0	88.2	88.4	96.9	97.5	95.9	87.2	44.9
1952	86.3	61.3	88.3	88.1	97.5	97.8	96.2	87.5	42.6
1953	86.0	60.7	88.0	87.7	97.4	98.2	96.5	87.9	41.6
1954	85.5	58.0	87.8	86.9	97.3	98.1	96.5	88.7	40.5
1955	85.4	58.9	87.6	86.9	97.6	98.1	96.4	87.9	39.6
1956	85.5	60.5	87.6	87.8	97.3	97.9	96.6	88.5	40.0
1957	84.8	59.1	86.9	87.1	97.1	97.9	96.3	87.5	37.5
1958	84.2	56.6	86.6	86.9	97.1	97.9	96.3	87.8	35.6
1959	83.7	55.8	86.3	87.8	97.4	97.8	96.0	87.4	34.2
1960	83.3	56.1	86.0	88.1	97.5	97.7	95.7	86.8	33.1
1961	82.9	54.6	85.7	87.8	97.5	97.6	95.6	87.3	31.7
1962	82.0	53.8	84.8	86.9	97.2	97.6	95.6	86.2	30.3
1963	81.4	52.9	84.4	86.1	97.1	97.5	95.7	86.2	28.4
1964	81.0	52.4	84.2	86.1	97.3	97.3	95.7	85.6	28.0
1965	80.7	53.8	83.9	85.8	97.2	97.3	95.6	84.6	27.9
1966	80.4	55.3	83.6	85.1	97.3	97.2	95.3	84.5	27.1
1967	80.4	55.6	83.4	84.4	97.2	97.3	95.2	84.4	27.1
1968	80.1	55.1	83.1	82.8	96.9	97.1	94.9	84.3	27.3
1969	79.8	55.9	82.8	82.8	96.7	96.9	94.6	83.4	27.2
1970	79.7	56.1	82.6	83.3	96.4	96.9	94.3	83.0	26.8
1971	79.1	56.1	82.1	83.0	95.9	96.5	93.9	82.1	25.5
1972	78.9	58.1	81.6	83.9	95.7	96.4	93.2	80.4	24.3
1973	78.8	59.7	81.3	85.2	95.7	96.2	93.0	78.2	22.7
1974	78.7	60.7	81.0	85.9	95.8	96.0	92.2	77.3	22.4
1975	77.9	59.1	80.3	84.5	95.2	95.6	92.1	75.6	21.6
1976	77.5	59.3	79.8	85.2	95.2	95.4	91.6	74.3	20.2
1977	77.7	60.9	79.7	85.6	95.3	95.7	91.1	73.8	20.0
1978	77.9	62.0	79.8	85.9	95.3	95.7	91.3	73.3	20.4
1979	77.8	61.5	79.8	86.4	95.3	95.7	91.4	72.8	19.9
1980	77.4	60.5	79.4	85.9	95.2	95.5	91.2	72.1	19.0
1981	77.0	59.0	79.0	85.5	94.9	95.4	91.4	70.6	18.4
1982	76.6	56.7	78.7	84.9	94.7	95.3	91.2	70.2	17.8
1983	76.4	56.2	78.5	84.8	94.2	95.2	91.2	69.4	17.4
1984	76.4	56.0	78.3	85.0	94.4	95.4	91.2	68.5	16.3
1985	76.3	56.8	78.1	85.0	94.7	95.0	91.0	67.9	15.8
1986	76.3	56.4	78.1	85.8	94.6	94.8	91.0	67.3	16.0
1987	76.2	56.1	78.0	85.2	94.6	94.6	90.7	67.6	16.3
1988	76.2	56.9	77.9	85.0	94.3	94.5	90.9	67.0	16.5
1989	76.4	57.9	78.1	85.3	94.4	94.5	91.1	67.2	16.6
1990	76.4	55.7	78.2	84.4	94.1	94.3	90.7	67.8	16.3
1991	75.8	53.2	77.7	83.5	93.6	94.1	90.5	67.0	15.7
1992	75.8	53.4	77.7	83.3	93.8	93.7	90.7	67.0	16.1
1993	75.4	53.2	77.3	83.2	93.4	93.4	90.1	66.5	15.6
1994	75.1	54.1	76.8	83.1	92.6	92.8	89.1	65.5	16.8
1995	75.0	54.8	76.7	83.1	93.0	92.3	88.8	66.0	16.8

Civilian Labor Force Participation Rates by Sex, Race, Hispanic Origin, and Age, 1948-1995—Continued

(Percent)

Year, sex, race, and Hispanic origin	16 years and over	16 to 19 years	20 years and over						
			Total	20 to 24 years	25 to 34 years	35 to 44 years	45 to 54 years	55 to 64 years	65 years and over
WOMEN									
1948	32.7	42.0	31.8	45.3	33.2	36.9	35.0	24.3	9.1
1949	33.1	42.4	32.3	45.0	33.4	38.1	35.9	25.3	9.6
1950	33.9	41.0	33.3	46.0	34.0	39.1	37.9	27.0	9.7
1951	34.6	42.4	34.0	46.5	35.4	39.8	39.7	27.6	8.9
1952	34.7	42.2	34.1	44.7	35.4	40.4	40.1	28.7	9.1
1953	34.4	40.7	33.9	44.3	34.0	41.3	40.4	29.1	10.0
1954	34.6	39.4	34.2	45.1	34.4	41.2	41.2	30.0	9.3
1955	35.7	39.7	35.4	45.9	34.9	41.6	43.8	32.5	10.6
1956	36.9	42.2	36.4	46.3	35.4	43.1	45.5	34.9	10.8
1957	36.9	41.1	36.5	45.9	35.6	43.3	46.5	34.5	10.5
1958	37.1	39.0	36.9	46.3	35.6	43.4	47.8	35.2	10.3
1959	37.1	38.2	37.1	45.1	35.3	43.4	49.0	36.6	10.2
1960	37.7	39.3	37.6	46.1	36.0	43.4	49.9	37.2	10.8
1961	38.1	39.7	38.0	47.0	36.4	43.8	50.1	37.9	10.7
1962	37.9	39.0	37.8	47.3	36.3	44.1	50.0	38.7	10.0
1963	38.3	38.0	38.3	47.5	37.2	44.9	50.6	39.7	9.6
1964	38.7	37.0	38.9	49.4	37.2	45.0	51.4	40.2	10.1
1965	39.3	38.0	39.4	49.9	38.5	46.1	50.9	41.1	10.0
1966	40.3	41.4	40.1	51.5	39.8	46.8	51.7	41.8	9.6
1967	41.1	41.6	41.1	53.3	41.9	48.1	51.8	42.4	9.6
1968	41.6	41.9	41.6	54.5	42.6	48.9	52.3	42.4	9.6
1969	42.7	43.2	42.7	56.7	43.7	49.9	53.8	43.1	9.9
1970	43.3	44.0	43.3	57.7	45.0	51.1	54.4	43.0	9.7
1971	43.4	43.4	43.3	57.7	45.6	51.6	54.3	42.9	9.5
1972	43.9	45.8	43.7	59.1	47.8	52.0	53.9	42.1	9.3
1973	44.7	47.8	44.4	61.1	50.4	53.3	53.7	41.1	8.9
1974	45.7	49.1	45.3	63.1	52.6	54.7	54.6	40.7	8.1
1975	46.3	49.1	46.0	64.1	54.9	55.8	54.6	40.9	8.2
1976	47.3	49.8	47.0	65.0	57.3	57.8	55.0	41.0	8.2
1977	48.4	51.2	48.1	66.5	59.7	59.6	55.8	40.9	8.1
1978	50.0	53.7	49.6	68.3	62.2	61.6	57.1	41.3	8.3
1979	50.9	54.2	50.6	69.0	63.9	63.6	58.3	41.7	8.3
1980	51.5	52.9	51.3	68.9	65.5	65.5	59.9	41.3	8.1
1981	52.1	51.8	52.1	69.6	66.7	66.8	61.1	41.4	8.0
1982	52.6	51.4	52.7	69.8	68.0	68.0	61.6	41.8	7.9
1983	52.9	50.8	53.1	69.9	69.0	68.7	61.9	41.5	7.8
1984	53.6	51.8	53.7	70.4	69.8	70.1	62.9	41.7	7.5
1985	54.5	52.1	54.7	71.8	70.9	71.8	64.4	42.0	7.3
1986	55.3	53.0	55.5	72.4	71.6	73.1	65.9	42.3	7.4
1987	56.0	53.3	56.2	73.0	72.4	74.5	67.1	42.7	7.4
1988	56.6	53.6	56.8	72.7	72.7	75.2	69.0	43.5	7.9
1989	57.4	53.9	57.7	72.4	73.5	76.0	70.5	45.0	8.4
1990	57.5	51.6	58.0	71.3	73.5	76.4	71.2	45.2	8.6
1991	57.4	50.0	57.9	70.1	73.1	76.5	72.0	45.2	8.5
1992	57.8	49.1	58.5	70.9	73.9	76.7	72.6	46.5	8.3
1993	57.9	49.7	58.5	70.9	73.4	76.6	73.5	47.2	8.1
1994	58.8	51.3	59.3	71.0	74.0	77.1	74.6	48.9	9.2
1995	58.9	52.2	59.4	70.3	74.9	77.2	74.4	49.2	8.8

Civilian Labor Force Participation Rates by Sex, Race, Hispanic Origin, and Age, 1948-1995—Continued

(Percent)

Year, sex, race, and Hispanic origin	16 years and over	16 to 19 years	20 years and over						
			Total	20 to 24 years	25 to 34 years	35 to 44 years	45 to 54 years	55 to 64 years	65 years and over
WHITE									
1954	58.2	48.8	58.9	61.0	63.5	68.0	67.9	58.4	23.7
1955	58.7	49.3	59.5	62.4	64.0	68.3	69.2	59.3	23.9
1956	59.4	51.3	60.1	64.1	64.0	68.9	70.1	60.6	24.2
1957	59.1	50.3	59.8	63.7	64.1	68.8	70.5	59.9	22.8
1958	58.9	47.9	59.8	64.1	64.2	68.8	71.0	60.3	21.7
1959	58.7	47.4	59.7	63.7	64.3	68.7	71.5	60.7	21.0
1960	58.8	47.9	59.8	64.8	64.7	68.6	71.7	60.6	20.8
1961	58.8	47.4	59.9	65.5	64.8	68.8	71.7	61.3	20.0
1962	58.3	46.6	59.4	65.0	64.4	69.0	71.8	61.3	19.0
1963	58.2	45.7	59.4	64.9	64.8	69.4	72.3	61.8	17.9
1964	58.2	45.1	59.6	65.8	64.9	69.5	72.5	61.8	17.8
1965	58.4	46.5	59.7	65.7	65.6	70.1	72.2	61.7	17.7
1966	58.7	49.1	59.8	66.0	66.3	70.4	72.5	61.9	17.1
1967	59.2	49.2	60.3	66.8	67.4	71.2	72.5	62.3	17.0
1968	59.3	49.3	60.4	66.6	67.9	71.7	72.7	62.2	17.1
1969	59.9	50.6	60.9	67.9	68.4	72.3	73.3	62.1	17.2
1970	60.2	51.4	61.2	69.2	69.1	72.9	73.5	61.8	16.8
1971	60.1	51.6	61.1	69.6	69.3	73.0	73.4	61.3	16.1
1972	60.4	54.1	61.2	71.2	70.4	73.2	72.9	60.3	15.4
1973	60.8	56.0	61.4	73.3	72.0	73.9	72.7	58.6	14.4
1974	61.4	57.3	61.9	74.8	73.4	74.6	73.0	58.0	13.9
1975	61.5	56.7	62.0	75.2	74.4	75.1	73.0	57.4	13.6
1976	61.8	57.5	62.3	76.0	75.6	76.1	73.0	56.9	13.0
1977	62.5	59.3	62.9	77.1	77.0	77.1	73.2	56.6	12.9
1978	63.3	60.8	63.6	78.1	78.3	78.1	73.8	56.4	13.1
1979	63.9	61.1	64.2	78.9	79.4	79.3	74.6	56.5	12.9
1980	64.1	60.0	64.5	78.7	80.2	80.3	75.4	56.0	12.5
1981	64.3	58.9	64.8	79.1	81.0	81.0	76.2	55.2	12.2
1982	64.3	57.5	65.0	78.9	81.6	81.5	76.4	55.3	12.0
1983	64.3	56.9	65.0	79.0	81.8	81.9	76.5	54.7	11.8
1984	64.6	57.2	65.3	79.4	82.5	82.6	77.0	54.5	11.1
1985	65.0	57.5	65.7	79.9	83.1	83.4	77.8	54.4	10.7
1986	65.5	57.8	66.1	80.6	83.6	84.0	78.5	54.3	11.0
1987	65.8	57.7	66.5	80.7	84.0	84.7	79.1	54.6	11.1
1988	66.2	58.6	66.8	80.6	84.1	85.0	80.3	55.1	11.4
1989	66.7	59.1	67.3	80.2	84.5	85.5	81.2	56.2	11.8
1990	66.9	57.5	67.6	79.8	84.6	85.9	81.3	56.5	11.9
1991	66.6	55.8	67.4	78.9	84.3	85.9	81.8	56.0	11.6
1992	66.8	54.7	67.7	79.4	84.6	85.8	82.2	56.8	11.6
1993	66.8	55.1	67.6	79.5	84.5	85.7	82.5	57.1	11.4
1994	67.1	56.4	67.9	79.5	84.4	85.7	82.7	57.6	12.5
1995	67.1	57.1	67.8	78.7	84.9	85.5	82.5	58.0	12.3

Civilian Labor Force Participation Rates by Sex, Race, Hispanic Origin, and Age, 1948-1995—Continued

(Percent)

Year, sex, race, and Hispanic origin	16 years and over	16 to 19 years	20 years and over						
			Total	20 to 24 years	25 to 34 years	35 to 44 years	45 to 54 years	55 to 64 years	65 years and over
WHITE MEN									
1954	85.6	57.6	87.8	86.3	97.5	98.2	96.8	89.1	40.4
1955	85.4	58.6	87.5	86.5	97.8	98.2	96.7	88.4	39.6
1956	85.6	60.4	87.6	87.6	97.4	98.1	96.8	88.9	40.0
1957	84.8	59.2	86.9	86.6	97.2	98.0	96.7	88.0	37.7
1958	84.3	56.5	86.6	86.7	97.2	98.0	96.6	88.2	35.7
1959	83.8	55.9	86.3	87.3	97.5	98.0	96.3	87.9	34.3
1960	83.4	55.9	86.0	87.8	97.7	97.9	96.1	87.2	33.3
1961	83.0	54.5	85.7	87.6	97.7	97.9	95.9	87.8	31.9
1962	82.1	53.8	84.9	86.5	97.4	97.9	96.0	86.7	30.6
1963	81.5	53.1	84.4	85.8	97.4	97.8	96.2	86.6	28.4
1964	81.1	52.7	84.2	85.7	97.5	97.6	96.1	86.1	27.9
1965	80.8	54.1	83.9	85.3	97.4	97.7	95.9	85.2	27.9
1966	80.6	55.9	83.6	84.4	97.5	97.6	95.8	84.9	27.2
1967	80.6	56.3	83.5	84.0	97.5	97.7	95.6	84.9	27.1
1968	80.4	55.9	83.2	82.4	97.2	97.6	95.4	84.7	27.4
1969	80.2	56.8	83.0	82.6	97.0	97.4	95.1	83.9	27.3
1970	80.0	57.5	82.8	83.3	96.7	97.3	94.9	83.3	26.7
1971	79.6	57.9	82.3	83.2	96.3	97.0	94.7	82.6	25.6
1972	79.6	60.1	82.0	84.3	96.0	97.0	94.0	81.1	24.4
1973	79.4	62.0	81.6	85.8	96.2	96.8	93.5	78.9	22.7
1974	79.4	62.9	81.4	86.6	96.3	96.7	93.0	78.0	22.4
1975	78.7	61.9	80.7	85.5	95.8	96.4	92.9	76.4	21.7
1976	78.4	62.3	80.3	86.3	95.9	96.0	92.5	75.2	20.2
1977	78.5	64.0	80.2	86.8	96.0	96.2	92.1	74.6	20.0
1978	78.6	65.0	80.1	87.3	95.9	96.3	92.1	73.7	20.3
1979	78.6	64.8	80.1	87.6	96.0	96.4	92.2	73.4	20.0
1980	78.2	63.7	79.8	87.2	95.9	96.2	92.1	73.1	19.1
1981	77.9	62.4	79.5	87.0	95.8	96.1	92.4	71.5	18.5
1982	77.4	60.0	79.2	86.3	95.6	96.0	92.2	71.0	17.9
1983	77.1	59.4	78.9	86.1	95.2	96.0	91.9	70.0	17.7
1984	77.1	59.0	78.7	86.5	95.4	96.1	92.0	69.5	16.4
1985	77.0	59.7	78.5	86.4	95.7	95.7	92.0	68.8	15.9
1986	76.9	59.3	78.5	87.3	95.5	95.4	91.8	68.0	16.3
1987	76.8	59.0	78.4	86.9	95.5	95.4	91.6	68.1	16.5
1988	76.9	60.0	78.3	86.6	95.2	95.4	91.8	67.9	16.7
1989	77.1	61.0	78.5	86.8	95.4	95.3	92.2	68.3	16.8
1990	77.1	59.6	78.5	86.2	95.2	95.3	91.7	68.6	16.6
1991	76.5	57.3	78.0	85.4	94.9	95.0	91.4	67.7	15.9
1992	76.5	56.9	78.0	85.2	94.9	94.7	91.8	67.7	16.2
1993	76.2	56.6	77.7	85.5	94.7	94.5	91.3	67.3	15.9
1994	75.9	57.7	77.3	85.5	93.9	93.9	90.3	66.4	17.2
1995	75.7	58.5	77.1	85.1	94.1	93.4	90.0	67.1	16.9
WHITE WOMEN									
1954	33.3	40.6	32.7	44.4	32.5	39.3	39.8	29.1	9.1
1955	34.5	40.7	34.0	45.8	32.8	40.0	42.7	31.8	10.5
1956	35.7	43.1	35.1	46.5	33.2	41.5	44.4	34.0	10.6
1957	35.7	42.2	35.2	45.8	33.6	41.5	45.4	33.7	10.2
1958	35.8	40.1	35.5	46.0	33.6	41.4	46.5	34.5	10.1
1959	36.0	39.6	35.6	44.5	33.4	41.4	47.8	35.7	10.0
1960	36.5	40.3	36.2	45.7	34.1	41.5	48.6	36.2	10.6
1961	36.9	40.6	36.6	46.9	34.3	41.8	48.9	37.2	10.5
1962	36.7	39.8	36.5	47.1	34.1	42.2	48.9	38.0	9.8
1963	37.2	38.7	37.0	47.3	34.8	43.1	49.5	38.9	9.4
1964	37.5	37.8	37.5	48.8	35.0	43.3	50.2	39.4	9.9
1965	38.1	39.2	38.0	49.2	36.3	44.4	49.9	40.3	9.7
1966	39.2	42.6	38.8	51.0	37.7	45.0	50.6	41.1	9.4
1967	40.1	42.5	39.8	53.1	39.7	46.4	50.9	41.9	9.3
1968	40.7	43.0	40.4	54.0	40.6	47.5	51.5	42.0	9.4
1969	41.8	44.6	41.5	56.4	41.7	48.6	53.0	42.6	9.7
1970	42.6	45.6	42.2	57.7	43.2	49.9	53.7	42.6	9.5
1971	42.6	45.4	42.3	58.0	43.7	50.2	53.6	42.5	9.3
1972	43.2	48.1	42.7	59.4	46.0	50.7	53.4	41.9	9.0
1973	44.1	50.1	43.5	61.7	48.7	52.2	53.4	40.7	8.7
1974	45.2	51.7	44.4	63.9	51.3	53.6	54.3	40.4	8.0
1975	45.9	51.5	45.3	65.5	53.8	54.9	54.3	40.6	8.0
1976	46.9	52.8	46.2	66.3	56.0	57.1	54.7	40.7	7.9
1977	48.0	54.5	47.3	67.8	58.5	58.9	55.3	40.7	7.9
1978	49.4	56.7	48.7	69.3	61.2	60.7	56.7	41.1	8.1
1979	50.5	57.4	49.8	70.5	63.1	63.0	58.1	41.5	8.1
1980	51.2	56.2	50.6	70.6	64.8	65.0	59.6	40.9	7.9
1981	51.9	55.4	51.5	71.5	66.4	66.4	60.9	40.9	7.9
1982	52.4	55.0	52.2	71.8	67.8	67.5	61.4	41.5	7.8
1983	52.7	54.5	52.5	72.1	68.7	68.2	61.9	41.1	7.8
1984	53.3	55.4	53.1	72.5	69.8	69.6	62.7	41.2	7.5
1985	54.1	55.2	54.0	73.8	70.9	71.4	64.2	41.5	7.0
1986	55.0	56.3	54.9	74.1	71.8	72.9	65.8	42.1	7.3
1987	55.7	56.5	55.6	74.8	72.5	74.2	67.2	42.4	7.2
1988	56.4	57.2	56.3	74.9	73.0	74.9	69.2	43.6	7.7
1989	57.2	57.1	57.2	74.0	73.8	75.9	70.6	45.2	8.2
1990	57.4	55.3	57.6	73.4	74.1	76.6	71.3	45.5	8.5
1991	57.4	54.1	57.6	72.5	73.8	76.8	72.4	45.4	8.5
1992	57.7	52.5	58.1	73.5	74.4	77.0	72.8	46.8	8.2
1993	58.0	53.5	58.3	73.4	74.3	76.9	74.0	47.6	8.1
1994	58.9	55.1	59.2	73.4	74.9	77.5	75.2	49.4	9.2
1995	59.0	55.5	59.2	72.3	75.8	77.6	75.2	49.5	9.0

Civilian Labor Force Participation Rates by Sex, Race, Hispanic Origin, and Age, 1948-1995—Continued

(Percent)

Year, sex, race, and Hispanic origin	16 years and over	16 to 19 years	20 years and over						
			Total	20 to 24 years	25 to 34 years	35 to 44 years	45 to 54 years	55 to 64 years	65 years and over
BLACK									
1972	59.9	39.1	63.3						
1973	60.2	39.8	63.4						
1974	59.8	39.8	63.0						
1975	58.8	38.2	62.0						
1976	59.0	37.0	62.5						
1977	59.8	37.9	63.2						
1978	61.5	41.0	64.5						
1979	61.4	40.1	64.5						
1980	61.0	38.9	64.1						
1981	60.8	37.7	64.2						
1982	61.0	36.6	64.3						
1983	61.5	36.4	64.9						
1984	62.2	38.3	65.2						
1985	62.9	41.2	65.6						
1986	63.3	41.3	65.9						
1987	63.8	41.6	66.5						
1988	63.8	40.8	66.5						
1989	64.2	42.5	66.7						
1990	64.0	38.7	66.9						
1991	63.3	35.4	66.4						
1992	63.9	37.9	66.8						
1993	63.2	37.0	66.0						
1994	63.4	38.5	66.0						
1995	63.7	39.9	66.3						
BLACK MEN									
1972	73.6	46.3	78.5						
1973	73.4	45.7	78.4						
1974	72.9	46.7	77.6						
1975	70.9	42.6	76.0						
1976	70.0	41.3	75.4						
1977	70.6	43.2	75.6						
1978	71.5	44.9	76.2						
1979	71.3	43.6	76.3						
1980	70.3	43.2	75.1						
1981	70.0	41.6	74.5						
1982	70.1	39.8	74.7						
1983	70.6	39.9	75.2						
1984	70.8	41.7	74.8						
1985	70.8	44.6	74.4						
1986	71.2	43.7	74.8						
1987	71.1	43.6	74.7						
1988	71.0	43.8	74.6						
1989	71.0	44.6	74.4						
1990	71.0	40.7	75.0						
1991	70.4	37.3	74.6						
1992	70.7	40.6	74.3						
1993	69.6	39.5	73.2						
1994	69.1	40.8	72.5						
1995	69.0	40.1	72.5						
BLACK WOMEN									
1972	48.7	32.2	51.2						
1973	49.3	34.2	51.6						
1974	49.0	33.4	51.4						
1975	48.8	34.2	51.1						
1976	49.8	32.9	52.5						
1977	50.8	32.9	53.6						
1978	53.1	37.3	55.5						
1979	53.1	36.8	55.4						
1980	53.1	34.9	55.6						
1981	53.5	34.0	56.0						
1982	53.7	33.5	56.2						
1983	54.2	33.0	56.8						
1984	55.2	35.0	57.6						
1985	56.5	37.9	58.6						
1986	56.9	39.1	58.9						
1987	58.0	39.6	60.0						
1988	58.0	37.9	60.1						
1989	58.7	40.4	60.6						
1990	58.3	36.8	60.6						
1991	57.5	33.5	60.0						
1992	58.5	35.2	60.8						
1993	57.9	34.6	60.2						
1994	58.7	36.3	60.9						
1995	59.5	39.8	61.4						

Civilian Labor Force Participation Rates by Sex, Race, Hispanic Origin, and Age, 1948-1995—Continued

(Percent)

Year, sex, race, and Hispanic origin	16 years and over	16 to 19 years	20 years and over						
			Total	20 to 24 years	25 to 34 years	35 to 44 years	45 to 54 years	55 to 64 years	65 years and over
HISPANIC									
1980	64.0	50.3	66.1	72.7	73.5	73.9	72.2	52.9	12.2
1981	64.1	46.4	66.8	74.6	74.7	73.7	72.0	51.7	12.0
1982	63.6	44.8	66.3	72.6	75.4	73.8	70.5	50.5	11.3
1983	63.8	45.3	66.2	71.6	74.5	73.3	71.7	53.4	11.1
1984	64.9	47.5	67.1	72.0	75.6	75.6	71.4	53.9	10.4
1985	64.6	44.6	67.1	72.9	75.6	75.4	71.5	52.0	9.7
1986	65.4	43.9	68.0	74.5	76.5	76.5	73.3	50.0	9.6
1987	66.4	45.8	68.8	74.6	77.8	77.3	72.8	51.4	9.1
1988	67.4	49.6	69.4	76.3	77.7	77.8	73.0	53.6	11.2
1989	67.6	48.6	69.7	76.0	78.9	78.7	73.1	52.9	12.0
1990	67.4	47.8	69.8	75.7	78.2	79.5	72.7	51.9	10.1
1991	66.5	45.1	69.0	74.0	76.9	78.3	73.2	53.0	9.8
1992	66.8	45.8	69.2	74.3	77.8	79.1	72.8	52.0	10.0
1993	66.2	43.9	68.7	72.8	77.8	78.9	73.1	51.7	10.7
1994	66.1	44.4	68.5	74.0	77.3	78.9	73.1	49.8	10.7
1995	65.8	45.4	68.1	71.9	78.1	78.5	72.8	48.6	10.5
HISPANIC MEN									
1980	81.4	60.0	84.9	88.0	93.3	93.8	91.7	73.6	20.7
1981	80.6	54.2	84.7	88.8	93.8	92.6	90.6	70.9	19.4
1982	79.7	50.1	84.0	86.1	93.9	93.5	88.8	70.0	17.9
1983	80.3	52.6	84.1	85.8	93.5	93.0	89.4	71.3	17.4
1984	80.6	52.6	84.3	87.0	93.4	93.6	89.0	71.2	14.9
1985	80.3	51.0	84.0	87.3	93.1	92.4	89.5	69.6	14.9
1986	81.0	51.3	84.6	88.3	93.4	93.3	89.9	69.3	15.2
1987	81.0	51.4	84.5	87.8	93.6	93.0	88.0	70.2	14.4
1988	81.9	55.3	85.0	89.4	93.4	93.8	88.5	68.8	17.4
1989	82.0	56.2	85.0	90.5	94.2	93.2	88.8	69.7	16.4
1990	81.4	55.9	84.7	89.6	94.1	92.8	87.1	66.3	14.0
1991	80.3	51.6	83.8	88.5	92.6	91.1	87.6	67.6	14.1
1992	80.7	52.0	84.0	87.4	92.9	92.2	86.8	68.7	14.9
1993	80.2	50.9	83.5	87.9	92.9	92.4	87.3	65.6	15.2
1994	79.2	50.0	82.5	88.0	92.5	91.5	85.7	63.6	14.4
1995	79.1	50.2	82.4	86.2	92.9	91.3	85.6	62.4	15.8
HISPANIC WOMEN									
1980	47.4	40.2	48.5	57.0	54.0	55.3	54.4	34.7	5.7
1981	48.3	38.3	49.7	59.8	55.5	55.9	54.8	34.5	6.4
1982	48.1	39.3	49.3	58.4	56.4	55.2	53.6	33.2	6.4
1983	47.7	37.6	49.0	56.5	54.8	54.7	55.4	37.5	6.4
1984	49.6	42.3	50.5	56.2	56.9	58.6	55.2	38.5	7.2
1985	49.3	38.1	50.6	57.7	57.1	59.1	55.1	36.4	5.9
1986	50.1	36.5	51.7	58.9	59.0	60.6	57.4	33.9	5.5
1987	52.0	40.1	53.3	60.4	60.9	62.2	57.8	36.8	5.3
1988	53.2	43.7	54.2	62.3	60.9	62.1	57.9	41.5	6.5
1989	53.5	40.7	54.9	60.7	63.0	64.7	57.9	38.9	8.6
1990	53.1	38.7	54.8	59.2	61.3	66.0	58.8	39.6	7.2
1991	52.4	38.0	54.0	56.4	59.8	65.3	60.3	40.5	6.7
1992	52.8	39.2	54.3	59.2	60.8	66.0	59.4	38.1	6.6
1993	52.1	36.7	53.8	56.2	60.5	65.4	59.7	40.1	7.3
1994	52.9	38.7	54.4	57.9	60.5	66.4	61.4	38.1	7.9
1995	52.6	40.4	53.9	55.9	61.6	65.9	60.5	37.2	6.6

NOTE: Data beginning in 1994 are not strictly comparable with data for 1993 and earlier years because of the introduction of a major redesign of the survey and collection methodology. Beginning in 1990, data are not strictly comparable with previous years because of the introduction of 1990 census-based population controls adjusted for the estimated undercount.

Employed and Unemployed Full- and Part-time Workers by Sex and Age, 1968-1995

(Thousands of persons)

Year, sex, and age	Employed				Unemployed	
	Full-time			Part-time	Looking for full-time work	Looking for part-time work
	Total	Full-time schedules	Part-time for economic reasons, usually work full-time			
TOTAL						
1968	65 277	64 225	1 052	10 644	2 138	679
1969	66 596	65 503	1 093	11 306	2 142	689
1970	66 753	65 418	1 335	11 925	3 206	889
1971	66 973	65 658	1 315	12 393	3 968	1 047
1972	69 214	68 008	1 206	12 939	3 806	1 077
1973	71 803	70 594	1 209	13 262	3 344	1 023
1974	73 093	71 634	1 460	13 701	4 010	1 147
1975	71 586	69 790	1 796	14 260	6 523	1 408
1976	73 964	72 465	1 499	14 788	5 974	1 432
1977	76 625	75 204	1 421	15 391	5 548	1 443
1978	80 193	78 782	1 411	15 855	4 838	1 364
1979	82 654	81 179	1 475	16 171	4 787	1 351
1980	82 562	80 706	1 856	16 740	6 269	1 369
1981	83 243	81 358	1 885	17 154	6 795	1 477
1982	81 421	79 118	2 303	18 106	9 006	1 672
1983	82 322	80 395	1 927	18 511	9 075	1 642
1984	86 544	84 831	1 713	18 462	7 057	1 481
1985	88 534	86 795	1 739	18 615	6 793	1 519
1986	90 529	88 789	1 740	19 069	6 708	1 529
1987	92 957	91 251	1 706	19 483	5 979	1 446
1988	95 214	93 454	1 760	19 754	5 357	1 343
1989	97 369	95 639	1 730	19 973	5 211	1 317
1990	98 666	96 750	1 915	20 128	5 677	1 369
1991	97 190	94 959	2 231	20 528	7 088	1 540
1992	97 664	95 596	2 068	20 828	7 923	1 690
1993	99 114	97 078	2 036	21 145	7 305	1 635
1994	99 772	98 380	1 392	23 288	6 513	1 483
1995	101 679	100 211	1 468	23 220	5 909	1 495

Employed and Unemployed Full- and Part-time Workers by Sex and Age, 1968-1995—Continued

(Thousands of persons)

Year, sex, and age	Employed				Unemployed	
	Full-time			Part-time	Looking for full-time work	Looking for part-time work
	Total	Full-time schedules	Part-time for economic reasons, usually work full-time			
MEN, 16 YEARS AND OVER						
1968	44 384	43 754	630	3 730	1 124	296
1969	44 815	44 169	646	4 003	1 101	302
1970	44 825	44 012	813	4 166	1 832	406
1971	45 023	44 233	790	4 367	2 319	472
1972	46 373	45 638	735	4 523	2 170	489
1973	47 843	47 123	719	4 507	1 834	441
1974	48 378	47 500	878	4 646	2 225	489
1975	46 988	45 858	1 130	4 870	3 852	590
1976	48 150	47 221	929	4 988	3 421	615
1977	49 551	48 695	855	5 178	3 071	596
1978	51 281	50 450	831	5 198	2 587	554
1979	52 427	51 559	868	5 180	2 590	530
1980	51 717	50 583	1 134	5 471	3 703	563
1981	51 906	50 750	1 156	5 492	3 958	619
1982	50 334	48 899	1 435	5 937	5 485	694
1983	50 643	49 470	1 173	6 145	5 581	679
1984	53 070	52 043	1 027	6 020	4 142	602
1985	53 862	52 832	1 030	6 028	3 925	596
1986	54 685	53 644	1 041	6 207	3 916	614
1987	55 746	54 735	1 011	6 360	3 520	580
1988	56 816	55 780	1 036	6 457	3 116	539
1989	57 885	56 894	991	6 430	2 995	530
1990	58 501	57 358	1 142	6 604	3 351	555
1991	57 407	56 020	1 388	6 815	4 315	631
1992	57 363	56 068	1 295	7 077	4 814	709
1993	58 123	56 886	1 237	7 226	4 375	680
1994	58 832	57 956	876	7 617	3 745	622
1995	59 936	59 039	897	7 441	3 374	609
MEN, 20 YEARS AND OVER						
1968	42 720	42 164	556	2 139	896	96
1969	43 100	42 530	570	2 288	862	101
1970	43 138	42 404	734	2 443	1 502	137
1971	43 321	42 607	715	2 591	1 932	165
1972	44 476	43 827	649	2 654	1 777	171
1973	45 637	45 012	626	2 673	1 474	150
1974	46 158	45 384	774	2 765	1 786	172
1975	45 051	44 026	1 026	2 967	3 255	223
1976	46 175	45 348	827	3 015	2 870	228
1977	47 402	46 652	751	3 152	2 571	223
1978	49 007	48 285	722	3 136	2 136	192
1979	50 174	49 403	771	3 133	2 129	179
1980	49 698	48 671	1 028	3 403	3 167	186
1981	50 092	49 028	1 064	3 490	3 394	220
1982	48 895	47 550	1 345	3 996	4 829	260
1983	49 264	48 167	1 097	4 223	4 982	274
1984	51 624	50 674	950	4 145	3 685	247
1985	52 425	51 475	950	4 137	3 479	236
1986	53 317	52 356	961	4 252	3 508	243
1987	54 381	53 443	938	4 345	3 147	222
1988	55 353	54 390	963	4 427	2 778	209
1989	56 386	55 468	918	4 451	2 651	215
1990	57 055	55 987	1 067	4 623	3 000	239
1991	56 243	54 922	1 320	4 936	3 928	267
1992	56 274	55 035	1 239	5 223	4 430	287
1993	57 010	55 837	1 173	5 345	4 011	276
1994	57 707	56 879	828	5 587	3 359	269
1995	58 707	57 862	845	5 377	2 988	251

Employed and Unemployed Full- and Part-time Workers by Sex and Age, 1968-1995—Continued

(Thousands of persons)

Year, sex, and age	Employed				Unemployed	
	Full-time			Part-time	Looking for full-time work	Looking for part-time work
	Total	Full-time schedules	Part-time for economic reasons, usually work full-time			
WOMEN, 16 YEARS AND OVER						
1968	20 893	20 471	422	6 914	1 014	383
1969	21 781	21 334	447	7 303	1 041	387
1970	21 929	21 406	522	7 758	1 373	482
1971	21 950	21 425	525	8 026	1 650	576
1972	22 842	22 371	471	8 416	1 634	588
1973	23 960	23 470	490	8 756	1 509	581
1974	24 714	24 134	580	9 055	1 785	656
1975	24 598	23 932	666	9 391	2 668	818
1976	25 814	25 244	570	9 799	2 553	816
1977	27 076	26 510	566	10 213	2 478	847
1978	28 912	28 332	580	10 658	2 252	810
1979	30 227	29 620	606	10 990	2 197	821
1980	30 845	30 123	723	11 270	2 564	806
1981	31 337	30 608	729	11 664	2 837	858
1982	31 086	30 218	868	12 170	3 521	978
1983	31 679	30 925	754	12 367	3 494	963
1984	33 473	32 788	685	12 441	2 916	879
1985	34 672	33 963	709	12 587	2 868	923
1986	35 845	35 145	700	12 862	2 792	915
1987	37 210	36 515	695	13 124	2 458	866
1988	38 398	37 674	724	13 298	2 241	805
1989	39 484	38 745	739	13 544	2 216	787
1990	40 165	39 392	773	13 524	2 326	815
1991	39 783	38 939	843	13 713	2 774	909
1992	40 301	39 528	773	13 751	3 108	981
1993	40 991	40 192	799	13 919	2 930	955
1994	40 940	40 424	516	15 670	2 768	861
1995	41 743	41 172	571	15 779	2 535	886
WOMEN, 20 YEARS AND OVER						
1968	19 600	19 219	381	5 681	765	220
1969	20 454	20 053	401	5 944	801	214
1970	20 654	20 185	469	6 297	1 077	271
1971	20 769	20 299	470	6 477	1 320	338
1972	21 536	21 116	420	6 741	1 294	332
1973	22 495	22 066	428	6 991	1 184	324
1974	23 181	22 668	513	7 243	1 405	372
1975	23 242	22 644	598	7 484	2 210	474
1976	24 406	23 905	502	7 820	2 104	485
1977	25 587	25 094	493	8 187	2 045	491
1978	27 326	26 813	513	8 511	1 830	462
1979	28 623	28 079	544	8 812	1 796	479
1980	29 391	28 747	644	9 102	2 135	480
1981	30 041	29 380	661	9 549	2 394	502
1982	30 007	29 205	802	10 079	3 024	588
1983	30 680	29 978	702	10 324	3 042	589
1984	32 404	31 774	630	10 388	2 556	551
1985	33 604	32 946	658	10 551	2 536	593
1986	34 812	34 163	649	10 744	2 468	565
1987	36 121	35 487	634	10 953	2 178	530
1988	37 299	36 628	671	11 084	1 987	500
1989	38 408	37 718	690	11 337	1 963	504
1990	39 138	38 416	722	11 397	2 079	517
1991	38 960	38 160	800	11 673	2 502	572
1992	39 544	38 811	733	11 783	2 840	628
1993	40 209	39 456	753	11 890	2 670	619
1994	40 183	39 699	484	13 423	2 506	543
1995	40 943	40 401	542	13 453	2 265	554

Employed and Unemployed Full- and Part-time Workers by Sex and Age, 1968-1995—Continued

(Thousands of persons)

Year, sex, and age	Employed				Unemployed	
	Full-time			Part-time	Looking for full-time work	Looking for part-time work
	Total	Full-time schedules	Part-time for economic reasons, usually work full-time			
BOTH SEXES, 16-19 YEARS						
1968	2 956	2 842	114	2 823	477	363
1969	3 042	2 921	121	3 074	479	374
1970	2 960	2 828	132	3 184	626	480
1971	2 882	2 752	130	3 326	716	544
1972	3 201	3 065	137	3 543	735	574
1973	3 672	3 517	155	3 599	686	549
1974	3 754	3 582	172	3 695	819	603
1975	3 292	3 121	172	3 810	1 057	709
1976	3 384	3 213	171	3 953	999	720
1977	3 636	3 459	177	4 053	933	730
1978	3 861	3 685	177	4 208	873	709
1979	3 857	3 697	161	4 225	862	692
1980	3 474	3 289	185	4 237	966	701
1981	3 110	2 950	160	4 115	1 007	755
1982	2 517	2 362	155	4 031	1 153	824
1983	2 378	2 250	128	3 964	1 051	778
1984	2 516	2 384	132	3 928	816	683
1985	2 507	2 375	132	3 927	777	690
1986	2 400	2 270	130	4 073	733	721
1987	2 454	2 321	133	4 185	653	694
1988	2 562	2 436	126	4 243	592	634
1989	2 574	2 453	121	4 185	596	598
1990	2 473	2 347	126	4 107	598	614
1991	1 987	1 876	111	3 919	658	701
1992	1 846	1 750	96	3 822	653	775
1993	1 895	1 785	110	3 910	625	740
1994	1 883	1 803	80	4 278	648	672
1995	2 029	1 948	81	4 390	657	689

NOTE: Data beginning in 1994 are not strictly comparable with data for 1993 and earlier years because of the introduction of a major redesign of the survey and collection methodology. Beginning in 1990, data are not strictly comparable with previous years because of the introduction of 1990 census-based population controls adjusted for the estimated undercount.

Persons Not in the Labor Force by Desire and Availability for Work, Age, and Sex, 1994-1995

(Thousands of persons)

Category	Total		Age						Sex			
			16 to 24 years		25 to 54 years		55 years and over		Men		Women	
	1994	1995	1994	1995	1994	1995	1994	1995	1994	1995	1994	1995
TOTAL, NOT IN THE LABOR FORCE	65 758	66 280	10 937	10 922	18 720	18 854	36 101	36 503	23 538	23 818	42 221	42 462
Do not want a job now	59 540	60 610	8 635	8 807	15 790	16 246	35 116	35 557	21 089	21 536	38 452	39 074
Want a job	6 218	5 670	2 302	2 115	2 930	2 608	985	947	2 449	2 282	3 769	3 388
Did not search for work in previous year	3 588	3 286	1 263	1 153	1 611	1 436	714	697	1 311	1 231	2 277	2 054
Searched for work in previous year	2 630	2 384	1 040	963	1 319	1 172	272	250	1 138	1 050	1 492	1 334
Not available to work now	823	791	400	397	379	350	44	45	308	302	515	490
Available to work now	1 807	1 593	639	566	939	822	228	205	830	749	977	844
Reason not currently looking:												
Discouragement over job prospects	500	410	143	108	278	231	79	72	296	245	204	166
Reasons other than discouragement	1 307	1 182	496	458	661	591	149	133	534	504	772	679
Family responsibilities	213	185	44	39	153	131	17	15	31	26	183	159
In school or training	267	245	213	199	52	44	1	2	137	131	129	114
Ill health or disability	150	131	21	19	92	84	36	28	69	60	81	71
Other	677	621	219	201	364	331	94	89	298	287	379	334

NOTE: Data beginning in 1994 are not strictly comparable with data for 1993 and earlier years because of the introduction of a major redesign of the survey and collection methodology. Beginning in 1990, data are not strictly comparable with previous years because of the introduction of 1990 census-based population controls adjusted for the estimated undercount.

POPULATION, LABOR FORCE, AND EMPLOYMENT STATUS

Employed Civilians by Sex, Race, Hispanic Origin, and Age, 1948-1995

(Thousands of persons)

Year, sex, race, and Hispanic origin	16 years and over	16 to 19 years			20 years and over						
		Total	16 to 17 years	18 to 19 years	Total	20 to 24 years	25 to 34 years	35 to 44 years	45 to 54 years	55 to 64 years	65 years and over
TOTAL											
1948	58 343	4 026	1 600	2 426	54 318	6 937	13 801	13 050	10 624	7 103	2 804
1949	57 651	3 712	1 466	2 246	53 940	6 660	13 639	13 108	10 636	7 042	2 864
1950	58 918	3 703	1 433	2 270	55 218	6 746	13 917	13 424	10 966	7 265	2 899
1951	59 961	3 767	1 575	2 192	56 196	6 321	14 233	13 746	11 421	7 558	2 917
1952	60 250	3 719	1 626	2 092	56 536	5 572	14 515	14 058	11 687	7 785	2 919
1953	61 179	3 720	1 577	2 142	57 460	5 225	14 519	14 774	11 969	7 806	3 166
1954	60 109	3 475	1 422	2 053	56 634	4 971	14 190	14 541	11 976	7 895	3 060
1955	62 170	3 642	1 500	2 143	58 528	5 270	14 481	14 879	12 556	8 158	3 185
1956	63 799	3 818	1 647	2 171	59 983	5 545	14 407	15 218	12 978	8 519	3 314
1957	64 071	3 778	1 613	2 167	60 291	5 641	14 253	15 348	13 320	8 553	3 179
1958	63 036	3 582	1 519	2 063	59 454	5 571	13 675	15 157	13 448	8 559	3 045
1959	64 630	3 838	1 670	2 168	60 791	5 870	13 709	15 454	13 915	8 822	3 023
1960	65 778	4 129	1 770	2 360	61 648	6 119	13 630	15 598	14 238	8 989	3 073
1961	65 746	4 108	1 621	2 486	61 638	6 227	13 429	15 552	14 320	9 120	2 987
1962	66 702	4 195	1 607	2 588	62 508	6 446	13 311	15 901	14 491	9 346	3 013
1963	67 762	4 255	1 751	2 504	63 508	6 815	13 318	16 114	14 749	9 596	2 915
1964	69 305	4 516	2 013	2 503	64 789	7 303	13 449	16 166	15 094	9 804	2 973
1965	71 088	5 036	2 075	2 962	66 052	7 702	13 704	16 294	15 320	10 028	3 005
1966	72 895	5 721	2 269	3 452	67 178	7 964	14 017	16 312	15 615	10 310	2 961
1967	74 372	5 682	2 334	3 348	68 690	8 499	14 575	16 281	15 789	10 536	3 011
1968	75 920	5 781	2 403	3 377	70 141	8 762	15 265	16 220	16 083	10 745	3 065
1969	77 902	6 117	2 573	3 543	71 785	9 319	15 883	16 100	16 410	10 919	3 155
1970	78 678	6 144	2 598	3 546	72 534	9 731	16 318	15 922	16 473	10 974	3 118
1971	79 367	6 208	2 596	3 613	73 158	10 201	16 781	15 675	16 451	11 009	3 040
1972	82 153	6 746	2 787	3 959	75 407	10 999	18 082	15 822	16 457	11 044	3 003
1973	85 064	7 271	3 032	4 239	77 793	11 839	19 509	16 041	16 553	10 966	2 886
1974	86 794	7 448	3 111	4 338	79 347	12 101	20 610	16 203	16 633	10 964	2 835
1975	85 846	7 104	2 941	4 162	78 744	11 885	21 087	15 953	16 190	10 827	2 801
1976	88 752	7 336	2 972	4 363	81 416	12 570	22 493	16 468	16 224	10 912	2 747
1977	92 017	7 688	3 138	4 550	84 329	13 196	23 850	17 157	16 212	11 126	2 787
1978	96 048	8 070	3 330	4 739	87 979	13 887	25 281	18 128	16 338	11 400	2 946
1979	98 824	8 083	3 340	4 743	90 741	14 327	26 492	18 981	16 357	11 585	2 999
1980	99 303	7 710	3 106	4 605	91 593	14 087	27 204	19 523	16 234	11 586	2 960
1981	100 397	7 225	2 866	4 359	93 172	14 122	28 180	20 145	16 255	11 525	2 945
1982	99 526	6 549	2 505	4 044	92 978	13 690	28 149	20 879	15 923	11 414	2 923
1983	100 834	6 342	2 320	4 022	94 491	13 722	28 756	21 960	15 812	11 315	2 927
1984	105 005	6 444	2 404	4 040	98 562	14 207	30 348	23 598	16 178	11 395	2 835
1985	107 150	6 434	2 492	3 941	100 716	13 980	31 208	24 732	16 509	11 474	2 813
1986	109 597	6 472	2 622	3 850	103 125	13 790	32 201	25 861	16 949	11 405	2 919
1987	112 440	6 640	2 736	3 905	105 800	13 524	33 105	27 179	17 487	11 465	3 041
1988	114 968	6 805	2 713	4 092	108 164	13 244	33 574	28 269	18 447	11 433	3 197
1989	117 342	6 759	2 588	4 172	110 582	12 962	34 045	29 443	19 279	11 499	3 355
1990	118 793	6 581	2 410	4 171	112 213	13 401	33 935	30 817	19 525	11 189	3 346
1991	117 718	5 906	2 202	3 704	111 812	12 975	33 061	31 593	19 882	11 001	3 300
1992	118 492	5 669	2 128	3 540	112 824	12 872	32 667	31 923	21 022	10 998	3 341
1993	120 259	5 805	2 226	3 579	114 455	12 840	32 385	32 666	22 175	11 058	3 331
1994	123 060	6 161	2 510	3 651	116 899	12 758	32 286	33 599	23 348	11 228	3 681
1995	124 900	6 419	2 573	3 846	118 481	12 443	32 356	34 202	24 378	11 435	3 666

Employed Civilians by Sex, Race, Hispanic Origin, and Age, 1948-1995—Continued

(Thousands of persons)

Year, sex, race, and Hispanic origin	16 years and over	16 to 19 years			20 years and over						
		Total	16 to 17 years	18 to 19 years	Total	20 to 24 years	25 to 34 years	35 to 44 years	45 to 54 years	55 to 64 years	65 years and over
MEN											
1948	41 725	2 344	996	1 348	39 382	4 349	10 038	9 363	7 742	5 587	2 303
1949	40 925	2 124	911	1 213	38 803	4 197	9 879	9 308	7 661	5 438	2 329
1950	41 578	2 186	909	1 277	39 394	4 255	10 060	9 445	7 790	5 508	2 336
1951	41 780	2 156	979	1 177	39 626	3 780	10 134	9 607	8 012	5 711	2 382
1952	41 682	2 107	985	1 121	39 578	3 183	10 352	9 753	8 144	5 804	2 343
1953	42 430	2 136	976	1 159	40 296	2 901	10 500	10 229	8 374	5 808	2 483
1954	41 619	1 985	881	1 104	39 634	2 724	10 254	10 082	8 330	5 830	2 414
1955	42 621	2 095	936	1 159	40 526	2 973	10 453	10 267	8 553	5 857	2 424
1956	43 379	2 164	1 008	1 156	41 216	3 245	10 337	10 385	8 732	6 004	2 512
1957	43 357	2 115	987	1 130	41 239	3 346	10 222	10 427	8 851	6 002	2 394
1958	42 423	2 012	948	1 064	40 411	3 293	9 790	10 291	8 828	5 955	2 254
1959	43 466	2 198	1 015	1 183	41 267	3 597	9 862	10 492	9 048	6 058	2 210
1960	43 904	2 361	1 090	1 271	41 543	3 754	9 759	10 552	9 182	6 105	2 191
1961	43 656	2 315	989	1 325	41 342	3 795	9 591	10 505	9 195	6 155	2 098
1962	44 177	2 362	990	1 372	41 815	3 898	9 475	10 711	9 333	6 260	2 138
1963	44 657	2 406	1 073	1 334	42 251	4 118	9 431	10 801	9 478	6 385	2 038
1964	45 474	2 587	1 242	1 345	42 886	4 370	9 531	10 832	9 637	6 478	2 039
1965	46 340	2 918	1 285	1 634	43 422	4 583	9 611	10 837	9 792	6 542	2 057
1966	46 919	3 253	1 389	1 863	43 668	4 599	9 709	10 764	9 904	6 668	2 024
1967	47 479	3 186	1 417	1 769	44 294	4 809	9 988	10 674	9 990	6 774	2 058
1968	48 114	3 255	1 453	1 802	44 859	4 812	10 405	10 554	10 102	6 893	2 093
1969	48 818	3 430	1 526	1 904	45 388	5 012	10 736	10 401	10 187	6 931	2 122
1970	48 990	3 409	1 504	1 905	45 581	5 237	10 936	10 216	10 170	6 928	2 094
1971	49 390	3 478	1 510	1 968	45 912	5 593	11 218	10 028	10 139	6 916	2 019
1972	50 896	3 765	1 598	2 167	47 130	6 138	11 884	10 088	10 139	6 929	1 953
1973	52 349	4 039	1 721	2 318	48 310	6 655	12 617	10 126	10 197	6 857	1 856
1974	53 024	4 103	1 744	2 359	48 922	6 739	13 119	10 135	10 181	6 880	1 869
1975	51 857	3 839	1 621	2 219	48 018	6 484	13 205	9 891	9 902	6 722	1 811
1976	53 138	3 947	1 626	2 321	49 190	6 915	13 869	10 069	9 881	6 724	1 732
1977	54 728	4 174	1 733	2 441	50 555	7 232	14 483	10 399	9 832	6 848	1 761
1978	56 479	4 336	1 800	2 535	52 143	7 559	15 124	10 845	9 806	6 954	1 855
1979	57 607	4 300	1 799	2 501	53 308	7 791	15 688	11 202	9 735	7 015	1 876
1980	57 186	4 085	1 672	2 412	53 101	7 532	15 832	11 355	9 548	6 999	1 835
1981	57 397	3 815	1 526	2 289	53 582	7 504	16 266	11 613	9 478	6 909	1 812
1982	56 271	3 379	1 307	2 072	52 891	7 197	16 002	11 902	9 234	6 781	1 776
1983	56 787	3 300	1 213	2 087	53 487	7 232	16 216	12 450	9 133	6 686	1 770
1984	59 091	3 322	1 244	2 078	55 769	7 571	17 166	13 309	9 326	6 694	1 703
1985	59 891	3 328	1 300	2 029	56 562	7 339	17 564	13 800	9 411	6 753	1 695
1986	60 892	3 323	1 352	1 971	57 569	7 250	18 092	14 266	9 554	6 654	1 753
1987	62 107	3 381	1 393	1 988	58 726	7 058	18 487	14 898	9 750	6 682	1 850
1988	63 273	3 492	1 403	2 089	59 781	6 918	18 702	15 457	10 201	6 591	1 911
1989	64 315	3 477	1 327	2 150	60 837	6 799	18 952	16 002	10 569	6 548	1 968
1990	65 104	3 427	1 254	2 173	61 678	7 151	18 779	16 771	10 690	6 378	1 909
1991	64 223	3 044	1 135	1 909	61 178	6 909	18 265	17 086	10 813	6 245	1 860
1992	64 440	2 944	1 096	1 848	61 496	6 819	17 966	17 230	11 365	6 173	1 943
1993	65 349	2 994	1 155	1 839	62 355	6 805	17 877	17 665	11 927	6 166	1 916
1994	66 450	3 156	1 288	1 868	63 294	6 771	17 741	18 111	12 439	6 142	2 089
1995	67 377	3 292	1 316	1 977	64 085	6 665	17 709	18 374	12 958	6 272	2 108

Employed Civilians by Sex, Race, Hispanic Origin, and Age, 1948-1995—Continued

(Thousands of persons)

Year, sex, race, and Hispanic origin	16 years and over	16 to 19 years			20 years and over						
		Total	16 to 17 years	18 to 19 years	Total	20 to 24 years	25 to 34 years	35 to 44 years	45 to 54 years	55 to 64 years	65 years and over
WOMEN											
1948	16 617	1 682	604	1 078	14 936	2 588	3 763	3 687	2 882	1 516	501
1949	16 723	1 588	555	1 033	15 137	2 463	3 760	3 800	2 975	1 604	535
1950	17 340	1 517	524	993	15 824	2 491	3 857	3 979	3 176	1 757	563
1951	18 181	1 611	596	1 015	16 570	2 541	4 099	4 139	3 409	1 847	535
1952	18 568	1 612	641	971	16 958	2 389	4 163	4 305	3 543	1 981	576
1953	18 749	1 584	601	983	17 164	2 324	4 019	4 545	3 595	1 998	683
1954	18 490	1 490	541	949	17 000	2 247	3 936	4 459	3 646	2 065	646
1955	19 551	1 547	564	984	18 002	2 297	4 028	4 612	4 003	2 301	761
1956	20 419	1 654	639	1 015	18 767	2 300	4 070	4 833	4 246	2 515	802
1957	20 714	1 663	626	1 037	19 052	2 295	4 031	4 921	4 469	2 551	785
1958	20 613	1 570	571	999	19 043	2 278	3 885	4 866	4 620	2 604	791
1959	21 164	1 640	655	985	19 524	2 273	3 847	4 962	4 867	2 764	813
1960	21 874	1 768	680	1 089	20 105	2 365	3 871	5 046	5 056	2 884	882
1961	22 090	1 793	632	1 161	20 296	2 432	3 838	5 047	5 125	2 965	889
1962	22 525	1 833	617	1 216	20 693	2 548	3 836	5 190	5 158	3 086	875
1963	23 105	1 849	678	1 170	21 257	2 697	3 887	5 313	5 271	3 211	877
1964	23 831	1 929	771	1 158	21 903	2 933	3 918	5 334	5 457	3 326	934
1965	24 748	2 118	790	1 328	22 630	3 119	4 093	5 457	5 528	3 486	948
1966	25 976	2 468	880	1 589	23 510	3 365	4 308	5 548	5 711	3 642	937
1967	26 893	2 496	917	1 579	24 397	3 690	4 587	5 607	5 799	3 762	953
1968	27 807	2 526	950	1 575	25 281	3 950	4 860	5 666	5 981	3 852	972
1969	29 084	2 687	1 047	1 639	26 397	4 307	5 147	5 699	6 223	3 988	1 033
1970	29 688	2 735	1 094	1 641	26 952	4 494	5 382	5 706	6 303	4 046	1 023
1971	29 976	2 730	1 086	1 645	27 246	4 609	5 563	5 647	6 313	4 093	1 021
1972	31 257	2 980	1 188	1 792	28 277	4 861	6 197	5 734	6 318	4 115	1 051
1973	32 715	3 231	1 310	1 920	29 484	5 184	6 893	5 915	6 356	4 109	1 029
1974	33 769	3 345	1 367	1 978	30 424	5 363	7 492	6 068	6 451	4 084	966
1975	33 989	3 263	1 320	1 943	30 726	5 401	7 882	6 061	6 288	4 105	989
1976	35 615	3 389	1 346	2 043	32 226	5 655	8 624	6 400	6 343	4 188	1 017
1977	37 289	3 514	1 403	2 110	33 775	5 965	9 367	6 758	6 380	4 279	1 027
1978	39 569	3 734	1 530	2 204	35 836	6 328	10 157	7 282	6 532	4 446	1 091
1979	41 217	3 783	1 541	2 242	37 434	6 538	10 802	7 779	6 622	4 569	1 124
1980	42 117	3 625	1 433	2 192	38 492	6 555	11 370	8 168	6 686	4 587	1 125
1981	43 000	3 411	1 340	2 070	39 590	6 618	11 914	8 532	6 777	4 616	1 133
1982	43 256	3 170	1 198	1 972	40 086	6 492	12 147	8 977	6 689	4 634	1 147
1983	44 047	3 043	1 107	1 935	41 004	6 490	12 540	9 510	6 678	4 629	1 157
1984	45 915	3 122	1 161	1 962	42 793	6 636	13 182	10 289	6 852	4 700	1 133
1985	47 259	3 105	1 193	1 913	44 154	6 640	13 644	10 933	7 097	4 721	1 118
1986	48 706	3 149	1 270	1 879	45 556	6 540	14 109	11 595	7 395	4 751	1 165
1987	50 334	3 260	1 343	1 917	47 074	6 466	14 617	12 281	7 737	4 783	1 191
1988	51 696	3 313	1 310	2 003	48 383	6 326	14 872	12 811	8 246	4 841	1 286
1989	53 027	3 282	1 261	2 021	49 745	6 163	15 093	13 440	8 711	4 950	1 388
1990	53 689	3 154	1 156	1 998	50 535	6 250	15 155	14 046	8 835	4 811	1 437
1991	53 496	2 862	1 067	1 794	50 634	6 066	14 796	14 507	9 069	4 756	1 440
1992	54 052	2 724	1 032	1 692	51 328	6 053	14 701	14 693	9 657	4 825	1 398
1993	54 910	2 811	1 071	1 740	52 099	6 035	14 508	15 002	10 248	4 892	1 414
1994	56 610	3 005	1 222	1 783	53 606	5 987	14 545	15 488	10 908	5 085	1 592
1995	57 523	3 127	1 258	1 869	54 396	5 779	14 647	15 828	11 421	5 163	1 558

Employed Civilians by Sex, Race, Hispanic Origin, and Age, 1948-1995—Continued

(Thousands of persons)

Year, sex, race, and Hispanic origin	16 years and over	16 to 19 years			20 years and over						
		Total	16 to 17 years	18 to 19 years	Total	20 to 24 years	25 to 34 years	35 to 44 years	45 to 54 years	55 to 64 years	65 years and over
WHITE											
1954	53 957	3 078	1 257	1 822	50 879	4 358	12 616	13 000	10 811	7 262	2 831
1955	55 833	3 225	1 330	1 896	52 608	4 637	12 855	13 327	11 322	7 510	2 957
1956	57 269	3 389	1 465	1 922	53 880	4 897	12 748	13 637	11 706	7 822	3 068
1957	57 465	3 374	1 442	1 931	54 091	4 952	12 619	13 716	12 009	7 829	2 951
1958	56 613	3 216	1 370	1 847	53 397	4 908	12 128	13 571	12 113	7 849	2 828
1959	58 006	3 475	1 520	1 955	54 531	5 138	12 144	13 830	12 552	8 063	2 805
1960	58 850	3 700	1 598	2 103	55 150	5 331	12 021	13 930	12 820	8 192	2 855
1961	58 913	3 693	1 472	2 220	55 220	5 460	11 835	13 905	12 906	8 335	2 778
1962	59 698	3 774	1 447	2 327	55 924	5 676	11 703	14 173	13 066	8 511	2 795
1963	60 622	3 851	1 600	2 250	56 771	6 036	11 689	14 341	13 304	8 718	2 683
1964	61 922	4 076	1 846	2 230	57 846	6 444	11 794	14 380	13 596	8 916	2 717
1965	63 446	4 562	1 892	2 670	58 884	6 752	11 992	14 473	13 804	9 116	2 748
1966	65 021	5 176	2 052	3 124	59 845	6 986	12 268	14 449	14 072	9 356	2 713
1967	66 361	5 114	2 121	2 993	61 247	7 493	12 763	14 429	14 224	9 596	2 746
1968	67 750	5 195	2 193	3 002	62 555	7 687	13 410	14 386	14 487	9 781	2 804
1969	69 518	5 508	2 347	3 161	64 010	8 182	13 935	14 270	14 788	9 947	2 888
1970	70 217	5 571	2 386	3 185	64 645	8 559	14 326	14 092	14 854	9 979	2 835
1971	70 878	5 670	2 404	3 266	65 208	9 000	14 713	13 858	14 843	10 014	2 780
1972	73 370	6 173	2 581	3 592	67 197	9 718	15 904	13 940	14 845	10 077	2 714
1973	75 708	6 623	2 806	3 816	69 086	10 424	17 099	14 083	14 886	9 983	2 610
1974	77 184	6 796	2 881	3 916	70 388	10 676	18 040	14 196	14 948	9 958	2 568
1975	76 411	6 487	2 721	3 770	69 924	10 546	18 485	13 979	14 555	9 827	2 533
1976	78 853	6 724	2 762	3 962	72 129	11 119	19 662	14 407	14 549	9 923	2 470
1977	81 700	7 068	2 926	4 142	74 632	11 696	20 844	14 984	14 483	10 107	2 518
1978	84 936	7 367	3 085	4 282	77 569	12 251	22 008	15 809	14 550	10 311	2 642
1979	87 259	7 356	3 079	4 278	79 904	12 594	23 033	16 578	14 522	10 477	2 699
1980	87 715	7 021	2 861	4 161	80 694	12 405	23 653	17 071	14 405	10 475	2 684
1981	88 709	6 588	2 645	3 943	82 121	12 477	24 551	17 617	14 414	10 386	2 676
1982	87 903	5 984	2 317	3 667	81 918	12 097	24 531	18 268	14 083	10 283	2 656
1983	88 893	5 799	2 156	3 643	83 094	12 138	24 955	19 194	13 961	10 169	2 678
1984	92 120	5 836	2 209	3 627	86 284	12 451	26 235	20 552	14 239	10 227	2 580
1985	93 736	5 768	2 270	3 498	87 968	12 235	26 945	21 552	14 459	10 247	2 530
1986	95 660	5 792	2 386	3 406	89 869	12 027	27 746	22 515	14 750	10 176	2 654
1987	97 789	5 898	2 468	3 431	91 890	11 748	28 429	23 596	15 216	10 164	2 738
1988	99 812	6 030	2 424	3 606	93 782	11 438	28 796	24 468	16 054	10 153	2 874
1989	101 584	5 946	2 278	3 668	95 638	11 084	29 091	25 442	16 775	10 223	3 024
1990	102 261	5 779	2 141	3 638	96 481	11 498	28 773	26 282	16 933	9 960	3 035
1991	101 182	5 216	1 971	3 246	95 966	11 116	27 989	26 883	17 269	9 719	2 990
1992	101 669	4 985	1 904	3 081	96 684	11 031	27 552	27 097	18 285	9 701	3 019
1993	103 045	5 113	1 990	3 123	97 932	10 931	27 274	27 645	19 273	9 772	3 037
1994	105 190	5 398	2 210	3 188	99 792	10 736	27 101	28 442	20 247	9 912	3 354
1995	106 490	5 593	2 273	3 320	100 897	10 400	27 014	28 951	21 127	10 070	3 335

POPULATION, LABOR FORCE, AND EMPLOYMENT STATUS

Employed Civilians by Sex, Race, Hispanic Origin, and Age, 1948-1995—Continued

(Thousands of persons)

Year, sex, race, and Hispanic origin	16 years and over	16 to 19 years			20 years and over						
		Total	16 to 17 years	18 to 19 years	Total	20 to 24 years	25 to 34 years	35 to 44 years	45 to 54 years	55 to 64 years	65 years and over
WHITE MEN											
1954	37 846	1 723	771	953	36 123	2 394	9 287	9 175	7 614	5 412	2 241
1955	38 719	1 824	821	1 004	36 895	2 607	9 461	9 351	7 792	5 431	2 254
1956	39 368	1 893	890	1 002	37 475	2 850	9 330	9 449	7 950	5 559	2 336
1957	39 349	1 865	874	990	37 484	2 930	9 226	9 480	8 067	5 542	2 234
1958	38 591	1 783	852	932	36 808	2 896	8 861	9 386	8 061	5 501	2 103
1959	39 494	1 961	915	1 046	37 533	3 153	8 911	9 560	8 261	5 588	2 060
1960	39 755	2 092	973	1 119	37 663	3 264	8 777	9 589	8 372	5 618	2 043
1961	39 588	2 055	891	1 164	37 533	3 311	8 630	9 566	8 394	5 670	1 961
1962	40 016	2 098	883	1 215	37 918	3 426	8 514	9 718	8 512	5 749	1 998
1963	40 428	2 156	972	1 184	38 272	3 646	8 463	9 782	8 650	5 844	1 887
1964	41 115	2 316	1 128	1 188	38 799	3 856	8 538	9 800	8 787	5 945	1 872
1965	41 844	2 612	1 159	1 453	39 232	4 025	8 598	9 795	8 924	5 998	1 892
1966	42 331	2 913	1 245	1 668	39 418	4 028	8 674	9 719	9 029	6 096	1 871
1967	42 833	2 849	1 278	1 571	39 985	4 231	8 931	9 632	9 093	6 208	1 892
1968	43 411	2 908	1 319	1 589	40 503	4 226	9 315	9 522	9 198	6 316	1 926
1969	44 048	3 070	1 385	1 685	40 978	4 401	9 608	9 379	9 279	6 359	1 953
1970	44 178	3 066	1 374	1 692	41 112	4 601	9 784	9 202	9 271	6 340	1 914
1971	44 595	3 157	1 393	1 764	41 438	4 935	10 026	9 026	9 256	6 339	1 856
1972	45 944	3 416	1 470	1 947	42 528	5 431	10 664	9 047	9 236	6 363	1 786
1973	47 085	3 660	1 590	2 071	43 424	5 863	11 268	9 046	9 257	6 299	1 689
1974	47 674	3 728	1 611	2 117	43 946	5 965	11 701	9 027	9 242	6 304	1 706
1975	46 697	3 505	1 502	2 002	43 192	5 770	11 783	8 818	9 005	6 160	1 656
1976	47 775	3 604	1 501	2 103	44 171	6 140	12 362	8 944	8 968	6 176	1 579
1977	49 150	3 824	1 607	2 217	45 326	6 437	12 893	9 212	8 898	6 279	1 605
1978	50 544	3 950	1 664	2 286	46 594	6 717	13 413	9 608	8 840	6 339	1 677
1979	51 452	3 904	1 654	2 250	47 546	6 868	13 888	9 930	8 748	6 406	1 707
1980	51 127	3 708	1 534	2 174	47 419	6 652	14 009	10 077	8 586	6 412	1 684
1981	51 315	3 469	1 402	2 066	47 846	6 652	14 398	10 307	8 518	6 309	1 662
1982	50 287	3 079	1 214	1 865	47 209	6 372	14 164	10 593	8 267	6 188	1 624
1983	50 621	3 003	1 124	1 879	47 618	6 386	14 297	11 062	8 152	6 084	1 637
1984	52 462	3 001	1 140	1 861	49 461	6 647	15 045	11 776	8 320	6 108	1 564
1985	53 046	2 985	1 185	1 800	50 061	6 428	15 374	12 214	8 374	6 118	1 552
1986	53 785	2 966	1 225	1 741	50 818	6 340	15 790	12 620	8 442	6 012	1 612
1987	54 647	2 999	1 252	1 747	51 649	6 150	16 084	13 138	8 596	5 991	1 690
1988	55 550	3 084	1 248	1 836	52 466	5 987	16 241	13 590	8 992	5 909	1 748
1989	56 352	3 060	1 171	1 889	53 292	5 839	16 383	14 046	9 335	5 891	1 797
1990	56 703	3 018	1 119	1 899	53 685	6 179	16 124	14 496	9 383	5 744	1 760
1991	55 797	2 694	1 017	1 677	53 103	5 942	15 644	14 743	9 488	5 578	1 707
1992	55 959	2 602	990	1 612	53 357	5 855	15 357	14 842	10 027	5 503	1 772
1993	56 656	2 634	1 031	1 603	54 021	5 830	15 230	15 178	10 497	5 514	1 772
1994	57 452	2 776	1 144	1 632	54 676	5 738	15 052	15 562	10 910	5 490	1 925
1995	58 146	2 892	1 169	1 723	55 254	5 613	14 958	15 793	11 359	5 609	1 921
WHITE WOMEN											
1954	16 111	1 355	486	869	14 756	1 964	3 329	3 825	3 197	1 850	590
1955	17 114	1 401	509	892	15 713	2 030	3 394	3 976	3 530	2 079	703
1956	17 901	1 496	575	920	16 405	2 047	3 418	4 188	3 756	2 263	732
1957	18 116	1 509	568	941	16 607	2 022	3 393	4 236	3 942	2 287	717
1958	18 022	1 433	518	915	16 589	2 012	3 267	4 185	4 052	2 348	725
1959	18 512	1 514	605	909	16 998	1 985	3 233	4 270	4 291	2 475	745
1960	19 095	1 608	625	984	17 487	2 067	3 244	4 341	4 448	2 574	812
1961	19 325	1 638	581	1 056	17 687	2 149	3 205	4 339	4 512	2 665	817
1962	19 682	1 676	564	1 112	18 006	2 250	3 189	4 455	4 554	2 762	797
1963	20 194	1 695	628	1 066	18 499	2 390	3 226	4 559	4 654	2 874	796
1964	20 807	1 760	718	1 042	19 047	2 588	3 256	4 580	4 809	2 971	845
1965	21 602	1 950	733	1 217	19 652	2 727	3 394	4 678	4 880	3 118	856
1966	22 690	2 263	807	1 456	20 427	2 958	3 594	4 730	5 043	3 260	842
1967	23 528	2 265	843	1 422	21 263	3 262	3 832	4 797	5 131	3 388	854
1968	24 339	2 287	874	1 413	22 052	3 461	4 095	4 864	5 289	3 465	878
1969	25 470	2 438	962	1 476	23 032	3 781	4 327	4 891	5 509	3 588	935
1970	26 039	2 505	1 012	1 493	23 534	3 959	4 542	4 890	5 582	3 640	921
1971	26 283	2 513	1 011	1 502	23 770	4 065	4 687	4 831	5 588	3 675	924
1972	27 426	2 755	1 111	1 645	24 669	4 286	5 240	4 893	5 608	3 714	928
1973	28 623	2 962	1 217	1 746	25 661	4 562	5 831	5 036	5 628	3 684	920
1974	29 511	3 069	1 269	1 799	26 442	4 711	6 340	5 169	5 706	3 654	862
1975	29 714	2 983	1 215	1 767	26 731	4 775	6 701	5 161	5 550	3 667	877
1976	31 078	3 120	1 260	1 860	27 958	4 978	7 300	5 462	5 580	3 746	891
1977	32 550	3 244	1 319	1 923	29 306	5 259	7 950	5 772	5 585	3 829	912
1978	34 392	3 416	1 420	1 996	30 975	5 535	8 595	6 201	5 710	3 972	964
1979	35 807	3 451	1 423	2 027	32 357	5 726	9 145	6 648	5 773	4 071	993
1980	36 587	3 314	1 327	1 986	33 275	5 753	9 644	6 994	5 818	4 064	1 001
1981	37 394	3 119	1 242	1 877	34 275	5 826	10 153	7 311	5 896	4 077	1 013
1982	37 615	2 905	1 103	1 802	34 710	5 724	10 367	7 675	5 816	4 095	1 032
1983	38 272	2 796	1 032	1 764	35 476	5 751	10 659	8 132	5 809	4 084	1 041
1984	39 659	2 835	1 069	1 766	36 823	5 804	11 190	8 776	5 920	4 118	1 015
1985	40 690	2 783	1 085	1 698	37 907	5 807	11 571	9 338	6 084	4 128	978
1986	41 876	2 825	1 160	1 665	39 050	5 687	11 956	9 895	6 307	4 164	1 042
1987	43 142	2 900	1 216	1 684	40 242	5 598	12 345	10 459	6 620	4 172	1 047
1988	44 262	2 946	1 176	1 770	41 316	5 450	12 555	10 878	7 062	4 244	1 126
1989	45 232	2 886	1 107	1 779	42 346	5 245	12 708	11 395	7 440	4 332	1 227
1990	45 558	2 762	1 023	1 739	42 796	5 319	12 649	11 785	7 551	4 217	1 275
1991	45 385	2 523	954	1 569	42 862	5 174	12 344	12 139	7 781	4 141	1 283
1992	45 710	2 383	915	1 468	43 327	5 176	12 195	12 254	8 258	4 198	1 246
1993	46 390	2 479	959	1 520	43 910	5 101	12 044	12 467	8 776	4 258	1 265
1994	47 738	2 622	1 066	1 556	45 116	4 997	12 049	12 880	9 338	4 423	1 429
1995	48 344	2 701	1 104	1 597	45 643	4 787	12 056	13 157	9 768	4 461	1 415

Employed Civilians by Sex, Race, Hispanic Origin, and Age, 1948-1995—Continued

(Thousands of persons)

Year, sex, race, and Hispanic origin	16 years and over	16 to 19 years			20 years and over						
		Total	16 to 17 years	18 to 19 years	Total	20 to 24 years	25 to 34 years	35 to 44 years	45 to 54 years	55 to 64 years	65 years and over
BLACK											
1972	7 802	509	180	329	7 292	1 166	1 924	1 629	1 434	872	269
1973	8 128	570	194	378	7 559	1 258	2 062	1 659	1 460	872	249
1974	8 203	554	190	364	7 649	1 231	2 157	1 682	1 452	884	243
1975	7 894	507	183	325	7 386	1 115	2 145	1 617	1 393	874	241
1976	8 227	508	170	338	7 719	1 193	2 309	1 679	1 416	870	252
1977	8 540	508	169	339	8 031	1 244	2 443	1 754	1 448	892	251
1978	9 102	571	191	380	8 531	1 359	2 641	1 848	1 479	932	273
1979	9 359	579	204	376	8 780	1 424	2 759	1 902	1 502	927	266
1980	9 313	547	192	356	8 765	1 376	2 827	1 910	1 487	925	239
1981	9 355	505	170	335	8 849	1 346	2 872	1 957	1 489	954	231
1982	9 189	428	138	290	8 761	1 283	2 830	2 025	1 469	928	225
1983	9 375	416	123	294	8 959	1 280	2 976	2 107	1 456	937	204
1984	10 119	474	146	328	9 645	1 423	3 223	2 311	1 533	945	209
1985	10 501	532	175	356	9 969	1 399	3 325	2 427	1 598	985	235
1986	10 814	536	183	353	10 278	1 429	3 464	2 524	1 666	982	214
1987	11 309	587	203	385	10 722	1 421	3 614	2 695	1 714	1 036	241
1988	11 658	601	223	378	11 057	1 433	3 725	2 839	1 783	1 018	261
1989	11 953	625	237	388	11 328	1 467	3 801	2 981	1 844	970	265
1990	12 175	598	194	404	11 577	1 409	3 803	3 287	1 897	933	248
1991	12 074	494	161	334	11 580	1 373	3 714	3 401	1 892	957	243
1992	12 151	492	157	335	11 659	1 343	3 699	3 441	1 964	965	246
1993	12 382	494	171	323	11 888	1 377	3 700	3 584	2 059	941	226
1994	12 835	552	224	328	12 284	1 449	3 732	3 722	2 178	953	251
1995	13 279	586	223	363	12 693	1 443	3 844	3 861	2 288	1 004	253
BLACK MEN											
1972	4 368	309	114	195	4 058	648	1 074	890	793	499	156
1973	4 527	330	112	220	4 197	711	1 142	898	816	483	148
1974	4 527	322	114	209	4 204	668	1 176	912	803	500	145
1975	4 275	276	98	179	3 998	595	1 159	865	755	487	137
1976	4 404	283	100	184	4 120	635	1 217	897	763	472	137
1977	4 565	291	105	186	4 273	659	1 271	940	777	484	143
1978	4 796	312	106	206	4 483	697	1 357	969	788	516	155
1979	4 923	316	111	205	4 606	754	1 425	983	801	498	147
1980	4 798	299	109	191	4 498	713	1 438	975	770	478	126
1981	4 794	273	95	178	4 520	693	1 457	991	764	492	123
1982	4 637	223	65	158	4 414	660	1 414	997	750	471	122
1983	4 753	222	64	158	4 531	684	1 483	1 034	749	477	105
1984	5 124	252	79	173	4 871	750	1 635	1 138	780	460	108
1985	5 270	278	92	186	4 992	726	1 669	1 187	795	501	114
1986	5 428	278	96	182	5 150	732	1 756	1 211	831	507	112
1987	5 661	304	109	195	5 357	728	1 821	1 283	853	547	124
1988	5 824	316	122	193	5 509	736	1 881	1 348	878	536	131
1989	5 928	327	124	202	5 602	742	1 931	1 415	886	498	131
1990	5 995	303	99	204	5 692	702	1 895	1 586	926	469	114
1991	5 961	255	85	170	5 706	695	1 859	1 634	923	481	114
1992	5 930	249	78	170	5 681	679	1 819	1 650	930	478	124
1993	6 047	254	88	166	5 793	674	1 858	1 717	978	461	106
1994	6 241	276	107	169	5 964	718	1 850	1 795	1 030	455	115
1995	6 422	285	111	174	6 137	714	1 895	1 836	1 085	468	138
BLACK WOMEN											
1972	3 433	200	65	134	3 233	519	850	739	641	373	113
1973	3 601	239	81	158	3 362	546	920	761	644	389	101
1974	3 677	232	77	155	3 445	562	981	770	649	383	98
1975	3 618	231	85	146	3 388	520	985	752	638	387	104
1976	3 823	224	70	154	3 599	558	1 092	782	653	398	115
1977	3 975	217	64	153	3 758	585	1 172	814	671	408	109
1978	4 307	260	85	175	4 047	662	1 283	879	691	416	118
1979	4 436	263	92	171	4 174	670	1 333	919	702	428	119
1980	4 515	248	82	165	4 267	663	1 389	936	717	448	113
1981	4 561	232	75	157	4 329	653	1 415	966	725	462	108
1982	4 552	205	73	132	4 347	623	1 416	1 028	719	457	103
1983	4 622	194	59	136	4 428	596	1 493	1 073	707	460	99
1984	4 995	222	67	155	4 773	673	1 588	1 173	753	485	101
1985	5 231	254	83	171	4 977	673	1 656	1 240	804	484	121
1986	5 386	259	87	171	5 128	696	1 708	1 313	835	475	102
1987	5 648	283	93	190	5 365	693	1 793	1 412	860	489	117
1988	5 834	285	101	184	5 548	697	1 844	1 491	905	482	129
1989	6 025	298	113	185	5 727	725	1 870	1 566	959	472	134
1990	6 180	296	96	200	5 884	707	1 907	1 701	971	464	135
1991	6 113	239	76	164	5 874	677	1 855	1 768	969	476	129
1992	6 221	243	79	164	5 978	664	1 880	1 791	1 034	487	123
1993	6 334	239	82	157	6 095	703	1 842	1 867	1 081	480	121
1994	6 595	275	117	158	6 320	731	1 882	1 926	1 147	497	136
1995	6 857	301	112	189	6 556	729	1 949	2 025	1 202	536	114

Employed Civilians by Sex, Race, Hispanic Origin, and Age, 1948-1995—Continued

(Thousands of persons)

Year, sex, race, and Hispanic origin	16 years and over	16 to 19 years			20 years and over						
		Total	16 to 17 years	18 to 19 years	Total	20 to 24 years	25 to 34 years	35 to 44 years	45 to 54 years	55 to 64 years	65 years and over
HISPANIC											
1973	3 396	325	....	....	....	....	....	....	....	....	....
1974	3 687	355	....	....	....	....	....	....	....	....	....
1975	3 663	322	....	....	....	....	....	....	....	....	....
1976	3 720	341	124	230	3 436	614	1 135	803	573	269	42
1977	4 079	381	135	245	3 715	715	1 212	860	608	269	50
1978	4 527	423	159	264	4 104	803	1 330	942	661	307	62
1979	4 785	445	152	292	4 340	860	1 430	996	666	319	69
1980	5 527	500	174	325	5 028	998	1 675	1 074	811	389	80
1981	5 813	459	155	304	5 354	1 060	1 837	1 147	829	399	82
1982	5 805	410	119	291	5 394	1 030	1 896	1 173	816	399	80
1983	6 072	423	125	297	5 649	1 068	1 997	1 224	837	441	81
1984	6 651	468	148	320	6 182	1 160	2 201	1 385	883	474	79
1985	6 888	438	144	294	6 449	1 187	2 316	1 473	913	486	75
1986	7 219	430	146	284	6 789	1 231	2 427	1 570	1 011	474	76
1987	7 790	474	149	325	7 316	1 273	2 668	1 775	1 010	512	76
1988	8 250	523	171	353	7 727	1 341	2 749	1 876	1 078	585	97
1989	8 573	548	165	383	8 025	1 325	2 900	1 968	1 129	589	114
1990	9 845	668	208	460	9 177	1 672	3 327	2 229	1 235	611	103
1991	9 828	602	169	433	9 225	1 622	3 264	2 333	1 266	637	103
1992	10 027	577	169	408	9 450	1 575	3 350	2 468	1 316	628	112
1993	10 361	570	160	410	9 792	1 574	3 446	2 605	1 402	630	135
1994	10 788	609	195	415	10 178	1 643	3 517	2 737	1 495	647	139
1995	11 127	645	194	450	10 483	1 609	3 618	2 889	1 565	666	135
HISPANIC MEN											
1973	2 198	....	....	....	2 010	....	....	....	....	....	....
1974	2 369	....	....	....	2 165	....	....	....	....	....	....
1975	2 301	....	....	....	2 117	....	....	....	....	....	....
1976	2 303	199	74	125	2 109	364	708	504	369	173	30
1977	2 564	225	78	147	2 335	427	763	540	394	184	37
1978	2 808	241	93	147	2 568	494	824	590	405	207	47
1979	2 962	260	93	168	2 701	511	891	615	427	205	53
1980	3 448	306	109	198	3 142	611	1 065	662	491	254	58
1981	3 597	272	90	182	3 325	642	1 157	707	504	259	56
1982	3 583	229	66	162	3 354	621	1 192	729	498	261	53
1983	3 771	248	71	177	3 523	655	1 280	760	499	275	53
1984	4 083	258	78	180	3 825	718	1 398	841	530	292	46
1985	4 245	251	82	169	3 994	727	1 473	888	550	308	48
1986	4 428	254	82	172	4 174	773	1 510	929	614	297	51
1987	4 713	268	81	188	4 444	777	1 664	1 044	606	303	50
1988	4 972	292	87	205	4 680	815	1 706	1 120	645	331	64
1989	5 172	319	94	225	4 853	821	1 787	1 152	676	350	67
1990	6 021	412	126	286	5 609	1 083	2 076	1 312	722	355	61
1991	5 979	356	94	263	5 623	1 063	2 050	1 360	719	369	62
1992	6 093	336	97	238	5 757	985	2 127	1 437	768	372	69
1993	6 328	337	95	242	5 992	1 003	2 200	1 527	822	360	80
1994	6 530	341	109	233	6 189	1 056	2 227	1 600	847	379	....
1995	6 725	358	110	248	6 367	1 030	2 284	1 675	908	384	....
HISPANIC WOMEN											
1973	1 198	....	....	....	1 060	....	....	....	....	....	....
1974	1 319	....	....	....	1 166	....	....	....	....	....	....
1975	1 362	....	....	....	1 224	....	....	....	....	....	....
1976	1 417	155	50	106	1 288	249	427	300	204	96	12
1977	1 516	155	57	98	1 370	288	449	320	214	86	13
1978	1 719	182	65	117	1 537	308	506	352	256	99	15
1979	1 824	185	60	125	1 638	349	539	381	241	115	15
1980	2 079	193	65	128	1 886	387	610	412	320	136	22
1981	2 216	187	65	122	2 029	418	680	440	326	139	26
1982	2 222	181	52	129	2 040	409	704	444	318	139	26
1983	2 301	175	54	120	2 127	413	717	464	338	166	28
1984	2 568	211	71	140	2 357	442	804	544	354	181	33
1985	2 642	187	62	125	2 456	460	843	585	362	178	27
1986	2 791	176	64	112	2 615	458	917	641	397	177	25
1987	3 077	206	69	137	2 872	496	1 004	732	405	209	26
1988	3 278	231	84	147	3 047	526	1 042	756	434	254	33
1989	3 401	229	71	158	3 172	504	1 114	816	453	239	46
1990	3 823	256	82	174	3 567	588	1 251	917	513	256	42
1991	3 848	246	76	170	3 603	559	1 214	972	548	268	41
1992	3 934	242	72	170	3 693	591	1 223	1 031	548	256	43
1993	4 033	233	65	168	3 800	571	1 246	1 077	581	269	55
1994	4 258	268	86	182	3 989	587	1 290	1 137	648	268	....
1995	4 403	287	85	202	4 116	579	1 334	1 213	657	282	....

NOTE: Data beginning in 1994 are not strictly comparable with data for 1993 and earlier years because of the introduction of a major redesign of the survey and collection methodology. Beginning in 1990, data are not strictly comparable with previous years because of the introduction of 1990 census-based population controls adjusted for the estimated undercount.

Civilian Employment-Population Ratios by Sex, Race, Hispanic Origin, and Age, 1948-1995

(Percent)

Year, sex, race, and Hispanic origin	Total			Men			Women		
	16 years and over	16 to 19 years	20 years and over	16 years and over	16 to 19 years	20 years and over	16 years and over	16 to 19 years	20 years and over
TOTAL									
1948	56.6	47.7	57.4	83.5	57.5	85.8	31.3	38.5	30.7
1949	55.4	45.2	56.3	81.3	53.8	83.7	31.2	37.2	30.6
1950	56.1	45.5	57.0	82.0	55.2	84.2	32.0	36.3	31.6
1951	57.3	47.9	58.1	84.0	57.9	86.1	33.1	38.9	32.6
1952	57.3	46.9	58.1	83.9	55.9	86.2	33.4	38.8	33.0
1953	57.1	46.4	58.0	83.6	55.9	85.9	33.3	37.8	32.9
1954	55.5	42.3	56.6	81.0	50.2	83.5	32.5	34.9	32.3
1955	56.7	43.5	57.8	81.8	52.1	84.3	34.0	35.6	33.8
1956	57.5	45.3	58.5	82.3	53.8	84.6	35.1	37.5	34.9
1957	57.1	43.9	58.2	81.3	51.8	83.8	35.1	36.7	35.0
1958	55.4	39.9	56.8	78.5	46.9	81.2	34.5	33.5	34.6
1959	56.0	39.9	57.5	79.3	47.2	82.3	35.0	33.0	35.1
1960	56.1	40.5	57.6	78.9	47.6	81.9	35.5	33.8	35.7
1961	55.4	39.1	56.9	77.6	45.3	80.8	35.4	33.2	35.6
1962	55.5	39.4	57.1	77.7	45.9	80.9	35.6	33.3	35.8
1963	55.4	37.4	57.2	77.1	43.8	80.6	35.8	31.5	36.3
1964	55.7	37.3	57.7	77.3	44.1	80.9	36.3	30.9	36.9
1965	56.2	38.9	58.2	77.5	46.2	81.2	37.1	32.0	37.6
1966	56.9	42.1	58.7	77.9	48.9	81.5	38.3	35.6	38.6
1967	57.3	42.2	59.0	78.0	48.7	81.5	39.0	35.9	39.3
1968	57.5	42.2	59.3	77.8	48.7	81.3	39.6	36.0	40.0
1969	58.0	43.4	59.7	77.6	49.5	81.1	40.7	37.5	41.1
1970	57.4	42.3	59.2	76.2	47.7	79.7	40.8	37.1	41.2
1971	56.6	41.3	58.4	74.9	46.8	78.5	40.4	36.0	40.9
1972	57.0	43.5	58.6	75.0	48.9	78.4	41.0	38.2	41.3
1973	57.8	45.9	59.3	75.5	51.4	78.6	42.0	40.5	42.2
1974	57.8	46.0	59.2	74.9	51.2	77.9	42.6	41.0	42.8
1975	56.1	43.3	57.6	71.7	47.2	74.8	42.0	39.4	42.3
1976	56.8	44.2	58.3	72.0	47.9	75.1	43.2	40.5	43.5
1977	57.9	46.1	59.2	72.8	50.4	75.6	44.5	41.8	44.8
1978	59.3	48.3	60.6	73.8	52.2	76.4	46.4	44.5	46.6
1979	59.9	48.5	61.2	73.8	51.7	76.5	47.5	45.3	47.7
1980	59.2	46.6	60.6	72.0	49.5	74.6	47.7	43.8	48.1
1981	59.0	44.6	60.5	71.3	47.1	74.0	48.0	42.0	48.6
1982	57.8	41.5	59.4	69.0	42.9	71.8	47.7	40.2	48.4
1983	57.9	41.5	59.5	68.8	43.1	71.4	48.0	40.0	48.8
1984	59.5	43.7	61.0	70.7	45.0	73.2	49.5	42.5	50.1
1985	60.1	44.4	61.5	70.9	45.7	73.3	50.4	42.9	51.0
1986	60.7	44.6	62.1	71.0	45.7	73.3	51.4	43.6	52.0
1987	61.5	45.5	62.9	71.5	46.1	73.8	52.5	44.8	53.1
1988	62.3	46.8	63.6	72.0	47.8	74.2	53.4	45.9	54.0
1989	63.0	47.5	64.2	72.5	48.7	74.5	54.3	46.4	54.9
1990	62.8	45.3	64.3	72.0	46.6	74.3	54.3	44.0	55.2
1991	61.7	42.0	63.2	70.4	42.7	72.7	53.7	41.2	54.6
1992	61.5	41.0	63.0	69.8	41.9	72.1	53.8	40.0	54.8
1993	61.7	41.7	63.3	70.0	42.3	72.3	54.1	41.0	55.0
1994	62.5	43.4	64.0	70.4	43.8	72.6	55.3	43.0	56.2
1995	62.9	44.2	64.4	70.8	44.7	73.0	55.6	43.8	56.5

Civilian Employment-Population Ratios by Sex, Race, Hispanic Origin, and Age, 1948-1995—Continued

(Percent)

Year, sex, race, and Hispanic origin	Total			Men			Women		
	16 years and over	16 to 19 years	20 years and over	16 years and over	16 to 19 years	20 years and over	16 years and over	16 to 19 years	20 years and over
WHITE									
1954	55.2	42.9	56.2	81.5	49.9	84.0	31.4	36.4	31.1
1955	56.5	44.2	57.4	82.2	52.0	84.7	33.0	37.0	32.7
1956	57.3	46.1	58.2	82.7	54.1	85.0	34.2	38.9	33.8
1957	56.8	45.0	57.8	81.8	52.4	84.1	34.2	38.2	33.9
1958	55.3	41.0	56.5	79.2	47.6	81.8	33.6	35.0	33.5
1959	55.9	41.2	57.2	79.9	48.1	82.8	34.0	34.8	34.0
1960	55.9	41.5	57.2	79.4	48.1	82.4	34.6	35.1	34.5
1961	55.3	40.1	56.7	78.2	45.9	81.4	34.5	34.6	34.5
1962	55.4	40.4	56.9	78.4	46.4	81.5	34.7	34.8	34.7
1963	55.3	38.6	56.9	77.7	44.7	81.1	35.0	32.9	35.2
1964	55.5	38.4	57.3	77.8	45.0	81.3	35.5	32.2	35.8
1965	56.0	40.3	57.8	77.9	47.1	81.5	36.2	33.7	36.5
1966	56.8	43.6	58.3	78.3	50.1	81.7	37.5	37.5	37.5
1967	57.2	43.8	58.7	78.4	50.2	81.7	38.3	37.7	38.3
1968	57.4	43.9	59.0	78.3	50.3	81.6	38.9	37.8	39.1
1969	58.0	45.2	59.4	78.2	51.1	81.4	40.1	39.5	40.1
1970	57.5	44.5	59.0	76.8	49.6	80.1	40.3	39.5	40.4
1971	56.8	43.8	58.3	75.7	49.2	79.0	39.9	38.6	40.1
1972	57.4	46.4	58.6	76.0	51.5	79.0	40.7	41.3	40.6
1973	58.2	48.9	59.3	76.5	54.3	79.2	41.8	43.6	41.6
1974	58.3	49.3	59.3	75.9	54.4	78.6	42.4	44.3	42.2
1975	56.7	46.5	57.9	73.0	50.6	75.7	42.0	42.5	41.9
1976	57.5	47.8	58.6	73.4	51.5	76.0	43.2	44.2	43.1
1977	58.6	50.1	59.6	74.1	54.4	76.5	44.5	45.9	44.4
1978	60.0	52.4	60.8	75.0	56.3	77.2	46.3	48.5	46.1
1979	60.6	52.6	61.5	75.1	55.7	77.3	47.5	49.4	47.3
1980	60.0	50.7	61.0	73.4	53.4	75.6	47.8	47.9	47.8
1981	60.0	48.7	61.1	72.8	51.3	75.1	48.3	46.2	48.5
1982	58.8	45.8	60.1	70.6	47.0	73.0	48.1	44.6	48.4
1983	58.9	45.9	60.1	70.4	47.4	72.6	48.5	44.5	48.9
1984	60.5	48.0	61.5	72.1	49.1	74.3	49.8	47.0	50.0
1985	61.0	48.5	62.0	72.3	49.9	74.3	50.7	47.1	51.0
1986	61.5	48.8	62.6	72.3	49.6	74.3	51.7	47.9	52.0
1987	62.3	49.4	63.4	72.7	49.9	74.7	52.8	49.0	53.1
1988	63.1	50.9	64.1	73.2	51.7	75.1	53.8	50.2	54.0
1989	63.8	51.6	64.7	73.7	52.6	75.4	54.6	50.5	54.9
1990	63.7	49.7	64.8	73.3	51.0	75.1	54.7	48.3	55.2
1991	62.6	46.6	63.7	71.6	47.2	73.5	54.2	45.9	54.8
1992	62.4	45.3	63.6	71.1	46.4	73.1	54.2	44.2	54.9
1993	62.7	46.2	63.9	71.4	46.6	73.3	54.6	45.7	55.2
1994	63.5	47.9	64.7	71.8	48.3	73.6	55.8	47.5	56.4
1995	63.8	48.8	64.9	72.0	49.4	73.8	56.1	48.1	56.7

Civilian Employment-Population Ratios by Sex, Race, Hispanic Origin, and Age, 1948-1995—Continued

(Percent)

Year, sex, race, and Hispanic origin	Total			Men			Women		
	16 years and over	16 to 19 years	20 years and over	16 years and over	16 to 19 years	20 years and over	16 years and over	16 to 19 years	20 years and over
BLACK									
1972	53.7	25.2	58.3	66.8	31.6	73.0	43.0	19.2	46.5
1973	54.5	27.2	58.9	67.5	32.8	73.7	43.8	22.0	47.2
1974	53.5	25.9	58.0	65.8	31.4	71.9	43.5	20.9	46.9
1975	50.1	23.1	54.5	60.6	26.3	66.5	41.6	20.2	44.9
1976	50.8	22.4	55.4	60.6	25.8	66.8	42.8	19.2	46.4
1977	51.4	22.3	56.0	61.4	26.4	67.5	43.3	18.5	47.0
1978	53.6	25.2	58.0	63.3	28.5	69.1	45.8	22.1	49.3
1979	53.8	25.4	58.1	63.4	28.7	69.1	46.0	22.4	49.3
1980	52.3	23.9	56.4	60.4	27.0	65.8	45.7	21.0	49.1
1981	51.3	22.1	55.5	59.1	24.6	64.5	45.1	19.7	48.5
1982	49.4	19.0	53.6	56.0	20.3	61.4	44.2	17.7	47.5
1983	49.5	18.7	53.6	56.3	20.4	61.6	44.1	17.0	47.4
1984	52.3	21.9	56.1	59.2	23.9	64.1	46.7	20.1	49.8
1985	53.4	24.6	57.0	60.0	26.3	64.6	48.1	23.1	50.9
1986	54.1	25.1	57.6	60.6	26.5	65.1	48.8	23.8	51.6
1987	55.6	27.1	58.9	62.0	28.5	66.4	50.3	25.8	53.0
1988	56.3	27.6	59.7	62.7	29.4	67.1	51.2	25.8	53.9
1989	56.9	28.7	60.1	62.8	30.4	67.0	52.0	27.1	54.6
1990	56.7	26.7	60.2	62.6	27.7	67.1	51.9	25.8	54.7
1991	55.4	22.6	59.0	61.3	23.8	65.9	50.6	21.5	53.6
1992	54.9	22.8	58.3	59.9	23.6	64.3	50.8	22.1	53.6
1993	55.0	22.6	58.4	60.0	23.6	64.3	50.9	21.6	53.8
1994	56.1	24.9	59.4	60.8	25.4	65.0	52.3	24.5	55.0
1995	57.1	25.7	60.5	61.7	25.2	66.1	53.4	26.1	56.1
HISPANIC									
1973	55.6								
1974	56.2								
1975	53.4								
1976	53.8								
1977	55.4								
1978	57.2								
1979	58.3								
1980	57.6								
1981	57.4								
1982	54.9								
1983	55.1								
1984	57.9								
1985	57.8								
1986	58.5								
1987	60.5								
1988	61.9								
1989	62.2								
1990	61.9								
1991	59.8								
1992	59.1								
1993	59.1								
1994	59.5								
1995	59.7								

NOTE: Data beginning in 1994 are not strictly comparable with data for 1993 and earlier years because of the introduction of a major redesign of the survey and collection methodology. Beginning in 1990, data are not strictly comparable with previous years because of the introduction of 1990 census-based population controls adjusted for the estimated undercount.

Employed Civilians by Occupation, Sex, Race, and Hispanic Origin, 1983-1995

(Thousands of persons)

Occupation	1983						1984					
	Total	Men	Women	White	Black	Hispanic	Total	Men	Women	White	Black	Hispanic
TOTAL	100 834	56 787	44 047	88 893	9 375	6 072	105 005	59 091	45 915	92 120	10 119	6 651
Managerial and professional specialty	23 592	13 933	9 659	21 608	1 324	716	24 858	14 529	10 329	22 702	1 422	797
Executive, administrative, and managerial	10 772	7 282	3 490	10 016	504	349	11 571	7 683	3 889	10 704	582	417
Professional specialty	12 820	6 651	6 169	11 592	820	366	13 286	6 846	6 440	11 998	840	379
Technical, sales, and administrative support	31 265	11 078	20 187	28 159	2 380	1 539	32 476	11 556	20 920	29 082	2 592	1 677
Technicians and related support	11 818	6 201	5 617	10 999	558	499	3 172	1 646	1 527	2 783	262	142
Sales occupations	3 053	1 582	1 471	2 689	251	108	12 582	6 550	6 032	11 673	627	584
Administrative support, including clerical	16 395	3 295	13 100	14 471	1 571	933	16 722	3 361	13 361	14 626	1 703	951
Service occupations	13 857	5 530	8 326	11 123	2 295	1 073	14 151	5 545	8 607	11 214	2 478	1 174
Private household	980	38	942	686	272	95	993	38	955	667	301	107
Protective service	1 672	1 457	215	1 419	228	89	1 678	1 461	217	1 395	252	85
Other services	11 205	4 035	7 170	9 019	1 795	889	11 481	4 046	7 435	9 152	1 925	982
Precision production, craft, and repair	12 328	11 328	1 000	11 219	841	873	13 057	11 945	1 112	11 844	939	967
Operators, fabricators, and laborers	16 091	11 809	4 282	13 444	2 256	1 521	16 864	12 479	4 385	14 036	2 411	1 655
Machine operators, assemblers, and inspectors	7 744	4 484	3 259	6 414	1 081	829	7 984	4 702	3 282	6 600	1 132	888
Transportation and material moving occupations	4 201	3 875	326	3 592	547	285	4 467	4 098	369	3 782	625	304
Handlers, equipment cleaners, helpers, and laborers	4 147	3 450	697	3 438	628	408	4 413	3 679	734	3 655	654	463
Farming, forestry, and fishing	3 700	3 108	592	3 339	279	349	3 600	3 037	562	3 242	277	381

Occupation	1985						1986					
	Total	Men	Women	White	Black	Hispanic	Total	Men	Women	White	Black	Hispanic
TOTAL	107 150	59 891	47 259	93 736	10 501	6 888	109 597	60 892	48 706	95 660	10 814	7 219
Managerial and professional specialty	25 851	14 802	11 049	23 561	1 514	871	26 554	15 029	11 525	24 134	1 594	923
Executive, administrative, and managerial	12 221	7 871	4 351	11 256	649	442	12 642	7 990	4 653	11 649	658	466
Professional specialty	13 630	6 932	6 699	12 305	865	429	13 911	7 039	6 872	12 485	936	457
Technical, sales, and administrative support	33 231	11 725	21 507	29 553	2 785	1 705	34 354	12 130	22 223	30 497	2 923	1 812
Technicians and related support	3 255	1 719	1 537	2 823	291	134	3 364	1 783	1 581	2 953	277	134
Sales occupations	12 667	6 579	6 088	11 669	696	575	13 245	6 862	6 383	12 168	750	646
Administrative support, including clerical	17 309	3 427	13 882	15 061	1 798	995	17 745	3 485	14 260	15 377	1 896	1 032
Service occupations	14 441	5 695	8 747	11 432	2 522	1 211	14 680	5 775	8 905	11 685	2 480	1 298
Private household	1 006	38	968	692	291	101	981	39	942	721	235	127
Protective service	1 718	1 491	227	1 428	259	103	1 787	1 566	221	1 487	268	99
Other services	11 718	4 166	7 552	9 312	1 972	1 006	11 913	4 170	7 742	9 478	1 977	1 071
Precision production, craft, and repair	13 340	12 213	1 127	12 107	946	1 025	13 405	12 256	1 150	12 083	1 009	1 031
Operators, fabricators, and laborers	16 816	12 539	4 277	13 951	2 465	1 737	17 160	12 805	4 355	14 107	2 583	1 795
Machine operators, assemblers, and inspectors	7 840	4 681	3 159	6 483	1 120	944	7 911	4 725	3 187	6 462	1 167	956
Transportation and material moving occupations	4 535	4 160	375	3 849	620	328	4 564	4 158	406	3 847	641	344
Handlers, equipment cleaners, helpers, and laborers	4 441	3 697	744	3 618	725	466	4 685	3 923	762	3 798	776	494
Farming, forestry, and fishing	3 470	2 917	552	3 132	269	337	3 444	2 896	548	3 154	224	360

Occupation	1987						1988					
	Total	Men	Women	White	Black	Hispanic	Total	Men	Women	White	Black	Hispanic
TOTAL	112 440	62 107	50 334	97 789	11 309	7 790	114 968	63 273	51 696	99 812	11 658	8 250
Managerial and professional specialty	27 742	15 457	12 286	25 107	1 712	1 018	29 190	16 139	13 050	26 408	1 794	1 086
Executive, administrative, and managerial	13 316	8 263	5 053	12 200	741	509	14 216	8 626	5 590	13 022	789	570
Professional specialty	14 426	7 194	7 232	12 907	972	509	14 974	7 513	7 460	13 386	1 005	516
Technical, sales, and administrative support	35 082	12 378	22 704	30 949	3 099	1 969	35 532	12 494	23 038	31 178	3 239	2 064
Technicians and related support	3 346	1 721	1 624	2 914	283	130	3 521	1 833	1 688	3 019	329	152
Sales occupations	13 480	7 015	6 465	12 295	806	713	13 747	7 025	6 722	12 495	839	730
Administrative support, including clerical	18 256	3 642	14 614	15 740	2 010	1 126	18 264	3 636	14 628	15 664	2 071	1 182
Service occupations	15 054	5 924	9 130	11 916	2 614	1 369	15 332	6 056	9 275	12 105	2 698	1 560
Private household	934	34	900	703	211	120	909	34	875	687	205	152
Protective service	1 907	1 637	271	1 558	316	111	1 944	1 664	279	1 584	324	122
Other services	12 213	4 253	7 960	9 655	2 087	1 139	12 479	4 358	8 121	9 834	2 169	1 286
Precision production, craft, and repair	13 568	12 416	1 153	12 262	996	1 083	13 664	12 474	1 190	12 305	1 029	1 116
Operators, fabricators, and laborers	17 486	12 978	4 508	14 340	2 659	1 890	17 814	13 234	4 580	14 665	2 672	1 975
Machine operators, assemblers, and inspectors	7 994	4 699	3 295	6 498	1 195	1 001	8 117	4 806	3 311	6 642	1 197	1 079
Transportation and material moving occupations	4 712	4 317	395	3 934	699	360	4 831	4 397	434	4 027	719	343
Handlers, equipment cleaners, helpers, and laborers	4 779	3 962	817	3 909	765	528	4 866	4 031	835	3 997	755	552
Farming, forestry, and fishing	3 507	2 954	554	3 214	229	461	3 437	2 875	562	3 150	226	448

Employed Civilians by Occupation, Sex, Race, and Hispanic Origin, 1983-1995—Continued

(Thousands of persons)

Occupation	1989						1990					
	Total	Men	Women	White	Black	Hispanic	Total	Men	Women	White	Black	Hispanic
TOTAL	117 342	64 315	53 027	101 584	11 953	8 573	118 793	65 104	53 689	102 261	12 175	9 845
Managerial and professional specialty	30 398	16 652	13 746	27 459	1 862	1 126	30 602	16 601	14 001	27 416	1 945	1 208
Executive, administrative, and managerial	14 848	8 944	5 904	13 555	840	599	14 802	8 872	5 931	13 432	869	630
Professional specialty	15 550	7 708	7 842	13 903	1 022	527	15 800	7 729	8 071	13 984	1 076	578
Technical, sales, and administrative support	36 127	12 687	23 440	31 619	3 346	2 057	36 913	13 054	23 859	32 136	3 465	2 366
Technicians and related support	3 645	1 887	1 759	3 125	347	157	3 866	1 973	1 893	3 298	357	182
Sales occupations	14 065	7 124	6 941	12 741	906	730	14 285	7 247	7 038	12 871	937	848
Administrative support, including clerical	18 416	3 676	14 741	15 752	2 094	1 169	18 762	3 834	14 928	15 967	2 170	1 336
Service occupations	15 556	6 164	9 391	12 237	2 731	1 684	16 012	6 470	9 543	12 565	2 757	1 984
Private household	872	36	836	628	219	138	792	29	763	571	191	168
Protective service	1 960	1 654	305	1 594	329	113	2 000	1 708	293	1 618	334	131
Other services	12 724	4 474	8 250	10 016	2 184	1 433	13 220	4 732	8 488	10 376	2 233	1 685
Precision production, craft, and repair	13 818	12 627	1 190	12 369	1 089	1 173	13 745	12 580	1 166	12 255	1 083	1 301
Operators, fabricators, and laborers	18 022	13 327	4 695	14 752	2 714	2 059	18 071	13 494	4 577	14 732	2 715	2 436
Machine operators, assemblers, and inspectors	8 248	4 878	3 370	6 721	1 202	1 121	8 200	4 931	3 269	6 668	1 184	1 249
Transportation and material moving occupations	4 886	4 436	450	4 080	712	371	4 886	4 449	436	4 010	757	466
Handlers, equipment cleaners, helpers, and laborers	4 888	4 013	875	3 950	800	567	4 985	4 114	871	4 054	775	721
Farming, forestry, and fishing	3 421	2 857	565	3 149	210	474	3 450	2 907	544	3 157	209	550

Occupation	1991						1992					
	Total	Men	Women	White	Black	Hispanic	Total	Men	Women	White	Black	Hispanic
TOTAL	117 718	64 223	53 496	101 182	12 074	9 828	118 492	64 440	54 052	101 669	12 151	10 027
Managerial and professional specialty	30 934	16 623	14 311	27 706	1 972	1 259	31 085	16 387	14 698	27 719	2 044	1 322
Executive, administrative, and managerial	14 904	8 858	6 046	13 513	875	653	14 722	8 612	6 110	13 327	872	683
Professional specialty	16 030	7 765	8 265	14 193	1 097	606	16 363	7 775	8 588	14 393	1 172	639
Technical, sales, and administrative support	36 318	12 852	23 466	31 524	3 443	2 413	37 048	13 379	23 669	32 167	3 423	2 492
Technicians and related support	3 814	1 937	1 877	3 257	344	196	4 277	2 185	2 092	3 620	418	216
Sales occupations	14 052	7 180	6 872	12 590	955	867	14 014	7 286	6 728	12 576	891	882
Administrative support, including clerical	18 452	3 735	14 717	15 677	2 145	1 349	18 757	3 908	14 849	15 971	2 114	1 395
Service occupations	16 254	6 610	9 644	12 739	2 783	2 005	16 377	6 676	9 701	12 778	2 843	2 037
Private household	799	33	766	608	162	179	891	37	854	695	162	187
Protective service	2 083	1 765	318	1 682	351	144	2 114	1 760	354	1 669	383	168
Other services	13 372	4 812	8 560	10 449	2 270	1 682	13 373	4 879	8 493	10 414	2 298	1 682
Precision production, craft, and repair	13 250	12 112	1 138	11 824	1 039	1 269	13 225	12 087	1 137	11 798	1 016	1 345
Operators, fabricators, and laborers	17 456	13 075	4 380	14 205	2 613	2 311	17 247	12 954	4 294	14 018	2 599	2 243
Machine operators, assemblers, and inspectors	7 820	4 693	3 127	6 284	1 159	1 142	7 658	4 623	3 035	6 141	1 153	1 130
Transportation and material moving occupations	4 913	4 476	437	4 022	774	462	4 908	4 482	426	4 069	730	460
Handlers, equipment cleaners, helpers, and laborers	4 723	3 906	816	3 899	680	707	4 682	3 850	832	3 808	716	653
Farming, forestry, and fishing	3 506	2 951	556	3 184	224	570	3 510	2 957	553	3 188	226	588

Occupation	1993					
	Total	Men	Women	White	Black	Hispanic
TOTAL	120 259	65 349	54 910	103 045	12 382	10 361
Managerial and professional specialty	32 231	16 811	15 419	28 647	2 181	1 437
Executive, administrative, and managerial	15 338	8 897	6 441	13 783	977	762
Professional specialty	16 893	7 915	8 978	14 863	1 204	675
Technical, sales, and administrative support	37 058	13 417	23 641	32 096	3 501	2 578
Technicians and related support	4 039	2 000	2 039	3 433	395	223
Sales occupations	14 342	7 418	6 924	12 824	974	940
Administrative support, including clerical	18 677	3 999	14 679	15 839	2 132	1 415
Service occupations	16 821	6 867	9 953	13 145	2 901	2 069
Private household	928	45	883	735	154	214
Protective service	2 165	1 792	373	1 729	380	160
Other services	13 727	5 030	8 697	10 681	2 367	1 695
Precision production, craft, and repair	13 429	12 279	1 150	11 990	1 006	1 372
Operators, fabricators, and laborers	17 341	13 109	4 232	14 090	2 580	2 310
Machine operators, assemblers, and inspectors	7 553	4 642	2 911	6 066	1 117	1 140
Transportation and material moving occupations	5 036	4 570	465	4 195	706	481
Handlers, equipment cleaners, helpers, and laborers	4 753	3 897	856	3 829	757	689
Farming, forestry, and fishing	3 379	2 864	515	3 078	212	596

Employed Civilians by Occupation, Sex, Race, and Hispanic Origin, 1983-1995—Continued

(Thousands of persons)

Occupation	1994						1995					
	Total	Men	Women	White	Black	Hispanic	Total	Men	Women	White	Black	Hispanic
TOTAL	123 060	66 450	56 610	105 190	12 835	10 788	124 900	67 377	57 523	106 490	13 279	11 127
Managerial and professional specialty	33 847	17 583	16 264	30 045	2 405	1 517	35 318	18 378	16 940	31 323	2 651	1 548
Executive, administrative, and managerial	16 312	9 298	7 014	14 605	1 103	807	17 186	9 840	7 346	15 398	1 233	821
Professional specialty	17 536	8 285	9 250	15 439	1 302	709	18 132	8 539	9 593	15 924	1 418	727
Technical, sales, and administrative support	37 306	13 322	23 984	32 232	3 637	2 639	37 417	13 310	24 107	32 184	3 808	2 719
Technicians and related support	3 869	1 856	2 013	3 301	376	205	3 909	1 900	2 009	3 361	378	240
Sales occupations	14 817	7 543	7 273	13 235	1 056	1 010	15 119	7 634	7 485	13 366	1 183	1 048
Administrative support, including clerical	18 620	3 923	14 697	15 696	2 205	1 424	18 389	3 776	14 613	15 457	2 248	1 431
Service occupations	16 912	6 840	10 072	13 207	2 890	2 131	16 930	6 774	10 155	13 208	2 880	2 195
Private household	817	30	787	643	136	223	821	37	784	638	137	204
Protective service	2 249	1 873	376	1 778	407	167	2 237	1 881	356	1 772	406	166
Other services	13 847	4 938	8 909	10 787	2 346	1 741	13 872	4 857	9 015	10 799	2 337	1 825
Precision production, craft, and repair	13 489	12 241	1 248	11 974	1 040	1 407	13 524	12 323	1 201	11 949	1 073	1 430
Operators, fabricators, and laborers	17 876	13 535	4 341	14 416	2 677	2 474	18 068	13 675	4 393	14 496	2 712	2 577
Machine operators, assemblers, and inspectors	7 754	4 800	2 954	6 166	1 167	1 151	7 907	4 958	2 949	6 221	1 218	1 250
Transportation and material moving occupations	5 136	4 654	483	4 227	749	511	5 171	4 682	490	4 254	760	512
Handlers, equipment cleaners, helpers, and laborers	4 986	4 081	904	4 023	760	811	4 990	4 035	955	4 022	734	816
Farming, forestry, and fishing	3 629	2 928	701	3 315	187	620	3 642	2 916	726	3 330	154	658

NOTE: Data beginning in 1994 are not strictly comparable with data for 1993 and earlier years because of the introduction of a major redesign of the survey and collection methodology. Beginning in 1990, data are not strictly comparable with previous years because of the introduction of 1990 census-based population controls adjusted for the estimated undercount.

Employed Civilians by Industry and Occupation, 1984-1995

(Thousands of persons)

Industry	Total employed	Executive, administrative, and managerial	Professional specialty	Technicians and related support	Sales	Administrative support, including clerical	Private household	Other service occupations	Precision production, craft, and repair	Machine operators, assemblers, and inspectors	Transportation and material moving	Handlers, equipment cleaners, helpers, and laborers	Farming, forestry, and fishing
1984													
Agriculture	3 321	51	62	22	16	101	....	13	40	9	48	15	2 944
Mining	957	155	99	44	11	126	....	14	301	31	140	36	1
Construction	6 665	748	134	60	56	431	....	33	3 841	88	470	788	16
Manufacturing	20 995	2 206	1 569	739	747	2 544	....	386	4 025	6 737	877	1 074	90
Durable goods	12 606	1 370	1 083	530	307	1 494	....	213	2 821	3 718	469	521	81
Nondurable goods	8 389	836	486	209	440	1 051	....	174	1 204	3 019	408	553	10
Transportation and public utilities	7 358	752	423	222	264	1 964	....	245	1 332	114	1 603	426	11
Wholesale trade	4 212	438	77	39	1 651	785	....	47	294	137	417	311	14
Retail trade	17 767	1 296	311	48	7 553	1 381	....	4 096	1 131	141	395	1 393	21
Finance, insurance, and real estate	6 750	1 585	151	118	1 597	2 822	....	266	108	13	18	16	56
Services	32 214	3 325	9 817	1 673	661	5 244	993	6 926	1 748	678	444	312	392
Private households							993						
Other service industries	30 971	3 321	9 804	1 663	660	5 234		6 853	1 741	677	438	292	288
Professional services	21 174	1 885	8 855	1 411	129	3 855		4 066	376	170	255	80	91
Public administration	4 766	1 016	642	207	25	1 323	....	1 131	237	36	55	41	54
1985													
Agriculture	3 179	57	62	23	13	96	....	11	37	8	45	13	2 814
Mining	939	138	94	47	14	114	....	9	302	27	162	32	1
Construction	6 987	829	141	57	74	441	....	31	4 015	91	495	799	15
Manufacturing	20 879	2 288	1 637	746	715	2 528	....	399	4 018	6 589	824	1 051	84
Durable goods	12 586	1 419	1 148	540	300	1 464	....	226	2 854	3 641	424	498	73
Nondurable goods	8 293	869	489	206	415	1 065	....	173	1 164	2 949	400	553	10
Transportation and public utilities	7 548	791	435	232	307	2 041	....	237	1 311	112	1 611	458	13
Wholesale trade	4 341	470	67	37	1 696	826	....	41	303	130	438	320	12
Retail trade	17 955	1 369	336	45	7 470	1 458	....	4 189	1 151	140	417	1 358	22
Finance, insurance, and real estate	7 005	1 649	152	119	1 669	2 918	....	282	113	15	14	22	52
Services	33 321	3 562	10 045	1 722	683	5 492	1 006	7 073	1 836	693	471	346	393
Private households							1 006						
Other service industries	32 067	3 560	10 035	1 713	682	5 481		6 992	1 828	692	465	321	299
Professional services	21 563	2 014	8 984	1 431	128	4 008		4 022	389	171	248	83	85
Public administration	4 995	1 069	660	229	26	1 396	....	1 163	254	35	59	42	64
1986													
Agriculture	3 163	62	65	28	15	104	....	14	46	11	43	17	2 758
Mining	880	138	96	35	13	104	....	8	271	27	145	40	1
Construction	7 288	864	135	69	78	443	....	31	4 209	95	480	867	15
Manufacturing	20 962	2 295	1 701	765	720	2 485	....	388	4 020	6 615	784	1 103	87
Durable goods	12 605	1 416	1 192	567	295	1 425	....	211	2 833	3 671	401	518	75
Nondurable goods	8 357	878	510	198	425	1 060	....	177	1 187	2 944	383	584	12
Transportation and public utilities	7 650	844	439	234	328	2 089	....	236	1 263	105	1 635	465	12
Wholesale trade	4 416	459	71	41	1 735	835	....	36	304	129	465	329	12
Retail trade	18 397	1 359	321	54	7 763	1 484	....	4 210	1 158	162	434	1 432	19
Finance, insurance, and real estate	7 401	1 753	175	137	1 778	3 043	....	284	132	13	13	22	51
Services	34 337	3 795	10 218	1 778	792	5 746	981	7 260	1 765	713	506	358	425
Private households							981						
Other service industries	33 096	3 792	10 208	1 772	791	5 733		7 177	1 755	711	501	337	318
Professional services	22 174	2 105	9 124	1 470	149	4 197		4 111	371	182	273	92	102
Public administration	5 104	1 074	689	225	22	1 410	....	1 232	237	40	57	53	64
1987													
Agriculture	3 208	70	65	25	21	98	....	16	38	11	45	20	2 800
Mining	818	128	85	30	13	91	....	8	258	21	141	42	2
Construction	7 456	926	131	56	71	458	....	33	4 279	95	511	877	20
Manufacturing	20 935	2 315	1 688	698	704	2 470	....	360	3 990	6 640	806	1 182	81
Durable goods	12 478	1 421	1 166	496	292	1 410	....	196	2 785	3 663	422	556	72
Nondurable goods	8 456	894	522	202	412	1 060	....	164	1 205	2 978	384	626	9
Transportation and public utilities	7 880	861	455	252	302	2 154	....	265	1 267	118	1 719	472	13
Wholesale trade	4 580	492	77	40	1 774	833	....	41	343	140	482	340	17
Retail trade	18 812	1 442	335	60	7 895	1 565	....	4 281	1 197	168	455	1 389	25
Finance, insurance, and real estate	7 763	1 903	184	138	1 859	3 128	....	281	144	21	12	25	67
Services	35 743	4 082	10 695	1 834	817	6 002	934	7 541	1 805	741	486	379	426
Private households							934						
Other service industries	34 527	4 076	10 685	1 828	815	5 994		7 437	1 794	739	477	359	322
Professional services	22 963	2 269	9 511	1 504	136	4 312		4 197	395	178	276	97	88
Public administration	5 246	1 099	711	212	24	1 457	....	1 295	246	40	54	52	55

Employed Civilians by Industry and Occupation, 1984-1995—Continued

(Thousands of persons)

Industry	Total employed	Managerial and professional specialty		Technical, sales, and administrative support			Service occupations		Precision production, craft, and repair	Operators, fabricators, and laborers			Farming, forestry, and fishing
		Executive, administrative, and managerial	Professional specialty	Technicians and related support	Sales	Administrative support, including clerical	Private household	Other service occupations		Machine operators, assemblers, and inspectors	Transportation and material moving	Handlers, equipment cleaners, helpers, and laborers	
1988													
Agriculture	3 169	78	69	20	18	99	....	15	39	10	47	19	2 754
Mining	753	112	76	37	13	93	....	7	239	24	118	34	1
Construction	7 603	998	146	51	80	460	....	29	4 331	90	499	895	24
Manufacturing	21 320	2 461	1 781	706	746	2 416	....	342	4 070	6 751	802	1 150	93
Durable goods	12 642	1 501	1 205	494	313	1 347	....	191	2 807	3 713	424	564	85
Nondurable goods	8 678	960	577	212	434	1 069	....	152	1 263	3 038	378	586	9
Transportation and public utilities	8 064	915	455	260	314	2 152	....	257	1 275	120	1 800	505	11
Wholesale trade	4 578	514	87	45	1 764	807	....	49	300	138	497	361	16
Retail trade	19 085	1 520	350	72	8 034	1 556	....	4 274	1 173	168	487	1 427	24
Finance, insurance, and real estate	7 921	1 999	195	146	1 885	3 133	....	290	158	17	12	22	63
Services	37 043	4 461	11 062	1 931	863	6 072	909	7 827	1 834	768	509	409	399
Private households	....	....	....	....	....	....	909	....	....	....	....	....	....
Other service industries	35 880	4 460	11 054	1 923	862	6 061	....	7 725	1 823	767	502	383	320
Professional services	23 725	2 441	9 831	1 566	142	4 375	....	4 299	383	213	298	95	83
Public administration	5 432	1 158	751	252	30	1 476	....	1 332	244	31	60	45	53
1989													
Agriculture	3 199	78	72	29	21	114	....	18	45	11	51	22	2 738
Mining	719	105	63	31	9	81	....	9	232	34	123	30	1
Construction	7 680	1 024	145	54	66	444	....	35	4 410	114	533	837	17
Manufacturing	21 652	2 576	1 807	739	758	2 394	....	350	4 109	6 774	846	1 208	91
Durable goods	12 805	1 550	1 222	519	321	1 322	....	193	2 830	3 729	445	590	84
Nondurable goods	8 847	1 026	586	220	437	1 072	....	157	1 279	3 045	401	619	7
Transportation and public utilities	8 094	934	477	276	349	2 162	....	269	1 260	122	1 748	483	13
Wholesale trade	4 611	510	89	40	1 844	798	....	44	322	136	472	343	14
Retail trade	19 618	1 535	352	78	8 237	1 587	....	4 426	1 226	190	500	1 463	23
Finance, insurance, and real estate	7 989	2 115	205	140	1 865	3 121	....	274	142	20	16	25	65
Services	38 227	4 748	11 560	2 008	890	6 243	872	7 899	1 833	817	533	421	403
Private households	....	....	....	....	....	....	872	....	....	....	....	....	....
Other service industries	37 118	4 744	11 553	2 003	889	6 233	....	7 813	1 820	816	528	400	319
Professional services	24 609	2 640	10 215	1 624	142	4 490	....	4 397	391	226	295	100	90
Public administration	5 553	1 222	780	250	24	1 473	....	1 359	239	30	63	56	56
1990													
Agriculture	3 223	95	85	30	23	108	....	17	42	13	49	21	2 740
Mining	724	110	63	32	9	72	....	9	243	26	123	36	2
Construction	7 764	1 034	133	64	75	426	....	35	4 445	114	524	890	23
Manufacturing	21 346	2 530	1 794	765	779	2 363	....	374	3 964	6 696	805	1 173	102
Durable goods	12 630	1 521	1 225	533	326	1 363	....	197	2 721	3 685	416	552	91
Nondurable goods	8 717	1 010	569	232	453	1 000	....	178	1 243	3 011	389	621	11
Transportation and public utilities	8 168	915	459	306	340	2 166	....	293	1 259	122	1 812	481	14
Wholesale trade	4 669	528	88	50	1 862	788	....	39	323	138	464	380	10
Retail trade	19 953	1 557	379	89	8 295	1 633	....	4 584	1 181	197	512	1 498	27
Finance, insurance, and real estate	8 051	2 087	225	155	1 904	3 097	....	296	155	19	17	25	71
Services	39 267	4 745	11 786	2 125	971	6 561	792	8 194	1 898	831	521	436	408
Private households	....	....	....	....	....	....	792	....	....	....	....	....	....
Other service industries	38 231	4 742	11 773	2 121	969	6 552	....	8 098	1 881	829	514	417	336
Professional services	25 351	2 642	10 425	1 719	162	4 763	....	4 544	400	228	276	101	91
Public administration	5 627	1 199	788	251	26	1 549	....	1 380	235	43	60	44	53
1991													
Agriculture	3 269	91	78	31	22	102	....	18	41	12	54	16	2 803
Mining	732	112	65	37	8	81	....	12	244	24	115	34	1
Construction	7 140	969	137	53	71	386	....	29	4 077	100	497	797	24
Manufacturing	20 580	2 499	1 777	749	729	2 283	....	355	3 837	6 402	780	1 076	92
Durable goods	12 015	1 489	1 178	512	292	1 260	....	185	2 630	3 459	404	525	80
Nondurable goods	8 565	1 010	599	237	437	1 023	....	170	1 207	2 943	376	551	13
Transportation and public utilities	8 234	973	474	301	331	2 170	....	262	1 285	125	1 833	465	16
Wholesale trade	4 660	537	77	37	1 868	776	....	36	319	135	490	374	11
Retail trade	19 758	1 591	372	103	8 181	1 589	....	4 605	1 142	173	530	1 450	23
Finance, insurance, and real estate	7 806	2 027	216	133	1 849	3 022	....	270	167	18	14	20	69
Services	39 884	4 873	12 035	2 148	967	6 534	799	8 455	1 884	792	537	444	416
Private households	....	....	....	....	....	....	799	....	....	....	....	....	....
Other service industries	38 868	4 871	12 029	2 144	966	6 522	....	8 375	1 870	791	531	422	346
Professional services	25 853	2 706	10 629	1 742	162	4 788	....	4 749	393	211	295	87	92
Public administration	5 655	1 231	798	223	27	1 508	....	1 414	253	41	62	46	51

Employed Civilians by Industry and Occupation, 1984-1995—Continued

(Thousands of persons)

Industry	Total employed	Managerial and professional specialty		Technical, sales, and administrative support			Service occupations		Precision production, craft, and repair	Operators, fabricators, and laborers			Farming, forestry, and fishing
		Executive, administrative, and managerial	Professional specialty	Technicians and related support	Sales	Administrative support, including clerical	Private household	Other service occupations		Machine operators, assemblers, and inspectors	Transportation and material moving	Handlers, equipment cleaners, helpers, and laborers	
1992													
Agriculture	3 247	91	74	44	21	118	....	17	45	10	44	19	2 764
Mining	666	100	58	31	7	79	....	12	214	28	106	31	1
Construction	7 063	892	147	67	73	410	....	34	4 073	99	480	762	28
Manufacturing	20 124	2 401	1 640	758	768	2 268	....	330	3 808	6 244	749	1 074	84
Durable goods	11 561	1 405	1 069	525	306	1 251	....	158	2 569	3 344	374	485	75
Nondurable goods	8 563	996	571	234	462	1 017	....	172	1 239	2 901	375	589	8
Transportation and public utilities	8 284	946	461	375	250	2 281	....	274	1 227	114	1 874	464	18
Wholesale trade	4 783	556	85	46	1 883	820	....	42	302	118	490	405	38
Retail trade	19 938	1 603	374	146	8 229	1 591	....	4 717	1 117	180	530	1 428	25
Finance, insurance, and real estate	7 780	1 966	224	162	1 851	2 991	....	290	171	19	13	22	73
Services	40 967	4 937	12 473	2 379	908	6 728	891	8 368	2 022	810	563	440	449
Private households	....	....	....	....	....	....	891						
Other service industries	39 821	4 933	12 463	2 373	906	6 714	....	8 270	2 007	807	555	421	372
Professional services	27 713	3 150	11 168	2 040	175	5 032	....	5 017	411	208	314	102	95
Public administration	5 640	1 231	829	268	25	1 472	....	1 404	246	37	59	38	31
1993													
Agriculture	3 115	99	87	39	14	114	....	15	45	8	53	20	2 621
Mining	672	102	75	24	4	73	....	8	233	25	103	25	....
Construction	7 276	928	137	46	74	390	....	35	4 292	79	517	753	25
Manufacturing	19 711	2 432	1 688	693	739	2 161	....	312	3 744	6 124	710	1 012	95
Durable goods	11 385	1 415	1 085	463	282	1 181	....	161	2 553	3 352	361	446	87
Nondurable goods	8 326	1 017	603	231	457	981	....	151	1 191	2 772	349	566	9
Transportation and public utilities	8 526	975	500	329	241	2 318	....	266	1 271	131	2 000	479	18
Wholesale trade	4 622	533	85	49	1 819	771	....	40	296	115	492	378	44
Retail trade	20 521	1 652	351	129	8 543	1 571	....	4 873	1 095	179	543	1 563	23
Finance, insurance, and real estate	7 975	2 089	244	161	1 918	2 967	....	290	183	21	13	19	70
Services	42 059	5 234	12 864	2 300	963	6 841	928	8 579	2 047	831	551	467	453
Private households	....	....	....	....	....	....	928						
Other service industries	40 924	5 231	12 857	2 298	961	6 830	....	8 497	2 035	831	547	446	392
Professional services	28 365	3 299	11 476	1 969	176	5 111	....	5 163	419	223	314	108	105
Public administration	5 782	1 294	862	270	26	1 469	....	1 475	224	39	54	39	31
1994													
Agriculture	3 409	97	88	38	14	145	....	18	42	5	45	19	2 897
Mining	669	110	76	22	10	67	....	9	222	21	109	21	1
Construction	7 493	1 055	138	60	59	429	....	34	4 263	86	529	818	22
Manufacturing	20 157	2 588	1 814	611	745	2 093	....	290	3 803	6 298	744	1 082	89
Durable goods	11 792	1 555	1 170	412	310	1 146	....	152	2 622	3 415	416	514	80
Nondurable goods	8 365	1 033	644	200	435	946	....	138	1 181	2 883	328	569	9
Transportation and public utilities	8 692	1 065	486	329	248	2 337	....	246	1 270	120	2 049	528	15
Wholesale trade	4 713	531	89	37	1 880	775	....	34	296	150	464	398	60
Retail trade	20 986	1 704	402	119	8 772	1 555	....	4 948	1 145	197	548	1 569	27
Finance, insurance, and real estate	8 141	2 198	272	160	2 029	2 915	....	282	167	18	17	18	66
Services	42 986	5 649	13 319	2 274	1 032	6 864	817	8 654	2 071	825	567	493	421
Private households	....	....	....	....	....	....	817						
Other service industries	42 009	5 645	13 311	2 272	1 031	6 855	....	8 584	2 063	825	564	480	380
Professional services	29 030	3 559	11 888	1 968	193	5 083	....	5 134	470	222	314	94	105
Public administration	5 814	1 315	853	221	28	1 440	....	1 579	211	32	64	39	30
1995													
Agriculture	3 440	105	92	45	15	145	....	16	35	17	45	19	2 907
Mining	627	100	60	22	4	53	....	5	228	28	101	25	2
Construction	7 668	1 117	145	43	63	431	....	33	4 362	85	513	858	18
Manufacturing	20 493	2 804	1 787	615	756	2 108	....	294	3 837	6 386	728	1 067	111
Durable goods	12 015	1 683	1 160	404	311	1 117	....	156	2 660	3 498	390	535	100
Nondurable goods	8 478	1 121	627	211	445	991	....	138	1 177	2 888	338	532	11
Transportation and public utilities	8 709	1 124	510	310	259	2 337	....	247	1 223	121	2 079	487	12
Wholesale trade	4 986	554	108	48	1 979	792	....	37	308	187	488	423	62
Retail trade	21 086	1 740	425	141	8 949	1 501	....	4 844	1 111	214	578	1 548	34
Finance, insurance, and real estate	7 983	2 258	268	148	1 985	2 757	....	269	183	14	14	19	68
Services	43 953	6 029	13 755	2 307	1 086	6 848	821	8 789	2 008	824	572	510	405
Private households	....	....	....	....	....	....	821						
Other service industries	42 982	6 023	13 746	2 305	1 086	6 838	....	8 719	2 002	822	569	497	374
Professional services	29 661	3 721	12 233	1 974	199	5 114	....	5 284	465	178	312	87	94
Public administration	5 957	1 356	981	230	24	1 417	....	1 577	229	32	52	35	25

NOTE: Data beginning in 1994 are not strictly comparable with data for 1993 and earlier years because of the introduction of a major redesign of the survey and collection methodology. Beginning in 1990, data are not strictly comparable with previous years because of the introduction of 1990 census-based population controls adjusted for the estimated undercount.

Employed Civilians in Agriculture and Nonagricultural Industries by Class of Worker and Sex, 1976-1995

(Thousands of persons)

Year	Total employed	Agriculture				Nonagricultural industries						
		Total	Wage and salary workers	Self-employed workers	Unpaid family workers	Total	Wage and salary workers				Self-employed workers	Unpaid family workers
							Total	Government	Private household	Other private		
TOTAL												
1976	88 752	3 331	1 344	1 646	342	85 421	79 175	15 132	1 374	62 669	5 783	464
1977	92 017	3 283	1 360	1 580	343	88 734	82 121	15 361	1 395	65 364	6 114	498
1978	96 048	3 387	1 452	1 618	316	92 661	85 753	15 525	1 384	68 844	6 429	479
1979	98 824	3 347	1 451	1 593	304	95 477	88 222	15 635	1 264	71 323	6 791	463
1980	99 303	3 364	1 425	1 642	297	95 938	88 525	15 912	1 192	71 420	7 000	413
1981	100 397	3 368	1 464	1 638	266	97 030	89 543	15 689	1 208	72 645	7 097	390
1982	99 526	3 401	1 505	1 636	261	96 125	88 462	15 516	1 207	71 738	7 262	401
1983	100 834	3 383	1 579	1 565	240	97 450	89 500	15 537	1 244	72 716	7 575	376
1984	105 005	3 321	1 555	1 553	213	101 685	93 565	15 770	1 238	76 556	7 785	335
1985	107 150	3 179	1 535	1 458	185	103 971	95 871	16 031	1 249	78 592	7 811	289
1986	109 597	3 163	1 547	1 447	169	106 434	98 299	16 342	1 235	80 722	7 881	255
1987	112 440	3 208	1 632	1 423	153	109 232	100 771	16 800	1 208	82 762	8 201	260
1988	114 968	3 169	1 621	1 398	150	111 800	103 021	17 114	1 153	84 754	8 519	260
1989	117 342	3 199	1 665	1 403	131	114 142	105 259	17 469	1 101	86 689	8 605	279
1990	118 793	3 223	1 740	1 378	105	115 570	106 598	17 769	1 027	87 802	8 719	253
1991	117 718	3 269	1 729	1 423	118	114 449	105 373	17 934	1 010	86 428	8 851	226
1992	118 492	3 247	1 750	1 385	112	115 245	106 437	18 136	1 135	87 166	8 575	233
1993	120 259	3 115	1 689	1 320	106	117 144	107 966	18 579	1 126	88 261	8 959	218
1994	123 060	3 409	1 715	1 645	49	119 651	110 517	18 293	966	91 258	9 003	131
1995	124 900	3 440	1 814	1 580	45	121 460	112 448	18 362	963	93 123	8 902	110
MEN												
1976	53 138	2 744	1 096	1 532	115	50 394	46 110	7 778	198	38 134	4 233	52
1977	54 728	2 671	1 103	1 462	107	52 057	47 578	7 865	198	39 515	4 423	56
1978	56 479	2 718	1 162	1 465	91	53 761	49 103	7 836	181	41 086	4 614	44
1979	57 607	2 686	1 160	1 429	98	54 921	50 068	7 790	159	42 119	4 810	43
1980	57 186	2 709	1 149	1 458	101	54 477	49 517	7 822	149	41 546	4 904	56
1981	57 397	2 700	1 168	1 442	91	54 697	49 745	7 676	192	41 877	4 905	47
1982	56 271	2 736	1 208	1 433	95	53 534	48 529	7 598	188	40 742	4 954	52
1983	56 787	2 704	1 265	1 355	84	54 083	48 896	7 623	208	41 063	5 136	51
1984	59 091	2 668	1 254	1 350	65	56 423	51 151	7 720	178	43 253	5 219	52
1985	59 891	2 535	1 230	1 244	60	57 356	52 111	7 757	170	44 183	5 207	38
1986	60 892	2 511	1 230	1 227	54	58 381	53 075	7 805	180	45 089	5 271	35
1987	62 107	2 543	1 290	1 194	58	59 564	54 102	8 013	180	45 909	5 423	39
1988	63 273	2 493	1 268	1 174	50	60 780	55 177	8 074	157	46 946	5 564	39
1989	64 315	2 513	1 302	1 167	44	61 802	56 202	8 116	156	47 930	5 562	38
1990	65 104	2 546	1 355	1 151	39	62 559	56 913	8 245	149	48 520	5 597	48
1991	64 223	2 589	1 359	1 185	45	61 634	55 899	8 300	143	47 455	5 700	35
1992	64 440	2 575	1 371	1 164	40	61 866	56 212	8 348	156	47 709	5 613	41
1993	65 349	2 478	1 323	1 117	39	62 871	56 926	8 435	146	48 345	5 894	50
1994	66 450	2 554	1 330	1 197	27	63 896	58 300	8 327	99	49 873	5 560	37
1995	67 377	2 559	1 395	1 138	26	64 818	59 332	8 267	96	50 969	5 461	25
WOMEN												
1976	35 615	588	248	113	227	35 027	33 065	7 354	1 176	24 535	1 549	412
1977	37 289	612	258	118	236	36 677	34 544	7 496	1 196	25 850	1 692	442
1978	39 569	669	290	155	225	38 900	36 651	7 689	1 204	27 758	1 814	435
1979	41 217	661	290	165	206	40 556	38 154	7 845	1 105	29 204	1 982	419
1980	42 117	656	275	184	197	41 461	39 007	8 090	1 044	29 874	2 097	357
1981	43 000	667	296	196	176	42 333	39 798	8 013	1 016	30 769	2 192	343
1982	43 256	665	296	203	166	42 591	39 934	7 918	1 019	30 996	2 309	348
1983	44 047	680	314	210	156	43 367	40 603	7 913	1 036	31 653	2 439	325
1984	45 915	653	301	203	148	45 262	42 413	8 050	1 061	33 302	2 566	283
1985	47 259	644	305	214	125	46 615	43 761	8 274	1 078	34 409	2 603	251
1986	48 706	652	317	220	115	48 054	45 225	8 537	1 055	35 633	2 610	219
1987	50 334	666	342	229	95	49 668	46 669	8 788	1 029	36 853	2 778	221
1988	51 696	676	353	224	99	51 020	47 844	9 039	996	37 809	2 955	220
1989	53 027	687	363	236	87	52 341	49 057	9 353	945	38 758	3 043	240
1990	53 689	678	385	227	66	53 011	49 685	9 524	879	39 282	3 122	205
1991	53 496	680	369	237	73	52 815	49 474	9 635	867	38 972	3 150	191
1992	54 052	672	379	221	73	53 380	50 225	9 788	979	39 458	2 963	192
1993	54 910	637	367	204	67	54 273	51 040	10 144	980	39 917	3 065	168
1994	56 610	855	384	448	23	55 755	52 217	9 965	867	41 385	3 443	95
1995	57 523	881	419	442	20	56 642	53 115	10 095	867	42 153	3 440	86

NOTE: Data beginning in 1994 are not strictly comparable with data for 1993 and earlier years because of the introduction of a major redesign of the survey and collection methodology. Beginning in 1990, data are not strictly comparable with previous years because of the introduction of 1990 census-based population controls adjusted for the estimated undercount.

Persons on Part-time Schedules for Economic Reasons in Agriculture and Nonagricultural Industries by Sex and Age, 1957-1995

(Thousands of persons)

Year	Total	Agri-culture	Nonagricultural industries												
			Total	Men						Women					
				Total	16 to 17 years	18 to 24 years	25 to 44 years	45 to 64 years	65 years and over	Total	16 to 17 years	18 to 24 years	25 to 44 years	45 to 64 years	65 years and over
1957	2 469	300	2 169	1 263	99	181	488	418	76	906	58	117	383	315	32
1958	3 280	327	2 953	1 793	114	257	727	607	88	1 161	57	166	482	413	42
1959	2 640	304	2 336	1 320	115	223	494	419	67	1 016	62	140	405	367	41
1960	2 860	300	2 560	1 476	114	251	552	489	70	1 083	75	167	420	385	36
1961	3 142	329	2 813	1 625	127	305	598	527	66	1 188	65	178	460	443	40
1962	2 661	324	2 337	1 308	113	243	476	422	55	1 029	65	171	386	372	34
1963	2 620	329	2 291	1 263	106	255	436	407	59	1 025	65	183	384	355	38
1964	2 455	318	2 137	1 154	106	235	398	368	49	982	60	177	350	359	37
1965	2 209	281	1 928	1 005	108	226	322	310	40	923	55	205	308	325	30
1966	1 894	230	1 664	863	75	195	277	273	43	801	47	164	286	279	27
1967	2 163	250	1 913	987	81	214	331	310	51	925	52	199	312	331	33
1968	1 970	255	1 715	830	90	194	250	250	47	886	55	201	286	314	30
1969	2 056	246	1 810	888	98	210	284	252	45	921	64	212	311	308	27
1970	2 446	248	2 198	1 106	98	285	374	303	46	1 091	70	269	355	362	35
1971	2 688	237	2 451	1 209	104	338	404	317	46	1 241	79	322	410	391	40
1972	2 648	218	2 430	1 180	136	370	364	268	42	1 249	94	340	412	361	41
1973	2 554	211	2 343	1 118	126	355	358	241	38	1 224	96	361	397	331	38
1974	2 988	237	2 751	1 332	129	405	458	295	46	1 419	103	402	472	405	41
1975	3 804	262	3 542	1 763	135	537	635	410	48	1 778	112	540	613	477	37
1976	3 607	273	3 334	1 617	129	545	555	342	44	1 717	112	539	597	433	35
1977	3 608	239	3 369	1 574	141	546	540	301	47	1 795	113	577	642	422	41
1978	3 516	218	3 298	1 474	144	521	516	245	49	1 824	127	561	661	429	50
1979	3 577	204	3 373	1 494	135	503	523	277	53	1 880	112	581	714	424	48
1980	4 321	257	4 064	1 909	133	608	754	363	51	2 155	121	668	821	496	49
1981	4 768	269	4 499	2 079	133	678	809	407	51	2 421	122	723	976	551	49
1982	6 169	317	5 852	2 779	133	857	155	573	61	3 073	124	892	311	686	61
1983	6 266	269	5 997	2 758	125	929	136	508	59	3 240	119	1 001	386	675	59
1984	5 743	231	5 512	2 483	117	845	36	438	48	3 030	111	920	293	647	58
1985	5 590	256	5 334	2 373	114	777	19	422	43	2 960	114	816	335	634	61
1986	5 588	243	5 345	2 399	112	723	81	429	54	2 945	106	805	345	634	57
1987	5 402	280	5 122	2 299	108	657	51	424	57	2 823	107	731	314	614	57
1988	5 206	241	4 965	2 284	125	630	43	422	63	2 680	100	682	243	598	57
1989	4 894	237	4 657	2 109	96	582	989	386	58	2 547	78	595	203	607	65
1990	5 204	254	4 950	2 320	95	619	97	450	59	2 630	83	656	247	570	72
1991	6 161	287	5 874	2 879	85	767	431	529	66	2 995	74	712	438	697	74
1992	6 520	280	6 240	3 005	79	804	489	561	72	3 235	76	761	552	763	81
1993	6 481	251	6 230	2 925	93	749	456	559	68	3 305	88	766	581	792	78
1994	....	....	4 414	2 131	49	555	50	441	35	2 283	41	555	124	524	38
1995	....	....	4 279	2 056	53	541	983	437	42	2 223	47	516	85	542	34

NOTE: Data beginning in 1994 are not strictly comparable with data for 1993 and earlier years because of the introduction of a major redesign of the survey and collection methodology. Beginning in 1990, data are not strictly comparable with previous years because of the introduction of 1990 census-based population controls adjusted for the estimated undercount.

POPULATION, LABOR FORCE, AND EMPLOYMENT STATUS

Multiple Jobholders and Multiple Jobholding Rates, May, Selected Years, 1970-1991

(Numbers in thousands)

Date	Multiple jobholders				Multiple jobholding rate [1]				
	Total	Men	Women		Total	Men	Women	White	Black [2]
			Number	Percent of all multiple jobholders					
1970	4 048	3 412	636	15.7	5.2	7.0	2.2	5.3	4.4
1971	4 035	3 270	765	19.0	5.1	6.7	2.6	5.3	3.8
1972	3 770	3 035	735	19.5	4.6	6.0	2.4	4.8	3.7
1973	4 262	3 393	869	20.4	5.1	6.6	2.7	5.1	4.7
1974	3 889	3 022	867	22.3	4.5	5.8	2.6	4.6	3.8
1975	3 918	2 962	956	24.4	4.7	5.8	2.9	4.8	3.7
1976	3 948	3 037	911	23.1	4.5	5.8	2.6	4.7	2.8
1977	4 558	3 317	1 241	27.2	5.0	6.2	3.4	5.3	2.6
1978	4 493	3 212	1 281	28.5	4.8	5.8	3.3	5.0	3.1
1979	4 724	3 317	1 407	29.8	4.9	5.9	3.5	5.1	3.0
1980	4 759	3 210	1 549	32.5	4.9	5.8	3.8	5.1	3.2
1985	5 730	3 537	2 192	38.3	5.4	5.9	4.7	5.7	3.2
1989	7 225	4 115	3 109	43.0	6.2	6.4	5.9	6.5	4.3
1991	7 183	4 054	3 129	43.6	6.2	6.4	5.9	6.4	4.9

1. Multiple jobholders as a percent of all employed persons in specified group.
2. Data for years prior to 1977 refer to the black-and-other population group.
NOTE: Data prior to 1985 reflect 1970 census-based population controls; for 1985-91, 1980 census-based controls. Comprehensive surveys of multiple jobholders were not conducted in 1981-1984, 1986-1988, and 1990.

Multiple Jobholders by Sex, Age, Marital Status, Race, Hispanic Origin, and Job Status, 1994-1995

(Numbers in thousands)

Characteristic	Both sexes				Men				Women			
	Number		Rate[1]		Number		Rate[1]		Number		Rate[1]	
	1994	1995	1994	1995	1994	1995	1994	1995	1994	1995	1994	1995
AGE												
Total, 16 years and over	7 260	7 693	5.9	6.2	3 924	4 139	5.9	6.1	3 336	3 554	5.9	6.2
16 to 19 years	307	350	5.0	5.4	129	153	4.1	4.7	178	196	5.9	6.3
20 to 24 years	880	829	6.9	6.7	428	404	6.3	6.1	452	424	7.6	7.3
25 to 34 years	2 016	2 085	6.2	6.4	1 136	1 189	6.4	6.7	880	896	6.1	6.1
35 to 44 years	2 042	2 201	6.1	6.4	1 110	1 194	6.1	6.5	932	1 007	6.0	6.4
45 to 54 years	1 421	1 587	6.1	6.5	771	834	6.2	6.4	650	753	6.0	6.6
55 to 64 years	509	537	4.5	4.7	295	298	4.8	4.8	215	238	4.2	4.6
65 years and over	85	104	2.3	2.8	57	66	2.7	3.1	29	38	1.8	2.5
MARITAL STATUS												
Single	2 005	2 061	6.4	6.5	1 001	1 044	5.7	5.9	1 003	1 016	7.2	7.2
Married, spouse present	4 096	4 398	5.6	5.9	2 516	2 683	6.1	6.4	1 580	1 715	5.0	5.3
Widowed, divorced, or separated	1 159	1 235	6.2	6.5	407	412	5.5	5.5	752	823	6.7	7.2
RACE AND HISPANIC ORIGIN												
White	6 392	6 764	6.1	6.4	3 462	3 650	6.0	6.3	2 930	3 114	6.1	6.4
Black	630	688	4.9	5.2	337	362	5.4	5.6	293	326	4.4	4.8
Hispanic origin	394	430	3.7	3.9	243	252	3.7	3.8	151	178	3.6	4.0
FULL- OR PART-TIME STATUS												
Primary job full-time, secondary job part-time	4 182	4 446			2 509	2 664			1 673	1 781		
Primary and secondary jobs, both part-time	1 602	1 693			513	533			1 089	1 160		
Primary and secondary jobs, both full-time	242	257			179	185			63	72		
Hours vary on primary or secondary job	1 193	1 262			705	740			488	521		

1. Multiple jobholders as a percent of all employed persons in specified group.
NOTE: Detail for race and Hispanic-origin groups will not add to totals because data for other races are not presented and Hispanics are included in both the white and black population groups.

POPULATION, LABOR FORCE, AND EMPLOYMENT STATUS

Major Unemployment Indicators, 1948-1995

(Unemployment as percent of civilian labor force)

Year	All civilian workers	Men, 20 years and over	Women, 20 years and over	Both sexes, 16 to 19 years	Both sexes, 25 years and over	White	Black and other	Black	Hispanic	Full-time workers	Part-time workers	Women who maintain families	Married men, spouse present
1948	3.8	3.2	3.6	9.2	2.9								
1949	5.9	5.4	5.3	13.4	4.8								
1950	5.3	4.7	5.1	12.2	4.4								
1951	3.3	2.5	4.0	8.2	2.8								
1952	3.0	2.4	3.2	8.5	2.4								
1953	2.9	2.5	2.9	7.6	2.4								
1954	5.5	4.9	5.5	12.6	4.7	5.0	9.9						
1955	4.4	3.8	4.4	11.0	3.6	3.9	8.7						2.6
1956	4.1	3.4	4.2	11.1	3.3	3.6	8.3						2.3
1957	4.3	3.6	4.1	11.6	3.4	3.8	7.9						2.8
1958	6.8	6.2	6.1	15.9	5.6	6.1	12.6						5.1
1959	5.5	4.7	5.2	14.6	4.4	4.8	10.7						3.6
1960	5.5	4.7	5.1	14.7	4.4	5.0	10.2						3.7
1961	6.7	5.7	6.3	16.8	5.4	6.0	12.4						4.6
1962	5.5	4.6	5.4	14.7	4.4	4.9	10.9						3.6
1963	5.7	4.5	5.4	17.2	4.3	5.0	10.8			5.5	7.3		3.4
1964	5.2	3.9	5.2	16.2	3.8	4.6	9.6			4.9	7.2		2.8
1965	4.5	3.2	4.5	14.8	3.2	4.1	8.1			4.2	6.7		2.4
1966	3.8	2.5	3.8	12.8	2.6	3.4	7.3			3.5	6.2		1.9
1967	3.8	2.3	4.2	12.9	2.6	3.4	7.4			3.4	6.9	4.9	1.8
1968	3.6	2.2	3.8	12.7	2.3	3.2	6.7			3.2	6.0	4.4	1.6
1969	3.5	2.1	3.7	12.2	2.2	3.1	6.4			3.1	5.7	4.4	1.5
1970	4.9	3.5	4.8	15.3	3.3	4.5	8.2			4.6	6.9	5.4	2.6
1971	5.9	4.4	5.7	16.9	4.0	5.4	9.9			5.6	7.8	7.3	3.2
1972	5.6	4.0	5.4	16.2	3.6	5.1	10.0	10.4		5.2	7.7	7.2	2.8
1973	4.9	3.3	4.9	14.5	3.1	4.3	9.0	9.4	7.5	4.4	7.2	7.1	2.3
1974	5.6	3.8	5.5	16.0	3.6	5.0	9.9	10.5	8.1	5.2	7.7	7.0	2.7
1975	8.5	6.8	8.0	19.9	6.0	7.8	13.8	14.8	12.2	8.4	9.0	10.0	5.1
1976	7.7	5.9	7.4	19.0	5.5	7.0	13.1	14.0	11.5	7.5	8.8	10.1	4.2
1977	7.1	5.2	7.0	17.8	4.9	6.2	13.1	14.0	10.1	6.8	8.6	9.4	3.6
1978	6.1	4.3	6.0	16.4	4.1	5.2	11.9	12.8	9.1	5.7	7.9	8.5	2.8
1979	5.8	4.2	5.7	16.1	3.9	5.1	11.3	12.3	8.3	5.5	7.7	8.3	2.8
1980	7.1	5.9	6.4	17.8	5.1	6.3	13.1	14.3	10.1	7.1	7.6	9.2	4.2
1981	7.6	6.3	6.8	19.6	5.4	6.7	14.2	15.6	10.4	7.5	7.9	10.4	4.3
1982	9.7	8.8	8.3	23.2	7.4	8.6	17.3	18.9	13.8	10.0	8.5	11.7	6.5
1983	9.6	8.9	8.1	22.4	7.5	8.4	17.8	19.5	13.7	9.9	8.1	12.2	6.5
1984	7.5	6.6	6.8	18.9	5.8	6.5	14.4	15.9	10.7	7.5	7.4	10.3	4.6
1985	7.2	6.2	6.6	18.6	5.6	6.2	13.7	15.1	10.5	7.1	7.5	10.4	4.3
1986	7.0	6.1	6.2	18.3	5.4	6.0	13.1	14.5	10.6	6.9	7.4	9.8	4.4
1987	6.2	5.4	5.4	16.9	4.8	5.3	11.6	13.0	8.8	6.0	6.9	9.2	3.9
1988	5.5	4.8	4.9	15.3	4.3	4.7	10.4	11.7	8.2	5.3	6.4	8.1	3.3
1989	5.3	4.5	4.7	15.0	4.0	4.5	10.0	11.4	8.0	5.1	6.2	8.1	3.0
1990	5.6	5.0	4.9	15.5	4.4	4.8	10.1	11.4	8.2	5.4	6.4	8.3	3.4
1991	6.8	6.4	5.7	18.7	5.4	6.1	11.1	12.5	10.0	6.8	7.0	9.3	4.4
1992	7.5	7.1	6.3	20.1	6.1	6.6	12.7	14.2	11.6	7.5	7.5	10.0	5.1
1993	6.9	6.4	5.9	19.0	5.6	6.1	11.7	13.0	10.8	6.9	7.2	9.7	4.4
1994	6.1	5.4	5.4	17.6	4.8	5.3	10.5	11.5	9.9	6.1	6.0	8.9	3.7
1995	5.6	4.8	4.9	17.3	4.3	4.9	9.6	10.4	9.3	5.5	6.0	8.0	3.3

NOTE: Data beginning in 1994 are not strictly comparable with data for 1993 and earlier years because of the introduction of a major redesign of the survey and collection methodology. Beginning in 1990, data are not strictly comparable with previous years because of the introduction of 1990 census-based population controls adjusted for the estimated undercount.

Unemployed Persons by Sex, Race, Hispanic Origin, and Age, 1948-1995

(Thousands of persons)

Year, sex, race, and Hispanic origin	16 years and over	16 to 19 years			20 years and over						
		Total	16 to 17 years	18 to 19 years	Total	20 to 24 years	25 to 34 years	35 to 44 years	45 to 54 years	55 to 64 years	65 years and over
TOTAL											
1948	2 276	409	180	228	1 869	455	457	347	290	226	93
1949	3 637	576	238	337	3 060	680	776	603	471	384	146
1950	3 288	513	226	287	2 776	561	702	530	478	368	137
1951	2 055	336	168	168	1 718	273	435	354	318	238	103
1952	1 883	345	180	165	1 539	268	389	325	274	195	86
1953	1 834	307	150	157	1 529	256	379	325	280	218	70
1954	3 532	501	221	247	3 032	504	793	680	548	374	132
1955	2 852	450	211	239	2 403	396	577	521	436	355	120
1956	2 750	478	231	247	2 274	395	554	476	429	311	109
1957	2 859	497	230	266	2 362	430	573	499	448	300	111
1958	4 602	678	299	379	3 923	701	993	871	731	472	154
1959	3 740	654	301	354	3 085	543	726	673	603	405	135
1960	3 852	712	325	387	3 140	583	752	671	614	396	122
1961	4 714	828	363	465	3 886	723	890	850	751	516	159
1962	3 911	721	312	409	3 191	636	712	688	605	411	141
1963	4 070	884	420	462	3 187	658	732	674	589	410	126
1964	3 786	872	436	437	2 913	660	607	605	543	378	117
1965	3 366	874	411	463	2 491	557	529	546	436	322	103
1966	2 875	837	395	441	2 041	446	441	426	369	265	92
1967	2 975	839	400	438	2 140	511	480	422	383	256	86
1968	2 817	838	414	426	1 978	543	443	371	314	219	88
1969	2 832	853	436	416	1 978	560	453	358	320	216	72
1970	4 093	1 106	537	569	2 987	866	718	515	476	309	104
1971	5 016	1 262	596	665	3 755	1 130	933	630	573	381	109
1972	4 882	1 308	633	676	3 573	1 132	878	576	510	368	111
1973	4 365	1 235	634	600	3 130	1 008	866	451	430	290	88
1974	5 156	1 422	699	722	3 733	1 212	1 044	559	498	321	99
1975	7 929	1 767	799	968	6 161	1 865	1 776	951	893	520	155
1976	7 406	1 719	796	924	5 687	1 714	1 710	849	758	510	147
1977	6 991	1 663	781	881	5 330	1 629	1 650	785	666	450	147
1978	6 202	1 583	796	787	4 620	1 483	1 422	694	552	345	123
1979	6 137	1 555	739	816	4 583	1 442	1 446	705	540	346	104
1980	7 637	1 669	778	890	5 969	1 835	2 024	940	676	399	94
1981	8 273	1 763	781	981	6 510	1 976	2 211	1 065	715	444	98
1982	10 678	1 977	831	1 145	8 701	2 392	3 037	1 552	966	647	107
1983	10 717	1 829	753	1 076	8 888	2 330	3 078	1 650	1 039	677	114
1984	8 539	1 499	646	854	7 039	1 838	2 374	1 335	828	566	97
1985	8 312	1 468	662	806	6 844	1 738	2 341	1 340	813	518	93
1986	8 237	1 454	665	789	6 783	1 651	2 390	1 371	790	489	91
1987	7 425	1 347	648	700	6 077	1 453	2 129	1 281	723	412	78
1988	6 701	1 226	573	653	5 475	1 261	1 929	1 166	657	375	87
1989	6 528	1 194	537	657	5 333	1 218	1 851	1 159	637	379	91
1990	7 047	1 212	527	685	5 835	1 299	1 995	1 328	723	386	105
1991	8 628	1 359	587	772	7 269	1 573	2 447	1 719	946	473	113
1992	9 613	1 427	641	787	8 186	1 649	2 702	1 976	1 138	589	132
1993	8 940	1 365	606	759	7 575	1 514	2 395	1 896	1 121	541	108
1994	7 996	1 320	624	696	6 676	1 373	2 067	1 627	971	485	153
1995	7 404	1 346	652	695	6 058	1 244	1 841	1 549	844	425	153

POPULATION, LABOR FORCE, AND EMPLOYMENT STATUS

Unemployed Persons by Sex, Race, Hispanic Origin, and Age, 1948-1995—Continued

(Thousands of persons)

Year, sex, race, and Hispanic origin	16 years and over	16 to 19 years			20 years and over						
		Total	16 to 17 years	18 to 19 years	Total	20 to 24 years	25 to 34 years	35 to 44 years	45 to 54 years	55 to 64 years	65 years and over
MEN											
1948	1 559	256	113	142	1 305	324	289	233	201	177	81
1949	2 572	353	145	207	2 219	485	539	414	347	310	125
1950	2 239	318	139	179	1 922	377	467	348	327	286	117
1951	1 221	191	102	89	1 029	155	241	192	193	162	87
1952	1 185	205	116	89	980	155	233	192	182	145	73
1953	1 202	184	94	90	1 019	152	236	208	196	167	60
1954	2 344	310	142	168	2 035	327	517	431	372	275	112
1955	1 854	274	134	140	1 580	248	353	328	285	265	102
1956	1 711	269	134	135	1 442	240	348	278	270	216	90
1957	1 841	300	140	159	1 541	283	349	304	302	220	83
1958	3 098	416	185	231	2 681	478	685	552	492	349	124
1959	2 420	398	191	207	2 022	343	484	407	390	287	112
1960	2 486	426	200	225	2 060	369	492	415	392	294	96
1961	2 997	479	221	258	2 518	458	585	507	473	375	122
1962	2 423	408	188	220	2 016	381	445	404	382	300	103
1963	2 472	501	248	252	1 971	396	445	386	358	290	97
1964	2 205	487	257	230	1 718	384	345	324	319	263	85
1965	1 914	479	247	232	1 435	311	292	283	253	221	75
1966	1 551	432	220	212	1 120	221	239	219	196	179	65
1967	1 508	448	241	207	1 060	235	219	185	199	163	60
1968	1 419	426	234	193	993	258	205	171	165	132	61
1969	1 403	440	244	196	963	270	205	155	157	127	48
1970	2 238	599	306	294	1 638	479	391	253	247	198	71
1971	2 789	693	346	347	2 097	640	513	320	313	239	71
1972	2 659	711	357	355	1 948	628	466	284	272	227	73
1973	2 275	653	352	300	1 624	528	439	211	219	171	57
1974	2 714	757	394	362	1 957	649	546	266	250	183	63
1975	4 442	966	445	521	3 476	1 081	986	507	499	302	103
1976	4 036	939	443	496	3 098	951	914	431	411	296	94
1977	3 667	874	421	453	2 794	877	869	373	326	252	97
1978	3 142	813	426	388	2 328	768	691	314	277	198	81
1979	3 120	811	393	418	2 308	744	699	329	272	196	67
1980	4 267	913	429	485	3 353	1 076	1 137	482	357	243	58
1981	4 577	962	431	531	3 615	1 144	1 213	552	390	261	55
1982	6 179	1 090	469	621	5 089	1 407	1 791	879	550	393	69
1983	6 260	1 003	408	595	5 257	1 369	1 822	947	613	433	73
1984	4 744	812	348	464	3 932	1 023	1 322	728	450	356	53
1985	4 521	806	363	443	3 715	944	1 244	706	459	307	55
1986	4 530	779	355	424	3 751	899	1 291	763	440	301	58
1987	4 101	732	353	379	3 369	779	1 169	689	426	258	49
1988	3 655	667	311	356	2 987	676	1 040	617	366	240	49
1989	3 525	658	303	355	2 867	660	953	619	351	234	49
1990	3 906	667	283	384	3 239	715	1 092	711	413	249	59
1991	4 946	751	317	433	4 195	911	1 375	990	550	305	64
1992	5 523	806	357	449	4 717	951	1 529	1 118	675	378	67
1993	5 055	768	342	426	4 287	865	1 338	1 049	636	336	64
1994	4 367	740	342	398	3 627	768	1 113	855	522	281	88
1995	3 983	744	352	391	3 239	673	961	815	464	233	94

Unemployed Persons by Sex, Race, Hispanic Origin, and Age, 1948-1995—Continued

(Thousands of persons)

Year, sex, race, and Hispanic origin	16 years and over	16 to 19 years			20 years and over						
		Total	16 to 17 years	18 to 19 years	Total	20 to 24 years	25 to 34 years	35 to 44 years	45 to 54 years	55 to 64 years	65 years and over
WOMEN											
1948	717	153	67	86	564	131	168	114	89	49	12
1949	1 065	223	93	130	841	195	237	189	124	74	21
1950	1 049	195	87	108	854	184	235	182	151	82	20
1951	834	145	66	79	689	118	194	162	125	76	16
1952	698	140	64	76	559	113	156	133	92	50	13
1953	632	123	56	67	510	104	143	117	84	51	10
1954	1 188	191	79	79	997	177	276	249	176	99	20
1955	998	176	77	99	823	148	224	193	151	90	18
1956	1 039	209	97	112	832	155	206	198	159	95	19
1957	1 018	197	90	107	821	147	224	195	146	80	28
1958	1 504	262	114	148	1 242	223	308	319	239	123	30
1959	1 320	256	110	147	1 063	200	242	266	213	118	23
1960	1 366	286	125	162	1 080	214	260	256	222	102	26
1961	1 717	349	142	207	1 368	265	305	343	278	141	37
1962	1 488	313	124	189	1 175	255	267	284	223	111	38
1963	1 598	383	172	210	1 216	262	287	288	231	120	29
1964	1 581	385	179	207	1 195	276	262	281	224	115	32
1965	1 452	395	164	231	1 056	246	237	263	183	101	28
1966	1 324	405	175	229	921	225	202	207	173	86	27
1967	1 468	391	159	231	1 078	277	261	237	184	93	26
1968	1 397	412	180	233	985	285	238	200	149	87	27
1969	1 429	413	192	220	1 015	290	248	203	163	89	24
1970	1 855	506	231	275	1 349	387	327	262	229	111	33
1971	2 227	568	250	318	1 658	489	420	310	260	142	38
1972	2 222	598	276	322	1 625	503	413	293	237	141	38
1973	2 089	583	282	301	1 507	480	427	240	212	119	31
1974	2 441	665	305	360	1 777	564	497	294	248	137	36
1975	3 486	802	355	447	2 684	783	791	444	395	219	52
1976	3 369	780	352	429	2 588	763	795	417	346	214	53
1977	3 324	789	361	428	2 535	752	782	412	340	198	50
1978	3 061	769	370	399	2 292	714	731	381	275	148	43
1979	3 018	743	346	396	2 276	697	748	375	268	150	38
1980	3 370	755	349	407	2 615	760	886	459	318	155	36
1981	3 696	800	350	450	2 895	833	998	513	325	184	43
1982	4 499	886	362	524	3 613	985	1 246	673	416	254	38
1983	4 457	825	344	481	3 632	961	1 255	703	427	244	41
1984	3 794	687	298	390	3 107	815	1 052	607	378	211	45
1985	3 791	661	298	363	3 129	794	1 098	634	355	211	39
1986	3 707	675	310	365	3 032	752	1 099	609	350	189	33
1987	3 324	616	295	321	2 709	674	960	592	298	155	30
1988	3 046	558	262	297	2 487	585	889	550	291	136	38
1989	3 003	536	234	302	2 467	558	897	540	286	144	41
1990	3 140	544	243	301	2 596	584	902	617	310	137	46
1991	3 683	608	270	338	3 074	662	1 071	728	396	168	49
1992	4 090	621	283	338	3 469	698	1 173	858	463	210	66
1993	3 885	597	264	333	3 288	648	1 058	847	485	205	45
1994	3 629	580	282	298	3 049	605	954	772	449	204	66
1995	3 421	602	299	303	2 819	571	880	735	381	193	60

Unemployed Persons by Sex, Race, Hispanic Origin, and Age, 1948-1995—Continued

(Thousands of persons)

Year, sex, race, and Hispanic origin	16 years and over	16 to 19 years			20 years and over						
		Total	16 to 17 years	18 to 19 years	Total	20 to 24 years	25 to 34 years	35 to 44 years	45 to 54 years	55 to 64 years	65 years and over
WHITE											
1954	2 859	423	191	232	2 436	394	610	540	447	329	115
1955	2 252	373	181	191	1 879	304	412	402	358	300	105
1956	2 159	382	191	191	1 777	297	406	363	355	258	98
1957	2 289	401	195	204	1 888	331	425	401	373	262	98
1958	3 680	541	245	297	3 139	541	756	686	614	405	136
1959	2 946	525	255	270	2 421	406	526	525	496	348	120
1960	3 065	575	273	302	2 490	456	573	520	502	330	109
1961	3 743	669	295	374	3 074	566	668	652	611	438	139
1962	3 052	580	262	318	2 472	488	515	522	485	345	117
1963	3 208	708	350	358	2 500	501	540	518	485	349	107
1964	2 999	708	365	342	2 291	508	441	472	447	323	100
1965	2 691	705	329	374	1 986	437	399	427	358	276	91
1966	2 255	651	315	336	1 604	338	323	336	298	227	80
1967	2 338	635	311	325	1 703	393	360	336	321	221	75
1968	2 226	644	326	318	1 582	422	330	297	269	187	80
1969	2 260	660	351	309	1 601	432	354	294	269	185	66
1970	3 339	871	438	432	2 468	679	570	433	415	275	95
1971	4 085	1 011	491	521	3 074	887	732	517	500	338	100
1972	3 906	1 021	515	506	2 885	887	679	459	439	324	95
1973	3 442	955	513	443	2 486	758	664	358	371	257	77
1974	4 097	1 104	561	544	2 993	925	821	448	427	283	88
1975	6 421	1 413	657	755	5 007	1 474	1 413	774	753	460	136
1976	5 914	1 364	649	715	4 550	1 326	1 329	682	637	448	128
1977	5 441	1 284	636	648	4 157	1 195	1 255	621	569	388	129
1978	4 698	1 189	631	558	3 509	1 059	1 059	543	453	290	104
1979	4 664	1 193	589	603	3 472	1 038	1 068	545	443	290	87
1980	5 884	1 291	625	666	4 593	1 364	1 528	740	550	335	74
1981	6 343	1 374	629	745	4 968	1 449	1 658	827	578	379	77
1982	8 241	1 534	683	851	6 707	1 770	2 283	1 223	796	549	86
1983	8 128	1 387	609	778	6 741	1 678	2 282	1 294	837	563	88
1984	6 372	1 116	510	605	5 256	1 282	1 723	1 036	660	475	81
1985	6 191	1 074	507	567	5 117	1 235	1 695	1 039	642	432	75
1986	6 140	1 070	509	561	5 070	1 149	1 751	1 056	629	407	78
1987	5 501	995	495	500	4 506	1 017	1 527	984	576	333	68
1988	4 944	910	437	473	4 033	874	1 371	890	520	309	69
1989	4 770	863	407	456	3 908	856	1 297	871	503	311	70
1990	5 186	903	401	502	4 283	899	1 401	983	582	330	88
1991	6 560	1 029	461	568	5 532	1 132	1 805	1 330	759	410	96
1992	7 169	1 037	484	553	6 132	1 156	1 967	1 483	915	495	116
1993	6 655	992	468	523	5 663	1 057	1 754	1 411	907	442	92
1994	5 892	960	471	489	4 933	952	1 479	1 184	779	407	132
1995	5 459	952	476	476	4 507	866	1 311	1 161	676	362	131

Unemployed Persons by Sex, Race, Hispanic Origin, and Age, 1948-1995—Continued

(Thousands of persons)

Year, sex, race, and Hispanic origin	16 years and over	16 to 19 years			20 years and over						
		Total	16 to 17 years	18 to 19 years	Total	20 to 24 years	25 to 34 years	35 to 44 years	45 to 54 years	55 to 64 years	65 years and over
WHITE MEN											
1954	1 913	266	125	142	1 647	260	408	341	299	241	98
1955	1 478	232	114	117	1 246	196	260	246	233	223	89
1956	1 366	221	112	108	1 145	186	265	212	225	177	81
1957	1 477	243	118	124	1 234	222	257	239	250	193	73
1958	2 489	333	149	184	2 156	382	525	436	404	299	110
1959	1 903	318	162	156	1 585	256	350	316	320	245	98
1960	1 988	341	167	174	1 647	295	376	330	317	243	86
1961	2 398	384	176	208	2 014	370	442	395	382	318	107
1962	1 915	334	158	176	1 581	300	332	311	308	246	84
1963	1 976	407	211	196	1 569	309	342	297	294	246	80
1964	1 779	400	217	183	1 379	310	262	255	266	216	70
1965	1 556	387	200	186	1 169	254	226	228	206	190	67
1966	1 241	340	178	162	901	172	185	173	160	154	57
1967	1 208	342	186	156	866	185	171	153	167	140	52
1968	1 142	328	185	143	814	206	162	140	142	111	55
1969	1 137	343	198	145	794	214	165	130	134	108	43
1970	1 857	485	255	230	1 372	388	316	212	216	177	64
1971	2 309	562	288	275	1 747	513	418	268	272	211	66
1972	2 173	564	288	276	1 610	506	375	231	237	199	60
1973	1 836	513	284	229	1 323	411	353	166	188	153	51
1974	2 169	584	311	274	1 585	505	434	218	213	161	53
1975	3 627	785	369	416	2 841	871	796	412	411	265	86
1976	3 258	754	368	385	2 504	750	730	346	341	259	78
1977	2 883	672	342	330	2 211	660	682	297	276	213	82
1978	2 411	615	338	277	1 797	558	525	250	227	169	68
1979	2 405	633	319	313	1 773	553	526	253	220	165	56
1980	3 345	716	347	369	2 629	827	884	378	291	206	44
1981	3 580	755	349	406	2 825	869	943	433	317	221	42
1982	4 846	854	387	467	3 991	1 066	1 385	696	460	331	53
1983	4 859	761	328	433	4 098	1 019	1 410	755	497	362	54
1984	3 600	608	280	328	2 992	722	991	572	363	302	42
1985	3 426	592	282	310	2 834	694	931	553	356	257	43
1986	3 433	576	276	299	2 857	645	978	586	349	248	51
1987	3 132	548	272	276	2 584	568	879	536	350	209	43
1988	2 766	499	239	260	2 268	480	777	477	293	200	40
1989	2 636	487	230	257	2 149	476	694	470	280	191	38
1990	2 935	504	214	290	2 431	510	796	530	330	214	51
1991	3 859	575	249	327	3 284	677	1 064	780	438	269	55
1992	4 209	590	270	319	3 620	686	1 155	858	543	318	58
1993	3 828	565	261	305	3 263	619	1 015	793	512	270	53
1994	3 275	540	259	280	2 735	555	827	626	417	236	74
1995	2 999	535	260	275	2 465	483	711	621	371	200	79
WHITE WOMEN											
1954	946	157	66	90	789	134	202	199	148	88	17
1955	774	141	67	74	633	108	152	156	125	77	16
1956	793	161	79	83	632	111	141	151	130	81	17
1957	812	158	77	80	654	109	168	162	123	69	25
1958	1 191	208	96	113	983	159	231	250	210	106	26
1959	1 043	207	93	114	836	150	176	209	176	103	22
1960	1 077	234	106	128	843	161	197	190	185	87	23
1961	1 345	285	119	166	1 060	196	226	257	229	120	32
1962	1 137	246	104	142	891	188	183	211	177	99	33
1963	1 232	301	139	162	931	192	198	221	191	103	27
1964	1 220	308	148	159	912	198	179	217	181	107	30
1965	1 135	318	129	188	817	183	173	199	152	86	24
1966	1 014	311	137	174	703	166	138	163	138	73	23
1967	1 130	293	125	169	837	209	189	183	154	81	23
1968	1 084	316	141	175	768	216	168	157	127	76	25
1969	1 123	317	153	164	806	218	189	164	135	77	23
1970	1 482	386	183	202	1 096	291	254	221	199	98	31
1971	1 777	449	203	246	1 328	376	314	249	228	126	34
1972	1 733	457	227	230	1 275	381	304	227	202	125	35
1973	1 606	442	228	214	1 164	347	311	192	183	104	26
1974	1 927	519	250	270	1 408	420	387	230	214	122	35
1975	2 794	628	288	340	2 166	602	617	362	342	195	49
1976	2 656	611	280	330	2 045	577	598	336	296	188	49
1977	2 558	612	294	318	1 946	536	573	323	293	175	47
1978	2 287	574	292	281	1 713	500	533	294	226	122	37
1979	2 260	560	270	290	1 699	485	542	293	223	125	32
1980	2 540	576	278	298	1 964	537	645	362	259	129	31
1981	2 762	620	281	339	2 143	580	715	394	261	158	36
1982	3 395	680	296	384	2 715	704	898	527	337	217	33
1983	3 270	626	282	345	2 643	659	872	539	340	201	33
1984	2 772	508	231	277	2 264	559	731	464	297	173	39
1985	2 765	482	225	257	2 283	541	763	486	286	175	32
1986	2 708	495	233	262	2 213	504	773	470	281	159	27
1987	2 369	447	223	224	1 922	449	648	448	227	124	25
1988	2 177	412	198	214	1 766	393	594	413	227	110	30
1989	2 135	376	177	199	1 758	380	603	401	223	120	32
1990	2 251	399	187	212	1 852	389	605	453	251	116	37
1991	2 701	453	212	241	2 248	455	741	550	320	141	41
1992	2 959	447	214	233	2 512	469	811	625	372	177	58
1993	2 827	426	208	219	2 400	438	739	618	395	172	39
1994	2 617	420	211	208	2 197	397	652	558	361	170	58
1995	2 460	418	216	201	2 042	384	600	540	306	162	52

Unemployed Persons by Sex, Race, Hispanic Origin, and Age, 1948-1995—Continued

(Thousands of persons)

Year, sex, race, and Hispanic origin	16 years and over	16 to 19 years			20 years and over						
		Total	16 to 17 years	18 to 19 years	Total	20 to 24 years	25 to 34 years	35 to 44 years	45 to 54 years	55 to 64 years	65 years and over
BLACK											
1972	906	279	113	167	627	226	183	106	62	37	12
1973	846	262	114	148	584	231	181	82	53	29	9
1974	965	297	127	170	666	261	201	95	65	33	10
1975	1 369	330	130	200	1 040	362	321	157	126	54	17
1976	1 334	330	134	195	1 005	350	338	145	101	54	16
1977	1 393	354	135	218	1 040	397	355	140	81	51	16
1978	1 330	360	150	210	972	379	320	127	82	47	17
1979	1 319	333	137	197	986	369	335	137	82	48	15
1980	1 553	343	134	210	1 209	426	433	171	109	53	18
1981	1 731	357	138	219	1 374	483	493	207	119	55	17
1982	2 142	396	130	266	1 747	565	662	278	141	84	17
1983	2 272	392	125	267	1 879	591	700	299	174	95	21
1984	1 914	353	122	230	1 561	504	577	253	138	75	15
1985	1 864	357	135	221	1 507	455	562	254	143	74	18
1986	1 840	347	138	209	1 493	453	564	269	127	69	10
1987	1 684	312	134	178	1 373	397	533	247	124	62	10
1988	1 547	288	121	167	1 259	349	502	230	111	51	15
1989	1 544	300	116	184	1 245	322	494	246	109	53	20
1990	1 565	268	112	156	1 297	349	505	278	106	44	14
1991	1 723	280	105	175	1 443	378	539	318	151	44	13
1992	2 011	324	127	197	1 687	421	610	402	178	64	13
1993	1 844	313	112	201	1 530	387	532	376	153	72	11
1994	1 666	300	127	173	1 366	351	468	346	130	55	16
1995	1 538	325	143	182	1 213	311	423	303	116	42	18
BLACK MEN											
1972	448	143	66	77	305	113	84	45	31	23	9
1973	395	128	62	66	267	108	75	37	27	16	5
1974	494	159	75	82	336	129	103	41	35	19	8
1975	741	170	71	100	571	195	169	83	78	33	13
1976	698	170	69	103	528	185	166	73	60	32	13
1977	698	187	73	114	512	197	170	63	40	31	12
1978	641	180	80	101	462	185	148	53	40	24	11
1979	636	164	68	97	473	174	152	66	44	27	10
1980	815	179	72	108	636	222	222	88	60	32	12
1981	891	188	73	115	703	248	245	102	65	32	10
1982	1 167	213	72	141	954	304	355	154	74	54	12
1983	1 213	211	70	142	1 002	313	358	162	96	59	14
1984	1 003	188	62	126	815	272	289	132	67	45	9
1985	951	193	69	124	757	224	268	127	85	43	11
1986	946	180	68	112	765	225	273	148	70	44	5
1987	826	160	70	90	666	186	253	122	61	39	6
1988	771	154	64	90	617	177	233	111	58	30	8
1989	773	153	65	88	619	162	226	129	59	33	10
1990	806	142	62	80	664	177	247	146	62	27	6
1991	890	145	54	91	745	201	252	172	87	25	7
1992	1 067	180	71	109	886	221	301	208	107	42	6
1993	971	170	66	104	801	201	260	201	87	46	7
1994	848	167	69	97	682	173	218	180	72	29	10
1995	762	168	73	95	593	153	195	150	63	21	11
BLACK WOMEN											
1972	458	136	47	90	322	113	99	61	31	14	3
1973	451	134	51	82	317	123	105	45	26	13	4
1974	470	139	51	87	331	132	98	55	30	14	2
1975	629	160	60	100	469	167	153	75	48	22	4
1976	637	160	66	93	477	165	172	73	41	23	3
1977	695	167	63	104	528	200	185	77	41	21	4
1978	690	179	70	110	510	194	173	74	41	23	6
1979	683	169	69	100	513	195	183	71	38	21	5
1980	738	164	62	102	574	204	211	83	49	21	6
1981	840	169	65	104	671	235	248	105	54	23	7
1982	975	182	58	124	793	261	307	123	67	29	5
1983	1 059	181	56	125	878	278	342	137	77	36	7
1984	911	165	60	104	747	231	288	121	71	30	5
1985	913	164	66	98	750	231	295	127	58	31	7
1986	894	167	70	97	728	228	291	121	57	25	5
1987	858	152	64	88	706	211	280	125	63	23	4
1988	776	134	57	78	642	172	269	118	53	22	7
1989	772	147	51	96	625	160	267	118	50	21	9
1990	758	126	49	76	633	172	258	132	44	17	8
1991	833	135	51	84	698	177	288	145	64	19	6
1992	944	144	56	88	800	200	308	194	71	22	6
1993	872	143	46	97	729	186	272	175	66	26	5
1994	818	133	57	76	685	178	249	166	59	26	6
1995	777	157	....	87	620	158	228	153	53	20	....

Unemployed Persons by Sex, Race, Hispanic Origin, and Age, 1948-1995—Continued

(Thousands of persons)

Year, sex, race, and Hispanic origin	16 years and over	16 to 19 years			20 years and over						
		Total	16 to 17 years	18 to 19 years	Total	20 to 24 years	25 to 34 years	35 to 44 years	45 to 54 years	55 to 64 years	65 years and over
HISPANIC											
1976	485	106	51	55	385	116	113	72	53	26	6
1977	456	113	50	60	344	98	114	56	48	24	5
1978	452	110	63	47	342	98	116	65	41	16	5
1979	434	106	54	51	329	100	102	65	37	20	4
1980	620	145	66	79	474	138	168	90	49	24	5
1981	678	144	60	84	533	171	178	92	57	31	5
1982	929	175	73	102	754	221	267	140	75	45	5
1983	961	167	64	104	793	214	270	156	93	54	5
1984	800	149	60	88	651	164	235	124	71	51	5
1985	811	141	55	85	670	171	256	123	73	41	7
1986	857	141	57	84	716	183	258	143	85	38	9
1987	751	136	57	79	615	152	222	128	75	33	5
1988	732	148	63	84	585	145	209	120	69	36	6
1989	750	132	59	73	618	158	218	124	76	36	6
1990	876	161	68	94	714	167	263	156	85	36	7
1991	1 092	179	79	99	913	214	332	206	110	44	8
1992	1 311	219	94	124	1 093	240	390	267	126	59	10
1993	1 248	201	86	115	1 047	237	354	261	132	54	10
1994	1 187	198	90	108	989	220	348	227	132	51	12
1995	1 140	205	96	109	934	209	325	224	106	54	16
HISPANIC MEN											
1976	278	60	30	31	217	69	63	38	29	16	4
1977	253	60	27	33	195	57	65	28	22	15	4
1978	234	59	35	24	175	51	59	30	20	10	4
1979	223	55	29	27	168	52	50	33	19	11	3
1980	370	86	39	47	284	85	96	51	31	16	5
1981	408	87	40	47	321	105	113	49	31	19	4
1982	565	104	45	59	461	138	169	80	40	29	4
1983	591	100	38	62	491	134	168	92	57	36	4
1984	480	87	36	51	393	103	142	69	41	33	4
1985	483	82	34	49	401	108	156	69	40	23	5
1986	520	82	33	50	438	115	159	86	46	26	5
1987	451	77	32	45	374	88	137	77	46	22	4
1988	437	86	36	50	351	83	128	70	42	24	5
1989	423	81	36	45	342	88	113	69	43	25	4
1990	524	100	40	60	425	99	154	91	53	25	4
1991	685	110	47	62	575	139	210	126	62	33	5
1992	807	132	56	75	675	156	239	156	75	42	6
1993	747	118	50	68	629	144	217	148	79	33	8
1994	680	121	54	67	558	128	203	113	75	30	....
1995	651	121	59	63	530	123	185	120	57	33	....
HISPANIC WOMEN											
1976	207	45	22	24	166	47	52	33	22	10	2
1977	204	50	23	27	153	40	49	28	25	11	1
1978	219	51	28	23	168	46	58	36	20	8	1
1979	211	50	26	24	160	48	52	32	18	10	1
1980	249	59	28	31	190	53	72	39	18	8	0
1981	269	57	20	37	212	65	65	43	25	13	1
1982	364	71	28	43	293	83	98	60	35	16	1
1983	369	68	26	42	302	80	102	65	36	18	1
1984	320	62	25	37	258	61	93	55	30	17	1
1985	327	58	22	37	269	63	100	54	32	18	2
1986	337	59	25	35	278	68	99	57	39	12	3
1987	300	59	25	34	241	64	85	51	29	11	1
1988	296	62	27	34	234	63	81	50	27	12	1
1989	327	51	23	28	276	70	105	55	33	11	2
1990	351	62	28	34	289	68	109	65	32	11	3
1991	407	69	32	37	339	74	122	80	48	12	3
1992	504	87	38	49	418	84	151	111	51	17	4
1993	501	83	36	47	418	93	136	113	53	21	1
1994	508	77	36	40	431	92	145	115	57	21	....
1995	488	84	38	46	404	86	140	104	50	21	....

NOTE: Data beginning in 1994 are not strictly comparable with data for 1993 and earlier years because of the introduction of a major redesign of the survey and collection methodology. Beginning in 1990, data are not strictly comparable with previous years because of the introduction of 1990 census-based population controls adjusted for the estimated undercount.

POPULATION, LABOR FORCE, AND EMPLOYMENT STATUS

Unemployment Rates of Civilian Workers by Sex, Race, Hispanic Origin, and Age, 1948-1995

(Percent of civilian labor force)

Year, sex, race, and Hispanic origin	16 years and over	16 to 19 years			20 years and over						
		Total	16 to 17 years	18 to 19 years	Total	20 to 24 years	25 to 34 years	35 to 44 years	45 to 54 years	55 to 64 years	65 years and over
TOTAL											
1948	3.8	9.2	10.1	8.6	3.3	6.2	3.2	2.6	2.7	3.1	3.2
1949	5.9	13.4	14.0	13.0	5.4	9.3	5.4	4.4	4.2	5.2	4.9
1950	5.3	12.2	13.6	11.2	4.8	7.7	4.8	3.8	4.2	4.8	4.5
1951	3.3	8.2	9.6	7.1	3.0	4.1	3.0	2.5	2.7	3.1	3.4
1952	3.0	8.5	10.0	7.3	2.7	4.6	2.6	2.3	2.3	2.4	2.9
1953	2.9	7.6	8.7	6.8	2.6	4.7	2.5	2.2	2.3	2.7	2.2
1954	5.5	12.6	13.5	10.7	5.1	9.2	5.3	4.5	4.4	4.5	4.1
1955	4.4	11.0	12.3	10.0	3.9	7.0	3.8	3.4	3.4	4.2	3.6
1956	4.1	11.1	12.3	10.2	3.7	6.6	3.7	3.0	3.2	3.5	3.2
1957	4.3	11.6	12.5	10.9	3.8	7.1	3.9	3.1	3.3	3.4	3.4
1958	6.8	15.9	16.4	15.5	6.2	11.2	6.8	5.4	5.2	5.2	4.8
1959	5.5	14.6	15.3	14.0	4.8	8.5	5.0	4.2	4.2	4.4	4.3
1960	5.5	14.7	15.5	14.1	4.8	8.7	5.2	4.1	4.1	4.2	3.8
1961	6.7	16.8	18.3	15.8	5.9	10.4	6.2	5.2	5.0	5.4	5.1
1962	5.5	14.7	16.3	13.6	4.9	9.0	5.1	4.1	4.0	4.2	4.5
1963	5.7	17.2	19.3	15.6	4.8	8.8	5.2	4.0	3.8	4.1	4.1
1964	5.2	16.2	17.8	14.9	4.3	8.3	4.3	3.6	3.5	3.7	3.8
1965	4.5	14.8	16.5	13.5	3.6	6.7	3.7	3.2	2.8	3.1	3.3
1966	3.8	12.8	14.8	11.3	2.9	5.3	3.1	2.5	2.3	2.5	3.0
1967	3.8	12.9	14.6	11.6	3.0	5.7	3.2	2.5	2.4	2.4	2.8
1968	3.6	12.7	14.7	11.2	2.7	5.8	2.8	2.2	1.9	2.0	2.8
1969	3.5	12.2	14.5	10.5	2.7	5.7	2.8	2.2	1.9	1.9	2.2
1970	4.9	15.3	17.1	13.8	4.0	8.2	4.2	3.1	2.8	2.7	3.2
1971	5.9	16.9	18.7	15.5	4.9	10.0	5.3	3.9	3.4	3.3	3.5
1972	5.6	16.2	18.5	14.6	4.5	9.3	4.6	3.5	3.0	3.2	3.6
1973	4.9	14.5	17.3	12.4	3.9	7.8	4.2	2.7	2.5	2.6	3.0
1974	5.6	16.0	18.3	14.3	4.5	9.1	4.8	3.3	2.9	2.8	3.4
1975	8.5	19.9	21.4	18.9	7.3	13.6	7.8	5.6	5.2	4.6	5.2
1976	7.7	19.0	21.1	17.5	6.5	12.0	7.1	4.9	4.5	4.5	5.1
1977	7.1	17.8	19.9	16.2	5.9	11.0	6.5	4.4	3.9	3.9	5.0
1978	6.1	16.4	19.3	14.2	5.0	9.6	5.3	3.7	3.3	2.9	4.0
1979	5.8	16.1	18.1	14.7	4.8	9.1	5.2	3.6	3.2	2.9	3.4
1980	7.1	17.8	20.0	16.2	6.1	11.5	6.9	4.6	4.0	3.3	3.1
1981	7.6	19.6	21.4	18.4	6.5	12.3	7.3	5.0	4.2	3.7	3.2
1982	9.7	23.2	24.9	22.1	8.6	14.9	9.7	6.9	5.7	5.4	3.5
1983	9.6	22.4	24.5	21.1	8.6	14.5	9.7	7.0	6.2	5.6	3.7
1984	7.5	18.9	21.2	17.4	6.7	11.5	7.3	5.4	4.9	4.7	3.3
1985	7.2	18.6	21.0	17.0	6.4	11.1	7.0	5.1	4.7	4.3	3.2
1986	7.0	18.3	20.2	17.0	6.2	10.7	6.9	5.0	4.5	4.1	3.0
1987	6.2	16.9	19.1	15.2	5.4	9.7	6.0	4.5	4.0	3.5	2.5
1988	5.5	15.3	17.4	13.8	4.8	8.7	5.4	4.0	3.4	3.2	2.7
1989	5.3	15.0	17.2	13.6	4.6	8.6	5.2	3.8	3.2	3.2	2.6
1990	5.6	15.5	17.9	14.1	4.9	8.8	5.6	4.1	3.6	3.3	3.0
1991	6.8	18.7	21.0	17.2	6.1	10.8	6.9	5.2	4.5	4.1	3.3
1992	7.5	20.1	23.1	18.2	6.8	11.4	7.6	5.8	5.1	5.1	3.8
1993	6.9	19.0	21.4	17.5	6.2	10.5	6.9	5.5	4.8	4.7	3.2
1994	6.1	17.6	19.9	16.0	5.4	9.7	6.0	4.6	4.0	4.1	4.0
1995	5.6	17.3	20.2	15.3	4.9	9.1	5.4	4.3	3.3	3.6	4.0

Unemployment Rates of Civilian Workers by Sex, Race, Hispanic Origin, and Age, 1948-1995—Continued

(Percent of civilian labor force)

Year, sex, race, and Hispanic origin	16 years and over	16 to 19 years			20 years and over						
		Total	16 to 17 years	18 to 19 years	Total	20 to 24 years	25 to 34 years	35 to 44 years	45 to 54 years	55 to 64 years	65 years and over
MEN											
1948	3.6	9.8	10.2	9.5	3.2	6.9	2.8	2.4	2.5	3.1	3.4
1949	5.9	14.3	13.7	14.6	5.4	10.4	5.2	4.3	4.3	5.4	5.1
1950	5.1	12.7	13.3	12.3	4.7	8.1	4.4	3.6	4.0	4.9	4.8
1951	2.8	8.1	9.4	7.0	2.5	3.9	2.3	2.0	2.4	2.8	3.5
1952	2.8	8.9	10.5	7.4	2.4	4.6	2.2	1.9	2.2	2.4	3.0
1953	2.8	7.9	8.8	7.2	2.5	5.0	2.2	2.0	2.3	2.8	2.4
1954	5.3	13.5	13.9	13.2	4.9	10.7	4.8	4.1	4.3	4.5	4.4
1955	4.2	11.6	12.5	10.8	3.8	7.7	3.3	3.1	3.2	4.3	4.0
1956	3.8	11.1	11.7	10.5	3.4	6.9	3.3	2.6	3.0	3.5	3.5
1957	4.1	12.4	12.4	12.3	3.6	7.8	3.3	2.8	3.3	3.5	3.4
1958	6.8	17.1	16.3	17.8	6.2	12.7	6.5	5.1	5.3	5.5	5.2
1959	5.2	15.3	15.8	14.9	4.7	8.7	4.7	3.7	4.1	4.5	4.8
1960	5.4	15.3	15.5	15.0	4.7	8.9	4.8	3.8	4.1	4.6	4.2
1961	6.4	17.1	18.3	16.3	5.7	10.8	5.7	4.6	4.9	5.7	5.5
1962	5.2	14.7	16.0	13.8	4.6	8.9	4.5	3.6	3.9	4.6	4.6
1963	5.2	17.2	18.8	15.9	4.5	8.8	4.5	3.5	3.6	4.3	4.5
1964	4.6	15.8	17.1	14.6	3.9	8.1	3.5	2.9	3.2	3.9	4.0
1965	4.0	14.1	16.1	12.4	3.2	6.4	2.9	2.5	2.5	3.3	3.5
1966	3.2	11.7	13.7	10.2	2.5	4.6	2.4	2.0	1.9	2.6	3.1
1967	3.1	12.3	14.5	10.5	2.3	4.7	2.1	1.7	2.0	2.3	2.8
1968	2.9	11.6	13.9	9.7	2.2	5.1	1.9	1.6	1.6	1.9	2.8
1969	2.8	11.4	13.8	9.3	2.1	5.1	1.9	1.5	1.5	1.8	2.2
1970	4.4	15.0	16.9	13.4	3.5	8.4	3.5	2.4	2.4	2.8	3.3
1971	5.3	16.6	18.7	15.0	4.4	10.3	4.4	3.1	3.0	3.3	3.4
1972	5.0	15.9	18.3	14.1	4.0	9.3	3.8	2.7	2.6	3.2	3.6
1973	4.2	13.9	17.0	11.4	3.3	7.3	3.4	2.0	2.1	2.4	3.0
1974	4.9	15.6	18.4	13.3	3.8	8.8	4.0	2.6	2.4	2.6	3.3
1975	7.9	20.1	21.6	19.0	6.8	14.3	6.9	4.9	4.8	4.3	5.4
1976	7.1	19.2	21.4	17.6	5.9	12.1	6.2	4.1	4.0	4.2	5.1
1977	6.3	17.3	19.5	15.6	5.2	10.8	5.7	3.5	3.2	3.6	5.2
1978	5.3	15.8	19.1	13.3	4.3	9.2	4.4	2.8	2.7	2.8	4.2
1979	5.1	15.9	17.9	14.3	4.2	8.7	4.3	2.9	2.7	2.7	3.4
1980	6.9	18.3	20.4	16.7	5.9	12.5	6.7	4.1	3.6	3.4	3.1
1981	7.4	20.1	22.0	18.8	6.3	13.2	6.9	4.5	4.0	3.6	2.9
1982	9.9	24.4	26.4	23.1	8.8	16.4	10.1	6.9	5.6	5.5	3.7
1983	9.9	23.3	25.2	22.2	8.9	15.9	10.1	7.1	6.3	6.1	3.9
1984	7.4	19.6	21.9	18.3	6.6	11.9	7.2	5.2	4.6	5.0	3.0
1985	7.0	19.5	21.9	17.9	6.2	11.4	6.6	4.9	4.6	4.3	3.1
1986	6.9	19.0	20.8	17.7	6.1	11.0	6.7	5.1	4.4	4.3	3.2
1987	6.2	17.8	20.2	16.0	5.4	9.9	5.9	4.4	4.2	3.7	2.6
1988	5.5	16.0	18.2	14.6	4.8	8.9	5.3	3.8	3.5	3.5	2.5
1989	5.2	15.9	18.6	14.2	4.5	8.8	4.8	3.7	3.2	3.5	2.4
1990	5.7	16.3	18.4	15.0	5.0	9.1	5.5	4.1	3.7	3.8	3.0
1991	7.2	19.8	21.8	18.5	6.4	11.6	7.0	5.5	4.8	4.6	3.3
1992	7.9	21.5	24.6	19.5	7.1	12.2	7.8	6.1	5.6	5.8	3.3
1993	7.2	20.4	22.9	18.8	6.4	11.3	7.0	5.6	5.1	5.2	3.2
1994	6.2	19.0	21.0	17.6	5.4	10.2	5.9	4.5	4.0	4.4	4.0
1995	5.6	18.4	21.1	16.5	4.8	9.2	5.1	4.2	3.5	3.6	4.3

Unemployment Rates of Civilian Workers by Sex, Race, Hispanic Origin, and Age, 1948-1995—Continued

(Percent of civilian labor force)

Year, sex, race, and Hispanic origin	16 years and over	16 to 19 years			20 years and over						
		Total	16 to 17 years	18 to 19 years	Total	20 to 24 years	25 to 34 years	35 to 44 years	45 to 54 years	55 to 64 years	65 years and over
WOMEN											
1948	4.1	8.3	10.0	7.4	3.6	4.8	4.3	3.0	3.0	3.1	2.3
1949	6.0	12.3	14.4	11.2	5.3	7.3	5.9	4.7	4.0	4.4	3.8
1950	5.7	11.4	14.2	9.8	5.1	6.9	5.7	4.4	4.5	4.5	3.4
1951	4.4	8.3	10.0	7.2	4.0	4.4	4.5	3.8	3.5	4.0	2.9
1952	3.6	8.0	9.1	7.3	3.2	4.5	3.6	3.0	2.5	2.5	2.2
1953	3.3	7.2	8.5	6.4	2.9	4.3	3.4	2.5	2.3	2.5	1.4
1954	6.0	11.4	12.7	7.7	5.5	7.3	6.6	5.3	4.6	4.6	3.0
1955	4.9	10.2	12.0	9.1	4.4	6.1	5.3	4.0	3.6	3.8	2.3
1956	4.8	11.2	13.2	9.9	4.2	6.3	4.8	3.9	3.6	3.6	2.3
1957	4.7	10.6	12.6	9.4	4.1	6.0	5.3	3.8	3.2	3.0	3.4
1958	6.8	14.3	16.6	12.9	6.1	8.9	7.3	6.2	4.9	4.5	3.7
1959	5.9	13.5	14.4	13.0	5.2	8.1	5.9	5.1	4.2	4.1	2.8
1960	5.9	13.9	15.5	12.9	5.1	8.3	6.3	4.8	4.2	3.4	2.9
1961	7.2	16.3	18.3	15.1	6.3	9.8	7.4	6.4	5.1	4.5	4.0
1962	6.2	14.6	16.7	13.5	5.4	9.1	6.5	5.2	4.1	3.5	4.2
1963	6.5	17.2	20.2	15.2	5.4	8.9	6.9	5.1	4.2	3.6	3.2
1964	6.2	16.6	18.8	15.2	5.2	8.6	6.3	5.0	3.9	3.3	3.3
1965	5.5	15.7	17.2	14.8	4.5	7.3	5.5	4.6	3.2	2.8	2.9
1966	4.8	14.1	16.6	12.6	3.8	6.3	4.5	3.6	2.9	2.3	2.8
1967	5.2	13.5	14.8	12.8	4.2	7.0	5.4	4.1	3.1	2.4	2.7
1968	4.8	14.0	15.9	12.9	3.8	6.7	4.7	3.4	2.4	2.2	2.7
1969	4.7	13.3	15.5	11.8	3.7	6.3	4.6	3.4	2.6	2.2	2.3
1970	5.9	15.6	17.4	14.4	4.8	7.9	5.7	4.4	3.5	2.7	3.1
1971	6.9	17.2	18.7	16.2	5.7	9.6	7.0	5.2	4.0	3.3	3.6
1972	6.6	16.7	18.8	15.2	5.4	9.4	6.2	4.9	3.6	3.3	3.5
1973	6.0	15.3	17.7	13.5	4.9	8.5	5.8	3.9	3.2	2.8	2.9
1974	6.7	16.6	18.2	15.4	5.5	9.5	6.2	4.6	3.7	3.2	3.6
1975	9.3	19.7	21.2	18.7	8.0	12.7	9.1	6.8	5.9	5.1	5.0
1976	8.6	18.7	20.8	17.4	7.4	11.9	8.4	6.1	5.2	4.9	5.0
1977	8.2	18.3	20.5	16.9	7.0	11.2	7.7	5.7	5.1	4.4	4.7
1978	7.2	17.1	19.5	15.3	6.0	10.1	6.7	5.0	4.0	3.2	3.8
1979	6.8	16.4	18.3	15.0	5.7	9.6	6.5	4.6	3.9	3.2	3.3
1980	7.4	17.2	19.6	15.6	6.4	10.4	7.2	5.3	4.5	3.3	3.1
1981	7.9	19.0	20.7	17.9	6.8	11.2	7.7	5.7	4.6	3.8	3.6
1982	9.4	21.9	23.2	21.0	8.3	13.2	9.3	7.0	5.9	5.2	3.2
1983	9.2	21.3	23.7	19.9	8.1	12.9	9.1	6.9	6.0	5.0	3.4
1984	7.6	18.0	20.4	16.6	6.8	10.9	7.4	5.6	5.2	4.3	3.8
1985	7.4	17.6	20.0	16.0	6.6	10.7	7.4	5.5	4.8	4.3	3.3
1986	7.1	17.6	19.6	16.3	6.2	10.3	7.2	5.0	4.5	3.8	2.8
1987	6.2	15.9	18.0	14.3	5.4	9.4	6.2	4.6	3.7	3.1	2.4
1988	5.6	14.4	16.6	12.9	4.9	8.5	5.6	4.1	3.4	2.7	2.9
1989	5.4	14.0	15.7	13.0	4.7	8.3	5.6	3.9	3.2	2.8	2.9
1990	5.5	14.7	17.4	13.1	4.9	8.5	5.6	4.2	3.4	2.8	3.1
1991	6.4	17.5	20.2	15.9	5.7	9.8	6.8	4.8	4.2	3.4	3.3
1992	7.0	18.6	21.5	16.6	6.3	10.3	7.4	5.5	4.6	4.2	4.5
1993	6.6	17.5	19.8	16.1	5.9	9.7	6.8	5.3	4.5	4.0	3.1
1994	6.0	16.2	18.7	14.3	5.4	9.2	6.2	4.7	4.0	3.9	4.0
1995	5.6	16.1	19.2	14.0	4.9	9.0	5.7	4.4	3.2	3.6	3.7

Unemployment Rates of Civilian Workers by Sex, Race, Hispanic Origin, and Age, 1948-1995—Continued

(Percent of civilian labor force)

Year, sex, race, and Hispanic origin	16 years and over	16 to 19 years			20 years and over						
		Total	16 to 17 years	18 to 19 years	Total	20 to 24 years	25 to 34 years	35 to 44 years	45 to 54 years	55 to 64 years	65 years and over
WHITE											
1954	5.0	12.1	13.2	11.3	4.6	8.3	4.6	4.0	4.0	4.3	3.9
1955	3.9	10.4	12.0	9.2	3.4	6.2	3.1	2.9	3.1	3.8	3.4
1956	3.6	10.1	11.5	9.0	3.2	5.7	3.1	2.6	2.9	3.2	3.1
1957	3.8	10.6	11.9	9.6	3.4	6.3	3.3	2.8	3.0	3.2	3.2
1958	6.1	14.4	15.2	13.9	5.6	9.9	5.9	4.8	4.8	4.9	4.6
1959	4.8	13.1	14.4	12.1	4.3	7.3	4.2	3.7	3.8	4.1	4.1
1960	5.0	13.5	14.6	12.6	4.3	7.9	4.5	3.6	3.8	3.9	3.7
1961	6.0	15.3	16.7	14.4	5.3	9.4	5.3	4.5	4.5	5.0	4.8
1962	4.9	13.3	15.3	12.0	4.2	7.9	4.2	3.6	3.6	3.9	4.0
1963	5.0	15.5	17.9	13.7	4.2	7.7	4.4	3.5	3.5	3.8	3.8
1964	4.6	14.8	16.5	13.3	3.8	7.3	3.6	3.2	3.2	3.5	3.5
1965	4.1	13.4	14.8	12.3	3.3	6.1	3.2	2.9	2.5	2.9	3.2
1966	3.4	11.2	13.3	9.7	2.6	4.6	2.6	2.3	2.1	2.4	2.9
1967	3.4	11.0	12.8	9.8	2.7	5.0	2.7	2.3	2.2	2.3	2.7
1968	3.2	11.0	12.9	9.6	2.5	5.2	2.4	2.0	1.8	1.9	2.8
1969	3.1	10.7	13.0	8.9	2.4	5.0	2.5	2.0	1.8	1.8	2.2
1970	4.5	13.5	15.5	11.9	3.7	7.3	3.8	3.0	2.7	2.7	3.2
1971	5.4	15.1	17.0	13.8	4.5	9.0	4.7	3.6	3.3	3.3	3.5
1972	5.1	14.2	16.6	12.3	4.1	8.4	4.1	3.2	2.9	3.1	3.4
1973	4.3	12.6	15.4	10.4	3.5	6.8	3.7	2.5	2.4	2.5	2.9
1974	5.0	14.0	16.3	12.2	4.1	8.0	4.4	3.1	2.8	2.8	3.3
1975	7.8	17.9	19.5	16.7	6.7	12.3	7.1	5.2	4.9	4.5	5.1
1976	7.0	16.9	19.0	15.3	5.9	10.7	6.3	4.5	4.2	4.3	4.9
1977	6.2	15.4	17.9	13.5	5.3	9.3	5.7	4.0	3.8	3.7	4.9
1978	5.2	13.9	17.0	11.5	4.3	8.0	4.6	3.3	3.0	2.7	3.8
1979	5.1	14.0	16.1	12.4	4.2	7.6	4.4	3.2	3.0	2.7	3.1
1980	6.3	15.5	17.9	13.8	5.4	9.9	6.1	4.2	3.7	3.1	2.7
1981	6.7	17.3	19.2	15.9	5.7	10.4	6.3	4.5	3.9	3.5	2.8
1982	8.6	20.4	22.8	18.8	7.6	12.8	8.5	6.3	5.4	5.1	3.1
1983	8.4	19.3	22.0	17.6	7.5	12.1	8.4	6.3	5.7	5.2	3.2
1984	6.5	16.0	18.8	14.3	5.7	9.3	6.2	4.8	4.4	4.4	3.0
1985	6.2	15.7	18.3	13.9	5.5	9.2	5.9	4.6	4.3	4.0	2.9
1986	6.0	15.6	17.6	14.1	5.3	8.7	5.9	4.5	4.1	3.8	2.9
1987	5.3	14.4	16.7	12.7	4.7	8.0	5.1	4.0	3.7	3.2	2.4
1988	4.7	13.1	15.3	11.6	4.1	7.1	4.5	3.5	3.1	3.0	2.4
1989	4.5	12.7	15.2	11.1	3.9	7.2	4.3	3.3	2.9	3.0	2.3
1990	4.8	13.5	15.8	12.1	4.3	7.3	4.6	3.6	3.3	3.2	2.8
1991	6.1	16.5	19.0	14.9	5.5	9.2	6.1	4.7	4.2	4.0	3.1
1992	6.6	17.2	20.3	15.2	6.0	9.5	6.7	5.2	4.8	4.9	3.7
1993	6.1	16.2	19.0	14.4	5.5	8.8	6.0	4.9	4.5	4.3	3.0
1994	5.3	15.1	17.6	13.3	4.7	8.1	5.2	4.0	3.7	3.9	3.8
1995	4.9	14.5	17.3	12.5	4.3	7.7	4.6	3.9	3.1	3.5	3.8

Unemployment Rates of Civilian Workers by Sex, Race, Hispanic Origin, and Age, 1948-1995—Continued

(Percent of civilian labor force)

Year, sex, race, and Hispanic origin	16 years and over	16 to 19 years			20 years and over						
		Total	16 to 17 years	18 to 19 years	Total	20 to 24 years	25 to 34 years	35 to 44 years	45 to 54 years	55 to 64 years	65 years and over
WHITE MEN											
1954	4.8	13.4	14.0	13.0	4.4	9.8	4.2	3.6	3.8	4.3	4.2
1955	3.7	11.3	12.2	10.4	3.3	7.0	2.7	2.6	2.9	3.9	3.8
1956	3.4	10.5	11.2	9.7	3.0	6.1	2.8	2.2	2.8	3.1	3.4
1957	3.6	11.5	11.9	11.1	3.2	7.0	2.7	2.5	3.0	3.4	3.2
1958	6.1	15.7	14.9	16.5	5.5	11.7	5.6	4.4	4.8	5.2	5.0
1959	4.6	14.0	15.0	13.0	4.1	7.5	3.8	3.2	3.7	4.2	4.5
1960	4.8	14.0	14.6	13.5	4.2	8.3	4.1	3.3	3.6	4.1	4.0
1961	5.7	15.7	16.5	15.2	5.1	10.1	4.9	4.0	4.4	5.3	5.2
1962	4.6	13.7	15.2	12.7	4.0	8.1	3.8	3.1	3.5	4.1	4.0
1963	4.7	15.9	17.8	14.2	3.9	7.8	3.9	2.9	3.3	4.0	4.1
1964	4.1	14.7	16.1	13.3	3.4	7.4	3.0	2.5	2.9	3.5	3.6
1965	3.6	12.9	14.7	11.3	2.9	5.9	2.6	2.3	2.3	3.1	3.4
1966	2.8	10.5	12.5	8.9	2.2	4.1	2.1	1.7	1.7	2.5	3.0
1967	2.7	10.7	12.7	9.0	2.1	4.2	1.9	1.6	1.8	2.2	2.7
1968	2.6	10.1	12.3	8.3	2.0	4.6	1.7	1.4	1.5	1.7	2.8
1969	2.5	10.0	12.5	7.9	1.9	4.6	1.7	1.4	1.4	1.7	2.2
1970	4.0	13.7	15.7	12.0	3.2	7.8	3.1	2.3	2.3	2.7	3.2
1971	4.9	15.1	17.1	13.5	4.0	9.4	4.0	2.9	2.9	3.2	3.4
1972	4.5	14.2	16.4	12.4	3.6	8.5	3.4	2.5	2.5	3.0	3.3
1973	3.8	12.3	15.2	10.0	3.0	6.6	3.0	1.8	2.0	2.4	2.9
1974	4.4	13.5	16.2	11.5	3.5	7.8	3.6	2.4	2.2	2.5	3.0
1975	7.2	18.3	19.7	17.2	6.2	13.1	6.3	4.5	4.4	4.1	5.0
1976	6.4	17.3	19.7	15.5	5.4	10.9	5.6	3.7	3.7	4.0	4.7
1977	5.5	15.0	17.6	13.0	4.7	9.3	5.0	3.1	3.0	3.3	4.9
1978	4.6	13.5	16.9	10.8	3.7	7.7	3.8	2.5	2.5	2.6	3.9
1979	4.5	13.9	16.1	12.2	3.6	7.5	3.7	2.5	2.5	2.5	3.2
1980	6.1	16.2	18.5	14.5	5.3	11.1	5.9	3.6	3.3	3.1	2.5
1981	6.5	17.9	19.9	16.4	5.6	11.6	6.1	4.0	3.6	3.4	2.4
1982	8.8	21.7	24.2	20.0	7.8	14.3	8.9	6.2	5.3	5.1	3.2
1983	8.8	20.2	22.6	18.7	7.9	13.8	9.0	6.4	5.7	5.6	3.2
1984	6.4	16.8	19.7	15.0	5.7	9.8	6.2	4.6	4.2	4.7	2.6
1985	6.1	16.5	19.2	14.7	5.4	9.7	5.7	4.3	4.1	4.0	2.7
1986	6.0	16.3	18.4	14.7	5.3	9.2	5.8	4.4	4.0	4.0	3.0
1987	5.4	15.5	17.9	13.7	4.8	8.4	5.2	3.9	3.9	3.4	2.5
1988	4.7	13.9	16.1	12.4	4.1	7.4	4.6	3.4	3.2	3.3	2.2
1989	4.5	13.7	16.4	12.0	3.9	7.5	4.1	3.2	2.9	3.1	2.1
1990	4.9	14.3	16.1	13.2	4.3	7.6	4.7	3.5	3.4	3.6	2.8
1991	6.5	17.6	19.7	16.3	5.8	10.2	6.4	5.0	4.4	4.6	3.1
1992	7.0	18.5	21.5	16.5	6.4	10.5	7.0	5.5	5.1	5.5	3.2
1993	6.3	17.7	20.2	16.0	5.7	9.6	6.2	5.0	4.7	4.7	2.9
1994	5.4	16.3	18.5	14.7	4.8	8.8	5.2	3.9	3.7	4.1	3.7
1995	4.9	15.6	18.2	13.8	4.3	7.9	4.5	3.8	3.2	3.4	4.0
WHITE WOMEN											
1954	5.5	10.4	12.0	9.4	5.1	6.4	5.7	4.9	4.4	4.5	2.8
1955	4.3	9.1	11.6	7.7	3.9	5.1	4.3	3.8	3.4	3.6	2.2
1956	4.2	9.7	12.1	8.3	3.7	5.1	4.0	3.5	3.3	3.5	2.3
1957	4.3	9.5	11.9	7.8	3.8	5.1	4.7	3.7	3.0	2.9	3.4
1958	6.2	12.7	15.6	11.0	5.6	7.3	6.6	5.6	4.9	4.3	3.5
1959	5.3	12.0	13.3	11.1	4.7	7.0	5.2	4.7	3.9	4.0	2.9
1960	5.3	12.7	14.5	11.5	4.6	7.2	5.7	4.2	4.0	3.3	2.8
1961	6.5	14.8	17.0	13.6	5.7	8.4	6.6	5.6	4.8	4.3	3.8
1962	5.5	12.8	15.6	11.3	4.7	7.7	5.4	4.5	3.7	3.5	4.0
1963	5.8	15.1	18.1	13.2	4.8	7.4	5.8	4.6	3.9	3.5	3.3
1964	5.5	14.9	17.1	13.2	4.6	7.1	5.2	4.5	3.6	3.5	3.4
1965	5.0	14.0	15.0	13.4	4.0	6.3	4.9	4.1	3.0	2.7	2.7
1966	4.3	12.1	14.5	10.7	3.3	5.3	3.7	3.3	2.7	2.2	2.7
1967	4.6	11.5	12.9	10.6	3.8	6.0	4.7	3.7	2.9	2.3	2.6
1968	4.3	12.1	13.9	11.0	3.4	5.9	3.9	3.1	2.3	2.1	2.8
1969	4.2	11.5	13.7	10.0	3.4	5.5	4.2	3.2	2.4	2.1	2.4
1970	5.4	13.4	15.3	11.9	4.4	6.9	5.3	4.3	3.4	2.6	3.3
1971	6.3	15.1	16.7	14.1	5.3	8.5	6.3	4.9	3.9	3.3	3.6
1972	5.9	14.2	17.0	12.3	4.9	8.2	5.5	4.4	3.5	3.3	3.7
1973	5.3	13.0	15.8	10.9	4.3	7.1	5.1	3.7	3.2	2.7	2.8
1974	6.1	14.5	16.4	13.0	5.1	8.2	5.8	4.3	3.6	3.2	3.9
1975	8.6	17.4	19.2	16.1	7.5	11.2	8.4	6.5	5.8	5.0	5.3
1976	7.9	16.4	18.2	15.1	6.8	10.4	7.6	5.8	5.0	4.8	5.3
1977	7.3	15.9	18.2	14.2	6.2	9.3	6.7	5.3	5.0	4.4	4.9
1978	6.2	14.4	17.1	12.4	5.2	8.3	5.8	4.5	3.8	3.0	3.7
1979	5.9	14.0	15.9	12.5	5.0	7.8	5.6	4.2	3.7	3.0	3.1
1980	6.5	14.8	17.3	13.1	5.6	8.5	6.3	4.9	4.3	3.1	3.0
1981	6.9	16.6	18.4	15.3	5.9	9.1	6.6	5.1	4.2	3.7	3.4
1982	8.3	19.0	21.2	17.6	7.3	10.9	8.0	6.4	5.5	5.0	3.1
1983	7.9	18.3	21.4	16.4	6.9	10.3	7.6	6.2	5.5	4.7	3.1
1984	6.5	15.2	17.8	13.6	5.8	8.8	6.1	5.0	4.8	4.0	3.7
1985	6.4	14.8	17.2	13.1	5.7	8.5	6.2	4.9	4.5	4.1	3.1
1986	6.1	14.9	16.7	13.6	5.4	8.1	6.1	4.5	4.3	3.7	2.6
1987	5.2	13.4	15.5	11.7	4.6	7.4	5.0	4.1	3.3	2.9	2.4
1988	4.7	12.3	14.4	10.8	4.1	6.7	4.5	3.7	3.1	2.5	2.6
1989	4.5	11.5	13.8	10.1	4.0	6.8	4.5	3.4	2.9	2.7	2.5
1990	4.7	12.6	15.5	10.9	4.1	6.8	4.6	3.7	3.2	2.7	2.8
1991	5.6	15.2	18.2	13.3	5.0	8.1	5.7	4.3	4.0	3.3	3.1
1992	6.1	15.8	18.9	13.7	5.5	8.3	6.2	4.9	4.3	4.0	4.5
1993	5.7	14.7	17.8	12.6	5.2	7.9	5.8	4.7	4.3	3.9	3.0
1994	5.2	13.8	16.6	11.8	4.6	7.4	5.1	4.2	3.7	3.7	3.9
1995	4.8	13.4	16.4	11.2	4.3	7.4	4.7	3.9	3.0	3.5	3.5

Unemployment Rates of Civilian Workers by Sex, Race, Hispanic Origin, and Age, 1948-1995—Continued

(Percent of civilian labor force)

Year, sex, race, and Hispanic origin	16 years and over	16 to 19 years			20 years and over						
		Total	16 to 17 years	18 to 19 years	Total	20 to 24 years	25 to 34 years	35 to 44 years	45 to 54 years	55 to 64 years	65 years and over
BLACK											
1972	10.4	35.4	38.7	33.6	7.9	16.3	8.7	6.1	4.2	4.1	4.3
1973	9.4	31.5	37.0	28.1	7.2	15.5	8.1	4.7	3.5	3.2	3.5
1974	10.5	35.0	40.0	31.8	8.0	17.5	8.5	5.4	4.3	3.6	3.9
1975	14.8	39.5	41.6	38.1	12.3	24.5	13.0	8.9	8.3	5.9	6.6
1976	14.0	39.3	44.2	36.7	11.5	22.7	12.8	8.0	6.7	5.9	5.9
1977	14.0	41.1	44.5	39.2	11.5	24.2	12.7	7.4	5.3	5.5	5.9
1978	12.8	38.7	43.9	35.7	10.2	21.8	10.8	6.4	5.2	4.8	5.8
1979	12.3	36.5	40.2	34.4	10.1	20.6	10.8	6.7	5.2	4.9	5.3
1980	14.3	38.5	41.1	37.1	12.1	23.6	13.3	8.2	6.8	5.4	6.9
1981	15.6	41.4	44.8	39.5	13.4	26.4	14.7	9.5	7.4	5.5	7.0
1982	18.9	48.0	48.6	47.8	16.6	30.6	19.0	12.1	8.7	8.3	7.1
1983	19.5	48.5	50.5	47.6	17.3	31.6	19.0	12.4	10.7	9.2	9.2
1984	15.9	42.7	45.7	41.2	13.9	26.1	15.2	9.9	8.2	7.4	6.5
1985	15.1	40.2	43.6	38.3	13.1	24.5	14.5	9.5	8.2	7.0	7.0
1986	14.5	39.3	43.0	37.2	12.7	24.1	14.0	9.6	7.1	6.6	4.5
1987	13.0	34.7	39.7	31.6	11.3	21.8	12.8	8.4	6.8	5.6	3.9
1988	11.7	32.4	35.1	30.7	10.2	19.6	11.9	7.5	5.9	4.8	5.5
1989	11.4	32.4	32.9	32.2	9.9	18.0	11.5	7.6	5.6	5.2	6.9
1990	11.4	30.9	36.5	27.8	10.1	19.9	11.7	7.8	5.3	4.6	5.3
1991	12.5	36.1	39.5	34.4	11.1	21.6	12.7	8.5	7.4	4.4	5.2
1992	14.2	39.7	44.7	37.1	12.6	23.8	14.2	10.5	8.3	6.2	4.9
1993	13.0	38.8	39.7	38.4	11.4	21.9	12.6	9.5	6.9	7.1	4.7
1994	11.5	35.2	36.1	34.6	10.0	19.5	11.1	8.5	5.6	5.4	6.2
1995	10.4	35.7	39.1	33.4	8.7	17.7	9.9	7.3	4.8	4.0	6.7
BLACK MEN											
1972	9.3	31.7	36.7	28.4	7.0	14.9	7.2	4.8	3.8	4.4	5.4
1973	8.0	27.8	35.7	23.0	6.0	13.2	6.2	3.9	3.2	3.2	3.3
1974	9.8	33.1	39.9	28.3	7.4	16.2	8.1	4.3	4.2	3.6	5.3
1975	14.8	38.1	41.9	35.9	12.5	24.7	12.7	8.7	9.3	6.3	8.7
1976	13.7	37.5	40.8	36.0	11.4	22.6	12.0	7.5	7.3	6.3	8.7
1977	13.3	39.2	41.0	38.2	10.7	23.0	11.8	6.2	4.9	6.0	7.8
1978	11.8	36.7	43.0	32.9	9.3	21.0	9.8	5.1	4.9	4.4	6.6
1979	11.4	34.2	37.9	32.2	9.3	18.7	9.6	6.3	5.2	5.1	6.4
1980	14.5	37.5	39.7	36.2	12.4	23.7	13.4	8.2	7.2	6.2	8.7
1981	15.7	40.7	43.2	39.2	13.5	26.4	14.4	9.3	7.8	6.1	7.5
1982	20.1	48.9	52.7	47.1	17.8	31.5	20.1	13.4	9.0	10.3	9.3
1983	20.3	48.8	52.2	47.3	18.1	31.4	19.4	13.5	11.4	11.0	11.8
1984	16.4	42.7	44.0	42.2	14.3	26.6	15.0	10.4	7.9	8.9	7.9
1985	15.3	41.0	42.9	40.0	13.2	23.5	13.8	9.6	9.7	7.9	8.9
1986	14.8	39.3	41.4	38.2	12.9	23.5	13.5	10.9	7.8	8.0	4.3
1987	12.7	34.4	39.0	31.6	11.1	20.3	12.2	8.7	6.7	6.6	4.3
1988	11.7	32.7	34.4	31.7	10.1	19.4	11.0	7.6	6.2	5.2	5.6
1989	11.5	31.9	34.4	30.3	10.0	17.9	10.5	8.4	6.2	6.2	7.4
1990	11.9	31.9	38.8	28.0	10.4	20.1	11.5	8.4	6.3	5.4	4.6
1991	13.0	36.3	39.0	34.8	11.5	22.4	11.9	9.5	8.6	5.0	6.1
1992	15.2	42.0	47.5	39.1	13.5	24.6	14.2	11.2	10.3	8.1	4.9
1993	13.8	40.1	42.7	38.6	12.1	23.0	12.3	10.5	8.1	9.0	5.8
1994	12.0	37.6	39.3	36.5	10.3	19.4	10.6	9.1	6.5	6.0	8.2
1995	10.6	37.1	39.7	35.4	8.8	17.6	9.3	7.6	5.5	4.4	7.6
BLACK WOMEN											
1972	11.8	40.5	42.0	40.1	9.0	17.9	10.5	7.6	4.6	3.7	2.6
1973	11.1	36.1	38.6	34.2	8.6	18.4	10.3	5.6	3.9	3.3	3.7
1974	11.3	37.4	40.2	36.0	8.8	19.0	9.0	6.6	4.4	3.6	1.9
1975	14.8	41.0	41.2	40.6	12.2	24.3	13.4	9.0	7.0	5.3	3.6
1976	14.3	41.6	48.4	37.6	11.7	22.8	13.6	8.5	5.9	5.4	2.4
1977	14.9	43.4	49.5	40.4	12.3	25.5	13.6	8.7	5.8	4.8	3.4
1978	13.8	40.8	45.0	38.7	11.2	22.7	11.9	7.8	5.6	5.2	4.7
1979	13.3	39.1	42.7	36.9	10.9	22.6	12.1	7.2	5.2	4.7	3.9
1980	14.0	39.8	42.9	38.2	11.9	23.5	13.2	8.2	6.4	4.5	4.9
1981	15.6	42.2	46.5	39.8	13.4	26.4	14.9	9.8	6.9	4.7	6.0
1982	17.6	47.1	44.2	48.6	15.4	29.6	17.8	10.7	8.5	6.1	4.5
1983	18.6	48.2	48.6	48.0	16.5	31.8	18.6	11.4	9.9	7.3	6.3
1984	15.4	42.6	47.5	40.2	13.5	25.6	15.4	9.4	8.6	5.9	4.9
1985	14.9	39.2	44.3	36.4	13.1	25.6	15.1	9.3	6.8	6.0	5.2
1986	14.2	39.2	44.6	36.1	12.4	24.7	14.6	8.5	6.4	5.0	4.9
1987	13.2	34.9	40.5	31.7	11.6	23.3	13.5	8.1	6.9	4.5	3.4
1988	11.7	32.0	35.9	29.6	10.4	19.8	12.7	7.4	5.6	4.3	5.4
1989	11.4	33.0	31.1	34.0	9.8	18.1	12.5	7.0	5.0	4.2	6.4
1990	10.9	29.9	34.1	27.6	9.7	19.6	11.9	7.2	4.3	3.6	5.9
1991	12.0	36.0	40.1	33.9	10.6	20.7	13.4	7.6	6.2	3.8	4.4
1992	13.2	37.2	41.7	34.8	11.8	23.1	14.1	9.8	6.4	4.2	5.0
1993	12.1	37.4	36.1	38.1	10.7	20.9	12.9	8.6	5.8	5.1	3.6
1994	11.0	32.6	32.9	32.5	9.8	19.6	11.7	8.0	4.9	4.9	4.4
1995	10.2	34.3	....	31.5	8.6	17.8	10.5	7.0	4.2	3.6	....

POPULATION, LABOR FORCE, AND EMPLOYMENT STATUS

Unemployment Rates of Civilian Workers by Sex, Race, Hispanic Origin, and Age, 1948-1995—Continued

(Percent of civilian labor force)

Year, sex, race, and Hispanic origin	16 years and over	16 to 19 years			20 years and over						
		Total	16 to 17 years	18 to 19 years	Total	20 to 24 years	25 to 34 years	35 to 44 years	45 to 54 years	55 to 64 years	65 years and over
HISPANIC											
1973	7.5	19.7	23.4	17.3	6.0	8.5	5.7	5.6	4.7	5.5	3.9
1974	8.1	19.8	23.5	17.2	6.6	9.8	6.3	5.9	4.6	6.1	6.3
1975	12.2	27.7	30.0	26.5	10.3	16.7	9.9	8.6	8.1	7.7	9.9
1976	11.5	23.8	29.2	19.2	10.1	15.9	9.1	8.2	8.4	8.8	12.6
1977	10.1	22.9	27.0	19.6	8.5	12.0	8.6	6.1	7.3	8.2	9.2
1978	9.1	20.7	28.3	15.1	7.7	10.9	8.0	6.5	5.8	5.0	7.5
1979	8.3	19.2	26.0	14.9	7.0	10.4	6.7	6.2	5.2	6.0	5.7
1980	10.1	22.5	27.6	19.5	8.6	12.1	9.1	7.7	5.7	5.9	6.0
1981	10.4	23.9	28.0	21.7	9.1	13.9	8.8	7.4	6.4	7.3	5.4
1982	13.8	29.9	38.1	25.9	12.3	17.7	12.3	10.7	8.4	10.1	6.5
1983	13.7	28.4	33.8	25.8	12.3	16.7	11.9	11.3	10.0	10.9	5.8
1984	10.7	24.1	28.9	21.6	9.5	12.4	9.7	8.2	7.5	9.7	6.1
1985	10.5	24.3	27.8	22.5	9.4	12.6	9.9	7.7	7.4	7.8	8.1
1986	10.6	24.7	28.1	22.9	9.5	12.9	9.6	8.4	7.8	7.3	10.1
1987	8.8	22.3	27.7	19.5	7.8	10.6	7.7	6.7	6.9	6.0	6.5
1988	8.2	22.0	27.1	19.3	7.0	9.8	7.1	6.0	6.0	5.8	5.6
1989	8.0	19.4	26.4	16.0	7.2	10.7	7.0	5.9	6.3	5.8	5.3
1990	8.2	19.5	24.5	16.9	7.2	9.1	7.3	6.6	6.4	5.6	6.0
1991	10.0	22.9	31.9	18.7	9.0	11.6	9.2	8.1	8.0	6.5	7.0
1992	11.6	27.5	35.7	23.4	10.4	13.2	10.4	9.8	8.8	8.6	8.1
1993	10.8	26.1	35.1	21.8	9.7	13.1	9.3	9.1	8.6	8.0	6.6
1994	9.9	24.5	31.7	20.6	8.9	11.8	9.0	7.7	8.1	7.3	7.9
1995	9.3	24.1	33.1	19.5	8.2	11.5	8.2	7.2	6.4	7.5	10.6
HISPANIC MEN											
1973	6.7	19.0	20.9	17.7	5.4	8.2	5.0	4.2	4.5	5.4	....
1974	7.3	19.0	22.0	17.1	6.0	9.9	5.5	5.0	4.3	5.4	....
1975	11.4	27.6	29.3	26.5	9.6	16.3	9.6	7.9	7.0	6.8	....
1976	10.8	23.3	28.7	19.7	9.4	16.0	8.1	7.0	7.4	8.7	....
1977	9.0	20.9	25.9	18.2	7.7	11.7	7.9	4.9	5.4	7.4	....
1978	7.7	19.7	27.5	13.9	6.4	9.4	6.6	4.8	4.8	4.4	....
1979	7.0	17.5	23.5	13.8	5.8	9.2	5.3	5.1	4.4	5.0	....
1980	9.7	21.9	26.2	19.3	8.3	12.2	8.3	7.1	6.0	5.9	....
1981	10.2	24.3	30.9	20.3	8.8	14.1	8.9	6.5	5.9	6.7	....
1982	13.6	31.3	40.2	26.8	12.1	18.2	12.4	9.9	7.5	10.0	....
1983	13.6	28.7	34.7	25.9	12.2	17.0	11.6	10.8	10.3	11.7	....
1984	10.5	25.2	31.5	22.2	9.3	12.5	9.2	7.6	7.2	10.2	....
1985	10.2	24.7	29.1	22.4	9.1	12.9	9.6	7.2	6.8	7.0	....
1986	10.5	24.5	28.5	22.4	9.5	13.0	9.5	8.5	7.0	8.0	....
1987	8.7	22.2	28.2	19.3	7.8	10.2	7.6	6.9	7.1	6.7	....
1988	8.1	22.7	29.5	19.5	7.0	9.2	7.0	5.9	6.1	6.7	....
1989	7.6	20.2	27.6	16.8	6.6	9.7	5.9	5.7	6.0	6.6	....
1990	8.0	19.5	24.0	17.4	7.0	8.4	6.9	6.5	6.8	6.5	....
1991	10.3	23.5	33.6	19.2	9.3	11.6	9.3	8.5	7.9	8.1	....
1992	11.7	28.2	36.6	24.0	10.5	13.7	10.1	9.8	8.9	10.2	....
1993	10.6	25.9	34.5	21.9	9.5	12.6	9.0	8.8	8.8	8.5	....
1994	9.4	26.3	33.3	22.5	8.3	10.8	8.4	6.6	8.1	7.4	....
1995	8.8	25.3	34.8	20.2	7.7	10.6	7.5	6.7	5.9	7.9	....
HISPANIC WOMEN											
1973	9.0	20.7	26.8	16.7	7.3	9.0	6.9	8.3	5.1	5.6	....
1974	9.4	20.8	25.3	17.4	7.7	9.7	7.7	7.5	5.3	7.5	....
1975	13.5	27.9	31.0	26.4	11.5	17.2	10.5	9.9	10.0	9.3	....
1976	12.7	22.2	30.3	18.7	11.4	15.8	10.8	10.0	9.8	9.0	....
1977	11.9	24.4	28.5	21.9	10.1	12.1	9.8	8.2	10.6	11.0	....
1978	11.3	21.8	29.9	16.6	9.8	13.0	10.3	9.2	7.4	7.2	....
1979	10.3	21.2	30.0	15.8	8.9	12.1	8.9	7.7	7.1	7.9	....
1980	10.7	23.4	29.7	19.8	9.2	12.0	10.6	8.6	5.3	5.8	....
1981	10.8	23.4	23.5	23.4	9.5	13.5	8.7	8.9	7.2	8.4	....
1982	14.1	28.2	35.1	25.0	12.5	16.8	12.2	11.9	9.9	10.4	....
1983	13.8	28.0	32.5	25.7	12.4	16.2	12.5	12.2	9.7	9.6	....
1984	11.1	22.8	26.1	21.0	9.9	12.2	10.3	9.1	7.9	8.8	....
1985	11.0	23.8	26.2	22.6	9.9	12.1	10.6	8.5	8.1	9.2	....
1986	10.8	25.1	27.6	23.6	9.6	12.9	9.8	8.2	8.9	6.2	....
1987	8.9	22.4	27.1	19.9	7.7	11.4	7.8	6.5	6.7	5.0	....
1988	8.3	21.0	24.5	18.9	7.1	10.7	7.2	6.2	5.9	4.6	....
1989	8.8	18.2	24.7	14.9	8.0	12.2	8.6	6.3	6.7	4.5	....
1990	8.4	19.4	25.4	16.2	7.5	10.4	8.0	6.7	6.0	4.3	....
1991	9.6	21.9	29.6	17.9	8.6	11.7	9.1	7.6	8.1	4.1	....
1992	11.4	26.4	34.5	22.4	10.2	12.4	11.0	9.7	8.5	6.2	....
1993	11.0	26.3	36.0	21.7	9.9	14.0	9.9	9.5	8.3	7.2	....
1994	10.7	22.2	29.7	18.1	9.8	13.5	10.1	9.2	8.0	7.1	....
1995	10.0	22.6	30.7	18.7	8.9	13.0	9.5	7.9	7.0	6.8	....

NOTE: Data beginning in 1994 are not strictly comparable with data for 1993 and earlier years because of the introduction of a major redesign of the survey and collection methodology. Beginning in 1990, data are not strictly comparable with previous years because of the introduction of 1990 census-based population controls adjusted for the estimated undercount.

Unemployed Persons and Unemployment Rates by Occupation, 1982-1995

(Numbers in thousands; Percent of civilian labor force)

Occupation	1982	1983	1984	1985	1986	1987	1988	1989	1990	1991	1992	1993	1994	1995
UNEMPLOYED PERSONS														
Total, 16 years and over	10 678	10 717	8 539	8 312	8 237	7 425	6 701	6 528	7 047	8 628	9 613	8 940	7 996	7 404
Managerial and professional specialty	789	795	663	645	653	650	577	613	666	889	1 009	984	907	880
Executive, administrative, and managerial	398	396	320	329	336	350	311	348	350	494	576	527	454	420
Professional specialty	391	399	343	316	317	300	266	265	316	395	433	457	453	460
Technical, sales, and administrative support	2 014	2 116	1 706	1 694	1 700	1 595	1 479	1 470	1 641	1 977	2 308	2 111	1 962	1 744
Technicians and related support	135	152	96	110	114	104	95	90	116	133	176	165	127	113
Sales occupations	743	850	715	702	718	691	652	643	720	857	985	927	907	795
Administrative support, including clerical	1 136	1 114	896	882	868	799	732	738	804	988	1 147	1 020	928	836
Service occupation	1 628	1 697	1 413	1 386	1 381	1 259	1 136	1 088	1 139	1 330	1 461	1 401	1 471	1 378
Private household	69	79	74	69	69	55	54	55	47	56	66	65	91	99
Protective service	116	120	102	85	90	94	81	74	74	101	108	108	96	86
Service, except private household and protective	1 444	1 498	1 237	1 233	1 223	1 110	1 000	960	1 018	1 172	1 287	1 228	1 285	1 193
Precision production, craft, and repair	1 403	1 466	1 051	1 038	1 038	875	773	762	861	1 149	1 294	1 155	910	860
Mechanics and repairers	316	344	229	225	226	191	166	161	175	246	281	258	201	182
Construction trades	714	709	560	531	522	470	405	428	483	655	730	631	518	501
Other precision production, craft, and repair	373	413	262	282	290	214	202	173	203	248	283	266	191	177
Operators, fabricators, and laborers	3 314	2 955	2 193	2 140	2 089	1 820	1 620	1 578	1 714	2 062	2 151	1 926	1 761	1 618
Machine operators, assemblers, and inspectors	1 623	1 411	954	980	907	777	673	678	727	903	922	816	672	629
Transportation and material moving occupations	626	596	454	422	431	366	317	306	329	398	428	404	364	329
Handlers, equipment cleaners, helpers, and laborers	1 066	948	785	739	752	677	630	594	657	761	802	706	725	660
Construction laborers	220	207	194	186	198	189	192	152	177	204	200	172	172	179
Other handlers, equipment cleaners, helpers, and laborers	846	740	591	553	554	488	439	442	481	556	601	534	552	481
Farming, forestry, and fishing	349	407	332	315	293	268	260	234	237	299	320	310	333	311
UNEMPLOYMENT RATES														
Total, 16 years and over	9.7	9.6	7.5	7.2	7.0	6.2	5.5	5.3	5.6	6.8	7.5	6.9	6.1	5.6
Managerial and professional specialty	3.3	3.3	2.6	2.4	2.4	2.3	1.9	2.0	2.1	2.8	3.1	3.0	2.6	2.4
Executive, administrative, and managerial	3.6	3.5	2.7	2.6	2.6	2.6	2.1	2.3	2.3	3.2	3.8	3.3	2.7	2.4
Professional specialty	3.0	3.0	2.5	2.3	2.2	2.0	1.7	1.7	2.0	2.4	2.6	2.6	2.5	2.5
Technical, sales, and administrative support	6.1	6.3	5.0	4.9	4.7	4.3	4.0	3.9	4.3	5.2	5.9	5.4	5.0	4.5
Technicians and related support	4.3	4.7	2.9	3.3	3.3	3.0	2.6	2.4	2.9	3.4	4.0	3.9	3.2	2.8
Sales occupations	6.2	6.7	5.4	5.3	5.1	4.9	4.5	4.4	4.8	5.7	6.6	6.1	5.8	5.0
Administrative support, including clerical	6.4	6.4	5.1	4.9	4.7	4.2	3.9	3.9	4.1	5.1	5.8	5.2	4.7	4.3
Service occupation	10.8	10.9	9.1	8.8	8.6	7.7	6.9	6.5	6.6	7.6	8.2	7.7	8.0	7.5
Private household	6.2	7.4	6.9	6.4	6.5	5.6	5.7	5.9	5.6	6.5	6.9	6.5	10.0	10.7
Protective service	6.7	6.7	5.7	4.7	4.8	4.7	4.0	3.6	3.6	4.6	4.9	4.7	4.1	3.7
Service, except private household and protective	11.8	11.8	9.7	9.5	9.3	8.3	7.4	7.0	7.1	8.1	8.8	8.2	8.5	7.9
Precision production, craft, and repair	10.6	10.6	7.5	7.2	7.2	6.1	5.4	5.2	5.9	8.0	8.9	7.9	6.3	6.0
Mechanics and repairers	7.5	7.6	5.0	4.8	4.9	4.1	3.6	3.4	3.8	5.2	5.9	5.5	4.3	4.0
Construction trades	15.3	14.2	10.9	10.1	9.6	8.6	7.4	7.7	8.5	11.9	13.1	11.1	9.4	9.0
Other precision production, craft, and repair	8.7	9.6	6.0	6.4	6.6	5.0	4.7	4.0	4.7	5.9	6.7	6.3	4.5	4.2
Operators, fabricators, and laborers	16.7	15.5	11.5	11.3	10.9	9.4	8.3	8.0	8.7	10.6	11.1	10.0	9.0	8.2
Machine operators, assemblers, and inspectors	17.1	15.4	10.7	11.1	10.3	8.9	7.7	7.6	8.1	10.4	10.7	9.7	8.0	7.4
Transportation and material moving occupations	13.0	12.4	9.2	8.5	8.6	7.2	6.2	5.9	6.3	7.5	8.0	7.4	6.6	6.0
Handlers, equipment cleaners, helpers, and laborers	19.2	18.6	15.1	14.3	13.8	12.4	11.5	10.8	11.6	13.9	14.6	12.9	12.7	11.7
Construction laborers	28.2	25.8	22.5	21.3	21.0	19.8	19.4	16.8	18.1	22.1	22.9	20.3	18.9	18.7
Other handlers, equipment cleaners, helpers, and laborers	17.8	17.2	13.6	12.8	12.3	10.8	9.7	9.7	10.3	12.2	13.0	11.6	11.5	10.3
Farming, forestry, and fishing	8.5	9.9	8.5	8.3	7.8	7.1	7.0	6.4	6.4	7.9	8.3	8.4	8.4	7.9

NOTE: Data beginning in 1994 are not strictly comparable with data for 1993 and earlier years because of the introduction of a major redesign of the survey and collection methodology. Beginning in 1990, data are not strictly comparable with previous years because of the introduction of 1990 census-based population controls adjusted for the estimated undercount.

POPULATION, LABOR FORCE, AND EMPLOYMENT STATUS

Unemployed Persons by Industry and Class of Worker, 1948-1995

(Thousands of persons)

Year	All civilian workers	Experienced wage and salary workers												Government
		Total	Agri-culture	Wage and salary workers in private nonagricultural industries, except private households										
				Total	Mining	Construc-tion	Manufacturing			Transpor-tation and public util-ities	Whole-sale and retail trade	Finance, insurance, and real estate	Services, except private house-holds	
							Total	Durable goods	Nondurable goods					
1948	2 276	2 046	96	1 756	28	232	678	339	339	149	415	30	224	118
1949	3 637	3 310	132	2 871	73	380	1 242	652	590	252	578	36	310	175
1950	3 288	2 990	162	2 512	61	348	981	466	515	189	580	40	313	178
1951	2 055	1 857	71	1 578	36	218	637	271	366	95	373	27	192	111
1952	1 883	1 707	73	1 453	35	218	573	266	307	95	326	33	173	103
1953	1 834	1 671	81	1 419	45	227	536	253	283	90	315	34	172	100
1954	3 532	3 230	133	2 827	106	386	1 232	720	512	231	549	46	277	151
1955	2 852	2 568	124	2 188	69	337	821	436	385	163	464	49	285	140
1956	2 750	2 443	126	2 081	50	313	832	448	384	127	459	39	261	118
1957	2 859	2 542	118	2 181	41	349	901	502	399	139	461	42	248	139
1958	4 602	4 096	180	3 584	72	523	1 605	1 036	569	246	705	68	365	190
1959	3 740	3 252	158	2 782	59	466	1 055	611	444	178	617	63	344	175
1960	3 852	3 337	159	2 847	59	463	1 103	626	477	193	637	63	329	191
1961	4 714	4 061	173	3 516	67	544	1 376	835	541	218	783	91	437	212
1962	3 911	3 342	127	2 889	46	466	1 045	575	470	166	678	82	406	188
1963	4 070	3 415	158	2 916	41	456	1 061	573	488	170	689	75	424	201
1964	3 786	3 134	158	2 643	37	390	941	498	443	143	649	75	408	198
1965	3 366	2 732	114	2 320	29	364	775	382	393	118	585	70	379	191
1966	2 875	2 331	89	1 957	20	286	651	325	326	88	528	62	322	194
1967	2 975	2 489	96	2 098	19	257	775	418	357	100	521	80	346	210
1968	2 817	2 356	86	1 971	16	247	691	368	323	87	513	74	343	218
1969	2 832	2 372	76	1 997	15	225	705	382	323	99	530	73	350	229
1970	4 093	3 526	94	3 070	16	380	1 195	719	475	150	732	102	495	282
1971	5 016	4 300	100	3 731	23	428	1 401	841	559	178	948	128	625	388
1972	4 882	4 122	103	3 537	19	450	1 154	653	501	168	994	138	613	409
1973	4 365	3 646	95	3 091	19	407	939	500	439	143	896	117	570	385
1974	5 156	4 391	110	3 769	20	486	1 257	703	554	162	1 058	139	648	442
1975	7 929	6 970	151	6 110	31	807	2 333	1 431	902	278	1 493	217	952	620
1976	7 406	6 387	180	5 421	37	694	1 700	987	714	246	1 527	200	1 017	698
1977	6 991	5 915	171	4 987	33	593	1 474	805	669	242	1 473	186	986	677
1978	6 202	5 220	142	4 359	37	530	1 244	661	583	201	1 295	161	891	637
1979	6 137	5 217	148	4 391	45	541	1 306	702	603	206	1 250	165	879	608
1980	7 637	6 634	175	5 710	65	740	1 991	1 254	736	280	1 443	188	1 004	681
1981	8 273	7 129	201	6 089	70	809	1 915	1 139	777	304	1 609	199	1 182	767
1982	10 678	9 275	260	8 128	154	1 031	2 771	1 788	983	397	2 066	276	1 433	799
1983	10 717	9 276	300	7 985	182	1 005	2 454	1 562	892	424	2 109	272	1 539	875
1984	8 539	7 236	243	6 145	103	817	1 654	955	699	330	1 710	232	1 299	739
1985	8 312	7 074	233	6 088	96	778	1 694	1 004	690	316	1 679	228	1 297	651
1986	8 237	7 019	222	6 097	134	809	1 559	910	650	313	1 706	239	1 336	603
1987	7 425	6 313	191	5 434	87	724	1 305	749	556	277	1 582	225	1 234	603
1988	6 701	5 718	192	4 943	62	669	1 161	653	508	246	1 433	221	1 151	497
1989	6 528	5 616	176	4 866	42	634	1 140	634	506	251	1 412	230	1 157	493
1990	7 047	6 104	190	5 354	36	718	1 289	762	527	252	1 551	221	1 287	492
1991	8 628	7 512	231	6 593	60	946	1 572	950	621	353	1 851	290	1 522	611
1992	9 613	8 361	251	7 344	56	1 020	1 663	979	685	373	2 097	332	1 802	675
1993	8 940	7 708	224	6 751	52	874	1 487	842	645	352	1 964	303	1 719	641
1994	7 996	7 092	218	6 113	37	724	1 154	630	524	340	1 899	271	1 688	645
1995	7 404	6 533	225	5 636	34	737	1 030	534	496	314	1 682	240	1 599	552

NOTE: Data beginning in 1994 are not strictly comparable with data for 1993 and earlier years because of the introduction of a major redesign of the survey and collection methodology. Beginning in 1990, data are not strictly comparable with previous years because of the introduction of 1990 census-based population controls adjusted for the estimated undercount.

Unemployment Rates by Industry and Class of Worker, 1948-1995

(Percent of civilian labor force)

Year	All civilian workers	Experienced wage and salary workers												
		Total	Agri-culture	Wage and salary workers in private nonagricultural industries, except private households										Govern-ment
				Total	Mining	Construc-tion	Manufacturing			Transpor-tation and public util-ities	Whole-sale and retail trade	Finance, insurance, and real estate	Services, except private house-holds	
							Total	Durable goods	Nondurable goods					
1948	3.8	4.3	5.5	4.5	3.1	8.7	4.2	4.0	4.4	3.5	4.7	1.8	5.0	2.2
1949	5.9	6.8	7.1	7.3	8.9	14.0	8.0	8.1	7.8	5.9	6.2	2.1	6.5	3.1
1950	5.3	6.0	9.0	6.2	6.9	12.2	6.2	5.7	6.7	4.6	6.0	2.2	6.2	3.0
1951	3.3	3.7	4.4	3.9	4.0	7.2	3.9	3.1	4.7	2.3	3.9	1.5	4.0	1.8
1952	3.0	3.4	4.8	3.6	3.8	6.7	3.5	3.0	4.1	2.3	3.5	1.8	3.4	1.6
1953	2.9	3.2	5.6	3.4	4.6	7.2	3.1	2.6	3.8	2.2	3.4	1.8	3.3	1.5
1954	5.5	6.2	9.0	6.7	14.4	12.9	7.1	7.3	6.9	5.6	5.7	2.3	5.2	2.2
1955	4.4	4.8	7.2	5.1	9.1	10.9	4.7	4.4	5.2	4.0	4.7	2.4	5.1	2.0
1956	4.1	4.4	7.4	4.7	6.8	10.0	4.7	4.4	5.2	3.0	4.5	1.8	4.4	1.7
1957	4.3	4.6	6.9	4.9	5.9	10.9	5.1	4.9	5.3	3.3	4.5	1.8	4.0	1.9
1958	6.8	7.3	10.3	8.0	11.0	15.3	9.3	10.6	7.7	6.1	6.8	2.9	5.6	2.5
1959	5.5	5.7	9.1	6.2	9.7	13.4	6.1	6.2	6.0	4.4	5.8	2.5	5.1	2.2
1960	5.5	5.7	8.3	6.2	9.7	13.5	6.2	6.4	6.1	4.6	5.9	2.4	4.8	2.4
1961	6.7	6.8	9.6	7.5	11.1	15.7	7.8	8.5	6.8	5.3	7.3	3.3	6.0	2.5
1962	5.5	5.6	7.5	6.2	7.8	13.5	5.8	5.7	6.0	4.1	6.3	3.0	5.4	2.1
1963	5.7	5.6	9.2	6.1	7.2	13.3	5.7	5.5	6.0	4.2	6.2	2.7	5.6	2.2
1964	5.2	5.0	9.7	5.4	6.7	11.2	5.0	4.7	5.4	3.5	5.7	2.6	5.2	2.1
1965	4.5	4.3	7.6	4.6	5.4	10.1	4.0	3.5	4.7	2.9	5.0	2.3	4.6	1.9
1966	3.8	3.5	6.6	3.8	3.7	8.0	3.2	2.8	3.8	2.1	4.4	2.1	3.8	1.8
1967	3.8	3.6	6.9	3.9	3.4	7.4	3.7	3.4	4.1	2.4	4.2	2.5	3.9	1.8
1968	3.6	3.4	6.3	3.6	3.1	6.9	3.3	3.0	3.7	2.0	4.0	2.2	3.7	1.8
1969	3.5	3.3	6.1	3.5	2.9	6.0	3.3	3.0	3.7	2.2	4.1	2.1	3.5	1.9
1970	4.9	4.8	7.5	5.3	3.1	9.7	5.6	5.7	5.4	3.2	5.3	2.8	4.7	2.2
1971	5.9	5.7	7.9	6.3	4.0	10.4	6.8	7.0	6.5	3.8	6.4	3.3	5.8	2.9
1972	5.6	5.3	7.7	5.8	3.2	10.3	5.6	5.5	5.8	3.5	6.4	3.4	5.4	3.0
1973	4.9	4.5	7.0	4.9	2.9	8.9	4.4	3.9	5.0	3.0	5.7	2.7	4.8	2.7
1974	5.6	5.3	7.5	5.8	3.0	10.7	5.8	5.4	6.3	3.3	6.5	3.1	5.2	3.0
1975	8.5	8.2	10.4	9.2	4.1	18.0	10.9	11.3	10.4	5.6	8.7	4.9	7.2	4.1
1976	7.7	7.3	11.8	8.0	4.6	15.5	7.9	7.7	8.2	5.0	8.6	4.3	7.3	4.4
1977	7.1	6.6	11.2	7.1	3.8	12.7	6.7	6.2	7.4	4.7	8.0	3.8	6.8	4.2
1978	6.1	5.6	8.9	6.0	4.2	10.6	5.5	5.0	6.3	3.7	6.9	3.1	5.8	3.9
1979	5.8	5.5	9.3	5.8	4.9	10.3	5.6	5.0	6.5	3.7	6.5	3.0	5.5	3.7
1980	7.1	6.9	11.0	7.4	6.4	14.1	8.5	8.9	7.9	4.9	7.4	3.4	6.0	4.1
1981	7.6	7.3	12.1	7.7	6.0	15.6	8.3	8.2	8.4	5.2	8.1	3.5	6.7	4.7
1982	9.7	9.3	14.7	10.2	13.4	20.0	12.3	13.3	10.8	6.8	10.0	4.7	7.7	4.9
1983	9.6	9.2	16.0	9.9	17.0	18.4	11.2	12.1	10.0	7.4	10.0	4.5	7.9	5.3
1984	7.5	7.1	13.5	7.4	10.0	14.3	7.5	7.2	7.8	5.5	8.0	3.7	6.5	4.5
1985	7.2	6.8	13.2	7.2	9.5	13.1	7.7	7.6	7.8	5.1	7.6	3.5	6.2	3.9
1986	7.0	6.6	12.5	7.0	13.5	13.1	7.1	6.9	7.4	5.1	7.6	3.5	6.1	3.6
1987	6.2	5.8	10.5	6.2	10.0	11.6	6.0	5.8	6.3	4.5	6.9	3.1	5.4	3.5
1988	5.5	5.2	10.6	5.5	7.9	10.6	5.3	5.0	5.7	3.9	6.2	3.0	4.8	2.8
1989	5.3	5.0	9.6	5.3	5.8	10.0	5.1	4.8	5.5	3.9	6.0	3.1	4.7	2.7
1990	5.6	5.3	9.8	5.7	4.8	11.1	5.8	5.8	5.8	3.9	6.4	3.0	5.0	2.7
1991	6.8	6.6	11.8	7.1	7.8	15.5	7.3	7.5	6.9	5.3	7.6	4.0	5.8	3.3
1992	7.5	7.2	12.5	7.8	8.0	16.8	7.8	8.0	7.6	5.5	8.4	4.6	6.5	3.6
1993	6.9	6.6	11.7	7.1	7.4	14.4	7.2	7.1	7.4	5.1	7.8	4.1	6.1	3.3
1994	6.1	5.9	11.3	6.3	5.4	11.8	5.6	5.2	6.0	4.8	7.4	3.6	5.7	3.4
1995	5.6	5.4	11.1	5.7	5.2	11.5	4.9	4.4	5.7	4.5	6.5	3.3	5.2	2.9

NOTE: Data beginning in 1994 are not strictly comparable with data for 1993 and earlier years because of the introduction of a major redesign of the survey and collection methodology. Beginning in 1990, data are not strictly comparable with previous years because of the introduction of 1990 census-based population controls adjusted for the estimated undercount.

POPULATION, LABOR FORCE, AND EMPLOYMENT STATUS

Unemployed Persons by Duration of Unemployment, 1948-1995

(Thousands of persons)

| Year | Total | Less than 5 weeks | 5 to 14 weeks | 15 weeks and over | | | Average duration | Median duration |
				Total	15 to 26 weeks	27 weeks and over		
1948	2 276	1 300	669	309	193	116	8.6	
1949	3 637	1 756	1 194	684	428	256	10.0	
1950	3 288	1 450	1 055	782	425	357	12.1	
1951	2 055	1 177	574	303	166	137	9.7	
1952	1 883	1 135	516	232	148	84	8.4	
1953	1 834	1 142	482	210	132	78	8.0	
1954	3 532	1 605	1 116	812	495	317	11.8	
1955	2 852	1 335	815	702	366	336	13.0	
1956	2 750	1 412	805	533	301	232	11.3	
1957	2 859	1 408	891	560	321	239	10.5	
1958	4 602	1 753	1 396	1 452	785	667	13.9	
1959	3 740	1 585	1 114	1 040	469	571	14.4	
1960	3 852	1 719	1 176	957	503	454	12.8	
1961	4 714	1 806	1 376	1 532	728	804	15.6	
1962	3 911	1 663	1 134	1 119	534	585	14.7	
1963	4 070	1 751	1 231	1 088	535	553	14.0	
1964	3 786	1 697	1 117	973	491	482	13.3	
1965	3 366	1 628	983	755	404	351	11.8	
1966	2 875	1 573	779	526	287	239	10.4	
1967	2 975	1 634	893	448	271	177	8.7	2.3
1968	2 817	1 594	810	412	256	156	8.4	4.5
1969	2 832	1 629	827	375	242	133	7.8	4.4
1970	4 093	2 139	1 290	663	428	235	8.6	4.9
1971	5 016	2 245	1 585	1 187	668	519	11.3	6.3
1972	4 882	2 242	1 472	1 167	601	566	12.0	6.2
1973	4 365	2 224	1 314	826	483	343	10.0	5.2
1974	5 156	2 604	1 597	955	574	381	9.8	5.2
1975	7 929	2 940	2 484	2 505	1 303	1 203	14.2	8.4
1976	7 406	2 844	2 196	2 366	1 018	1 348	15.8	8.2
1977	6 991	2 919	2 132	1 942	913	1 028	14.3	7.0
1978	6 202	2 865	1 923	1 414	766	648	11.9	5.9
1979	6 137	2 950	1 946	1 241	706	535	10.8	5.4
1980	7 637	3 295	2 470	1 871	1 052	820	11.9	6.5
1981	8 273	3 449	2 539	2 285	1 122	1 162	13.7	6.9
1982	10 678	3 883	3 311	3 485	1 708	1 776	15.6	8.7
1983	10 717	3 570	2 937	4 210	1 652	2 559	20.0	10.1
1984	8 539	3 350	2 451	2 737	1 104	1 634	18.2	7.9
1985	8 312	3 498	2 509	2 305	1 025	1 280	15.6	6.8
1986	8 237	3 448	2 557	2 232	1 045	1 187	15.0	6.9
1987	7 425	3 246	2 196	1 983	943	1 040	14.5	6.5
1988	6 701	3 084	2 007	1 610	801	809	13.5	5.9
1989	6 528	3 174	1 978	1 375	730	646	11.9	4.8
1990	7 047	3 265	2 257	1 525	822	703	12.0	5.3
1991	8 628	3 480	2 791	2 357	1 246	1 111	13.7	6.8
1992	9 613	3 376	2 830	3 408	1 453	1 954	17.7	8.7
1993	8 940	3 262	2 584	3 094	1 297	1 798	18.0	8.3
1994	7 996	2 728	2 408	2 860	1 237	1 623	18.8	9.2
1995	7 404	2 700	2 342	2 363	1 085	1 278	16.6	8.3

NOTE: Data beginning in 1994 are not strictly comparable with data for 1993 and earlier years because of the introduction of a major redesign of the survey and collection methodology. Beginning in 1990, data are not strictly comparable with previous years because of the introduction of 1990 census-based population controls adjusted for the estimated undercount.

Long Term Unemployment by Industry and Occupation, 1982-1995

(Thousands of persons)

Industry and occupation	1982	1983	1984	1985	1986	1987	1988	1989	1990	1991	1992	1993	1994	1995
UNEMPLOYED 15 WEEKS AND OVER														
Total	3 485	4 210	2 737	2 305	2 232	1 983	1 610	1 375	1 525	2 357	3 408	3 094	2 860	2 363
WAGE AND SALARY WORKERS BY INDUSTRY														
Agriculture	59	75	61	54	51	42	39	32	31	47	57	56	72	58
Mining	52	100	49	41	57	42	28	15	11	23	25	27	21	13
Construction	376	425	279	230	234	209	169	153	162	285	402	330	238	233
Manufacturing	1 093	1 292	685	598	547	449	361	299	353	525	725	655	482	371
Durable goods	758	904	429	387	354	273	228	177	221	334	457	394	283	198
Nondurable goods	335	388	255	212	193	176	133	123	132	192	268	262	199	172
Transportation and public utilities	164	220	148	114	114	99	86	74	75	130	190	171	171	135
Wholesale and retail trade	605	745	495	413	423	387	295	268	303	448	699	630	628	493
Finance and services	692	858	617	532	501	457	405	350	403	615	921	840	825	711
Public administration	106	126	89	74	69	79	55	42	36	66	71	85	79	57
EXPERIENCED WORKERS BY OCCUPATION														
Managerial and professional speciality	261	340	224	196	190	202	164	156	184	310	473	429	371	320
Executive, administrative, and managerial	146	185	124	110	103	116	98	95	101	184	284	244	203	170
Professional speciality	115	154	99	85	87	86	66	61	83	126	189	185	168	150
Technical, sales, and administrative support	611	775	501	421	419	403	338	281	352	543	858	773	699	553
Technicians and related support	45	64	30	30	35	31	31	18	31	45	74	67	48	43
Sales occupations	221	280	187	163	166	173	141	114	141	210	338	296	303	231
Administrative support, including clerical	344	430	284	228	218	200	166	149	180	288	446	410	347	279
Service occupations	473	585	419	363	345	293	232	209	215	308	427	404	470	407
Precision production, craft, and repair	500	669	386	330	335	266	215	193	211	363	533	460	335	287
Operators, fabricators, and laborers	1 276	1 401	832	708	667	576	462	376	413	618	810	722	640	517
Machine operators, assemblers, and inspectors	631	715	377	327	297	254	198	164	180	275	354	312	237	204
Transportation and material moving occupations	252	283	174	144	145	126	93	75	84	127	172	167	143	99
Handlers, equipment cleaners, helpers, and laborers	394	402	281	238	225	195	171	137	148	216	284	244	260	215
Farming, forestry, and fishing	95	112	92	76	73	65	63	48	43	62	75	82	113	81
UNEMPLOYED 27 WEEKS AND OVER														
Total	1 776	2 559	1 634	1 280	1 187	1 040	809	646	703	1 111	1 954	1 798	1 623	1 278
WAGE AND SALARY WORKERS BY INDUSTRY														
Agriculture	25	36	28	27	26	19	16	13	13	17	26	26	36	27
Mining	26	64	34	26	32	28	17	8	5	13	19	16	14	9
Construction	182	251	148	112	114	101	78	66	69	125	219	188	125	125
Manufacturing	584	865	451	344	318	249	194	146	168	255	455	392	282	203
Durable goods	413	628	298	234	209	159	128	85	102	160	294	237	170	108
Nondurable goods	171	237	153	110	109	90	66	62	65	95	162	155	113	95
Transportation and public utilities	86	141	90	66	57	52	46	39	34	67	120	102	107	77
Wholesale and retail trade	292	419	282	231	212	189	154	120	139	203	378	368	350	259
Finance and services	359	496	359	295	264	239	191	160	179	293	527	492	452	380
Public administration	61	75	52	40	37	43	28	22	20	32	45	53	50	32
EXPERIENCED WORKERS BY OCCUPATION														
Managerial and professional speciality	141	191	134	108	97	107	73	73	86	153	290	266	214	181
Executive, administrative, and managerial	80	104	74	63	52	60	43	42	48	88	175	151	115	96
Professional speciality	61	87	59	45	45	47	30	31	38	66	115	115	99	85
Technical, sales, and administrative support	289	436	282	225	201	198	162	119	152	247	498	460	389	289
Technicians and related support	17	36	17	15	18	16	14	8	14	19	48	41	29	26
Sales occupations	103	151	101	88	78	82	71	48	62	91	183	175	170	117
Administrative support, including clerical	169	250	164	122	105	100	77	62	76	136	267	244	189	146
Service occupations	243	345	248	209	190	157	125	97	104	146	231	234	268	228
Precision production, craft, and repair	255	430	232	176	191	143	108	98	95	169	308	270	184	156
Operators, fabricators, and laborers	678	911	524	410	362	312	247	183	197	302	480	416	373	276
Machine operators, assemblers, and inspectors	335	471	242	189	167	135	107	83	86	140	217	186	143	105
Transportation and material moving occupations	138	179	103	81	71	70	52	37	41	60	102	98	86	51
Handlers, equipment cleaners, helpers, and laborers	205	262	179	140	124	107	88	64	70	102	161	132	144	119
Farming, forestry, and fishing	44	59	46	37	36	33	29	22	17	25	33	39	57	41

NOTE: Data beginning in 1994 are not strictly comparable with data for 1993 and earlier years because of the introduction of a major redesign of the survey and collection methodology. Beginning in 1990, data are not strictly comparable with previous years because of the introduction of 1990 census-based population controls adjusted for the estimated undercount.

Unemployed Persons and Unemployment Rates by Sex, Age, Race, and Reason for Unemployment, 1967-1995

(Numbers in thousands; Percent of civilian labor force)

Year, sex, and race	Number unemployed					Unemployment rate			
				Entrants				Entrants	
	Total	Job losers	Job leavers	Reentrants	New entrants	Job losers	Job leavers	Reentrants	New entrants
TOTAL									
1967	2 975	1 229	438	945	396	1.6	0.6	1.2	0.5
1968	2 817	1 070	431	909	407	1.4	0.5	1.2	0.5
1969	2 832	1 017	436	965	413	1.3	0.5	1.2	0.5
1970	4 093	1 811	550	1 228	504	2.2	0.7	1.5	0.6
1971	5 016	2 323	590	1 472	630	2.8	0.7	1.7	0.7
1972	4 882	2 108	641	1 456	677	2.4	0.7	1.7	0.8
1973	4 365	1 694	683	1 340	649	1.9	0.8	1.5	0.7
1974	5 156	2 242	768	1 463	681	2.4	0.8	1.6	0.7
1975	7 929	4 386	827	1 892	823	4.7	0.9	2.0	0.9
1976	7 406	3 679	903	1 928	895	3.8	0.9	2.0	0.9
1977	6 991	3 166	909	1 963	953	3.2	0.9	2.0	1.0
1978	6 202	2 585	874	1 857	885	2.5	0.9	1.8	0.9
1979	6 137	2 635	880	1 806	817	2.5	0.8	1.7	0.8
1980	7 637	3 947	891	1 927	872	3.7	0.8	1.8	0.8
1981	8 273	4 267	923	2 102	981	3.9	0.8	1.9	0.9
1982	10 678	6 268	840	2 384	1 185	5.7	0.8	2.2	1.1
1983	10 717	6 258	830	2 412	1 216	5.6	0.7	2.2	1.1
1984	8 539	4 421	823	2 184	1 110	3.9	0.7	1.9	1.0
1985	8 312	4 139	877	2 256	1 039	3.6	0.8	2.0	0.9
1986	8 237	4 033	1 015	2 160	1 029	3.4	0.9	1.8	0.9
1987	7 425	3 566	965	1 974	920	3.0	0.8	1.6	0.8
1988	6 701	3 092	983	1 809	816	2.5	0.8	1.5	0.7
1989	6 528	2 983	1 024	1 843	677	2.4	0.8	1.5	0.5
1990	7 047	3 387	1 041	1 930	688	2.7	0.8	1.5	0.5
1991	8 628	4 694	1 004	2 139	792	3.7	0.8	1.7	0.6
1992	9 613	5 389	1 002	2 285	937	4.2	0.8	1.8	0.7
1993	8 940	4 848	976	2 198	919	3.8	0.8	1.7	0.7
1994	7 996	3 815	791	2 786	604	2.9	0.6	2.1	0.5
1995	7 404	3 476	824	2 525	579	2.6	0.6	1.9	0.4
MEN, 20 YEARS AND OVER									
1967	1 060	678	165	194	25	1.5	0.4	0.4	0.1
1968	993	599	167	205	22	1.3	0.4	0.4	0.1
1969	963	556	164	216	27	1.2	0.4	0.5	0.1
1970	1 638	1 066	209	318	44	2.2	0.4	0.7	0.1
1971	2 097	1 391	239	411	57	2.9	0.5	0.9	0.1
1972	1 948	1 219	248	420	60	2.5	0.5	0.9	0.1
1973	1 624	959	258	350	56	1.9	0.5	0.7	0.1
1974	1 957	1 276	276	356	48	2.5	0.5	0.7	0.1
1975	3 476	2 598	298	506	76	5.0	0.6	1.0	0.1
1976	3 098	2 167	323	521	86	4.1	0.6	1.0	0.2
1977	2 794	1 816	335	540	103	3.4	0.6	1.0	0.2
1978	2 328	1 433	337	471	86	2.6	0.6	0.9	0.2
1979	2 308	1 464	325	446	73	2.6	0.6	0.8	0.1
1980	3 353	2 389	359	516	90	4.2	0.6	0.9	0.2
1981	3 615	2 565	356	592	102	4.5	0.6	1.0	0.2
1982	5 089	3 965	327	678	119	6.8	0.6	1.2	0.2
1983	5 257	4 088	336	695	138	6.9	0.6	1.2	0.2
1984	3 932	2 800	324	663	146	4.7	0.5	1.1	0.2
1985	3 715	2 568	352	671	124	4.3	0.6	1.1	0.2
1986	3 751	2 568	444	611	128	4.1	0.7	1.0	0.2
1987	3 369	2 289	413	558	108	3.7	0.7	0.9	0.2
1988	2 987	1 939	416	534	98	3.1	0.7	0.9	0.2
1989	2 867	1 843	394	541	88	2.9	0.6	0.8	0.1
1990	3 239	2 100	431	626	82	3.2	0.7	1.0	0.1
1991	4 195	2 982	411	698	105	4.6	0.6	1.1	0.2
1992	4 717	3 420	421	765	111	5.2	0.6	1.2	0.2
1993	4 287	2 996	429	747	114	4.5	0.6	1.1	0.2
1994	3 627	2 296	367	898	65	3.4	0.5	1.3	0.1
1995	3 239	2 051	356	775	57	3.0	0.5	1.2	0.1

Unemployed Persons and Unemployment Rates by Sex, Age, Race, and Reason for Unemployment, 1967-1995—Continued

(Numbers in thousands; Percent of civilian labor force)

Year, sex, and race	Number unemployed					Unemployment rate			
	Total	Job losers	Job leavers	Entrants		Job losers	Job leavers	Entrants	
				Reentrants	New entrants			Reentrants	New entrants
WOMEN, 20 YEARS AND OVER									
1967	1 078	401	179	454	54	1.6	0.7	1.8	0.2
1968	985	341	167	422	55	1.3	0.6	1.6	0.2
1969	1 015	335	171	455	55	1.2	0.6	1.7	0.2
1970	1 349	546	214	531	58	1.9	0.8	1.9	0.2
1971	1 658	700	235	651	72	2.5	0.8	2.3	0.2
1972	1 625	641	264	641	80	2.2	0.9	2.1	0.3
1973	1 507	522	280	625	80	1.6	0.9	2.0	0.3
1974	1 777	685	319	673	100	2.1	1.0	2.1	0.3
1975	2 684	1 339	375	858	114	4.0	1.1	2.6	0.3
1976	2 588	1 124	427	912	126	3.2	1.2	2.6	0.4
1977	2 535	1 031	419	945	140	2.8	1.2	2.6	0.4
1978	2 292	852	371	930	138	2.2	1.0	2.4	0.4
1979	2 276	851	370	908	145	2.1	0.9	2.3	0.4
1980	2 615	1 170	376	930	139	2.8	0.9	2.3	0.3
1981	2 895	1 317	404	1 023	151	3.1	1.0	2.4	0.4
1982	3 613	1 844	379	1 197	192	4.2	0.9	2.7	0.4
1983	3 632	1 801	384	1 235	212	4.0	0.9	2.8	0.5
1984	3 107	1 350	386	1 151	220	2.9	0.8	2.5	0.5
1985	3 129	1 296	412	1 195	227	2.7	0.9	2.5	0.5
1986	3 032	1 225	426	1 175	206	2.5	0.9	2.4	0.4
1987	2 709	1 067	406	1 041	194	2.2	0.8	2.1	0.4
1988	2 487	946	408	965	168	1.9	0.8	1.9	0.3
1989	2 467	942	430	958	137	1.8	0.8	1.8	0.3
1990	2 596	1 054	429	966	146	2.0	0.8	1.8	0.3
1991	3 074	1 423	413	1 075	163	2.6	0.8	2.0	0.3
1992	3 469	1 710	433	1 142	183	3.1	0.8	2.1	0.3
1993	3 288	1 619	395	1 098	176	2.9	0.7	2.0	0.3
1994	3 049	1 334	339	1 253	122	2.4	0.6	2.2	0.2
1995	2 819	1 211	366	1 135	107	2.1	0.6	2.0	0.2
BOTH SEXES, 16 TO 19 YEARS									
1967	839	151	95	297	317	2.3	1.5	4.6	4.9
1968	838	130	97	281	330	2.0	1.5	4.2	5.0
1969	853	127	101	295	331	1.8	1.5	4.2	4.8
1970	1 106	200	126	378	401	2.8	1.7	5.2	5.5
1971	1 262	233	117	410	501	3.1	1.6	5.5	6.7
1972	1 308	248	129	395	536	3.1	1.6	4.9	6.6
1973	1 235	212	146	364	513	2.4	1.7	4.3	6.0
1974	1 422	280	173	436	533	3.1	2.0	4.9	6.0
1975	1 767	450	155	529	634	5.1	1.7	6.0	7.1
1976	1 719	387	153	496	683	4.3	1.7	5.5	7.5
1977	1 663	318	156	477	711	3.4	1.7	5.1	7.6
1978	1 583	300	167	455	660	3.1	1.7	4.7	6.8
1979	1 555	319	184	452	599	3.3	1.9	4.7	6.2
1980	1 669	388	156	481	643	4.1	1.7	5.1	6.9
1981	1 763	385	162	487	728	4.3	1.8	5.4	8.1
1982	1 977	460	134	509	874	5.4	1.6	6.0	10.2
1983	1 829	370	110	482	867	4.6	1.3	5.9	10.6
1984	1 499	271	114	370	745	3.4	1.4	4.7	9.4
1985	1 468	275	113	390	689	3.5	1.4	4.9	8.7
1986	1 454	240	145	374	695	3.0	1.8	4.7	8.8
1987	1 347	210	146	375	617	2.7	1.8	4.7	7.7
1988	1 226	207	159	310	550	2.6	2.0	3.9	6.8
1989	1 194	198	200	345	452	2.5	2.5	4.3	5.7
1990	1 212	233	181	338	460	3.0	2.3	4.3	5.9
1991	1 359	289	180	365	524	4.0	2.5	5.0	7.2
1992	1 427	259	149	377	643	3.6	2.1	5.3	9.1
1993	1 365	233	151	353	628	3.3	2.1	4.9	8.8
1994	1 320	185	84	634	416	2.5	1.1	8.5	5.6
1995	1 346	214	102	615	415	2.8	1.3	7.9	5.3

POPULATION, LABOR FORCE, AND EMPLOYMENT STATUS

Unemployed Persons and Unemployment Rates by Sex, Age, Race, and Reason for Unemployment, 1967-1995—Continued

(Numbers in thousands; Percent of civilian labor force)

Year, sex, and race	Number unemployed					Unemployment rate			
				Entrants				Entrants	
	Total	Job losers	Job leavers	Reentrants	New entrants	Job losers	Job leavers	Reentrants	New entrants
WHITE									
1967	2 338	987	347	740	293	....	0.5	1.1	0.4
1968	2 226	849	346	718	313	....	0.5	1.0	0.5
1969	2 260	816	357	767	321	....	0.5	1.1	0.4
1970	3 339	1 503	456	983	396	....	0.6	1.3	0.5
1971	4 085	1 928	486	1 179	492	....	0.6	1.6	0.7
1972	3 906	1 719	531	1 136	520	....	0.7	1.5	0.7
1973	3 442	1 371	557	1 032	480	....	0.7	1.3	0.6
1974	4 097	1 813	641	1 145	498	....	0.8	1.4	0.6
1975	6 421	3 593	706	1 508	615	....	0.9	1.8	0.7
1976	5 914	2 999	766	1 484	664	3.5	0.9	1.8	0.8
1977	5 441	2 529	771	1 467	675	2.9	0.9	1.7	0.8
1978	4 698	2 008	723	1 369	598	2.2	0.8	1.5	0.7
1979	4 664	2 033	730	1 338	562	2.2	0.8	1.5	0.6
1980	5 884	3 100	733	1 447	603	3.3	0.8	1.5	0.6
1981	6 343	3 335	758	1 565	684	3.5	0.8	1.6	0.7
1982	8 241	4 949	698	1 785	809	5.2	0.7	1.9	0.8
1983	8 128	4 896	683	1 722	827	5.1	0.7	1.8	0.9
1984	6 372	3 406	680	1 566	719	3.4	0.7	1.6	0.7
1985	6 191	3 146	727	1 635	682	3.2	0.7	1.6	0.7
1986	6 140	3 076	825	1 560	680	3.0	0.8	1.5	0.7
1987	5 501	2 704	784	1 401	613	2.7	0.8	1.4	0.6
1988	4 944	2 338	776	1 298	532	2.3	0.7	1.2	0.5
1989	4 770	2 240	812	1 303	416	2.1	0.8	1.2	0.4
1990	5 186	2 570	803	1 368	445	2.4	0.7	1.3	0.4
1991	6 560	3 661	811	1 554	535	3.4	0.8	1.4	0.5
1992	7 169	4 167	775	1 625	601	3.8	0.7	1.5	0.6
1993	6 655	3 722	757	1 567	609	3.4	0.7	1.4	0.6
1994	5 892	2 972	638	1 898	385	2.7	0.6	1.7	0.3
1995	5 459	2 710	660	1 728	361	2.4	0.6	1.5	0.3
BLACK AND OTHER									
1974	1 058	243	91	205	103	....	1.1	3.3	1.8
1975	1 507	221	85	190	94	....	1.2	3.3	1.8
1976	1 492	200	79	198	93	6.0	1.2	3.9	2.0
1977	1 550	309	93	245	107	5.4	1.2	4.2	2.3
1978	1 505	395	104	294	138	4.6	1.2	3.9	2.3
1979	1 473	389	111	320	157	4.6	1.1	3.6	2.0
1980	1 752	322	126	308	168	6.3	1.2	3.6	2.0
1981	1 930	429	127	319	184	6.8	1.2	3.9	2.2
1982	2 437	793	121	385	208	9.4	1.0	4.3	2.7
1983	2 588	680	137	444	231	9.3	1.0	4.7	2.7
1984	2 167	637	138	496	278	6.7	1.0	4.1	2.6
1985	2 121	577	151	489	287	6.4	1.0	4.0	2.3
1986	2 097	602	149	469	254	5.9	1.2	3.7	2.2
1987	1 924	847	157	480	270	5.2	1.1	3.5	1.9
1988	1 757	932	164	537	296	4.5	1.2	3.0	1.7
1989	1 757	1 319	142	599	377	....	....	....	....
1990	1 860	1 362	147	690	389	....	....	....	....
1991	2 068	1 015	144	617	391	....	....	....	....
1992	2 444	993	150	620	357	....	....	....	....
1993	2 285	957	190	600	349	....	....	....	....
1994	2 104	862	182	573	307	....	....	....	....
1995	1 945	754	207	511	284	....	....	....	....

NOTE: Data beginning in 1994 are not strictly comparable with data for 1993 and earlier years because of the introduction of a major redesign of the survey and collection methodology. Beginning in 1990, data are not strictly comparable with previous years because of the introduction of 1990 census-based population controls adjusted for the estimated undercount.

Percent of the Population with Work Experience During the Year by Sex and Age, 1987-1994

Year	Total	16 to 17 years	18 to 19 years	20 to 24 years	25 to 34 years	35 to 44 years	45 to 54 years	55 to 59 years	60 to 64 years	65 to 69 years	70 years and over
TOTAL											
1987	69.7	51.8	76.6	85.5	85.7	86.1	81.6	69.4	51.3	26.2	10.2
1988	70.2	50.6	75.5	85.7	86.0	86.8	82.2	70.5	52.2	27.9	10.3
1989	70.5	51.9	75.4	84.9	86.6	86.9	82.8	70.4	52.5	28.4	10.0
1990	70.2	48.6	74.2	84.1	86.2	87.0	82.8	70.9	53.4	28.3	10.2
1991	69.5	43.4	70.8	83.4	85.9	86.6	83.0	70.3	52.9	27.2	9.8
1992	69.1	43.8	69.9	82.7	85.2	85.9	82.8	70.8	53.5	25.5	9.8
1993	69.2	42.1	70.4	82.0	85.0	85.3	82.8	71.6	51.6	27.5	10.7
1994	69.6	44.1	71.5	82.5	85.5	85.6	83.8	72.2	52.8	27.5	10.0
MEN											
1987	78.9	52.4	77.4	90.4	94.3	94.1	91.9	83.3	63.2	34.2	15.4
1988	79.1	51.8	78.9	90.7	94.3	94.6	91.6	82.1	63.1	35.6	15.6
1989	79.4	53.2	77.7	89.9	94.7	94.7	91.9	82.0	64.2	35.4	15.1
1990	78.9	50.3	76.7	88.7	94.4	94.7	91.3	82.0	65.8	35.8	14.0
1991	77.9	45.4	72.2	87.9	93.5	93.6	91.3	81.5	63.6	35.0	14.4
1992	77.4	46.6	73.7	87.1	93.3	92.8	89.9	80.9	63.2	32.4	14.3
1993	76.8	43.9	71.4	86.6	92.5	92.0	89.3	79.8	59.1	34.3	15.3
1994	77.2	44.4	74.7	87.2	92.9	92.0	90.0	81.3	61.4	33.9	14.8
WOMEN											
1987	61.3	51.1	75.8	81.0	77.3	78.5	71.9	56.7	41.0	19.6	6.8
1988	62.1	49.3	72.2	81.0	78.1	79.4	73.5	60.0	42.5	21.4	6.8
1989	62.3	50.6	73.1	80.2	78.6	79.3	74.2	59.9	42.4	22.5	6.7
1990	62.2	46.8	71.7	79.6	78.0	79.6	74.9	60.4	42.5	22.1	7.7
1991	61.8	41.4	69.4	79.0	78.3	79.9	75.3	59.9	43.6	20.6	6.7
1992	61.5	40.9	66.1	78.4	77.2	79.1	76.1	61.5	44.4	20.0	6.7
1993	62.1	40.3	69.4	77.5	77.6	78.7	76.5	63.9	44.7	22.1	7.7
1994	62.5	43.7	68.4	77.8	78.1	79.4	78.0	63.9	45.0	22.2	6.8

NOTE: Data beginning in 1994 are not strictly comparable with data for 1993 and earlier years because of the introduction of a major redesign of the survey and collection methodology.
Beginning in 1990, data are not strictly comparable with previous years because of the introduction of 1990 census-based population controls adjusted for the estimated undercount.

Number of Persons with Work Experience During the Year by Sex and Extent of Employment, 1987-1994

(Thousands of persons)

Year and sex	Total	Full-time				Part-time			
		Total	50-52 weeks	27-49 weeks	1-26 weeks	Total	50-52 weeks	27-49 weeks	1-26 weeks
TOTAL									
1987	128 315	100 288	77 015	13 361	9 912	28 027	10 973	6 594	10 460
1988	130 451	102 131	79 627	12 875	9 629	28 320	11 384	6 624	10 312
1989	132 817	104 876	81 117	14 271	9 488	27 941	11 275	6 987	9 679
1990	133 535	105 323	80 932	14 758	9 633	28 212	11 507	7 012	9 693
1991	133 410	104 472	80 385	14 491	9 596	28 938	11 946	7 003	9 989
1992	133 912	104 813	81 523	13 587	9 703	29 099	12 326	6 841	9 932
1993	136 354	106 299	83 384	13 054	9 861	30 055	12 818	6 777	10 460
1994	138 468	108 141	85 764	13 051	9 326	30 327	12 936	6 956	10 435
MEN									
1987	69 144	59 736	47 040	7 503	5 193	9 408	3 260	2 191	3 957
1988	70 021	60 504	48 299	7 329	4 876	9 517	3 468	2 199	3 850
1989	71 640	62 108	49 693	7 642	4 773	9 532	3 619	2 254	3 659
1990	71 953	62 319	49 175	8 188	4 956	9 634	3 650	2 322	3 662
1991	71 700	61 636	47 895	8 324	5 417	10 064	3 820	2 342	3 902
1992	72 007	61 722	48 300	7 965	5 457	10 285	3 864	2 354	4 067
1993	72 872	62 513	49 832	7 317	5 364	10 359	4 005	2 144	4 210
1994	73 958	63 634	51 582	7 094	4 958	10 324	3 948	2 358	4 018
WOMEN									
1987	59 171	40 552	29 975	5 858	4 719	18 619	7 713	4 403	6 503
1988	60 430	41 627	31 328	5 546	4 753	18 803	7 916	4 425	6 462
1989	61 178	42 768	31 424	6 629	4 715	18 410	7 656	4 733	6 021
1990	61 582	43 004	31 757	6 570	4 677	18 578	7 857	4 690	6 031
1991	61 712	42 837	32 491	6 167	4 179	18 875	8 126	4 662	6 087
1992	61 904	43 090	33 223	5 621	4 246	18 814	8 462	4 487	5 865
1993	63 481	43 785	33 552	5 736	4 497	19 696	8 813	4 633	6 250
1994	64 511	44 508	34 182	5 957	4 369	20 003	8 988	4 598	6 417

NOTE: Data beginning in 1994 are not strictly comparable with data for 1993 and earlier years because of the introduction of a major redesign of the survey and collection methodology. Beginning in 1990, data are not strictly comparable with previous years because of the introduction of 1990 census-based population controls adjusted for the estimated undercount.

Percent Distribution of the Population with Work Experience During the Year by Sex and Extent of Employment, 1987-1994

Year and sex	Total	Full-time				Part-time			
		Total	50-52 weeks	27-49 weeks	1-26 weeks	Total	50-52 weeks	27-49 weeks	1-26 weeks
TOTAL									
1987	100.0	78.1	60.0	10.4	7.7	21.9	8.6	5.1	8.2
1988	100.0	78.3	61.0	9.9	7.4	21.7	8.7	5.1	7.9
1989	100.0	78.9	61.1	10.7	7.1	21.1	8.5	5.3	7.3
1990	100.0	78.9	60.6	11.1	7.2	21.2	8.6	5.3	7.3
1991	100.0	78.4	60.3	10.9	7.2	21.7	9.0	5.2	7.5
1992	100.0	78.2	60.9	10.1	7.2	21.7	9.2	5.1	7.4
1993	100.0	78.0	61.2	9.6	7.2	22.1	9.4	5.0	7.7
1994	100.0	78.0	61.9	9.4	6.7	21.8	9.3	5.0	7.5
MEN									
1987	100.0	86.4	68.0	10.9	7.5	13.6	4.7	3.2	5.7
1988	100.0	86.5	69.0	10.5	7.0	13.6	5.0	3.1	5.5
1989	100.0	86.8	69.4	10.7	6.7	13.3	5.1	3.1	5.1
1990	100.0	86.6	68.3	11.4	6.9	13.4	5.1	3.2	5.1
1991	100.0	86.0	66.8	11.6	7.6	14.0	5.3	3.3	5.4
1992	100.0	85.8	67.1	11.1	7.6	14.3	5.4	3.3	5.6
1993	100.0	85.8	68.4	10.0	7.4	14.2	5.5	2.9	5.8
1994	100.0	86.0	69.7	9.6	6.7	13.9	5.3	3.2	5.4
WOMEN									
1987	100.0	68.6	50.7	9.9	8.0	31.4	13.0	7.4	11.0
1988	100.0	68.9	51.8	9.2	7.9	31.1	13.1	7.3	10.7
1989	100.0	69.9	51.4	10.8	7.7	30.0	12.5	7.7	9.8
1990	100.0	69.9	51.6	10.7	7.6	30.2	12.8	7.6	9.8
1991	100.0	69.4	52.6	10.0	6.8	30.7	13.2	7.6	9.9
1992	100.0	69.7	53.7	9.1	6.9	30.4	13.7	7.2	9.5
1993	100.0	69.0	52.9	9.0	7.1	31.0	13.9	7.3	9.8
1994	100.0	69.0	53.0	9.2	6.8	30.9	13.9	7.1	9.9

NOTE: Data beginning in 1994 are not strictly comparable with data for 1993 and earlier years because of the introduction of a major redesign of the survey and collection methodology. Beginning in 1990, data are not strictly comparable with previous years because of the introduction of 1990 census-based population controls adjusted for the estimated undercount.

POPULATION, LABOR FORCE, AND EMPLOYMENT STATUS

Extent of Unemployment During the Year by Sex, 1987-1994

(Thousands of persons; percent)

Sex and extent of unemployment	1987	1988	1989	1990	1991	1992	1993	1994
TOTAL								
Total who worked or looked for work	130 353	132 185	134 394	135 408	135 826	136 654	139 786	141 325
Percent with unemployment	14.1	12.9	12.9	14.6	15.7	15.7	14.7	13.4
Total with unemployment	18 399	17 096	17 273	19 809	21 276	21 455	20 527	18 966
Did not work but looked for work	2 037	1 735	1 577	1 874	2 415	2 742	3 432	2 857
Worked during the year	16 362	15 362	15 697	17 936	18 861	18 714	17 094	16 109
Year-round workers with 1 or 2 weeks of unemployment	792	830	833	1 056	966	871	688	746
Part-year workers with unemployment	15 570	14 532	14 864	16 880	17 895	17 843	16 406	15 363
1 to 4 weeks	3 363	3 256	3 489	3 645	3 224	2 944	2 626	2 788
5 to 10 weeks	3 191	3 148	3 359	3 669	3 655	3 496	2 898	2 983
11 to 14 weeks	2 258	2 128	2 235	2 501	2 587	2 574	2 300	2 265
15 to 26 weeks	3 904	3 479	3 600	4 316	4 927	4 877	4 549	4 158
27 weeks or more	2 854	2 521	2 181	2 749	3 502	3 952	4 033	3 169
With 2 spells or more of unemployment	5 149	5 136	5 073	5 811	5 864	5 734	5 338	4 783
2 spells	2 442	2 460	2 460	2 855	2 738	2 698	2 572	2 207
3 spells or more	2 707	2 676	2 613	2 956	3 126	3 036	2 766	2 576
MEN								
Total who worked or looked for work	69 995	70 738	72 362	72 844	72 909	73 387	74 516	75 244
Percent with unemployment	15.0	13.7	13.5	15.5	17.3	17.5	15.7	14.1
Total with unemployment	10 504	9 696	9 792	11 307	12 642	12 844	11 723	10 582
Did not work but looked for work	852	717	723	891	1 210	1 379	1 641	1 286
Worked during the year	9 653	8 978	9 071	10 415	11 432	11 466	10 082	9 296
Year-round workers with 1 or 2 weeks of unemployment	536	585	568	711	612	567	449	527
Part-year workers with unemployment	9 117	8 393	8 503	9 704	10 820	10 899	9 633	8 769
1 to 4 weeks	1 561	1 633	1 742	1 819	1 591	1 563	1 343	1 365
5 to 10 weeks	1 824	1 808	1 890	2 041	2 111	2 039	1 647	1 666
11 to 14 weeks	1 415	1 279	1 365	1 462	1 659	1 615	1 354	1 370
15 to 26 weeks	2 514	2 124	2 188	2 645	3 206	3 165	2 862	2 449
27 weeks or more	1 803	1 549	1 318	1 737	2 253	2 517	2 427	1 919
With 2 spells or more of unemployment	3 300	3 366	3 178	3 689	3 886	3 889	3 451	2 940
2 spells	1 488	1 560	1 517	1 676	1 742	1 781	1 580	1 266
3 spells or more	1 812	1 806	1 661	2 013	2 144	2 108	1 871	1 674
WOMEN								
Total who worked or looked for work	60 357	61 447	62 032	62 564	62 917	63 267	65 270	66 081
Percent with unemployment	13.1	12.0	12.1	13.6	13.7	13.6	13.5	12.7
Total with unemployment	7 895	7 400	7 481	8 502	8 634	8 611	8 804	8 383
Did not work but looked for work	1 185	1 017	854	982	1 205	1 363	1 791	1 570
Worked during the year	6 710	6 382	6 628	7 520	7 427	7 247	7 014	6 813
Year-round workers with 1 or 2 weeks of unemployment	255	244	265	344	354	304	239	219
Part-year workers with unemployment	6 455	6 138	6 363	7 176	7 073	6 943	6 775	6 594
1 to 4 weeks	1 802	1 623	1 747	1 827	1 633	1 380	1 284	1 422
5 to 10 weeks	1 368	1 340	1 469	1 627	1 544	1 457	1 252	1 317
11 to 14 weeks	844	849	870	1 038	927	959	946	896
15 to 26 weeks	1 391	1 354	1 413	1 671	1 720	1 712	1 687	1 708
27 weeks or more	1 050	972	864	1 013	1 249	1 435	1 606	1 251
With 2 spells or more of unemployment	1 849	1 769	1 895	2 122	1 979	1 844	1 887	1 843
2 spells	954	899	943	1 179	997	916	992	941
3 spells or more	895	870	952	943	982	928	895	902

NOTE: Data beginning in 1994 are not strictly comparable with data for 1993 and earlier years because of the introduction of a major redesign of the survey and collection methodology. Beginning in 1990, data are not strictly comparable with previous years because of the introduction of 1990 census-based population controls adjusted for the estimated undercount.

Percent Distribution of Persons with Unemployment During the Year by Sex, 1987-1994

Sex and extent of unemployment	1987	1988	1989	1990	1991	1992	1993	1994
TOTAL								
Total with unemployment who worked during the year	100.0	100.0	100.0	100.0	100.0	100.0	100.0	100.0
Year-round workers with 1 or 2 weeks of unemployment	4.8	5.4	5.3	5.9	5.1	4.7	4.0	3.2
Part-year workers with unemployment	95.2	94.5	94.6	94.1	94.8	95.4	96.1	96.7
1 to 4 weeks	20.6	21.2	22.2	20.3	17.1	15.7	15.4	20.9
5 to 10 weeks	19.5	20.5	21.4	20.5	19.4	18.7	17.0	19.3
11 to 14 weeks	13.8	13.8	14.2	13.9	13.7	13.8	13.5	13.1
15 to 26 weeks	23.9	22.6	22.9	24.1	26.1	26.1	26.6	25.1
27 weeks or more	17.4	16.4	13.9	15.3	18.5	21.1	23.6	18.3
With 2 spells or more of unemployment	31.4	33.4	32.3	32.4	31.1	30.6	31.2	27.0
2 spells	14.9	16.0	15.7	15.9	14.5	14.4	15.0	13.8
3 spells or more	16.5	17.4	16.6	16.5	16.6	16.2	16.2	13.2
MEN								
Total with unemployment who worked during the year	100.0	100.0	100.0	100.0	100.0	100.0	100.0	100.0
Year-round workers with 1 or 2 weeks of unemployment	5.6	6.5	6.3	6.8	5.4	4.9	4.4	5.7
Part-year workers with unemployment	94.5	93.4	93.7	93.2	94.6	95.0	95.5	94.3
1 to 4 weeks	16.2	18.2	19.2	17.5	13.9	13.6	13.3	14.7
5 to 10 weeks	18.9	20.1	20.8	19.6	18.5	17.8	16.3	17.9
11 to 14 weeks	14.7	14.2	15.1	14.0	14.5	14.1	13.4	14.7
15 to 26 weeks	26.0	23.7	24.1	25.4	28.0	27.6	28.4	26.4
27 weeks or more	18.7	17.2	14.5	16.7	19.7	21.9	24.1	20.6
With 2 spells or more of unemployment	34.2	37.5	35.0	35.4	34.0	33.9	34.3	31.6
2 spells	15.4	17.4	16.7	16.1	15.2	15.5	15.7	13.6
3 spells or more	18.8	20.1	18.3	19.3	18.8	18.4	18.6	18.0
WOMEN								
Total with unemployment who worked during the year	100.0	100.0	100.0	100.0	100.0	100.0	100.0	100.0
Year-round workers with 1 or 2 weeks of unemployment	3.8	3.8	4.0	4.6	4.8	4.2	3.4	3.2
Part-year workers with unemployment	96.3	96.1	96.0	95.3	95.3	95.7	96.6	96.7
1 to 4 weeks	26.9	25.4	26.4	24.3	22.0	19.0	18.3	20.9
5 to 10 weeks	20.4	21.0	22.2	21.6	20.8	20.1	17.8	19.3
11 to 14 weeks	12.6	13.3	13.1	13.8	12.5	13.2	13.5	13.1
15 to 26 weeks	20.7	21.2	21.3	22.2	23.2	23.6	24.1	25.1
27 weeks or more	15.7	15.2	13.0	13.4	16.8	19.8	22.9	18.3
With 2 spells or more of unemployment	27.5	27.7	28.6	28.2	26.6	25.4	26.9	27.0
2 spells	14.2	14.1	14.2	15.7	13.4	12.6	14.1	13.8
3 spells or more	13.3	13.6	14.4	12.5	13.2	12.8	12.8	13.2

NOTE: Data beginning in 1994 are not strictly comparable with data for 1993 and earlier years because of the introduction of a major redesign of the survey and collection methodology. Beginning in 1990, data are not strictly comparable with previous years because of the introduction of 1990 census-based population controls adjusted for the estimated undercount.

Persons with Work Experience During the Year by Industry and Class of Worker of Job Held the Longest, 1987-1994

(Thousands of persons)

Industry and class of worker	1987	1988	1989	1990	1991	1992	1993	1994
TOTAL	128 316	130 450	132 817	133 534	133 410	133 912	136 354	138 469
Agriculture	3 832	3 754	3 770	3 743	3 555	3 793	3 844	3 924
Wage and salary workers	2 238	2 262	2 197	2 149	2 150	2 286	2 186	2 364
Self-employed workers	1 419	1 359	1 453	1 458	1 313	1 398	1 591	1 502
Unpaid family workers	176	133	120	136	92	109	67	58
Nonagricultural industries	124 484	126 696	129 047	129 791	129 856	130 118	132 510	134 544
Wage and salary workers	115 594	117 757	120 019	120 416	120 734	120 924	123 314	125 591
Mining	769	807	735	858	775	719	709	683
Construction	6 937	7 235	7 491	7 236	6 896	6 610	6 690	7 137
Manufacturing	22 563	22 957	22 764	22 435	21 635	21 195	21 198	21 490
Durable goods	13 268	13 196	13 379	13 155	12 363	11 994	12 309	12 082
Lumber and wood products	770	789	840	797	639	632	653	752
Furniture and fixtures	670	727	683	621	600	694	757	651
Stone, clay, and glass products	694	628	721	691	594	549	629	656
Primary metal industries	764	768	892	852	830	823	784	733
Fabricated metal products	1 402	1 367	1 386	1 348	1 375	1 293	1 325	1 339
Machinery except electrical	2 600	2 778	2 601	2 631	2 442	2 264	2 445	2 557
Electrical equipment	2 295	2 231	2 280	2 281	2 142	1 925	1 857	1 945
Transportation equipment	2 745	2 693	2 669	2 661	2 483	2 460	2 476	2 124
Automobiles	1 278	1 284	1 273	1 206	1 157	1 214	1 205	1 102
Other transportation equipment	1 467	1 409	1 396	1 455	1 326	1 246	1 271	1 022
Other durable goods	1 329	1 215	1 307	1 274	1 248	1 344	1 383	1 324
Nondurable goods	9 295	9 761	9 385	9 280	9 272	9 201	8 889	9 408
Food and kindred products	2 033	2 083	2 048	2 000	1 920	2 028	1 879	1 906
Textile mill products	797	785	747	800	716	639	694	807
Apparel and related products	1 321	1 343	1 214	1 174	1 172	1 290	1 189	1 235
Printing and publishing	1 874	1 951	2 018	1 880	2 013	1 933	1 905	2 055
Chemicals and allied products	1 270	1 533	1 404	1 356	1 405	1 276	1 396	1 402
Other nondurable goods	1 999	2 066	1 953	2 069	2 046	2 025	1 827	2 002
Transportation and public utilities	8 188	8 195	8 267	8 364	8 499	8 510	8 639	8 569
Transportation	4 778	4 856	4 952	5 021	5 066	5 219	5 411	5 375
Communications and utilities	3 410	3 339	3 315	3 343	3 425	3 276	3 227	3 194
Wholesale and retail trade	26 069	26 078	26 387	26 879	26 864	26 968	27 328	27 843
Wholesale trade	4 599	4 454	4 642	4 809	4 829	4 588	4 509	4 933
Retail trade	21 470	21 624	21 745	22 070	22 035	22 380	22 819	22 910
Finance and services	44 919	46 321	47 370	47 587	49 143	49 827	51 659	52 371
Finance, insurance, and real estate	7 937	7 980	8 091	7 760	7 741	7 633	7 971	7 869
Business and repair services	6 299	6 646	6 985	7 040	6 140	6 315	6 849	7 007
Private households	1 493	1 535	1 238	1 161	1 266	1 395	1 254	1 241
Personal services, except private	2 943	3 019	3 196	3 177	3 110	3 003	3 272	3 181
Entertainment and recreation	1 575	1 568	1 673	1 752	2 235	2 296	2 371	2 407
Medical and other health services	8 843	9 247	9 389	9 904	10 457	10 573	10 979	11 030
Social services	2 083	2 092	2 264	2 335	2 479	2 606	2 752	2 632
Educational services	9 622	9 895	10 094	9 976	10 328	10 705	10 882	11 454
Other professional services	4 018	4 181	4 270	4 296	5 251	5 079	5 144	5 403
Forestry and fisheries	107	160	169	186	125	198	184	148
Public administration	6 147	6 163	7 005	7 057	6 917	7 097	7 088	7 498
Self-employed workers	8 588	8 580	8 717	9 120	8 855	8 965	8 992	8 818
Unpaid family workers	302	359	312	255	267	229	204	135

NOTE: Data beginning in 1994 are not strictly comparable with data for 1993 and earlier years because of the introduction of a major redesign of the survey and collection methodology. Beginning in 1990, data are not strictly comparable with previous years because of the introduction of 1990 census-based population controls adjusted for the estimated undercount.

Number and Median Annual Earnings of Year-round Full-time Wage and Salary Workers by Age, Sex, and Race, 1987-1994

(Thousands of persons)

Age, sex, and race	1987	1988	1989	1990	1991	1992	1993	1994
NUMBER								
Total, 16 years and over	71 069	73 598	74 898	74 728	74 449	75 517	77 427	79 875
16 to 24 years	7 563	7 400	7 471	6 978	6 571	6 224	6 685	6 684
25 to 44 years	42 211	44 036	45 082	45 086	44 811	45 022	45 951	47 150
25 to 34 years	22 884	23 727	23 721	23 201	22 541	22 469	22 637	23 193
35 to 44 years	19 327	20 309	21 361	21 885	22 270	22 553	23 314	23 957
45 to 54 years	12 764	13 506	13 848	14 070	14 718	15 652	16 424	17 366
55 to 64 years	7 406	7 529	7 321	7 458	7 219	7 590	7 208	7 500
65 years and over	1 125	1 127	1 177	1 137	1 130	1 029	1 159	1 174
Men, 16 years and over	42 490	43 785	45 107	44 574	43 523	43 894	45 494	47 255
16 to 24 years	4 145	4 165	4 223	3 982	3 596	3 457	3 853	3 918
25 to 44 years	25 293	26 246	27 321	27 069	26 353	26 335	27 161	28 000
25 to 34 years	13 659	14 163	14 439	13 941	13 303	13 146	13 400	13 749
35 to 44 years	11 634	12 083	12 882	13 128	13 050	13 189	13 761	14 251
45 to 54 years	7 726	8 086	8 276	8 168	8 479	8 908	9 522	10 120
55 to 64 years	4 654	4 616	4 562	4 650	4 403	4 588	4 238	4 460
65 years and over	672	672	725	705	694	606	719	757
Women, 16 years and over	28 579	29 812	29 791	30 155	30 925	31 622	31 933	32 619
16 to 24 years	3 418	3 235	3 249	2 995	2 976	2 767	2 832	2 767
25 to 44 years	16 918	17 790	17 760	18 017	18 458	18 688	18 790	19 150
25 to 34 years	9 225	9 564	9 282	9 260	9 238	9 323	9 237	9 444
35 to 44 years	7 693	8 226	8 478	8 757	9 220	9 365	9 553	9 706
45 to 54 years	5 037	5 420	5 572	5 902	6 239	6 744	6 902	7 246
55 to 64 years	2 752	2 913	2 758	2 808	2 816	3 002	2 970	3 040
65 years and over	453	455	451	433	436	423	439	417
White, 16 years and over	61 546	63 357	64 246	64 128	63 926	64 706	65 656	67 370
Men	37 461	38 449	39 430	38 915	38 018	38 267	39 347	40 589
Women	24 085	24 908	24 815	25 213	25 908	26 439	26 309	26 782
Black, 16 years and over	7 440	7 907	8 140	8 027	7 941	7 995	8 478	9 074
Men	3 838	3 976	4 219	4 162	4 001	4 011	4 259	4 598
Women	3 602	3 931	3 920	3 865	3 940	3 984	4 219	4 476
MEDIAN ANNUAL EARNINGS								
Total, 16 years and over	$21 000	$22 000	$23 000	$24 000	$25 000	$25 871	$26 000	$26 620
16 to 24 years	13 000	13 500	14 000	14 400	14 100	15 000	15 000	15 000
25 to 34 years	20 000	21 000	22 000	22 000	23 000	24 000	24 000	24 480
35 to 44 years	25 000	26 000	27 000	27 970	28 000	29 483	30 000	30 000
45 to 54 years	25 000	26 000	27 000	28 000	29 000	30 000	30 500	32 343
55 to 64 years	23 000	24 000	26 000	26 000	27 000	27 430	28 000	30 000
65 years and over	18 000	19 500	23 000	23 841	22 000	24 000	24 000	24 377
Men, 16 years and over	25 900	26 570	27 300	28 000	29 120	30 000	30 000	30 000
16 to 24 years	14 000	14 200	15 000	15 000	15 000	15 000	15 000	15 000
25 to 34 years	23 000	24 000	24 000	25 000	25 000	26 000	25 000	26 000
35 to 44 years	30 000	31 000	32 000	32 000	33 000	34 000	35 000	35 000
45 to 54 years	31 200	32 000	34 000	35 000	36 000	37 000	38 000	40 000
55 to 64 years	29 181	30 000	32 000	31 875	33 000	33 000	34 000	36 000
65 years and over	24 000	25 000	30 000	29 000	28 000	30 000	28 000	30 000
Women, 16 years and over	17 000	18 000	18 574	20 000	20 000	21 500	22 000	22 150
16 to 24 years	12 000	13 000	13 167	13 392	13 800	14 000	14 872	14 560
25 to 34 years	17 000	18 000	19 000	19 500	20 000	21 000	21 000	22 000
35 to 44 years	19 000	20 000	20 200	22 000	22 510	23 397	24 000	25 000
45 to 54 years	18 148	19 000	20 000	21 000	22 000	24 000	24 000	25 000
55 to 64 years	17 000	17 000	18 000	19 000	20 000	22 000	21 500	22 000
65 years and over	16 000	15 600	17 566	18 586	17 000	18 500	20 000	19 000
White, 16 years and over	22 000	23 000	24 000	25 000	25 000	26 200	27 000	28 000
Men	26 500	27 489	28 500	29 000	30 000	31 000	30 700	32 000
Women	17 000	18 000	19 000	20 000	20 500	22 000	22 000	23 000
Black, 16 years and over	17 000	18 000	19 000	19 350	20 000	21 000	20 800	21 000
Men	18 850	20 000	20 000	20 800	22 000	22 312	23 000	23 500
Women	15 500	16 200	17 115	18 000	18 500	20 000	19 843	20 000

NOTE: Data beginning in 1994 are not strictly comparable with data for 1993 and earlier years because of the introduction of a major redesign of the survey and collection methodology. Beginning in 1990, data are not strictly comparable with previous years because of the introduction of 1990 census-based population controls adjusted for the estimated undercount.

Number and Median Annual Earnings of Year-round Full-time Wage and Salary Workers by Sex and Occupation of Job Held the Longest, 1987-1994

(Thousands of persons)

Sex and occupation	1987	1988	1989	1990	1991	1992	1993	1994
TOTAL, NUMBER OF WORKERS								
Managerial and professional specialty	20 802	22 213	21 972	21 996	22 037	23 479	23 682	24 816
Executive, administrative, and managerial	10 776	11 715	11 735	11 662	11 644	12 167	12 361	12 954
Professional specialty	10 026	10 498	10 237	10 334	10 393	11 312	11 321	11 862
Technical sales and administrative support	22 010	22 280	23 119	22 889	23 749	23 193	23 353	23 525
Technicians and related support	2 594	2 716	2 893	2 842	3 163	2 963	2 972	2 962
Sales occupations	7 381	7 565	7 856	7 605	7 665	7 826	8 120	8 484
Administrative support including clerical	12 035	11 999	12 370	12 442	12 921	12 404	12 261	12 079
Service occupations	6 651	6 857	7 118	7 264	7 392	7 721	7 823	8 257
Private household	194	236	215	192	165	227	206	218
Protective service	1 398	1 551	1 637	1 639	1 674	1 761	1 748	1 776
Service, except private household and protective	5 059	5 070	5 266	5 433	5 553	5 733	5 869	6 263
Precision production, craft, and repair	9 348	9 640	9 542	9 373	8 710	8 570	9 226	9 420
Mechanics and repairers	3 466	3 550	3 395	3 519	3 345	3 168	3 449	3 420
Construction trades	2 693	2 877	2 880	2 850	2 412	2 431	2 540	2 940
Other precision production, craft, and repair	3 189	3 213	3 267	3 004	2 953	2 971	3 237	3 060
Operators, fabricators, and laborers	11 228	11 584	11 278	11 343	10 790	10 717	11 471	11 887
Machine operators, assemblers, and inspectors	5 806	5 989	5 664	5 733	5 341	5 231	5 534	5 821
Transportation and material moving occupations	3 017	3 187	3 168	3 165	3 025	3 129	3 364	3 370
Handlers, equipment cleaners, helpers, and laborers	2 405	2 408	2 446	2 445	2 424	2 357	2 573	2 696
Farming, forestry, and fishing	896	916	993	995	926	1 067	1 059	1 145
Armed Forces	135	106	876	869	845	769	813	824
TOTAL, MEDIAN ANNUAL EARNINGS								
Managerial and professional specialty	$30 000	$30 000	$33 000	$34 000	$35 000	$35 624	$37 000	$38 300
Executive, administrative, and managerial	30 000	30 000	33 000	33 372	35 000	35 200	36 000	38 000
Professional specialty	30 000	30 200	32 645	34 000	35 000	36 000	37 953	38 500
Technical sales and administrative support	19 000	19 800	20 000	21 000	22 000	23 200	24 000	24 000
Technicians and related support	24 200	25 000	25 400	27 000	27 000	28 000	30 000	30 000
Sales occupations	22 000	22 000	23 400	24 000	25 000	26 000	26 000	27 000
Administrative support including clerical	17 000	17 500	18 200	19 500	20 000	21 000	21 000	21 700
Service occupations	13 050	14 000	15 000	15 000	15 000	16 000	16 000	16 400
Private household	6 240	7 600	7 200	7 280	9 100	10 000	8 000	10 000
Protective service	25 000	26 000	27 000	26 000	27 000	30 000	30 000	30 700
Service, except private household and protective	12 000	12 000	13 000	13 000	13 800	14 000	14 847	15 000
Precision production, craft, and repair	24 000	25 000	25 600	26 000	27 000	28 000	27 387	29 000
Mechanics and repairers	24 810	25 432	26 000	27 000	28 000	30 000	28 000	30 000
Construction trades	24 000	24 000	25 000	25 000	27 000	27 200	26 000	28 343
Other precision production, craft, and repair	24 000	25 000	26 000	25 000	27 000	28 000	27 000	28 542
Operators, fabricators, and laborers	18 000	18 045	19 500	20 000	20 000	20 770	20 000	21 000
Machine operators, assemblers, and inspectors	17 000	17 100	19 000	18 458	19 200	20 000	20 000	20 658
Transportation and material moving occupations	22 000	22 700	23 000	24 000	24 000	25 000	25 000	25 000
Handlers, equipment cleaners, helpers, and laborers	16 000	16 000	17 200	17 000	17 000	18 000	17 000	17 000
Farming, forestry, and fishing	12 000	13 000	13 600	14 000	14 400	15 000	15 600	15 028
Armed Forces	13 000	13 000	19 700	19 751	20 000	22 000	24 000	25 000
MEN, NUMBER OF WORKERS								
Managerial and professional specialty	12 275	12 846	12 860	12 597	12 301	12 860	13 168	13 898
Executive, administrative, and managerial	6 656	7 070	7 187	7 061	6 887	7 100	7 166	7 554
Professional specialty	5 619	5 776	5 673	5 536	5 414	5 760	6 002	6 344
Technical sales and administrative support	8 736	8 856	9 320	9 048	9 322	9 306	9 312	9 562
Technicians and related support	1 468	1 524	1 561	1 567	1 666	1 585	1 454	1 540
Sales occupations	4 622	4 652	4 876	4 671	4 784	4 798	4 950	5 202
Administrative support including clerical	2 646	2 680	2 883	2 810	2 872	2 923	2 908	2 820
Service occupations	3 435	3 540	3 804	3 947	3 938	3 933	4 066	4 210
Private household	6	13	17	9	22	25	16	13
Protective service	1 279	1 373	1 459	1 442	1 416	1 528	1 508	1 560
Service, except private household and protective	2 150	2 154	2 328	2 496	2 500	2 380	2 542	2 637
Precision production, craft, and repair	8 587	8 887	8 749	8 610	8 021	7 891	8 316	8 651
Mechanics and repairers	3 334	3 416	3 271	3 385	3 227	3 057	3 280	3 272
Construction trades	2 663	2 806	2 825	2 815	2 391	2 410	2 491	2 890
Other precision production, craft, and repair	2 590	2 665	2 653	2 410	2 403	2 424	2 545	2 489
Operators, fabricators, and laborers	8 525	8 747	8 653	8 699	8 295	8 197	8 940	9 149
Machine operators, assemblers, and inspectors	3 612	3 681	3 554	3 657	3 443	3 295	3 608	3 787
Transportation and material moving occupations	2 876	3 029	2 990	3 002	2 872	2 935	3 150	3 141
Handlers, equipment cleaners, helpers, and laborers	2 037	2 037	2 109	2 040	1 980	1 967	2 182	2 221
Farming, forestry, and fishing	810	817	891	887	847	979	948	1 022
Armed Forces	123	91	830	787	801	728	745	762

Number and Median Annual Earnings of Year-round Full-time Wage and Salary Workers by Sex and Occupation of Job Held the Longest, 1987-94—Continued

(Thousands of persons)

Sex and occupation	1987	1988	1989	1990	1991	1992	1993	1994
MEN, MEDIAN ANNUAL EARNINGS								
Managerial and professional specialty	$36 000	$37 000	$39 500	$40 000	$42 000	$43 000	$44 000	$45 613
Executive, administrative, and managerial	37 000	37 299	40 000	41 000	42 000	44 000	45 000	46 000
Professional specialty	35 000	36 500	38 000	40 000	42 000	42 270	43 995	45 000
Technical sales and administrative support	26 000	26 050	28 000	29 000	30 000	30 000	31 000	31 197
Technicians and related support	29 000	30 000	31 000	30 300	31 100	33 000	34 000	35 000
Sales occupations	27 500	27 000	29 000	30 000	30 000	32 000	33 000	34 000
Administrative support including clerical	23 860	24 000	25 000	25 220	27 000	27 000	26 632	27 000
Service occupations	17 466	18 000	18 400	18 000	19 315	20 000	20 000	20 500
Private household	....	....	....	....	....			
Protective service	25 800	27 000	28 000	27 000	28 500	30 000	30 000	32 800
Service, except private household and protective	14 000	15 000	15 000	15 000	16 000	15 600	16 000	17 000
Precision production, craft, and repair	25 000	25 434	26 000	27 000	28 000	29 000	28 000	30 000
Mechanics and repairers	24 403	25 000	26 000	27 000	28 000	30 000	28 000	30 000
Construction trades	24 000	24 500	25 000	25 000	27 000	27 116	26 000	28 600
Other precision production, craft, and repair	26 000	27 000	29 000	28 000	30 000	30 000	30 000	30 000
Operators, fabricators, and laborers	20 000	20 500	21 000	22 000	22 000	23 000	23 000	23 000
Machine operators, assemblers, and inspectors	20 246	21 000	22 000	22 000	23 500	24 000	23 400	24 000
Transportation and material moving occupations	22 071	23 800	23 200	24 000	24 960	25 000	26 000	25 500
Handlers, equipment cleaners, helpers, and laborers	16 500	16 858	18 000	18 000	17 053	18 144	17 623	18 000
Farming, forestry, and fishing	12 000	13 400	14 000	14 000	15 000	15 000	15 600	16 000
Armed Forces	13 000	12 725	20 000	19 200	20 700	22 202	24 748	25 000
WOMEN, NUMBER OF WORKERS								
Managerial and professional specialty	8 527	9 367	9 113	9 398	9 736	10 618	10 515	10 918
Executive, administrative, and managerial	4 120	4 645	4 548	4 600	4 757	5 067	5 195	5 400
Professional specialty	4 407	4 722	4 565	4 798	4 979	5 551	5 320	5 518
Technical sales and administrative support	13 273	13 425	13 800	13 842	14 427	13 888	14 041	13 962
Technicians and related support	1 126	1 192	1 332	1 275	1 497	1 379	1 518	1 422
Sales occupations	2 759	2 913	2 981	2 934	2 882	3 028	3 170	3 281
Administrative support including clerical	9 388	9 320	9 487	9 633	10 048	9 481	9 353	9 259
Service occupations	3 216	3 318	3 313	3 318	3 455	3 787	3 758	4 048
Private household	188	224	197	183	144	202	190	206
Protective service	119	179	178	197	258	232	241	216
Service, except private household and protective	2 909	2 915	2 938	2 938	3 053	3 353	3 327	3 626
Precision production, craft, and repair	761	753	793	764	689	679	910	770
Mechanics and repairers	132	134	124	134	118	111	169	148
Construction trades	30	71	55	36	21	21	49	50
Other precision production, craft, and repair	599	548	614	594	550	547	692	572
Operators, fabricators, and laborers	2 703	2 836	2 625	2 644	2 495	2 521	2 531	2 738
Machine operators, assemblers, and inspectors	2 194	2 308	2 110	2 076	1 898	1 936	1 926	2 034
Transportation and material moving occupations	141	157	178	163	153	195	214	229
Handlers, equipment cleaners, helpers, and laborers	368	371	337	405	444	390	391	475
Farming, forestry, and fishing	87	99	102	108	79	88	111	123
Armed Forces	13	15	45	83	45	41	68	62
WOMEN, MEDIAN ANNUAL EARNINGS								
Managerial and professional specialty	$23 000	$25 000	$26 000	$27 500	$29 000	$29 863	$30 000	$31 000
Executive, administrative, and managerial	22 000	23 500	24 755	25 400	27 000	28 000	29 000	30 000
Professional specialty	24 328	25 000	28 000	29 000	30 000	30 000	32 000	32 000
Technical sales and administrative support	16 000	16 600	17 594	18 500	19 111	20 000	20 000	21 000
Technicians and related support	19 000	20 500	21 800	24 000	22 270	24 353	26 000	27 000
Sales occupations	14 263	15 000	15 500	17 000	18 000	18 000	18 720	19 000
Administrative support including clerical	16 000	16 376	17 500	18 000	19 000	20 000	20 000	20 260
Service occupations	10 600	11 000	12 000	12 444	12 000	13 000	13 513	13 500
Private household	6 240	7 000	7 000	7 280	7 800	9 200	8 000	10 000
Protective service	20 000	22 000	21 267	22 314	23 000	23 570	26 000	23 550
Service, except private household and protective	10 700	11 000	12 000	12 050	12 000	13 000	13 000	13 200
Precision production, craft, and repair	17 500	17 000	17 836	18 852	18 707	20 000	21 000	22 000
Mechanics and repairers	26 011	28 000	26 000	26 500	30 000	29 000	30 000	33 000
Construction trades	....	....	....	....	....	....	....	....
Other precision production, craft, and repair	15 600	15 000	16 000	17 900	17 000	18 000	20 000	20 000
Operators, fabricators, and laborers	13 000	13 000	14 000	14 300	15 000	15 000	15 000	16 000
Machine operators, assemblers, and inspectors	13 000	13 000	14 000	14 374	15 000	15 000	15 000	16 000
Transportation and material moving occupations	13 300	13 000	15 000	16 100	19 000	20 000	19 000	24 000
Handlers, equipment cleaners, helpers, and laborers	13 800	13 500	13 500	13 441	15 000	14 200	14 520	14 600
Farming, forestry, and fishing	10 000	10 400	12 000	11 799	12 200	13 000	15 600	10 700
Armed Forces	....	....	....	....	....	....	....	....

NOTE: Data beginning in 1994 are not strictly comparable with data for 1993 and earlier years because of the introduction of a major redesign of the survey and collection methodology. Beginning in 1990, data are not strictly comparable with previous years because of the introduction of 1990 census-based population controls adjusted for the estimated undercount.

POPULATION, LABOR FORCE, AND EMPLOYMENT STATUS

Employment Status of the Population by Marital Status and Sex, March 1988-1995

(Thousands of persons; percent)

Marital status and year	Men						Women					
	Popu-lation	Labor force					Popu-lation	Labor force				
		Total		Em-ployed	Unemployed			Total		Em-ployed	Unemployed	
		Number	Percent of population		Number	Percent of labor force		Number	Percent of population		Number	Percent of labor force
SINGLE												
1988	25 475	18 353	72.0	16 189	2 164	11.8	21 105	13 792	65.3	12 605	1 187	8.6
1989	25 714	18 867	73.4	16 999	1 868	9.9	21 153	13 969	66.0	12 843	1 126	8.1
1990	25 757	18 829	73.1	16 893	1 936	10.3	21 088	14 003	66.4	12 856	1 147	8.2
1991	26 220	19 014	72.5	16 418	2 596	13.7	21 688	14 125	65.1	12 887	1 238	8.8
1992	26 529	19 229	72.5	16 401	2 828	14.7	21 738	14 072	64.7	12 793	1 279	9.1
1993	26 951	19 625	72.8	16 858	2 767	14.1	21 848	14 091	64.5	12 711	1 380	9.8
1994	28 350	20 365	71.8	17 826	2 539	12.5	22 885	14 903	65.1	13 419	1 484	10.0
1995	28 318	20 449	72.2	18 286	2 163	10.6	22 853	14 974	65.5	13 673	1 301	8.7
MARRIED, SPOUSE PRESENT												
1988	51 678	40 449	78.3	38 897	1 552	3.8	52 469	29 678	56.6	28 500	1 178	4.0
1989	52 155	40 912	78.4	39 516	1 396	3.4	52 889	30 489	57.6	29 446	1 043	3.4
1990	52 464	41 020	78.2	39 562	1 458	3.6	53 207	30 967	58.2	29 870	1 097	3.5
1991	52 460	40 883	77.9	38 843	2 040	5.0	53 176	31 103	58.5	29 668	1 435	4.6
1992	52 780	40 930	77.5	38 650	2 280	5.6	53 464	31 686	59.3	30 130	1 556	4.9
1993	53 488	41 255	77.1	39 069	2 186	5.3	54 146	32 158	59.4	30 757	1 401	4.4
1994	53 436	40 993	76.7	39 085	1 908	4.7	54 198	32 863	60.6	31 397	1 466	4.5
1995	54 166	41 806	77.2	40 262	1 544	3.7	54 902	33 563	61.1	32 267	1 296	3.9
WIDOWED, DIVORCED, OR SEPARATED												
1988	10 442	6 968	66.7	6 438	530	7.6	22 942	10 565	46.1	9 947	618	5.8
1989	10 641	7 108	66.8	6 552	556	7.8	23 346	10 733	46.0	10 119	614	5.7
1990	11 152	7 513	67.4	6 959	554	7.4	23 857	11 168	46.8	10 530	638	5.7
1991	11 588	7 804	67.3	6 985	819	10.5	24 105	11 145	46.2	10 386	759	6.8
1992	11 927	8 049	67.5	7 140	909	11.3	24 582	11 486	46.7	10 610	876	7.6
1993	11 861	7 956	67.1	7 055	901	11.3	24 661	11 308	45.9	10 528	780	6.9
1994	12 239	8 156	66.6	7 382	774	9.5	25 098	11 879	47.3	10 995	884	7.4
1995	12 410	8 315	67.0	7 632	683	8.2	25 373	12 001	47.3	11 308	693	5.8
WIDOWED												
1988	2 285	523	22.9	486	37	7.1	11 294	2 259	20.0	2 162	97	4.3
1989	2 279	536	23.5	521	15	2.8	11 493	2 309	20.1	2 231	78	3.4
1990	2 331	519	22.3	490	29	5.6	11 477	2 243	19.5	2 149	94	4.2
1991	2 385	486	20.4	448	38	7.8	11 288	2 150	19.0	2 044	106	4.9
1992	2 529	566	22.4	501	65	11.5	11 325	2 131	18.8	2 029	102	4.8
1993	2 468	596	24.1	535	61	10.2	11 214	1 961	17.5	1 856	105	5.4
1994	2 220	474	21.4	440	34	7.2	11 073	1 945	17.6	1 825	120	6.2
1995	2 282	496	21.7	469	27	5.4	11 080	1 941	17.5	1 844	97	5.0
DIVORCED												
1988	5 754	4 609	80.1	4 269	340	7.4	8 211	6 220	75.8	5 899	321	5.2
1989	6 023	4 819	80.0	4 433	386	8.0	8 521	6 396	75.1	6 035	361	5.6
1990	6 256	5 004	80.0	4 639	365	7.3	8 845	6 678	75.5	6 333	345	5.2
1991	6 586	5 262	79.9	4 722	540	10.3	9 152	6 779	74.1	6 365	414	6.1
1992	6 743	5 418	80.3	4 823	595	11.0	9 569	7 076	73.9	6 578	498	7.0
1993	6 770	5 330	78.7	4 736	594	11.1	9 879	7 183	72.7	6 736	447	6.2
1994	7 222	5 548	76.8	5 028	520	9.4	10 113	7 473	73.9	6 962	511	6.8
1995	7 343	5 739	78.2	5 266	473	8.2	10 262	7 559	73.7	7 206	353	4.7
SEPARATED												
1988	2 403	1 836	76.4	1 683	153	8.3	3 437	2 086	60.7	1 886	200	9.6
1989	2 339	1 753	74.9	1 598	155	8.8	3 332	2 028	60.9	1 853	175	8.6
1990	2 565	1 990	77.6	1 830	160	8.0	3 535	2 247	63.6	2 048	199	8.9
1991	2 616	2 057	78.6	1 816	241	11.7	3 665	2 216	60.5	1 977	239	10.8
1992	2 655	2 065	77.8	1 816	249	12.1	3 688	2 279	61.8	2 003	276	12.1
1993	2 623	2 030	77.4	1 784	246	12.1	3 568	2 165	60.7	1 937	228	10.5
1994	2 797	2 134	76.3	1 914	220	10.3	3 911	2 461	62.9	2 208	253	10.3
1995	2 784	2 081	74.7	1 898	183	8.8	4 031	2 501	62.0	2 258	243	9.7

NOTE: Data beginning in 1994 are not strictly comparable with data for 1993 and earlier years because of the introduction of a major redesign of the survey and collection methodology. Beginning in 1990, data are not strictly comparable with previous years because of the introduction of 1990 census-based population controls adjusted for the estimated undercount.

Employment Status of All Women and Single Women by Presence and Age of Children, March 1988-1995

(Thousands of persons; percent)

Age of children and year	All women							Single women						
	Civilian labor force	Civilian labor force as percent of population	Employed number	Employed percent full-time	Employed percent part-time	Unemployed number	Unemployed percent of labor force	Civilian labor force	Civilian labor force as percent of population	Employed number	Employed percent full-time	Employed percent part-time	Unemployed number	Unemployed percent of labor force
WITH NO CHILDREN UNDER 18														
1988	32 490	51.2	30 911	73.6	26.4	1 580	4.9	12 417	67.3	11 538	66.7	33.3	880	7.1
1989	33 255	51.9	31 761	73.7	26.3	1 495	4.5	12 445	67.8	11 643	66.1	33.9	803	6.5
1990	33 942	52.3	32 391	74.4	25.6	1 551	4.6	12 478	68.1	11 611	65.9	34.1	866	6.9
1991	34 047	52.0	32 167	74.0	26.0	1 880	5.5	12 472	67.0	11 529	66.2	33.8	943	7.6
1992	34 487	52.3	32 481	74.3	25.7	2 006	5.8	12 355	66.9	11 374	66.6	33.4	982	7.9
1993	34 495	52.1	32 476	74.6	25.4	2 020	5.9	12 223	66.4	11 201	66.1	33.9	1 022	8.4
1994	35 454	53.1	33 343	72.7	27.3	2 110	6.0	12 737	66.8	11 674	64.5	35.5	1 063	8.3
1995	35 843	52.9	34 054	72.9	27.1	1 789	5.0	12 870	67.1	11 919	64.5	35.5	951	7.4
WITH CHILDREN UNDER 18														
1988	21 545	65.1	20 141	73.0	27.0	1 404	6.5	1 375	51.6	1 068	79.8	20.2	308	22.4
1989	20 936	65.7	20 647	72.8	27.2	1 289	6.2	1 524	54.7	1 200	79.0	21.0	324	21.3
1990	22 196	66.7	20 865	73.0	27.0	1 331	6.0	1 525	55.2	1 244	79.1	20.9	280	18.4
1991	22 327	66.6	20 774	73.0	27.0	1 552	7.0	1 654	53.6	1 358	76.4	23.6	296	17.9
1992	22 756	67.2	21 052	73.8	26.2	1 704	7.5	1 716	52.5	1 420	75.9	24.1	297	17.3
1993	23 063	66.9	21 521	73.9	26.1	1 541	6.7	1 869	54.4	1 510	74.8	25.2	359	19.2
1994	24 191	68.4	22 467	70.8	29.2	1 724	7.1	2 166	56.9	1 745	73.9	26.1	421	19.4
1995	24 695	69.7	23 195	71.7	28.3	1 500	6.1	2 104	57.5	1 754	73.6	26.4	350	16.6
WITH CHILDREN UNDER 6														
1988	8 862	56.1	8 099	69.5	30.5	763	8.6	831	44.9	621	78.8	21.2	211	25.4
1989	9 136	56.7	8 478	68.8	31.2	657	7.2	966	48.9	722	79.2	20.8	244	25.3
1990	9 397	58.2	8 732	69.6	30.4	664	7.1	929	48.7	736	75.0	25.0	194	20.9
1991	9 636	58.4	8 758	69.5	30.5	878	9.1	1 050	48.8	819	72.2	27.8	231	22.0
1992	9 573	58.0	8 662	70.2	29.8	911	9.5	1 029	45.8	829	73.2	26.8	200	19.4
1993	9 621	57.9	8 764	70.1	29.9	857	8.9	1 125	47.4	869	70.0	30.0	257	22.8
1994	10 328	60.3	9 394	67.1	32.9	935	9.1	1 379	52.2	1 062	70.0	30.0	317	23.0
1995	10 395	62.3	9 587	67.5	32.5	809	7.8	1 328	53.0	1 069	68.6	31.4	259	19.5

NOTE: Data beginning in 1994 are not strictly comparable with data for 1993 and earlier years because of the introduction of a major redesign of the survey and collection methodology. Beginning in 1990, data are not strictly comparable with previous years because of the introduction of 1990 census-based population controls adjusted for the estimated undercount.

POPULATION, LABOR FORCE, AND EMPLOYMENT STATUS

Employment Status of Ever-Married Women and Married Women, Spouse Present, by Presence and Age of Children, March 1988-1995

(Thousands of persons; percent)

Age of children and year	Ever-married women							Married women, spouse present						
	Civilian labor force	Civilian labor force as percent of population	Employed number	Employed percent full-time	Employed percent part-time	Unemployed number	Unemployed as percent of labor force	Civilian labor force	Civilian labor force as percent of population	Employed number	Employed percent full-time	Employed percent part-time	Unemployed number	Unemployed as percent of labor force
WITH NO CHILDREN UNDER 18														
1988	20 073	44.6	19 373	77.7	22.3	700	3.5	13 460	48.9	13 058	76.3	23.7	401	3.0
1989	20 810	45.6	20 118	78.1	21.9	692	3.3	14 044	50.5	13 633	77.2	22.8	411	2.9
1990	21 464	46.1	20 779	79.1	20.9	685	3.2	14 467	51.1	14 068	77.3	22.7	399	2.8
1991	21 575	46.1	20 637	78.4	21.6	937	4.3	14 529	51.2	13 976	77.6	22.4	552	3.8
1992	22 132	46.6	21 108	78.5	21.5	1 024	4.6	14 851	51.9	14 247	77.8	22.2	604	4.1
1993	22 273	46.6	21 275	79.0	21.0	998	4.5	15 211	52.4	14 630	77.6	22.4	581	3.8
1994	22 716	47.6	21 669	77.1	22.9	1 047	4.6	15 234	53.2	14 641	75.6	24.4	593	3.9
1995	22 973	47.3	22 134	77.4	22.6	839	3.7	15 594	53.2	15 072	76.3	23.7	522	3.3
WITH CHILDREN UNDER 18														
1988	20 170	66.3	19 074	72.6	27.4	1 096	5.4	16 218	65.0	15 441	69.6	30.4	776	4.8
1989	20 411	66.7	19 446	72.5	27.5	965	4.7	16 445	65.6	15 813	69.6	30.4	632	3.8
1990	20 671	67.8	19 621	72.6	27.4	1 051	5.1	16 500	66.3	15 803	69.8	30.2	698	4.2
1991	20 673	67.9	19 416	72.8	27.2	1 257	6.1	16 575	66.8	15 692	70.1	29.9	883	5.3
1992	21 040	68.8	19 633	73.6	26.4	1 407	6.7	16 835	67.8	15 884	71.3	28.7	952	5.7
1993	21 194	68.3	20 011	73.9	26.1	1 183	5.6	16 947	67.5	16 127	71.4	28.6	820	4.8
1994	22 025	69.8	20 722	70.5	29.5	1 303	5.9	17 628	69.0	16 755	68.0	32.0	873	5.0
1995	22 591	71.1	21 441	71.5	28.5	1 150	5.1	17 969	70.2	17 195	68.8	31.2	774	4.3
WITH CHILDREN UNDER 6														
1988	8 031	57.6	7 478	68.7	31.3	552	6.9	6 950	57.1	6 527	66.4	33.6	422	6.1
1989	8 169	57.8	7 756	67.8	32.2	413	5.1	7 034	57.4	6 749	66.0	34.0	285	4.1
1990	8 467	59.5	7 996	69.1	30.9	471	5.6	7 247	58.9	6 901	67.4	32.6	346	4.8
1991	8 585	59.9	7 938	69.2	30.8	647	7.5	7 434	59.9	6 933	67.5	32.5	501	6.7
1992	8 544	60.0	7 832	69.9	30.1	711	8.3	7 333	59.9	6 819	68.5	31.5	514	7.0
1993	8 496	59.6	7 895	70.2	29.8	600	7.1	7 289	59.6	6 840	68.8	31.2	450	6.2
1994	8 949	61.8	8 332	66.7	33.3	617	6.9	7 723	61.7	7 291	65.4	34.6	432	5.6
1995	9 067	63.9	8 517	67.4	32.6	550	6.1	7 759	63.5	7 349	66.1	33.9	409	5.3

NOTE: Data beginning in 1994 are not strictly comparable with data for 1993 and earlier years because of the introduction of a major redesign of the survey and collection methodology. Beginning in 1990, data are not strictly comparable with previous years because of the introduction of 1990 census-based population controls adjusted for the estimated undercount.

Employment Status of Women Who Maintain Families by Marital Status and Presence and Age of Children, March 1988-1995

(Thousands of persons; percent)

Family status, age of children, and year	Civilian, noninstitutional population	Civilian labor force					Not in labor force
		Number	Percent of population	Employed	Unemployed		
					Number	Percent of labor force	
WOMEN WHO MAINTAIN FAMILIES, TOTAL							
1988	11 074	6 851	61.9	6 296	555	8.1	4 222
1989	11 280	6 999	62.0	6 420	579	8.3	4 281
1990	11 309	7 088	62.7	6 471	617	8.7	4 221
1991	11 765	7 329	62.3	6 657	672	9.2	4 436
1992	12 214	7 517	61.5	6 798	719	9.6	4 697
1993	12 489	7 777	62.3	7 093	684	8.8	4 712
1994	12 963	8 214	63.4	7 413	801	9.8	4 750
1995	12 762	8 192	64.2	7 527	665	8.1	4 570
WOMEN WITH NO CHILDREN UNDER 18							
1988	4 315	2 299	53.3	2 213	86	3.7	2 015
1989	4 375	2 291	52.4	2 213	78	3.4	2 084
1990	4 290	2 227	51.9	2 132	95	4.3	2 062
1991	4 447	2 364	53.2	2 231	133	5.6	2 083
1992	4 651	2 427	52.2	2 307	120	4.9	2 223
1993	4 708	2 466	52.4	2 339	127	5.2	2 242
1994	4 758	2 609	54.8	2 489	120	4.6	2 149
1995	4 610	2 471	53.6	2 394	77	3.1	2 139
WOMEN WITH CHILDREN UNDER 18							
1988	6 759	4 552	67.3	4 083	469	10.3	2 207
1989	6 905	4 707	68.2	4 206	501	10.6	2 197
1990	7 018	4 860	69.3	4 338	522	10.7	2 159
1991	7 318	4 965	67.8	4 426	539	10.9	2 353
1992	7 564	5 090	67.3	4 491	599	11.8	2 473
1993	7 781	5 311	68.3	4 755	556	10.5	2 470
1994	8 205	5 604	68.3	4 924	680	12.1	2 601
1995	8 152	5 720	70.2	5 132	588	10.3	2 431
SINGLE WOMEN WHO MAINTAIN FAMILIES, TOTAL							
1988	2 387	1 377	57.7	1 169	208	15.1	1 012
1989	2 586	1 582	61.2	1 357	225	14.2	1 003
1990	2 595	1 545	59.5	1 299	246	15.9	1 050
1991	2 890	1 656	57.3	1 426	230	13.9	1 235
1992	3 121	1 761	56.4	1 542	219	12.4	1 361
1993	3 197	1 945	60.8	1 655	290	14.9	1 252
1994	3 494	2 115	60.5	1 779	336	15.9	1 378
1995	3 392	2 044	60.3	1 769	275	13.5	1 347
SINGLE WOMEN WITH NO CHILDREN UNDER 18							
1988	609	427	70.1	415	12	2.8	183
1989	665	466	70.1	452	14	3.0	198
1990	642	450	70.1	425	25	5.6	192
1991	682	469	68.8	441	28	6.0	214
1992	745	505	67.8	475	30	5.9	241
1993	752	531	70.6	494	37	7.0	221
1994	704	490	69.6	451	39	8.0	213
1995	779	534	68.5	508	26	4.9	245
SINGLE WOMEN WITH CHILDREN UNDER 18							
1988	1 778	950	53.4	754	196	20.6	829
1989	1 921	1 116	58.1	905	211	18.9	805
1990	1 953	1 095	56.1	874	221	20.2	858
1991	2 208	1 187	53.8	985	202	17.0	1 021
1992	2 376	1 256	52.9	1 067	189	15.0	1 120
1993	2 445	1 414	57.8	1 161	253	17.9	1 031
1994	2 790	1 625	58.2	1 328	297	18.3	1 165
1995	2 613	1 510	57.8	1 261	249	16.5	1 102
WIDOWED, DIVORCED, OR SEPARATED WOMEN WHO MAINTAIN FAMILIES, TOTAL							
1988	8 686	5 474	63.0	5 127	347	6.3	3 212
1989	8 694	5 416	62.3	5 063	353	6.5	3 278
1990	8 713	5 543	63.6	5 172	371	6.7	3 171
1991	8 874	5 674	63.9	5 232	442	7.8	3 200
1992	9 092	5 757	63.3	5 256	501	8.7	3 335
1993	9 292	5 832	62.8	5 439	393	6.7	3 460
1994	9 469	6 097	64.4	5 633	464	7.6	3 372
1995	9 370	6 148	65.6	5 758	390	6.3	3 223
WIDOWED, DIVORCED, OR SEPARATED WOMEN WITH NO CHILDREN UNDER 18							
1988	3 705	1 872	50.5	1 798	74	4.0	1 833
1989	3 711	1 825	49.2	1 761	64	3.5	1 886
1990	3 648	1 778	48.7	1 708	70	3.9	1 870
1991	3 765	1 896	50.4	1 791	105	5.5	1 869
1992	3 905	1 923	49.2	1 832	91	4.7	1 982
1993	3 956	1 935	48.9	1 845	90	4.7	2 021
1994	4 054	2 118	52.2	2 037	81	3.8	1 936
1995	3 831	1 938	50.6	1 887	51	2.6	1 894
WIDOWED, DIVORCED, OR SEPARATED WOMEN WITH CHILDREN UNDER 18							
1988	4 981	3 602	72.3	3 329	273	7.6	1 379
1989	4 983	3 591	72.1	3 302	289	8.0	1 392
1990	5 065	3 765	74.3	3 464	301	8.0	1 301
1991	5 109	3 778	73.9	3 441	337	8.9	1 331
1992	5 187	3 834	73.9	3 424	410	10.7	1 353
1993	5 336	3 897	73.0	3 594	303	7.8	1 439
1994	5 415	3 979	73.5	3 596	383	9.6	1 436
1995	5 539	4 210	76.0	3 871	339	8.1	1 329

NOTE: Data beginning in 1994 are not strictly comparable with data for 1993 and earlier years because of the introduction of a major redesign of the survey and collection methodology. Beginning in 1990, data are not strictly comparable with previous years because of the introduction of 1990 census-based population controls adjusted for the estimated undercount.

Number and Age of Children in Families by Type of Family and Labor Force Status of Mother, March 1988-1995

(Thousands of children)

Age of children and year	Total children	Mother in labor force	Mother not in labor force	Married-couple families			Families maintained by women			Families maintained by men
				Total	Mother in labor force	Mother not in labor force	Total	Mother in labor force	Mother not in labor force	
UNDER 18 YEARS										
1988	58 716	35 279	21 799	45 474	28 091	17 384	11 603	7 188	4 415	1 638
1989	59 483	36 050	21 757	45 988	28 673	17 315	11 819	7 377	4 442	1 676
1990	59 596	36 712	21 110	45 898	29 077	16 820	11 925	7 635	4 290	1 774
1991	60 330	36 968	21 526	45 912	29 056	16 856	12 582	7 912	4 670	1 836
1992	61 262	38 081	21 176	45 966	29 882	16 084	13 291	8 199	5 093	2 005
1993	62 020	38 542	21 444	46 499	30 054	16 445	13 487	8 488	4 999	2 034
1994	63 407	40 186	21 188	47 247	31 279	15 968	14 127	8 907	5 220	2 033
1995	63 989	41 365	20 421	47 675	32 190	15 486	14 111	9 176	4 935	2 202
6 TO 17 YEARS										
1988	38 744	24 957	12 614	29 304	19 394	9 910	8 268	5 563	2 705	1 172
1989	39 084	25 421	12 451	29 637	19 861	9 777	8 235	5 561	2 674	1 212
1990	39 095	25 805	12 079	29 726	20 067	9 659	8 157	5 737	2 420	1 211
1991	39 470	25 806	12 392	29 598	19 907	9 691	8 599	5 899	2 701	1 272
1992	40 064	26 666	12 067	29 673	20 586	9 087	9 060	6 079	2 980	1 331
1993	40 622	27 046	12 291	30 233	20 796	9 437	9 104	6 249	2 854	1 285
1994	41 795	28 179	12 287	30 895	21 663	9 233	9 570	6 516	3 054	1 329
1995	42 423	28 931	12 000	31 298	22 239	9 059	9 633	6 692	2 941	1 492
UNDER 6 YEARS										
1988	19 972	10 321	9 185	16 171	8 696	7 474	3 335	1 625	1 711	466
1989	20 399	10 628	9 306	16 351	8 812	7 539	3 584	1 816	1 767	465
1990	20 502	10 907	9 031	16 171	9 010	7 161	3 767	1 897	1 870	563
1991	20 860	11 162	9 134	16 313	9 148	7 165	3 983	2 013	1 969	563
1992	21 198	11 415	9 109	16 293	9 296	6 997	4 232	2 119	2 112	674
1993	21 398	11 496	9 153	16 266	9 258	7 008	4 383	2 239	2 145	749
1994	21 612	12 007	8 901	16 352	9 617	6 735	4 556	2 391	2 166	704
1995	21 566	12 435	8 421	16 377	9 951	6 427	4 478	2 484	1 995	710

NOTE: Data beginning in 1994 are not strictly comparable with data for 1993 and earlier years because of the introduction of a major redesign of the survey and collection methodology. Beginning in 1990, data are not strictly comparable with previous years because of the introduction of 1990 census-based population controls adjusted for the estimated undercount.

Number of Families and Median Family Income by Type of Family and Earner Status of Members, 1987-1994

(Thousands of families)

Number of families and median family income	1987	1988	1989	1990	1991	1992	1993	1994
NUMBER OF FAMILIES								
Married-couple families, total	51 720	52 149	52 385	52 241	52 549	53 254	53 248	53 929
No earners	6 648	6 751	6 812	6 765	7 101	7 250	7 281	7 225
One earner	12 083	11 938	11 737	11 630	11 553	12 053	11 806	11 715
Husband	9 651	9 508	9 196	9 110	8 907	9 182	8 715	8 673
Wife	1 765	1 782	1 844	1 816	1 987	2 145	2 405	2 364
Other family member	667	648	697	703	659	726	686	678
Two earners	24 968	25 397	25 681	25 896	26 037	26 344	26 742	27 263
Husband and wife	22 623	23 237	23 534	23 697	23 880	24 255	24 543	25 123
Husband and other family member(s)	1 826	1 652	1 718	1 711	1 633	1 447	1 582	1 565
Husband not an earner	519	509	429	487	524	642	617	574
Three earners or more	8 020	8 062	8 155	7 950	7 858	7 606	7 419	7 727
Husband and wife	7 027	7 140	7 245	7 029	7 052	6 882	6 723	6 987
Husband an earner, not wife	823	744	761	756	595	550	535	543
Husband not an earner	170	178	150	165	211	175	162	196
Families maintained by women, total	11 087	11 288	11 310	11 771	12 214	12 504	12 982	12 771
No earners	2 607	2 547	2 496	2 623	2 925	2 968	3 100	2 848
One earner	5 141	5 390	5 467	5 672	5 926	6 184	6 407	6 506
Householder	4 060	4 300	4 396	4 585	4 812	5 042	5 278	5 415
Other family member	1 081	1 090	1 071	1 087	1 114	1 142	1 129	1 091
Two earners or more	3 339	3 350	3 347	3 476	3 363	3 352	3 476	3 417
Householder and other family member(s)	3 020	3 022	2 975	3 146	3 058	2 998	3 139	3 126
Householder not an earner	318	328	372	330	305	354	337	291
Families maintained by men, total	2 859	2 874	2 929	2 948	3 079	3 094	2 992	3 287
No earners	312	296	281	296	310	345	329	383
One earner	1 288	1 263	1 350	1 396	1 541	1 544	1 593	1 705
Householder	1 054	992	1 103	1 133	1 289	1 305	1 352	1 428
Other family member	234	271	247	263	253	239	241	277
Two earners or more	1 258	1 315	1 298	1 257	1 228	1 204	1 070	1 198
Householder and other family member(s)	1 173	1 242	1 225	1 180	1 157	1 117	1 002	1 128
Householder not an earner	85	....	....	76	....	88	....	....
MEDIAN FAMILY INCOME								
Married-couple families, total	$34 834	$36 267	$38 415	$39 802	$40 746	$42 000	$43 000	$44 893
No earners	16 338	17 000	17 820	19 221	20 415	20 023	19 983	20 604
One earner	28 000	28 701	30 700	31 020	31 671	32 500	32 084	33 393
Husband	29 225	30 030	32 236	32 422	33 208	34 714	34 401	35 000
Wife	22 700	23 771	24 000	25 228	26 500	27 343	27 502	28 661
Other family member	25 640	27 840	29 992	33 262	33 042	33 622	30 254	32 578
Two earners	38 100	40 033	42 208	44 000	45 359	47 737	49 650	51 190
Husband and wife	38 074	40 050	42 285	44 031	45 516	48 050	49 980	51 500
Husband and other family member(s)	40 400	41 388	43 000	42 602	45 000	45 694	48 862	48 517
Husband not an earner	32 184	33 333	35 201	39 494	40 495	40 124	38 800	42 800
Three earners or more	53 150	54 556	56 500	59 336	61 120	61 640	63 535	66 172
Husband and wife	53 324	54 672	56 980	55 846	61 448	62 674	64 099	66 674
Husband an earner, not wife	53 000	56 600	53 928	59 675	60 592	57 015	60 712	63 633
Husband not an earner	40 500	40 900	47 656	49 107	44 874	47 551	54 805	54 655
Families maintained by women, total	14 183	14 935	15 800	16 351	16 054	16 431	16 800	17 600
No earners	5 184	5 396	5 618	5 880	6 060	5 964	6 492	6 805
One earner	14 000	14 235	15 187	15 987	16 284	16 468	16 745	17 226
Householder	13 385	13 754	14 700	15 001	15 542	15 905	15 700	16 603
Other family member	15 851	16 580	18 628	20 173	20 220	19 709	20 800	21 300
Two earners or more	27 154	28 302	30 038	30 500	31 508	32 705	33 300	33 820
Householder and other family member(s)	27 150	28 000	30 000	30 367	31 550	33 280	33 165	33 357
Householder not an earner	27 535	33 590	33 524	32 800	29 477	30 460	35 394	37 531
Families maintained by men, total	25 000	26 610	27 600	28 493	28 000	27 400	25 856	27 486
No earners	10 800	10 200	9 800	11 386	11 196	9 416	10 900	11 293
One earner	20 305	22 357	22 732	25 000	23 715	23 020	22 300	24 011
Householder	20 391	23 053	23 000	24 150	23 309	23 000	22 079	24 000
Other family member	19 681	19 869	21 196	27 620	25 720	24 359	26 916	26 253
Two earners or more	33 750	36 500	37 601	40 000	37 700	39 000	38 000	41 439
Householder and other family member(s)	33 846	36 525	37 859	40 256	37 550	39 300	38 363	41 534
Householder not an earner	32 560	....	....	34 064	....	36 445	....	....

NOTE: Data beginning in 1994 are not strictly comparable with data for 1993 and earlier years because of the introduction of a major redesign of the survey and collection methodology. Beginning in 1990, data are not strictly comparable with previous years because of the introduction of 1990 census-based population controls adjusted for the estimated undercount.

Percent Distribution of the Civilian Labor Force 25 to 64 Years of Age by Educational Attainment, Sex, and Race, March 1988-1995

Sex, race, and year	Civilian labor force (thousands)	Percent distribution				
		Total	Less than four years of high school	Four years of high school only	One to three years of college	Four or more years of college
TOTAL						
1988	94 922	100.0	14.7	39.9	19.7	25.7
1989	97 318	100.0	14.0	39.6	20.0	26.4
1990	99 175	100.0	13.4	39.5	20.7	26.4
1991	100 480	100.0	13.0	39.4	21.1	26.5
1992	102 387	100.0	12.2	36.2	25.2	26.4
1993	103 504	100.0	11.5	35.2	26.3	27.0
1994	104 868	100.0	11.0	34.0	27.7	27.3
1995	106 519	100.0	10.8	33.1	27.8	28.3
MEN						
1988	52 653	100.0	16.5	37.2	18.5	27.7
1989	53 668	100.0	15.7	36.9	19.2	28.2
1990	54 476	100.0	15.1	37.2	19.7	28.0
1991	55 165	100.0	14.7	37.5	20.2	27.6
1992	55 917	100.0	13.9	34.7	23.8	27.5
1993	56 544	100.0	13.2	33.9	24.7	28.1
1994	56 633	100.0	12.7	32.9	25.8	28.6
1995	57 454	100.0	12.2	32.3	25.7	29.7
WOMEN						
1988	42 269	100.0	12.5	43.3	21.1	23.1
1989	43 650	100.0	11.9	42.9	20.9	24.3
1990	44 699	100.0	11.3	42.4	21.9	24.5
1991	45 315	100.0	10.9	41.6	22.2	25.2
1992	46 469	100.0	10.2	37.9	26.9	25.0
1993	46 961	100.0	9.3	36.7	28.2	25.8
1994	48 235	100.0	9.1	35.3	29.8	25.8
1995	49 065	100.0	9.1	34.1	30.2	26.6
WHITE						
1988	81 902	100.0	13.8	40.0	19.7	26.4
1989	83 694	100.0	13.0	39.7	20.0	27.2
1990	85 238	100.0	12.6	39.6	20.6	27.1
1991	86 344	100.0	12.2	39.3	21.1	27.4
1992	87 656	100.0	11.3	36.1	25.5	27.1
1993	88 457	100.0	10.7	35.0	26.4	27.9
1994	89 009	100.0	10.5	33.7	27.7	28.1
1995	90 192	100.0	10.0	32.8	27.8	29.3
BLACK						
1988	10 032	100.0	22.6	43.2	19.2	15.0
1989	10 358	100.0	21.7	42.3	20.5	15.6
1990	10 537	100.0	19.9	42.5	22.1	15.5
1991	10 650	100.0	19.5	42.9	22.1	15.4
1992	10 936	100.0	19.2	40.3	24.9	15.6
1993	11 051	100.0	16.8	39.5	27.6	16.1
1994	11 368	100.0	14.5	39.3	29.2	17.0
1995	11 695	100.0	14.1	38.6	29.6	17.7

NOTE: Data beginning in 1994 are not strictly comparable with data for 1993 and earlier years because of the introduction of a major redesign of the survey and collection methodology. Beginning in 1990, data are not strictly comparable with previous years because of the introduction of 1990 census-based population controls adjusted for the estimated undercount.

Labor Force Participation Rates of Persons 25 to 64 Years of Age by Educational Attainment, Sex, and Race, March 1988-1995

(Civilian labor force as percent of civilian noninstitutional population)

Sex, race, and year	Participation rates				
	Total	Less than four years of high school	Four years of high school only	One to three years of college	Four or more years of college
TOTAL					
1988	77.5	60.9	76.9	82.4	88.4
1989	78.2	60.5	77.9	83.3	88.4
1990	78.6	60.7	78.2	83.3	88.4
1991	78.6	60.7	78.1	83.2	88.4
1992	79.0	60.3	78.3	83.5	88.4
1993	78.9	59.6	77.7	82.9	88.3
1994	78.9	58.3	77.8	83.2	88.2
1995	79.3	59.8	77.3	83.2	88.7
MEN					
1988	88.6	76.6	89.4	91.2	94.4
1989	88.8	75.9	89.6	91.8	94.5
1990	88.8	75.1	89.9	91.5	94.5
1991	88.6	75.1	89.3	92.0	94.2
1992	88.6	75.1	89.0	91.8	93.7
1993	88.1	74.9	88.1	90.6	93.7
1994	87.0	71.5	86.8	90.3	93.2
1995	87.4	72.0	86.9	90.1	93.8
WOMEN					
1988	67.1	45.5	66.9	74.6	80.7
1989	68.3	45.5	68.5	75.4	81.1
1990	68.9	46.2	68.7	75.9	81.1
1991	69.1	46.2	68.6	75.2	81.8
1992	70.0	45.6	69.1	76.2	82.2
1993	70.0	44.2	68.8	76.1	82.2
1994	71.1	44.7	70.0	77.0	82.5
1995	71.5	47.2	68.9	77.3	82.8
WHITE					
1988	78.1	62.3	76.9	82.2	88.6
1989	78.7	61.6	77.8	83.2	88.5
1990	79.2	62.5	78.4	83.3	88.3
1991	79.4	62.5	78.3	83.1	88.6
1992	79.8	61.5	78.7	83.8	88.7
1993	79.7	61.1	78.2	83.1	88.8
1994	79.8	60.3	78.3	83.5	88.5
1995	80.1	61.6	77.9	83.4	88.8
BLACK					
1988	74.4	56.4	78.0	85.6	90.7
1989	74.9	56.7	78.9	83.9	90.4
1990	74.6	54.5	78.2	84.2	92.0
1991	73.9	53.9	77.1	84.1	90.2
1992	74.4	55.4	76.9	83.4	89.1
1993	73.8	53.4	74.7	83.0	89.6
1994	73.5	49.4	75.2	82.4	89.5
1995	74.2	51.0	74.5	82.8	90.9

NOTE: Data beginning in 1994 are not strictly comparable with data for 1993 and earlier years because of the introduction of a major redesign of the survey and collection methodology. Beginning in 1990, data are not strictly comparable with previous years because of the introduction of 1990 census-based population controls adjusted for the estimated undercount.

Unemployment Rates of Persons 25 to 64 Years of Age by Educational Attainment, Sex, and Race, March 1988-1995

(Unemployment as percent of civilian labor force)

Sex, race, and year	Unemployment rates				
	Total	Less than four years of high school	Four years of high school only	One to three years of college	Four or more years of college
TOTAL					
1988	4.8	9.5	5.5	3.7	1.8
1989	4.4	8.9	4.8	3.4	2.2
1990	4.5	9.6	4.9	3.7	1.9
1991	6.1	12.3	6.7	5.0	2.9
1992	6.7	13.5	7.7	5.9	2.9
1993	6.4	13.0	7.3	5.5	3.2
1994	5.8	12.6	6.7	5.0	2.9
1995	4.8	10.0	5.2	4.5	2.5
MEN					
1988	5.2	10.1	6.3	3.9	1.7
1989	4.7	9.4	5.4	3.2	2.3
1990	4.8	9.6	5.3	3.9	2.1
1991	6.8	13.4	7.7	5.2	3.2
1992	7.5	14.8	8.8	6.4	3.2
1993	7.3	14.1	8.7	6.3	3.4
1994	6.2	12.8	7.2	5.3	2.9
1995	5.1	10.9	5.7	4.4	2.6
WOMEN					
1988	4.2	8.6	4.6	3.5	1.9
1989	4.0	8.1	4.2	3.7	2.0
1990	4.2	9.5	4.6	3.5	1.7
1991	5.2	10.7	5.5	4.8	2.5
1992	5.7	11.4	6.5	5.3	2.5
1993	5.2	11.2	5.8	4.6	2.9
1994	5.4	12.4	6.2	4.7	2.9
1995	4.4	8.6	4.6	4.5	2.4
WHITE					
1988	4.1	8.5	4.6	3.3	1.5
1989	3.8	7.7	4.2	3.0	2.0
1990	4.0	8.3	4.4	3.3	1.8
1991	5.6	11.6	6.2	4.6	2.7
1992	6.0	12.9	6.8	5.3	2.7
1993	5.8	12.4	6.5	5.0	3.1
1994	5.2	11.7	5.8	4.5	2.6
1995	4.3	9.2	4.6	4.2	2.3
BLACK					
1988	10.1	14.5	11.3	7.5	3.4
1989	9.2	14.6	9.2	6.9	4.7
1990	8.6	15.9	8.6	6.5	1.9
1991	10.1	15.9	10.3	8.0	5.2
1992	12.4	17.2	14.1	10.7	4.8
1993	10.9	17.3	12.4	8.7	4.1
1994	10.6	17.4	12.2	8.3	4.9
1995	7.7	13.7	8.4	6.3	4.1

NOTE: Data beginning in 1994 are not strictly comparable with data for 1993 and earlier years because of the introduction of a major redesign of the survey and collection methodology. Beginning in 1990, data are not strictly comparable with previous years because of the introduction of 1990 census-based population controls adjusted for the estimated undercount.

Part Two

Employment, Hours, and Earnings, Nonagricultural Payrolls

Employment, Hours, and Earnings, Nonagricultural Payrolls

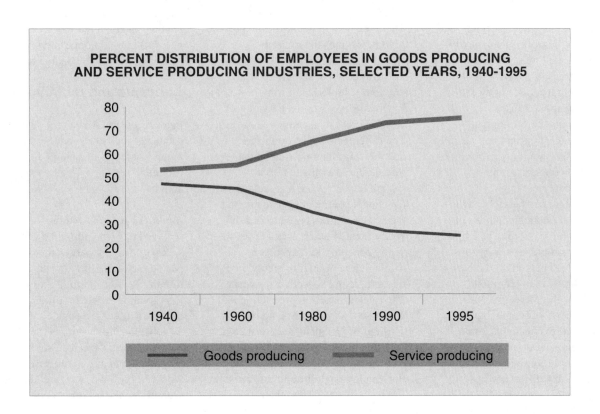

PERCENT DISTRIBUTION OF EMPLOYEES IN GOODS PRODUCING AND SERVICE PRODUCING INDUSTRIES, SELECTED YEARS, 1940-1995

Goods producing · Service producing

As evidenced by the graph, there has been a dramatic decline in the proportion of total private employment in goods-producing industries. Concurrently, there has been an increase in the proportion of employees in service-producing industries. Within the goods-producing sector, there has been an actual employment decline in manufacturing and mining, while construction employment continues to hold steady. Employment in all of the service-producing industries—transportation and public utilities; wholesale and retail trade; finance, insurance, and real estate; and other services—has increased.

NOTES

Employment, Hours, and Earnings, Nonagricultural Payrolls

(Establishment Survey)

Collection and Coverage

Statistics on employment, hours, and earnings are compiled from payroll records reported monthly on a voluntary basis to the Bureau of Labor Statistics and its cooperating state agencies by about 390,000 establishments representing all industries except agriculture. In most industries, the sampling probabilities are based on the size of the establishment; most large establishments are therefore in the sample. (An establishment is not necessarily a firm; it may be a branch plant, for example, or a warehouse.) Self-employed persons and others not on a regular civilian payroll are outside the scope of the survey because they are excluded from establishment records. The exclusion of farm employment, self-employment, and domestic service employment accounts for much of the difference in employment figures between the household and establishment surveys. The payroll survey also excludes persons on leave without pay, who are counted as employed in the household survey. Persons who worked in more than one establishment during the reporting period are counted each time their names appear on payrolls, whereas such persons are only counted once in the household survey.

Industries are classified in accordance with the 1987 *Standard Industrial Classification (SIC) Manual.*

Establishment survey data are annually adjusted to accord with comprehensive counts of employment in March of the preceding year, called "benchmarks". The adjustments are published with the release of May data each year. The benchmarks are derived mainly from employment reports from all employers subject to unemployment insurance. The employment count for the previous March becomes the revised employment number for that month; the difference between it and the previous sample-based March estimate is spread back over the previous 11 months, creating a continuous series. The difference is also projected forward and the "bias factors" that adjust recent sample-based estimates for known systematic biases are recalculated. (The main source of systematic bias is the failure of the sample to pick up newly-created businesses.) Thus, each year's benchmarking results in recalculation of employment data for the current and two previous years. The related series on production and nonsupervisory workers, hours, and earnings are recalculated consistently with the employment benchmarks.

For employment, the sum of the state figures will differ from the official U.S. national totals because of the effects of differing industrial and geographic stratifications used in the process of expanding sample totals to universe estimates, as well as differences in the timing of benchmark adjustments. The national estimation procedures used by BLS are designed to produce accurate national data by detailed industry; the state estimation procedures are designed to produce accurate data for each individual state. State estimates are not forced to sum to national totals nor vice versa. Because each state series is subject to larger sampling and nonsampling errors than the national series, summing them cumulates individual state level errors and can cause distortions at an aggregate level, particularly at turning points for the economy.

The data include Alaska and Hawaii beginning in 1959. This inclusion resulted in an increase of 212,000 (0.4 percent) in total nonfarm employment for the March 1959 benchmark.

Concepts and Definitions

Establishment. An economic unit that produces goods or services (such as a factory or store) at a single location and is engaged in one type of economic activity.

Employed persons. All persons who received pay (including holiday and sick pay) for any part of the payroll period including the 12th day of the month. Persons holding more than one job (about five percent of all persons in the labor force) are counted in each establishment that reports them. The data exclude proprietors, the self-employed, unpaid volunteer or family workers, farm workers, and domestic workers. Salaried officers of corporations are included. Government employment covers only civilian employees and excludes military personnel. Employees of the Central Intelligence Agency and the National Security Agency are also excluded.

Production or nonsupervisory workers. A subgroup of employment accounting for about four-fifths of total employment on private nonagricultural payrolls, consisting of production workers in manufacturing and mining, construction workers in construction, and nonsupervisory employees elsewhere. Separate employment figures are tabulated for this group and the data on hours and earnings refer to this group only.

Manufacturing and mining production workers. Working supervisors and nonsupervisory workers closely associated with production operations, including those engaged in fabricating, processing, assembling, inspecting, receiving, storing, handling, packing, warehousing, shipping, trucking, hauling, maintenance, repair, janitorial and guard services, product development, and recordkeeping.

Construction workers in construction. Working supervisors and others engaged in new work, alterations, demolition, repair, maintenance, etc., whether working at the site or in shops or yards at jobs ordinarily performed by members of the construction trades.

Nonsupervisory workers are enumerated in the following industries. Transportation and public utilities; wholesale and retail trade; finance, insurance, and real estate; and services. The category includes employees not above the working supervisory level such as office and clerical workers, repairers, salespersons, operators, drivers, physicians, lawyers, accountants, nurses, social workers, research aides, teachers, drafters, photographers, beauticians, musicians, restaurant workers, custodial workers, attendants, line installers and repairers, laborers, janitors, guards, and other employees at similar occupational levels whose services are closely associated with those of the employees listed.

Earnings. The payments that production or nonsupervisory workers receive during the survey period, including premium pay for overtime or late-shift work and holiday, vacation, and sick pay paid directly by the firm. Earnings exclude irregular bonuses, retroactive pay, tips, and payments in kind. Earnings also exclude employee benefits such as health or other insurance and contributions to Social Security and other retirement funds paid by the employer. Payroll earnings are reported before deductions of any kind, e.g., the employee share of Social Security contributions, group insurance, withholding tax, bonds, or union dues. Real earnings are earnings adjusted to reflect the effects of changes in consumer prices using the Consumer Price Index for Urban Wage Earners and Clerical Workers (CPI-W). Since the price index used is calculated with the year 1982 set equal to 100, the real earnings are expressed in 1982 dollars.

Hours. Hours paid for during the pay period including the 12th of the month for production or nonsupervisory workers. Includes hours paid for holidays, vacations, and sick leave.

Average weekly hours. For any industry grouping, total production or nonsupervisory hours paid for divided by total reported production or nonsupervisory employment. Will not be the same as standard or scheduled hours, reflecting such factors as unpaid absenteeism, labor turnover, part-time work, and work stoppages. Industry and total averages will reflect changes in the workweeks of component industries and also shifts in the composition of employment between industries and employees with shorter and longer workweeks. Because the survey reports multiple jobholders separately at each job, average hours refer to jobs and not to individuals. Thus, if a worker with a full-time job takes a part-time job and nothing changes for any other worker, the average workweek will decline, even though every person is working the same or longer hours.

Indexes of aggregate weekly hours. For individual industries, the hours aggregates are the products of average hours and production worker or nonsupervisory worker employment. At all higher levels of industry aggregation, hours aggregates are the sum of the component aggregates. They are published in the form of indexes, 1982=100, which are calculated by dividing each year's aggregate by the average of the 12 monthly figures for 1982 and expressing the result in percentage form. Thus, these indexes measure changes in the labor inputs of production or nonsupervisory workers.

Average overtime hours. The portion of average weekly hours which exceed regular hours and for which overtime premiums were paid.

Average hourly earnings. Reflect not only changes in basic hourly and incentive wage rates but also such variable factors as premium pay for overtime and late-shift work and changes in output of workers paid on an incentive plan. They also reflect shifts in the number of employees between relatively high-paid and low-paid work as well as changes in workers' earnings in individual establishments. Averages for groups and divisions (such as total private industry, total goods-producing, and total service-producing) further reflect shifts among component industries as well as changes in average hourly earnings for individual industries. Average hourly earnings do not measure the level of total labor costs to the employer since the following are excluded: irregular bonuses, retroactive items, payments of employee welfare benefits, payroll taxes paid by employers, and earnings for those employees not covered under production worker, construction worker, or nonsupervisory employee definitions.

Average weekly earnings. Derived by multiplying average weekly hours estimates by average hourly earnings estimates. Therefore, weekly earnings are affected not only by changes in average hourly earnings but also by changes in the length of the workweek. Average weekly earnings are per job and will not necessarily reflect trends in income per worker (because of multiple jobholders) or per family (because of families with more than one earner).

For further details on estimation methods and relation to the household data, see the Bureau of Labor Statistics, *Employment and Earnings*, June 1996 issue.

Employees on Nonagricultural Payrolls by Industry, Selected Years, 1919-1995

(Thousands of persons)

Year	Total	Total private	Goods-producing					
			Total	Mining	Construction	Manufacturing		
						Total	Durable goods	Nondurable goods
1919	27 078	24 402	12 828	1 133	1 036	10 659	....	....
1920	27 340	24 737	12 760	1 239	863	10 658	....	....
1925	28 766	25 966	12 489	1 089	1 461	9 939	....	....
1930	29 409	26 261	11 958	1 009	1 387	9 562	....	....
1935	27 039	23 558	10 893	897	927	9 069	....	....
1940	32 361	28 159	13 221	925	1 311	10 985	5 401	5 584
1945	40 374	34 431	17 507	836	1 147	15 524	9 108	6 415
1950	45 197	39 170	18 506	901	2 364	15 241	8 066	7 175
1955	50 641	43 727	20 513	792	2 839	16 882	9 511	7 370
1960	54 189	45 836	20 434	712	2 926	16 796	9 429	7 367
1961	53 999	45 404	19 857	672	2 859	16 326	9 041	7 285
1962	55 549	46 660	20 451	650	2 948	16 853	9 450	7 403
1963	56 653	47 429	20 640	635	3 010	16 995	9 586	7 410
1964	58 283	48 686	21 005	634	3 097	17 274	9 785	7 489
1965	60 765	50 689	21 926	632	3 232	18 062	10 374	7 688
1966	63 901	53 116	23 158	627	3 317	19 214	11 250	7 963
1967	65 803	54 413	23 308	613	3 248	19 447	11 408	8 039
1968	67 897	56 058	23 737	606	3 350	19 781	11 594	8 187
1969	70 384	58 189	24 361	619	3 575	20 167	11 862	8 304
1970	70 880	58 325	23 578	623	3 588	19 367	11 176	8 190
1971	71 214	58 331	22 935	609	3 704	18 623	10 604	8 019
1972	73 675	60 341	23 668	628	3 889	19 151	11 022	8 129
1973	76 790	63 058	24 893	642	4 097	20 154	11 863	8 291
1974	78 265	64 095	24 794	697	4 020	20 077	11 897	8 181
1975	76 945	62 259	22 600	752	3 525	18 323	10 662	7 661
1976	79 382	64 511	23 352	779	3 576	18 997	11 051	7 946
1977	82 471	67 344	24 346	813	3 851	19 682	11 570	8 112
1978	86 697	71 026	25 585	851	4 229	20 505	12 245	8 259
1979	89 823	73 876	26 461	958	4 463	21 040	12 730	8 310
1980	90 406	74 166	25 658	1 027	4 346	20 285	12 159	8 127
1981	91 152	75 121	25 497	1 139	4 188	20 170	12 082	8 089
1982	89 544	73 707	23 812	1 128	3 904	18 780	11 014	7 766
1983	90 152	74 282	23 330	952	3 946	18 432	10 707	7 725
1984	94 408	78 384	24 718	966	4 380	19 372	11 476	7 896
1985	97 387	80 992	24 842	927	4 668	19 248	11 458	7 790
1986	99 344	82 651	24 533	777	4 810	18 947	11 195	7 752
1987	101 958	84 948	24 674	717	4 958	18 999	11 154	7 845
1988	105 210	87 824	25 125	713	5 098	19 314	11 363	7 951
1989	107 895	90 117	25 254	692	5 171	19 391	11 394	7 997
1990	109 419	91 115	24 905	709	5 120	19 076	11 109	7 968
1991	108 256	89 854	23 745	689	4 650	18 406	10 569	7 837
1992	108 604	89 959	23 231	635	4 492	18 104	10 277	7 827
1993	110 730	91 889	23 352	610	4 668	18 075	10 221	7 854
1994	114 172	95 044	23 908	601	4 986	18 321	10 448	7 873
1995	117 203	97 892	24 206	580	5 158	18 468	10 654	7 814

NOTE: Data include Alaska and Hawaii beginning in 1959.

Employees on Nonagricultural Payrolls by Industry, Selected Years, 1919-1995—Continued

(Thousands of persons)

Year	Service-producing									
	Total	Transportation and public utilities	Wholesale trade	Retail trade	Finance, insurance, and real estate	Services	Government			
							Total	Federal	State	Local
1919	14 250	3 711	....	....	....	....	2 676	....	....	....
1920	14 580	3 998	....	....	....	....	2 603	....	....	....
1925	16 277	3 826	....	....	....	....	2 800	....	....	....
1930	17 451	3 685	....	....	....	....	3 148	....	....	....
1935	16 146	2 786	....	....	....	....	3 481	....	....	....
1940	19 140	3 038	1 841	4 909	1 485	3 665	4 202	996	....	....
1945	22 867	3 906	1 955	5 359	1 481	4 222	5 944	2 808	....	....
1950	26 691	4 034	2 643	6 743	1 888	5 356	6 026	1 928	....	....
1955	30 128	4 141	2 934	7 601	2 298	6 240	6 914	2 187	1 168	3 558
1960	33 755	4 004	3 153	8 238	2 628	7 378	8 353	2 270	1 536	4 547
1961	34 142	3 903	3 142	8 195	2 688	7 619	8 594	2 279	1 607	4 708
1962	35 098	3 906	3 207	8 359	2 754	7 982	8 890	2 340	1 668	4 881
1963	36 013	3 903	3 258	8 520	2 830	8 277	9 225	2 358	1 747	5 121
1964	37 278	3 951	3 347	8 812	2 911	8 660	9 596	2 348	1 856	5 392
1965	38 839	4 036	3 477	9 239	2 977	9 036	10 074	2 378	1 996	5 700
1966	40 743	4 158	3 608	9 637	3 058	9 498	10 784	2 564	2 141	6 080
1967	42 495	4 268	3 700	9 906	3 185	10 045	11 391	2 719	2 302	6 371
1968	44 160	4 318	3 791	10 308	3 337	10 567	11 839	2 737	2 442	6 660
1969	46 023	4 442	3 919	10 785	3 512	11 169	12 195	2 758	2 533	6 904
1970	47 302	4 515	4 006	11 034	3 645	11 548	12 554	2 731	2 664	7 158
1971	48 278	4 476	4 014	11 338	3 772	11 797	12 881	2 696	2 747	7 437
1972	50 007	4 541	4 127	11 822	3 908	12 276	13 334	2 684	2 859	7 790
1973	51 897	4 656	4 291	12 315	4 046	12 857	13 732	2 663	2 923	8 146
1974	53 471	4 725	4 447	12 539	4 148	13 441	14 170	2 724	3 039	8 407
1975	54 345	4 542	4 430	12 630	4 165	13 892	14 686	2 748	3 179	8 758
1976	56 030	4 582	4 562	13 193	4 271	14 551	14 871	2 733	3 273	8 865
1977	58 125	4 713	4 723	13 792	4 467	15 302	15 127	2 727	3 377	9 023
1978	61 113	4 923	4 985	14 556	4 724	16 252	15 672	2 753	3 474	9 446
1979	63 363	5 136	5 221	14 972	4 975	17 112	15 947	2 773	3 541	9 633
1980	64 748	5 146	5 292	15 018	5 160	17 890	16 241	2 866	3 610	9 765
1981	65 655	5 165	5 375	15 171	5 298	18 615	16 031	2 772	3 640	9 619
1982	65 732	5 081	5 295	15 158	5 340	19 021	15 837	2 739	3 640	9 458
1983	66 821	4 952	5 283	15 587	5 466	19 664	15 869	2 774	3 662	9 434
1984	69 690	5 156	5 568	16 512	5 684	20 746	16 024	2 807	3 734	9 482
1985	72 544	5 233	5 727	17 315	5 948	21 927	16 394	2 875	3 832	9 687
1986	74 811	5 247	5 761	17 880	6 273	22 957	16 693	2 899	3 893	9 901
1987	77 284	5 362	5 848	18 422	6 533	24 110	17 010	2 943	3 967	10 100
1988	80 086	5 514	6 030	19 023	6 630	25 504	17 386	2 971	4 076	10 339
1989	82 642	5 625	6 187	19 475	6 668	26 907	17 779	2 988	4 182	10 609
1990	84 514	5 793	6 173	19 601	6 709	27 934	18 304	3 085	4 305	10 914
1991	84 511	5 762	6 081	19 284	6 646	28 336	18 402	2 966	4 355	11 081
1992	85 373	5 721	5 997	19 356	6 602	29 052	18 645	2 969	4 408	11 267
1993	87 378	5 829	5 981	19 773	6 757	30 197	18 841	2 915	4 488	11 438
1994	90 264	5 993	6 162	20 507	6 896	31 579	19 128	2 870	4 576	11 682
1995	92 997	6 165	6 412	21 173	6 830	33 107	19 310	2 822	4 642	11 847

NOTE: Data include Alaska and Hawaii beginning in 1959.

Production or Nonsupervisory Workers on Private Nonagricultural Payrolls by Industry, 1947-1995
(Thousands of persons)

Year	Total private	Mining	Construction	Manufacturing			Transportation and public utilities	Wholesale trade	Retail trade	Finance, insurance, and real estate	Services
				Total	Durable goods	Nondurable goods					
1947	33 747	871	1 786	12 990	7 064	5 926	....	2 255	6 000	1 436	....
1948	34 489	906	1 954	12 910	6 962	5 950	....	2 368	6 275	1 496	....
1949	33 159	839	1 949	11 790	6 158	5 633	....	2 361	6 248	1 517	....
1950	34 349	816	2 101	12 523	6 741	5 781	....	2 390	6 368	1 565	....
1951	36 225	840	2 343	13 368	7 514	5 854	....	2 464	6 642	1 622	....
1952	36 643	801	2 360	13 359	7 583	5 777	....	2 541	6 807	1 683	....
1953	37 694	765	2 341	14 055	8 186	5 869	....	2 562	6 964	1 742	....
1954	36 276	686	2 316	12 817	7 226	5 591	....	2 544	6 928	1 807	....
1955	37 500	680	2 477	13 288	7 580	5 708	....	2 583	7 109	1 889	....
1956	38 495	702	2 653	13 436	7 701	5 735	....	2 654	7 296	1 961	....
1957	38 384	695	2 577	13 189	7 581	5 607	....	2 647	7 292	1 998	....
1958	36 608	611	2 420	11 997	6 611	5 387	....	2 580	7 174	2 029	....
1959	38 080	590	2 577	12 603	7 065	5 538	....	2 669	7 434	2 086	....
1960	38 516	570	2 497	12 586	7 060	5 526	....	2 714	7 618	2 145	....
1961	37 989	532	2 426	12 083	6 650	5 433	....	2 692	7 558	2 189	....
1962	38 979	512	2 500	12 488	6 967	5 521	....	2 735	7 682	2 237	....
1963	39 553	498	2 562	12 555	7 059	5 495	....	2 767	7 811	2 291	....
1964	40 560	497	2 637	12 781	7 245	5 537	3 490	2 832	8 037	2 346	7 939
1965	42 278	494	2 749	13 434	7 746	5 688	3 561	2 932	8 426	2 388	8 295
1966	44 249	487	2 818	14 296	8 400	5 895	3 638	3 033	8 787	2 441	8 749
1967	45 137	469	2 741	14 308	8 396	5 912	3 718	3 095	9 026	2 533	9 246
1968	46 473	461	2 822	14 514	8 489	6 024	3 757	3 164	9 378	2 651	9 727
1969	48 208	472	3 012	14 767	8 683	6 084	3 863	3 271	9 822	2 797	10 205
1970	48 156	473	2 990	14 044	8 088	5 956	3 914	3 340	10 034	2 879	10 481
1971	48 148	455	3 071	13 544	7 697	5 847	3 872	3 327	10 288	2 936	10 655
1972	49 937	475	3 257	14 045	8 025	6 022	3 943	3 418	10 717	3 024	11 059
1973	52 201	486	3 405	14 834	8 699	6 138	4 034	3 560	11 155	3 121	11 606
1974	52 809	530	3 294	14 638	8 634	6 004	4 079	3 683	11 316	3 169	12 100
1975	50 991	571	2 808	13 043	7 532	5 510	3 894	3 650	11 373	3 173	12 479
1976	52 897	592	2 814	13 638	7 888	5 750	3 918	3 759	11 890	3 243	13 043
1977	55 179	618	3 021	14 135	8 280	5 855	4 008	3 892	12 424	3 397	13 683
1978	58 156	638	3 354	14 734	8 777	5 956	4 142	4 109	13 110	3 593	14 476
1979	60 367	719	3 565	15 068	9 082	5 986	4 299	4 290	13 458	3 776	15 193
1980	60 331	762	3 421	14 214	8 416	5 798	4 293	4 328	13 484	3 907	15 921
1981	60 923	841	3 261	14 020	8 270	5 751	4 283	4 375	13 582	3 999	16 562
1982	59 468	821	2 998	12 742	7 290	5 451	4 190	4 261	13 594	3 996	16 867
1983	60 028	673	3 031	12 528	7 095	5 433	4 072	4 239	13 989	4 066	17 429
1984	63 339	686	3 404	13 280	7 715	5 565	4 258	4 466	14 736	4 226	18 284
1985	65 475	658	3 655	13 084	7 618	5 466	4 335	4 607	15 421	4 410	19 305
1986	66 866	545	3 770	12 864	7 399	5 465	4 339	4 623	15 925	4 637	20 163
1987	68 771	511	3 870	12 952	7 409	5 543	4 446	4 685	16 378	4 797	21 132
1988	71 106	512	3 980	13 193	7 582	5 611	4 562	4 858	16 869	4 811	22 323
1989	73 034	493	4 035	13 230	7 594	5 636	4 671	4 981	17 262	4 829	23 532
1990	73 800	509	3 974	12 947	7 363	5 584	4 807	4 959	17 358	4 860	24 387
1991	72 650	489	3 549	12 434	6 967	5 467	4 792	4 872	17 006	4 795	24 712
1992	72 930	448	3 431	12 287	6 822	5 466	4 780	4 817	17 048	4 772	25 347
1993	74 777	431	3 589	12 341	6 849	5 492	4 878	4 823	17 428	4 908	26 380
1994	77 610	427	3 858	12 632	7 104	5 528	5 015	4 972	18 056	5 018	27 632
1995	80 123	424	3 992	12 787	7 298	5 489	5 164	5 191	18 624	4 978	28 965

NOTE: Data include Alaska and Hawaii beginning in 1959.

Total Employees on Durable Goods Manufacturing Payrolls by Industry, Selected Years, 1939-1995

(Thousands of persons)

Year	Total	Lumber and wood products	Furniture and fixtures	Stone, clay, and glass products	Primary metal industries		Fabricated metal products	Industrial machinery and equipment	Electrical and electronic equipment	Transportation equipment		Instruments and related products	Miscellaneous manufacturing
					Total	Blast furnaces and basic steel products				Total	Motor vehicles and equipment		
1939	4 754	....	....	350.0	....	515.5	....	....	369.0	638.0	460.7	....	....
1940	5 401	....	....	366.0	....	590.5	....	....	413.0	824.0	526.0	....	....
1945	9 108	....	....	386.0	....	600.7	....	....	820.0	2 517.0	656.0	....	....
1950	8 066	846.0	346.0	518.0	1 194.0	674.4	1 042.0	1 221.0	819.0	1 253.0	816.2	427.0	400.0
1955	9 511	780.9	346.5	557.0	1 266.9	706.9	1 221.5	1 465.4	1 039.3	1 874.1	891.2	563.4	396.2
1956	9 802	772.8	357.7	573.1	1 298.4	706.6	1 239.9	1 588.5	1 106.1	1 871.1	792.5	591.7	403.0
1957	9 825	697.2	356.5	563.6	1 298.4	719.9	1 267.3	1 603.3	1 123.3	1 927.8	769.3	599.8	387.2
1958	8 801	655.3	343.4	532.5	1 106.5	601.1	1 169.9	1 378.2	1 045.1	1 634.5	606.5	562.8	373.0
1959	9 342	703.4	366.5	571.9	1 133.2	587.3	1 218.9	1 469.1	1 165.6	1 714.5	692.3	611.3	387.7
1960	9 429	670.1	364.9	572.0	1 184.8	651.4	1 230.0	1 496.1	1 220.9	1 668.1	724.1	632.2	389.9
1961	9 041	624.3	350.0	551.1	1 100.1	595.5	1 180.9	1 435.4	1 221.6	1 574.4	632.3	624.6	378.2
1962	9 450	634.3	366.8	561.0	1 120.9	592.8	1 237.7	1 511.2	1 295.9	1 682.8	691.7	650.3	389.6
1963	9 586	641.4	371.3	569.0	1 127.3	589.9	1 263.8	1 547.5	1 282.4	1 748.6	741.3	647.7	386.8
1964	9 785	657.8	386.5	581.2	1 187.8	629.2	1 295.0	1 627.0	1 273.1	1 732.1	752.9	646.7	397.6
1965	10 374	665.1	410.2	595.1	1 252.8	657.3	1 372.1	1 753.9	1 367.6	1 853.1	842.7	684.3	419.5
1966	11 250	677.4	439.6	610.3	1 296.5	651.9	1 489.0	1 931.1	1 571.3	2 031.0	861.6	770.0	433.7
1967	11 408	661.5	434.1	595.4	1 267.0	635.2	1 556.1	1 991.1	1 614.6	2 058.4	815.8	801.1	428.4
1968	11 594	674.0	449.5	602.1	1 261.0	635.9	1 609.2	1 988.2	1 629.1	2 132.8	873.7	814.4	433.4
1969	11 862	690.8	461.3	622.0	1 305.0	643.8	1 665.0	2 054.7	1 664.3	2 120.0	911.4	838.3	441.0
1970	11 176	658.1	439.9	609.8	1 260.4	627.0	1 559.1	2 003.0	1 583.6	1 832.9	799.0	803.6	425.7
1971	10 604	680.9	443.6	610.6	1 171.0	573.9	1 479.4	1 833.7	1 476.7	1 743.0	848.5	753.1	411.7
1972	11 022	740.2	483.3	644.6	1 173.3	568.4	1 540.9	1 908.8	1 535.0	1 776.7	874.8	786.2	433.3
1973	11 863	774.1	506.8	680.4	1 259.1	604.6	1 644.9	2 110.8	1 667.2	1 914.5	976.5	850.8	454.4
1974	11 897	726.6	489.3	672.8	1 288.8	609.5	1 632.2	2 230.0	1 666.4	1 853.0	907.7	885.4	452.0
1975	10 662	626.9	416.9	597.8	1 139.0	548.2	1 452.9	2 076.2	1 441.5	1 700.4	792.4	803.7	406.8
1976	11 051	692.5	444.3	612.7	1 154.9	549.4	1 505.2	2 084.6	1 502.7	1 784.8	881.0	839.8	429.1
1977	11 570	736.0	464.3	635.7	1 181.6	554.3	1 576.9	2 194.7	1 590.5	1 857.1	947.3	894.9	438.4
1978	12 245	769.8	494.1	663.7	1 214.9	560.5	1 666.7	2 346.9	1 699.0	1 986.6	1 004.9	951.9	451.5
1979	12 730	781.8	497.8	673.5	1 253.9	570.5	1 712.6	2 507.7	1 793.1	2 058.9	990.4	1 006.3	444.8
1980	12 159	704.2	465.8	628.9	1 142.2	511.9	1 609.0	2 517.0	1 770.9	1 880.5	788.8	1 021.9	418.0
1981	12 082	679.8	464.3	606.1	1 122.4	506.1	1 586.3	2 520.7	1 773.6	1 878.9	788.7	1 041.3	408.3
1982	11 014	610.3	432.0	547.5	921.9	396.2	1 424.4	2 264.3	1 700.5	1 717.6	699.3	1 013.3	382.1
1983	10 707	670.5	448.0	540.7	831.8	340.8	1 368.4	2 052.6	1 703.8	1 730.4	753.6	990.2	370.3
1984	11 476	717.9	486.4	561.6	857.4	334.1	1 461.6	2 217.9	1 868.5	1 882.8	861.5	1 040.4	381.6
1985	11 458	711.1	492.9	557.1	807.9	302.6	1 463.9	2 194.7	1 859.0	1 959.6	883.1	1 044.7	366.5
1986	11 195	724.0	497.5	553.9	751.4	273.4	1 422.4	2 073.7	1 790.1	2 002.6	871.8	1 018.4	360.7
1987	11 154	753.8	514.8	554.3	746.2	268.3	1 399.4	2 027.8	1 749.6	2 027.5	865.9	1 011.1	369.5
1988	11 363	767.3	526.7	567.4	770.3	278.4	1 428.4	2 088.6	1 764.1	2 036.1	856.4	1 031.0	382.8
1989	11 394	756.2	524.3	568.4	771.8	279.1	1 445.4	2 124.9	1 744.3	2 051.5	858.5	1 025.9	381.2
1990	11 109	733.3	505.8	556.2	756.2	276.2	1 419.0	2 094.6	1 673.4	1 988.9	812.1	1 005.9	375.3
1991	10 569	675.2	474.7	521.5	722.6	262.7	1 355.1	1 999.6	1 591.1	1 890.0	788.8	974.0	365.5
1992	10 277	679.9	477.7	513.3	694.5	250.3	1 329.1	1 928.6	1 528.1	1 829.6	812.5	928.5	367.6
1993	10 221	709.1	486.9	517.0	683.1	240.3	1 338.5	1 930.6	1 525.7	1 756.2	836.6	895.5	378.3
1994	10 448	754.3	504.6	531.6	697.7	239.2	1 388.1	1 989.5	1 570.6	1 761.1	909.3	861.1	389.0
1995	10 654	764.2	508.7	538.1	710.4	240.7	1 437.9	2 059.2	1 624.7	1 784.8	968.0	836.8	389.4

NOTE: Data include Alaska and Hawaii beginning in 1959.

EMPLOYMENT, HOURS, AND EARNINGS, NONAGRICULTURAL PAYROLLS

Production Workers on Durable Goods Manufacturing Payrolls by Industry, Selected Years, 1939-1995

(Thousands of persons)

Year	Total	Lumber and wood products	Furniture and fixtures	Stone, clay, and glass products	Primary metal industries Total	Blast furnaces and basic steel products	Fabricated metal products	Industrial machinery and equipment	Electrical and electronic equipment	Transportation equipment Total	Motor vehicles and equipment	Instruments and related products	Miscellaneous manufacturing
1939	3 926	....	....	297.0	....	452.6	....	....	....	540.0	388.3	....	....
1940	4 506	....	....	311.0	....	519.6	....	....	....	711.0	448.6	....	....
1945	7 571	....	....	334.0	....	527.3	....	....	....	2 057.0	519.7	....	....
1950	6 741	777.0	302.0	448.0	1 031.0	586.8	862.0	939.0	....	1 016.0	677.1	....	344.0
1955	7 580	706.3	292.6	469.1	1 069.4	604.5	974.5	1 082.1	....	1 418.1	718.3		330.4
1956	7 701	696.0	300.6	479.9	1 084.6	595.4	977.0	1 170.9	....	1 366.2	619.5		333.1
1957	7 581	622.0	298.2	466.5	1 071.4	600.1	989.1	1 155.6	....	1 394.5	601.7		315.3
1958	6 611	581.8	284.4	433.5	890.8	486.5	892.2	956.3	....	1 128.8	452.5		299.5
1959	7 065	628.5	305.7	469.7	914.2	470.9	939.5	1 038.9	....	1 183.8	537.5		312.9
1960	7 060	595.8	303.5	465.5	956.9	528.4	943.4	1 047.4	....	1 134.6	563.3		314.3
1961	6 650	551.4	289.5	444.4	880.8	478.4	896.5	987.3	....	1 029.2	479.1		303.5
1962	6 967	562.7	304.5	452.3	901.5	476.3	944.8	1 049.4	....	1 096.5	534.0		313.2
1963	7 059	565.8	308.7	458.1	911.7	479.1	965.4	1 070.9	....	1 142.9	573.6		310.4
1964	7 245	574.8	320.9	467.4	967.1	515.6	992.2	1 131.8	....	1 144.7	579.2		317.9
1965	7 746	579.3	340.3	477.8	1 022.7	538.4	1 059.5	1 227.4	....	1 259.2	658.9		335.5
1966	8 400	587.4	364.4	489.9	1 055.5	530.9	1 158.9	1 358.1	....	1 385.3	670.3		346.1
1967	8 396	570.6	357.6	473.5	1 015.7	509.5	1 204.8	1 383.2	....	1 390.9	626.9		338.3
1968	8 489	581.0	371.5	482.0	1 002.6	506.2	1 243.5	1 357.5	....	1 449.9	680.8		340.4
1969	8 683	594.3	382.9	498.5	1 042.2	513.6	1 283.6	1 397.1	....	1 443.3	708.0		344.6
1970	8 088	563.5	362.4	484.9	999.7	499.7	1 188.3	1 335.8	....	1 222.7	605.3		328.7
1971	7 697	588.4	364.5	485.5	923.3	454.6	1 128.0	1 195.1	....	1 196.1	655.4		317.6
1972	8 025	636.7	400.4	515.5	932.9	452.6	1 189.1	1 258.4	....	1 225.7	676.0		339.9
1973	8 699	664.9	420.0	545.8	1 010.5	484.8	1 276.7	1 415.9	....	1 324.1	754.9		356.4
1974	8 634	618.1	401.9	539.1	1 029.5	487.3	1 255.9	1 494.3	....	1 256.3	687.5		353.8
1975	7 532	525.6	337.3	472.7	886.6	428.1	1 089.6	1 350.2	....	1 141.7	602.4		310.6
1976	7 888	585.4	364.0	486.2	904.4	430.5	1 138.2	1 352.0	....	1 222.5	682.4		328.7
1977	8 280	625.8	381.8	504.6	922.1	432.6	1 197.5	1 434.7	....	1 277.0	734.7		334.2
1978	8 777	656.5	406.3	524.9	954.3	441.7	1 269.3	1 540.0	....	1 369.5	781.7		344.5
1979	9 082	663.7	405.9	529.1	986.4	451.3	1 298.3	1 648.2	....	1 408.5	764.4		338.8
1980	8 416	587.2	375.8	486.0	877.6	395.7	1 194.3	1 614.4	....	1 220.3	575.4		313.1
1981	8 270	562.5	373.8	464.8	861.9	391.6	1 170.6	1 592.4	....	1 206.8	586.0		302.1
1982	7 290	496.7	341.8	412.7	683.4	293.9	1 027.5	1 367.1	....	1 067.7	511.9		276.4
1983	7 095	555.3	356.1	411.6	619.8	256.3	993.6	1 206.9	....	1 084.8	568.3		266.7
1984	7 715	598.2	389.9	431.0	651.4	256.8	1 078.4	1 342.3	....	1 202.5	663.9		277.5
1985	7 618	592.2	393.6	426.7	611.4	231.5	1 082.9	1 319.8	....	1 243.6	684.5		264.0
1986	7 399	605.0	397.4	426.2	565.3	208.7	1 051.0	1 233.7	....	1 258.0	670.2		261.6
1987	7 409	627.8	412.0	428.7	562.2	202.8	1 037.6	1 203.4	....	1 278.2	673.1		269.4
1988	7 582	638.9	420.2	442.7	589.0	215.4	1 061.5	1 256.1	1 112.3	1 272.8	667.4	508.0	280.3
1989	7 594	625.7	417.7	443.6	588.9	215.2	1 070.4	1 281.5	1 101.7	1 277.7	663.8	509.4	277.6
1990	7 363	603.2	399.5	432.1	573.9	211.9	1 044.5	1 260.1	1 054.6	1 223.6	617.1	499.1	272.3
1991	6 967	552.5	372.6	402.5	544.8	199.6	991.0	1 193.2	999.0	1 169.2	601.5	479.4	262.9
1992	6 822	558.0	376.6	396.2	525.1	188.8	975.2	1 151.9	970.8	1 146.6	621.9	456.5	264.7
1993	6 849	583.8	384.7	398.6	520.3	183.2	988.1	1 169.5	974.5	1 120.0	642.0	438.2	270.9
1994	7 104	622.9	399.6	410.7	536.9	182.1	1 037.2	1 233.0	1 010.4	1 154.3	703.9	422.1	276.8
1995	7 298	628.3	402.3	416.8	551.5	183.9	1 080.4	1 289.0	1 044.8	1 195.9	758.9	413.7	275.3

NOTE: Data include Alaska and Hawaii beginning in 1959.

Total Employees on Nondurable Goods Manufacturing Payrolls by Industry, Selected Years, 1939-1995

(Thousands of persons)

Year	Total	Food and kindred products	Tobacco products	Textile mill products	Apparel and other textile products	Paper and allied products	Printing and publishing	Chemicals and allied products	Petroleum and coal products	Rubber and miscellaneous plastics products	Leather and leather products
1939	5 524	1 393.0	....	1 193.0	924.0	318.0	569.0	371.0	139.0	184.0	386.0
1940	5 584	1 414.0	....	1 176.0	929.0	331.0	570.0	399.0	146.0	198.0	374.0
1945	6 415	1 691.0	....	1 139.0	1 060.0	389.0	577.0	668.0	186.0	308.0	358.0
1950	7 175	1 790.0	103.0	1 256.0	1 202.0	482.0	748.0	640.0	218.0	342.0	395.0
1955	7 370	1 824.7	102.5	1 050.2	1 219.2	546.4	834.7	773.1	237.1	396.7	385.9
1956	7 442	1 841.9	99.6	1 032.0	1 223.4	564.1	862.0	796.5	235.5	403.8	382.7
1957	7 351	1 805.4	97.0	981.1	1 210.1	566.8	870.0	810.0	232.2	406.0	372.7
1958	7 144	1 772.8	94.5	918.8	1 171.8	560.4	872.6	794.1	223.8	376.2	359.2
1959	7 333	1 789.6	94.5	945.7	1 225.9	583.3	888.5	809.2	215.5	407.0	374.0
1960	7 367	1 790.0	94.0	924.4	1 233.2	597.2	911.3	828.2	211.9	413.3	363.4
1961	7 285	1 775.2	90.7	893.4	1 214.5	597.4	917.3	828.2	201.9	408.3	358.2
1962	7 403	1 763.0	90.5	902.3	1 263.7	610.4	926.4	848.5	195.3	442.0	360.7
1963	7 410	1 752.0	88.6	885.4	1 282.8	614.5	930.6	865.3	188.7	452.6	349.2
1964	7 489	1 750.4	90.2	892.0	1 302.5	621.4	951.5	878.6	183.9	470.8	347.6
1965	7 688	1 756.7	86.8	925.6	1 354.2	634.9	979.4	907.8	182.9	506.5	352.9
1966	7 963	1 777.2	84.3	963.5	1 401.9	662.5	1 016.9	961.4	184.2	547.4	363.6
1967	8 039	1 786.3	86.5	958.5	1 397.5	674.6	1 047.8	1 001.4	183.2	552.4	350.9
1968	8 187	1 781.5	84.6	993.9	1 405.8	686.7	1 065.1	1 029.9	186.8	597.5	355.2
1969	8 304	1 790.8	83.0	1 002.5	1 409.1	706.4	1 093.6	1 059.9	182.3	633.6	343.2
1970	8 190	1 786.2	82.9	974.8	1 363.8	700.9	1 104.3	1 049.3	191.2	616.7	319.5
1971	8 019	1 765.6	77.1	954.7	1 342.6	677.4	1 080.5	1 010.7	194.2	616.9	299.1
1972	8 129	1 745.2	74.9	985.7	1 382.7	678.8	1 094.0	1 009.2	195.4	666.9	296.0
1973	8 291	1 714.8	77.5	1 009.8	1 438.1	694.4	1 110.7	1 037.6	192.9	731.1	284.0
1974	8 181	1 706.7	77.1	965.0	1 362.6	696.1	1 111.3	1 060.5	197.0	733.4	271.1
1975	7 661	1 657.5	75.5	867.9	1 243.3	633.4	1 083.4	1 014.7	194.4	642.7	248.2
1976	7 946	1 688.9	76.6	918.8	1 318.1	666.4	1 099.2	1 042.5	198.5	674.7	262.7
1977	8 112	1 711.0	70.7	910.2	1 316.3	682.1	1 141.4	1 073.7	202.3	749.9	254.8
1978	8 259	1 724.1	70.6	899.1	1 332.3	688.8	1 192.0	1 095.5	207.7	792.6	256.8
1979	8 310	1 732.5	70.0	885.1	1 304.3	697.3	1 235.1	1 109.3	209.8	820.6	245.7
1980	8 127	1 708.0	68.9	847.7	1 263.5	684.6	1 252.1	1 107.4	197.9	763.8	232.9
1981	8 089	1 671.1	70.4	823.0	1 244.4	680.5	1 266.3	1 109.0	214.0	772.3	237.7
1982	7 766	1 635.8	68.7	749.4	1 161.1	655.4	1 271.4	1 075.1	200.8	729.3	218.9
1983	7 725	1 614.4	67.9	741.3	1 163.2	653.9	1 298.2	1 042.8	195.6	742.8	204.9
1984	7 896	1 611.4	64.2	746.1	1 184.8	673.8	1 375.2	1 049.0	188.9	813.2	189.4
1985	7 790	1 600.9	63.9	702.2	1 120.4	670.9	1 426.1	1 043.5	179.3	818.2	164.9
1986	7 752	1 606.7	58.5	702.9	1 099.6	667.1	1 456.0	1 021.0	168.8	822.5	149.0
1987	7 845	1 616.8	55.0	725.3	1 096.9	674.0	1 502.7	1 024.6	163.9	842.1	143.3
1988	7 951	1 626.1	54.4	728.3	1 085.1	688.8	1 542.9	1 057.3	160.1	865.6	142.6
1989	7 997	1 644.4	49.9	719.8	1 075.7	695.7	1 555.9	1 073.9	156.0	888.0	137.6
1990	7 968	1 660.5	49.1	691.4	1 036.2	696.7	1 569.4	1 086.1	157.4	887.6	133.1
1991	7 837	1 666.9	49.0	670.0	1 006.0	687.9	1 535.6	1 075.9	160.0	861.9	123.7
1992	7 827	1 662.5	47.5	674.1	1 007.2	690.3	1 506.5	1 084.1	157.6	877.6	119.9
1993	7 854	1 679.6	43.7	675.1	989.1	691.7	1 516.7	1 080.5	151.5	909.0	117.2
1994	7 873	1 678.0	42.9	676.4	974.0	692.3	1 537.2	1 057.0	149.1	953.1	112.9
1995	7 814	1 680.4	41.9	666.5	930.4	691.5	1 542.6	1 034.9	144.4	975.6	105.6

NOTE: Data include Alaska and Hawaii beginning in 1959.

Production Workers on Nondurable Goods Manufacturing Payrolls by Industry, Selected Years, 1939-1995

(Thousands of persons)

Year	Total	Food and kindred products	Tobacco products	Textile mill products	Apparel and other textile products	Paper and allied products	Printing and publishing	Chemicals and allied products	Petroleum and coal products	Rubber and miscellaneous plastics products	Leather and leather products
1939	4 392	989.0	....	1 108.0	814.0	264.6	320.0	252.0	100.0	149.0	349.0
1940	4 434	1 003.0	....	1 090.0	819.0	276.8	321.0	274.0	105.0	161.0	337.0
1945	5 438	1 380.0	....	1 074.0	973.0	342.8	381.0	518.0	148.0	255.0	325.0
1950	5 781	1 331.0	95.0	1 169.0	1 080.0	413.0	494.0	461.0	165.0	279.0	355.0
1955	5 708	1 291.7	94.4	961.6	1 086.4	450.6	539.0	518.1	163.2	316.3	344.0
1956	5 735	1 302.1	90.1	944.3	1 088.1	461.5	559.6	525.7	161.2	319.5	340.9
1957	5 607	1 263.2	85.3	893.3	1 072.0	460.3	563.7	519.7	156.6	318.1	331.0
1958	5 387	1 222.0	84.1	832.5	1 039.5	451.2	563.2	493.7	146.9	290.2	318.2
1959	5 538	1 222.1	83.9	857.4	1 091.4	468.7	575.1	505.6	139.9	317.7	332.9
1960	5 526	1 211.8	83.3	835.1	1 098.2	476.5	588.9	509.9	137.9	320.5	320.9
1961	5 433	1 191.1	79.6	805.0	1 079.6	474.9	591.7	505.0	129.9	314.7	316.4
1962	5 521	1 178.4	78.7	812.1	1 122.9	482.8	594.5	519.3	125.5	343.3	318.9
1963	5 495	1 167.1	76.6	793.4	1 138.0	483.2	590.3	525.3	119.9	349.8	307.8
1964	5 537	1 157.3	78.4	798.2	1 158.3	485.6	602.1	529.4	114.2	364.1	305.5
1965	5 688	1 159.1	74.8	826.7	1 205.6	494.4	620.6	546.1	112.9	394.3	310.0
1966	5 895	1 180.0	71.8	858.8	1 245.7	514.9	646.4	574.3	114.7	427.1	318.5
1967	5 912	1 187.3	73.9	850.2	1 237.2	522.9	661.6	592.3	114.7	425.3	303.7
1968	6 024	1 191.6	71.9	880.7	1 240.1	532.7	667.0	609.9	118.0	463.2	306.3
1969	6 084	1 201.8	69.6	884.0	1 237.9	547.0	681.7	621.9	112.2	491.3	294.4
1970	5 956	1 206.9	69.0	855.0	1 196.4	539.6	679.0	604.0	118.2	472.7	273.4
1971	5 847	1 203.2	63.4	837.2	1 177.5	518.4	658.0	587.8	124.1	478.5	257.1
1972	6 022	1 191.8	62.2	866.6	1 208.0	528.1	664.2	592.8	125.1	524.8	256.4
1973	6 138	1 166.8	64.8	886.2	1 249.7	539.6	669.6	610.5	123.9	579.1	245.0
1974	6 004	1 163.6	63.8	842.6	1 174.9	540.8	660.4	623.0	126.1	576.5	232.3
1975	5 510	1 120.3	62.4	752.4	1 066.6	476.6	624.0	579.6	123.0	492.7	212.6
1976	5 750	1 145.1	63.6	800.4	1 134.3	505.0	624.7	600.1	127.8	521.6	227.0
1977	5 855	1 161.0	57.0	792.3	1 129.4	514.8	646.5	616.0	131.3	587.7	218.4
1978	5 956	1 173.9	56.2	783.1	1 144.6	521.3	671.9	627.6	135.5	622.1	220.4
1979	5 986	1 190.8	55.5	770.9	1 116.8	532.1	697.2	633.3	137.1	643.0	209.1
1980	5 798	1 174.6	53.6	736.9	1 079.4	519.3	698.9	625.8	124.7	588.2	196.6
1981	5 751	1 149.5	54.7	712.5	1 059.5	515.0	699.3	628.3	133.9	596.8	201.1
1982	5 451	1 125.5	53.4	642.1	981.2	490.7	699.1	598.6	119.9	557.8	182.9
1983	5 433	1 113.5	52.0	639.2	983.5	491.2	711.5	578.6	118.0	574.2	171.1
1984	5 565	1 118.9	48.6	645.6	1 002.1	508.1	757.7	582.8	111.3	632.2	158.0
1985	5 466	1 117.0	48.0	606.3	943.9	508.4	787.9	577.4	108.5	631.7	136.6
1986	5 465	1 129.4	44.1	608.1	926.0	507.2	815.7	567.6	105.9	638.5	122.7
1987	5 543	1 145.1	41.5	629.5	921.7	512.3	839.4	574.6	106.8	652.6	119.7
1988	5 611	1 154.8	40.7	631.8	912.4	516.3	863.6	596.0	104.3	673.5	117.8
1989	5 636	1 176.2	37.0	621.9	906.8	520.5	863.2	603.1	101.8	691.5	114.1
1990	5 584	1 193.8	36.3	592.9	868.5	522.3	871.2	599.6	102.9	686.9	109.4
1991	5 467	1 205.2	36.3	574.1	841.1	517.4	847.0	579.7	103.4	662.0	100.2
1992	5 466	1 211.9	35.7	577.1	843.9	519.8	833.1	567.1	103.3	677.1	96.9
1993	5 492	1 227.8	32.8	574.5	828.6	521.6	838.5	572.6	98.9	703.3	93.7
1994	5 528	1 230.9	33.0	574.5	814.7	524.2	845.5	577.5	96.6	741.8	89.6
1995	5 489	1 238.0	31.9	563.1	771.6	524.5	846.1	578.0	93.3	759.5	82.8

NOTE: Data include Alaska and Hawaii beginning in 1959.

Women Employees on Nonagricultural Payrolls by Industry, 1960-1995

(Thousands of persons)

| Year | Total | Mining | Con-struc-tion | Manufacturing | | | Trans-porta-tion and public utilities | Whole-sale trade | Retail trade | Fi-nance, insur-ance, and real estate | Serv-ices | Government | | | |
				Total	Durable goods	Nondurable goods						Total	Federal	State	Local
1960	....	36	....	4 371	1 702	2 670	....	717	3 579	....	....	....	....	....	....
1961	....	35	....	4 292	1 662	2 630	....	703	3 564	....	....	....	....	....	....
1962	....	35	....	4 474	1 770	2 705	....	712	3 643	....	....	....	....	....	....
1963	....	35	....	4 482	1 767	2 715	....	720	3 708	....	....	....	....	....	....
1964	19 662	34	152	4 537	1 777	2 760	723	741	3 878	1 464	4 415	3 718	530	708	2 480
1965	20 660	34	152	4 768	1 911	2 857	748	768	4 113	1 496	4 611	3 970	542	768	2 660
1966	22 168	34	156	5 213	2 204	3 009	786	809	4 315	1 549	4 931	4 375	610	841	2 924
1967	23 272	35	158	5 353	2 300	3 053	835	832	4 465	1 624	5 267	4 703	674	931	3 099
1968	24 395	36	164	5 490	2 361	3 129	860	857	4 669	1 709	5 632	4 979	710	1 013	3 256
1969	25 595	37	174	5 667	2 469	3 197	911	904	4 937	1 819	5 994	5 153	723	1 087	3 343
1970	26 132	37	186	5 448	2 307	3 141	957	924	5 083	1 907	6 224	5 365	723	1 126	3 517
1971	26 466	37	199	5 229	2 152	3 078	955	917	5 211	1 978	6 438	5 502	715	1 118	3 669
1972	27 541	40	219	5 470	2 280	3 190	953	939	5 410	2 032	6 718	5 759	747	1 162	3 849
1973	28 988	43	241	5 865	2 567	3 298	987	996	5 686	2 138	7 023	6 010	780	1 216	4 014
1974	30 124	49	262	5 849	2 618	3 230	1 018	1 050	5 928	2 245	7 454	6 270	798	1 287	4 185
1975	30 178	55	256	5 257	2 271	2 985	996	1 053	5 998	2 287	7 822	6 454	805	1 373	4 276
1976	31 570	60	281	5 607	2 444	3 163	1 010	1 100	6 301	2 371	8 256	6 586	808	1 448	4 329
1977	33 252	65	304	5 880	2 645	3 235	1 051	1 153	6 611	2 511	8 771	6 907	856	1 510	4 540
1978	35 349	76	331	6 237	2 894	3 343	1 133	1 243	7 036	2 708	9 368	7 216	866	1 537	4 813
1979	37 096	91	355	6 466	3 085	3 380	1 237	1 328	7 369	2 882	9 919	7 450	860	1 572	5 018
1980	38 186	105	372	6 317	3 003	3 314	1 292	1 371	7 480	3 039	10 452	7 759	908	1 632	5 219
1981	39 035	129	380	6 341	3 029	3 312	1 340	1 404	7 585	3 158	10 969	7 730	878	1 659	5 193
1982	39 041	134	377	5 990	2 822	3 168	1 339	1 424	7 653	3 198	11 330	7 595	883	1 637	5 075
1983	39 826	117	388	5 964	2 788	3 176	1 313	1 463	7 912	3 277	11 755	7 637	939	1 584	5 114
1984	42 022	118	427	6 295	3 031	3 265	1 386	1 557	8 519	3 430	12 413	7 878	975	1 678	5 224
1985	43 851	120	463	6 230	3 022	3 208	1 448	1 632	9 037	3 634	13 129	8 159	1 009	1 776	5 374
1986	45 476	106	495	6 181	2 974	3 207	1 480	1 684	9 404	3 886	13 819	8 420	1 031	1 848	5 541
1987	47 188	95	523	6 242	2 987	3 255	1 532	1 736	9 764	4 076	14 549	8 672	1 048	1 919	5 705
1988	49 026	96	539	6 352	3 032	3 320	1 592	1 815	10 113	4 134	15 454	8 931	1 060	2 000	5 870
1989	50 672	94	547	6 399	3 048	3 351	1 625	1 891	10 384	4 188	16 296	9 248	1 105	2 070	6 073
1990	51 877	95	552	6 285	2 969	3 316	1 698	1 892	10 445	4 239	16 958	9 714	1 258	2 141	6 315
1991	51 986	97	532	6 067	2 824	3 243	1 692	1 864	10 304	4 215	17 352	9 862	1 226	2 177	6 460
1992	52 449	93	511	5 964	2 736	3 228	1 676	1 838	10 312	4 192	17 830	10 033	1 226	2 202	6 606
1993	53 531	88	521	5 933	2 710	3 222	1 710	1 826	10 471	4 279	18 507	10 197	1 211	2 245	6 742
1994	55 126	85	546	5 987	2 761	3 226	1 761	1 890	10 834	4 354	19 271	10 397	1 197	2 289	6 911
1995	56 637	81	573	5 992	2 808	3 185	1 826	1 971	11 162	4 309	20 132	10 591	1 201	2 339	7 051

NOTE: Data include Alaska and Hawaii beginning in 1959.

EMPLOYMENT, HOURS, AND EARNINGS, NONAGRICULTURAL PAYROLLS

Average Weekly Hours of Production or Nonsupervisory Workers on Private Nonagricultural Payrolls by Industry, 1964-1995

Year	Total private	Mining	Construction	Manufacturing			Transportation and public utilities	Wholesale trade	Retail trade	Finance, insurance, and real estate	Services
				Total	Durable goods	Nondurable goods					
1964	38.7	41.9	37.2	40.7	41.5	39.7	41.1	40.7	37.0	37.3	36.1
1965	38.8	42.3	37.4	41.2	42.0	40.1	41.3	40.8	36.6	37.2	35.9
1966	38.6	42.7	37.6	41.4	42.1	40.2	41.2	40.7	35.9	37.3	35.5
1967	38.0	42.6	37.7	40.6	41.2	39.7	40.5	40.3	35.3	37.1	35.1
1968	37.8	42.6	37.3	40.7	41.4	39.8	40.6	40.1	34.7	37.0	34.7
1969	37.7	43.0	37.9	40.6	41.3	39.7	40.7	40.2	34.2	37.1	34.7
1970	37.1	42.7	37.3	39.8	40.3	39.1	40.5	39.9	33.8	36.7	34.4
1971	36.9	42.4	37.2	39.9	40.3	39.3	40.1	39.4	33.7	36.6	33.9
1972	37.0	42.6	36.5	40.5	41.2	39.7	40.4	39.4	33.4	36.6	33.9
1973	36.9	42.4	36.8	40.7	41.4	39.6	40.5	39.2	33.1	36.6	33.8
1974	36.5	41.9	36.6	40.0	40.6	39.1	40.2	38.8	32.7	36.5	33.6
1975	36.1	41.9	36.4	39.5	39.9	38.8	39.7	38.6	32.4	36.5	33.5
1976	36.1	42.4	36.8	40.1	40.6	39.4	39.8	38.7	32.1	36.4	33.3
1977	36.0	43.4	36.5	40.3	41.0	39.4	39.9	38.8	31.6	36.4	33.0
1978	35.8	43.4	36.8	40.4	41.1	39.4	40.0	38.8	31.0	36.4	32.8
1979	35.7	43.0	37.0	40.2	40.8	39.3	39.9	38.8	30.6	36.2	32.7
1980	35.3	43.3	37.0	39.7	40.1	39.0	39.6	38.4	30.2	36.2	32.6
1981	35.2	43.7	36.9	39.8	40.2	39.2	39.4	38.5	30.1	36.3	32.6
1982	34.8	42.7	36.7	38.9	39.3	38.4	39.0	38.3	29.9	36.2	32.6
1983	35.0	42.5	37.1	40.1	40.7	39.4	39.0	38.5	29.8	36.2	32.7
1984	35.2	43.3	37.8	40.7	41.4	39.7	39.4	38.5	29.8	36.5	32.6
1985	34.9	43.4	37.7	40.5	41.2	39.6	39.5	38.4	29.4	36.4	32.5
1986	34.8	42.2	37.4	40.7	41.3	39.9	39.2	38.3	29.2	36.4	32.5
1987	34.8	42.4	37.8	41.0	41.5	40.2	39.2	38.1	29.2	36.3	32.5
1988	34.7	42.3	37.9	41.1	41.8	40.2	38.8	38.1	29.1	35.9	32.6
1989	34.6	43.0	37.9	41.0	41.6	40.2	38.9	38.0	28.9	35.8	32.6
1990	34.5	44.1	38.2	40.8	41.3	40.0	38.9	38.1	28.8	35.8	32.5
1991	34.3	44.4	38.1	40.7	41.1	40.2	38.7	38.1	28.6	35.7	32.4
1992	34.4	43.9	38.0	41.0	41.5	40.4	38.9	38.2	28.8	35.8	32.5
1993	34.5	44.3	38.5	41.4	42.1	40.6	39.6	38.2	28.8	35.8	32.5
1994	34.7	44.8	38.9	42.0	42.9	40.9	39.9	38.4	28.9	35.8	32.5
1995	34.5	44.7	38.8	41.6	42.4	40.5	39.5	38.3	28.8	35.9	32.4

Note: Data include Alaska and Hawaii beginning in 1959.

Average Weekly Hours of Production Workers on Manufacturing Payrolls by Industry, 1947-1995

Year	Durable goods										
	Total	Lumber and wood products	Furniture and fix-tures	Stone, clay, and glass products	Primary metal industries	Fab-ricated metal products	Industrial machinery and equip-ment	Electrical and elec-tronic equip-ment	Transpor-tation equip-ment	Instru-ments and related products	Mis-cellane-ous manufac-turing
1947	40.5	40.3	41.5	41.0	39.9	40.9	41.5	40.3	39.7	40.4	40.5
1948	40.4	40.0	41.0	40.7	40.2	40.7	41.3	....	39.4	....	40.6
1949	39.4	39.2	40.0	39.7	38.4	39.7	39.6	....	39.6	....	39.6
1950	41.1	39.5	41.8	41.1	40.9	41.5	41.9	41.1	41.4	41.3	40.8
1951	41.5	39.3	41.1	41.4	41.6	41.8	43.5	....	41.2	....	40.5
1952	41.4	39.7	41.4	41.1	40.8	41.7	43.0	....	41.8	....	40.7
1953	41.2	39.3	40.9	40.8	41.0	41.8	42.4	....	41.6	....	40.5
1954	40.1	39.1	40.0	40.5	38.8	40.8	40.7	....	40.9	....	39.6
1955	41.3	39.5	41.4	41.4	41.3	41.7	41.9	40.7	42.3	40.9	40.3
1956	41.0	38.9	40.7	41.1	41.0	41.3	42.3	....	41.4	....	40.0
1957	40.3	38.4	39.9	40.4	39.6	40.9	41.1	....	40.8	....	39.7
1958	39.5	38.6	39.3	40.0	38.3	39.9	39.8	....	40.0	....	39.2
1959	40.7	39.7	40.7	41.2	40.5	40.9	41.5	....	40.7	....	39.9
1960	40.1	39.1	40.0	40.6	39.0	40.5	41.0	39.8	40.7	40.4	39.3
1961	40.2	39.5	40.0	40.7	39.5	40.5	40.9	40.2	40.5	40.7	39.5
1962	40.9	39.8	40.7	41.0	40.2	41.1	41.7	40.6	42.0	40.9	39.7
1963	41.1	40.2	40.9	41.4	41.0	41.3	41.8	40.3	42.0	40.8	39.6
1964	41.5	40.4	41.2	41.7	41.7	41.7	42.4	40.5	42.1	40.8	39.6
1965	42.0	40.9	41.5	42.0	42.1	42.1	43.1	41.0	42.9	41.4	39.9
1966	42.1	40.8	41.5	42.0	42.1	42.4	43.8	41.2	42.6	42.1	40.0
1967	41.2	40.3	40.4	41.6	41.1	41.5	42.5	40.2	41.4	41.2	39.4
1968	41.4	40.6	40.6	41.8	41.6	41.7	42.0	40.3	42.2	40.5	39.4
1969	41.3	40.2	40.4	41.9	41.8	41.6	42.5	40.4	41.5	40.7	39.0
1970	40.3	39.6	39.2	41.2	40.4	40.7	41.1	39.8	40.3	40.2	38.7
1971	40.3	39.8	39.8	41.6	40.1	40.4	40.6	39.9	40.7	39.8	38.9
1972	41.2	40.4	40.2	42.0	41.4	41.2	42.1	40.4	41.7	40.6	39.5
1973	41.4	40.0	40.0	41.9	42.3	41.6	42.8	40.4	42.1	40.9	39.0
1974	40.6	39.2	39.1	41.3	41.6	40.8	42.1	39.7	40.5	40.4	38.7
1975	39.9	38.8	38.0	40.4	40.0	40.1	40.8	39.5	40.4	39.5	38.5
1976	40.6	39.9	38.8	41.1	40.8	40.8	41.2	40.0	41.7	40.3	38.8
1977	41.0	39.9	39.0	41.3	41.3	41.0	41.5	40.4	42.5	40.6	38.8
1978	41.1	39.8	39.3	41.6	41.8	41.0	42.0	40.3	42.2	40.9	38.8
1979	40.8	39.5	38.7	41.5	41.4	40.7	41.7	40.3	41.1	40.8	38.8
1980	40.1	38.6	38.1	40.8	40.1	40.4	41.0	39.8	40.6	40.5	38.7
1981	40.2	38.7	38.4	40.6	40.5	40.3	40.9	40.0	40.9	40.4	38.8
1982	39.3	38.1	37.2	40.1	38.6	39.2	39.7	39.3	40.5	39.8	38.4
1983	40.7	40.1	39.4	41.5	40.5	40.6	40.5	40.5	42.1	40.4	39.1
1984	41.4	39.9	39.7	42.0	41.7	41.4	41.9	41.0	42.7	41.3	39.4
1985	41.2	39.9	39.4	41.9	41.5	41.3	41.5	40.6	42.6	41.0	39.4
1986	41.3	40.4	39.8	42.2	41.9	41.3	41.6	41.0	42.3	41.0	39.6
1987	41.5	40.6	40.0	42.3	43.1	41.6	42.2	40.9	42.0	41.4	39.4
1988	41.8	40.1	39.4	42.3	43.5	41.9	42.7	41.0	42.7	41.5	39.2
1989	41.6	40.1	39.5	42.3	43.0	41.6	42.4	40.8	42.4	41.1	39.4
1990	41.3	40.2	39.1	42.0	42.7	41.3	41.9	40.8	42.0	41.1	39.5
1991	41.1	40.0	38.9	41.7	42.2	41.2	41.7	40.7	41.9	41.0	39.7
1992	41.5	40.6	39.7	42.2	43.0	41.6	42.2	41.2	41.8	41.1	39.9
1993	42.1	40.8	40.1	42.7	43.7	42.1	43.0	41.8	43.0	41.1	39.8
1994	42.8	41.2	40.4	43.4	44.7	42.9	43.7	42.2	44.3	41.7	40.0
1995	42.4	40.6	39.6	43.0	44.0	42.3	43.4	41.6	43.8	41.4	39.9

NOTE: Data include Alaska and Hawaii beginning in 1959.

Average Weekly Hours of Production Workers on Manufacturing Payrolls by Industry, 1947-1995—Continued

Year	Nondurable goods										
	Total	Food and kindred products	Tobacco manufactures	Textile mill products	Apparel and other textile products	Paper and allied products	Printing and publishing	Chemicals and allied products	Petroleum and coal products	Rubber and miscellaneous plastics products	Leather and leather products
1947	40.2	43.2	38.9	39.6	36.0	43.1	40.2	41.2	40.6	40.0	38.6
1948	39.6	42.4	38.3	39.2	35.8	42.8	39.4	41.2	40.6	39.3	37.2
1949	38.9	41.9	37.3	37.7	35.4	41.7	38.8	40.7	40.3	38.5	36.6
1950	39.7	41.9	38.1	39.6	36.0	43.3	38.9	41.2	40.8	41.0	37.6
1951	39.6	42.1	38.5	38.8	35.6	43.1	38.9	41.3	40.8	40.8	36.9
1952	39.7	41.9	38.4	39.1	36.3	42.8	38.9	40.9	40.5	40.9	38.4
1953	39.6	41.5	38.1	39.1	36.1	43.0	39.0	41.0	40.7	40.4	37.7
1954	39.0	41.3	37.6	38.3	35.3	42.3	38.5	40.8	40.7	39.8	36.9
1955	39.9	41.5	38.7	40.1	36.3	43.1	38.9	41.1	40.9	41.7	37.9
1956	39.6	41.3	38.8	39.7	36.0	42.8	38.9	41.1	41.0	40.4	37.6
1957	39.2	40.8	38.4	38.9	35.7	42.3	38.6	40.9	40.8	40.6	37.4
1958	38.8	40.8	39.1	38.6	35.1	41.9	38.0	40.7	40.9	39.3	36.7
1959	30.7	41.0	39.1	40.4	36.3	42.8	38.5	41.4	41.2	41.3	37.9
1960	39.2	40.8	38.2	39.5	35.5	42.1	38.4	41.3	41.1	40.0	36.9
1961	39.3	40.9	39.0	39.9	35.4	42.5	38.2	41.4	41.2	40.4	37.4
1962	39.7	41.0	38.6	40.6	36.2	42.6	38.3	41.6	41.6	41.0	37.6
1963	39.6	41.0	38.7	40.6	36.1	42.7	38.3	41.6	41.7	40.9	37.5
1964	39.7	41.0	38.8	41.0	35.9	42.8	38.5	41.6	41.8	41.3	37.9
1965	40.1	41.1	37.9	41.7	36.4	43.1	38.6	41.9	42.2	42.0	38.2
1966	40.2	41.2	38.9	41.9	36.4	43.4	38.8	42.0	42.4	42.0	38.6
1967	39.7	40.9	38.6	40.9	36.0	42.8	38.4	41.6	42.7	41.4	38.2
1968	39.8	40.8	37.9	41.2	36.1	42.9	38.3	41.8	42.5	41.5	38.3
1969	39.7	40.8	37.4	40.8	35.9	43.0	38.3	41.8	42.6	41.2	37.2
1970	39.1	40.5	37.8	39.9	35.3	41.9	37.7	41.6	42.8	40.3	37.2
1971	39.3	40.3	37.8	40.6	35.6	42.1	37.5	41.6	42.8	40.4	37.7
1972	39.7	40.5	37.6	41.3	36.0	42.8	37.7	41.7	42.7	41.2	38.3
1973	39.6	40.4	38.6	40.9	35.9	42.9	37.7	41.8	42.4	41.2	37.8
1974	39.1	40.4	38.3	39.5	35.2	42.2	37.5	41.5	42.1	40.6	36.9
1975	38.8	40.3	38.2	39.3	35.2	41.6	36.9	41.0	41.2	39.9	37.1
1976	39.4	40.5	37.5	40.1	35.8	42.5	37.5	41.6	42.1	40.7	37.4
1977	39.4	40.0	37.8	40.4	35.6	42.9	37.7	41.7	42.7	41.1	36.9
1978	39.4	39.7	38.1	40.4	35.6	42.9	37.6	41.9	43.6	40.9	37.1
1979	39.3	39.9	38.0	40.4	35.3	42.6	37.5	41.9	43.8	40.6	36.5
1980	39.0	39.7	38.1	40.1	35.4	42.2	37.1	41.5	41.8	40.0	36.7
1981	39.2	39.7	38.8	39.6	35.7	42.5	37.3	41.6	43.2	40.3	36.7
1982	38.4	39.4	37.8	37.5	34.7	41.8	37.1	40.9	43.9	39.6	35.6
1983	39.4	39.5	37.4	40.4	36.2	42.6	37.6	41.6	43.9	41.2	36.8
1984	39.7	39.8	38.9	39.9	36.4	43.1	37.9	41.9	43.7	41.7	36.8
1985	39.6	40.0	37.2	39.7	36.4	43.1	37.8	41.9	43.0	41.1	37.2
1986	39.9	40.0	37.4	41.1	36.7	43.2	38.0	41.9	43.8	41.4	36.9
1987	40.2	40.2	39.0	41.8	37.0	43.4	38.0	42.3	44.0	41.6	38.2
1988	40.2	40.3	39.8	41.0	37.0	43.3	38.0	42.2	44.4	41.7	37.5
1989	40.2	40.7	38.6	40.9	36.9	43.3	37.9	42.4	44.3	41.4	37.9
1990	40.0	40.8	39.2	39.9	36.4	43.3	37.9	42.6	44.6	41.1	37.4
1991	40.2	40.6	39.1	40.6	37.0	43.3	37.7	42.9	44.1	41.1	37.5
1992	40.4	40.6	38.6	41.1	37.2	43.6	38.1	43.1	43.8	41.7	38.0
1993	40.6	40.7	37.4	41.4	37.2	43.6	38.3	43.1	44.2	41.8	38.6
1994	40.9	41.3	39.3	41.6	37.5	43.9	38.6	43.2	44.4	42.2	38.6
1995	40.5	41.1	39.6	40.8	37.0	43.1	38.2	43.2	43.7	41.5	38.0

NOTE: Data include Alaska and Hawaii beginning in 1959.

Average Weekly Overtime Hours of Production Workers on Manufacturing Payrolls by Industry, Selected Years, 1956-1995

| Year | Manufac-turing | Durable goods | | | | | | | | | | | | | |
| | | Total | Lumber and wood products | Furniture and fix-tures | Stone, clay, and glass products | Primary metal industries | | Fab-ricated metal products | Industrial machinery and equip-ment | Electrical and elec-tronic equip-ment | Transportation equipment | | Instru-ments and relat-ed prod-ucts | Mis-cellane-ous man-ufacturing |
						Total	Blast fur-nace and basic steel products				Total	Motor ve-hicles and equip-ment		
1956	2.8	3.0	2.6	2.3	3.3	2.8	....	3.1	3.9	2.6	3.1	....	2.5	2.8
1957	2.3	2.4	2.2	1.9	2.8	2.0	....	2.8	2.8	....	2.5	....	....	2.4
1958	2.0	1.9	2.3	2.0	2.8	1.4	0.9	2.1	1.8	....	2.1	2.3	....	1.9
1959	2.7	2.7	3.2	2.8	3.6	2.6	2.2	2.8	2.9	....	2.6	3.1	....	2.4
1960	2.5	2.4	2.9	2.5	3.1	1.8	1.3	2.6	2.7	1.9	2.7	3.2	2.1	2.1
1961	2.4	2.4	2.9	2.4	3.2	1.9	1.3	2.4	2.5	1.9	2.5	2.6	2.1	2.2
1962	2.8	2.8	3.2	2.9	3.4	2.2	1.4	2.9	3.1	2.2	3.5	4.1	2.4	2.3
1963	2.8	3.0	3.3	3.0	3.7	2.7	1.9	3.0	3.2	2.0	3.6	4.4	2.4	2.2
1964	3.1	3.3	3.4	3.2	3.9	3.2	2.4	3.4	3.9	2.3	3.9	5.0	2.4	2.4
1965	3.6	3.9	3.8	3.6	4.2	3.8	2.8	4.0	4.6	2.8	4.8	6.2	3.0	2.7
1966	3.9	4.3	4	3.8	4.5	4.0	2.7	4.5	5.5	3.4	4.7	4.9	3.8	3.0
1967	3.4	3.5	3.6	3.0	4.2	3.2	2.1	3.8	4.4	2.5	3.7	3.4	3.1	2.6
1968	3.6	3.8	3.9	3.4	4.5	3.8	2.9	4.1	4.0	2.6	4.6	5.8	2.7	2.5
1969	3.6	3.8	3.8	3.3	4.8	4.1	3.2	4.2	4.5	2.8	3.8	4.2	3.0	2.6
1970	3.0	3.0	3.3	2.3	4.2	3.0	2.3	3.3	3.2	2.3	2.9	3.2	2.3	2.2
1971	2.9	2.9	3.6	2.6	4.5	3.0	2.3	2.8	2.6	2.1	3.1	3.6	2.1	2.2
1972	3.5	3.6	4.0	3.1	4.8	3.6	2.6	3.5	3.8	2.7	4.3	5.3	2.7	2.7
1973	3.8	4.1	3.9	3.1	5.0	4.5	3.5	4.1	4.8	3.1	4.9	6.1	3.1	2.6
1974	3.3	3.4	3.3	2.4	4.4	3.9	3.1	3.5	4.2	2.4	3.4	3.5	2.7	2.2
1975	2.6	2.6	2.9	1.8	3.7	2.6	1.9	2.6	2.9	1.9	2.8	2.6	1.8	1.9
1976	3.1	3.2	3.5	2.0	4.1	3.3	2.5	3.2	3.3	2.3	4.2	5.4	2.3	2.2
1977	3.5	3.7	3.7	2.4	4.6	3.7	2.8	3.6	4.0	2.6	5.0	6.4	2.4	2.2
1978	3.6	3.8	3.7	2.7	4.8	4.2	3.5	3.8	4.3	2.8	5.0	6.1	2.6	2.4
1979	3.3	3.5	3.5	2.2	4.5	3.9	3.4	3.4	4.0	2.7	4.2	4.4	2.5	2.2
1980	2.8	2.8	2.8	1.7	3.8	2.8	2.2	2.8	3.4	2.3	3.2	2.6	2.3	1.9
1981	2.8	2.8	2.6	1.8	3.8	3.0	2.7	2.7	3.2	2.2	3.2	3.0	2.2	1.9
1982	2.3	2.2	2.3	1.5	3.5	2.0	1.5	2.0	2.2	1.8	2.7	2.5	1.7	1.6
1983	3.0	3.0	3.1	2.3	4.1	3.0	2.3	2.9	2.7	2.6	3.9	4.8	2.0	2.0
1984	3.4	3.6	3.2	2.5	4.8	3.9	3.1	3.6	3.7	3.1	4.7	5.6	2.5	2.2
1985	3.3	3.5	3.2	2.4	4.8	3.8	3.2	3.5	3.4	2.7	4.8	5.4	2.5	2.2
1986	3.4	3.5	3.5	2.6	4.9	4.1	3.8	3.5	3.4	2.8	4.3	4.4	2.7	2.4
1987	3.7	3.8	3.8	2.8	5.1	4.9	5.0	3.8	4.0	3.0	4.2	4.3	3.0	2.6
1988	3.9	4.1	3.6	2.7	5.2	5.5	5.8	4.1	4.4	3.4	4.7	5.2	3.1	2.5
1989	3.8	3.9	3.5	2.7	5.1	5.2	5.5	3.9	4.3	3.2	4.6	4.7	2.8	2.5
1990	3.6	3.7	3.5	2.4	4.9	5.0	5.6	3.6	3.9	3.1	4.0	4.1	2.8	2.5
1991	3.6	3.5	3.3	2.4	4.6	4.6	4.8	3.5	3.7	3.2	3.8	4.0	2.9	2.6
1992	3.8	3.7	3.8	2.8	4.9	5.0	5.3	3.8	4.0	3.4	3.8	4.1	2.8	2.8
1993	4.1	4.3	4.1	3.1	5.2	5.6	5.8	4.3	4.7	3.9	4.8	5.8	2.8	2.8
1994	4.7	5.0	4.5	3.4	5.8	6.6	6.5	5.1	5.4	4.3	6.2	7.6	3.3	3.1
1995	4.4	4.7	4.1	3.0	5.5	6.1	6.4	4.7	5.1	4.0	5.8	6.6	3.4	3.0

NOTE: Data include Alaska and Hawaii beginning in 1959.

Average Weekly Overtime Hours of Production Workers on Manufacturing Payrolls by Industry, Selected Years, 1956-1995—Continued

Year	Nondurable goods										
	Total	Food and kindred products	Tobacco manufactures	Textile mill products	Apparel and other textile products	Paper and allied products	Printing and publishing	Chemicals and allied products	Petroleum and coal products	Rubber and miscellaneous plastics products	Leather and leather products
1956	2.4	3.1	1.3	2.6	1.0	4.5	3.1	2.1	2.2	2.2	1.4
1957	2.3	2.9	1.4	2.2	1.0	4.2	2.9	2.0	2.0	2.2	1.3
1958	2.2	3.1	1.3	2.1	1.0	3.9	2.5	1.9	1.8	2.0	1.1
1959	2.7	3.3	1.2	3.1	1.3	4.5	2.8	2.5	2.0	3.5	1.4
1960	2.5	3.3	1.0	2.6	1.2	4.1	2.9	2.3	2.0	2.4	1.2
1961	2.5	3.3	1.1	2.7	1.1	4.2	2.7	2.3	2.0	2.7	1.4
1962	2.7	3.4	1.0	3.2	1.3	4.4	2.8	2.5	2.3	3.1	1.4
1963	2.7	3.4	1.1	3.2	1.3	4.5	2.7	2.5	2.3	3.0	1.4
1964	2.9	3.6	1.6	3.6	1.3	4.7	2.9	2.7	2.5	3.5	1.7
1965	3.2	3.8	1.1	4.2	1.4	5.0	3.1	3.0	2.8	4.1	1.8
1966	3.4	4.0	1.4	4.4	1.5	5.5	3.5	3.3	3.2	4.4	2.1
1967	3.1	4.0	1.8	3.7	1.3	5.0	3.2	3.0	3.5	4.0	1.9
1968	3.3	4.1	1.8	4.1	1.4	5.3	3.1	3.3	3.6	4.2	2.1
1969	3.4	4.2	1.4	3.9	1.3	5.5	3.4	3.4	3.9	4.2	1.8
1970	3.0	4.0	1.7	3.3	1.1	4.6	2.8	3.1	3.8	3.4	1.7
1971	3.0	3.8	1.7	3.8	1.2	4.6	2.6	3.1	3.7	3.3	1.9
1972	3.3	4.0	1.6	4.5	1.5	4.9	2.9	3.2	3.8	4.0	2.3
1973	3.4	4.1	2.4	4.4	1.5	5.2	3.0	3.5	3.9	4.3	2.1
1974	3.0	4.1	2.1	3.3	1.2	4.6	2.7	3.3	3.9	3.5	1.8
1975	2.7	3.9	2.0	3.1	1.2	4.0	2.2	2.7	3.0	2.9	1.9
1976	3.0	4.1	1.3	3.4	1.3	4.8	2.5	3.2	3.5	3.6	1.9
1977	3.2	4.1	1.9	3.5	1.3	4.8	2.8	3.4	4.0	3.7	1.8
1978	3.2	4.0	2.1	3.6	1.3	5.1	3.0	3.5	4.3	3.7	1.8
1979	3.1	4.0	1.3	3.5	1.0	4.8	2.8	3.5	4.3	3.1	1.4
1980	2.8	3.8	1.7	3.2	1.0	4.3	2.5	3.1	3.7	2.7	1.5
1981	2.8	3.7	2.0	3.0	1.1	4.5	2.4	3.3	3.8	3.1	1.4
1982	2.5	3.6	1.4	2.2	1.0	4.1	2.3	2.8	3.9	2.7	1.2
1983	3.0	3.6	1.2	3.5	1.3	4.6	2.6	3.1	4.0	3.5	1.4
1984	3.1	3.8	1.4	3.2	1.4	4.9	2.8	3.4	4.2	3.9	1.4
1985	3.1	3.8	1.1	3.2	1.4	4.7	2.7	3.3	4.2	3.6	1.5
1986	3.3	3.9	1.4	4.0	1.6	4.8	2.9	3.6	4.5	3.8	1.5
1987	3.6	4.1	2.8	4.4	1.8	5.2	3.1	4.0	5.0	4.1	2.2
1988	3.6	4.2	2.6	4.0	1.8	5.0	3.1	4.1	5.5	4.1	2.0
1989	3.6	4.4	2.1	4.0	1.9	4.5	3.0	4.2	5.8	3.8	2.0
1990	3.6	4.5	2.3	3.6	1.6	4.8	3.0	4.4	6.1	3.6	1.8
1991	3.7	4.5	2.0	4.1	1.8	4.9	2.7	4.5	6.2	3.6	1.9
1992	3.8	4.5	2.1	4.3	1.8	5.3	2.9	4.8	6.2	4.1	2.1
1993	4.0	4.6	1.9	4.4	1.8	5.4	3.1	4.8	6.0	4.4	2.3
1994	4.3	4.9	3.7	4.7	2.1	5.6	3.4	5.0	6.4	4.7	2.5
1995	4.0	4.8	4.7	4.2	1.8	5.2	3.1	4.9	6.1	4.1	2.0

Note: Data include Alaska and Hawaii beginning in 1959.

Indexes of Aggregate Weekly Hours of Production or Nonsupervisory Workers on Private Nonagricultural Payrolls by Industry, 1947-1995

(1982=100)

Year	Total private	Goods-producing						Service-producing					
		Total	Mining	Construction	Manufacturing			Total	Transportation and public utilities	Wholesale trade	Retail trade	Finance, insurance, and real estate	Services
					Total	Durable Goods	Nondurable Goods						
1947	....	98.0	101.4	62.0	105.8	99.2	114.9	....	....	56.8	....	....	....
1948	....	97.8	101.9	67.6	104.2	97.4	113.8	....	....	59.5	....	....	....
1949	....	88.2	86.8	66.7	93.0	84.0	105.6	....	....	59.0	....	....	....
1950	....	96.1	88.3	71.3	102.2	96.0	110.8	....	....	59.7	....	....	....
1951	....	103.7	91.9	81.0	109.6	108.0	111.7	....	....	61.7	....	....	....
1952	....	103.9	88.2	83.3	109.6	108.9	110.6	....	....	63.3	....	....	....
1953	....	107.3	84.8	80.5	114.8	116.9	112.0	....	....	63.7	....	....	....
1954	....	96.8	75.5	78.2	102.4	100.5	105.3	....	....	63.1	....	....	....
1955	....	103.0	78.9	83.4	109.0	108.5	109.8	....	....	64.4	....	....	....
1956	....	104.7	81.5	90.2	109.5	109.5	109.5	....	....	65.9	....	....	....
1957	....	101.1	79.6	86.6	105.9	105.8	106.0	....	....	65.4	....	....	....
1958	....	90.9	67.9	80.8	94.8	90.4	100.9	....	....	63.6	....	....	....
1959	....	97.8	68.1	86.7	102.3	99.6	106.1	....	....	66.4	....	....	....
1960	....	95.8	65.7	83.2	100.7	98.1	104.4	....	....	67.3	....	....	....
1961	....	92.4	61.5	81.4	97.0	92.8	103.0	....	....	66.8	....	....	....
1962	....	96.3	59.8	83.9	101.6	98.8	105.6	....	....	68.1	....	....	....
1963	....	97.4	59.1	86.8	102.4	100.6	105.0	....	....	68.8	....	....	....
1964	75.8	99.7	59.4	89.1	104.9	104.1	106.1	65.1	87.7	70.6	73.2	60.4	51.9
1965	79.1	105.6	59.6	93.4	111.5	112.7	109.9	67.3	89.9	73.3	75.9	61.4	54.0
1966	82.5	112.0	59.3	96.3	119.2	122.7	114.4	69.3	91.7	75.7	77.6	62.8	56.4
1967	82.9	109.8	57.0	93.8	117.1	119.8	113.3	70.8	92.1	76.5	78.3	64.8	58.9
1968	84.9	111.7	56.0	95.6	119.2	121.7	115.7	72.8	93.4	77.7	80.1	67.8	61.3
1969	87.7	114.5	57.9	103.6	121.0	124.2	116.5	75.7	96.3	80.6	82.6	71.6	64.2
1970	86.3	107.8	57.6	101.3	112.8	113.0	112.4	76.7	96.9	81.7	83.4	73.0	65.3
1971	85.8	105.0	54.9	103.6	108.8	107.4	110.8	77.2	95.1	80.4	85.3	74.3	65.6
1972	89.2	110.5	57.8	107.9	114.8	115.4	114.1	79.6	97.3	82.5	88.2	76.5	68.0
1973	93.2	116.9	58.8	113.7	121.7	125.8	116.0	82.5	99.9	85.6	90.9	78.9	71.3
1974	93.2	113.7	63.4	109.5	118.1	122.4	112.1	84.0	100.4	87.6	91.0	79.8	73.9
1975	88.8	99.9	68.3	92.7	103.8	104.9	102.1	83.9	94.6	86.4	90.6	79.9	76.0
1976	92.3	105.4	71.5	94.0	110.3	111.9	108.1	86.4	95.5	89.1	93.9	81.5	78.8
1977	96.0	110.3	76.5	100.2	115.0	118.4	110.2	89.5	97.9	92.5	96.5	85.4	82.0
1978	100.7	116.5	79.0	112.2	120.1	125.9	112.0	93.6	101.3	97.7	100.0	90.3	86.3
1979	104.0	119.9	88.2	119.9	122.1	129.1	112.3	96.9	104.9	102.0	101.5	94.4	90.2
1980	102.8	112.9	94.1	115.1	113.8	117.8	108.1	98.3	104.1	101.9	100.1	97.8	94.3
1981	104.1	111.6	104.8	109.3	112.5	116.1	107.6	100.8	103.3	103.3	100.6	105.5	98.2
1982	100.0	100.0	100.0	100.0	100.0	100.0	100.0	100.0	100.0	100.0	100.0	100.0	100.0
1983	101.5	100.5	81.5	102.2	101.4	100.7	102.4	102.0	97.3	99.9	102.7	101.6	103.6
1984	107.7	109.0	84.9	116.8	109.0	111.5	105.5	107.1	102.8	105.3	108.2	106.4	108.2
1985	110.5	108.7	81.4	125.3	106.9	109.5	103.4	111.3	104.6	108.4	111.7	110.9	114.0
1986	112.3	107.3	65.7	128.2	105.7	106.8	104.2	114.6	104.0	108.5	114.3	116.7	119.2
1987	115.6	109.0	61.8	132.7	107.0	107.4	106.6	118.5	106.5	109.4	117.9	120.1	124.9
1988	119.3	111.4	61.7	136.9	109.3	110.5	107.7	122.8	108.2	113.3	121.0	119.2	132.2
1989	122.1	111.7	60.5	138.9	109.3	110.1	108.2	126.8	111.1	116.1	122.9	119.5	139.3
1990	123.0	109.5	63.9	138.0	106.4	106.1	106.8	129.1	114.5	115.7	123.0	120.2	144.2
1991	120.4	103.4	62.0	122.8	102.1	99.3	105.9	128.0	113.4	113.7	119.5	118.3	145.3
1992	121.2	102.1	56.2	118.4	101.7	98.2	106.6	129.7	113.6	112.8	120.6	118.1	149.3
1993	124.6	104.2	54.3	125.4	103.1	100.0	107.4	133.7	118.2	112.8	123.4	121.2	155.4
1994	130.0	109.2	54.6	136.3	107.0	105.5	109.2	139.3	122.4	116.9	128.6	124.0	162.9
1995	133.5	110.0	54.0	140.7	107.2	107.2	107.2	144.0	124.9	121.8	132.1	123.3	170.4

NOTE: Data include Alaska and Hawaii beginning in 1959.

Indexes of Aggregate Weekly Hours of Production Workers on Manufacturing Payrolls by Industry, 1947-1995

(1982=100)

Year	Durable goods										
	Total	Lumber and wood products	Furniture and fixtures	Stone, clay, and glass products	Primary metal industries	Fabricated metal products	Industrial machinery and equipment	Electrical and electronic equipment	Transportation equipment	Instruments and related products	Miscellaneous manufacturing
1947	99.2	173.6	92.0	110.4	161.7	89.1	83.9		94.3		140.1
1948	97.4	167.0	93.3	111.7	163.5	87.0	82.4		92.6		139.1
1949	84.0	146.9	82.0	100.4	135.0	74.9	66.3		88.3		121.9
1950	96.0	162.4	99.2	111.1	159.7	88.8	72.5		97.4		131.8
1951	108.0	167.4	94.5	120.2	177.4	98.4	91.4		115.6		132.1
1952	108.9	158.2	94.7	112.7	160.7	97.7	93.1		130.8		127.3
1953	116.9	152.8	96.7	115.3	174.6	107.8	93.6		151.5		136.0
1954	100.5	139.1	86.3	107.6	143.5	94.1	79.5		127.4		121.6
1955	108.5	147.5	95.1	117.5	167.3	100.9	83.7		138.7		125.2
1956	109.5	143.1	96.1	119.2	168.7	100.2	91.4		130.8		125.4
1957	105.8	126.3	93.5	113.9	161.0	100.6	87.5		131.7		117.6
1958	90.4	118.9	87.9	104.8	129.1	88.5	70.2		104.4		110.5
1959	99.6	132.0	97.7	117.0	140.2	95.6	79.4		111.4		117.6
1960	98.1	123.1	95.4	114.1	141.4	95.0	79.2		106.8		116.4
1961	92.8	115.2	90.9	109.3	132.0	90.2	74.5		96.4		113.0
1962	98.8	118.5	97.5	112.0	137.4	96.5	80.7		106.6		117.1
1963	100.6	120.2	99.2	114.6	141.7	99.2	82.5		111.2		115.7
1964	104.1	122.8	103.8	117.9	153.0	102.8	88.5		111.5		118.3
1965	112.7	125.3	111.1	121.2	163.2	110.8	97.6		125.0		126.0
1966	122.7	126.9	118.8	124.4	168.4	122.1	109.6		136.7		130.3
1967	119.8	121.5	113.5	119.1	158.1	124.2	108.5		133.2		125.6
1968	121.7	124.8	118.6	121.9	158.1	128.8	105.2		141.7		126.1
1969	124.2	126.5	121.5	126.4	165.1	132.6	109.4		138.5		126.5
1970	113.0	117.9	111.6	120.9	152.9	120.3	101.2		114.1		119.8
1971	107.4	123.8	114.0	122.2	140.5	113.2	89.5		112.6		116.2
1972	115.4	136.1	126.6	131.1	146.3	121.9	97.8		118.4		126.2
1973	125.8	140.6	132.0	138.4	161.8	131.8	111.8		129.1		130.9
1974	122.4	128.2	123.4	134.5	162.4	127.4	116.1		117.9		128.8
1975	104.9	107.8	100.7	115.6	134.3	108.4	101.6		106.8		112.5
1976	111.9	123.5	111.0	120.8	140.0	115.3	102.6		117.9		120.1
1977	118.4	132.0	117.2	125.9	144.2	121.9	109.8		125.6		122.2
1978	125.9	138.3	125.6	132.1	151.3	129.3	119.4		133.6		125.9
1979	129.1	138.6	123.5	132.8	154.8	131.4	126.9		134.1		123.8
1980	117.8	119.9	112.4	119.8	133.4	119.8	122.1		114.6		113.9
1981	116.1	115.1	112.7	114.1	132.5	117.1	120.2		114.2		110.5
1982	100.0	100.0	100.0	100.0	100.0	100.0	100.0		100.0		100.0
1983	100.7	117.7	110.3	103.2	95.2	100.3	90.1		105.7		98.1
1984	111.5	126.3	121.6	109.5	102.9	111.0	103.8		118.9		102.9
1985	109.5	124.9	121.9	108.1	96.1	111.2	101.0		122.7		97.8
1986	106.8	129.2	124.2	108.7	89.8	107.8	94.7		123.3		97.5
1987	107.4	134.9	129.5	109.7	91.8	107.1	93.8		124.3		99.9
1988	110.5	135.6	130.1	113.3	97.2	110.5	98.8	113.1	125.8	89.9	103.5
1989	110.1	132.6	129.6	113.5	96.0	110.6	100.3	111.5	125.3	89.6	103.0
1990	106.1	128.2	122.8	109.7	93.0	107.1	97.5	106.5	119.1	87.6	101.1
1991	99.3	116.9	113.9	101.4	87.2	101.4	91.8	100.7	113.3	84.0	98.1
1992	98.2	119.9	117.6	101.2	85.6	100.7	89.6	99.1	110.9	80.2	99.4
1993	100.0	126.1	121.3	102.9	86.2	103.3	92.7	100.9	111.4	77.0	101.6
1994	105.5	135.9	127.0	107.9	90.9	110.5	99.1	105.7	118.5	75.2	104.2
1995	107.2	135.0	125.3	108.5	91.9	113.7	102.4	107.8	121.2	73.2	103.3

NOTE: Data include Alaska and Hawaii beginning in 1959.

Indexes of Aggregate Weekly Hours of Production Workers on Manufacturing Payrolls by Industry,1947-1995—Continued

(1982=100)

Year	Nondurable goods										
	Total	Food and kindred products	Tobacco manufac- tures	Textile mill products	Apparel and other textile products	Paper and allied products	Printing and pub- lishing	Chemi- cals and allied products	Petroleum and coal products	Rubber and mis- cellane- ous plas- tics prod- ucts	Leather and leather products
1947	114.9	136.0	212.3	200.9	110.6	84.8	75.6	82.2	131.0	52.6	221.8
1948	113.8	131.3	202.2	203.3	112.7	84.6	75.0	81.6	135.3	50.0	211.2
1949	105.6	126.6	186.4	172.6	109.4	78.6	73.1	74.7	129.7	43.8	195.8
1950	110.8	125.7	178.9	192.5	114.0	87.1	74.2	77.6	127.7	51.7	205.0
1951	111.7	127.1	182.8	184.8	113.0	90.9	75.8	84.7	133.9	55.2	193.1
1952	110.6	125.7	184.8	174.5	115.8	87.5	76.6	84.6	130.0	55.0	203.0
1953	112.0	124.5	180.5	172.9	118.2	92.3	78.5	87.6	134.0	57.8	202.2
1954	105.3	120.7	177.2	151.7	109.1	90.4	78.0	83.9	129.1	51.1	188.4
1955	109.8	120.8	180.7	160.3	115.9	94.6	81.0	87.0	127.0	59.8	200.0
1956	109.5	121.2	173.0	155.6	114.9	96.3	84.0	88.2	125.6	58.5	196.9
1957	106.0	116.3	162.2	144.3	112.4	94.9	83.9	86.7	121.6	58.4	190.4
1958	100.9	112.3	162.7	133.7	107.2	92.1	82.6	82.1	114.3	51.6	179.3
1959	106.1	112.8	162.2	144.1	116.3	97.7	85.4	85.6	109.5	59.4	193.6
1960	104.4	111.5	157.6	137.1	114.3	97.9	87.4	86.0	107.7	58.0	181.9
1961	103.0	109.8	153.7	133.4	112.1	98.4	87.3	85.3	101.9	57.5	181.6
1962	105.6	108.8	150.4	137.0	119.4	100.2	87.9	88.1	99.2	63.7	184.4
1963	105.0	107.8	146.5	133.8	120.7	100.7	87.2	89.2	94.9	64.8	177.2
1964	106.1	107.0	150.8	136.1	122.1	101.3	89.4	89.9	90.9	68.2	177.7
1965	109.9	107.4	140.3	143.4	128.7	104.0	92.4	93.5	90.6	75.0	182.0
1966	114.4	109.5	138.2	149.5	133.2	109.0	96.8	98.6	92.4	81.3	188.8
1967	113.3	109.4	141.0	144.4	130.8	109.1	97.9	100.6	93.0	79.7	178.0
1968	115.7	109.5	134.8	150.6	131.3	111.4	98.5	104.1	95.4	87.0	180.0
1969	116.5	110.5	128.8	150.0	130.5	114.6	100.9	106.2	90.9	91.6	168.1
1970	112.4	110.2	129.2	141.8	123.9	110.2	98.9	102.5	96.2	86.3	156.4
1971	110.8	109.3	118.7	141.3	122.9	106.4	95.3	99.8	100.9	87.5	148.7
1972	114.1	108.7	115.9	148.9	127.8	110.3	96.5	100.9	101.5	97.8	150.7
1973	116.0	106.3	124.0	150.7	131.7	112.7	97.4	104.2	99.9	107.9	142.3
1974	112.1	106.0	120.9	138.5	121.3	111.2	95.5	105.7	100.9	105.8	131.8
1975	102.1	101.8	118.1	122.9	110.2	96.8	88.9	97.1	96.3	89.0	121.3
1976	108.1	104.4	118.2	133.3	119.3	104.7	90.3	102.0	102.3	96.1	130.6
1977	110.2	104.6	106.8	132.9	117.9	107.6	94.1	105.0	106.6	109.2	123.9
1978	112.0	105.1	106.1	131.6	119.5	109.0	97.5	107.4	112.2	115.3	125.5
1979	112.3	107.0	104.4	129.3	115.6	110.5	101.0	108.3	114.0	118.2	117.1
1980	108.1	105.1	101.2	122.7	112.2	106.9	100.1	106.0	99.1	106.7	110.7
1981	107.6	102.8	105.1	117.3	111.0	106.8	100.6	106.8	110.0	109.0	113.6
1982	100.0	100.0	100.0	100.0	100.0	100.0	100.0	100.0	100.0	100.0	100.0
1983	102.4	99.1	96.3	107.4	104.5	102.1	103.3	98.3	98.4	107.2	96.8
1984	105.5	100.3	93.5	107.0	107.2	106.8	110.9	99.8	92.5	119.6	89.3
1985	103.4	100.6	88.4	100.1	100.7	106.8	114.9	98.9	88.7	117.6	78.1
1986	104.2	101.7	81.6	103.8	99.7	106.9	119.6	97.3	88.1	119.6	69.5
1987	106.6	103.7	80.1	109.4	100.1	108.5	123.2	99.3	89.4	123.1	70.3
1988	107.7	105.0	80.1	107.7	99.0	108.9	126.7	102.9	88.1	127.3	67.9
1989	108.2	107.8	70.6	105.6	98.3	109.9	126.2	104.5	85.7	129.6	66.4
1990	106.8	109.7	70.6	98.4	92.9	110.4	127.5	104.3	87.2	127.9	62.8
1991	105.9	110.2	70.2	97.0	91.3	109.3	123.3	101.6	86.7	123.2	57.7
1992	106.6	110.9	68.2	98.6	92.2	110.5	122.3	100.0	86.0	127.8	56.6
1993	107.4	112.6	60.7	98.9	90.4	110.9	123.9	100.9	83.1	133.2	55.6
1994	109.2	114.6	64.1	99.4	89.7	112.3	125.9	102.0	81.4	141.9	53.0
1995	107.2	114.7	62.5	95.4	83.7	110.3	124.7	102.1	77.5	142.8	48.3

NOTE: Data include Alaska and Hawaii beginning in 1959.

Average Hourly Earnings of Production or Nonsupervisory Workers on Private Nonagricultural Payrolls by Industry, 1939-1995

(Dollars)

Year	Total private	Mining	Construction	Manufacturing			Transportation and public Utilities	Wholesale trade	Retail trade	Finance, insurance, and real estate	Services
				Total	Durable goods	Nondurable goods					
1939	...	...	...	...	0.69	0.57	...	...	...	...	...
1940	...	...	...	0.66	0.72	0.59	...	...	...	...	...
1941	...	...	...	0.73	0.80	0.63	...	...	...	...	...
1942	...	...	...	0.85	0.94	0.71	...	...	...	...	...
1943	...	...	...	0.96	1.05	0.79	...	...	...	...	...
1944	...	...	...	1.01	1.10	0.85	...	...	...	...	...
1945	...	...	...	1.02	1.10	0.89	...	...	...	...	...
1946	...	...	...	1.08	1.14	1.00	...	...	...	...	...
1947	...	1.47	1.54	1.22	1.28	1.15	...	1.22	0.84	1.14	...
1948	...	1.66	1.71	1.33	1.39	1.25	...	1.31	0.90	1.20	...
1949	...	1.72	1.79	1.38	1.45	1.30	...	1.36	0.95	1.26	...
1950	1.34	1.77	1.86	1.44	1.45	1.30	...	1.36	0.98	1.26	...
1951	1.45	1.93	2.02	1.56	1.65	1.45	...	1.52	1.06	1.45	...
1952	1.52	2.01	2.13	1.64	1.74	1.51	...	1.61	1.09	1.51	...
1953	1.61	2.14	2.28	1.74	1.85	1.58	...	1.69	1.16	1.58	...
1954	1.65	2.14	2.38	1.78	1.89	1.62	...	1.76	1.20	1.65	...
1955	1.71	2.20	2.45	1.85	1.98	1.68	...	1.83	1.25	1.70	...
1956	1.80	2.33	2.57	1.95	2.08	1.77	...	1.93	1.30	1.78	...
1957	1.89	2.45	2.71	2.04	2.18	1.85	...	2.02	1.37	1.84	...
1958	1.95	2.47	2.82	2.10	2.25	1.92	...	2.09	1.42	1.89	...
1959	2.02	2.56	2.93	2.19	2.35	1.98	...	2.18	1.47	1.95	...
1960	2.09	2.60	3.07	2.26	2.42	2.05	...	2.24	1.52	2.02	...
1961	2.14	2.64	3.20	2.32	2.48	2.11	...	2.31	1.56	2.09	...
1962	2.22	2.70	3.31	2.39	2.55	2.17	...	2.37	1.63	2.17	...
1963	2.28	2.75	3.41	2.45	2.63	2.22	...	2.45	1.68	2.25	...
1964	2.36	2.81	3.55	2.53	2.70	2.29	2.89	2.52	1.75	2.30	1.94
1965	2.46	2.92	3.70	2.61	2.78	2.36	3.03	2.60	1.82	2.39	2.05
1966	2.56	3.05	3.89	2.71	2.89	2.45	3.11	2.73	1.91	2.47	2.17
1967	2.68	3.19	4.11	2.82	2.99	2.57	3.23	2.87	2.01	2.58	2.29
1968	2.85	3.35	4.41	3.01	3.18	2.74	3.42	3.04	2.16	2.75	2.42
1969	3.04	3.60	4.79	3.19	3.38	2.91	3.63	3.23	2.30	2.93	2.61
1970	3.23	3.85	5.24	3.35	3.55	3.08	3.85	3.43	2.44	3.07	2.81
1971	3.45	4.06	5.69	3.57	3.79	3.27	4.21	3.64	2.60	3.22	3.04
1972	3.70	4.44	6.06	3.82	4.07	3.48	4.65	3.85	2.75	3.36	3.27
1973	3.94	4.75	6.41	4.09	4.35	3.70	5.02	4.07	2.91	3.53	3.47
1974	4.24	5.23	6.81	4.42	4.70	4.01	5.41	4.38	3.14	3.77	3.75
1975	4.53	5.95	7.31	4.83	5.15	4.37	5.88	4.72	3.36	4.06	4.02
1976	4.86	6.46	7.71	5.22	5.57	4.71	6.45	5.02	3.57	4.27	4.31
1977	5.25	6.94	8.10	5.68	6.06	5.11	6.99	5.39	3.85	4.54	4.65
1978	5.69	7.67	8.66	6.17	6.58	5.54	7.57	5.88	4.20	4.89	4.99
1979	6.16	8.49	9.27	6.70	7.12	6.01	8.16	6.39	4.53	5.27	5.36
1980	6.66	9.17	9.94	7.27	7.75	6.56	8.87	6.95	4.88	5.79	5.85
1981	7.25	10.04	10.82	7.99	8.53	7.19	9.70	7.55	5.25	6.31	6.41
1982	7.68	10.77	11.63	8.49	9.03	7.75	10.32	8.08	5.48	6.78	6.92
1983	8.02	11.28	11.94	8.83	9.38	8.09	10.79	8.54	5.74	7.29	7.31
1984	8.32	11.63	12.13	9.19	9.73	8.39	11.12	8.88	5.85	7.63	7.59
1985	8.57	11.98	12.32	9.54	10.09	8.72	11.40	9.15	5.94	7.94	7.90
1986	8.76	12.46	12.48	9.73	10.28	8.95	11.70	9.34	6.03	8.36	8.18
1987	8.98	12.54	12.71	9.91	10.43	9.19	12.03	9.59	6.12	8.73	8.49
1988	9.28	12.80	13.08	10.19	10.71	9.45	12.26	9.98	6.31	9.06	8.88
1989	9.66	13.26	13.54	10.48	11.01	9.75	12.60	10.39	6.53	9.53	9.38
1990	10.01	13.68	13.77	10.83	11.35	10.12	12.97	10.79	6.75	9.97	9.83
1991	10.32	14.19	14.00	11.18	11.75	10.44	13.22	11.15	6.94	10.39	10.23
1992	10.57	14.54	14.15	11.46	12.02	10.73	13.45	11.39	7.12	10.82	10.54
1993	10.83	14.60	14.38	11.74	12.33	10.98	13.62	11.74	7.29	11.35	10.78
1994	11.12	14.88	14.73	12.07	12.68	11.24	13.86	12.06	7.49	11.83	11.04
1995	11.44	15.30	15.08	12.37	12.93	11.58	14.23	12.43	7.69	12.33	11.39

NOTE: Data include Alaska and Hawaii beginning in 1959.

Average Hourly Earnings of Production Workers on Manufacturing Payrolls by Industry, 1947-1995
(Dollars)

Year	Durable goods												
	Total	Lumber and wood products	Furniture and fixtures	Stone, clay, and glass products	Primary metal industries		Fab-ricated metal products	Industrial machinery and equip-ment	Electrical and electronic equip-ment	Transportation equipment		Instru-ments and related products	Mis-cellane-ous manufac-turing
					Total	Blast fur-nace and basic steel products				Total	Motor vehicles and equip-ment		
1947	1.28	1.09	1.10	1.19	1.39	1.44	1.27	1.34	1.25	1.44	1.47	1.20	1.11
1948	1.39	1.19	1.19	1.31	1.52	1.59	1.39	1.46	....	1.57	1.61	....	1.18
1949	1.45	1.23	1.23	1.37	1.59	1.65	1.45	1.52	....	1.64	1.70	....	1.22
1950	1.45	1.30	1.28	1.44	1.64	1.70	1.52	1.60	1.44	1.72	1.78	1.45	1.28
1951	1.65	1.41	1.39	1.54	1.81	1.90	1.64	1.75	....	1.84	1.91	....	1.36
1952	1.74	1.49	1.47	1.61	1.90	2.00	1.72	1.85	....	1.95	2.05	....	1.45
1953	1.85	1.56	1.54	1.72	2.06	2.18	1.83	1.95	....	2.05	2.14	....	1.52
1954	1.89	1.57	1.57	1.77	2.10	2.22	1.88	2.00	....	2.11	2.20	....	1.56
1955	1.98	1.62	1.62	1.86	2.24	2.39	1.96	2.08	1.84	2.21	2.29	1.87	1.61
1956	2.08	1.69	1.69	1.96	2.37	2.54	2.05	2.20	....	2.29	2.35	....	1.69
1957	2.18	1.74	1.75	2.05	2.50	2.70	2.16	2.29	....	2.39	2.46	....	1.75
1958	2.25	1.80	1.78	2.12	2.64	2.88	2.26	2.37	....	2.51	2.55	....	1.79
1959	2.35	1.87	1.83	2.22	2.77	3.06	2.35	2.48	....	2.64	2.71	....	1.84
1960	2.42	1.90	1.88	2.28	2.81	3.04	2.43	2.55	2.28	2.74	2.81	2.31	1.89
1961	2.48	1.95	1.91	2.34	2.90	3.16	2.49	2.62	2.35	2.80	2.86	2.38	1.92
1962	2.55	1.99	1.95	2.41	2.98	3.25	2.55	2.71	2.40	2.91	2.99	2.44	1.98
1963	2.63	2.05	2.00	2.48	3.04	3.31	2.61	2.78	2.46	3.01	3.10	2.49	2.03
1964	2.70	2.12	2.05	2.53	3.11	3.36	2.68	2.87	2.51	3.09	3.21	2.54	2.08
1965	2.78	2.18	2.12	2.62	3.18	3.42	2.76	2.95	2.58	3.21	3.34	2.62	2.14
1966	2.89	2.26	2.21	2.72	3.28	3.53	2.88	3.08	2.65	3.33	3.44	2.73	2.22
1967	2.99	2.38	2.33	2.82	3.34	3.57	2.98	3.19	2.77	3.44	3.55	2.85	2.35
1968	3.18	2.58	2.47	2.99	3.55	3.76	3.16	3.36	2.93	3.69	3.89	2.98	2.50
1969	3.38	2.75	2.62	3.19	3.79	4.02	3.34	3.58	3.09	3.89	4.10	3.15	2.66
1970	3.55	2.97	2.77	3.40	3.93	4.16	3.53	3.77	3.28	4.06	4.22	3.34	2.83
1971	3.79	3.18	2.90	3.67	4.23	4.49	3.77	4.02	3.49	4.45	4.72	3.50	2.97
1972	4.07	3.34	3.08	3.94	4.66	5.08	4.05	4.32	3.71	4.81	5.13	3.66	3.11
1973	4.35	3.62	3.29	4.22	5.04	5.51	4.29	4.60	3.91	5.15	5.46	3.83	3.29
1974	4.70	3.90	3.53	4.54	5.60	6.27	4.61	4.94	4.21	5.54	5.87	4.11	3.53
1975	5.15	4.28	3.78	4.92	6.18	6.94	5.05	5.37	4.64	6.07	6.44	4.53	3.81
1976	5.57	4.74	3.99	5.33	6.77	7.59	5.50	5.79	4.96	6.62	7.09	4.93	4.04
1977	6.06	5.11	4.34	5.81	7.40	8.36	5.91	6.26	5.39	7.29	7.85	5.29	4.36
1978	6.58	5.62	4.68	6.32	8.20	9.39	6.35	6.78	5.82	7.91	8.50	5.71	4.69
1979	7.12	6.08	5.06	6.85	8.98	10.41	6.85	7.32	6.32	8.53	9.06	6.17	5.03
1980	7.75	6.57	5.49	7.50	9.77	11.39	7.45	8.00	6.94	9.35	9.85	6.80	5.46
1981	8.53	7.02	5.91	8.27	10.81	12.60	8.20	8.81	7.62	10.39	11.02	7.40	5.97
1982	9.03	7.46	6.31	8.87	11.33	13.35	8.77	9.26	8.21	11.11	11.62	8.06	6.42
1983	9.38	7.82	6.62	9.27	11.35	12.89	9.12	9.56	8.67	11.67	12.14	8.48	6.81
1984	9.73	8.05	6.84	9.57	11.47	12.98	9.40	9.97	9.04	12.20	12.73	8.84	7.05
1985	10.09	8.25	7.17	9.84	11.67	13.33	9.71	10.30	9.46	12.71	13.39	9.17	7.30
1986	10.28	8.37	7.46	10.04	11.86	13.73	9.89	10.58	9.65	12.81	13.45	9.47	7.55
1987	10.43	8.43	7.67	10.25	11.94	13.77	10.01	10.73	9.88	12.94	13.53	9.72	7.76
1988	10.71	8.59	7.95	10.56	12.16	13.98	10.29	11.08	9.79	13.29	13.99	9.98	8.00
1989	11.01	8.84	8.25	10.82	12.43	14.25	10.57	11.40	10.05	13.67	14.25	10.83	8.29
1990	11.35	9.08	8.52	11.12	12.92	14.82	10.83	11.77	10.30	14.08	14.56	11.29	8.61
1991	11.75	9.24	8.76	11.36	13.33	15.36	11.19	12.15	10.70	14.75	15.23	11.64	8.85
1992	12.02	9.44	9.01	11.60	13.66	15.87	11.42	12.41	11.00	15.20	15.45	11.89	9.15
1993	12.33	9.61	9.27	11.85	13.99	16.36	11.69	12.73	11.24	15.80	16.10	12.23	9.39
1994	12.68	9.84	9.55	12.13	14.34	16.85	11.93	13.00	11.50	16.51	17.02	12.47	9.67
1995	12.93	10.12	9.82	12.41	14.62	17.35	12.12	13.24	11.67	16.75	17.36	12.71	10.06

NOTE: Data include Alaska and Hawaii beginning in 1959.

Average Hourly Earnings of Production Workers on Manufacturing Payrolls by Industry, 1947-1995—Continued

(Dollars)

Year	Nondurable goods										
	Total	Food and kindred products	Tobacco manufactures	Textile mill products	Apparel and other textile products	Paper and allied products	Printing and publishing	Chemicals and allied products	Petroleum and coal products	Rubber and miscellaneous plastics products	Leather and leather products
1947	1.15	1.06	0.90	1.04	1.16	1.15	1.48	1.22	1.50	1.29	1.04
1948	1.25	1.15	0.96	1.16	1.22	1.28	1.65	1.34	1.71	1.36	1.11
1949	1.30	1.25	1.00	1.18	1.21	1.33	1.77	1.42	1.80	1.41	1.12
1950	1.30	1.26	1.08	1.23	1.24	1.40	1.83	1.50	1.84	1.47	1.17
1951	1.45	1.35	1.14	1.32	1.31	1.51	1.91	1.62	1.99	1.58	1.25
1952	1.51	1.44	1.18	1.34	1.32	1.59	2.02	1.69	2.10	1.70	1.30
1953	1.58	1.53	1.25	1.36	1.35	1.67	2.11	1.81	2.22	1.79	1.35
1954	1.62	1.59	1.30	1.36	1.37	1.73	2.18	1.89	2.29	1.83	1.36
1955	1.68	1.66	1.34	1.38	1.37	1.81	2.26	1.97	2.37	1.95	1.39
1956	1.77	1.76	1.45	1.44	1.47	1.92	2.33	2.09	2.54	2.02	1.48
1957	1.85	1.85	1.53	1.49	1.51	2.02	2.40	2.20	2.66	2.11	1.52
1958	1.92	1.94	1.59	1.49	1.54	2.10	2.49	2.29	2.73	2.18	1.56
1959	1.98	2.02	1.65	1.56	1.56	2.18	2.59	2.40	2.85	2.27	1.59
1960	2.05	2.11	1.70	1.61	1.59	2.26	2.68	2.50	2.89	2.32	1.64
1961	2.11	2.17	1.78	1.63	1.64	2.34	2.75	2.58	3.01	2.38	1.68
1962	2.17	2.24	1.85	1.68	1.69	2.40	2.82	2.65	3.05	2.44	1.72
1963	2.22	2.30	1.91	1.71	1.73	2.48	2.89	2.72	3.16	2.47	1.76
1964	2.29	2.37	1.95	1.79	1.79	2.56	2.97	2.80	3.20	2.54	1.83
1965	2.36	2.44	2.09	1.87	1.83	2.65	3.06	2.89	3.28	2.61	1.88
1966	2.45	2.52	2.19	1.96	1.89	2.75	3.16	2.98	3.41	2.68	1.94
1967	2.57	2.64	2.27	2.06	2.03	2.87	3.28	3.10	3.58	2.75	2.07
1968	2.74	2.80	2.48	2.21	2.21	3.05	3.48	3.26	3.75	2.93	2.23
1969	2.91	2.96	2.62	2.35	2.31	3.24	3.69	3.47	4.00	3.08	2.36
1970	3.08	3.16	2.91	2.45	2.39	3.44	3.92	3.69	4.28	3.21	2.49
1971	3.27	3.38	3.16	2.57	2.49	3.67	4.20	3.97	4.57	3.41	2.59
1972	3.48	3.60	3.47	2.75	2.60	3.95	4.51	4.26	4.96	3.63	2.68
1973	3.70	3.85	3.76	2.95	2.76	4.20	4.75	4.51	5.28	3.84	2.79
1974	4.01	4.19	4.12	3.20	2.97	4.53	5.03	4.88	5.68	4.09	2.99
1975	4.37	4.61	4.55	3.42	3.17	5.01	5.38	5.39	6.48	4.42	3.21
1976	4.71	4.98	4.98	3.69	3.40	5.47	5.71	5.91	7.21	4.71	3.40
1977	5.11	5.37	5.54	3.99	3.62	5.96	6.12	6.43	7.83	5.21	3.61
1978	5.54	5.80	6.13	4.30	3.94	6.52	6.51	7.02	8.63	5.57	3.89
1979	6.01	6.27	6.67	4.66	4.23	7.13	6.94	7.60	9.36	6.02	4.22
1980	6.56	6.85	7.74	5.07	4.56	7.84	7.53	8.30	10.10	6.58	4.58
1981	7.19	7.44	8.88	5.52	4.97	8.60	8.19	9.12	11.38	7.22	4.99
1982	7.75	7.92	9.79	5.83	5.20	9.32	8.74	9.96	12.46	7.70	5.33
1983	8.09	8.19	10.38	6.18	5.38	9.93	9.11	10.58	13.28	8.06	5.54
1984	8.39	8.39	11.22	6.46	5.55	10.41	9.41	11.07	13.44	8.35	5.71
1985	8.72	8.57	11.96	6.70	5.73	10.83	9.71	11.56	14.06	8.60	5.83
1986	8.95	8.75	12.88	6.93	5.84	11.18	9.99	11.98	14.19	8.79	5.92
1987	9.19	8.93	14.07	7.17	5.94	11.43	10.28	12.37	14.58	8.98	6.08
1988	9.45	9.12	14.67	7.38	6.12	11.69	10.53	12.71	14.97	9.19	6.28
1989	9.75	9.38	15.31	7.67	6.35	11.96	10.88	13.09	15.41	9.46	6.59
1990	10.12	9.62	16.23	8.02	6.57	12.31	11.24	13.54	16.24	9.76	6.91
1991	10.44	9.90	16.77	8.30	6.77	12.72	11.48	14.04	17.04	10.07	7.18
1992	10.73	10.20	16.92	8.60	6.95	13.07	11.74	14.51	17.90	10.36	7.42
1993	10.98	10.45	16.89	8.88	7.09	13.42	11.93	14.82	18.53	10.57	7.63
1994	11.24	10.66	19.07	9.13	7.34	13.77	12.14	15.13	19.07	10.70	7.97
1995	11.58	10.94	19.48	9.41	7.64	14.23	12.33	15.63	19.36	10.92	8.17

NOTE: Data include Alaska and Hawaii beginning in 1959.

Average Hourly Earnings Excluding Overtime of Production Workers on Manufacturing Payrolls by Industry, 1956-1995

(Dollars)

| Year | Manufac-turing total | Durable goods | | | | | | | | | | |
		Total	Lumber and wood products	Furniture and fix-tures	Stone, clay and glass products	Primary metal industries	Fabricated metal prod-ucts	Industrial machinery and equip-ment	Electrical and elec-tronic equipment	Transpor-tation equipment	Instru-ments and related products	Miscellane-ous manufac-turing
1956	1.89	2.00	1.64	1.65	1.89	2.29	1.98	2.10	....	2.20	....	1.63
1957	1.98	2.12	1.69	1.71	1.98	2.44	2.09	2.21	....	2.32	....	1.70
1958	2.05	2.20	1.75	1.74	2.05	2.59	2.20	2.31	....	2.44	....	1.74
1959	2.12	2.27	1.80	1.77	2.13	2.68	2.27	2.40	....	2.56	....	1.79
1960	2.19	2.35	1.83	1.82	2.20	2.75	2.36	2.47	2.22	2.65	2.25	1.84
1961	2.25	2.41	1.88	1.86	2.25	2.84	2.41	2.54	2.29	2.72	2.32	1.87
1962	2.31	2.47	1.92	1.89	2.31	2.90	2.46	2.61	2.34	2.80	2.37	1.92
1963	2.37	2.53	1.97	1.93	2.37	2.94	2.51	2.68	2.40	2.89	2.42	1.98
1964	2.43	2.59	2.03	1.97	2.42	2.99	2.57	2.75	2.44	2.96	2.47	2.02
1965	2.50	2.66	2.08	2.03	2.49	3.04	2.64	2.80	2.49	3.04	2.53	2.07
1966	2.59	2.75	2.15	2.11	2.58	3.13	2.73	2.90	2.54	3.15	2.61	2.15
1967	2.71	2.87	2.27	2.24	2.68	3.21	2.85	3.03	2.69	3.29	2.75	2.27
1968	2.88	3.05	2.46	2.38	2.84	3.40	3.01	3.21	2.84	3.50	2.89	2.43
1969	3.05	3.23	2.62	2.52	3.01	3.61	3.18	3.40	2.98	3.72	3.04	2.57
1970	3.23	3.42	2.85	2.69	3.23	3.79	3.39	3.63	3.19	3.92	3.25	2.75
1971	3.45	3.66	3.04	2.81	3.49	4.08	3.64	3.89	3.40	4.29	3.41	2.89
1972	3.66	3.89	3.19	2.97	3.73	4.47	3.88	4.13	3.59	4.57	3.54	3.01
1973	3.91	4.14	3.45	3.16	3.98	4.79	4.09	4.35	3.77	4.86	3.69	3.19
1974	4.25	4.51	3.74	3.42	4.31	5.35	4.42	4.70	4.08	5.32	3.98	3.43
1975	4.67	4.99	4.12	3.69	4.71	5.98	4.89	5.19	4.54	5.87	4.43	3.72
1976	5.02	5.36	4.54	3.89	5.08	6.51	5.29	5.56	4.82	6.30	4.79	3.93
1977	5.44	5.80	4.88	4.21	5.50	7.08	5.66	5.97	5.22	6.88	5.14	4.24
1978	5.91	6.28	5.36	4.52	5.98	7.81	6.07	6.45	5.63	7.47	5.54	4.55
1979	6.43	6.83	5.83	4.92	6.49	8.57	6.57	6.99	6.11	8.12	5.99	4.89
1980	7.02	7.48	6.34	5.37	7.17	9.44	7.20	7.68	6.75	8.99	6.61	5.33
1981	7.72	8.24	6.79	5.77	7.90	10.41	7.93	8.48	7.42	10.00	7.20	5.82
1982	8.25	8.79	7.24	6.19	8.50	11.04	8.55	9.01	8.02	10.75	7.90	6.29
1983	8.52	9.05	7.53	6.43	8.83	10.94	8.81	9.25	8.40	11.15	8.27	6.64
1984	8.82	9.33	7.74	6.63	9.05	10.96	9.01	9.54	8.71	11.57	8.58	6.86
1985	9.16	9.68	7.93	6.96	9.31	11.16	9.32	9.90	9.16	12.03	8.89	7.10
1986	9.34	9.86	8.02	7.22	9.50	11.30	9.49	10.16	9.32	12.19	9.17	7.33
1987	9.48	9.97	8.06	7.41	9.67	11.29	9.57	10.24	9.75	12.32	9.39	7.51
1988	9.73	10.22	8.22	7.69	9.95	11.44	9.80	10.53	9.40	12.60	10.23	7.76
1989	10.02	10.52	8.46	7.98	10.20	11.72	10.10	10.84	9.67	12.98	10.47	8.03
1990	10.37	10.86	8.70	8.26	10.51	12.21	10.37	11.25	9.92	13.44	10.91	8.34
1991	10.71	11.27	8.88	8.49	10.77	12.65	10.74	11.64	10.30	14.11	11.24	8.57
1992	10.95	11.50	9.02	8.71	10.96	12.91	10.93	11.85	10.56	14.55	11.51	8.85
1993	11.18	11.73	9.15	8.93	11.17	13.15	11.12	12.07	10.75	14.96	11.83	9.07
1994	11.43	11.97	9.34	9.16	11.38	13.35	11.26	12.24	10.94	15.43	12.00	9.31
1995	11.74	12.25	9.63	9.46	11.66	13.67	11.48	12.50	11.13	15.71	12.21	9.69

NOTE: Data include Alaska and Hawaii beginning in 1959.

Average Hourly Earnings Excluding Overtime of Production Workers on Manufacturing Payrolls by Industry, 1956-1995—Continued

(Dollars)

Year	Nondurable Goods										
	Total	Food and kindred products	Tobacco manufac-tures	Textile mill products	Apparel and other textile products	Paper and allied prod-ucts	Printing and publishing	Chemicals and allied products	Petroleum and coal products	Rubber and mis-cellaneous plastics products	Leather and leather products
1956	1.72	1.70	1.43	1.40	1.45	1.82	....	2.04	2.48	1.97	1.45
1957	1.80	1.79	1.50	1.45	1.49	1.92	....	2.15	2.60	2.05	1.50
1958	1.86	1.87	1.56	1.45	1.52	2.01	....	2.24	2.67	2.13	1.53
1959	1.92	1.94	1.62	1.50	1.53	2.07	2.50	2.33	2.79	2.18	1.56
1960	1.99	2.02	1.68	1.56	1.57	2.15	2.58	2.43	2.82	2.25	1.61
1961	2.05	2.09	1.75	1.58	1.62	2.22	2.65	2.51	2.94	2.30	1.64
1962	2.10	2.15	1.83	1.62	1.66	2.29	2.72	2.57	2.97	2.35	1.69
1963	2.15	2.21	1.88	1.65	1.70	2.35	2.79	2.64	3.07	2.38	1.73
1964	2.21	2.27	1.91	1.71	1.76	2.43	2.86	2.72	3.11	2.44	1.79
1965	2.27	2.33	2.06	1.78	1.79	2.50	2.94	2.79	3.18	2.49	1.84
1966	2.35	2.40	2.15	1.87	1.85	2.59	3.03	2.87	3.29	2.54	1.89
1967	2.48	2.52	2.22	1.97	1.99	2.71	3.15	3.00	3.43	2.63	2.02
1968	2.63	2.66	2.43	2.10	2.17	2.87	3.34	3.14	3.60	2.79	2.17
1969	2.79	2.82	2.57	2.24	2.26	3.05	3.54	3.33	3.83	2.93	2.31
1970	2.97	3.01	2.85	2.36	2.35	3.26	3.78	3.56	4.09	3.08	2.43
1971	3.15	3.23	3.09	2.46	2.44	3.48	4.06	3.83	4.38	3.28	2.53
1972	3.34	3.43	3.40	2.61	2.54	3.73	4.34	4.10	4.75	3.46	2.60
1973	3.55	3.67	3.65	2.80	2.71	3.97	4.57	4.33	5.05	3.65	2.72
1974	3.86	3.99	4.01	3.07	2.93	4.30	4.85	4.69	5.43	3.92	2.92
1975	4.22	4.40	4.43	3.29	3.12	4.78	5.22	5.22	6.25	4.27	3.13
1976	4.53	4.74	4.89	3.54	3.35	5.18	5.52	5.69	6.93	4.51	3.32
1977	4.92	5.11	5.40	3.82	3.56	5.64	5.90	6.18	7.48	4.98	3.52
1978	5.32	5.53	5.96	4.11	3.87	6.16	6.26	6.73	8.23	5.32	3.80
1979	5.79	5.97	6.55	4.47	4.17	6.75	6.69	7.30	8.92	5.80	4.14
1980	6.33	6.54	7.57	4.88	4.50	7.46	7.28	8.00	9.67	6.36	4.49
1981	6.94	7.10	8.66	5.32	4.90	8.17	7.93	8.77	10.90	6.96	4.90
1982	7.50	7.58	9.62	5.67	5.13	8.89	8.48	9.64	11.93	7.45	5.24
1983	7.79	7.84	10.22	5.92	5.28	9.42	8.81	10.20	12.70	7.73	5.44
1984	8.07	8.01	11.03	6.21	5.45	9.85	9.07	10.64	12.82	7.97	5.60
1985	8.39	8.17	11.78	6.44	5.63	10.27	9.38	11.12	13.41	8.24	5.71
1986	8.60	8.34	12.64	6.60	5.72	10.59	9.63	11.48	13.50	8.41	5.80
1987	8.79	8.50	13.59	6.81	5.79	10.79	9.88	11.82	13.79	8.56	5.91
1988	9.04	8.67	14.20	7.04	5.97	11.04	10.12	12.12	14.09	8.76	6.12
1989	9.33	8.89	14.90	7.31	6.19	11.37	10.47	12.47	14.47	9.05	6.43
1990	9.69	9.11	15.77	7.67	6.44	11.67	10.82	12.88	15.20	9.35	6.74
1991	9.99	9.39	16.34	7.91	6.61	12.04	11.08	13.34	15.91	9.65	7.01
1992	10.24	9.66	16.47	8.17	6.78	12.33	11.31	13.75	16.71	9.88	7.22
1993	10.47	9.89	16.48	8.43	6.92	12.64	11.47	14.04	17.35	10.05	7.40
1994	10.69	10.06	18.22	8.64	7.15	12.94	11.63	14.30	17.78	10.13	7.73
1995	11.04	10.33	18.39	8.95	7.46	13.42	11.85	14.79	18.10	10.40	7.96

NOTE: Data include Alaska and Hawaii beginning in 1959.

Average Weekly Earnings of Production or Nonsupervisory Workers on Private Nonagricultural Payrolls by Industry, 1947-1995
(Dollars)

Year	Total private	Mining	Construction	Manufacturing			Transportation and public utilities	Wholesale trade	Retail trade	Finance, insurance, and real estate	Services
				Total	Durable goods	Nondurable goods					
1947	45.58	59.89	58.83	49.13	51.64	46.03	....	50.06	33.77	43.21	....
1948	49.00	65.52	65.23	53.08	56.24	49.54	....	53.59	36.22	45.48	....
1949	50.24	62.33	67.56	53.80	57.13	50.41	....	55.45	38.42	47.63	....
1950	53.13	67.16	69.68	58.28	59.60	51.45	....	55.31	39.71	47.50	....
1951	57.86	74.11	76.96	63.34	68.48	57.42	....	62.02	42.82	54.67	....
1952	60.65	77.59	82.86	66.75	72.04	59.95	....	65.53	43.38	57.08	....
1953	63.76	83.03	86.41	70.47	76.22	62.57	....	68.61	45.36	59.57	....
1954	64.52	82.60	88.54	70.49	75.79	63.18	....	71.28	47.04	62.04	....
1955	67.72	89.54	90.90	75.30	81.77	67.03	....	74.48	48.75	63.92	....
1956	70.74	95.06	96.38	78.78	85.28	70.09	....	78.17	50.18	65.68	....
1957	73.33	98.25	100.27	81.19	87.85	72.52	....	81.41	52.20	67.53	....
1958	75.08	96.08	103.78	82.32	88.88	74.50	....	84.02	54.10	70.12	....
1959	78.78	103.68	108.41	88.26	95.65	78.61	....	88.51	56.15	72.74	....
1960	80.67	105.04	112.67	89.72	97.04	80.36	....	90.72	57.76	75.14	....
1961	82.60	106.92	118.08	92.34	99.70	82.92	....	93.56	58.66	77.12	....
1962	85.91	110.70	122.47	96.56	104.30	86.15	....	96.22	60.96	80.94	....
1963	88.46	114.40	127.19	99.23	108.09	87.91	....	99.47	62.66	84.38	....
1964	91.33	117.74	132.06	102.97	112.05	90.91	118.78	102.56	64.75	85.79	70.03
1965	95.45	123.52	138.38	107.53	116.76	94.64	125.14	106.08	66.61	88.91	73.60
1966	98.82	130.24	146.26	112.19	121.67	98.49	128.13	111.11	68.57	92.13	77.04
1967	101.84	135.89	154.95	114.49	123.19	102.03	130.82	115.66	70.95	95.72	80.38
1968	107.73	142.71	164.49	122.51	131.65	109.05	138.85	121.90	74.95	101.75	83.97
1969	114.61	154.80	181.54	129.51	139.59	115.53	147.74	129.85	78.66	108.70	90.57
1970	119.83	164.40	195.45	133.33	143.07	120.43	155.93	136.86	82.47	112.67	96.66
1971	127.31	172.14	211.67	142.44	152.74	128.51	168.82	143.42	87.62	117.85	103.06
1972	136.90	189.14	221.19	154.71	167.68	138.16	187.86	151.69	91.85	122.98	110.85
1973	145.39	201.40	235.89	166.46	180.09	146.52	203.31	159.54	96.32	129.20	117.29
1974	154.76	219.14	249.25	176.80	190.82	156.79	217.48	169.94	102.68	137.61	126.00
1975	163.53	249.31	266.08	190.79	205.49	169.56	233.44	182.19	108.86	148.19	134.67
1976	175.45	273.90	283.73	209.32	226.14	185.57	256.71	194.27	114.60	155.43	143.52
1977	189.00	301.20	295.65	228.90	248.46	201.33	278.90	209.13	121.66	165.26	153.45
1978	203.70	332.88	318.69	249.27	270.44	218.28	302.80	228.14	130.20	178.00	163.67
1979	219.91	365.07	342.99	269.34	290.50	236.19	325.58	247.93	138.62	190.77	175.27
1980	235.10	397.06	367.78	288.62	310.78	255.84	351.25	266.88	147.38	209.60	190.71
1981	255.20	438.75	399.26	318.00	342.91	281.85	382.18	290.68	158.03	229.05	208.97
1982	267.26	459.88	426.82	330.26	354.88	297.60	402.48	309.46	163.85	245.44	225.59
1983	280.70	479.40	442.97	354.08	381.77	318.75	420.81	328.79	171.05	263.90	239.04
1984	292.86	503.58	458.51	374.03	402.82	333.08	438.13	341.88	174.33	278.50	247.43
1985	299.09	519.93	464.46	386.37	415.71	345.31	450.30	351.36	174.64	289.02	256.75
1986	304.85	525.81	466.75	396.01	424.56	357.11	458.64	357.72	176.08	304.30	265.85
1987	312.50	531.70	480.44	406.31	432.85	369.44	471.58	365.38	178.70	316.90	275.93
1988	322.02	541.44	495.73	418.81	447.68	379.89	475.69	380.24	183.62	325.25	289.49
1989	334.24	570.18	513.17	429.68	458.02	391.95	490.14	394.82	188.72	341.17	305.79
1990	345.35	603.29	526.01	441.86	468.76	404.80	504.53	411.10	194.40	356.93	319.48
1991	353.98	630.04	533.40	455.03	482.93	419.69	511.61	424.82	198.48	370.92	331.45
1992	363.61	638.31	537.70	469.86	498.83	433.49	523.21	435.10	205.06	387.36	342.55
1993	373.64	646.78	553.63	486.04	519.09	445.79	539.35	448.47	209.95	406.33	350.35
1994	385.86	666.62	573.00	506.94	543.97	459.72	553.01	463.10	216.46	423.51	358.80
1995	394.68	683.91	585.10	514.59	548.23	468.99	562.09	476.07	221.47	442.65	369.04

NOTE: Data include Alaska and Hawaii beginning in 1959.

EMPLOYMENT, HOURS, AND EARNINGS, NONAGRICULTURAL PAYROLLS

Average Weekly Earnings of Production Workers on Manufacturing Payrolls by Industry, 1947-1995
(Dollars)

Year	Total manufac-turing	Durable goods				Primary metal industries		Fab-ricated metal products	Industrial machinery and equip-ment	Electrical and elec-tronic equip-ment	Transportation equipment		Instru-ments and related products	Mis-cellane-ous man-ufacturing
		Total	Lumber and wood products	Furniture and fixtures	Stone, clay, and glass products	Total	Blast fur-nace and basic steel products				Total	Motor ve-hicles and equip-ment		
1947	49.13	51.64	43.93	45.53	48.95	55.38	56.51	51.74	55.78	50.21	56.97	58.63	48.36	44.75
1948	53.08	56.24	47.64	48.83	53.20	61.14	62.84	56.37	60.38	....	61.70	63.15	....	48.03
1949	53.80	57.13	48.10	49.36	54.27	60.90	63.34	57.45	60.27	....	65.10	67.33	....	48.23
1950	58.28	59.60	51.31	53.55	59.06	67.36	67.95	63.04	67.04	59.31	71.29	74.85	59.80	52.02
1951	63.34	68.48	55.41	57.13	63.76	75.30	77.71	68.55	76.13	....	75.81	77.16		55.08
1952	66.75	72.04	59.15	60.86	66.17	77.52	80.00	71.72	79.55	....	81.51	84.87		59.02
1953	70.47	76.22	61.31	62.99	70.18	84.46	88.29	76.49	82.68	....	85.28	89.88		61.56
1954	70.49	75.79	61.39	62.80	71.69	81.48	83.92	76.70	81.40	....	86.30	91.30		61.78
1955	75.30	81.77	63.99	67.07	77.00	92.51	96.80	81.73	87.15	74.89	93.48	99.84	76.48	64.88
1956	78.78	85.28	65.74	68.78	80.56	97.17	102.87	84.67	93.06	....	94.81	96.82		67.60
1957	81.19	87.85	66.82	69.83	82.82	99.00	105.57	88.34	94.12	....	97.51	100.61		69.48
1958	82.32	88.88	69.48	69.95	84.80	101.11	108.00	90.17	94.33	....	100.40	101.24		70.17
1959	88.26	95.65	74.24	74.48	91.46	112.19	122.71	96.12	102.92	....	107.45	111.38		73.42
1960	89.72	97.04	74.29	75.20	92.57	109.59	116.13	98.42	104.55	90.74	111.52	115.21	93.32	74.28
1961	92.34	99.70	77.03	76.40	95.24	114.55	122.92	100.85	107.16	94.47	113.40	114.69	96.87	75.84
1962	96.56	104.30	79.20	79.37	98.81	119.80	127.40	104.81	113.01	97.44	122.22	127.67	99.80	78.61
1963	99.23	108.09	82.41	81.80	102.67	124.64	133.06	107.79	116.20	99.14	126.42	132.68	101.59	80.39
1964	102.97	112.05	85.65	84.46	105.50	129.69	138.43	111.76	121.69	101.66	130.09	138.03	103.63	82.37
1965	107.53	116.76	89.16	87.98	110.04	133.88	140.90	116.20	127.15	105.78	137.71	147.63	108.47	85.39
1966	112.19	121.67	92.21	91.72	114.24	138.09	144.73	122.11	134.90	109.18	141.86	147.23	114.93	88.80
1967	114.49	123.19	95.91	94.13	117.31	137.27	143.51	123.67	135.58	111.35	142.42	144.84	117.42	92.59
1968	122.51	131.65	104.75	100.28	124.98	147.68	154.16	131.77	141.12	118.08	155.72	168.09	120.69	98.50
1969	129.51	139.59	110.55	105.85	133.66	158.42	166.03	138.94	152.15	124.84	161.44	170.56	128.21	103.74
1970	133.33	143.07	117.61	108.58	140.08	158.77	166.40	143.67	154.95	130.54	163.62	170.07	134.27	109.52
1971	142.44	152.74	126.56	115.42	152.67	169.62	177.80	152.31	163.21	139.25	181.12	194.46	139.30	115.53
1972	154.71	167.68	134.94	123.82	165.48	192.92	206.25	166.86	181.87	149.88	200.58	220.59	148.60	122.85
1973	166.46	180.09	144.80	131.60	176.82	213.19	229.77	178.46	196.88	157.96	216.82	237.51	156.65	128.31
1974	176.80	190.82	152.88	138.02	187.50	232.96	258.95	188.09	207.97	167.14	224.37	238.32	166.04	136.61
1975	190.79	205.49	166.06	143.64	198.77	247.20	274.13	202.51	219.10	183.28	245.23	259.53	178.94	146.69
1976	209.32	226.14	189.13	154.81	219.06	276.22	305.88	224.40	238.55	198.40	276.05	304.16	198.68	156.75
1977	228.90	248.46	203.89	169.26	239.95	305.62	338.58	242.31	259.79	217.76	309.83	345.40	214.77	169.17
1978	249.27	270.44	223.68	183.92	262.91	342.76	389.69	260.35	284.76	234.55	333.80	368.05	233.54	181.97
1979	269.34	290.50	240.16	195.82	284.28	371.77	428.89	278.80	305.24	254.70	350.58	372.37	251.74	195.16
1980	288.62	310.78	253.60	209.17	306.00	391.78	448.77	300.98	328.00	276.00	379.61	394.00	275.40	211.30
1981	318.00	342.91	271.67	226.94	335.76	437.81	509.04	330.46	360.33	21.00	424.95	450.72	298.96	231.64
1982	330.26	354.88	284.23	234.73	355.69	437.34	505.97	343.78	367.62	304.80	449.96	470.61	320.79	246.53
1983	354.08	381.77	313.58	260.83	384.71	459.68	509.16	370.27	387.18	322.65	491.31	525.66	342.59	266.27
1984	374.03	402.82	321.20	271.55	401.94	478.30	528.29	389.16	417.74	351.14	520.94	557.57	365.09	277.77
1985	386.37	415.71	329.18	282.50	412.30	484.31	547.86	401.02	427.45	370.64	541.45	582.47	375.97	287.62
1986	396.01	424.56	338.15	296.91	423.69	496.93	572.54	408.46	440.13	384.08	541.86	572.97	388.27	298.98
1987	406.31	432.85	342.26	306.80	433.58	514.61	597.62	416.42	452.81	395.65	543.48	570.97	402.41	305.74
1988	418.81	447.68	344.46	313.23	446.69	528.96	615.12	431.15	473.12	401.39	567.48	608.57	438.84	313.60
1989	429.68	458.02	354.48	325.88	457.69	534.49	618.45	439.71	483.36	410.04	579.61	614.18	445.11	326.63
1990	441.86	468.76	365.02	333.13	467.04	551.68	643.19	447.28	493.16	420.24	591.36	617.34	464.02	340.10
1991	455.03	482.93	369.60	340.76	473.71	562.53	655.87	461.03	506.66	435.49	618.03	644.23	477.24	351.35
1992	469.86	498.83	383.26	357.70	489.52	587.38	690.35	475.07	523.70	453.20	635.36	655.08	488.68	365.09
1993	486.04	519.09	392.09	371.73	506.00	611.36	721.48	492.15	547.39	469.83	679.40	713.23	502.65	373.72
1994	506.94	543.97	405.41	385.82	526.44	641.00	756.57	511.80	568.10	485.30	731.39	782.92	520.00	386.80
1995	514.59	548.23	410.87	388.87	533.63	643.28	770.34	512.68	574.62	485.47	733.65	779.46	526.19	401.39

NOTE: Data include Alaska and Hawaii beginning in 1959.

Average Weekly Earnings of Production Workers on Manufacturing Payrolls by Industry, 1947-1995—Continued

(Dollars)

Year	Nondurable goods										
	Total	Food and kindred products	Tobacco manufac-tures	Textile mill products	Apparel and other textile products	Paper and allied products	Printing and pub-lishing	Chemi-cals and allied products	Petroleum and coal products	Rubber and mis-cellane-ous plas-tics prod-ucts	Leather and leather products
1947	46.03	45.92	35.17	40.99	41.80	49.69	59.30	50.26	60.94	51.60	40.07
1948	49.54	48.84	36.58	45.28	43.68	54.70	65.13	55.29	69.30	53.29	41.11
1949	50.41	50.49	37.26	44.52	42.76	55.42	68.60	57.67	72.42	54.13	41.03
1950	51.45	52.88	41.00	48.59	44.60	60.53	71.23	61.64	75.11	60.27	43.95
1951	57.42	56.84	43.89	51.22	46.64	65.08	74.30	66.91	81.19	64.46	46.13
1952	59.95	60.34	45.31	52.39	47.92	68.05	78.58	69.12	85.05	69.53	49.92
1953	62.57	63.50	47.63	53.18	48.74	71.81	82.29	74.21	90.35	72.32	50.90
1954	63.18	65.67	48.88	52.09	48.36	73.18	83.93	77.11	93.20	72.83	50.18
1955	67.03	68.89	51.86	55.34	49.73	78.01	87.91	80.97	96.93	81.32	52.68
1956	70.09	72.69	56.26	57.17	52.92	82.18	90.64	85.90	104.14	81.61	55.65
1957	72.52	75.48	58.75	57.96	53.91	85.45	92.64	89.98	108.53	85.67	56.85
1958	74.50	79.15	62.17	57.51	54.05	87.99	94.62	93.20	111.66	85.67	57.25
1959	78.61	82.82	64.52	63.02	56.63	93.30	99.72	99.36	117.42	93.75	60.26
1960	80.36	86.09	64.94	63.60	56.45	95.15	102.91	103.25	118.78	92.80	60.52
1961	82.92	88.75	69.42	65.04	58.06	99.45	105.05	106.81	124.01	96.15	62.83
1962	86.15	91.84	71.41	68.21	61.18	102.24	108.01	110.24	126.88	100.04	64.67
1963	87.91	94.30	73.92	69.43	62.45	105.90	110.69	113.15	131.77	101.02	66.00
1964	90.91	97.17	75.66	73.39	64.26	109.57	114.35	116.48	133.76	104.90	69.36
1965	94.64	100.28	79.21	77.98	66.61	114.22	118.12	121.09	138.42	109.62	71.82
1966	98.49	103.82	85.19	82.12	68.80	119.35	122.61	125.16	144.58	112.56	74.88
1967	102.03	107.98	87.62	84.25	73.08	122.84	125.95	128.96	152.87	113.85	79.07
1968	109.05	114.24	93.99	91.05	79.78	130.85	133.28	136.27	159.38	121.60	85.41
1969	115.53	120.77	97.99	95.88	82.93	139.32	141.33	145.05	170.40	126.90	87.79
1970	120.43	127.98	110.00	97.76	84.37	144.14	147.78	153.50	183.18	129.36	92.63
1971	128.51	136.21	119.45	104.34	88.64	154.51	157.50	165.15	195.60	137.76	97.64
1972	138.16	145.80	130.47	113.58	93.60	169.06	170.03	177.64	211.79	149.56	102.64
1973	146.52	155.54	145.14	120.66	99.08	180.18	179.08	188.52	223.87	158.21	105.46
1974	156.79	169.28	157.80	126.40	104.54	191.17	188.63	202.52	239.13	166.05	110.33
1975	169.56	185.78	173.81	134.41	111.58	208.42	198.52	220.99	266.98	176.36	119.09
1976	185.57	201.69	186.75	147.97	121.72	232.48	214.13	245.86	303.54	191.70	127.16
1977	201.33	214.80	209.41	161.20	128.87	255.68	230.72	268.13	334.34	214.13	133.21
1978	218.28	230.26	233.55	173.72	140.26	279.71	244.78	294.14	376.27	227.81	144.32
1979	236.19	250.17	253.46	188.26	149.32	303.74	260.25	318.44	409.97	244.41	154.03
1980	255.84	271.95	294.89	203.31	161.42	330.85	279.36	344.45	422.18	263.20	168.09
1981	281.85	295.37	344.54	218.59	177.43	365.50	305.49	379.39	491.62	290.97	183.13
1982	297.60	312.05	370.06	218.63	180.44	389.58	324.25	407.36	546.99	304.92	189.75
1983	318.75	323.51	388.21	249.67	194.76	423.02	342.54	440.13	582.99	332.07	203.87
1984	333.08	333.92	436.46	257.75	202.02	448.67	356.64	463.83	587.33	348.20	210.13
1985	345.31	342.80	444.91	265.99	208.57	466.77	367.04	484.36	604.58	353.46	216.88
1986	357.11	350.00	481.71	284.82	214.33	482.98	379.62	501.96	621.52	363.91	218.45
1987	369.44	358.99	548.73	299.71	219.78	496.06	390.64	523.25	641.52	373.57	232.26
1988	379.89	367.54	583.87	302.58	226.44	506.18	400.14	536.36	664.67	383.22	235.50
1989	391.95	381.77	590.97	313.70	234.32	517.87	412.35	555.02	682.66	391.64	249.76
1990	404.80	392.50	636.22	320.00	239.15	533.02	426.00	576.80	724.30	401.14	258.43
1991	419.69	401.94	655.71	336.98	250.49	550.78	432.80	602.32	751.46	413.88	269.25
1992	433.49	414.12	653.11	353.46	258.54	569.85	447.29	625.38	784.02	432.01	281.96
1993	445.79	425.32	631.69	367.63	263.75	585.11	456.92	638.74	819.03	441.83	294.52
1994	459.72	440.26	749.45	379.81	275.25	604.50	468.60	653.62	846.71	451.54	306.85
1995	468.99	449.63	771.41	383.93	282.68	613.31	471.01	675.22	846.03	452.77	310.46

NOTE: Data include Alaska and Hawaii beginning in 1959.

Average Weekly Earnings of Production or Nonsupervisory Workers on Private Nonagricultural Payrolls, in Current and Constant Dollars, 1947-1995

Year	Total private		Mining		Construction		Manufacturing		Transportation and public utilities	
	Current dollars	1982 dollars	Current dollars	1982 dollars	Current dollars	1982 dollars	Current dollars	1982 dollars	Current dollars	1982 dollars
1947	45.58	196.47	59.89	258.15	58.83	253.58	49.13	211.77		
1948	49.00	196.00	65.52	262.08	65.23	260.92	53.08	212.32		
1949	50.24	202.58	62.33	251.33	67.56	272.42	53.80	216.94		
1950	53.13	212.52	67.16	268.64	69.68	278.72	58.28	233.12		
1951	57.86	215.09	74.11	275.50	76.96	286.10	63.34	235.46		
1952	60.65	219.75	77.59	281.12	82.86	300.22	66.75	241.85		
1953	63.76	229.35	83.03	298.67	86.41	310.83	70.47	253.49		
1954	64.52	231.25	82.60	296.06	88.54	317.35	70.49	252.65		
1955	67.72	243.60	89.54	322.09	90.90	326.98	75.30	270.86		
1956	70.74	250.85	95.06	337.09	96.38	341.77	78.78	279.36		
1957	73.33	251.13	98.25	336.47	100.27	343.39	81.19	278.05		
1958	75.08	250.27	96.08	320.27	103.78	345.93	82.32	274.40		
1959	78.78	260.86	103.68	343.31	108.41	358.97	88.26	292.25		
1960	80.67	261.92	105.04	341.04	112.67	365.81	89.72	291.30		
1961	82.60	265.59	106.92	343.79	118.08	379.68	92.34	296.91		
1962	85.91	273.60	110.70	352.55	122.47	390.03	96.56	307.52		
1963	88.46	278.18	114.40	359.75	127.19	399.97	99.23	312.04		
1964	91.33	283.63	117.74	365.65	132.06	410.12	102.97	319.78	118.78	368.88
1965	95.45	291.90	123.52	377.74	138.38	423.18	107.53	328.84	125.14	382.69
1966	98.82	294.11	130.24	387.62	146.26	435.30	112.19	333.90	128.13	381.34
1967	101.84	293.49	135.89	391.61	154.95	446.54	114.49	329.94	130.82	377.00
1968	107.73	298.42	142.71	395.32	164.49	455.65	122.51	339.36	138.85	384.63
1969	114.61	300.81	154.80	406.30	181.54	476.48	129.51	339.92	147.74	387.77
1970	119.83	298.08	164.40	408.96	195.45	486.19	133.33	331.67	155.93	387.89
1971	127.31	303.12	172.14	409.86	211.67	503.98	142.44	339.14	168.82	401.95
1972	136.90	315.44	189.14	435.81	221.19	509.65	154.71	356.47	187.86	432.86
1973	145.39	315.38	201.40	436.88	235.89	511.69	166.46	361.08	203.31	441.02
1974	154.76	302.27	219.14	428.01	249.25	486.82	176.80	345.31	217.48	424.77
1975	163.53	293.06	249.31	446.79	266.08	476.85	190.79	341.92	233.44	418.35
1976	175.45	297.37	273.90	464.24	283.73	480.90	209.32	354.78	256.71	435.10
1977	189.00	300.96	301.20	479.62	295.65	470.78	228.90	364.49	278.90	444.11
1978	203.70	300.89	332.88	491.70	318.69	470.74	249.27	368.20	302.80	447.27
1979	219.91	291.66	365.07	484.18	342.99	454.89	269.34	357.21	325.58	431.80
1980	235.10	274.65	397.06	463.86	367.78	429.65	288.62	337.17	351.25	410.34
1981	255.20	270.63	438.75	465.27	399.26	423.39	318.00	337.22	382.18	405.28
1982	267.26	267.26	459.88	459.88	426.82	426.82	330.26	330.26	402.48	402.48
1983	280.70	272.52	479.40	465.44	442.97	430.07	354.08	343.77	420.81	408.55
1984	292.86	274.73	503.58	472.40	458.51	430.12	374.03	350.87	438.13	411.00
1985	299.09	271.16	519.93	471.38	464.46	421.09	386.37	350.29	450.30	408.25
1986	304.85	271.94	525.81	469.05	466.75	416.37	396.01	353.26	458.64	409.13
1987	312.50	269.16	531.70	457.97	480.44	413.82	406.31	349.97	471.58	406.18
1988	322.02	266.79	541.44	448.58	495.73	410.71	418.81	346.98	475.69	394.11
1989	334.24	264.22	570.18	450.74	513.17	405.67	429.68	339.67	490.14	387.46
1990	345.35	259.47	603.29	453.26	526.01	395.20	441.86	331.98	504.53	379.06
1991	353.98	255.40	630.04	454.57	533.40	384.85	455.03	328.30	511.61	369.13
1992	363.61	254.99	638.31	447.62	537.70	377.07	469.86	329.50	523.21	366.91
1993	373.64	254.87	646.78	441.19	553.63	377.65	486.04	331.54	539.35	367.91
1994	385.86	256.73	666.62	443.53	573.00	381.24	506.94	337.29	553.01	367.94
1995	394.68	255.29	683.91	442.37	585.10	378.46	514.59	332.85	562.09	363.58

NOTE: Data include Alaska and Hawaii beginning in 1959.

Average Weekly Earnings of Production or Nonsupervisory Workers on Private Nonagricultural Payrolls, in Current and Constant Dollars, 1947-1995—Continued

Year	Wholesale trade		Retail trade		Finance, insurance, and real estate		Services	
	Current dollars	1982 dollars	Current dollars	1982 dollars	Current dollars	1982 dollars	Current dollars	1982 dollars
1947	50.06	215.95	33.77	145.56	43.21	186.25	....	....
1948	53.59	214.12	36.22	144.88	45.48	181.92	....	....
1949	55.45	223.59	38.42	154.92	47.63	192.06	....	....
1950	55.31	232.40	39.71	158.84	47.50	202.08	....	....
1951	62.02	230.93	42.82	159.18	54.67	203.20	....	....
1952	65.53	237.17	43.38	157.17	57.08	206.81	....	....
1953	68.61	246.94	45.36	163.17	59.57	214.28	....	....
1954	71.28	255.02	47.04	168.60	62.04	222.37	....	....
1955	74.48	268.02	48.75	175.36	63.92	229.93	....	....
1956	78.17	277.77	50.18	177.94	65.68	232.91	....	....
1957	81.41	278.73	52.20	178.77	67.53	231.27	....	....
1958	84.02	280.47	54.10	180.33	70.12	233.73	....	....
1959	88.51	292.78	56.15	185.93	72.74	240.83	....	....
1960	90.72	293.93	57.76	187.53	75.14	243.96	....	....
1961	93.56	299.87	58.66	188.62	77.12	247.97	....	....
1962	96.22	306.43	60.96	194.14	80.94	257.77	....	....
1963	99.47	312.61	62.66	197.04	84.38	265.35	....	....
1964	102.56	317.89	64.75	201.27	85.79	266.37	70.03	217.55
1965	106.08	324.98	66.61	203.82	88.91	271.71	73.60	225.08
1966	111.11	330.60	68.57	203.87	92.13	274.43	77.04	228.93
1967	115.66	333.86	70.95	204.21	95.72	275.79	80.38	231.41
1968	121.90	337.65	74.95	207.56	101.75	281.72	83.97	232.91
1969	129.85	340.52	78.66	206.48	108.70	284.93	90.57	237.85
1970	136.86	340.57	82.47	204.75	112.67	280.57	96.66	240.10
1971	143.42	342.10	87.62	208.36	117.85	281.00	103.06	245.33
1972	151.69	348.89	91.85	212.05	122.98	283.27	110.85	254.88
1973	159.54	346.51	96.32	209.22	129.20	280.56	117.29	254.86
1974	169.94	332.25	102.68	200.29	137.61	268.91	126.00	246.52
1975	182.19	326.92	108.86	194.68	148.19	265.04	134.67	241.45
1976	194.27	329.07	114.60	194.17	155.43	263.58	143.52	243.27
1977	209.13	332.42	121.66	193.54	165.26	263.41	153.45	244.57
1978	228.14	336.59	130.20	192.23	178.00	262.97	163.67	242.08
1979	247.93	328.45	138.62	184.12	190.77	253.21	175.27	232.57
1980	266.88	312.07	147.38	172.01	209.60	244.95	190.71	223.11
1981	290.68	308.25	158.03	167.58	229.05	242.90	208.97	221.60
1982	309.46	309.46	163.85	163.85	245.44	245.44	225.59	225.59
1983	328.79	319.21	171.05	166.07	263.90	256.21	239.04	232.08
1984	341.88	320.71	174.33	163.54	278.50	261.26	247.43	232.11
1985	351.36	318.55	174.64	158.33	289.02	262.03	256.75	232.77
1986	357.72	319.11	176.08	157.07	304.30	271.45	265.85	237.15
1987	365.38	314.71	178.70	153.92	316.90	272.95	275.93	237.67
1988	380.24	315.03	183.62	152.13	325.25	269.47	289.49	239.84
1989	394.82	312.11	188.72	149.19	341.17	269.70	305.79	241.73
1990	411.10	308.87	194.40	146.06	356.93	268.17	319.48	240.03
1991	424.82	306.51	198.48	143.20	370.92	267.62	331.45	239.14
1992	435.10	305.12	205.06	143.80	387.36	271.64	342.55	240.22
1993	448.47	305.91	209.95	143.21	406.33	277.17	350.35	238.98
1994	463.10	308.12	216.46	144.02	423.51	281.78	358.80	238.72
1995	476.07	307.94	221.47	143.25	442.65	286.32	369.04	238.71

NOTE: Data include Alaska and Hawaii beginning in 1959.

Employees on Nonagricultural Payrolls by State, 1960-1995

(Thousands of persons)

State	1960	1961	1962	1963	1964	1965	1966	1967	1968	1969	1970	1971
Alabama	776.4	774.6	791.8	812.5	843.8	886.5	935.6	951.8	970.1	1 000.2	1 010.5	1 021.9
Alaska	56.6	57.1	58.9	62.1	65.4	70.5	73.1	76.9	79.9	86.8	93.1	97.8
Arizona	333.8	347.1	364.8	377.2	389.1	403.7	434.8	445.6	473.4	517.2	547.4	581.4
Arkansas	367.6	378.0	399.7	416.3	431.8	458.8	489.8	501.0	514.6	533.8	536.2	551.0
California	4 896.0	4 996.1	5 217.7	5 412.3	5 606.5	5 800.3	6 145.2	6 367.6	6 642.1	6 931.5	6 946.2	6 917.0
Colorado	520.9	542.8	557.5	571.7	583.2	598.9	631.2	655.8	686.6	720.7	750.2	787.0
Connecticut	915.4	922.6	949.8	969.3	991.2	1 032.9	1 095.4	1 130.1	1 158.0	1 194.1	1 197.5	1 164.3
Delaware	153.9	151.9	156.4	163.6	170.8	184.1	193.2	197.4	202.9	211.9	216.8	224.9
District of Columbia	501.6	511.4	527.2	542.5	551.5	572.5	587.0	594.7	582.8	575.0	566.7	566.6
Florida	1 320.6	1 333.9	1 387.8	1 447.4	1 526.5	1 619.1	1 726.8	1 816.4	1 932.3	2 069.9	2 152.1	2 276.4
Georgia	1 051.1	1 050.7	1 092.7	1 139.7	1 186.7	1 257.1	1 337.9	1 394.7	1 455.6	1 531.7	1 557.5	1 602.9
Hawaii	188.8	193.8	195.2	199.6	207.8	219.4	232.1	241.7	255.3	275.9	293.7	301.5
Idaho	155.2	159.1	164.6	164.7	168.6	177.6	184.8	187.7	192.9	201.4	207.8	217.1
Illinois	3 537.9	3 502.5	3 572.5	3 614.4	3 712.2	3 880.4	4 095.3	4 209.7	4 284.9	4 376.1	4 345.6	4 296.4
Indiana	1 431.4	1 408.4	1 461.3	1 498.7	1 545.7	1 631.1	1 737.2	1 777.0	1 817.4	1 880.3	1 849.0	1 841.1
Iowa	680.1	678.5	685.2	699.8	718.3	752.2	803.8	832.8	852.1	873.4	876.9	882.7
Kansas	560.2	562.4	573.5	574.2	587.2	600.4	634.3	652.8	672.1	686.4	678.8	677.8
Kentucky	653.6	648.0	673.7	702.9	721.7	758.9	803.8	836.5	868.6	895.5	910.1	931.5
Louisiana	783.0	774.0	790.1	810.3	849.4	898.4	957.9	997.3	1 020.5	1 032.7	1 033.6	1 055.9
Maine	277.5	277.1	279.5	279.6	285.1	295.4	309.2	316.9	323.2	330.0	332.2	332.3
Maryland	894.7	908.7	946.7	978.6	1 009.7	1 057.6	1 132.0	1 178.6	1 223.9	1 272.4	1 349.2	1 371.5
Massachusetts	1 901.0	1 911.1	1 942.7	1 943.2	1 958.1	2 015.8	2 097.4	2 147.9	2 187.9	2 249.4	2 243.5	2 211.4
Michigan	2 349.8	2 244.9	2 334.9	2 410.4	2 512.9	2 685.3	2 861.0	2 900.5	2 959.7	3 081.1	2 999.0	2 995.0
Minnesota	958.8	956.6	984.5	1 001.7	1 028.0	1 080.6	1 148.3	1 199.8	1 243.5	1 299.8	1 315.3	1 310.2
Mississippi	404.0	408.7	425.7	443.7	460.2	486.6	521.6	535.1	551.9	573.0	583.9	602.2
Missouri	1 350.1	1 332.5	1 357.2	1 383.5	1 418.3	1 478.3	1 554.1	1 595.5	1 631.3	1 672.1	1 668.0	1 660.8
Montana	165.0	165.2	169.7	172.6	174.2	179.2	184.6	188.0	192.5	195.5	199.1	204.8
Nebraska	384.4	390.5	396.4	401.9	408.9	418.7	434.1	449.3	458.8	474.4	484.3	490.8
Nevada	103.4	109.6	126.9	142.8	149.3	157.4	162.0	166.1	177.3	193.5	203.3	210.5
New Hampshire	200.7	201.9	207.9	208.8	212.8	220.8	235.2	244.0	251.8	259.2	258.5	259.9
New Jersey	2 017.1	2 033.6	2 095.8	2 129.4	2 168.7	2 259.0	2 359.1	2 421.5	2 485.2	2 569.6	2 606.2	2 607.6
New Mexico	236.3	236.2	242.6	248.6	255.7	262.5	271.7	272.6	276.6	287.5	292.6	305.7
New York	6 181.9	6 157.1	6 261.3	6 273.7	6 370.7	6 518.7	6 709.5	6 858.3	7 001.7	7 182.0	7 156.4	7 011.4
North Carolina	1 195.5	1 209.1	1 258.5	1 298.6	1 353.7	1 431.2	1 534.2	1 600.9	1 678.5	1 747.0	1 782.7	1 813.8
North Dakota	126.8	127.0	131.3	136.7	142.6	146.1	148.3	151.5	155.6	157.8	163.6	167.0
Ohio	3 147.3	3 044.3	3 099.2	3 145.2	3 216.3	3 364.3	3 537.3	3 619.8	3 750.8	3 887.3	3 880.7	3 839.6
Oklahoma	577.1	582.1	596.7	606.7	619.3	642.5	676.0	699.7	720.4	748.3	762.6	774.4
Oregon	509.7	509.9	529.0	549.5	573.9	608.4	640.4	652.1	679.2	708.5	710.5	729.1
Pennsylvania	3 715.4	3 634.1	3 694.9	3 694.8	3 777.1	3 917.5	4 077.1	4 171.3	4 263.5	4 374.9	4 351.6	4 291.3
Rhode Island	291.7	291.6	298.3	298.1	303.9	316.3	330.0	338.3	343.0	346.4	344.1	342.8
South Carolina	582.5	587.0	609.8	630.6	651.4	686.0	734.9	754.4	782.9	819.8	842.0	862.6
South Dakota	142.7	148.0	153.9	152.6	152.2	155.5	160.1	163.9	167.8	172.9	175.4	179.0
Tennessee	925.4	934.0	969.4	1 002.5	1 045.5	1 108.5	1 184.4	1 218.8	1 264.0	1 309.8	1 327.6	1 356.8
Texas	2 539.5	2 549.5	2 631.2	2 706.5	2 808.0	2 932.4	3 108.7	3 259.4	3 424.3	3 597.1	3 624.9	3 683.5
Utah	263.1	272.1	286.1	293.7	293.2	299.8	317.4	326.6	335.1	348.2	357.0	369.3
Vermont	107.9	107.3	110.5	111.5	113.7	121.3	130.8	136.3	140.3	145.5	147.9	148.1
Virginia	1 017.6	1 034.8	1 081.8	1 123.8	1 163.0	1 218.9	1 285.3	1 330.2	1 385.1	1 436.4	1 518.9	1 567.2
Washington	812.7	818.5	856.8	850.6	854.7	896.4	988.4	1 045.3	1 099.4	1 120.1	1 079.4	1 064.5
West Virginia	460.0	448.1	447.5	449.9	460.9	476.6	495.1	503.6	508.4	512.3	516.5	520.0
Wisconsin	1 191.9	1 179.9	1 207.2	1 233.5	1 270.9	1 331.7	1 394.1	1 430.5	1 472.1	1 525.1	1 530.4	1 525.4
Wyoming	96.5	96.3	95.5	96.2	97.2	96.6	97.2	99.0	102.9	106.9	108.3	111.0
Puerto Rico	....	....	....	....	....	....	....	....	....	....	....	....
Virgin Islands	....	....	....	....	....	....	....	....	....	....	....	....

Employees on Nonagricultural Payrolls by State, 1960-1995—Continued

(Thousands of persons)

State	1972	1973	1974	1975	1976	1977	1978	1979	1980	1981	1982	1983
Alabama	1 072.3	1 135.5	1 169.8	1 155.4	1 207.0	1 269.2	1 336.5	1 362.0	1 356.1	1 347.6	1 312.5	1 328.8
Alaska	103.5	110.0	127.9	161.8	171.7	163.3	163.5	166.9	169.4	186.1	200.4	214.3
Arizona	646.3	714.5	746.0	729.1	758.7	809.3	895.4	979.9	1 014.0	1 040.8	1 029.8	1 077.8
Arkansas	581.5	614.5	640.7	623.8	660.0	695.6	732.7	749.4	742.3	740.1	720.1	741.3
California	7 209.9	7 621.9	7 834.3	7 847.2	8 154.2	8 599.7	9 199.8	9 664.6	9 848.8	9 985.3	9 810.3	9 917.8
Colorado	869.4	936.0	959.7	963.5	1 003.4	1 058.1	1 150.0	1 218.0	1 251.1	1 295.2	1 316.6	1 327.2
Connecticut	1 190.4	1 238.7	1 264.0	1 223.4	1 239.7	1 282.3	1 346.1	1 398.0	1 426.8	1 438.3	1 428.5	1 444.2
Delaware	232.4	239.4	233.1	229.9	236.7	238.8	247.8	256.7	259.2	259.2	259.2	266.1
District of Columbia	572.0	573.7	580.1	576.5	575.8	578.7	596.3	612.5	616.1	611.0	597.9	596.6
Florida	2 513.1	2 778.6	2 863.8	2 746.4	2 784.3	2 933.2	3 180.6	3 381.2	3 576.2	3 736.0	3 761.9	3 905.4
Georgia	1 695.2	1 802.5	1 827.5	1 755.7	1 839.1	1 926.4	2 050.1	2 127.5	2 159.4	2 198.6	2 201.5	2 279.5
Hawaii	312.7	327.5	335.9	342.8	349.2	359.4	377.3	394.0	404.1	404.8	399.4	406.2
Idaho	236.5	251.7	266.8	273.0	291.0	307.4	331.3	338.0	330.0	327.8	312.2	317.9
Illinois	4 314.8	4 466.9	4 545.7	4 418.9	4 565.7	4 655.5	4 788.8	4 880.0	4 850.3	4 732.3	4 593.3	4 530.6
Indiana	1 921.9	2 028.1	2 031.4	1 941.7	2 023.8	2 114.0	2 205.5	2 236.3	2 129.5	2 114.4	2 028.0	2 029.5
Iowa	912.3	961.3	999.0	998.7	1 036.9	1 079.2	1 119.2	1 131.7	1 109.9	1 088.6	1 041.9	1 040.4
Kansas	717.5	763.3	790.0	801.2	834.8	871.0	912.5	946.8	944.7	949.7	921.4	921.6
Kentucky	988.3	1 038.6	1 065.9	1 057.6	1 103.1	1 148.3	1 209.9	1 245.4	1 210.0	1 196.0	1 160.7	1 152.3
Louisiana	1 128.6	1 176.1	1 220.8	1 249.5	1 314.4	1 364.6	1 463.5	1 517.4	1 578.9	1 630.5	1 607.0	1 565.2
Maine	343.7	354.8	361.5	356.9	375.3	387.8	405.6	415.9	418.3	419.2	415.5	425.0
Maryland	1 415.0	1 471.5	1 493.6	1 479.3	1 498.3	1 545.6	1 625.8	1 691.3	1 711.8	1 715.8	1 675.8	1 724.1
Massachusetts	2 251.7	2 333.5	2 353.7	2 273.1	2 323.5	2 416.0	2 526.3	2 603.5	2 654.3	2 671.8	2 642.0	2 696.5
Michigan	3 118.9	3 284.3	3 277.6	3 136.6	3 283.0	3 442.3	3 609.4	3 637.1	3 442.8	3 364.4	3 193.3	3 223.1
Minnesota	1 357.1	1 436.1	1 481.0	1 474.4	1 520.9	1 597.3	1 689.3	1 767.0	1 770.2	1 761.3	1 707.3	1 718.4
Mississippi	649.3	693.2	710.8	692.3	727.5	765.9	813.7	838.1	829.3	819.1	790.9	792.8
Missouri	1 700.1	1 770.6	1 789.5	1 740.6	1 797.8	1 861.8	1 953.1	2 011.1	1 969.8	1 956.3	1 922.4	1 937.0
Montana	215.3	224.2	234.0	238.1	251.1	264.8	280.4	283.8	280.4	281.8	273.7	276.0
Nebraska	517.0	541.3	562.1	557.8	572.1	593.7	609.9	631.2	627.6	623.2	609.8	610.8
Nevada	223.4	244.6	256.1	263.1	279.8	308.2	350.3	383.7	399.9	411.2	401.1	402.8
New Hampshire	278.5	297.8	300.3	292.8	313.4	337.1	359.6	378.5	385.4	394.6	394.4	409.5
New Jersey	2 672.5	2 759.7	2 783.0	2 699.9	2 753.7	2 836.9	2 961.9	3 027.2	3 060.4	3 098.9	3 092.7	3 165.1
New Mexico	327.5	346.0	360.2	370.2	390.0	415.4	444.3	461.0	465.4	475.5	473.6	479.5
New York	7 038.5	7 132.2	7 077.1	6 829.9	6 789.5	6 857.6	7 044.5	7 179.4	7 207.1	7 287.3	7 254.6	7 313.3
North Carolina	1 911.9	2 018.1	2 048.2	1 979.9	2 082.7	2 170.4	2 277.4	2 373.0	2 380.0	2 391.6	2 347.0	2 419.2
North Dakota	176.1	183.9	193.8	203.6	215.0	221.1	234.0	244.2	245.2	249.4	249.7	250.6
Ohio	3 938.4	4 112.9	4 169.4	4 016.2	4 094.6	4 230.1	4 394.9	4 484.8	4 367.4	4 317.7	4 124.3	4 092.5
Oklahoma	811.9	851.9	886.9	899.7	931.1	971.5	1 035.7	1 087.9	1 138.1	1 201.2	1 216.9	1 170.6
Oregon	774.7	816.2	838.2	837.4	878.5	936.9	1 009.2	1 056.0	1 044.6	1 018.7	961.1	966.7
Pennsylvania	4 400.0	4 506.5	4 514.6	4 435.8	4 512.8	4 565.2	4 716.2	4 806.1	4 753.1	4 728.9	4 580.1	4 524.3
Rhode Island	358.1	365.9	367.0	349.2	366.7	381.7	395.8	400.0	398.3	401.4	390.5	396.3
South Carolina	920.3	984.0	1 015.8	982.6	1 038.1	1 081.7	1 137.5	1 176.0	1 188.8	1 196.4	1 162.3	1 189.0
South Dakota	189.9	199.1	206.6	209.3	218.6	226.6	236.6	241.4	238.0	236.0	230.2	235.3
Tennessee	1 450.1	1 531.1	1 558.2	1 505.7	1 575.4	1 648.1	1 737.0	1 777.3	1 746.6	1 755.4	1 703.0	1 719.0
Texas	3 884.4	4 141.7	4 360.2	4 462.9	4 683.7	4 906.8	5 271.6	5 601.8	5 851.2	6 180.0	6 263.4	6 193.6
Utah	393.0	414.8	434.1	440.3	462.8	488.7	525.4	548.4	550.8	558.0	560.9	566.9
Vermont	153.6	161.3	162.8	162.1	168.4	178.4	190.6	197.9	200.1	204.3	202.9	206.4
Virginia	1 655.2	1 753.4	1 804.3	1 778.7	1 848.1	1 930.4	2 033.5	2 115.0	2 157.2	2 160.8	2 146.4	2 206.9
Washington	1 100.1	1 152.3	1 199.1	1 225.7	1 282.9	1 367.0	1 485.4	1 581.2	1 608.3	1 612.0	1 568.6	1 586.1
West Virginia	540.5	561.6	572.4	574.7	596.3	611.6	633.1	658.6	645.9	628.5	607.8	582.3
Wisconsin	1 580.8	1 660.5	1 703.4	1 676.8	1 725.9	1 798.9	1 887.0	1 960.2	1 938.1	1 923.2	1 866.7	1 867.3
Wyoming	117.3	126.1	136.5	146.0	156.5	170.5	187.4	200.7	210.2	223.5	217.7	202.5
Puerto Rico	....	....	....	....	....	....	....	....	693.1	679.7	641.6	645.6
Virgin Islands	....	....	....	33.1	31.3	32.2	33.8	36.1	37.3	37.7	36.5	36.4

EMPLOYMENT, HOURS, AND EARNINGS, NONAGRICULTURAL PAYROLLS

Employees on Nonagricultural Payrolls by State, 1960-1995—Continued

(Thousands of persons)

State	1984	1985	1986	1987	1988	1989	1990	1991	1992	1993	1994	1995
Alabama	1 387.7	1 427.1	1 463.3	1 507.7	1 558.7	1 601.2	1 635.7	1 642.0	1 674.5	1 716.8	1 758.5	1 803.4
Alaska	225.7	230.7	220.7	210.1	213.7	227.0	238.1	242.8	247.2	252.9	259.3	262.1
Arizona	1 181.9	1 278.6	1 337.8	1 385.8	1 419.3	1 454.5	1 483.0	1 491.4	1 517.0	1 586.2	1 692.2	1 783.1
Arkansas	780.2	797.1	813.8	836.6	865.4	893.4	923.5	936.4	963.1	994.0	1 034.1	1 068.6
California	10 390.0	10 769.8	11 085.5	11 472.6	11 911.5	12 238.5	12 499.9	12 359.0	12 153.5	12 045.3	12 159.5	12 433.8
Colorado	1 402.3	1 418.7	1 408.3	1 412.6	1 436.1	1 482.3	1 520.9	1 545.0	1 596.9	1 670.7	1 755.9	1 839.2
Connecticut	1 517.3	1 558.2	1 598.4	1 638.2	1 667.4	1 665.6	1 623.5	1 555.2	1 526.2	1 531.1	1 543.7	1 563.9
Delaware	280.0	293.4	303.2	320.7	334.2	344.5	347.6	341.8	341.3	348.6	356.0	366.1
District of Columbia	613.8	629.0	640.0	655.6	673.6	680.6	686.1	677.3	673.6	670.3	658.8	643.3
Florida	4 204.2	4 410.0	4 599.4	4 848.1	5 066.6	5 260.9	5 387.4	5 294.3	5 358.7	5 571.4	5 799.4	6 000.4
Georgia	2 448.7	2 569.8	2 672.4	2 782.0	2 875.9	2 941.1	2 991.8	2 937.5	2 987.2	3 109.2	3 265.9	3 416.6
Hawaii	412.7	425.7	438.6	460.0	478.1	505.5	528.4	539.1	542.8	538.8	536.2	532.7
Idaho	330.5	336.0	328.2	333.4	348.5	365.8	384.9	398.1	416.4	436.5	460.9	476.9
Illinois	4 672.3	4 755.3	4 790.7	4 928.3	5 097.5	5 213.9	5 288.3	5 231.5	5 234.9	5 330.5	5 462.9	5 598.6
Indiana	2 122.3	2 168.6	2 221.8	2 304.9	2 395.6	2 479.3	2 521.9	2 507.3	2 554.2	2 626.9	2 712.7	2 780.7
Iowa	1 074.7	1 074.2	1 073.8	1 109.1	1 156.2	1 200.1	1 226.3	1 238.1	1 252.6	1 278.6	1 319.9	1 357.2
Kansas	960.8	967.9	984.8	1 005.1	1 035.4	1 064.2	1 088.5	1 095.4	1 115.0	1 133.3	1 165.8	1 200.5
Kentucky	1 213.8	1 250.3	1 274.1	1 328.2	1 381.9	1 433.0	1 470.5	1 474.7	1 508.5	1 547.9	1 597.2	1 643.2
Louisiana	1 601.5	1 591.2	1 518.5	1 483.6	1 511.6	1 538.5	1 589.9	1 613.0	1 626.9	1 658.6	1 722.1	1 774.5
Maine	445.7	458.4	477.4	501.1	527.1	541.8	534.9	513.4	511.9	519.4	531.6	541.6
Maryland	1 814.0	1 887.8	1 952.0	2 028.0	2 102.3	2 155.2	2 171.2	2 099.8	2 081.3	2 102.4	2 145.8	2 181.0
Massachusetts	2 855.8	2 930.0	2 988.8	3 065.8	3 130.8	3 108.6	2 984.8	2 821.2	2 795.1	2 840.2	2 903.8	2 974.4
Michigan	3 381.0	3 561.5	3 657.3	3 735.8	3 819.2	3 922.3	3 969.6	3 891.1	3 927.4	4 005.8	4 146.8	4 251.9
Minnesota	1 819.8	1 865.5	1 892.5	1 962.5	2 028.1	2 086.8	2 126.7	2 136.8	2 184.9	2 242.7	2 310.4	2 374.1
Mississippi	820.8	838.9	848.2	864.4	896.2	919.3	936.6	937.5	960.3	1 002.3	1 055.5	1 075.1
Missouri	2 032.7	2 094.7	2 142.6	2 197.8	2 258.9	2 315.0	2 345.0	2 309.1	2 333.7	2 394.5	2 470.5	2 520.6
Montana	281.1	279.1	275.4	274.1	282.9	291.0	297.3	303.7	316.6	325.6	340.2	350.6
Nebraska	635.4	650.5	652.5	667.2	688.1	708.0	730.1	739.2	750.1	767.2	796.1	815.1
Nevada	426.0	446.4	468.1	500.2	537.6	581.2	620.9	628.7	638.7	671.4	738.0	789.1
New Hampshire	441.5	466.0	490.1	512.8	529.0	529.1	508.0	482.1	487.0	502.4	523.1	538.8
New Jersey	3 329.2	3 414.1	3 488.1	3 576.3	3 651.0	3 689.8	3 635.1	3 498.7	3 457.9	3 493.1	3 552.8	3 605.8
New Mexico	502.8	520.2	525.9	529.3	547.5	562.2	580.4	585.4	601.5	626.2	657.2	689.7
New York	7 570.4	7 751.3	7 907.9	8 059.4	8 186.9	8 246.8	8 212.4	7 886.7	7 729.9	7 752.0	7 818.7	7 871.3
North Carolina	2 565.2	2 651.2	2 744.1	2 862.6	2 986.6	3 073.9	3 117.7	3 072.2	3 125.5	3 244.7	3 358.9	3 454.6
North Dakota	252.5	252.0	249.9	252.8	256.7	260.4	265.9	270.6	277.2	284.8	294.9	302.1
Ohio	4 260.2	4 372.9	4 471.4	4 582.6	4 700.6	4 817.4	4 882.3	4 818.6	4 847.7	4 918.3	5 076.0	5 232.1
Oklahoma	1 180.3	1 165.3	1 124.4	1 108.5	1 131.5	1 163.8	1 195.9	1 211.0	1 221.7	1 247.0	1 279.5	1 314.3
Oregon	1 006.9	1 030.0	1 058.5	1 100.1	1 152.8	1 205.8	1 247.1	1 244.7	1 267.6	1 308.4	1 362.9	1 417.0
Pennsylvania	4 654.8	4 730.3	4 790.9	4 915.1	5 041.7	5 138.5	5 170.1	5 083.7	5 075.5	5 122.8	5 192.4	5 248.2
Rhode Island	416.4	429.2	442.5	451.9	459.4	461.9	451.2	421.5	424.8	430.0	1 607.2	1 648.2
South Carolina	1 262.5	1 296.2	1 338.0	1 392.2	1 449.0	1 499.7	1 545.0	1 513.4	1 527.7	1 570.1	332.0	344.2
South Dakota	247.0	249.4	251.9	256.9	266.1	276.0	288.7	296.4	308.7	318.7	2 423.0	2 502.7
Tennessee	1 812.0	1 867.8	1 929.8	2 011.6	2 092.1	2 167.2	2 193.2	2 183.6	2 245.0	2 328.5	7 750.9	8 026.7
Texas	6 492.4	6 663.1	6 564.2	6 516.9	6 677.8	6 840.0	7 095.4	7 174.7	7 269.1	7 481.5	859.7	908.4
Utah	601.2	624.3	634.1	640.0	660.0	691.1	723.6	745.2	768.7	809.8	263.8	270.2
Vermont	214.9	224.7	234.4	245.6	256.1	261.8	257.5	248.9	251.0	257.2	3 003.6	3 068.2
Virginia	2 333.3	2 454.7	2 557.7	2 680.4	2 772.5	2 861.9	2 896.3	2 828.9	2 848.4	2 918.9	2 304.3	2 348.5
Washington	1 659.6	1 710.4	1 769.9	1 851.8	1 941.4	2 046.8	2 143.0	2 177.4	2 222.4	2 253.0	2 490.8	2 554.9
West Virginia	596.6	597.2	597.5	599.0	609.8	614.7	630.1	629.1	640.0	652.6	216.8	220.0
Wisconsin	1 949.2	1 983.1	2 023.9	2 089.6	2 168.5	2 236.4	2 291.5	2 302.0	2 357.9	2 412.7	2 490.8	2 554.9
Wyoming	204.3	206.9	196.3	182.6	189.0	192.8	198.5	203.1	205.6	210.3	216.8	220.0
Puerto Rico	684.2	692.5	728.0	763.8	817.8	837.4	843.8	835.6	855.8	869.4	434.2	440.5
Virgin Islands	36.6	36.9	37.7	39.6	41.5	42.0	43.1	43.8	44.8	48.6	674.6	687.6

Employees on Manufacturing Payrolls by State, 1960-1995

(Thousands of persons)

State	1960	1961	1962	1963	1964	1965	1966	1967	1968	1969	1970	1971
Alabama	238.7	232.8	242.2	249.4	259.2	279.2	296.9	300.6	310.0	327.3	327.2	322.7
Alaska	5.8	5.2	5.5	5.7	5.6	6.3	6.6	6.6	6.9	7.3	8.6	7.8
Arizona	49.3	51.0	55.2	58.0	59.5	64.9	77.7	79.1	84.9	94.2	91.2	89.2
Arkansas	103.0	105.6	114.0	119.4	126.7	135.9	149.7	153.4	159.0	169.1	168.6	172.5
California	1 317.2	1 318.0	1 382.5	1 394.3	1 389.4	1 411.2	1 531.3	1 594.0	1 639.7	1 661.3	1 558.0	1 473.2
Colorado	90.6	94.8	96.1	96.4	93.5	92.6	102.7	106.1	110.5	118.3	120.8	123.5
Connecticut	407.2	403.6	418.3	420.8	421.0	436.1	471.4	479.5	474.3	471.7	441.9	399.0
Delaware	58.9	55.4	56.1	59.1	61.9	67.8	71.0	71.7	72.9	73.6	71.1	68.8
District of Columbia	21.0	20.6	20.6	20.6	20.7	21.1	21.7	22.0	21.4	20.8	19.3	18.5
Florida	207.5	211.8	223.1	229.3	237.9	252.6	276.1	293.8	311.4	329.2	322.5	322.7
Georgia	341.6	333.9	350.5	363.8	378.9	403.9	431.5	438.9	452.9	477.6	467.1	461.7
Hawaii	25.7	25.7	25.0	25.0	25.2	24.5	24.2	24.7	23.8	25.2	25.6	25.2
Idaho	28.8	29.9	30.5	30.4	31.8	33.3	35.6	35.3	37.9	39.9	40.3	41.2
Illinois	1 225.4	1 179.3	1 214.0	1 218.6	1 253.3	1 318.4	1 410.5	1 409.6	1 404.0	1 417.4	1 358.6	1 282.4
Indiana	593.9	568.2	601.8	614.5	630.9	673.6	719.7	716.0	722.9	752.3	710.2	683.4
Iowa	177.1	171.6	174.8	179.0	183.5	192.9	212.1	219.3	223.1	225.4	216.0	209.8
Kansas	118.4	117.2	120.4	117.9	123.1	124.7	142.3	149.3	151.0	150.6	137.2	132.5
Kentucky	173.2	167.4	176.4	184.7	194.0	207.8	228.6	234.2	242.9	250.4	255.4	253.3
Louisiana	144.9	138.7	141.9	148.9	155.4	161.1	168.3	176.7	181.9	184.6	179.0	177.7
Maine	104.5	103.2	104.3	102.8	104.0	108.0	115.0	116.3	118.0	115.7	110.4	102.7
Maryland	259.9	256.7	258.6	260.4	258.2	264.8	279.8	283.3	280.6	281.7	271.4	252.4
Massachusetts	698.0	684.9	687.6	663.5	649.9	668.2	699.1	700.8	689.5	681.5	648.2	605.7
Michigan	976.3	887.3	952.2	989.6	1 032.0	1 112.4	1 179.6	1 148.8	1 172.5	1 203.8	1 081.1	1 059.2
Minnesota	229.2	228.9	239.1	242.1	246.4	261.6	287.4	302.2	314.7	331.4	318.7	298.8
Mississippi	120.2	119.0	128.0	134.5	140.4	153.0	166.6	167.4	175.5	182.5	182.1	189.5
Missouri	395.6	378.5	390.3	396.8	405.7	420.1	448.7	457.4	462.7	465.7	449.4	430.3
Montana	20.3	20.3	21.9	22.3	21.4	22.1	22.9	22.4	23.2	24.1	23.9	23.9
Nebraska	66.5	66.3	67.6	66.2	67.2	68.7	74.7	79.7	82.8	86.2	84.5	82.6
Nevada	5.4	5.7	6.0	6.8	6.9	7.1	7.1	6.8	7.1	8.2	8.6	8.8
New Hampshire	87.0	85.9	88.6	85.9	85.6	89.8	96.0	97.6	99.7	97.9	91.6	86.3
New Jersey	808.8	791.5	812.8	809.4	806.7	837.5	879.3	882.8	893.7	892.5	860.7	818.3
New Mexico	17.1	16.6	17.6	17.2	17.9	17.6	18.6	18.3	18.5	20.7	21.4	22.6
New York	1 878.7	1 823.0	1 837.9	1 804.1	1 794.8	1 838.1	1 894.5	1 885.7	1 879.0	1 870.8	1 760.6	1 633.5
North Carolina	504.5	504.3	525.6	537.0	557.1	590.6	638.1	657.5	686.1	714.0	713.0	716.2
North Dakota	6.5	6.3	7.0	7.8	8.4	8.7	8.9	8.6	8.9	9.0	9.9	10.2
Ohio	1 264.8	1 183.2	1 218.2	1 236.6	1 259.1	1 326.0	1 404.4	1 401.4	1 433.5	1 471.0	1 409.9	1 333.8
Oklahoma	86.6	86.5	90.4	90.9	96.6	103.0	113.3	116.4	121.7	129.9	134.1	132.7
Oregon	144.4	139.1	143.4	145.1	151.7	158.2	167.2	165.4	173.7	180.5	172.3	174.3
Pennsylvania	1 444.5	1 383.0	1 403.9	1 401.0	1 434.8	1 494.1	1 565.3	1 562.4	1 570.0	1 588.9	1 528.8	1 438.1
Rhode Island	119.7	116.8	118.9	115.5	116.0	121.0	127.6	127.4	127.4	127.9	120.9	115.2
South Carolina	244.6	246.5	260.1	269.6	277.7	293.0	313.7	319.0	327.3	341.5	340.3	337.2
South Dakota	13.0	13.7	14.0	14.8	13.3	13.5	14.3	15.4	15.9	15.9	15.8	16.5
Tennessee	315.0	313.1	331.6	344.7	361.5	386.6	424.2	434.8	454.3	469.0	463.8	459.5
Texas	487.7	484.4	502.1	516.5	540.5	572.1	622.1	661.9	709.4	750.2	734.3	710.5
Utah	47.5	50.5	54.3	55.5	52.5	50.0	51.2	50.9	51.9	54.8	56.0	56.5
Vermont	35.3	33.8	35.6	34.9	34.7	38.6	43.4	44.2	43.7	43.4	40.5	37.9
Virginia	275.0	276.0	292.4	297.5	308.6	322.5	340.0	346.0	362.7	371.0	366.0	366.2
Washington	216.6	217.5	232.6	224.0	219.3	227.0	265.2	277.1	286.9	278.5	239.5	214.7
West Virginia	124.6	120.1	122.6	124.2	126.2	129.2	133.0	133.2	132.4	131.0	126.5	122.9
Wisconsin	460.4	439.0	455.9	461.4	469.6	491.9	508.6	508.7	510.3	520.9	500.9	479.6
Wyoming	8.4	8.4	7.5	7.2	7.7	7.1	6.8	7.1	6.8	7.4	7.4	7.5
Puerto Rico	....	....	....	....	....	....	....	....	....	....	....	....
Virgin Islands	....	....	....	....	....	....	....	....	....	....	....	....

Employees on Manufacturing Payrolls by State, 1960-1995—Continued

(Thousands of persons)

State	1972	1973	1974	1975	1976	1977	1978	1979	1980	1981	1982	1983
Alabama	333.4	350.9	353.7	321.9	340.2	354.3	368.9	374.9	363.1	362.0	337.8	340.9
Alaska	8.1	9.5	9.7	9.6	10.3	10.9	11.6	12.7	13.4	14.0	12.6	11.9
Arizona	98.7	110.2	112.9	99.8	105.6	113.9	126.9	144.1	154.4	160.6	154.5	155.8
Arkansas	185.2	200.4	203.9	179.2	195.1	209.3	217.5	217.8	209.1	209.7	195.2	200.3
California	1 542.7	1 660.7	1 701.3	1 593.7	1 659.8	1 737.8	1 884.6	2 012.7	2 018.2	2 032.3	1 957.7	1 927.0
Colorado	131.5	143.3	146.6	137.2	144.5	152.8	168.2	180.6	180.4	186.2	183.3	180.7
Connecticut	400.1	420.2	430.9	389.8	397.0	406.7	419.6	436.5	440.8	439.0	418.7	403.2
Delaware	69.4	73.7	70.8	65.7	68.2	67.6	69.0	70.2	70.9	71.0	67.9	68.2
District of Columbia	17.8	17.4	17.0	15.5	15.3	14.8	15.0	15.3	15.4	14.5	13.7	14.2
Florida	351.3	380.6	375.9	339.4	354.0	380.9	415.5	443.6	456.4	472.2	456.7	464.3
Georgia	476.6	494.5	483.7	439.3	476.3	494.1	515.8	528.5	519.2	524.6	500.3	511.1
Hawaii	24.9	23.8	22.7	23.7	23.4	23.2	23.7	24.0	23.3	23.0	22.4	22.4
Idaho	43.6	46.9	48.0	47.8	52.0	54.1	58.1	58.3	53.3	52.7	47.8	51.4
Illinois	1 284.2	1 353.5	1 345.1	1 199.8	1 215.2	1 241.3	1 276.0	1 271.6	1 208.2	1 131.4	1 013.4	955.8
Indiana	709.4	758.2	737.2	647.2	685.1	713.2	741.5	733.2	657.0	652.6	589.0	581.6
Iowa	222.9	241.3	249.9	230.4	234.0	245.6	252.5	259.8	244.8	236.5	209.8	202.3
Kansas	145.7	164.5	169.2	164.2	166.6	172.9	185.9	198.9	190.5	188.6	168.8	164.7
Kentucky	268.3	288.3	290.9	259.7	273.3	284.9	292.2	297.2	276.2	270.5	244.8	242.5
Louisiana	183.2	190.5	192.5	186.2	195.4	203.3	209.5	213.6	214.2	222.1	202.6	180.1
Maine	102.4	104.5	105.1	96.3	102.5	105.9	111.3	114.6	113.2	113.5	108.6	109.2
Maryland	248.8	257.0	254.5	230.0	232.4	235.1	241.5	246.9	236.7	231.7	215.3	214.1
Massachusetts	610.2	634.7	639.3	577.8	593.6	621.0	652.1	672.8	673.3	668.0	636.5	629.0
Michigan	1 097.4	1 178.8	1 114.0	983.7	1 061.7	1 128.4	1 179.6	1 160.2	998.9	979.0	876.9	880.5
Minnesota	310.2	331.2	340.7	313.0	321.7	339.3	360.4	381.6	371.2	364.0	346.8	346.4
Mississippi	207.7	221.0	220.0	201.8	218.9	230.1	235.3	235.2	221.8	220.3	203.2	204.7
Missouri	441.5	459.7	451.6	405.3	424.9	439.6	456.8	464.4	437.0	427.5	406.8	405.4
Montana	24.5	24.8	24.5	22.1	23.7	25.1	26.3	27.0	24.2	23.2	20.6	22.1
Nebraska	85.0	90.5	93.4	85.4	87.9	90.6	94.1	99.6	96.4	94.9	87.9	84.7
Nevada	9.8	11.8	12.3	12.2	13.0	15.1	17.8	19.4	19.2	20.1	18.8	19.1
New Hampshire	90.8	96.0	94.2	85.1	94.5	101.4	109.8	116.5	116.6	116.6	111.7	113.3
New Jersey	823.3	842.6	825.9	747.9	756.2	767.4	786.8	799.1	781.0	771.1	729.6	715.1
New Mexico	26.1	28.9	29.6	28.6	30.3	32.2	33.4	34.8	34.4	34.3	34.1	34.4
New York	1 602.2	1 619.1	1 574.6	1 421.9	1 438.9	1 459.6	1 481.2	1 492.8	1 445.1	1 433.3	1 352.5	1 302.4
North Carolina	756.8	796.9	789.6	715.5	756.3	780.9	807.2	826.8	820.0	820.7	782.2	796.1
North Dakota	10.8	12.6	14.7	16.2	16.2	15.3	15.7	16.7	15.6	15.3	14.9	14.8
Ohio	1 346.8	1 426.3	1 416.6	1 267.5	1 295.3	1 344.1	1 377.2	1 382.3	1 264.3	1 232.6	1 099.9	1 066.0
Oklahoma	141.1	151.9	156.7	150.7	156.1	163.2	172.7	184.4	191.3	200.0	180.6	166.2
Oregon	184.2	196.9	197.1	182.3	193.7	206.1	219.1	228.3	215.1	202.7	185.7	188.8
Pennsylvania	1 444.0	1 480.1	1 464.5	1 334.8	1 335.2	1 341.9	1 367.8	1 386.8	1 328.2	1 299.0	1 170.5	1 095.8
Rhode Island	121.0	125.6	126.0	112.7	122.9	128.8	134.4	132.6	128.2	127.7	116.6	116.2
South Carolina	354.3	374.9	375.9	339.9	371.0	380.2	391.1	399.5	391.9	390.2	364.3	362.4
South Dakota	18.4	19.8	20.9	19.8	22.2	23.4	24.9	27.5	26.1	25.9	24.8	25.9
Tennessee	489.2	519.4	513.3	459.0	486.1	507.5	526.0	524.7	502.1	506.9	466.7	468.6
Texas	738.7	790.2	831.3	815.9	862.3	893.5	962.8	1 021.9	1 056.9	1 115.3	1 045.2	963.7
Utah	60.5	65.1	70.4	67.5	70.7	74.5	80.3	86.8	87.7	89.6	85.7	85.5
Vermont	38.5	41.6	42.8	39.5	41.0	43.4	47.7	50.8	50.9	51.3	48.6	47.6
Virginia	387.8	401.8	401.9	371.5	387.7	400.8	409.4	413.8	413.8	414.0	397.2	403.6
Washington	224.1	244.2	253.6	244.0	247.4	260.0	284.7	309.6	308.7	305.2	289.0	278.4
West Virginia	123.3	129.0	132.1	121.1	124.4	123.8	126.6	126.1	117.2	111.5	98.1	89.8
Wisconsin	495.4	531.7	546.1	507.0	519.4	540.4	569.7	591.3	558.0	543.5	498.2	486.7
Wyoming	7.9	8.4	8.4	8.3	8.4	9.0	9.6	10.1	9.6	9.9	9.1	8.2
Puerto Rico	....	....	....	....	....	....	....	....	154.6	153.1	142.7	143.7
Virgin Islands	....	....	....	3.1	3.1	3.1	2.9	3.2	3.2	3.1	2.7	2.5

Employees on Manufacturing Payrolls by State, 1960-1995—Continued

(Thousands of persons)

State	1984	1985	1986	1987	1988	1989	1990	1991	1992	1993	1994	1995
Alabama	359.8	358.1	358.6	368.8	380.6	385.6	384.5	379.3	380.7	384.2	386.4	390.7
Alaska	11.3	12.1	12.6	12.9	15.0	15.7	17.2	18.0	18.0	17.1	16.6	16.9
Arizona	172.8	181.6	184.6	187.4	189.0	188.2	185.3	176.1	173.2	176.4	190.1	192.6
Arkansas	213.0	209.6	211.8	219.6	226.3	231.0	232.8	233.7	237.0	244.3	254.0	258.9
California	2 004.1	2 024.2	2 039.1	2 060.1	2 096.7	2 107.0	2 068.8	1 970.9	1 890.5	1 805.1	1 777.3	1 790.4
Colorado	195.3	192.2	185.3	184.5	189.6	193.4	193.2	185.6	185.9	188.1	190.9	191.3
Connecticut	415.1	408.0	394.0	384.2	372.3	359.3	341.0	322.5	305.7	294.1	285.1	280.4
Delaware	70.6	72.2	68.7	70.5	70.3	73.1	71.8	70.1	67.4	65.6	63.5	61.9
District of Columbia	14.5	14.8	15.7	16.1	16.3	15.8	15.7	14.6	14.0	13.8	13.0	13.0
Florida	501.9	514.4	517.2	531.0	539.6	537.9	522.1	492.8	482.9	485.2	484.0	482.4
Georgia	546.5	557.1	564.6	571.2	574.3	568.3	561.1	541.0	545.2	558.2	577.3	588.4
Hawaii	21.9	21.9	22.0	21.9	22.0	21.5	21.1	20.5	19.7	19.2	17.8	17.0
Idaho	54.8	54.7	52.1	54.3	57.9	60.5	62.9	63.3	65.7	69.2	71.9	71.1
Illinois	997.0	970.7	925.8	940.2	975.2	986.6	982.7	940.8	919.3	933.1	952.1	966.7
Indiana	620.5	609.8	604.0	616.6	636.7	646.3	638.0	618.7	628.6	642.9	664.4	683.6
Iowa	211.9	204.7	201.7	213.5	226.4	234.8	236.4	232.5	230.2	236.1	244.9	250.3
Kansas	176.4	174.4	175.7	176.2	181.6	184.4	186.0	183.9	182.7	183.5	187.9	191.9
Kentucky	257.4	255.3	253.8	262.5	274.1	284.2	287.5	281.4	286.9	294.6	305.1	313.7
Louisiana	182.4	178.0	166.0	164.5	171.5	176.3	184.4	186.4	185.0	185.4	186.5	188.4
Maine	110.6	105.9	103.6	104.1	108.0	105.5	101.9	95.2	92.2	90.9	91.4	91.6
Maryland	219.4	217.2	210.2	208.4	210.2	209.8	205.9	191.7	183.7	180.2	178.2	175.7
Massachusetts	667.6	649.7	614.4	599.1	584.7	561.1	521.3	485.0	465.7	454.8	447.2	445.3
Michigan	962.8	1 002.4	1 000.4	972.5	955.4	971.3	943.6	896.7	900.6	908.3	951.5	974.9
Minnesota	373.8	375.4	369.1	376.4	394.1	399.8	400.8	395.2	397.1	406.5	414.7	425.9
Mississippi	218.7	221.6	223.7	228.6	238.8	243.6	246.5	246.9	251.9	255.7	261.0	258.0
Missouri	433.8	430.3	424.7	424.0	433.9	440.6	438.1	415.6	412.0	411.1	414.1	421.1
Montana	22.5	21.8	21.1	20.8	21.3	22.3	22.3	21.7	22.5	23.0	23.0	23.3
Nebraska	90.5	88.4	86.0	88.6	93.6	94.7	97.8	99.6	100.7	103.8	108.8	111.8
Nevada	21.0	21.9	22.3	23.3	24.9	25.4	26.2	25.9	26.1	29.5	33.7	36.7
New Hampshire	123.4	122.5	118.1	117.5	117.9	113.6	105.6	98.2	97.4	97.6	100.3	102.1
New Jersey	726.7	712.8	689.7	672.2	662.1	639.6	596.6	558.4	530.3	516.6	509.3	500.2
New Mexico	36.5	37.3	37.4	38.3	40.4	42.6	43.4	41.8	41.0	42.7	44.7	45.3
New York	1 326.3	1 293.1	1 251.6	1 218.4	1 212.5	1 189.0	1 131.4	1 059.6	1 014.4	980.5	956.1	944.3
North Carolina	835.6	828.6	832.8	856.0	867.5	871.1	861.5	826.1	834.4	847.8	859.9	860.7
North Dakota	15.5	15.4	15.3	15.8	16.4	16.5	17.4	17.9	18.3	19.5	21.4	21.2
Ohio	1 127.0	1 124.2	1 109.8	1 098.9	1 110.6	1 122.6	1 112.3	1 066.9	1 050.6	1 049.7	1 070.2	1 101.3
Oklahoma	175.0	172.0	160.4	156.8	161.4	164.4	168.8	168.8	163.8	168.6	169.8	169.8
Oregon	201.1	199.3	198.4	206.2	214.2	218.4	220.3	211.7	209.0	211.7	221.3	227.6
Pennsylvania	1 121.9	1 089.5	1 048.9	1 044.0	1 055.2	1 047.0	1 019.0	973.0	953.0	943.1	942.0	938.9
Rhode Island	121.7	119.2	118.9	116.3	112.4	108.3	99.7	91.7	89.5	88.1	86.8	84.6
South Carolina	377.6	365.4	365.2	374.0	385.0	389.6	383.3	369.2	371.0	374.8	377.4	377.9
South Dakota	29.2	27.5	28.2	29.3	31.6	32.3	34.4	35.0	37.0	39.6	43.5	46.3
Tennessee	497.1	492.4	490.5	497.4	511.9	524.5	520.3	502.7	514.5	528.4	538.9	542.1
Texas	1 004.3	998.6	951.1	932.0	962.6	979.1	997.4	981.0	969.6	987.6	1 009.0	1 030.2
Utah	94.0	94.0	92.0	92.1	99.0	103.1	107.3	105.8	106.9	110.7	116.7	123.7
Vermont	49.0	49.8	49.5	49.6	49.7	48.6	46.4	44.2	43.7	43.6	43.9	45.1
Virginia	421.3	423.4	424.7	428.9	427.4	429.6	426.4	412.0	407.4	405.1	404.3	402.0
Washington	288.1	295.6	305.0	318.4	341.6	361.6	369.4	351.9	347.7	340.8	336.9	332.0
West Virginia	91.5	89.5	86.8	86.2	87.0	87.8	87.5	83.2	82.2	82.9	81.6	82.3
Wisconsin	518.9	513.9	514.5	528.7	551.5	558.5	558.6	546.2	549.6	561.8	583.9	600.9
Wyoming	8.0	8.0	7.9	8.2	8.7	8.9	9.5	9.3	9.3	9.6	9.9	9.8
Puerto Rico	150.1	147.5	148.8	151.3	154.5	157.3	154.9	151.6	151.7	150.2	151.0	152.9
Virgin Islands	2.3	2.2	1.8	2.1	2.4	2.3	2.4	2.7	2.8	2.8	2.9	2.5

EMPLOYMENT, HOURS, AND EARNINGS, NONAGRICULTURAL PAYROLLS

Employees on Government Payrolls by State, 1960-1995

(Thousands of persons)

State	1960	1961	1962	1963	1964	1965	1966	1967	1968	1969	1970	1971
Alabama	159.8	165.9	167.8	170.0	173.3	179.1	191.6	197.7	201.4	204.7	209.5	213.6
Alaska	22.5	23.8	25.0	27.1	28.1	29.7	30.8	31.8	32.2	33.3	35.6	37.9
Arizona	68.0	72.6	77.7	81.6	85.3	92.2	98.9	104.7	110.0	113.4	119.5	129.5
Arkansas	70.2	72.9	76.1	74.6	76.5	84.9	91.6	93.4	97.0	100.9	102.7	104.9
California	874.0	920.3	962.8	1 001.6	1 043.5	1 105.4	1 196.7	1 274.3	1 335.8	1 391.7	1 424.7	1 446.3
Colorado	111.1	118.3	123.5	128.6	132.0	137.7	148.2	157.7	162.4	166.9	177.2	184.7
Connecticut	93.7	96.4	98.7	103.3	109.0	115.9	122.5	131.5	140.0	150.9	157.9	160.9
Delaware	18.7	19.4	20.9	22.6	23.9	25.0	26.3	27.9	29.3	31.9	35.0	36.8
District of Columbia	228.7	232.9	240.8	249.5	251.3	262.7	274.6	278.0	264.6	254.4	249.7	256.7
Florida	220.5	232.3	247.4	262.5	278.7	301.2	326.2	342.3	361.8	377.9	397.8	419.1
Georgia	186.1	191.9	197.2	204.0	210.8	222.8	243.9	263.0	275.3	286.1	297.5	309.6
Hawaii	49.5	50.4	51.2	52.9	54.4	57.8	62.6	66.3	69.1	71.1	73.7	78.2
Idaho	32.7	34.4	36.4	37.8	38.1	39.6	41.9	44.3	45.2	46.8	49.1	51.3
Illinois	416.9	433.8	447.0	459.3	475.0	502.4	536.5	572.0	593.4	615.6	638.9	648.6
Indiana	188.5	194.0	201.3	209.7	219.2	232.2	254.1	271.4	285.3	280.9	286.4	296.3
Iowa	117.2	122.3	125.4	129.5	133.1	138.8	148.8	157.1	163.8	171.7	176.0	178.3
Kansas	114.1	116.4	118.9	120.6	126.2	130.2	137.0	143.2	146.0	149.6	153.3	155.1
Kentucky	110.1	114.6	120.2	125.2	128.4	135.2	145.2	155.5	163.3	166.1	172.1	180.5
Louisiana	145.2	150.3	154.4	158.3	163.4	171.7	185.4	197.4	201.8	208.2	213.2	216.0
Maine	48.2	49.5	50.3	51.5	52.9	54.3	57.4	59.5	61.6	64.3	66.4	68.7
Maryland	142.8	151.2	159.4	166.0	174.1	183.8	201.9	218.2	232.3	243.2	301.0	314.9
Massachusetts	248.0	255.5	261.7	267.5	272.7	278.5	286.2	297.1	302.5	310.7	319.9	330.6
Michigan	333.3	337.5	343.2	359.8	373.3	395.4	433.0	455.0	471.3	494.5	506.6	509.4
Minnesota	149.5	153.7	162.2	171.8	179.3	189.9	201.6	214.1	215.4	224.1	234.9	239.7
Mississippi	87.5	90.8	94.2	97.2	99.5	105.2	114.3	120.6	125.1	128.0	131.2	133.7
Missouri	190.3	192.7	198.0	202.9	210.6	225.4	244.7	260.3	269.1	276.1	284.1	292.9
Montana	38.5	40.0	41.1	43.0	44.7	45.9	48.1	51.8	53.3	52.1	52.6	54.3
Nebraska	80.8	83.6	85.4	87.7	89.1	92.5	93.3	97.6	97.4	100.9	104.7	109.1
Nevada	18.8	20.2	22.0	24.2	26.4	28.6	30.3	32.3	34.1	35.8	36.9	38.1
New Hampshire	25.6	26.4	27.0	28.0	29.0	30.1	31.4	33.4	34.4	35.5	37.3	38.8
New Jersey	242.1	253.6	262.8	272.1	280.0	295.4	312.0	329.2	344.4	360.1	374.8	388.0
New Mexico	63.5	65.3	67.7	70.3	71.8	75.4	81.0	83.4	85.0	86.3	89.2	92.3
New York	837.7	850.3	875.7	897.2	924.1	958.6	1 012.4	1 073.1	1 123.8	1 176.0	1 218.1	1 239.8
North Carolina	164.2	171.0	178.8	185.6	192.7	201.6	217.4	231.6	244.4	254.3	264.2	268.4
North Dakota	31.5	32.3	33.9	36.4	38.8	40.3	42.1	44.4	47.2	48.4	49.3	49.3
Ohio	399.2	412.5	424.2	431.7	440.3	458.6	483.0	509.5	528.3	544.8	565.5	577.2
Oklahoma	124.7	127.0	131.0	134.9	136.9	145.8	158.8	168.2	171.9	175.5	176.7	179.0
Oregon	95.3	100.2	103.4	107.9	111.3	118.2	125.3	132.4	136.1	140.8	146.7	152.0
Pennsylvania	436.1	451.0	465.1	474.8	488.6	508.4	536.1	567.2	588.1	609.4	618.7	629.2
Rhode Island	40.1	41.2	41.9	42.4	43.4	46.1	48.7	51.2	52.3	52.8	53.6	55.9
South Carolina	96.2	98.3	99.5	103.1	106.8	111.1	121.0	128.4	134.0	140.8	149.9	156.7
South Dakota	38.9	40.2	42.2	43.0	44.4	46.6	48.2	49.3	50.3	53.0	53.1	52.6
Tennessee	146.3	151.9	157.4	163.5	173.3	185.1	195.3	201.8	208.2	214.2	225.9	231.9
Texas	431.0	444.5	461.2	480.7	500.0	525.6	567.1	607.1	630.1	651.4	662.3	684.2
Utah	62.3	65.1	68.6	71.6	73.7	79.4	90.7	98.0	98.8	99.6	100.1	103.2
Vermont	17.3	17.8	18.2	18.9	19.5	20.3	21.2	22.3	23.4	24.4	26.2	27.2
Virginia	191.1	199.6	207.7	215.7	221.2	232.2	251.2	270.5	283.6	292.4	355.1	371.9
Washington	166.6	170.1	175.4	179.9	184.6	193.1	206.2	218.5	230.1	237.4	244.5	252.4
West Virginia	67.5	71.5	71.4	72.1	75.3	81.7	88.5	92.1	94.9	95.0	95.9	98.0
Wisconsin	163.2	170.4	174.6	181.7	190.4	201.0	215.2	230.3	244.6	255.3	265.5	270.2
Wyoming	21.3	22.5	22.8	23.8	24.6	25.6	26.9	28.4	28.1	28.1	28.4	29.4
Puerto Rico	....	....	....	....	....	....	....	....	....	....	....	....
Virgin Islands	....	....	....	....	....	....	....	....	....	....	....	....

Employees on Government Payrolls by State, 1960-1995—Continued

(Thousands of persons)

State	1972	1973	1974	1975	1976	1977	1978	1979	1980	1981	1982	1983
Alabama	220.9	225.7	235.1	247.5	252.9	266.3	285.9	291.6	297.4	291.3	290.1	292.7
Alaska	40.5	41.5	43.8	47.7	48.2	50.1	51.6	54.4	55.0	57.1	59.6	63.0
Arizona	139.2	147.6	161.0	169.7	177.3	181.9	194.8	196.2	201.8	199.5	199.9	203.1
Arkansas	108.5	110.1	115.6	120.9	125.3	128.6	135.9	139.1	141.1	138.1	136.0	137.3
California	1 492.7	1 524.8	1 586.0	1 670.6	1 695.6	1 740.7	1 753.1	1 735.0	1 763.9	1 756.4	1 735.2	1 724.3
Colorado	190.8	197.2	204.0	216.6	219.5	221.1	234.0	238.8	243.6	241.7	238.6	240.7
Connecticut	165.2	167.7	171.0	178.7	175.1	175.6	179.2	181.3	185.2	182.4	179.6	181.9
Delaware	39.0	39.2	39.1	40.3	40.6	41.4	42.8	44.4	45.2	44.5	43.8	43.4
District of Columbia	260.2	259.6	265.3	269.7	275.9	275.6	281.6	284.5	282.2	273.2	260.8	258.8
Florida	437.9	469.9	510.5	546.0	542.8	565.7	601.8	600.5	618.8	620.1	632.5	639.3
Georgia	320.9	328.2	340.5	354.8	366.1	384.0	407.9	418.7	429.2	431.1	434.0	437.6
Hawaii	79.4	78.0	78.8	82.0	84.8	85.7	87.1	86.5	89.0	89.0	90.3	91.3
Idaho	54.5	56.2	59.7	62.3	64.5	67.3	69.8	69.6	70.5	69.2	67.8	67.8
Illinois	654.3	666.5	680.9	714.5	717.2	717.8	728.0	739.8	749.4	734.5	717.9	701.6
Indiana	301.4	303.8	308.0	323.3	332.5	342.0	349.1	347.6	346.6	339.7	328.7	327.0
Iowa	180.2	182.8	186.7	192.0	197.0	202.5	208.2	204.5	207.4	203.1	202.0	203.4
Kansas	162.8	166.5	164.0	168.7	171.6	176.9	180.0	183.3	187.4	185.9	183.8	182.9
Kentucky	188.5	194.3	198.5	208.3	213.0	212.0	220.3	230.4	230.9	224.3	218.9	216.6
Louisiana	227.9	233.2	241.6	248.7	253.0	257.4	280.3	289.7	300.8	303.8	307.3	315.0
Maine	69.4	70.7	72.9	74.8	75.2	77.7	81.5	82.6	83.3	82.6	82.1	83.1
Maryland	327.0	338.1	349.1	366.1	372.1	378.1	401.9	418.7	434.8	415.9	393.2	379.6
Massachusetts	343.1	351.6	354.3	365.1	375.8	407.9	429.2	416.7	412.3	394.6	374.7	375.4
Michigan	526.8	534.4	562.5	583.1	594.5	596.7	611.4	621.0	627.8	598.4	577.8	569.8
Minnesota	246.2	256.6	263.8	271.5	276.0	286.3	292.8	295.6	300.6	299.0	289.6	286.6
Mississippi	139.4	145.0	150.4	153.5	156.2	163.9	181.8	192.2	194.5	185.9	180.0	181.1
Missouri	297.5	306.9	312.9	316.0	316.5	321.5	335.6	338.5	339.2	326.6	328.2	323.2
Montana	55.4	55.4	58.2	64.9	65.7	70.0	71.7	70.1	70.2	69.3	67.4	68.4
Nebraska	114.3	116.9	121.4	124.7	124.3	129.2	130.3	130.6	130.8	129.7	129.3	130.2
Nevada	39.7	41.4	43.0	45.6	46.8	49.2	52.2	54.7	57.0	57.1	58.2	58.0
New Hampshire	41.2	43.4	45.6	48.0	49.9	53.8	54.3	55.1	57.3	56.7	55.9	56.1
New Jersey	405.3	417.1	439.9	470.2	480.5	504.0	523.0	517.8	529.7	529.0	524.6	521.2
New Mexico	96.0	99.5	102.5	104.8	108.0	111.0	116.6	120.5	125.0	125.8	125.6	127.2
New York	1 243.9	1 268.6	1 301.9	1 328.7	1 273.6	1 270.8	1 315.1	1 311.3	1 314.4	1 300.3	1 293.7	1 299.6
North Carolina	275.3	281.8	303.2	328.3	347.9	367.6	386.4	397.2	409.9	403.7	400.3	407.1
North Dakota	51.3	52.2	53.3	54.5	56.2	57.5	60.0	60.6	60.9	60.5	60.3	61.3
Ohio	589.1	597.8	613.1	626.4	632.2	642.3	667.5	674.0	689.9	676.0	659.6	656.1
Oklahoma	184.9	192.2	199.0	206.3	207.0	212.4	218.4	224.0	228.5	235.7	237.2	245.2
Oregon	157.5	160.3	168.5	177.1	181.6	186.8	197.1	200.7	203.2	202.6	195.5	192.3
Pennsylvania	651.9	658.7	682.0	721.4	722.1	710.9	720.7	720.7	723.3	703.4	682.5	673.7
Rhode Island	56.8	55.5	55.1	56.6	57.0	58.2	59.8	59.3	59.2	58.5	57.8	56.9
South Carolina	165.6	170.7	182.2	199.8	203.3	213.7	223.8	228.8	236.4	233.0	228.1	230.3
South Dakota	53.7	53.8	54.9	55.7	55.9	56.6	58.1	58.3	58.6	57.8	56.6	56.9
Tennessee	240.6	246.2	256.4	271.3	283.1	291.2	305.6	313.9	317.2	311.7	297.5	294.1
Texas	714.8	745.3	776.0	815.8	847.0	875.5	923.7	953.2	978.1	1 000.8	1 023.6	1 042.0
Utah	105.5	105.7	108.2	110.3	112.2	115.8	121.0	123.2	125.0	125.1	126.4	128.8
Vermont	28.2	28.7	29.3	30.5	30.9	34.3	35.1	35.8	37.0	36.2	36.0	36.3
Virginia	380.0	391.2	405.9	422.8	436.6	453.6	482.7	493.5	511.2	506.6	500.1	500.9
Washington	258.7	259.0	269.3	280.5	284.8	294.9	308.0	315.5	330.8	326.4	318.5	324.0
West Virginia	99.4	104.2	106.4	108.1	109.6	111.0	120.3	130.1	133.1	130.2	126.8	127.8
Wisconsin	275.8	276.3	276.9	285.4	288.6	287.1	298.2	310.1	321.1	318.0	314.1	312.5
Wyoming	30.5	31.3	32.4	34.5	36.1	38.0	39.1	40.8	43.0	44.5	46.0	48.9
Puerto Rico	....	....	....	....	....	....	....	246.0	254.4	244.6	236.7	240.1
Virgin Islands	....	....	....	11.7	11.3	11.9	12.8	13.5	13.4	13.9	13.5	14.0

Employees on Government Payrolls by State, 1960-1995—Continued

(Thousands of persons)

State	1984	1985	1986	1987	1988	1989	1990	1991	1992	1993	1994	1995
Alabama	293.4	295.9	298.0	300.6	309.5	317.9	326.7	332.6	337.9	340.7	346.0	342.9
Alaska	66.5	68.3	68.0	65.8	66.5	68.7	71.0	71.6	73.3	74.6	73.9	72.9
Arizona	207.5	218.1	225.0	232.0	237.2	246.4	258.9	271.1	276.7	287.8	286.4	298.6
Arkansas	139.5	143.0	145.1	146.1	150.0	154.2	159.3	163.2	167.1	169.8	173.0	177.1
California	1 747.4	1 792.8	1 838.8	1 883.7	1 934.1	1 998.7	2 074.8	2 090.6	2 095.6	2 080.6	2 093.2	2 101.6
Colorado	244.4	248.9	256.0	262.2	266.7	271.4	276.8	283.3	291.1	296.7	299.3	302.7
Connecticut	185.2	188.8	195.3	201.2	206.3	207.7	210.4	207.6	207.4	210.7	217.2	221.1
Delaware	43.7	44.8	46.1	46.6	47.5	47.1	47.9	48.0	48.6	49.7	50.4	50.1
District of Columbia	260.6	265.0	266.9	270.6	276.1	276.8	277.3	281.2	285.8	285.3	270.5	254.3
Florida	649.5	674.4	701.9	731.8	773.0	800.1	846.7	859.3	870.1	881.6	910.6	923.6
Georgia	442.0	448.7	462.2	476.6	494.1	512.2	531.9	536.6	537.1	548.1	564.0	575.2
Hawaii	91.8	93.3	93.9	96.1	99.5	101.6	105.6	108.9	111.1	111.5	111.8	111.1
Idaho	68.9	70.2	70.9	73.3	76.0	77.9	81.3	84.3	88.1	90.4	92.9	95.5
Illinois	687.9	697.8	714.8	724.5	738.8	744.4	766.0	770.6	773.9	774.4	786.0	801.2
Indiana	328.1	332.9	339.7	347.2	354.5	366.6	378.6	379.9	387.6	391.3	300.7	388.5
Iowa	204.5	206.8	207.3	210.2	212.1	216.7	219.0	220.6	221.0	222.5	226.9	230.1
Kansas	185.2	188.7	194.1	199.0	204.4	209.1	214.4	219.0	225.7	229.5	233.4	237.5
Kentucky	223.0	230.0	236.0	240.2	246.1	253.3	260.2	267.3	273.3	276.6	280.6	287.0
Louisiana	318.6	322.4	319.3	313.1	312.6	315.7	326.2	332.3	339.5	342.0	351.5	357.2
Maine	83.9	84.9	86.7	88.4	91.6	94.1	95.8	95.9	95.7	95.4	94.1	93.3
Maryland	387.9	393.6	391.6	392.9	399.1	411.3	419.3	416.3	414.8	417.4	420.1	422.3
Massachusetts	375.4	385.3	393.0	401.2	411.3	408.8	402.2	389.9	382.6	387.5	390.0	394.1
Michigan	567.2	580.7	598.6	611.6	623.5	623.2	633.9	635.8	639.0	639.4	638.9	638.5
Minnesota	293.7	301.2	307.9	313.8	320.8	328.7	337.7	341.8	346.1	352.1	359.5	380.8
Mississippi	183.2	188.5	189.5	191.1	196.0	199.8	203.4	203.9	207.9	210.1	213.7	217.4
Missouri	321.8	334.1	338.5	344.0	351.8	359.3	369.7	370.7	370.7	376.8	384.9	390.3
Montana	68.7	69.9	70.2	69.4	70.7	70.3	71.4	71.9	74.2	74.1	76.3	76.8
Nebraska	131.1	133.8	134.9	135.3	137.8	139.7	143.4	145.6	147.6	149.0	151.6	150.5
Nevada	58.9	60.5	61.6	64.1	67.0	70.8	75.6	81.3	86.0	88.6	92.3	96.5
New Hampshire	57.5	60.0	62.0	65.4	68.7	71.2	72.7	72.4	73.1	74.4	76.2	75.6
New Jersey	522.1	531.1	535.6	541.8	550.9	559.0	571.6	566.7	566.8	565.6	568.4	568.9
New Mexico	129.7	132.8	135.9	137.6	141.6	144.9	149.7	152.3	156.1	159.1	163.1	165.2
New York	1 318.2	1 353.6	1 382.3	1 402.1	1 433.2	1 447.6	1 473.4	1 445.1	1 427.6	1 425.4	1 423.3	1 393.8
North Carolina	413.7	420.5	430.9	442.3	458.7	477.2	492.0	501.7	502.5	527.1	538.6	549.7
North Dakota	62.2	63.6	64.4	64.6	64.8	65.6	65.4	65.7	66.8	67.1	67.2	71.2
Ohio	655.2	665.2	678.9	687.3	693.8	706.4	722.2	727.9	735.1	735.6	741.0	749.0
Oklahoma	241.4	245.7	246.8	245.4	248.5	257.2	261.9	264.9	270.1	269.8	270.2	269.7
Oregon	194.1	197.7	200.2	205.6	211.2	215.6	223.5	226.4	231.0	232.6	234.7	238.8
Pennsylvania	672.9	680.2	679.8	688.7	694.6	697.9	706.3	701.9	699.9	709.0	713.6	720.0
Rhode Island	57.4	57.7	58.0	58.2	58.9	59.1	62.5	60.9	61.2	61.4	61.7	61.2
South Carolina	237.3	244.8	251.4	258.0	261.5	273.1	282.2	285.7	291.9	295.8	295.3	294.4
South Dakota	57.2	57.9	58.8	58.9	60.1	61.6	62.7	63.4	65.4	66.6	67.1	70.9
Tennessee	296.1	304.2	312.4	321.2	328.4	344.3	351.4	353.2	356.9	362.0	370.7	376.4
Texas	1 063.5	1 088.9	1 118.8	1 142.7	1 175.5	1 206.6	1 263.4	1 287.5	1 334.3	1 376.0	1 413.7	1 449.4
Utah	131.5	137.8	141.2	141.5	142.7	146.3	150.5	153.9	156.9	159.5	161.4	163.4
Vermont	36.5	37.4	38.2	39.0	40.9	42.0	43.5	43.8	43.7	44.0	44.7	45.0
Virginia	505.0	515.6	519.9	530.3	544.4	562.6	578.4	580.5	589.4	597.8	603.2	597.3
Washington	334.5	342.8	348.9	357.2	368.8	379.9	397.6	411.6	423.6	430.0	437.2	443.9
West Virginia	130.7	127.5	128.9	128.2	129.3	125.9	127.4	127.7	132.3	132.8	136.5	136.6
Wisconsin	314.7	320.6	325.6	325.0	327.8	335.0	342.9	346.4	356.9	361.5	367.1	378.1
Wyoming	50.9	52.2	53.1	50.5	54.1	54.3	55.3	55.8	56.8	57.2	58.2	58.1
Puerto Rico	253.2	255.4	267.7	281.2	298.5	298.1	294.6	290.6	295.8	289.9	300.1	304.7
Virgin Islands	13.8	13.5	13.1	12.8	13.2	13.6	13.6	13.4	13.9	13.9	13.8	13.7

Average Weekly Hours of Production Workers on Manufacturing Payrolls by State, 1970-1995

State	1970	1971	1972	1973	1974	1975	1976	1977	1978	1979	1980	1981	1982
Alabama	40.3	40.9	41.0	41.0	40.5	39.5	40.6	40.5	40.6	40.7	40.1	39.9	38.5
Alaska			40.1	36.6	40.5	36.6	40.5	43.3	42.4	43.9	42.7	40.0	38.6
Arizona			40.5	39.8	39.2	39.0	39.5	40.1	40.3	40.6	40.1	39.6	38.9
Arkansas			40.2	39.9	39.2	38.8	39.6	39.7	39.3	39.6	39.3	39.4	38.6
California	39.6	39.5	40.1	40.3	39.7	39.4	39.7	40.1	40.1	39.9	39.5	39.6	39.2
Colorado								39.4	39.3	39.5	39.8	39.8	39.2
Connecticut	40.9	40.5	41.5	42.1	41.4	40.5	40.8	41.5	42.0	42.0	41.8	41.6	40.5
Delaware			40.1	40.3	39.4	39.3	40.0	39.6	40.0	39.5	40.5	40.3	39.2
District of Columbia													
Florida	41.1	40.8	41.2	41.0	40.2	40.0	40.4	40.7	40.9	40.5	40.8	40.6	39.9
Georgia	39.8	40.4	41.0	40.5	39.8	39.5	40.1	40.5	40.1	40.4	40.2	40.1	38.6
Hawaii			39.5	39.9	39.4	39.1	39.0	38.0	38.6	38.3	37.8	38.5	37.9
Idaho			39.4	38.8	39.0	38.8	38.7	39.3	38.8	38.3	37.1	37.8	36.7
Illinois			41.0	41.2	40.4	39.7	40.4	40.6	40.1	40.7	39.8	40.0	39.2
Indiana						39.8	40.6	41.2	41.2	40.5	39.8	40.1	39.2
Iowa	39.9	40.1	40.1	40.5	39.6	39.5	38.7	39.8	40.2	40.2	40.6	41.3	41.4
Kansas											40.7	40.4	40.4
Kentucky	39.4	39.2	40.4	40.3	39.6	38.7	39.4	39.5	39.6	39.4	39.1	39.3	38.4
Louisiana			42.3	41.4	40.1	42.8	41.3	41.8	41.6	41.3	41.2	42.2	41.0
Maine	40.1	39.8	40.7	40.8	40.3	39.9	39.9	39.8	40.2	40.1	40.0	40.4	40.0
Maryland			40.2	40.5	39.9	39.1	39.6	39.9	39.9	40.0	39.6	39.9	39.2
Massachusetts			40.1	40.5	39.9	39.1	39.7	39.9	40.2	40.1	39.6	40.0	39.2
Michigan							42.7	43.3	43.0	41.2	40.1	40.5	40.2
Minnesota			40.7	41.0	39.9	39.2	39.8	40.0	40.2	40.0	39.4	39.4	39.1
Mississippi	40.2	40.4	41.1	40.3	39.3	39.3	40.0	40.1	39.9	39.6	39.3	39.3	38.1
Missouri			39.8	39.8	39.3	39.0	39.8	40.2	40.0	39.5	39.2	39.2	38.6
Montana			40.3	39.3	38.8	38.0	39.8	41.8	42.7	42.9	43.2	41.0	39.3
Nebraska			41.7	41.8	41.2	40.5	41.1	40.8	41.1	41.3	40.6	40.3	39.9
Nevada			40.2	40.0	38.8	38.2	38.9	38.8	38.5	38.5	38.2	38.6	37.3
New Hampshire			39.8	39.8	39.3	39.1	39.6	40.0	40.3	40.1	39.8	39.9	39.6
New Jersey	40.3	40.4	40.9	41.4	40.7	39.9	40.4	41.1	40.8	41.2	40.7	40.6	39.9
New Mexico	39.0	39.4	40.1	39.4	38.4	39.0	39.5	38.8	39.2	39.5	39.8	39.5	39.2
New York	38.9	39.1	39.6	39.9	39.4	38.9	39.4	39.6	39.8	39.6	39.4	39.4	38.8
North Carolina	39.5	40.0	40.7	40.1	39.1	38.4	39.4	39.6	39.8	39.6	39.3	39.1	37.3
North Dakota			40.2	40.4	40.2	39.9	39.1	38.6	39.7	39.1	37.5	38.1	37.6
Ohio	40.6	40.7	41.6	42.3	41.2	40.3	41.4	42.0	42.1	41.5	40.6	40.9	40.1
Oklahoma	40.8	40.3	40.5	40.6	40.5	40.0	40.3	40.4	40.2	40.5	40.1	40.1	39.5
Oregon			39.4	39.3	38.8	38.4	38.9	38.6	39.0	38.5	38.1	37.5	37.9
Pennsylvania			39.8	40.2	39.6	38.8	39.2	39.5	40.0	39.9	38.8	39.2	38.4
Rhode Island	39.2	40.0	40.1	40.4	39.9	40.6	40.7	40.5	40.3	40.1	39.2	39.3	39.5
South Carolina	40.2	40.9	41.4	40.5	39.8	39.4	40.4	40.6	40.8	40.8	40.3	40.4	38.2
South Dakota			43.3	42.6	41.7	40.7	39.9	39.3	41.7	41.9	40.9	41.6	41.1
Tennessee	39.9	40.1	40.6	40.4	39.9	39.8	40.3	40.2	39.6	39.7	39.7	39.9	38.6
Texas							40.9	41.1	41.3	41.1	41.2	41.3	40.0
Utah			38.5	38.8	38.7	38.1	39.2	40.0	39.5	39.0	39.1	39.7	38.5
Vermont			41.0	41.2	41.5	41.5	41.1	40.4	41.0	40.8	41.0	40.8	40.6
Virginia			40.0	40.2	40.8	40.6	39.8	39.2	39.9	39.9	39.8	39.7	39.3
Washington			39.6	39.2	38.9	38.7	39.1	39.2	39.3	38.6	38.4	38.8	38.5
West Virginia	39.8	39.6	40.0	40.0	39.6	39.0	39.2	39.5	39.6	39.6	39.2	39.4	38.8
Wisconsin	40.4	40.5	41.3	41.4	41.1	40.4	40.6	40.6	41.0	40.9	40.2	40.1	39.6
Wyoming			38.6	38.6	38.0	38.6	40.2	39.8	38.6	37.6	38.9	40.0	38.2
Puerto Rico											38.0	38.2	37.5
Virgin Islands									40.9	40.9	41.1	42.3	42.3

Average Weekly Hours of Production Workers on Manufacturing Payrolls by State, 1970-1995—Continued

State	1983	1984	1985	1986	1987	1988	1989	1990	1991	1992	1993	1994	1995
Alabama	40.7	41.0	40.8	41.1	41.4	41.4	41.2	41.0	40.8	41.2	41.2	41.9	41.7
Alaska	36.2	39.3	40.7	41.1	42.7	42.1	44.4	44.9	46.4	45.5	45.0	47.4	47.8
Arizona	40.5	40.8	40.9	41.0	40.6	41.1	41.2	40.7	40.7	40.8	40.7	42.3	42.2
Arkansas	40.1	40.5	40.2	40.4	41.0	40.9	40.8	41.0	41.2	41.4	41.4	41.8	41.0
California	40.0	40.3	40.2	40.3	40.3	40.7	40.7	40.6	40.6	40.6	40.9	41.4	41.2
Colorado	39.9	40.9	40.2	39.9	40.2	40.4	40.2	41.2	40.4	40.5	41.2	41.3	41.0
Connecticut	41.3	42.5	41.9	41.8	42.1	42.2	42.2	42.0	41.8	41.7	42.1	42.8	42.8
Delaware	40.6	41.5	41.1	41.3	40.7	40.0	41.5	41.3	40.8	40.8	42.1	42.8	40.9
District of Columbia	....	....	....	....	....	....	....	....	....	....	....	....	....
Florida	40.7	41.2	41.3	40.8	40.8	40.7	40.9	40.7	40.7	40.9	41.2	41.4	41.4
Georgia	41.1	41.0	40.6	40.9	41.6	41.4	41.1	40.9	41.0	41.4	41.7	42.4	42.3
Hawaii	38.6	38.1	37.4	38.9	39.4	40.0	40.0	40.3	39.8	40.0	39.8	38.3	37.5
Idaho	37.4	37.6	37.8	38.2	38.1	38.1	38.9	38.9	39.1	39.2	40.1	40.0	39.3
Illinois	40.6	40.6	40.6	40.9	41.6	42.3	41.9	41.4	41.2	41.0	41.5	41.9	41.7
Indiana	41.0	41.7	40.9	41.5	41.9	41.8	41.6	41.3	41.2	42.0	42.7	43.3	42.2
Iowa	40.8	40.5	40.5	41.3	41.6	42.4	41.9	....	....	....	....	....	....
Kansas	39.2	39.1	40.1	39.5	40.3	40.8	40.7	40.2	40.3	40.3	40.9	41.6	41.6
Kentucky	39.2	39.2	38.9	39.2	40.5	40.5	40.0	40.1	40.3	40.3	40.5	41.3	41.3
Louisiana	40.0	41.6	41.7	41.8	41.8	42.5	42.6	42.9	42.7	42.6	42.5	43.4	43.2
Maine	39.9	39.9	40.0	40.6	41.5	41.0	40.2	41.1	40.0	40.2	40.8	40.6	39.8
Maryland	40.0	41.0	40.3	40.5	40.8	41.5	41.1	40.8	40.6	40.8	41.1	41.5	41.5
Massachusetts	39.9	40.1	40.7	41.3	41.0	40.7	40.7	40.7	41.0	41.0	41.3	41.6	41.7
Michigan	42.5	43.2	43.1	42.6	42.2	43.3	42.9	41.8	41.5	41.8	43.1	44.9	44.3
Minnesota	39.7	40.3	40.3	40.6	40.9	40.8	40.5	40.3	40.4	40.8	41.1	41.6	41.5
Mississippi	40.1	40.6	40.6	40.2	40.3	40.3	40.0	39.4	39.7	40.3	41.0	41.7	41.0
Missouri	39.9	40.5	40.2	40.5	40.6	40.8	40.7	40.7	40.4	40.6	41.4	42.0	41.3
Montana	39.7	39.2	39.1	39.4	38.6	38.7	39.2	39.0	39.1	38.9	38.6	39.3	39.4
Nebraska	40.3	40.5	40.3	40.4	40.5	41.1	40.7	40.8	40.4	41.1	41.5	42.1	41.5
Nevada	38.8	39.8	40.4	40.2	40.3	39.7	40.9	40.7	40.6	40.7	41.4	41.1	41.4
New Hampshire	40.5	41.0	40.7	41.2	41.2	40.7	41.2	40.8	41.2	41.6	42.1	42.3	41.6
New Jersey	40.6	41.1	40.8	41.2	41.2	41.0	41.0	41.4	41.4	41.5	41.5	41.8	41.8
New Mexico	39.7	39.9	39.8	39.5	39.7	40.5	40.0	40.7	40.1	40.0	40.9	40.9	40.0
New York	39.3	39.8	39.8	39.9	39.9	39.9	40.0	39.6	39.8	40.0	40.4	41.0	40.9
North Carolina	40.0	39.9	39.6	40.7	41.2	40.5	40.3	39.9	40.1	40.7	40.8	41.1	40.6
North Dakota	38.0	38.4	38.6	38.2	38.7	38.7	39.8	39.8	39.8	40.4	41.2	42.3	40.7
Ohio	41.4	42.3	42.0	42.1	42.6	43.0	42.7	42.4	42.2	42.2	43.0	43.9	43.4
Oklahoma	40.5	41.6	41.3	41.3	41.2	41.1	41.6	41.1	41.0	41.2	41.9	43.1	41.9
Oregon	38.9	39.2	38.7	39.0	39.2	39.3	39.4	39.3	39.4	39.5	39.5	40.4	40.1
Pennsylvania	39.2	40.2	39.9	40.2	40.9	41.1	41.0	40.7	40.4	40.8	41.2	41.6	41.3
Rhode Island	39.3	39.2	38.9	39.5	39.1	38.9	39.1	39.3	39.3	38.6	39.0	40.9	40.2
South Carolina	40.6	40.8	40.4	41.1	41.7	41.1	41.3	41.0	41.3	41.7	41.6	41.8	41.9
South Dakota	41.6	42.1	41.8	42.1	41.7	42.5	41.8	40.6	41.2	41.2	41.3	42.0	41.2
Tennessee	40.5	40.9	41.0	41.2	41.6	41.6	40.8	38.6	39.6	40.3	40.8	40.9	40.4
Texas	40.9	41.7	41.2	41.4	41.6	41.7	41.8	41.8	42.1	42.5	42.8	43.1	42.8
Utah	39.4	39.9	40.1	40.0	39.5	40.3	40.0	39.8	39.9	40.3	39.6	40.6	39.8
Vermont	40.0	39.0	40.0	40.6	40.7	40.7	40.6	40.4	40.9	40.8	40.8	41.0	41.5
Virginia	39.7	38.4	39.7	40.3	40.1	40.4	41.1	40.8	40.9	40.4	40.5	41.0	41.0
Washington	38.9	38.8	39.0	39.4	39.9	40.1	39.4	40.6	39.9	40.0	40.2	40.5	40.8
West Virginia	39.6	40.3	39.9	40.3	40.6	40.6	40.7	40.7	40.6	40.6	40.9	41.3	41.8
Wisconsin	40.7	41.1	41.1	41.3	41.4	41.8	41.5	41.4	41.4	41.8	42.0	42.7	42.1
Wyoming	36.9	39.5	40.9	39.0	38.8	38.5	39.8	39.9	38.6	38.6	38.9	40.0	39.4
Puerto Rico	38.7	38.7	38.5	39.0	38.9	39.1	39.5	39.1	39.0	39.6	39.5	39.9	39.6
Virgin Islands	41.4	42.7	41.7	41.9	42.2	40.4	41.7	42.4	41.4	42.0	43.5	42.7	41.7

Average Hourly Earnings of Production Workers on Manufacturing Payrolls by State, 1970-1995
(Dollars)

State	1970	1971	1972	1973	1974	1975	1976	1977	1978	1979	1980	1981	1982
Alabama	2.90	3.03	3.25	3.42	3.73	4.10	4.46	4.89	5.40	5.95	6.49	7.01	7.33
Alaska			5.92	5.97	7.10	8.09	7.82	9.12	8.86	9.14	10.22	11.42	11.74
Arizona			3.85	4.03	4.40	4.85	5.19	5.55	6.03	6.62	7.29	8.02	8.73
Arkansas			2.79	2.99	3.30	3.69	3.91	4.30	4.72	5.19	5.71	6.26	6.69
California			4.25	4.44	4.76	5.22	5.59	6.00	6.43	7.03	7.70	8.56	9.24
Colorado			3.87	4.14	4.42	4.78	5.12	5.56	5.96	6.43	7.08	7.67	8.23
Connecticut	3.43	3.61	3.87	4.14	4.42	4.78	5.12	5.56	5.96	6.43	7.08	7.67	8.23
Delaware			4.04	4.29	4.62	5.02	5.51	5.94	6.58	7.04	7.58	8.28	8.64
District of Columbia													
Florida	2.89	3.07	3.20	3.45	3.76	4.11	4.36	4.63	5.07	5.48	5.98	6.53	7.02
Georgia	2.67	2.84	3.04	3.25	3.50	3.80	4.10	4.46	4.88	5.30	5.77	6.37	6.75
Hawaii			3.59	3.93	4.24	4.68	5.14	5.51	5.90	6.38	6.83	7.53	7.97
Idaho			3.69	4.05	4.41	4.77	5.29	5.82	6.53	6.92	7.55	8.23	8.62
Illinois			4.28	4.57	4.97	5.53	5.85	6.28	6.76	7.30	8.02	8.91	9.31
Indiana						5.49	6.00	6.60	7.17	7.79	8.49	9.37	9.79
Iowa							5.85	6.43	7.02	7.75	8.67	9.60	10.01
Kansas										6.71	7.37	8.05	8.80
Kentucky	3.27	3.44	3.70	4.00	4.36	4.77	5.15	5.69	6.26	6.77	7.34	7.86	8.38
Louisiana			3.68	3.98	4.40	4.88	5.33	5.75	6.42	6.97	7.74	8.58	9.38
Maine	2.71	2.86	3.03	3.23	3.51	3.81	4.16	4.52	4.91	5.42	6.00	6.66	7.22
Maryland			3.92	4.22	4.62	5.04	5.52	6.05	6.46	7.09	7.61	8.39	8.78
Massachusetts			3.65	3.89	4.16	4.48	4.79	5.13	5.54	5.98	6.51	7.01	7.58
Michigan							6.81	7.54	8.13	8.73	9.52	10.53	11.18
Minnesota			4.00	4.22	4.67	5.10	5.53	5.97	6.44	6.93	7.61	8.40	9.11
Mississippi	2.43	2.57	2.75	2.95	3.19	3.58	3.83	4.15	4.56	4.95	5.44	6.01	6.41
Missouri			3.78	4.05	4.39	4.80	5.20	5.75	6.21	6.70	7.26	7.90	8.46
Montana			4.11	4.53	5.05	5.53	5.93	6.53	7.81	8.44	8.78	9.09	9.86
Nebraska			3.55	3.75	4.15	4.63	4.93	5.39	5.83	6.53	7.38	8.01	8.47
Nevada			4.46	4.71	4.89	5.26	5.61	6.10	6.54	6.95	7.72	8.42	8.80
New Hampshire			3.20	3.39	3.65	3.97	4.26	4.56	4.94	5.37	5.87	6.41	6.94
New Jersey	3.46	3.72	3.99	4.26	4.57	4.99	5.33	5.82	6.28	6.71	7.31	8.05	8.66
New Mexico	2.68	2.86	2.88	3.08	3.31	3.63	4.07	4.43	4.79	5.36	5.79	6.54	7.22
New York	3.46	3.73	3.98	4.20	4.53	4.91	5.27	5.67	6.08	6.57	7.18	7.84	8.35
North Carolina	2.46	2.60	2.77	2.99	3.28	3.52	3.79	4.10	4.47	4.87	5.37	5.94	6.35
North Dakota			3.31	3.55	3.83	4.31	4.75	5.19	5.55	5.98	6.56	7.12	7.50
Ohio	3.81	4.11	4.45	4.76	5.13	5.57	6.10	6.74	7.29	7.84	8.57	9.53	10.07
Oklahoma	3.09	3.25	3.49	3.69	4.01	4.45	4.83	5.31	5.81	6.53	7.36	8.20	8.69
Oregon			4.30	4.60	5.01	5.53	6.07	6.67	7.23	7.92	8.65	9.47	10.02
Pennsylvania			3.88	4.16	4.57	4.98	5.36	5.85	6.37	6.97	7.59	8.30	8.63
Rhode Island	2.85	2.99	3.15	3.37	3.62	3.84	4.15	4.39	4.71	5.10	5.59	6.10	6.61
South Carolina	2.51	2.65	2.80	3.03	3.32	3.59	3.91	4.28	4.66	5.10	5.59	6.18	6.68
South Dakota			3.17	3.37	3.77	4.21	4.51	4.84	5.19	5.70	6.50	7.12	7.36
Tennessee	2.73	2.89	3.07	3.29	3.62	3.93	4.24	4.68	5.13	5.56	6.08	6.72	7.16
Texas							4.98	5.42	5.88	6.46	7.15	7.95	8.60
Utah			3.62	3.83	4.19	4.61	4.89	5.18	5.68	6.29	7.02	7.74	8.40
Vermont	2.93	3.12	3.28	3.50	3.78	4.07	4.40	4.70	5.10	5.53	6.14	6.79	7.35
Virginia	2.73	2.88	3.10	3.34	3.65	3.99	4.30	4.69	5.11	5.58	6.22	6.84	7.37
Washington			4.54	4.83	5.24	5.82	6.36	6.83	7.56	8.39	9.41	10.44	11.23
West Virginia	3.42	3.61	3.87	4.14	4.53	4.93	5.42	6.06	6.68	7.41	8.08	8.80	9.40
Wisconsin	3.61	3.86	4.15	4.45	4.81	5.26	5.69	6.16	6.69	7.27	8.03	8.80	9.37
Wyoming			3.45	4.03	4.52	4.92	5.43	5.70	6.18	6.68	7.01	7.89	8.62
Puerto Rico											4.02	4.39	4.64
Virgin Islands									6.12	6.70	7.18	8.50	9.76

Average Hourly Earnings of Production Workers on Manufacturing Payrolls by State, 1970-1995—Continued

(Dollars)

State	1983	1984	1985	1986	1987	1988	1989	1990	1991	1992	1993	1994	1995
Alabama	7.58	7.97	8.48	8.64	8.76	8.95	9.10	9.39	9.72	9.99	10.35	10.75	11.14
Alaska	12.33	12.25	12.19	11.62	11.79	11.98	12.01	12.46	11.40	10.75	11.14	10.96	11.00
Arizona	8.99	9.09	9.48	9.88	9.97	9.85	9.92	10.21	10.70	10.96	11.06	11.17	11.19
Arkansas	7.05	7.31	7.57	7.76	7.88	8.07	8.26	8.51	8.81	9.05	9.36	9.65	10.05
California	9.52	9.77	10.12	10.36	10.75	10.80	11.16	11.48	11.87	12.19	12.38	12.44	12.54
Colorado	8.76	9.22	9.57	10.07	10.46	10.78	11.21	11.53	11.99	12.46	13.01	13.53	13.72
Connecticut	8.76	9.22	9.57	10.07	10.46	10.78	11.21	11.53	11.99	12.46	13.01	13.53	13.72
Delaware	9.19	9.28	9.86	10.05	10.67	11.49	12.36	12.39	12.20	12.35	13.29	13.92	14.17
District of Columbia	....	....	....	....	....	....	....	....	....	....	....	....	....
Florida	7.33	7.62	7.86	8.02	8.16	8.39	8.67	8.98	9.30	9.59	9.76	9.97	10.19
Georgia	7.13	7.58	8.10	8.35	8.49	8.65	8.87	9.17	9.56	9.86	10.09	10.34	10.71
Hawaii	8.23	8.35	8.65	8.86	9.30	9.84	10.37	10.99	11.39	11.61	11.98	12.22	12.82
Idaho	8.98	9.34	9.41	9.66	9.75	10.00	10.21	10.60	11.11	11.42	11.88	11.88	11.46
Illinois	9.70	10.08	10.37	10.67	10.85	10.98	11.21	11.44	11.68	11.84	12.04	12.25	12.63
Indiana	10.10	10.45	10.71	10.81	11.06	11.38	11.70	12.03	12.43	12.79	13.17	13.55	13.92
Iowa	10.09	10.24	10.32	10.35	10.62	10.56	10.82	11.27	11.62	11.92	12.22	12.45	12.73
Kansas	9.23	9.38	9.45	9.76	9.97	10.24	10.68	10.94	11.24	11.60	11.99	12.15	12.40
Kentucky	8.79	9.28	9.53	9.86	10.02	10.16	10.37	10.70	11.00	11.28	11.47	11.81	12.22
Louisiana	9.79	10.06	10.43	10.60	10.90	10.94	11.13	11.61	11.86	12.19	12.66	13.11	13.43
Maine	7.61	8.05	8.40	8.65	8.77	9.31	9.92	10.59	11.08	11.40	11.63	11.91	12.39
Maryland	9.02	9.45	9.73	9.91	10.11	10.71	11.19	11.57	11.92	12.50	12.83	13.15	13.50
Massachusetts	8.01	8.50	9.00	9.24	9.77	10.40	10.87	11.39	11.81	12.15	12.36	12.59	12.79
Michigan	11.62	12.18	12.64	12.80	12.97	13.31	13.51	13.86	14.52	14.81	15.36	16.13	16.31
Minnesota	9.56	9.75	10.05	10.20	10.37	10.59	10.95	11.23	11.52	11.92	12.23	12.58	12.80
Mississippi	6.70	6.95	7.22	7.46	7.59	7.83	8.03	8.37	8.67	8.91	9.16	9.41	9.74
Missouri	8.89	9.31	9.57	9.83	10.00	10.24	10.49	10.74	10.86	11.24	11.55	11.77	12.18
Montana	10.44	10.76	10.95	10.94	10.61	10.68	11.15	11.51	11.57	12.18	12.40	12.49	12.92
Nebraska	8.76	8.93	9.02	9.26	9.33	9.38	9.53	9.66	9.84	10.22	10.46	10.94	11.20
Nevada	9.02	9.12	9.15	9.36	9.76	10.08	10.33	11.05	11.04	11.55	11.65	11.83	12.62
New Hampshire	7.42	7.86	8.39	8.77	9.29	9.97	10.37	10.83	10.84	11.22	11.62	11.74	11.93
New Jersey	9.11	9.50	9.86	10.12	10.40	10.86	11.17	11.76	12.17	12.57	12.98	13.36	13.56
New Mexico	7.60	7.97	8.41	8.75	8.74	8.87	8.74	9.04	9.40	9.68	9.74	10.13	10.70
New York	8.84	9.22	9.67	9.92	10.09	10.43	10.67	11.11	11.43	11.72	11.97	12.19	12.50
North Carolina	6.68	7.01	7.29	7.54	7.84	8.12	8.42	8.79	9.19	9.49	9.81	10.19	10.57
North Dakota	7.73	7.86	8.05	8.19	8.43	8.36	8.80	9.27	9.25	9.60	9.86	10.19	10.75
Ohio	10.56	10.96	11.38	11.56	11.73	12.00	12.26	12.64	13.12	13.49	14.05	14.40	14.42
Oklahoma	9.21	9.64	9.86	9.80	10.14	10.35	10.48	10.73	11.09	11.38	11.42	11.42	11.51
Oregon	10.25	10.44	10.50	10.57	10.56	10.60	10.81	11.15	11.53	11.97	12.18	12.31	12.76
Pennsylvania	8.95	9.28	9.57	9.74	9.98	10.33	10.66	11.04	11.46	11.78	12.11	12.49	12.81
Rhode Island	6.92	7.33	7.59	7.90	8.20	8.64	9.06	9.45	9.73	9.92	10.20	10.35	10.62
South Carolina	7.03	7.28	7.61	7.92	8.10	8.30	8.54	8.84	9.17	9.48	9.80	10.00	10.15
South Dakota	7.31	7.14	7.43	7.75	7.92	8.09	8.30	8.48	8.79	8.84	8.89	9.19	9.56
Tennessee	7.49	7.93	8.29	8.58	8.78	8.96	9.22	9.55	9.92	10.13	10.33	10.50	10.77
Texas	8.88	9.04	9.41	9.65	9.85	9.97	10.25	10.47	10.84	10.92	11.02	11.13	11.47
Utah	8.69	8.92	9.64	9.98	9.96	10.11	10.14	10.32	10.77	11.09	11.10	11.28	11.63
Vermont	7.66	8.03	8.41	8.83	9.12	9.47	9.99	10.52	11.00	11.52	12.09	11.96	12.21
Virginia	7.79	8.10	8.51	8.83	9.14	9.37	9.69	10.07	10.43	10.62	10.85	11.24	11.73
Washington	11.42	11.57	11.63	11.65	11.73	11.90	12.12	12.61	13.13	13.59	14.01	14.86	13.68
West Virginia	9.74	9.93	10.24	10.38	10.55	10.81	11.17	11.53	11.77	12.11	12.27	12.60	12.64
Wisconsin	9.78	10.03	10.26	10.35	10.55	10.61	10.77	11.11	11.47	11.85	12.17	12.41	12.76
Wyoming	8.73	9.14	9.64	9.68	9.75	10.27	10.58	10.83	10.98	11.10	11.53	11.79	11.97
Puerto Rico	4.83	5.02	5.19	5.31	5.43	5.56	5.77	6.04	6.32	6.63	6.98	7.22	7.41
Virgin Islands	10.03	9.51	9.44	9.60	9.40	9.86	10.87	11.85	12.52	13.68	14.97	15.16	15.82

Average Weekly Earnings of Production Workers on Manufacturing Payrolls by State, 1970-1995
(Dollars)

State	1970	1971	1972	1973	1974	1975	1976	1977	1978	1979	1980	1981	1982
Alabama	116.87	123.93	133.25	140.22	151.06	161.95	181.08	198.04	219.24	242.16	260.25	279.70	282.20
Alaska			237.39	239.40	287.55	296.09	316.71	394.90	375.66	401.25	436.49	456.80	453.16
Arizona			155.92	160.39	172.48	189.15	205.00	222.56	243.01	268.77	292.33	317.59	339.60
Arkansas			112.16	119.30	129.36	143.17	154.84	170.71	185.50	205.52	224.40	246.64	258.23
California	150.48	158.79	170.43	178.93	188.97	205.67	221.92	240.60	257.84	280.50	304.15	338.98	362.21
Colorado									228.52	244.05	273.74	303.67	329.54	338.30
Connecticut	140.29	146.21	160.61	174.29	182.99	193.59	208.90	230.74	250.32	270.06	295.94	319.07	333.32
Delaware			162.00	172.89	182.03	197.29	220.40	235.22	263.20	278.08	306.99	333.68	338.69
District of Columbia													
Florida	118.78	125.26	131.84	141.45	151.15	164.40	176.14	188.44	207.36	221.94	243.98	265.12	280.10
Georgia	106.27	114.74	124.64	131.63	139.30	150.10	164.41	180.63	195.69	214.12	231.95	255.44	260.55
Hawaii			141.81	156.81	167.06	182.99	200.46	209.38	227.74	244.35	258.17	289.90	302.06
Idaho			145.39	157.14	171.99	185.08	204.72	228.73	253.36	265.04	280.11	311.09	316.35
Illinois			175.55	187.85	200.69	219.13	236.11	254.91	271.42	296.66	319.20	356.23	364.86
Indiana					218.50	243.60	271.92	295.92	295.40	315.94	337.90	375.74	383.77
Iowa								233.42	257.84	281.50	313.88	343.33	379.20	387.39
Kansas										273.10	297.75	325.22	344.96
Kentucky	128.84	134.85	149.48	161.20	172.66	184.60	202.91	224.75	247.90	266.74	286.99	308.90	321.79
Louisiana			155.66	164.77	176.44	208.86	220.13	240.35	267.07	287.86	318.89	362.08	384.58
Maine	108.67	113.83	123.32	131.78	141.45	152.02	165.98	179.90	197.38	217.34	240.00	269.06	288.80
Maryland			157.58	170.91	184.34	197.06	218.59	241.40	257.75	283.60	301.36	334.76	344.18
Massachusetts			146.37	157.55	165.98	175.17	190.16	204.69	222.71	239.80	257.80	280.40	297.14
Michigan								290.97	326.27	349.50	359.72	381.87	426.27	449.33
Minnesota			162.80	173.02	186.33	199.92	220.09	238.80	258.89	277.20	299.83	330.96	356.20
Mississippi	97.69	103.83	113.03	118.89	125.37	140.69	153.20	166.42	181.94	196.02	213.79	236.19	244.22
Missouri			150.44	161.19	172.53	187.20	206.96	231.15	248.40	264.65	284.59	318.37	326.56
Montana			165.63	178.03	195.94	210.14	236.01	272.95	333.49	362.08	379.30	372.69	387.50
Nebraska			148.07	156.78	170.98	187.66	202.57	219.91	239.61	269.69	299.63	322.80	337.95
Nevada			179.29	188.40	189.73	200.93	218.23	236.68	251.79	267.58	294.90	325.01	328.24
New Hampshire			127.36	134.92	143.44	155.23	168.70	182.40	199.08	215.34	233.63	255.76	274.82
New Jersey	139.44	150.29	163.35	176.41	186.11	199.68	215.71	239.20	256.22	276.45	297.07	327.16	345.53
New Mexico	104.52	112.68	115.49	121.35	127.10	141.57	160.77	171.88	187.77	211.72	230.44	258.33	283.02
New York	134.59	145.84	157.61	167.58	178.48	191.00	207.64	224.53	241.98	260.17	282.89	308.90	323.98
North Carolina	97.17	104.00	112.74	119.90	128.25	135.17	149.33	162.36	177.91	192.85	211.04	232.25	236.86
North Dakota			133.06	143.42	153.97	171.97	185.73	200.33	220.34	233.82	246.00	271.27	282.00
Ohio			185.12	201.35	211.36	224.47	252.54	283.08	306.91	325.36	347.94	389.78	403.81
Oklahoma	126.07	130.98	141.34	149.81	162.40	178.00	194.65	214.52	233.56	264.46	295.14	328.82	343.26
Oregon			169.42	180.78	194.39	212.35	236.12	257.46	281.97	304.92	329.57	355.13	379.76
Pennsylvania			154.42	167.23	180.97	193.22	210.11	231.08	254.80	278.10	294.49	325.36	331.39
Rhode Island	111.72	117.51	124.43	132.44	141.90	149.04	163.93	171.65	183.22	199.41	219.69	239.73	255.16
South Carolina	100.90	108.38	115.92	122.72	132.14	141.45	157.96	173.77	190.13	208.08	225.28	249.67	255.18
South Dakota			137.26	143.56	157.21	171.35	179.95	190.21	216.42	238.83	265.85	296.19	302.50
Tennessee	108.93	115.89	124.64	132.92	144.44	156.41	170.87	188.14	203.15	220.73	241.38	268.13	276.38
Texas							203.68	222.76	242.84	265.51	294.58	328.34	344.00
Utah			139.56	148.62	162.02	175.77	191.69	207.15	224.36	245.31	274.48	307.28	323.40
Vermont	120.13	128.54	136.12	145.25	155.36	164.43	180.40	191.76	209.10	225.62	249.28	271.60	286.65
Virginia	109.20	115.78	126.48	135.60	145.27	156.41	171.57	187.13	203.38	221.53	244.45	271.55	283.01
Washington			179.78	189.34	203.84	225.23	248.68	267.74	297.11	323.85	361.34	405.07	432.36
West Virginia	136.12	142.96	154.80	165.60	179.39	192.27	212.46	239.37	264.53	293.44	316.74	346.72	364.72
Wisconsin	145.78	156.31	171.04	183.99	197.43	212.25	230.91	250.06	274.21	297.00	323.10	352.55	370.87
Wyoming			133.10	155.58	171.71	190.36	218.11	226.82	238.55	251.17	272.69	315.60	329.28
Puerto Rico											152.76	167.77	174.00
Virgin Islands									250.31	274.03	295.10	359.55	412.85

Average Weekly Earnings of Production Workers on Manufacturing Payrolls by State, 1970-1995—Continued

(Dollars)

State	1983	1984	1985	1986	1987	1988	1989	1990	1991	1992	1993	1994	1995
Alabama	308.51	326.77	345.98	355.10	362.66	370.53	374.92	384.99	396.58	411.59	426.42	450.43	464.54
Alaska	446.35	481.42	496.13	477.58	503.43	504.36	533.24	559.45	528.96	489.13	501.30	519.50	525.80
Arizona	364.10	370.87	387.73	405.08	404.78	404.84	408.70	415.55	435.49	447.17	450.14	472.49	472.22
Arkansas	282.71	296.06	304.31	313.50	323.08	330.06	337.01	348.91	362.97	374.67	387.50	403.37	412.05
California	380.80	393.73	406.82	417.51	433.23	439.56	454.21	466.09	481.92	494.91	506.34	515.02	516.65
Colorado	357.90	377.92	382.70	391.82	404.01	419.35	419.69	450.73	457.73	458.46	494.81	506.34	513.32
Connecticut	361.79	391.85	400.98	420.93	440.37	454.92	473.06	484.26	501.18	519.58	547.72	579.08	587.22
Delaware	373.11	385.12	405.25	415.07	434.27	459.60	512.94	511.71	497.76	503.88	559.50	595.78	579.55
District of Columbia	....	....	....	....	....	....	....	....	....	....	....	....	....
Florida	298.33	313.94	324.62	327.22	332.93	341.47	354.60	365.49	378.51	392.23	402.11	412.76	421.87
Georgia	293.04	310.78	328.86	341.52	353.18	358.11	364.56	375.05	391.96	408.20	420.75	438.42	453.03
Hawaii	317.68	318.14	323.51	344.65	366.42	393.60	414.80	442.90	453.32	464.40	476.80	468.03	480.75
Idaho	335.85	351.18	355.70	369.01	371.48	381.00	397.16	412.34	434.40	447.66	476.39	475.20	450.38
Illinois	393.59	409.35	421.02	436.40	451.36	464.45	469.70	473.62	481.22	485.44	499.66	513.28	526.67
Indiana	414.10	435.76	438.04	448.62	463.41	475.68	486.72	496.84	512.12	537.18	562.36	586.72	587.42
Iowa	401.58	411.65	414.86	420.21	438.61	437.18	441.46	456.44	470.61	492.30	508.35	527.88	533.39
Kansas	360.89	376.14	373.28	393.33	406.78	416.77	429.34	440.88	452.97	474.44	498.78	505.44	509.64
Kentucky	344.57	363.78	370.72	386.51	405.81	411.48	414.80	429.07	443.30	454.58	464.54	487.75	504.69
Louisiana	391.60	418.50	434.93	443.08	455.62	464.95	474.14	498.07	506.42	519.29	538.05	568.97	580.18
Maine	303.64	321.20	336.00	351.19	363.96	381.71	398.78	424.66	443.20	458.28	474.50	483.55	493.12
Maryland	360.80	387.45	392.12	401.36	412.49	444.47	459.91	472.06	483.95	510.00	527.31	545.73	560.25
Massachusetts	319.60	340.85	366.30	381.61	400.57	423.28	442.41	463.57	484.21	498.15	510.47	523.74	533.34
Michigan	494.02	526.18	544.78	545.28	547.33	576.32	579.58	579.35	602.58	619.06	662.02	724.24	722.53
Minnesota	379.53	392.93	405.02	414.12	424.13	432.07	443.48	452.57	465.41	486.34	502.65	523.33	531.20
Mississippi	268.67	282.17	293.13	299.89	305.88	315.55	321.20	329.78	344.20	359.07	375.56	392.40	399.34
Missouri	354.71	377.06	384.71	398.12	406.00	417.79	426.94	437.12	438.74	456.34	478.17	494.34	503.03
Montana	414.47	421.79	428.15	431.04	409.55	413.32	437.08	448.89	452.39	473.80	478.64	490.86	509.05
Nebraska	353.03	361.67	363.51	374.10	377.87	385.52	387.87	394.13	397.54	420.04	434.09	460.57	464.80
Nevada	349.98	362.98	369.66	376.27	393.33	400.18	422.50	449.74	448.22	470.09	482.31	486.21	522.47
New Hampshire	300.51	322.26	341.47	361.32	382.75	405.78	427.24	441.86	446.61	466.75	489.20	496.60	496.29
New Jersey	369.87	390.45	402.29	416.94	428.48	445.26	457.97	486.86	503.84	521.66	538.67	558.45	566.81
New Mexico	301.72	318.00	334.72	345.63	346.98	359.24	349.60	367.93	376.94	387.20	398.37	414.32	428.00
New York	347.41	366.96	384.87	395.81	402.59	416.16	426.80	439.96	454.91	468.80	483.59	499.79	511.25
North Carolina	267.20	279.70	288.68	306.88	323.01	328.86	339.33	350.72	368.52	386.24	400.25	418.81	429.14
North Dakota	293.74	301.82	310.73	312.86	326.24	323.53	350.24	368.95	368.15	387.84	406.23	431.04	437.53
Ohio	437.18	463.61	477.96	486.68	499.70	516.00	523.50	535.94	553.66	569.28	604.15	632.16	625.83
Oklahoma	373.01	401.02	407.22	404.74	417.77	425.39	435.97	441.00	454.69	468.86	478.50	492.20	482.27
Oregon	398.73	409.25	406.35	412.23	413.95	416.58	425.91	438.20	454.28	472.82	481.11	497.32	511.68
Pennsylvania	350.84	373.06	381.84	391.55	408.18	424.56	437.06	449.33	462.98	480.62	498.93	519.58	529.05
Rhode Island	269.88	299.80	305.11	319.16	328.00	343.01	356.06	375.17	389.20	397.79	405.96	417.11	430.11
South Carolina	285.30	297.07	307.44	325.51	337.77	341.13	352.70	362.44	378.72	395.32	407.68	418.00	425.29
South Dakota	304.10	300.59	310.57	326.28	330.26	343.83	346.94	344.29	362.15	364.21	367.16	385.98	393.87
Tennessee	303.34	324.34	339.72	353.50	365.25	372.74	376.18	368.63	392.83	408.24	421.46	429.45	435.11
Texas	363.19	376.97	387.69	399.51	409.76	415.75	428.45	437.65	456.36	464.10	471.66	479.70	490.92
Utah	342.39	355.91	386.56	399.20	393.42	407.43	405.60	410.74	429.72	446.93	439.56	457.97	462.87
Vermont	306.40	326.02	342.29	359.38	370.27	382.59	408.59	429.22	448.80	472.32	501.74	489.16	494.51
Virginia	309.26	326.43	341.25	356.73	375.65	382.30	396.32	406.83	422.42	435.42	444.85	468.71	489.14
Washington	444.24	448.92	453.57	459.01	468.03	477.19	477.53	511.97	523.89	543.60	563.20	601.83	558.14
West Virginia	385.70	400.18	408.58	418.31	428.33	438.89	454.62	469.27	477.86	491.67	501.84	520.38	528.35
Wisconsin	398.05	412.23	421.69	427.46	436.77	443.50	446.96	459.95	474.86	495.33	511.14	529.91	537.20
Wyoming	322.21	361.03	394.28	377.52	378.30	395.40	421.08	432.12	423.83	428.46	448.52	471.60	471.62
Puerto Rico	186.92	194.27	199.82	207.09	211.23	217.40	227.92	236.16	246.48	262.55	275.71	288.08	293.44
Virgin Islands	415.24	405.41	393.65	402.24	396.68	398.34	453.28	502.44	518.33	574.56	651.20	647.33	659.69

Part Three

Projections of Employment by Industry and Occupation

Projections of Employment by Industry and Occupation

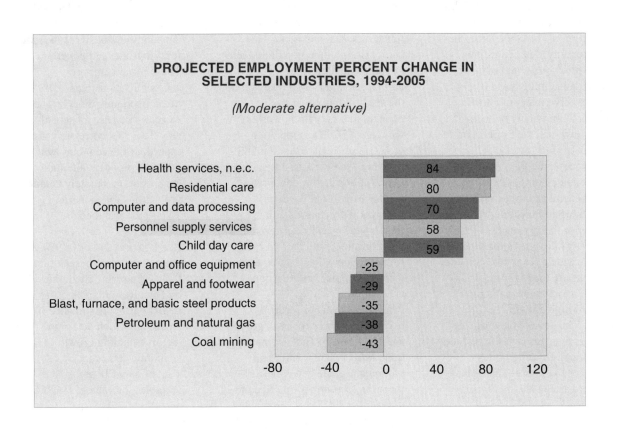

PROJECTED EMPLOYMENT PERCENT CHANGE IN SELECTED INDUSTRIES, 1994-2005

(Moderate alternative)

Industry	Percent change
Health services, n.e.c.	84
Residential care	80
Computer and data processing	70
Personnel supply services	58
Child day care	59
Computer and office equipment	-25
Apparel and footwear	-29
Blast, furnace, and basic steel products	-35
Petroleum and natural gas	-38
Coal mining	-43

nder the BLS moderate alternative, total employment is projected to grow at an average annual growth rate of 1.2 percent—a much slower pace of growth than the 2.0 percent rate of growth over the 1983-1994 period. All the projected growth in nonfarm wage and salary employment at the major industry division level occurs in the service-producing sector. This trend even carries over to the computer-related sector of the economy as shown in the chart above where the employment in the computer and office equipment industry is expected to decline as employment in the computer processing industry increases. All health-related services show substantial increases. Even the medical equipment industry shows a small increase.

NOTES
Projections of Employment by Industry and Occupation

Long-term projections of likely employment conditions in the U.S. economy have been developed by the Bureau of Labor Statistics since 1957. These projections cover the future size and composition of the labor force, the aggregate economy, detailed estimates of industrial production, and industrial and occupational employment. The resulting data serve many users who need information on likely patterns of economic growth and their effects on employment. To carry out the projection process, the BLS makes many underlying assumptions concerning general economic and social conditions and sets ranges of acceptability for the key results of the various stages of the projection process. In order to provide a range of estimates the projections are made for three economic scenarios representing low, moderate, and high growth possibilities. The development of alternative versions reflects some of the uncertainties and differing policy decisions about the future. The tables presented here are for the moderate growth alternative.

Projecting employment in industry and occupational detail requires an integrated projection of the total economy and its various sectors. BLS projections are developed in a series of six steps, each of which is based on separate projections procedures and models and various related assumptions. The six steps or analytical phases are: (1) labor force, (2) aggregate economy, (3) final demand (GDP) by sector and product, (4) inter-industry relationships (input-output), (5) industry output and employment, and (6) occupational employment. Each phase is solved separately, with the results of each used as input for the next phase, and with some results feeding back to earlier steps. In each phase, many iterations are made to ensure internal consistency as assumptions and results are reviewed and revised.

(1) *Labor force projections* are determined by projections of the future age, sex, and racial composition of the population and by trends in labor force participation rates—the percent of the specified group in the population who will be working or seeking work. The population projections, prepared by the U.S. Bureau of the Census, are based on trends in birth rates, death rates, and net migration. With the population projections in hand, BLS analyzes and projects changes in labor force participation rates for more than 100 age, sex, and race or Hispanic origin groups.

Projections of labor force participation rates for each group are developed by first estimating a trend rate of change based on participation rate behavior during the prior 15 year period. Second, the rate is modified when the time series projections for the specific group appear inconsistent with the results of cross-sectional and cohort analyses. This second step ensures consistency in the projections across various groups. Finally, the size of the labor force is derived by applying the participation rates to the population projections. The results are again reviewed for consistency.

(2) *Aggregate economic performance*—the second phase of the BLS projections process—develops projections of the gross domestic product (GDP) and major categories of demand and income. These results provide control totals that are consistent with each other and with the various assumptions and conditions of the projection scenarios. The values generated for each demand sector and subsector are then used in the next phase in developing detailed purchases for personal consumption, business investment, foreign trade, and government. These projections are accomplished using a macroeconomic model. The model basically consists of sets of equations that correlate various aspects of the economy with each other. It provides internally consistent, moderately detailed projections for each set of assumptions and goals.

Employment Outlook 1994-2005 projections were based upon a long-term macro model developed by Data Resources, Inc. This model has approximately 400 equations which determine those factors affecting growth in the U.S. economy. This model is driven by a set of over 200 exogenous variables, or values, which are specified by BLS.

(3) *Final demand.* The BLS projection proceeds then from the aggregate to the industrial level. For the industry output projections, the economy is disaggregated into 178 producing sectors that cover the U.S. industrial structure, both public and private. The framework for this procedure is an input-output model. The initial input-output data used by BLS are prepared by the Bureau of Economic Analysis, U.S. Department of Commerce.

The development of projections of industry output begins with aggregate demand projections from the Data Resources model. In this model, projections are made for seven major categories of consumption, six categories of investment, 13 end-use categories of foreign trade, and three categories of government spending. A further disaggregation of the values from the model is then undertaken. For example, personal consumption expenditures are estimated for 82 detailed categories.

Provision is made to allow for shifts in the commodity makeup of a given demand category. This is accomplished by projecting "bridge tables" relating individual types of demand to the actual industries supplying the goods. The bridge table is a percent distribution for each given demand category, such as the personal consumption or investment category, among each of the 178 sectors in the BLS input-output model. In projecting changes in these bridge tables, expected changes in technology, consumer tastes, or buying patterns, the commodity pattern of exports and imports, the future composition of business investment, and other structural factors are considered.

(4) *Input-output.* The next stage in the projections process is the estimation of the intermediate flows of goods and services required to produce the projected GDP. Only final sales are counted in the GDP to avoid repeated counting of intermediate inputs. An industry's total employment, however, depends on its total output, whether sold to another industry or used as a final good. The total output of each industry is projected using an inter-industry or input-output model. This model mathematically solves given industry relationships and final demand for all levels of intermediate inputs.

The BLS input-output model consists of two basic matrices for each year, a "use" and a "make" table. The principal table is the "use" table. This table shows the purchase of commodities by each industry as inputs into its production process. Projecting this table must take into account changes in the input pattern or the way in which goods or services are produced by each industry. In general, two types of changes in these input patterns are made in developing a future input-output table: (a) those made to the inputs of a specific industry (as, for example, the changes in inputs in the publishing industry); and, (b) those made to the inputs of a specific commodity in all or most industries (as, for example, increased use of business services across a wide spectrum of industries.) The "make" table shows the commodity output of each industry. It allocates commodity output to the industry to which it is primary and to all other industries where the commodity is produced as a secondary product. The "use" table is the basis for the direct requirements table of coefficients showing the inputs required to produce one dollar of that industry's output. The "make" table is used to create a "market shares" table, which shows the values of the "make" table as coefficients. The coefficient tables are used to calculate the total requirements tables which show the direct and indirect requirements to produce a dollar's worth of final demand. Projection tables are based on historical tables and on studies of specific industries.

(5) *Industry Employment.* The projected level of industry employment is based on the projected levels of industry output as well as other factors such as expected technological changes and their impact on labor productivity. After the initial industry output is calculated, employment is derived for each industry from the level of projected industry output based on trend analyses of industry employment, hours, and the ratio of output to hours. The employment projections by industry are constrained by the requirement that they sum to the aggregate employment level as determined by the aggregate projections. Employment for wage and salary workers is based on the Current Employment Statistics (payroll) Survey, which counts jobs, whereas self-employed, unpaid family worker, agricultural, and private household data are based on the Current Population Survey (Household Survey), which counts workers. Employment totals for 1983 and 1994, therefore, differ from the official employment estimates of the Bureau of Labor Statistics.

(6) *Occupational Employment.* The model used to develop the occupational employment projections is an industry-occupation matrix showing the distribution of employment for 258 industries and for more than 507 detailed occupations. Occupational staffing patterns for the industries are based on data collected by state employment security agencies and analyzed by the BLS.

Staffing patterns of industries in the base-year industry-occupation matrix are projected to the target year to account for changes expected to occur in technology, shifts in production mix, and other factors. For example, one would expect greater employment of computer specialists as computer technology spreads across industries. In projecting the staffing patterns, the changes introduced into the input-output model for expected change are also analyzed to account for the impact of that technological change on future occupational staffing patterns of industries. The projected industry total employment data are applied to the projected industry staffing patterns, yielding employment by occupation for each industry. These data are aggregated across all industries to yield total occupational employment for the projected year.

An important element of the projection system is its comprehensive structure. To ensure the internal consistency of this large structure, the BLS procedure encompasses detailed review and analysis of the results at each stage for reasonableness and for consistency with the results from other stages of the BLS projections. The final results reflect innumerable interactions among staff members who focus on particular variables in the model. Because of this review, the projection process at BLS converges to an internally consistent set of employment projections across a substantial number of industries and occupations.

A complete presentation of the projections including an analysis of results, additional tables, and a comprehensive description of the methodology is available in the *Monthly Labor Review*, November 1995. Once the target year is reached, BLS evaluates the projections and these evaluations generally appear in articles in the *Monthly Labor Review*.

Number Employed and Projected Employment by Detailed Industry, 1983, 1994, and 2005

(Numbers in thousands; percent)

Industry	Employment					Annual rate of growth[1]	
	1983	1994	2005			Employment 1994-2005	Output 1994-2005
			Low	Moderate	High		
TOTAL JOBS	102 404	127 014	140 261	144 708	150 212	1.2	2.2
Nonfarm wage and salary jobs, total	89 734	113 340	125 631	130 185	135 729	1.3	....
Mining	952	601	450	439	509	-2.8	-0.4
Metal mining	56	49	38	42	44	-1.5	1.4
Coal mining	194	112	63	70	77	-4.3	0.2
Crude petroleum, natural gas, and gas liquids	265	168	138	105	124	-4.2	-1.9
Oil and gas field services	333	168	127	136	173	-1.9	3.2
Nonmetallic minerals, except fuels	104	104	85	88	91	-1.5	0.9
Construction	3 946	5 010	5 193	5 500	5 966	0.9	1.5
Manufacturing	18 430	18 304	16 218	16 991	18 000	-0.7	2.0
Durable manufacturing	10 707	10 431	8 803	9 290	10 045	-1.0	2.2
Lumber and wood products	670	752	649	685	729	-0.9	0.9
Logging	83	82	73	74	75	-0.9	0.6
Sawmills and planing mills	193	189	140	150	161	-2.1	0.1
Millwork, plywood, and structural members	207	271	236	250	269	-0.7	1.3
Wood containers and miscellaneous wood products	119	138	133	139	147	0.0	2.2
Wood buildings and mobile homes	69	73	67	72	78	-0.1	0.0
Furniture and fixtures	448	502	486	515	581	0.2	1.3
Household furniture	279	284	264	280	327	-0.1	1.0
Partitions and fixtures	59	80	83	88	95	0.9	1.2
Office and miscellaneous furniture and fixtures	110	138	138	146	159	0.5	1.6
Stone, clay, and glass products	541	533	413	434	463	-1.8	0.5
Glass and glass products	165	153	118	125	133	-1.8	0.4
Hydraulic cement	25	18	14	14	14	-2.2	0.2
Stone, clay, and miscellaneous mineral products	167	164	115	124	136	-2.5	0.2
Concrete, gypsum, and plaster products	184	198	166	172	180	-1.3	0.9
Primary metal industries	832	699	508	532	565	-2.5	0.1
Blast furnaces and basic steel products	341	239	150	155	163	-3.9	-0.5
Iron and steel foundries	139	125	88	92	99	-2.7	-1.2
Primary nonferrous smelting and refining	50	41	32	36	39	-1.2	2.3
All other primary metals	41	44	40	40	40	-0.8	1.8
Nonferrous rolling and drawing	184	167	130	135	141	-1.9	0.0
Nonferrous foundries	78	84	68	74	82	-1.2	-0.2
Fabricated metal products	1 368	1 387	1 114	1 181	1 271	-1.5	0.5
Metal cans and shipping containers	60	42	27	27	27	-3.9	0.9
Cutlery, hand tools, and hardware	138	129	85	90	97	-3.2	-0.2
Plumbing and nonelectric heating equipment	62	60	46	48	52	-1.9	-0.3
Fabricated structural metal products	416	409	299	315	339	-2.3	0.4
Screw machine products, bolts, rivets, etc.	86	96	73	78	84	-1.8	0.5
Metal forgings and stampings	224	234	183	194	211	-1.7	0.2
Metal coating, engraving, and allied services	96	124	134	140	150	1.1	2.5
Ordnance and ammunition	67	54	49	51	51	-0.5	-0.8
Miscellaneous fabricated metal products	219	241	218	238	260	-0.1	0.9
Industrial machinery and equipment	2 052	1 985	1 687	1 769	1 904	-1.0	3.9
Engines and turbines	104	90	69	70	73	-2.2	0.2
Farm and garden machinery and equipment	107	105	84	87	91	-1.7	1.6
Construction and related machinery	245	210	182	188	204	-1.0	1.6
Metalworking machinery and equipment	298	322	283	291	304	-0.9	-0.4
Special industry machinery	151	155	149	150	151	-0.3	1.8
General industrial machinery and equipment	234	243	228	235	250	-0.3	-0.4
Computer and office equipment	474	351	240	263	293	-2.6	7.3
Refrigeration and service industry machinery	158	190	181	192	210	0.1	1.1
Industrial machinery, n.e.c.	282	319	273	292	329	-0.8	1.7
Electronic and other electric equipment	1 704	1 571	1 347	1 408	1 524	-1.0	3.5
Electric distribution equipment	103	82	69	70	71	-1.5	0.1
Electrical industrial apparatus	190	156	115	116	118	-2.7	0.3
Household appliances	138	123	92	98	109	-2.1	1.5
Electric lighting and wiring equipment	187	176	148	155	167	-1.2	1.3
Household audio and video equipment	87	89	55	55	54	-4.2	1.2
Communications equipment	279	244	200	210	225	-1.3	3.8
Electronic components and accessories	563	544	522	553	620	0.1	5.5
Miscellaneous electrical equipment	157	156	146	151	159	-0.3	1.9
Transportation equipment	1 731	1 749	1 455	1 567	1 744	-1.0	1.8
Motor vehicles and equipment	754	899	715	775	883	-1.3	1.6
Aerospace	702	587	517	552	605	-0.6	2.2
Ship and boat building and repairing	183	159	120	131	140	-1.8	-1.0
Railroad equipment	30	35	34	35	36	-0.1	3.6
Miscellaneous transportation equipment	62	69	69	75	81	0.8	3.5
Instruments and related products	990	863	771	798	836	-0.7	2.9
Search and navigation equipment	311	180	126	132	141	-2.8	0.5
Measuring and controlling devices	300	284	234	248	273	-1.2	1.9
Medical equipment, instruments, and supplies	198	265	305	306	307	1.3	5.7
Ophthalmic goods	38	37	36	37	38	-0.1	3.9
Photographic equipment and supplies	128	89	66	70	72	-2.2	2.1
Watches, clocks, and parts	16	8	4	5	5	-5.3	-0.5
Miscellaneous manufacturing industries	370	391	374	404	428	0.3	1.8
Jewelry, silverware, and plated ware	54	51	43	44	44	-1.5	-1.0
Toys and sporting goods	106	115	120	135	143	1.4	2.8
Manufactured products, n.e.c.	211	224	211	225	240	0.0	1.9

1. Based on moderate path.

Number Employed and Projected Employment by Detailed Industry, 1983, 1994, and 2005—Continued

(Numbers in thousands; percent)

Industry	Employment					Annual rate of growth[1]	
	1983	1994	2005			Employment 1994-2005	Output 1994-2005
			Low	Moderate	High		
Nondurable manufacturing	7 723	7 873	7 415	7 700	7 955	-0.2	1.8
Food and kindred products	1 612	1 680	1 693	1 696	1 696	0.1	1.3
Meat products	346	451	514	515	513	1.2	1.2
Dairy products	164	149	132	133	133	-1.0	1.9
Preserved fruits and vegetables	220	245	252	260	264	0.5	1.4
Grain mill products and fats and oils	170	160	166	161	158	0.0	1.4
Bakery products	220	213	196	195	194	-0.8	0.4
Sugar and confectionery products	103	99	89	90	90	-0.9	0.4
Beverages	222	178	130	132	134	-2.7	0.8
Miscellaneous food and kindred products	165	185	213	211	210	1.2	2.3
Tobacco products	68	42	28	26	26	-4.2	-0.4
Textile mill products	742	673	521	568	608	-1.5	0.2
Weaving, finishing, yarn, and thread mills	432	358	253	281	303	-2.2	-0.2
Knitting mills	207	199	157	173	187	-1.2	0.0
Carpets and rugs	49	64	64	65	68	0.1	1.0
Miscellaneous textile goods	55	52	47	49	51	-0.6	1.3
Apparel and other textile products	1 163	969	723	772	815	-2.1	0.5
Apparel	990	755	512	547	577	-2.9	-0.4
Miscellaneous fabricated textile products	173	215	211	225	238	0.4	2.6
Paper and allied products	654	691	674	708	730	0.2	2.5
Pulp, paper, and paperboard mills	249	232	211	218	222	-0.6	2.7
Paperboard containers and boxes	191	213	216	230	240	0.7	1.8
Converted paper products, except containers	214	246	247	260	267	0.5	2.9
Printing and publishing	1 298	1 542	1 576	1 627	1 676	0.5	2.5
Newspapers	426	450	400	413	424	-0.8	-0.4
Periodicals	100	135	156	163	169	1.7	2.1
Books	98	120	125	130	134	0.8	2.7
Miscellaneous publishing	56	84	84	85	86	0.1	3.6
Commercial printing and business forms	480	597	653	675	699	1.1	3.3
Greeting cards	23	29	33	32	32	1.0	4.7
Blankbooks and bookbinding	65	70	75	77	80	0.8	2.6
Service industries for the printing trade	49	57	51	53	54	-0.7	2.6
Chemicals and allied products	1 043	1 061	1 032	1 067	1 089	0.1	2.0
Industrial chemicals	314	277	253	259	260	-0.6	0.9
Plastics materials and synthetics	177	162	138	143	145	-1.1	1.4
Drugs	201	263	309	325	337	1.9	4.0
Soap cleaners and toilet goods	142	153	164	165	166	0.7	2.5
Paints and allied products	60	58	46	48	51	-1.6	1.4
Agricultural chemicals	61	55	39	43	44	-2.3	1.2
Miscellaneous chemical products	89	93	83	85	87	-0.9	0.9
Petroleum and coal products	196	149	142	140	137	-0.5	2.1
Petroleum refining	158	109	105	103	98	-0.5	2.2
Miscellaneous petroleum and coal products	37	40	37	38	39	-0.5	0.9
Rubber and miscellaneous plastics products	743	952	972	1 030	1 100	0.7	2.9
Tires and inner tubes	94	80	59	60	63	-2.5	0.2
Rubber products and plastic hose and footwear	171	182	158	170	185	-0.6	1.9
Miscellaneous plastics products, n.e.c.	478	690	755	800	853	1.4	3.4
Leather and leather products	205	114	54	65	79	-4.9	-1.9
Footwear, except rubber and plastic	136	61	20	29	40	-6.7	-5.0
Luggage, handbags, and leather products, n.e.c.	69	53	34	37	39	-3.3	-0.3
Transportation, communications, and utilities	4 958	6 006	6 145	6 431	6 723	0.6	3.2
Transportation	2 748	3 775	4 060	4 251	4 438	1.1	4.0
Railroad transportation	376	241	172	186	199	-2.3	1.3
Local and interurban passenger transit	257	410	474	490	499	1.6	0.0
Trucking and warehousing	1 222	1 797	1 903	2 000	2 099	1.0	5.0
Water transportation	189	169	158	165	175	-0.2	2.0
Air transportation	455	748	830	870	910	1.4	3.7
Pipelines, except natural gas	20	18	14	15	16	-1.6	-0.2
Transportation services	229	393	509	525	541	2.7	6.5
Passenger transportation arrangement	120	197	237	255	272	2.4	6.2
Miscellaneous transportation services	109	195	272	270	269	3.0	6.7
Communications	1 324	1 305	1 190	1 235	1 279	-0.5	3.1
Electric, gas, and sanitary services	887	927	895	945	1 007	0.2	2.0
Electric utilities	560	516	465	485	517	-0.6	2.2
Gas utilities	224	197	159	160	164	-1.9	1.5
Water and sanitation	102	213	272	300	327	3.2	2.7
Wholesale trade	5 283	6 140	6 389	6 559	6 765	0.6	2.2
Retail trade	15 587	20 438	22 781	23 094	23 417	1.1	2.4
Retail trade, except eating and drinking places	10 549	13 369	14 523	15 005	15 495	1.1	2.7
Eating and drinking places	5 038	7 069	8 258	8 089	7 922	1.2	1.1
Finance, insurance, and real estate	5 466	6 933	7 076	7 373	7 721	0.6	2.3
Depository institutions	2 048	2 076	1 812	1 886	1 961	-0.9	2.0
Nondepository; holding and investment offices	385	730	968	970	973	2.6	3.0
Security and commodity brokers	308	518	679	700	719	2.8	7.0
Insurance carriers	1 229	1 551	1 597	1 633	1 668	0.5	1.9
Insurance agents, brokers, and service	499	686	696	702	709	0.2	2.6
Real estate	997	1 373	1 324	1 482	1 691	0.7	2.2
Royalties	0	0	0	0	0	0.0	2.6
Owner-occupied dwellings	0	0	0	0	0	0.0	0.7

1. Based on moderate path.

Number Employed and Projected Employment by Detailed Industry, 1983, 1994, and 2005—Continued

(Numbers in thousands; percent)

Industry	Employment					Annual rate of growth[1]	
	1983	1994	2005			Employment 1994-2005	Output 1994-2005
			Low	Moderate	High		
Services	19 242	30 792	42 072	42 810	43 678	3.0	3.0
Hotels and other lodging places	1 172	1 618	1 875	1 899	1 926	1.5	1.5
Personal services	869	1 139	1 372	1 374	1 373	1.7	1.0
Laundry, cleaning, and shoe repair	356	428	487	500	510	1.4	0.5
Personal services, n.e.c.	118	225	331	314	299	3.1	2.3
Beauty and barber shops	323	397	455	460	462	1.3	0.6
Funeral service and crematories	72	89	98	100	102	1.1	-1.0
Business services	2 948	6 239	9 796	10 032	10 313	4.4	4.5
Advertising	171	224	250	250	250	1.0	1.4
Services to buildings	559	855	1 325	1 350	1 379	4.2	3.6
Miscellaneous equipment rental and leasing	111	216	319	325	332	3.8	0.3
Personnel supply services	619	2 254	3 507	3 564	3 635	4.3	6.0
Computer and data processing services	416	950	1 516	1 611	1 725	4.9	4.9
Miscellaneous business services	1 074	1 741	2 880	2 932	2 992	4.9	4.7
Auto repair, services, and garages	619	971	1 304	1 345	1 368	3.0	2.3
Automotive rentals, without drivers	126	174	222	227	231	2.4	2.6
Automobile parking, repair, and services	493	796	1 082	1 119	1 137	3.1	2.0
Miscellaneous repair shops	287	334	393	400	407	1.7	2.2
Electrical repair shops	91	105	123	125	127	1.6	1.8
Watch, jewelry, and furniture repair	28	26	25	25	25	-0.5	3.2
Miscellaneous repair services	169	202	245	250	255	1.9	2.2
Motion pictures	268	471	588	591	596	2.1	3.1
Motion picture production, distribution, and theatres	214	333	433	426	419	2.2	3.0
Video tape rental	54	138	155	165	177	1.7	3.2
Amusement and recreation services	853	1 344	1 846	1 844	1 848	2.9	2.4
Producers, orchestras, and entertainers	94	148	197	200	204	2.8	3.0
Bowling centers	97	85	73	73	73	-1.5	-1.8
Commercial sports	76	106	147	137	131	2.4	1.1
Amusement and recreation services, n.e.c.	586	1 005	1 431	1 434	1 441	3.3	2.6
Health services	5 986	9 001	11 985	12 075	12 321	2.7	2.9
Offices of health practitioners	1 503	2 546	3 560	3 525	3 472	3.0	3.4
Nursing and personal care facilities	1 106	1 649	2 377	2 400	2 474	3.5	3.1
Hospitals, private	3 037	3 774	4 175	4 250	4 451	1.1	1.6
Health services, n.e.c.	341	1 032	1 873	1 900	1 925	5.7	6.2
Legal services	602	927	1 240	1 270	1 300	2.9	2.9
Educational services	1 225	1 822	2 336	2 400	2 437	2.5	2.8
Social services	1 188	2 181	3 637	3 639	3 623	4.8	3.3
Individual and miscellaneous social services	464	779	1 273	1 314	1 335	4.9	3.8
Job training and related services	190	298	443	425	411	3.3	0.7
Child day care services	284	502	840	800	766	4.3	1.0
Residential care	251	602	1 082	1 100	1 111	5.6	5.4
Museums, botanical, zoological gardens	43	79	112	112	112	3.2	4.7
Membership organizations	1 510	2 059	2 156	2 336	2 488	1.2	2.6
Engineering, management, and related services	1 673	2 607	3 431	3 494	3 565	2.7	2.5
Engineering and architectural services	576	775	1 008	1 044	1 086	2.7	2.0
Research and testing services	384	563	743	745	747	2.6	5.0
Management and public relations	327	716	1 037	1 049	1 062	3.5	1.7
Accounting, auditing, and other services	387	553	642	656	670	1.6	1.4
Government	15 870	19 117	19 307	20 990	22 951	0.9	1.0
Federal government	2 774	2 870	2 607	2 635	2 667	-0.8	0.2
Federal enterprises	890	1 017	898	935	976	-0.8	2.3
US Postal Service	685	818	726	760	797	-0.7	2.8
Federal electric utilities	43	27	24	25	27	-0.9	0.5
Federal government enterprises, n.e.c.	162	172	148	150	152	-1.2	2.2
Federal general government	1 884	1 853	1 709	1 700	1 691	-0.8	-0.7
State and local government	13 096	16 247	16 701	18 355	20 284	1.1	1.4
State and local enterprises	782	941	1 073	1 113	1 146	1.5	2.2
Local government passenger transit	180	214	249	260	266	1.8	-0.1
State and local electric utilities	73	86	102	100	98	1.3	1.6
State and local government enterprises, n.e.c.	529	641	722	753	782	1.5	2.7
State and local general government	12 314	15 306	15 628	17 242	19 138	1.1	1.2
State and local government hospitals	1 115	1 081	994	1 090	1 202	0.1	-0.2
State and local government education	6 589	8 365	9 058	10 000	11 108	1.6	1.8
State and local general government, n.e.c.	4 610	5 860	5 576	6 152	6 829	0.4	0.4
Agriculture	3 508	3 623	3 431	3 399	3 361	-0.6	1.0
Agricultural production	2 727	2 326	1 813	1 799	1 783	-2.3	0.9
Agricultural services	699	1 197	1 528	1 514	1 494	2.2	2.2
Forestry, fishing, hunting, and trapping	82	100	90	87	84	-1.3	-2.3
Private household wage and salary	1 247	966	818	800	779	-1.7	0.4
Nonagricultural self-employed and unpaid family	7 914	9 085	10 382	10 324	10 343	1.2	....

1. Based on moderate path.

Number Employed and Projected Employment by Detailed Occupation, 1994 and 2005

(Numbers in thousands; percent)

Occupation	1994	2005 Low	2005 Moderate	2005 High	Percent Low	Percent Moderate	Percent High	Number, moderate	Total job openings due to growth and net replacement [1]
TOTAL, ALL OCCUPATIONS	127 014	140 261	144 708	150 212	10	14	18	17 694	49 631
Executive, administrative, and managerial occupations	12 903	14 621	15 071	15 638	13	17	21	2 168	4 844
Managerial and administrative occupations	9 058	10 267	10 575	10 965	13	17	21	1 517	3 467
Administrative services managers	279	296	307	320	6	10	15	28	87
Communication, transportation, and utilities operations managers	154	129	135	141	-16	-12	-8	-19	32
Construction managers	197	240	253	274	21	28	39	56	97
Education administrators	393	431	459	491	10	17	25	66	176
Engineering, mathematical, and natural science managers	337	415	432	453	23	28	35	95	165
Financial managers	768	919	950	988	20	24	29	182	324
Food service and lodging managers	579	776	771	769	34	33	33	192	313
Funeral directors and morticians	26	28	29	29	9	11	13	3	8
General managers and top executives	3 046	3 403	3 512	3 641	12	15	20	466	1 104
Government chief executives and legislators	91	86	94	104	-5	4	14	4	26
Industrial production managers	206	183	191	202	-11	-7	-2	-15	43
Marketing, advertising, and public relations managers	461	558	575	595	21	25	29	114	211
Personnel, training, and labor relations managers	206	243	252	262	18	22	27	46	104
Property and real estate managers	261	281	298	321	8	14	23	37	81
Purchasing managers	226	228	235	244	1	4	8	9	55
All other managers and administrators	1 829	2 051	2 081	2 129	12	14	16	252	639
Management support occupations	3 845	4 354	4 496	4 673	13	17	22	651	1 377
Accountants and auditors	962	1 056	1 083	1 119	10	13	16	121	312
Budget analysts	66	71	74	78	8	12	17	8	19
Claims examiners, property and casualty insurance	56	64	65	66	13	15	18	9	14
Construction and building inspectors	64	74	79	84	15	22	31	14	28
Cost estimators	179	199	210	225	12	17	26	31	48
Credit analysts	39	47	48	49	21	24	27	9	16
Employment interviewers, private or public employment service	77	102	104	107	33	36	39	27	43
Inspectors and compliance officers, except construction	157	165	175	186	6	12	18	18	50
Loan officers and counselors	214	258	264	269	21	23	26	50	85
Management analysts	231	308	312	319	33	35	38	82	109
Personnel, training, and labor relations specialists	307	360	374	391	17	22	27	67	129
Purchasing agents, except wholesale, retail, and farm products	215	218	226	238	2	5	11	12	64
Tax examiners, collectors, and revenue agents	63	60	63	66	-5	0	6	0	14
Underwriters	96	101	103	105	5	7	9	7	25
Wholesale and retail buyers, except farm products	180	173	178	183	-4	-2	1	-3	50
All other management support workers	940	1 098	1 138	1 188	17	21	26	198	371
Professional specialty occupations	17 314	21 430	22 387	23 540	24	29	36	5 073	8 376
Engineers	1 327	1 516	1 573	1 658	14	19	25	246	581
Aeronautical and astronautical engineers	56	57	59	62	2	6	12	3	16
Chemical engineers	50	56	57	59	10	13	16	7	21
Civil engineers, including traffic engineers	184	209	219	231	13	19	25	34	90
Electrical and electronics engineers	349	402	417	439	15	20	26	69	157
Industrial engineers, except safety engineers	115	125	131	139	8	13	21	15	47
Mechanical engineers	231	266	276	290	15	19	26	45	98
Metallurgists and metallurgical, ceramic, and materials engineers	19	19	20	20	2	5	10	1	6
Mining engineers, including mine safety engineers	3	3	3	3	-22	-18	-12	-1	1
Nuclear engineers	15	15	15	16	1	4	8	1	5
Petroleum engineers	14	12	11	13	-11	-21	-8	-3	4
All other engineers	292	353	367	387	21	26	33	75	136
Architects and surveyors	200	209	215	222	4	7	11	14	70
Architects, except landscape and marine	91	104	106	109	14	17	20	15	35
Landscape architects	14	16	16	16	16	17	18	2	5
Surveyors	96	89	92	97	-7	-3	1	-3	30
Life scientists	186	222	230	239	20	24	29	44	94
Agricultural and food scientists	26	30	31	31	16	19	22	5	12
Biological scientists	82	100	103	107	21	25	30	21	43
Foresters and conservation scientists	41	47	49	50	15	18	22	8	18
Medical scientists	36	45	47	49	25	31	38	11	21
All other life scientists	1	1	1	1	0	1	2	0	0
Computer, mathematical, and operations research occupations	917	1 629	1 696	1 781	78	85	94	779	863
Actuaries	17	18	18	18	2	4	6	1	4
Computer systems analysts, engineers, and scientists	828	1 519	1 583	1 663	84	91	101	755	819
Computer engineers and scientists	345	626	655	691	82	90	101	310	338
Computer engineers	195	355	372	394	82	90	102	177	191
All other computer scientists	149	271	283	297	81	89	99	134	147
Systems analysts	483	893	928	972	85	92	101	445	481
Statisticians	14	14	15	15	1	3	5	0	3
Mathematicians and all other mathematical scientists	14	14	15	15	1	5	10	1	3
Operations research analysts	44	65	67	69	46	50	56	22	35
Physical scientists	209	245	250	257	17	19	23	41	104
Chemists	97	112	115	118	15	19	22	18	45
Geologists, geophysicists, and oceanographers	46	54	54	57	17	17	22	8	24
Meteorologists	7	7	7	7	4	7	10	0	2
Physicists and astronomers	20	18	18	19	-12	-9	-6	-2	5
All other physical scientists	40	55	56	57	39	41	43	16	27

1. Based on moderate path. Total job openings represent the sum of employment increases and net replacement. If employment change is negative, job openings due to growth are zero and total job openings equal net replacements.

Number Employed and Projected Employment by Detailed Occupation, 1994 and 2005—Continued

(Numbers in thousands; percent)

Occupation	1994	2005			1994-2005 change				Total job openings due to growth and net replacement [1]
		Low	Moderate	High	Percent			Number, moderate	
					Low	Moderate	High		
Social scientists	259	309	318	329	19	23	27	59	103
Economists	48	59	59	61	23	25	28	12	30
Psychologists	144	173	177	183	20	23	27	33	45
Urban and regional planners	29	33	35	38	15	24	34	7	13
All other social scientists	38	44	45	47	16	19	23	7	15
Social, recreational, and religious workers	1 387	1 836	1 924	2 010	32	39	45	536	810
Clergy	195	216	234	249	11	20	27	38	77
Directors, religious activities and education	81	89	96	102	10	19	27	15	31
Human services workers	168	284	293	303	69	75	80	125	170
Recreation workers	222	251	266	283	13	20	28	45	86
Residential counselors	165	284	290	295	73	76	79	126	158
Social workers	557	712	744	778	28	34	40	187	288
Lawyers and judicial workers	735	899	918	940	22	25	28	183	279
Judges, magistrates, and other judicial workers	79	75	79	84	-5	1	7	1	11
Lawyers	656	824	839	856	26	28	31	183	268
Teachers, librarians, and counselors	6 246	7 311	7 849	8 464	17	26	36	1 603	2 886
Teachers, preschool and kindergarten	462	588	602	620	27	30	34	140	215
Teachers, elementary	1 419	1 509	1 639	1 787	6	16	26	220	511
Teachers, secondary school	1 340	1 585	1 726	1 885	18	29	41	386	782
Teachers, special education	388	545	593	648	41	53	67	206	262
College and university faculty	823	893	972	1 062	9	18	29	150	395
Other teachers and instructors	886	1 100	1 151	1 210	24	30	37	265	331
Farm and home management advisors	14	13	14	15	-9	-1	8	0	1
Instructors and coaches, sports and physical training	282	365	381	399	29	35	41	98	119
Adult and vocational education teachers	590	723	757	796	23	28	35	167	211
Instructors, adult (nonvocational) education	290	366	376	387	26	29	33	85	107
Teachers and instructors, vocational education and training	299	356	381	409	19	27	37	81	104
All other teachers and instructors	596	720	769	826	21	29	38	173	251
Librarians, archivists, curators, and related workers	168	169	182	196	1	8	17	14	56
Curators, archivists, museum technicians, and restorers	19	22	23	24	14	19	24	4	9
Librarians, professional	148	147	159	172	-1	7	16	10	47
Counselors	165	202	215	230	23	31	40	50	83
Health diagnosing occupations	850	1 005	1 003	1 004	18	18	18	153	312
Chiropractors	42	54	54	53	30	29	28	12	20
Dentists	164	174	173	172	6	5	4	9	54
Optometrists	37	42	42	41	12	12	11	4	12
Physicians	539	659	659	661	22	22	23	120	205
Podiatrists	13	15	15	15	16	15	15	2	5
Veterinarians and veterinary inspectors	56	62	62	62	11	11	11	6	17
Health assessment and treating occupations	2 563	3 212	3 294	3 425	25	29	34	731	1 101
Dietitians and nutritionists	53	62	63	65	17	19	23	10	24
Pharmacists	168	190	196	203	14	17	21	28	54
Physician assistants	56	69	69	70	23	23	24	13	22
Registered nurses	1 906	2 318	2 379	2 481	22	25	30	473	740
Therapists	380	573	586	606	51	54	60	207	262
Occupational therapists	54	91	93	95	69	72	77	39	47
Physical therapists	102	182	183	185	79	80	82	81	96
Recreational therapists	31	37	37	39	20	22	27	7	11
Respiratory therapists	73	96	99	104	32	36	44	26	37
Speech-language pathologists and audiologists	85	120	125	130	40	46	53	39	52
All other therapists	36	48	50	52	34	39	45	14	19
Writers, artists, and entertainers	1 612	1 938	1 975	2 016	20	22	25	363	680
Artists and commercial artists	273	336	336	339	23	23	24	64	117
Athletes, coaches, umpires, and related workers	38	46	46	46	20	20	21	8	19
Dancers and choreographers	24	30	30	30	24	24	24	6	11
Designers	301	377	384	393	25	28	31	84	130
Designers, except interior designers	238	308	314	322	29	32	35	76	113
Interior designers	63	69	70	71	11	12	14	8	17
Musicians	256	304	317	329	19	24	29	62	105
Photographers and camera operators	139	173	172	173	24	24	25	34	61
Camera operators, television, motion picture, and video	18	19	19	19	5	6	6	1	5
Photographers	121	154	153	154	27	27	27	32	57
Producers, directors, actors, and entertainers	93	120	121	121	30	30	30	28	47
Public relations specialists and publicity writers	107	123	128	133	16	20	24	21	44
Radio and TV announcers and newscasters	50	49	51	52	-3	1	4	0	21
Reporters and correspondents	59	55	57	58	-6	-4	-1	-2	13
Writers and editors, including technical writers	272	324	332	340	19	22	25	59	111
All other professional workers	822	1 097	1 142	1 194	33	39	45	319	494

1. Based on moderate path. Total job openings represent the sum of employment increases and net replacement. If employment change is negative, job openings due to growth are zero and total job openings equal net replacements.

Number Employed and Projected Employment by Detailed Occupation, 1994 and 2005—Continued

(Numbers in thousands; percent)

Occupation	1994	2005			1994-2005 change				Total job openings due to growth and net replacement [1]
		Low	Moderate	High	Percent			Number, moderate	
					Low	Moderate	High		
Technicians and related support occupations	4 439	5 161	5 316	5 526	16	20	24	876	1 798
Health technicians and technologists	2 197	2 754	2 815	2 905	25	28	32	618	1 024
Cardiology technologists	14	17	17	18	18	22	29	3	6
Clinical laboratory technologists and technicians	274	300	307	317	10	12	16	33	86
Dental hygienists	127	182	180	178	43	42	40	53	74
Electroneurodiagnostic technologists	6	8	8	9	25	28	34	2	3
EKG technicians	16	11	11	12	-31	-30	-27	-5	3
Emergency medical technicians	138	178	187	197	29	36	43	49	72
Licensed practical nurses	702	882	899	927	26	28	32	197	341
Medical records technicians	81	125	126	130	54	56	60	45	59
Nuclear medicine technologists	13	16	16	17	22	26	32	3	5
Opticians, dispensing and measuring	63	75	76	76	20	21	22	13	28
Pharmacy technicians	81	98	101	104	21	24	28	20	33
Psychiatric technicians	72	78	80	84	8	11	16	8	18
Radiologic technologists and technicians	167	222	226	232	33	35	39	59	82
Surgical technologists	46	64	65	68	39	43	49	19	27
Veterinary technicians and technologists	22	26	26	26	17	18	17	4	8
All other health professionals and paraprofessionals	374	472	488	510	26	30	36	114	179
Engineering and science technicians and technologists	1 220	1 265	1 312	1 376	4	8	13	92	357
Engineering technicians	685	718	746	786	5	9	15	61	207
Electrical and electronic technicians and technologists	314	336	349	367	7	11	17	35	108
All other engineering technicians and technologists	371	382	397	419	3	7	13	26	99
Drafters	304	294	304	318	-3	0	5	1	70
Science and mathematics technicians	231	254	262	272	10	13	18	31	79
Technicians, except health and engineering and science	1 023	1 142	1 189	1 245	12	16	22	167	418
Aircraft pilots and flight engineers	91	93	97	101	3	8	12	7	32
Air traffic controllers and airplane dispatchers	29	29	29	29	0	0	1	0	6
Broadcast technicians	42	39	40	41	-6	-4	-2	-2	9
Computer programmers	537	577	601	631	7	12	18	65	228
Legal assistants and technicians, except clerical	219	291	301	311	33	38	42	82	103
Paralegals	110	170	175	179	54	58	62	64	74
Title examiners and searchers	28	27	28	29	-3	0	5	0	3
All other legal assistants, including law clerks	80	94	98	103	17	22	28	18	27
Programmers, numerical, tool, and process control	7	6	6	7	-13	-9	-2	-1	2
Technical assistants, library	75	84	91	99	11	21	31	16	32
All other technicians	24	22	24	25	-5	0	6	0	5
Marketing and sales occupations	13 990	16 107	16 502	16 944	15	18	21	2 512	6 706
Cashiers	3 005	3 493	3 567	3 645	16	19	21	562	1 772
Counter and rental clerks	341	438	451	464	28	32	36	109	203
Insurance sales workers	418	432	436	441	3	4	6	18	88
Marketing and sales worker supervisors	2 293	2 628	2 673	2 728	15	17	19	380	788
Real estate agents, brokers, and appraisers	374	395	407	426	6	9	14	33	113
Brokers, real estate	67	72	75	79	8	12	18	8	22
Real estate appraisers	47	50	53	58	6	13	22	6	16
Sales agents, real estate	260	273	279	289	5	7	11	19	75
Salespersons, retail	3 842	4 244	4 374	4 508	10	14	17	532	1 821
Securities and financial services sales workers	246	328	335	343	34	37	40	90	126
Travel agents	122	141	150	159	16	23	30	28	55
All other sales and related workers	3 349	4 008	4 109	4 230	20	23	26	760	1 741

1. Based on moderate path. Total job openings represent the sum of employment increases and net replacement. If employment change is negative, job openings due to growth are zero and total job openings equal net replacements.

Number Employed and Projected Employment by Detailed Occupation, 1994 and 2005—Continued

(Numbers in thousands; percent)

Occupation	1994	2005			1994-2005 change				Total job openings due to growth and net replacement [1]
		Low	Moderate	High	Percent			Number, moderate	
					Low	Moderate	High		
Administrative support occupations, including clerical	23 178	23 332	24 172	25 147	1	4	8	994	6 991
Adjusters, investigators, and collectors	1 229	1 465	1 507	1 553	19	23	26	277	399
Adjustment clerks	373	505	521	540	35	40	45	148	175
Bill and account collectors	250	334	342	351	33	36	40	91	112
Insurance claims and policy processing occupations	461	487	495	503	6	8	9	35	92
Insurance adjusters, examiners, and investigators	162	189	192	196	17	19	21	30	45
Insurance claims clerks	119	133	135	137	12	13	15	16	27
Insurance policy processing clerks	179	165	168	171	-8	-6	-5	-12	20
Welfare eligibility workers and interviewers	104	101	108	116	-3	4	12	4	16
All other adjusters and investigators	41	38	40	43	-6	-1	6	0	4
Communications equipment operators	319	259	266	275	-19	-17	-14	-53	83
Telephone operators	310	253	260	268	-18	-16	-14	-50	81
Central office operators	48	14	14	15	-71	-70	-69	-34	12
Directory assistance operators	33	10	10	10	-71	-70	-69	-24	8
Switchboard operators	228	230	236	243	1	3	6	7	62
All other communications equipment operators	9	6	6	6	-33	-31	-30	-3	2
Computer operators and peripheral equipment operators	289	169	175	182	-41	-39	-37	-114	62
Computer operators, except peripheral equipment	259	157	162	168	-40	-38	-35	-98	56
Peripheral EDP equipment operators	30	13	13	14	-57	-55	-52	-16	6
Information clerks	1 477	1 790	1 832	1 879	21	24	27	355	699
Hotel desk clerks	136	161	163	165	18	20	22	27	84
Interviewing clerks, except personnel and social welfare	69	80	83	87	16	20	26	14	36
New accounts clerks, banking	114	112	116	121	-2	2	6	2	40
Receptionists and information clerks	1 019	1 311	1 337	1 367	29	31	34	318	508
Reservation and transportation ticket agents and travel clerks	139	126	133	139	-9	-4	0	-6	31
Mail clerks and messengers	260	249	256	265	-4	-1	2	-4	70
Mail clerks, except mail machine operators and postal service	127	113	116	120	-11	-8	-5	-10	35
Messengers	133	136	140	145	2	5	8	7	35
Postal clerks and mail carriers	474	459	481	504	-3	1	6	7	126
Postal mail carriers	320	305	320	335	-5	0	5	-1	85
Postal service clerks	154	154	161	169	0	5	10	7	41
Material recording, scheduling, dispatching, and distributing occupations	3 556	3 559	3 688	3 836	0	4	8	132	863
Dispatchers	224	244	258	273	9	15	22	34	65
Dispatchers, except police, fire, and ambulance	141	162	168	175	14	19	24	27	46
Dispatchers, police, fire, and ambulance	83	83	90	98	0	8	18	7	18
Meter readers, utilities	57	43	46	50	-25	-19	-13	-11	13
Order fillers, wholesale and retail sales	215	225	231	239	5	8	11	16	63
Procurement clerks	57	50	52	54	-12	-9	-6	-5	13
Production, planning, and expediting clerks	239	241	251	263	1	5	10	12	56
Stock clerks	1 759	1 743	1 800	1 863	-1	2	6	41	443
Traffic, shipping, and receiving clerks	798	798	827	861	0	4	8	29	150
Weighers, measurers, checkers, and samplers, recordkeeping	45	44	46	48	-2	3	7	1	12
All other material recording, scheduling, and distribution workers	161	171	177	184	6	10	14	16	47
Records processing occupations	3 733	3 338	3 438	3 559	-11	-8	-5	-294	877
Advertising clerks	17	18	18	19	2	5	8	1	5
Brokerage clerks	73	71	73	75	-2	1	4	1	9
Correspondence clerks	29	26	27	28	-10	-8	-5	-2	6
File clerks	278	232	236	241	-17	-15	-13	-42	102
Financial records processing occupations	2 757	2 438	2 506	2 591	-12	-9	-6	-250	573
Billing, cost, and rate clerks	323	321	328	336	0	2	4	5	98
Billing, posting, and calculating machine operators	96	32	32	33	-67	-67	-66	-64	40
Bookkeeping, accounting, and auditing clerks	2 181	1 946	2 003	2 073	-11	-8	-5	-178	400
Payroll and timekeeping clerks	157	139	144	150	-12	-9	-5	-14	35
Library assistants and bookmobile drivers	121	117	127	139	-3	5	15	7	57
Order clerks, materials, merchandise, and service	310	327	337	348	6	9	12	27	95
Personnel clerks, except payroll and timekeeping	123	95	98	101	-23	-21	-18	-26	27
Statement clerks	25	15	16	16	-40	-38	-35	-9	3
Secretaries, stenographers, and typists	4 100	4 123	4 276	4 457	1	4	9	175	1 230
Secretaries	3 349	3 605	3 739	3 898	8	12	16	390	1 102
Legal secretaries	281	341	350	358	21	24	27	68	128
Medical secretaries	226	280	281	282	24	24	25	55	103
Secretaries, except legal and medical	2 842	2 983	3 109	3 258	5	9	15	267	871
Stenographers	105	99	102	107	-6	-3	1	-3	22
Typists and word processors	646	418	434	452	-35	-33	-30	-212	106
Other clerical and administrative support workers	7 740	7 921	8 253	8 638	2	7	12	513	2 582
Bank tellers	559	391	407	423	-30	-27	-24	-152	244
Clerical supervisors and managers	1 340	1 550	1 600	1 658	16	19	24	261	613
Court clerks	51	54	59	64	5	15	26	8	12
Credit authorizers, credit checkers, and loan and credit clerks	258	261	267	274	1	4	6	9	49
Credit authorizers	15	18	19	19	21	24	28	4	5
Credit checkers	40	34	35	36	-16	-14	-12	-6	3
Loan and credit clerks	187	192	196	201	3	5	8	10	37
Loan interviewers	16	17	17	18	7	10	12	2	4
Customer service representatives, utilities	150	171	179	187	14	19	24	29	61
Data entry keyers, except composing	395	359	370	383	-9	-6	-3	-25	17
Data entry keyers, composing	19	6	6	7	-68	-67	-65	-13	1
Duplicating, mail, and other office machine operators	222	160	166	172	-28	-25	-23	-56	99
General office clerks	2 946	2 959	3 071	3 204	0	4	9	126	908
Municipal clerks	22	19	21	23	-11	-3	7	-1	2
Proofreaders and copy markers	26	20	20	21	-23	-20	-18	-5	7
Real estate clerks	24	22	25	28	-5	5	20	1	8
Statistical clerks	75	65	68	72	-13	-10	-5	-7	11
Teacher aides and educational assistants	932	1 211	1 296	1 393	30	39	49	364	480
All other clerical and administrative support workers	721	672	698	729	-7	-3	1	-23	69

1. Based on moderate path. Total job openings represent the sum of employment increases and net replacement. If employment change is negative, job openings due to growth are zero and total job openings equal net replacements.

Number Employed and Projected Employment by Detailed Occupation, 1994 and 2005—Continued

(Numbers in thousands; percent)

Occupation	1994	2005			1994-2005 change				Total job openings due to growth and net replacement[1]
		Low	Moderate	High	Percent			Number, moderate	
					Low	Moderate	High		
Service occupations	20 239	24 465	24 832	25 318	21	23	25	4 593	9 813
Cleaning and building service occupations, except private household	3 450	3 935	4 071	4 235	14	18	23	621	1 293
Institutional cleaning supervisors	125	144	147	151	16	18	21	22	58
Janitors and cleaners, including maids and housekeeping cleaners	3 043	3 483	3 602	3 745	14	18	23	559	1 140
Pest controllers and assistants	56	75	76	78	33	36	39	20	31
All other cleaning and building service workers	226	232	245	261	3	8	15	19	63
Food preparation and service occupations	7 964	9 094	9 057	9 037	14	14	13	1 093	3 498
Chefs, cooks, and other kitchen workers	3 237	3 737	3 739	3 751	15	16	16	502	1 102
Cooks, except short order	1 286	1 484	1 492	1 503	15	16	17	206	524
Bakers, bread and pastry	170	226	230	235	33	35	38	60	102
Cooks, institution or cafeteria	412	419	435	454	2	6	10	23	125
Cooks, restaurant	704	839	827	815	19	17	16	123	297
Cooks, short order and fast food	760	884	869	855	16	14	12	109	297
Food preparation workers	1 190	1 368	1 378	1 393	15	16	17	187	282
Food and beverage service occupations	4 514	5 098	5 051	5 009	13	12	11	537	2 263
Bartenders	373	348	347	346	-7	-7	-7	-25	138
Dining room and cafeteria attendants and bar helpers	416	415	416	419	0	0	1	0	157
Food counter, fountain, and related workers	1 630	1 680	1 669	1 661	3	2	2	40	463
Hosts and hostesses, restaurant, lounge, or coffee shop	248	293	292	292	18	18	18	44	114
Waiters and waitresses	1 847	2 361	2 326	2 291	28	26	24	479	1 390
All other food preparation and service workers	213	259	267	278	21	25	30	54	132
Health service occupations	2 086	2 807	2 846	2 919	35	36	40	759	1 131
Ambulance drivers and attendants, except EMTs	18	20	21	21	10	15	20	3	8
Dental assistants	190	271	269	266	43	42	40	79	137
Medical assistants	206	329	327	324	60	59	58	121	155
Nursing aides and psychiatric aides	1 370	1 737	1 770	1 834	27	29	34	400	594
Nursing aides, orderlies, and attendants	1 265	1 624	1 652	1 709	28	31	35	387	566
Psychiatric aides	105	113	118	126	7	12	19	13	28
Occupational therapy assistants and aides	16	28	29	29	80	82	86	13	16
Pharmacy assistants	52	62	64	68	20	23	29	12	22
Physical and corrective therapy assistants and aides	78	141	142	143	82	83	85	64	87
All other health service workers	157	218	224	233	39	43	49	67	112
Personal service occupations	2 530	3 682	3 719	3 761	45	47	49	1 189	1 670
Amusement and recreation attendants	267	398	406	414	49	52	55	139	211
Baggage porters and bellhops	35	44	44	45	24	26	29	9	16
Barbers	64	60	60	60	-6	-6	-6	-4	20
Child care workers	757	1 009	1 005	1 006	33	33	33	248	321
Cosmetologists and related workers	645	751	754	757	16	17	17	109	273
Hairdressers, hairstylists, and cosmetologists	595	675	677	680	13	14	14	82	233
Manicurists	38	63	64	64	69	69	70	26	36
Shampooers	12	13	13	13	7	8	8	1	4
Flight attendants	105	128	135	141	23	28	34	30	49
Homemaker-home health aides	598	1 214	1 238	1 260	103	107	111	640	747
Home health aides	420	832	848	863	98	102	106	428	488
Personal and home care aides	179	382	391	397	114	119	122	212	259
Ushers, lobby attendants, and ticket takers	59	77	77	77	30	29	29	17	33
Private household workers	808	697	682	664	-14	-16	-18	-126	245
Child care workers, private household	283	284	278	270	0	-2	-4	-5	139
Cleaners and servants, private household	496	396	387	378	-20	-22	-24	-108	100
Cooks, private household	9	5	5	4	-48	-49	-51	-4	2
Housekeepers and butlers	20	13	12	12	-36	-37	-39	-7	4
Protective service occupations	2 381	3 017	3 199	3 410	27	34	43	818	1 514
Firefighting occupations	284	301	328	359	6	16	27	44	169
Fire fighters	219	237	258	283	8	18	29	40	138
Fire fighting and prevention supervisors	52	51	56	61	-2	7	18	4	24
Fire inspection occupations	13	13	14	15	-2	7	18	1	6
Law enforcement occupations	992	1 210	1 316	1 439	22	33	45	324	610
Correction officers	310	430	468	513	39	51	65	158	194
Police and detectives	682	780	848	927	14	24	36	166	416
Police and detective supervisors	87	86	93	102	-1	7	16	6	45
Police detectives and investigators	66	75	80	85	13	20	29	13	40
Police patrol officers	400	469	511	560	17	28	40	112	271
Sheriffs and deputy sheriffs	86	101	110	121	18	29	41	25	42
Other law enforcement occupations	43	49	54	59	15	25	37	11	19
Other protective service workers	1 106	1 506	1 554	1 612	36	41	46	449	735
Detectives, except public	55	77	79	80	42	44	47	24	35
Guards	867	1 248	1 282	1 322	44	48	53	415	580
Crossing guards	58	55	60	66	-5	3	13	2	17
All other protective service workers	126	125	133	143	-1	6	14	8	104
All other service workers	1 020	1 234	1 259	1 290	21	23	27	240	462
Agriculture, forestry, fishing, and related occupations	3 762	3 635	3 650	3 676	-3	-3	-2	-112	988
Animal breeders and trainers	16	15	15	15	-5	-5	-5	-1	3
Animal caretakers, except farm	125	157	158	160	26	26	28	33	62
Farm workers	906	871	870	868	-4	-4	-4	-36	263
Gardening, nursery, and greenhouse and lawn service occupations	844	971	986	1 006	15	17	19	142	271
Gardeners and groundskeepers, except farm	569	609	623	641	7	9	13	54	128
Lawn maintenance workers	96	127	127	127	32	32	32	31	43
Lawn service managers	36	48	47	47	33	33	33	12	18
Nursery and greenhouse managers	19	26	26	26	38	37	37	7	11
Nursery workers	83	107	109	111	29	31	34	26	50
Pruners	26	34	34	34	32	32	32	8	14
Sprayers/applicators	15	20	20	20	32	32	32	5	7
Farm operators and managers	1 327	1 057	1 050	1 048	-20	-21	-21	-277	221
Farmers	1 276	1 011	1 003	1 002	-21	-21	-21	-273	211
Farm managers	51	47	46	46	-9	-9	-9	-5	10
Fishers, hunters, and trappers	49	48	47	47	-3	-4	-5	-2	11
Captains and other officers, fishing vessels	7	6	6	6	-10	-11	-12	-1	2
Fishers, hunters, and trappers	42	41	41	41	-2	-3	-4	-1	9
Forestry and logging occupations	124	116	118	120	-6	-5	-3	-6	34
Forest and conservation workers	42	41	42	44	-1	1	4	1	12
Timber cutting and logging occupations	82	75	76	77	-9	-8	-7	-7	22
Fallers and buckers	29	27	27	27	-9	-9	-9	-3	8
Logging tractor operators	20	20	20	20	-3	-1	0	0	4
Log handling equipment operators	16	14	15	15	-11	-9	-6	-1	5
All other timber cutting and related logging workers	17	14	15	15	-14	-13	-12	-2	5
Supervisors, farming, forestry, and agricultural related occupations	85	90	91	92	6	7	8	6	22
Veterinary assistants	31	36	37	36	19	19	19	6	13
All other agricultural, forestry, fishing, and related workers	255	273	278	283	7	9	11	23	87

1. Based on moderate path. Total job openings represent the sum of employment increases and net replacement. If employment change is negative, job openings due to growth are zero and total job openings equal net replacements.

Number Employed and Projected Employment by Detailed Occupation, 1994 and 2005—Continued

(Numbers in thousands; percent)

Occupation	1994	2005			1994-2005 change				Total job openings due to growth and net replacement [1]
		Low	Moderate	High	Percent			Number, moderate	
					Low	Moderate	High		
Precision production, craft, and repair occupations	14 047	14 312	14 880	15 659	2	6	11	833	4 489
Blue collar worker supervisors	1 884	1 822	1 894	1 990	-3	1	6	11	480
Construction trades	3 616	3 806	3 956	4 182	5	9	16	340	1 183
Bricklayers and stone masons	147	155	162	171	6	10	17	15	43
Carpenters	992	1 044	1 074	1 122	5	8	13	82	290
Carpet installers	66	72	72	73	9	9	11	6	28
Ceiling tile installers and acoustical carpenters	16	14	14	16	-15	-10	-2	-2	3
Concrete and terrazzo finishers	126	134	141	151	6	12	20	15	41
Drywall installers and finishers	133	138	143	151	3	7	13	9	50
Electricians	528	529	554	591	0	5	12	25	152
Glaziers	34	33	34	36	-2	2	8	1	9
Hard tile setters	27	27	28	29	-2	1	6	0	7
Highway maintenance workers	167	167	182	199	0	9	20	15	62
Insulation workers	64	73	77	83	14	20	29	13	34
Painters and paperhangers, construction and maintenance	439	497	509	529	13	16	21	70	174
Paving, surfacing, and tamping equipment operators	73	87	93	101	19	26	37	19	37
Pipelayers and pipelaying fitters	57	60	63	69	6	12	21	7	23
Plasterers	30	32	33	36	7	11	19	3	11
Plumbers, pipefitters, and steamfitters	375	374	390	413	0	4	10	15	92
Roofers	126	138	143	151	9	13	19	17	42
Structural and reinforcing metal workers	61	60	64	69	-1	5	14	3	19
All other construction trades workers	155	174	181	191	12	17	24	26	68
Extractive and related workers, including blasters	220	196	204	226	-11	-7	2	-16	59
Oil and gas extraction occupations	66	39	39	49	-41	-41	-25	-27	12
Roustabouts	28	13	13	16	-54	-55	-44	-16	5
All other oil and gas extraction occupations	38	26	26	33	-31	-30	-12	-11	7
Mining, quarrying, and tunneling occupations	18	11	12	13	-40	-34	-28	-6	3
All other extraction and related workers	136	146	153	163	7	12	20	17	43
Mechanics, installers, and repairers	5 012	5 372	5 586	5 842	7	11	17	574	1 950
Communications equipment mechanics, installers, and repairers	118	75	78	80	-37	-34	-32	-41	26
Central office and PBX installers and repairers	84	50	51	53	-41	-39	-37	-33	17
Radio mechanics	7	6	6	6	-18	-16	-14	-1	2
All other communications equipment mechanics, installers and repairers	27	19	20	21	-28	-25	-22	-7	6
Electrical and electronic equipment mechanics, installers, and repairers	554	534	555	581	-4	0	5	1	175
Data processing equipment repairers	75	100	104	108	33	38	44	29	49
Electrical powerline installers and repairers	112	117	123	130	5	10	17	11	37
Electronic home entertainment equipment repairers	34	30	30	31	-11	-10	-8	-3	9
Electronics repairers, commercial and industrial equipment	66	66	68	70	0	2	5	1	20
Station installers and repairers, telephone	37	10	11	11	-71	-70	-69	-26	7
Telephone and cable TV line installers and repairers	191	174	181	191	-9	-5	0	-9	43
All other electrical and electronic equipment mechanics, installers, and repairers	39	37	38	39	-7	-3	0	-1	10
Machinery and related mechanics, installers, and repairers	1 815	1 974	2 072	2 196	9	14	21	258	700
Industrial machinery mechanics	464	480	502	529	3	8	14	38	173
Maintenance repairers, general utility	1 273	1 431	1 505	1 597	12	18	25	231	508
Millwrights	77	63	66	70	-19	-15	-9	-11	20
Vehicle and mobile equipment mechanics and repairers	1 502	1 685	1 736	1 788	12	16	19	234	655
Aircraft mechanics, including engine specialists	119	129	134	140	8	13	18	15	49
Aircraft engine specialists	23	24	25	26	3	8	13	2	8
Aircraft mechanics	96	105	109	114	9	14	19	13	40
Automotive body and related repairers	209	237	243	248	14	17	19	35	92
Automotive mechanics	736	840	862	882	14	17	20	126	347
Bus and truck mechanics and diesel engine specialists	250	281	293	306	12	17	22	42	100
Farm equipment mechanics	41	46	47	48	11	14	17	6	17
Mobile heavy equipment mechanics	101	106	110	115	5	9	14	9	37
Motorcycle, boat, and small engine mechanics	46	47	48	49	2	4	6	2	14
Motorcycle repairers	11	11	12	12	2	4	6	0	4
Small engine specialists	35	36	36	37	2	4	6	1	11
Other mechanics, installers, and repairers	1 023	1 105	1 145	1 197	8	12	17	122	394
Bicycle repairers	40	44	44	44	10	10	11	4	13
Camera and photographic equipment repairers	11	12	12	12	10	9	9	1	4
Coin and vending machine servicers and repairers	19	16	17	17	-16	-14	-12	-3	4
Electric meter installers and repairers	12	9	10	11	-23	-18	-12	-2	3
Electromedical and biomedical equipment repairers	10	11	11	12	14	17	23	2	4
Elevator installers and repairers	24	26	28	30	10	15	24	4	10
Heat, air conditioning, and refrigeration mechanics and installers	233	286	299	319	23	29	37	66	125
Home appliance and power tool repairers	70	64	66	68	-8	-6	-3	-4	19
Locksmiths and safe repairers	20	21	21	22	7	10	13	2	7
Musical instrument repairers and tuners	10	11	11	11	14	15	16	1	4
Office machine and cash register servicers	59	61	63	64	4	6	10	4	29
Precision instrument repairers	40	38	40	41	-3	0	4	0	10
Riggers	11	10	11	11	-8	-4	1	0	2
Tire repairers and changers	89	92	95	98	4	7	10	6	42
Watchmakers	6	5	5	5	-16	-15	-14	-1	2
All other mechanics, installers, and repairers	371	397	412	432	7	11	16	42	116

1. Based on moderate path. Total job openings represent the sum of employment increases and net replacement. If employment change is negative, job openings due to growth are zero and total job openings equal net replacements.

PROJECTIONS OF EMPLOYMENT BY OCCUPATION AND INDUSTRY

Number Employed and Projected Employment by Detailed Occupation, 1994 and 2005—Continued

(Numbers in thousands; percent)

Occupation	1994	2005			1994-2005 change			Number, moderate	Total job openings due to growth and net replacement[1]
		Low	Moderate	High	Percent				
					Low	Moderate	High		
Production occupations, precision	2 986	2 796	2 906	3 066	-6	-3	3	-80	730
Assemblers, precision	324	300	315	340	-7	-3	5	-9	91
Aircraft assemblers, precision	20	17	19	20	-14	-8	1	-2	4
Electrical and electronic equipment assemblers, precision	144	121	127	138	-16	-12	-5	-17	36
Electromechanical equipment assemblers, precision	47	42	44	48	-10	-6	2	-3	12
Fitters, structural metal, precision	14	9	9	10	-38	-35	-29	-5	3
Machine builders and other precision machine assemblers	58	62	65	69	6	11	19	6	18
All other precision assemblers	40	48	50	54	21	26	36	11	18
Food workers, precision	292	278	282	285	-5	-4	-2	-11	81
Bakers, manufacturing	36	40	40	40	12	12	11	4	12
Butchers and meatcutters	219	198	202	206	-9	-8	-6	-17	58
All other precision food and tobacco workers	38	39	39	39	4	4	4	2	11
Inspectors, testers, and graders, precision	654	602	629	663	-8	-4	1	-25	138
Metal workers, precision	885	788	824	878	-11	-7	-1	-61	190
Boilermakers	20	19	19	20	-8	-4	2	-1	4
Jewelers and silversmiths	30	32	32	33	5	6	8	2	8
Machinists	369	335	349	372	-9	-5	1	-20	79
Sheet metal workers and duct installers	222	194	205	220	-12	-8	-1	-17	45
Shipfitters	12	10	11	11	-17	-10	-4	-1	2
Tool and die makers	142	121	127	136	-15	-11	-4	-15	34
All other precision metal workers	90	78	82	86	-13	-9	-4	-8	18
Printing workers, precision	150	152	157	162	1	4	8	7	53
Bookbinders	6	6	6	6	-7	-4	-1	0	1
Prepress printing workers, precision	131	128	132	136	-2	1	4	1	43
Compositors and typesetters, precision	11	8	8	8	-24	-23	-21	-2	2
Job printers	14	10	11	11	-29	-27	-24	-4	3
Paste-up workers	22	16	16	17	-30	-28	-26	-6	4
Electronic pagination systems workers	18	32	33	34	77	83	88	15	19
Photoengravers	7	5	5	5	-22	-20	-17	-1	1
Camera operators	15	13	14	14	-9	-6	-3	-1	3
Strippers, printing	31	33	34	35	6	9	12	3	9
Platemakers	13	11	11	12	-18	-15	-13	-2	2
All other printing workers, precision	13	19	19	20	40	44	48	6	8
Textile, apparel, and furnishings workers, precision	240	211	219	229	-12	-9	-4	-21	40
Custom tailors and sewers	84	63	63	64	-25	-25	-24	-21	10
Patternmakers and layout workers, fabric and apparel	17	21	23	25	22	31	41	5	7
Shoe and leather workers and repairers, precision	24	16	17	19	-34	-28	-19	-7	2
Upholsterers	63	62	64	69	-2	1	8	1	9
All other precision textile, apparel, and furnishings workers	51	49	51	53	-4	0	3	0	11
Woodworkers, precision	241	266	277	297	10	15	23	36	86
Cabinetmakers and bench carpenters	131	145	151	161	11	15	23	20	45
Furniture finishers	38	39	40	43	3	6	13	2	12
Wood machinists	50	56	59	65	13	19	30	10	19
All other precision woodworkers	22	25	26	28	13	19	28	4	10
Other precision workers	199	198	204	211	-1	2	6	5	52
Dental laboratory technicians, precision	49	47	47	47	-5	-5	-4	-2	11
Optical goods workers, precision	19	21	22	22	8	12	16	2	7
Photographic process workers, precision	14	16	16	16	15	15	15	2	6
All other precision workers	117	114	119	125	-2	2	7	3	28
Plant and system occupations	330	321	334	354	-3	1	7	4	87
Chemical plant and system operators	37	35	36	37	-6	-3	-2	-1	8
Electric power generating plant operators, distributors, and dispatchers	43	39	42	44	-9	-3	3	-1	10
Power distributors and dispatchers	18	15	15	16	-17	-14	-10	-2	4
Power generating and reactor plant operators	26	25	26	28	-3	4	11	1	6
Gas and petroleum plant and system occupations	31	30	28	29	-4	-10	-6	-3	7
Stationary engineers	30	26	27	28	-14	-10	-6	-3	7
Water and liquid waste treatment plant and system operators	95	96	104	114	1	9	19	9	30
All other plant and system operators	93	94	97	102	1	5	10	4	25

1. Based on moderate path. Total job openings represent the sum of employment increases and net replacement. If employment change is negative, job openings due to growth are zero and total job openings equal net replacements.

Number Employed and Projected Employment by Detailed Occupation, 1994 and 2005—Continued

(Numbers in thousands; percent)

Occupation	1994	2005			1994-2005 change			Number, moderate	Total job openings due to growth and net replacement [1]
		Low	Moderate	High	Percent				
					Low	Moderate	High		
Operators, fabricators, and laborers	17 142	17 197	17 898	18 764	0	4	9	757	5 626
Machine setters, set-up operators, operators, and tenders	4 779	4 304	4 505	4 749	-10	-6	-1	-274	1 353
Numerical control machine tool operators and tenders, metal and plastic ..	75	90	94	103	20	26	38	20	34
Combination machine tool setters, set-up operators, operators, and tenders	106	116	123	133	10	16	26	17	38
Machine tool cut and form setters, operators, and tenders, metal and plastic	709	563	593	638	-21	-16	-10	-116	175
Drilling and boring machine tool setters and set-up operators, metal and plastic	45	28	30	32	-38	-35	-30	-16	9
Grinding machine setters and set-up operators, metal and plastic	64	50	52	56	-22	-18	-12	-12	13
Lathe, turning machine tool setters and set-up operators, metal and plastic	71	47	50	54	-34	-31	-25	-22	14
Machine forming operators and tenders, metal and plastic	171	144	151	161	-15	-11	-6	-19	58
Machine tool cutting operators and tenders, metal and plastic	119	80	85	92	-33	-29	-23	-34	23
Punching machine setters and set-up operators, metal and plastic	48	35	37	41	-25	-21	-15	-10	12
All other machine tool cutting and forming, etc.	191	178	188	202	-6	-1	6	-2	46
Metal fabricating machine setters, operators, and related workers	157	130	138	150	-17	-12	-5	-19	39
Metal fabricators, structural metal products	44	41	43	47	-8	-3	5	-1	9
Soldering and brazing machine operators and tenders	10	8	8	9	-21	-17	-10	-2	3
Welding machine setters, operators, and tenders	103	82	87	94	-20	-16	-8	-16	28
Metal and plastic processing machine setters, operators, and related workers ..	425	420	444	477	-1	4	12	19	152
Electrolytic plating machine operators and tenders, setters and set-up operators, metal and plastic	42	43	45	48	1	6	14	2	14
Foundry mold assembly and shakeout workers	10	8	8	9	-27	-23	-18	-2	4
Furnace operators and tenders	20	18	19	20	-13	-8	-3	-2	4
Heat treating machine operators and tenders, metal and plastic	20	17	17	19	-15	-12	-6	-2	5
Metal molding machine operators and tenders, setters and set-up operators	40	38	40	44	-5	0	9	0	14
Plastic molding machine operators and tenders, setters and set-up operators	165	167	177	190	1	7	15	12	68
All other metal and plastic machine setters, operators, and related workers	127	130	137	148	2	8	16	10	44
Printing, binding, and related workers	384	373	387	401	-3	1	4	3	108
Bindery machine operators and set-up operators	72	75	77	79	3	7	10	5	18
Prepress printing workers, production	25	9	9	9	-65	-64	-63	-16	5
Photoengraving and lithographic machine operators and tenders	5	3	3	3	-34	-32	-30	-2	1
Typesetting and composing machine operators and tenders	20	6	6	6	-72	-71	-70	-14	4
Printing press operators	218	215	223	230	-1	2	6	5	62
Letterpress operators	14	4	4	4	-72	-71	-71	-10	3
Offset lithographic press operators	79	82	84	87	3	7	10	5	22
Printing press machine setters, operators, and tenders	113	115	119	124	2	6	10	6	31
All other printing press setters and set-up operators	13	15	16	16	22	24	27	3	6
Screen printing machine setters and set-up operators	26	29	30	32	9	16	22	4	10
All other printing, binding, and related workers	43	46	48	50	5	10	15	5	13
Textile and related setters, operators, and related workers	1 018	778	829	878	-24	-19	-14	-188	222
Extruding and forming machine operators and tenders, synthetic or glass fibers	22	27	28	29	23	28	32	6	11
Pressing machine operators and tenders, textile, garment, and related materials	77	74	76	78	-5	-1	1	-1	19
Sewing machine operators, garment	531	367	391	412	-31	-26	-22	-140	106
Sewing machine operators, non-garment	129	111	117	127	-14	-9	-2	-12	26
Textile bleaching and dyeing machine operators and tenders	30	34	37	39	13	24	32	7	14
Textile draw-out and winding machine operators and tenders	190	132	143	153	-31	-25	-20	-47	38
Textile machine setters and set-up operators	39	33	36	39	-14	-6	0	-2	8
Woodworking machine setters, operators, and other related workers	126	92	97	105	-27	-23	-17	-29	32
Head sawyers and sawing machine operators and tenders, setters, and set-up operators	62	45	47	51	-28	-24	-18	-15	16
Woodworking machine operators and tenders, setters and set-up operators	64	48	50	54	-26	-22	-15	-14	16
Other machine setters, set-up operators, operators, and tenders	1 779	1 741	1 799	1 865	-2	1	5	20	554
Boiler operators and tenders, low pressure	18	12	12	13	-35	-32	-29	-6	4
Cement and gluing machine operators and tenders	36	24	25	27	-34	-30	-25	-11	9
Chemical equipment controllers, operators, and tenders	75	65	67	68	-13	-11	-9	-8	28
Cooking and roasting machine operators and tenders, food and tobacco ...	28	30	30	30	8	8	7	2	9
Crushing and mixing machine operators and tenders	137	131	136	141	-4	-1	3	-1	36
Cutting and slicing machine setters, operators, and tenders	92	99	103	108	7	12	17	11	29
Dairy processing equipment operators, including setters	14	14	14	14	-2	-1	-1	0	5
Electronic semiconductor processors	33	32	34	38	-2	4	16	1	10
Extruding and forming machine operators, operators, and tenders	102	91	95	99	-11	-8	-3	-8	27
Furnace, kiln, or kettle operators and tenders	28	23	24	25	-17	-13	-8	-4	5
Laundry and drycleaning machine operators and tenders, except pressing	175	195	198	203	11	13	15	23	68
Motion picture projectionists	8	4	4	4	-46	-47	-48	-4	2
Packaging and filling machine operators and tenders	329	351	359	367	7	9	12	30	119
Painting and coating machine operators	155	151	159	169	-3	2	9	3	47
Coating, painting, and spraying machine operators, tenders, setters, and set-up operators	111	104	110	119	-6	-1	7	-1	31
Painters, transportation equipment	45	47	49	50	5	9	13	4	16
Paper goods machine setters and set-up operators	51	40	42	44	-20	-16	-14	-8	13
Photographic processing machine operators and tenders	43	49	49	50	13	15	16	6	17
Separating and still machine operators and tenders	20	19	19	19	-8	-6	-4	-1	8
Shoe sewing machine operators and tenders	14	4	5	7	-71	-64	-54	-9	2
Tire building machine operators	14	13	13	14	-9	-6	-2	-1	4
All other machine operators, tenders, setters, and set-up operators	407	395	409	427	-3	1	5	2	111
Hand workers, including assemblers and fabricators	2 605	2 557	2 665	2 819	-2	2	8	60	784
Cannery workers	73	81	82	83	10	12	13	9	29
Coil winders, tapers, and finishers	21	15	15	16	-28	-26	-21	-5	5
Cutters and trimmers, hand	51	44	47	50	-13	-8	0	-4	14
Electrical and electronic assemblers	212	173	182	197	-18	-14	-7	-30	52
Grinders and polishers, hand	74	66	70	75	-11	-6	1	-4	21
Machine assemblers	51	52	55	60	3	8	17	4	17
Meat, poultry, and fish cutters and trimmers, hand	132	168	168	168	27	28	27	36	74
Painting, coating, and decorating workers, hand	33	35	36	38	6	10	15	3	13
Pressers, hand	16	15	15	16	-8	-4	-2	-1	5
Sewers, hand	19	16	17	18	-14	-9	-5	-2	2
Solderers and brazers	27	30	31	33	13	17	23	5	12
Welders and cutters	314	303	316	335	-3	1	7	3	88
All other assemblers, fabricators, and hand workers	1 583	1 558	1 630	1 731	-2	3	9	46	453

1. Based on moderate path. Total job openings represent the sum of employment increases and net replacement. If employment change is negative, job openings due to growth are zero and total job openings equal net replacements.

Number Employed and Projected Employment by Detailed Occupation, 1994 and 2005—Continued

(Numbers in thousands; percent)

| Occupation | 1994 | 2005 | | | 1994-2005 change | | | | Total job openings due to growth and net replacement [1] |
| | | Low | Moderate | High | Percent | | | Number, moderate | |
					Low	Moderate	High		
Transportation and material moving machine and vehicle operators	4 959	5 259	5 459	5 694	6	10	15	500	1 434
Motor vehicle operators	3 620	3 906	4 045	4 200	8	12	16	425	1 066
Bus drivers	568	623	663	704	10	17	24	95	193
Bus drivers, except school	165	184	193	201	12	17	22	29	57
Bus drivers, school	404	439	470	503	9	16	25	66	136
Taxi drivers and chauffeurs	129	156	157	159	20	22	23	28	43
Truck drivers	2 897	3 099	3 196	3 307	7	10	14	299	823
Driver/sales workers	331	355	359	364	7	8	10	28	122
Truck drivers light and heavy	2 565	2 744	2 837	2 944	7	11	15	271	701
All other motor vehicle operators	26	28	29	29	9	11	13	3	8
Rail transportation workers	86	70	75	81	-18	-12	-6	-10	15
Locomotive engineers	22	18	19	20	-20	-14	-8	-3	3
Railroad brake, signal, and switch operators	19	12	13	14	-36	-31	-26	-6	3
Railroad conductors and yardmasters	26	23	25	26	-13	-6	0	-2	4
Rail yard engineers, dinkey operators, and hostlers	6	3	4	4	-44	-40	-37	-2	1
Subway and streetcar operators	12	14	15	17	13	23	34	3	5
Water transportation and related workers	48	46	48	51	-4	0	6	0	10
Able seamen, ordinary seamen, and marine oilers	20	19	20	21	-7	-3	3	-1	4
Captains and pilots, ship	13	12	13	13	-4	0	6	0	3
Mates, ship, boat, and barge	7	7	8	8	1	6	12	0	2
Ship engineers	8	8	8	8	-1	3	9	0	2
Material moving equipment operators	1 061	1 084	1 129	1 193	2	6	12	69	298
Crane and tower operators	45	40	42	45	-10	-6	0	-3	11
Excavation and loading machine operators	88	95	100	107	8	13	21	11	31
Grader, dozer, and scraper operators	108	107	113	122	0	5	14	6	27
Hoist and winch operators	9	8	9	9	-9	-5	2	0	2
Industrial truck and tractor operators	464	474	493	515	2	6	11	29	132
Operating engineers	146	145	154	165	-1	5	13	7	37
All other material moving equipment operators	201	214	219	229	7	9	14	18	59
All other transportation and material moving equipment operators	145	154	161	170	6	11	17	16	44
Helpers, laborers, and material movers, hand	4 799	5 078	5 270	5 502	6	10	15	471	2 056
Freight, stock, and material movers, hand	765	707	728	754	-8	-5	-1	-36	306
Hand packers and packagers	942	1 070	1 102	1 137	14	17	21	160	429
Helpers, construction trades	513	549	581	630	7	13	23	68	240
Machine feeders and offbearers	262	232	242	253	-11	-8	-3	-20	80
Parking lot attendants	64	75	76	77	18	20	21	13	25
Refuse collectors	111	107	115	123	-3	4	12	4	31
Service station attendants	167	143	148	151	-15	-12	-10	-20	67
Vehicle washers and equipment cleaners	249	290	299	306	16	20	23	50	133
All other helpers, laborers, and material movers, hand	1 727	1 905	1 980	2 070	10	15	20	253	744

1. Based on moderate path. Total job openings represent the sum of employment increases and net replacement. If employment change is negative, job openings due to growth are zero and total job openings equal net replacements.

Part Four

Productivity and Related Costs

Productivity and Related Costs

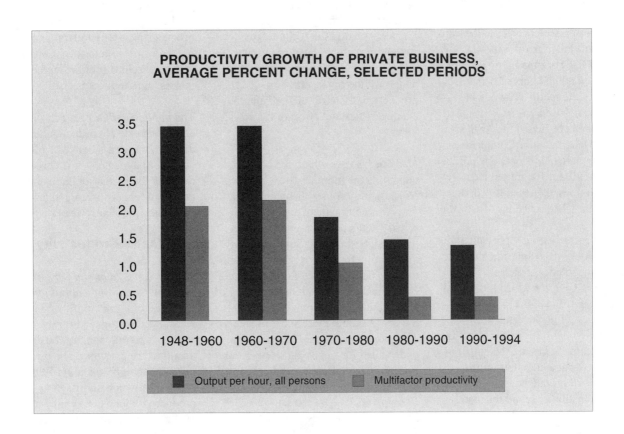

PRODUCTIVITY GROWTH OF PRIVATE BUSINESS,
AVERAGE PERCENT CHANGE, SELECTED PERIODS

The relatively high productivity increase of the post-World War II period that this bar chart displays, has not been achieved since 1970. Multifactor productivity, which includes capital input, is always lower than the measure of output per man hour. However, both measures follow the same trend. While manufacturing productivity has shown recent substantial gains, the influence of that sector on total private business productivity has declined. Measurement problems in the service sectors of the economy are among the factors believed to account for the slower growth in total productivity.

NOTES
Productivity and Related Costs

Output per Hour—Business and Manufacturing

The *measures of output per hour* for the business, nonfarm business, and manufacturing sectors refer to the ratio of constant-dollar gross domestic product (GDP) originating in a sector to the corresponding hours of persons engaged in the sector. The output measures are based on series prepared by the Bureau of Economic Analysis of the U.S. Department of Commerce as part of the national income and product accounts (NIPA). The output measures have been revised to accord with the most recent NIPA revisions of the GDP.

Business sector output represents about 76 percent of gross domestic product (GDP). It excludes some activities included in GDP for which theoretical or practical difficulties make the computation of meaningful productivity measures impossible. The omitted output series are the output of general government, output of paid employees of private households and nonprofit institutions, and the rental value of owner-occupied dwellings. Conforming adjustments are also made to the labor input measures. The nonfarm business sector accounts for about 75 percent of the GDP. The manufacturing output measures are derived directly from Census Bureau data by the BLS. All of these output measures are chain-type annual-weighted indexes. That means that the relative prices (weights) used to combine output changes into an aggregate output measure are changed each year, minimizing the bias that arises from using fixed weights over long periods of time.

The *productivity measures* show the changes from period to period in the amount of goods and services produced per hour. Although these measures relate output to hours of persons engaged in a sector, they do not measure only the specific contributions of labor, capital, or any other factor of production. Rather, they reflect the joint effects of many influences, including changes in technology; capital investment; level of output; utilization of capacity, energy, and materials; the organization of production; managerial skill; and the characteristics and effort of the work force.

Measures of labor input are based mainly on the monthly BLS Survey of Nonagricultural Establishments which measures employment and average weekly hours paid for employees of these establishments. Supplementary information for farm workers, the self-employed, and unpaid family workers is obtained from the monthly Survey of Households, the Current Population Survey. Without these supplementary data, labor input would be seriously understated for family farms, in retail trade, and for self-employed individuals in all occupations.

The *indexes of hourly compensation and unit labor costs in the business sectors* are developed from hours measured based mainly on the establishment series and employee compensation data from the NIPA.

Compensation includes wages and salaries and supplemental payments such as contributions by employers to Social Security and private health and pension funds. The all persons' compensation data include measures of proprietors' salaries and contributions for supplementary benefits. Real compensation per hour is derived by adjusting the compensation data by the Consumer Price Index for All Urban Consumers to reflect changes in purchasing power.

The *indexes of unit labor costs* are computed by dividing compensation per hour by output per hour. *Nonlabor payments* are calculated by subtracting total compensation from gross domestic product (in current dollars) originating in the business sector of the economy, and thus include profits, depreciation, interest, and indirect taxes.

The *implicit deflator* reflects changes in all of the costs of production and distribution (unit labor costs plus unit nonlabor payments). It is derived by dividing the current-dollar measure of gross product originating in a sector by the constant-dollar series.

Multifactor Productivity

The *measures of output per unit of combined labor and capital input* (multifactor productivity) and related measures are produced for the private business, private nonfarm business, and manufacturing sectors. The *private business* and *private nonfarm business* sectors for which multifactor productivity indexes are prepared exclude government enterprises, and thus differ from the business and nonfarm business sectors described above. The manufacturing sector coverage is the same in the multifactor and labor productivity series.

Multifactor productivity measures refer to the ratio of an output to an index of combined labor and capital services inputs. *Multifactor productivity growth* reflects the amount of output growth which cannot be accounted for by the growth of weighted labor and capital inputs as they have been measured. The weights are associated cost shares: *labor's* share is the ratio of compensation to current-dollar output; *capital's* share is equal to the ratio of capital cost to current-dollar output. As is the case with the output measures, the weights are updated annually.

Capital services measure the services derived from the stock of physical assets. The assets included are fixed business equipment, structures, inventories, and land. Structures include nonresidential structures and residential capital which is rented out by profit-making firms or persons. Financial assets are excluded as are owner-occupied residential structures. The aggregate capital measures are obtained by weighting the capital stocks for each asset type within each of 53 industries using estimated rental prices for each asset type. Data on investments in physical assets and gross product originating by industry, used in measuring the rental prices, are obtained from the Bureau of Economic Analysis (BEA).

Labor input in private business and private nonfarm business is obtained by weighting the hours worked by all persons, classified by education, work experience, and gender, by their shares of labor compensation. Additional information concerning data sources and methods of measuring labor composition can be found in *BLS Bulletin 2426* (December 1993), *Labor Composition and U.S. Productivity Growth, 1948-1990.*

The *manufacturing multifactor productivity index* is derived by dividing an output index by a weighted index of combined hours, capital services, energy, materials, and purchased business services. Weights (shares of total costs) are updated annually. The labor hours for the manufacturing measure are directly added and thus do not include the effect of changing labor composition, unlike those used for business multifactor productivity.

Output per Hour in Selected Industries

The BLS industry productivity data supplement the measures for the business economy and major sectors with annual measures of labor productivity for selected industries. The

industry measures differ in methodology and data sources from the productivity measures for the major sectors.

Data on *output-per-employee-hour in selected industries* contain indexes of output, employee hours, and output per employee hour for selected U.S. manufacturing and nonmanufacturing industries. The industries included are not necessarily a representative cross-section of U.S. industry, and their output-per-employee-hour indexes therefore should not be combined to obtain an overall measure for the entire economy or any other sector. These data series are annually extended and published in the *BLS Bulletin, Productivity Measures for Selected Industries and Government Services,* which contains more complete historical data for the industries.

An *output index* for an industry is calculated with a formula that aggregates the growth rates of the various industry products between two periods with weights based on the products' shares in industry value of production (the weight for each product equals its average value share in the two periods). When quantity of production data are not available, values of production, adjusted to eliminate the effects of price change, are substituted. For most industries, output indexes are developed in two stages. First, comprehensive data from the economic censuses that are conducted by the Bureau of the Census every five years are used to develop benchmark indexes for the census years. Second, less comprehensive data are used to prepare annual indexes. The latter indexes are adjusted to the benchmark indexes by means of linear interpolation. For the period following the last census year, annual indexes are linked to the most recent benchmark index.

Indexes of employee hours are computed by dividing the aggregate employee hours for each year by the base period aggregate. Employee hours

are treated as homogeneous and additive. Some of the employee hour indexes are based on hours paid and some on plant hours.

Output per employee hour indexes are obtained by dividing an output index by an index of aggregate employee hours.

Although the measures relate output to one input—labor time—they do not measure the specific contribution of labor or any other factor of production. Rather, they reflect the joint effect of a number of interrelated influences, such as changes in technology, capital investment per worker, and capacity utilization. Industry output-per-employee measures are limited to the extent that they do not account adequately for quality changes, and often do not adequately reflect changes in the degree of vertical integration in industry. In addition, there is not always strict comparability between output and labor input estimates. Finally, year to year changes in output-per-employee-hour are irregular and, therefore, not necessarily indicative of basic changes in long-term trends. Conversely, long-term trends are not necessarily applicable to any one year or period in the future.

180 PRODUCTIVITY AND RELATED COSTS

Indexes of Productivity and Related Data, 1949-1995

(1992=100)

Year	Output per hour, all persons			Hourly compensation			Real hourly compensation			Output per person		
	Business	Nonfarm business	Manufac- turing	Business	Nonfarm business	Manufac- turing	Business	Nonfarm business	Manufac- turing	Business	Nonfarm business	Manufac- turing
1949	....	....	33.5	....	....	8.3	....	....	48.8	....	....	33.2
1950	....	....	34.1	....	....	8.7	....	....	50.6	....	....	34.6
1951	....	....	33.8	....	....	9.6	....	....	51.7	....	....	34.4
1952	....	....	35.0	....	....	10.2	....	....	54.0	....	....	35.7
1953	....	....	36.1	....	....	10.8	....	....	56.6	....	....	36.7
1954	....	....	37.0	....	....	11.3	....	....	58.7	....	....	36.9
1955	....	....	38.7	....	....	11.7	....	....	61.2	....	....	39.3
1956	....	....	38.4	....	....	12.4	....	....	64.2	....	....	38.9
1957	....	....	39.2	....	....	13.2	....	....	65.8	....	....	39.2
1958	....	....	39.8	....	....	13.8	....	....	67.0	....	....	39.3
1959	49.8	54.1	40.5	12.9	13.7	14.3	62.1	65.8	69.0	57.3	61.6	40.8
1960	50.5	54.7	41.2	13.4	14.3	14.9	63.7	67.6	70.6	57.9	62.0	41.1
1961	52.2	56.4	42.5	14.0	14.7	15.3	65.5	69.2	72.0	59.6	63.7	42.5
1962	54.8	59.0	43.6	14.6	15.3	15.9	67.9	71.3	74.0	62.6	66.8	44.0
1963	56.9	61.0	45.4	15.2	15.9	16.4	69.6	72.9	75.2	65.0	69.0	45.9
1964	59.6	63.7	47.4	16.0	16.6	17.1	72.3	75.3	77.4	67.9	72.0	48.2
1965	61.8	65.7	48.4	16.6	17.2	17.5	73.9	76.5	77.8	70.6	74.4	49.7
1966	64.4	68.0	49.0	17.7	18.2	18.2	76.8	78.7	79.0	73.1	76.7	50.5
1967	65.9	69.2	50.9	18.7	19.2	19.2	78.7	80.8	80.8	73.5	76.7	51.6
1968	68.2	71.6	52.7	20.3	20.8	20.7	81.7	83.7	83.5	75.6	78.9	53.3
1969	68.7	71.7	53.4	21.7	22.2	22.2	83.1	84.8	85.0	75.5	78.4	53.6
1970	69.8	72.6	55.0	23.4	23.8	23.8	84.6	86.0	86.1	75.5	78.2	54.1
1971	72.7	75.6	58.6	24.9	25.3	25.3	86.2	87.7	87.5	78.4	81.0	57.7
1972	75.2	78.2	60.7	26.5	27.0	26.6	88.9	90.5	89.2	81.0	83.8	60.8
1973	77.6	80.7	62.5	28.8	29.2	28.6	90.9	92.2	90.5	83.2	86.1	62.5
1974	76.6	79.4	63.2	31.6	32.1	31.8	89.9	91.2	90.5	80.9	83.5	62.1
1975	79.0	81.5	65.1	34.8	35.3	35.7	90.7	92.1	93.0	82.4	84.6	62.9
1976	82.2	84.5	67.8	38.0	38.4	38.6	93.6	94.6	95.3	85.6	87.7	66.3
1977	83.8	85.8	70.2	41.0	41.4	42.0	95.0	95.9	97.2	87.1	88.7	68.9
1978	84.5	87.0	71.1	44.7	45.2	45.4	96.3	97.3	97.6	87.3	89.5	69.8
1979	84.3	86.4	70.7	49.1	49.5	49.8	94.9	95.7	96.3	86.7	88.4	69.0
1980	84.1	86.0	71.2	54.4	54.8	55.8	92.7	93.4	94.9	85.5	87.1	68.6
1981	85.8	87.0	72.1	59.6	60.2	61.3	92.0	92.9	94.6	86.9	87.8	69.5
1982	85.2	86.3	75.5	64.1	64.6	67.2	93.1	93.9	97.7	85.7	86.4	71.4
1983	88.0	89.9	78.4	66.7	67.3	69.0	93.9	94.9	97.3	89.1	90.8	76.2
1984	90.2	91.5	80.7	69.6	70.2	71.4	94.0	94.8	96.4	91.9	93.0	79.6
1985	91.9	92.4	83.7	73.1	73.5	75.3	95.3	95.8	98.1	93.2	93.6	82.6
1986	94.2	94.9	87.5	76.9	77.3	78.6	98.4	98.9	100.6	94.6	95.2	86.3
1987	94.1	94.7	89.8	79.9	80.2	80.9	98.6	99.0	99.9	94.8	95.3	89.1
1988	94.6	95.3	91.0	83.5	83.6	84.0	99.0	99.2	99.6	95.5	96.1	91.2
1989	95.4	95.8	92.5	85.8	85.8	86.7	97.1	97.1	98.1	96.6	97.0	92.7
1990	96.2	96.3	94.2	90.8	90.6	90.9	97.4	97.3	97.6	96.7	96.8	93.7
1991	96.7	96.9	96.5	95.1	95.1	95.7	97.9	97.9	98.6	96.4	96.6	95.4
1992	100.0	100.0	100.0	100.0	100.0	100.0	100.0	100.0	100.0	100.0	100.0	100.0
1993	100.2	100.2	102.1	102.6	102.3	102.4	99.6	99.3	99.4	100.6	100.7	103.4
1994	101.0	100.7	106.3	104.8	104.5	105.3	99.2	98.9	99.7	101.8	101.7	108.8
1995	101.9	101.8	110.3	108.5	108.2	108.5	99.9	99.6	99.9	102.2	102.3	112.1

Indexes of Productivity and Related Data, 1949-1995—Continued

(1992=100)

Year	Deflators and costs								
	Business			Nonfarm business			Manufacturing		
	Implict price deflator	Unit labor cost	Unit nonlabor payments	Implict price deflator	Unit labor cost	Unit nonlabor payments	Implict price deflator	Unit labor cost	Unit nonlabor payments
1949	....	....	....	....	....	....	24.3	24.7	24.1
1950	....	....	....	....	....	....	24.9	25.5	24.5
1951	....	....	....	....	....	....	27.2	28.4	26.4
1952	....	....	....	....	....	....	27.1	29.1	25.9
1953	....	....	....	....	....	....	27.1	29.8	25.3
1954	....	....	....	....	....	....	27.5	30.4	25.6
1955	....	....	....	....	....	....	27.7	30.2	26.0
1956	....	....	....	....	....	....	28.7	32.4	26.3
1957	....	....	....	....	....	....	29.8	33.6	27.3
1958	....	....	....	....	....	....	30.5	34.7	27.9
1959	25.5	25.9	24.9	25.0	25.3	24.6	30.5	35.3	27.4
1960	25.8	26.6	24.5	25.3	26.1	23.9	30.4	36.2	26.8
1961	26.1	26.7	25.0	25.5	26.2	24.4	30.5	36.1	27.0
1962	26.4	26.7	25.7	25.8	26.0	25.3	30.5	36.5	26.7
1963	26.5	26.7	26.3	26.0	26.1	25.8	30.5	36.1	26.9
1964	26.8	26.8	26.9	26.3	26.1	26.6	30.5	36.1	27.0
1965	27.3	26.8	28.1	26.7	26.2	27.7	30.9	36.1	27.6
1966	28.0	27.5	28.8	27.3	26.7	28.3	31.8	37.3	28.3
1967	28.8	28.4	29.4	28.2	27.8	28.9	32.2	37.8	28.7
1968	29.9	29.7	30.2	29.3	29.0	29.9	33.1	39.3	29.1
1969	31.1	31.7	30.2	30.5	30.9	29.7	34.2	41.6	29.5
1970	32.6	33.5	30.8	31.9	32.7	30.3	35.4	43.3	30.4
1971	34.0	34.2	33.6	33.3	33.5	33.0	36.7	43.1	32.5
1972	35.2	35.2	35.1	34.3	34.5	34.0	37.9	43.8	34.1
1973	37.0	37.1	36.9	35.5	36.1	34.4	40.7	45.8	37.5
1974	40.4	41.2	38.7	39.1	40.4	36.7	47.7	50.3	46.0
1975	44.3	44.1	44.7	43.2	43.3	43.0	53.4	54.8	52.5
1976	46.6	46.2	47.2	45.6	45.4	46.2	55.6	57.0	54.7
1977	49.3	48.9	49.9	48.6	48.3	49.2	59.0	59.8	58.5
1978	53.1	53.0	53.4	51.9	52.0	51.9	63.0	63.8	62.4
1979	57.7	58.3	56.6	56.4	57.3	54.8	69.9	70.5	69.6
1980	62.9	64.7	59.5	61.9	63.8	58.5	79.5	78.3	80.3
1981	68.6	69.5	67.0	67.9	69.1	65.6	86.4	85.0	87.4
1982	72.6	75.2	67.9	72.2	74.9	67.2	89.0	89.0	89.0
1983	75.3	75.7	74.4	74.7	74.9	74.2	89.6	88.1	90.5
1984	77.7	77.2	78.6	77.0	76.8	77.5	91.3	88.5	93.0
1985	79.9	79.5	80.4	79.7	79.5	80.0	90.6	89.9	90.9
1986	81.6	81.6	81.7	81.4	81.4	81.3	87.8	89.9	86.4
1987	83.8	84.9	81.9	83.5	84.7	81.4	89.6	90.0	89.4
1988	86.8	88.2	84.2	86.4	87.8	83.8	92.0	92.3	91.8
1989	90.5	89.9	91.4	90.0	89.6	90.8	95.7	93.7	97.0
1990	94.0	94.3	93.5	93.8	94.1	93.2	99.0	96.5	100.6
1991	97.7	98.3	96.5	97.6	98.1	96.7	99.6	99.1	99.9
1992	100.0	100.0	100.0	100.0	100.0	100.0	100.0	100.0	100.0
1993	102.5	102.4	102.8	102.5	102.1	103.4	100.8	100.3	101.1
1994	104.8	103.8	106.5	104.9	103.8	106.9	....	99.0	....
1995	107.1	106.5	108.2	107.2	106.3	108.7	....	98.4	....

PRODUCTIVITY AND RELATED COSTS

Indexes of Productivity and Related Data, 1949-1995—Continued

(1992=100)

Year	Output in 1992 dollars			Hours			Employment			Compensation in current dollars			Nonlabor payments in current dollars		
	Business	Nonfarm business	Manu-facturing	Business	Nonfarm business	Manu-facturing	Business	Nonfarm business	Manu-facturing	Business	Nonfarm business	Manu-facturing	Business	Nonfarm business	Manu-facturing
1949	....	....	26.6	....	....	79.3	....	....	80.1	....	....	6.6	....	....	6.4
1950	....	....	29.2	....	....	85.7	....	....	84.4	....	....	7.5	....	....	7.2
1951	....	....	31.2	....	....	92.3	....	....	90.6	....	....	8.8	....	....	8.2
1952	....	....	32.8	....	....	93.5	....	....	91.9	....	....	9.5	....	....	8.5
1953	....	....	35.5	....	....	98.3	....	....	96.8	....	....	10.6	....	....	9.0
1954	....	....	33.2	....	....	89.9	....	....	90.1	....	....	10.1	....	....	8.5
1955	....	....	36.6	....	....	94.8	....	....	93.1	....	....	11.1	....	....	9.5
1956	....	....	37.0	....	....	96.2	....	....	95.1	....	....	12.0	....	....	9.7
1957	....	....	37.1	....	....	94.7	....	....	94.7	....	....	12.5	....	....	10.1
1958	....	....	34.5	....	....	86.8	....	....	88.0	....	....	12.0	....	....	9.6
1959	33.8	33.5	37.5	67.8	61.9	92.6	58.9	54.3	91.9	8.7	8.5	13.3	8.4	8.2	10.3
1960	34.3	34.0	38.0	67.9	62.3	92.3	59.2	54.9	92.6	9.1	8.9	13.8	8.4	8.1	10.2
1961	34.9	34.7	38.2	66.8	61.5	89.9	58.6	54.5	90.0	9.3	9.1	13.8	8.7	8.5	10.3
1962	37.1	37.1	40.9	67.8	62.8	93.6	59.3	55.5	92.9	9.9	9.6	14.9	9.6	9.4	10.9
1963	38.8	38.7	43.0	68.2	63.5	94.5	59.7	56.1	93.5	10.3	10.1	15.5	10.2	10.0	11.6
1964	41.3	41.4	45.7	69.2	65.0	96.5	60.8	57.4	94.9	11.1	10.8	16.5	11.1	11.0	12.4
1965	44.2	44.3	49.4	71.4	67.4	102.1	62.6	59.5	99.3	11.8	11.6	17.8	12.4	12.2	13.6
1966	47.1	47.4	53.3	73.1	69.7	108.8	64.5	61.8	105.4	13.0	12.7	19.8	13.6	13.4	15.1
1967	48.0	48.2	55.1	72.9	69.7	108.1	65.3	62.9	106.7	13.7	13.4	20.8	14.1	14.0	15.8
1968	50.4	50.8	57.8	73.9	70.9	109.7	66.7	64.4	108.5	15.0	14.7	22.7	15.2	15.2	16.8
1969	52.0	52.3	59.3	75.7	72.9	111.0	68.8	66.7	110.6	16.5	16.2	24.7	15.7	15.5	17.5
1970	51.8	52.2	57.5	74.3	71.8	104.5	68.6	66.7	106.3	17.4	17.1	24.9	16.0	15.8	17.5
1971	53.8	54.1	59.0	74.0	71.6	100.7	68.6	66.8	102.2	18.4	18.1	25.4	18.1	17.9	19.2
1972	57.4	57.9	63.9	76.3	74.0	105.2	70.8	69.0	105.0	20.2	19.9	28.0	20.1	19.7	21.8
1973	61.3	62.1	69.1	79.0	76.9	110.5	73.8	72.1	110.5	22.7	22.4	31.7	22.6	21.3	25.9
1974	60.6	61.1	68.4	79.1	77.0	108.1	74.9	73.2	110.1	25.0	24.7	34.4	23.5	22.4	31.5
1975	59.9	60.1	63.4	75.8	73.7	97.4	72.6	71.0	100.7	26.4	26.0	34.7	26.8	25.9	33.3
1976	64.0	64.3	69.1	77.9	76.1	101.9	74.8	73.4	104.3	29.6	29.2	39.4	30.3	29.7	37.8
1977	67.8	68.0	74.5	80.9	79.2	106.2	77.9	76.6	108.2	33.2	32.8	44.6	33.9	33.4	43.6
1978	71.6	72.3	78.7	84.8	83.2	110.6	82.0	80.8	112.7	37.9	37.6	50.2	38.3	37.5	49.1
1979	73.8	74.3	79.7	87.5	86.1	112.8	85.1	84.1	115.6	43.0	42.6	56.2	41.8	40.7	55.5
1980	72.9	73.5	76.6	86.8	85.4	107.6	85.3	84.4	111.6	47.2	46.8	60.0	43.4	43.0	61.5
1981	74.9	74.8	77.2	87.3	86.0	107.0	86.2	85.2	111.0	52.0	51.7	65.6	50.2	49.1	67.4
1982	72.6	72.4	74.0	85.2	83.9	98.0	84.7	83.8	103.5	54.6	54.2	65.9	49.3	48.6	65.8
1983	76.2	76.8	77.6	86.6	85.4	99.0	85.5	84.6	101.8	57.7	57.5	68.4	56.7	57.0	70.2
1984	82.5	82.8	85.0	91.5	90.5	105.4	89.8	89.1	106.8	63.7	63.6	75.3	64.8	64.2	79.1
1985	85.9	85.8	87.6	93.4	92.8	104.6	92.1	91.6	106.0	68.3	68.2	78.8	69.1	68.6	79.6
1986	88.6	88.7	90.2	94.0	93.5	103.1	93.6	93.2	104.5	72.3	72.3	81.1	72.4	72.2	77.9
1987	91.1	91.4	93.3	96.8	96.5	103.8	96.1	95.8	104.7	77.3	77.4	84.0	74.6	74.3	83.4
1988	94.6	95.1	97.2	100.0	99.8	106.8	99.1	98.9	106.6	83.4	83.5	89.7	79.6	79.7	89.2
1989	97.8	98.1	99.2	102.5	102.4	107.2	101.2	101.2	107.0	87.9	87.9	93.0	89.4	89.1	96.2
1990	98.7	98.8	98.8	102.6	102.7	104.9	102.0	102.1	105.5	93.1	93.0	95.4	92.2	92.1	99.4
1991	96.9	97.1	97.1	100.3	100.2	100.6	100.5	100.5	101.8	95.3	95.3	96.2	93.5	93.8	97.0
1992	100.0	100.0	100.0	100.0	100.0	100.0	100.0	100.0	100.0	100.0	100.0	100.0	100.0	100.0	100.0
1993	102.6	102.9	103.5	102.4	102.7	101.4	102.0	102.2	100.1	105.1	105.0	103.8	105.5	106.4	104.7
1994	106.9	106.9	110.2	105.9	106.2	103.6	105.0	105.1	101.2	111.0	111.0	109.1	113.8	114.4	....
1995	109.6	109.8	114.1	107.6	107.9	103.5	107.2	107.3	101.8	116.7	116.7	112.3	118.5	119.3	....

Annual Indexes of Multifactor Productivity and Related Measures, Selected Years, 1948-1994

(1987=100)

Item	1948	1950	1960	1970	1975	1980	1981	1982	1983	1984
PRIVATE BUSINESS										
Productivity										
Output per hour of all persons	35.9	40.5	53.5	74.8	84.4	89.1	90.9	90.5	93.1	95.6
Output per unit of capital services	116.5	119.8	115.9	115.1	107.1	105.8	103.3	96.3	97.9	102.2
Multifactor productivity	55.6	60.5	70.5	87.2	92.8	96.0	96.3	93.3	95.3	98.3
Output	25.6	28.1	37.8	57.4	66.0	79.9	82.1	79.6	83.3	90.4
Inputs										
Hours of all persons	64.1	63.0	66.7	74.2	75.7	86.8	88.0	86.6	88.5	93.7
Capital services	22.0	23.5	32.6	49.9	61.6	75.5	79.5	82.7	85.0	88.5
Combined units of labor and capital inputs	46.0	46.5	53.6	65.8	71.1	83.2	85.3	85.3	87.4	92.0
Capital per hour of all persons	30.8	33.9	46.2	65.0	78.8	84.2	88.0	94.0	95.0	93.5
PRIVATE NONFARM BUSINESS										
Productivity										
Output per hour of all persons	41.6	46.3	57.7	77.3	86.4	90.6	91.9	91.4	94.5	96.4
Output per unit of capital services	122.9	126.5	122.6	120.5	110.3	108.2	104.8	97.3	99.5	103.3
Multifactor productivity	61.5	66.5	74.9	89.9	94.9	97.7	97.3	94.1	96.7	99.2
Output	24.7	27.2	37.4	57.4	65.8	80.2	82.0	79.4	83.6	90.6
Inputs										
Hours of all persons	54.2	53.8	61.4	72.0	73.9	85.7	87.0	85.6	87.6	93.0
Capital services	20.1	21.5	30.5	47.7	59.7	74.2	78.2	81.6	84.1	87.7
Combined units of labor and capital inputs	40.2	40.9	49.9	63.9	69.4	82.1	84.3	84.4	86.5	91.3
Capital per hour of all persons	33.8	36.6	47.0	64.1	78.4	83.8	87.7	93.9	95.0	93.4
MANUFACTURING										
Productivity										
Output per hour of all persons	....	37.9	45.9	61.3	72.3	79.1	80.3	84.2	87.2	89.7
Output per unit of capital services	....	136.6	122.7	116.6	105.4	102.5	98.7	91.0	94.1	100.0
Multifactor productivity	....	61.0	67.6	80.1	81.7	86.4	87.6	88.8	91.1	94.0
Output	....	31.3	40.8	61.6	67.9	82.1	82.8	79.3	83.2	91.2
Inputs										
Hours of all persons	....	82.6	88.9	100.6	94.0	103.8	103.0	94.2	95.5	101.7
Capital services	....	22.9	33.2	52.8	64.4	80.1	83.8	87.1	88.4	91.2

Annual Indexes of Multifactor Productivity and Related Measures, Selected Years, 1948-1994—Continued

(1987=100)

Item	1985	1986	1987	1988	1989	1990	1991	1992	1993	1994
PRIVATE BUSINESS										
Productivity										
Output per hour of all persons	97.0	99.6	100.0	100.9	101.0	101.9	102.9	105.9	106.4	107.3
Output per unit of capital services	101.2	99.7	100.0	101.3	101.3	99.8	97.0	98.1	99.1	100.7
Multifactor productivity	98.8	99.8	100.0	100.5	100.2	100.1	99.1	100.5	101.0	101.8
Output	93.7	96.7	100.0	104.3	107.0	107.9	106.5	109.3	112.5	117.4
Inputs										
Hours of all persons	95.8	96.8	100.0	104.2	107.2	107.8	106.5	107.5	110.4	114.8
Capital services	92.6	96.9	100.0	102.9	105.7	108.1	109.8	111.4	113.5	116.6
Combined units of labor and capital inputs	94.8	96.8	100.0	103.8	106.7	107.9	107.5	108.7	111.3	115.4
Capital per hour of all persons	95.9	99.9	100.0	99.6	99.7	102.1	106.1	108.0	107.4	106.6
PRIVATE NONFARM BUSINESS										
Productivity										
Output per hour of all persons	97.2	99.8	100.0	100.9	100.7	101.3	102.5	105.1	105.6	106.4
Output per unit of capital services	101.7	100.0	100.0	101.3	100.8	99.1	96.2	96.9	98.1	99.3
Multifactor productivity	99.1	100.0	100.0	100.5	99.9	99.4	98.5	99.6	100.2	100.7
Output	93.5	96.7	100.0	104.5	107.1	107.8	106.4	108.9	112.4	117.1
Inputs										
Hours of all persons	95.5	96.6	100.0	104.4	107.6	108.3	106.8	108.0	111.2	115.6
Capital services	92.0	96.7	100.0	103.2	106.2	108.8	110.6	112.4	114.7	118
Combined units of labor and capital inputs	94.4	96.7	100.0	104.0	107.2	108.5	107.9	109.3	112.2	116.3
Capital per hour of all persons	95.6	99.9	100.0	99.6	99.9	102.2	106.6	108.5	107.7	107.1
MANUFACTURING										
Productivity										
Output per hour of all persons	93.0	97.2	100.0	101.1	102.8	104.7	107.2	111.1	113.4	....
Output per unit of capital services	99.0	99.0	100.0	101.6	100.6	97.0	93.0	93.5	94.5	....
Multifactor productivity	95.3	97.1	100.0	100.6	100.3	99.8	99.7	102.4	103.5	....
Output	93.9	96.7	100.0	104.2	106.4	105.9	104.1	107.2	111.0	....
Inputs										
Hours of all persons	100.9	99.5	100.0	103.1	103.5	101.2	97.1	96.5	97.8	....
Capital services	94.8	97.6	100.0	102.6	105.8	109.2	111.9	114.6	117.4	....

Annual Indexes of Output per Employee-hour for Selected Industries, 1984-1994

(1987=100)

Industry	SIC	1984	1985	1986	1987	1988	1989	1990	1991	1992	1993	1994
Iron mining, usable ore	101	70.0	76.1	79.3	100.0	103.1	98.4	88.5	85.0	83.3	86.9	82.2
Copper mining, recoverable metal	102	75.9	93.6	109.7	100.0	109.1	106.5	102.7	100.5	115.2	118.1	123.6
Coal mining	12	83.4	85.1	92.4	100.0	110.5	116.4	118.3	122.1	132.7	145.4	150.4
Crude petroleum and natural gas production	131	81.9	83.0	90.3	100.0	100.9	98.0	96.9	97.9	102.1	106.5	113.1
Nonmetallic minerals, except fuels	14	94.0	95.1	95.1	100.0	101.0	99.6	101.4	98.5	102.7	100.2	103.9
Meat packing plants	2011	93.6	98.3	98.7	100.0	100.9	97.9	96.8	100.2	104.5	105.1	101.2
Sausages and other prepared meats	2013	99.3	97.8	98.6	100.0	107.1	105.9	97.4	95.9	104.6	105.0	101.6
Poultry dressing and processing	2015	99.1	100.5	95.6	100.0	96.2	105.2	108.6	115.4	119.6	119.8	119.9
Cheese, natural and processed	2022	85.1	88.2	93.5	100.0	99.8	102.6	108.2	114.6	121.8	115.5	117.5
Fluid milk	2026	88.9	92.0	96.0	100.0	102.3	103.7	103.3	104.3	104.0	107.1	113.3
Canned fruits and vegetables	2033	87.4	92.8	99.1	100.0	98.7	92.9	93.8	100.1	101.5	106.6	101.9
Frozen fruits and vegetables	2037	99.7	95.2	103.3	100.0	94.0	98.0	90.0	94.6	96.4	102.8	109.6
Flour and other grain mill products	2041	91.7	95.8	95.9	100.0	102.5	102.5	107.9	108.3	111.9	122.2	126.8
Cereal breakfast foods	2043	92.8	97.1	98.6	100.0	98.6	95.5	100.2	102.3	99.1	95.5	106.6
Rice milling	2044	63.8	68.6	72.7	100.0	83.1	97.5	104.9	99.3	101.4	129.5	109.2
Wet corn milling	2046	74.9	74.6	97.3	100.0	96.1	103.6	103.8	100.4	101.8	111.9	110.0
Prepared feeds for animals and fowls	2047,48	89.2	96.9	95.2	100.0	101.5	103.7	107.0	108.0	108.1	110.7	108.5
Bakery products	205	93.4	95.6	100.1	100.0	93.4	91.0	93.2	89.2	89.4	90.3	91.0
Raw and refined cane sugar	2061,62	89.1	96.6	96.9	100.0	99.7	101.8	107.7	110.3	111.7	120.2	111.8
Beet sugar	2063	79.7	73.4	80.8	100.0	97.6	92.1	97.6	102.3	110.8	109.8	122.7
Malt beverages	2082	77.7	73.7	85.0	100.0	99.1	105.2	110.6	109.6	113.4	112.5	116.8
Bottled and canned soft drinks	2086	81.6	85.2	91.4	100.0	109.8	119.4	126.7	135.1	144.2	144.7	147.8
Fresh or frozen prepared fish	2092	89.4	87.8	91.2	100.0	100.0	94.6	88.9	87.4	95.6	100.1	94.3
Cigarettes, chewing and smoking tobacco	211,3	91.3	93.6	95.4	100.0	104.8	106.7	109.9	111.6	113.4	101.6	....
Cotton and synthetic broadwoven fabrics	221,2	91.1	94.8	101.1	100.0	100.0	103.9	108.1	113.8	118.4	125.8	133.8
Hosiery	2251,52	102.4	100.9	102.5	100.0	108.1	110.9	109.2	115.7	122.2	117.3	126.1
Yarn spinning mills	2281	86.2	89.6	93.2	100.0	98.5	103.3	106.0	105.5	114.1	120.0	126.9
Men's and boys' suits and coats	231	93.2	106.3	103.5	100.0	102.4	101.9	98.7	91.4	102.4	109.0	130.1
Housefurnishings, except curtains and draperies	2392	83.6	92.4	93.6	100.0	99.8	96.8	101.3	110.9	117.9	118.7	115.4
Sawmills and planing mills, general	2421	89.7	93.5	102.3	100.0	101.2	100.1	99.9	102.9	108.9	101.5	102.6
Hardwood dimension and flooring mills	2426	85.6	95.1	98.8	100.0	97.5	96.9	95.7	98.6	105.4	111.2	111.5
Millwork	2431	100.4	97.4	102.2	100.0	98.2	97.8	97.8	95.7	93.4	92.6	89.7
Wood kitchen cabinets	2434	91.6	87.1	85.2	100.0	97.7	91.1	93.6	92.3	102.0	101.9	95.9
Hardwood veneer and plywood	2435	83.9	84.5	83.2	100.0	99.0	98.9	92.2	93.3	104.1	105.8	94.4
Softwood veneer and plywood	2436	87.1	88.3	90.4	100.0	100.6	102.6	108.3	114.3	109.2	103.4	101.9
Wood containers	244	103.4	99.6	98.7	100.0	103.2	108.8	111.6	113.5	109.8	100.5	101.8
Wood household furniture	2511,17	96.9	95.0	99.6	100.0	100.8	101.2	102.5	101.3	106.5	106.2	106.4
Upholstered household furniture	2512	96.2	96.3	101.7	100.0	98.8	101.2	107.7	115.1	120.0	120.0	130.2
Metal household furniture	2514	84.9	89.4	95.3	100.0	100.2	100.7	101.4	107.2	109.5	106.8	99.5
Mattresses and bedsprings	2515	84.1	79.5	85.5	100.0	92.5	106.5	106.2	108.9	103.4	104.4	105.9
Wood office furniture	2521	99.3	99.4	96.2	100.0	95.4	95.4	97.4	101.3	107.1	104.4	104.0
Office furniture, except wood	2522	97.6	96.9	100.6	100.0	96.0	98.7	95.6	92.9	93.9	94.3	94.3
Pulp, paper, and paperboard mills	261,2,3	89.7	87.6	93.3	100.0	103.1	103.2	102.6	102.1	104.7	104.5	111.4
Corrugated and solid fiber boxes	2653	96.7	99.6	102.8	100.0	99.8	98.1	100.9	100.8	101.9	105.5	110.6
Folding paperboard boxes	2657	93.4	90.0	88.5	100.0	101.6	105.4	105.3	110.9	116.4	117.9	122.2
Paper and plastic bags	2673,74	99.9	99.7	101.8	100.0	97.7	93.7	92.2	89.5	93.9	92.0	96.0
Alkalies and chlorine	2812	66.6	70.8	97.7	100.0	101.6	92.5	92.3	86.2	87.7	84.8	84.1
Inorganic pigments	2816	81.4	84.4	88.6	100.0	103.3	107.8	104.5	98.9	107.8	107.9	113.2
Industrial inorganic chemicals, n.e.c.	2819 pt.	88.4	87.3	88.6	100.0	97.5	105.9	109.0	102.3	104.9	110.7	111.1
Synthetic fibers	2823,24	79.8	79.3	90.8	100.0	102.9	104.1	98.7	97.5	99.3	112.3	119.4
Soaps and detergents	2841	90.5	91.5	92.3	100.0	102.4	109.4	128.2	126.4	115.3	112.6	111.2
Cosmetics and other toiletries	2844	87.3	90.3	96.6	100.0	105.2	102.7	101.1	103.9	108.4	108.5	111.8
Paints and allied products	285	93.6	96.9	98.0	100.0	101.4	103.3	106.3	104.3	102.9	108.7	116.5
Industrial organic chemicals, n.e.c.	2869	89.6	87.8	92.3	100.0	110.5	110.5	99.0	92.6	91.6	88.5	96.6
Nitrogenous fertilizers	2873	101.1	100.7	90.5	100.0	101.3	103.3	107.7	108.4	111.8	117.5	111.1
Fertilizers, mixing only	2875	97.8	100.8	95.1	100.0	104.7	112.4	112.8	114.6	127.1	139.1	118.9
Agricultural chemicals, n.e.c.	2879	98.8	92.9	93.2	100.0	108.4	108.9	106.2	102.2	108.4	111.0	115.6
Petroleum refining	291	78.7	84.7	94.9	100.0	105.3	109.6	109.2	106.6	111.3	120.1	123.8
Tires and inner tubes	301	88.8	89.3	92.6	100.0	102.9	103.8	103.0	102.4	107.8	116.5	119.9
Rubber and plastics hose and belting	3052	104.9	100.1	102.1	100.0	108.2	97.8	103.3	96.1	104.3	111.3	104.9
Miscellaneous plastics products, n.e.c.	308	86.4	88.2	88.9	100.0	100.1	101.1	105.3	107.5	114.0	116.2	119.7
Footwear, except rubber	314	98.8	100.3	101.9	100.0	102.3	100.9	92.4	93.1	93.3	97.2	102.7
Glass containers	3221	97.4	93.4	98.5	100.0	99.6	101.6	107.5	108.1	111.5	106.0	111.7
Cement, hydraulic	324	89.4	91.8	97.1	100.0	103.2	110.2	112.4	108.3	115.1	119.9	125.6
Clay construction products	3251,53,59	92.7	94.2	95.5	100.0	105.2	98.3	102.3	97.4	98.9	102.3	107.7
Clay refractories	3255	96.9	94.9	100.8	100.0	102.3	98.5	103.6	97.9	98.6	95.0	104.6
Concrete products	3271,72	98.3	99.5	104.4	100.0	102.1	104.8	103.8	104.9	103.2	109.3	107.9
Ready-mixed concrete	3273	92.9	93.6	96.0	100.0	100.2	101.0	100.2	96.7	98.2	96.9	93.1

PRODUCTIVITY AND RELATED COSTS

Annual Indexes of Output per Employee-hour for Selected Industries, 1984-1994—Continued

(1987=100)

Industry	SIC	1984	1985	1986	1987	1988	1989	1990	1991	1992	1993	1994
Steel	331	81.3	85.8	89.7	100.0	113.5	108.5	110.5	108.2	117.7	134.2	142.7
Gray and ductile iron foundries	3321	99.1	96.9	99.3	100.0	108.0	106.9	107.9	104.6	107.7	113.1	115.7
Steel foundries	3324,25	102.4	99.5	104.9	100.0	95.5	96.3	96.9	94.8	95.6	101.5	100.3
Primary copper	3331	57.6	73.8	88.7	100.0	103.8	94.7	84.9	82.5	71.9	86.9	73.9
Primary aluminum	3334	100.7	97.6	102.7	100.0	102.3	104.8	106.5	110.6	109.7	105.7	98.6
Copper rolling and drawing	3351	84.7	86.2	92.3	100.0	93.0	89.1	90.7	86.4	83.0	89.2	95.1
Aluminum rolling and drawing	3353,54,55	92.3	85.7	95.8	100.0	96.3	90.6	91.2	90.3	96.5	93.9	99.8
Metal cans	3411	101.1	99.2	95.9	100.0	106.9	108.1	117.5	123.8	129.7	134.6	140.7
Hand and edge tools, n.e.c.	3423	97.9	98.8	97.1	100.0	100.5	101.0	95.0	93.1	93.1	93.3	101.8
Heating equipment, except electric	3433	91.6	91.9	96.2	100.0	113.7	105.0	114.0	119.4	121.2	121.8	124.8
Fabricated structural metal	3441	91.2	99.0	99.0	100.0	100.4	97.6	101.2	104.5	103.6	108.1	109.6
Metal doors, sash, and trim	3442	101.4	104.8	102.0	100.0	104.6	105.8	103.1	103.0	106.7	105.4	103.2
Fabricated plate work	3443	88.3	87.5	86.4	100.0	96.2	90.3	94.1	94.3	98.3	98.3	108.4
Bolts, nuts, rivets, and washers	3452	85.3	88.8	91.0	100.0	97.0	93.8	93.7	96.1	91.9	92.8	95.6
Automotive stampings	3465	100.5	94.5	95.7	100.0	102.8	101.8	96.1	97.3	113.8	120.8	124.5
Metal stampings, n.e.c.	3469	94.3	88.6	93.9	100.0	98.0	95.3	90.4	89.5	98.8	104.8	109.3
Valves and pipe fittings	3491,92,94	95.0	94.4	93.9	100.0	101.4	101.2	102.1	101.7	100.4	104.2	110.1
Fabricated pipe and fittings	3498	130.0	120.0	121.4	100.0	99.6	102.3	107.0	114.2	109.6	113.3	110.3
Internal combustion engines, n.e.c.	3519	90.2	92.0	98.5	100.0	106.3	113.2	108.4	103.3	101.2	104.3	118.3
Farm machinery and equipment	3523	112.7	101.6	95.7	100.0	112.8	124.0	131.8	125.3	119.1	123.7	134.2
Lawn and garden equipment	3524	79.3	82.4	93.2	100.0	97.5	93.2	94.8	95.8	108.7	114.7	116.3
Construction machinery	3531	91.6	92.2	99.1	100.0	107.6	110.2	109.6	101.0	100.6	107.0	123.7
Mining machinery	3532	90.2	93.7	95.1	100.0	102.0	107.0	98.4	90.0	90.1	109.5	97.4
Oil and gas field machinery	3533	126.0	115.2	105.9	100.0	123.1	116.1	113.9	110.9	125.7	122.1	123.6
Metal cutting machine tools	3541	87.2	89.9	92.0	100.0	94.8	99.9	99.2	94.8	113.0	111.4	109.2
Metal forming machine tools	3542	90.7	93.1	93.7	100.0	113.1	107.9	97.7	88.4	102.5	115.0	103.0
Machine tool accessories	3545	94.6	92.3	95.0	100.0	98.2	102.5	104.1	104.6	96.8	101.5	112.6
Pumps and pumping equipment	3561,94	92.0	91.9	92.7	100.0	105.7	101.3	103.4	102.5	98.6	105.2	109.3
Ball and roller bearings	3562	95.4	91.6	94.1	100.0	102.9	99.0	93.1	89.6	97.8	103.8	107.2
Air and gas compressors	3563	90.1	92.2	96.0	100.0	103.7	105.3	107.8	110.2	112.7	111.4	116.5
Refrigeration and heating equipment	3585	100.1	98.1	95.8	100.0	104.0	109.0	106.3	104.8	107.6	111.8	115.8
Carburetors, pistons, rings, and valves	3592	95.1	98.8	95.7	100.0	109.9	119.4	114.1	115.1	126.4	136.5	139.8
Transformers, except electronic	3612	95.4	97.0	99.3	100.0	102.8	104.3	107.3	110.7	126.5	121.7	141.2
Switchgear and switchboard apparatus	3613	92.2	95.1	95.9	100.0	109.1	106.5	106.5	103.9	114.6	123.0	124.5
Motors and generators	3621	93.3	94.9	96.8	100.0	102.8	103.6	100.9	104.4	111.5	127.0	123.2
Household cooking equipment	3631	92.0	90.3	104.6	100.0	116.1	96.8	99.5	104.9	100.9	103.7	127.5
Household refrigerators and freezers	3632	97.5	104.1	101.2	100.0	103.3	105.2	107.3	111.8	116.0	116.8	126.7
Household laundry equipment	3633	92.8	93.8	97.4	100.0	106.1	98.7	104.0	111.0	115.9	144.8	150.5
Household appliances, n.e.c.	3639	85.9	86.3	89.1	100.0	100.6	96.3	91.8	80.5	91.6	117.6	119.1
Electric lamp bulbs and tubes	3641	86.4	94.2	91.5	100.0	100.3	92.7	98.0	101.8	112.8	100.9	97.7
Lighting fixtures and equipment	3645,46,47,48	91.3	96.7	103.0	100.0	98.1	97.3	96.0	94.3	98.9	103.7	109.6
Household audio and video equipment	3651	84.7	96.3	106.9	100.0	106.2	120.5	124.1	135.7	151.8	163.1	175.7
Motor vehicles and equipment	371	91.1	95.3	95.1	100.0	103.2	103.3	102.4	96.7	104.3	105.4	108.6
Aircraft	3721	84.7	94.2	93.5	100.0	105.8	107.5	112.9	131.4	141.7	142.4	131.7
Instruments to measure electricity	3825	96.2	95.4	90.4	100.0	106.1	105.2	106.2	108.3	119.0	122.4	145.0
Photographic equipment and supplies	386	88.2	86.1	94.1	100.0	105.6	113.0	107.8	110.2	116.4	126.6	131.9
Railroad transportation, revenue traffic	4011	78.0	81.5	89.2	100.0	108.4	114.6	118.5	127.8	139.6	....	....
Bus carriers, class I	411,13,14 pts	100.1	96.1	95.6	100.0	107.9	104.6	....	....	....	....	....
Trucking, except local	4213	97.3	93.8	96.8	100.0	105.2	109.4	....	....	....	....	....
Air transportation	4512,13,22 pts.	88.8	92.0	93.8	100.0	99.5	95.8	92.9	92.5	96.9	103.8	105.7
Petroleum pipelines	4612,13	99.4	99.9	102.0	100.0	104.8	103.2	102.5	99.0	100.2	104.4	105.1
Telephone communications	481	84.5	88.9	95.0	100.0	106.2	111.6	113.3	119.8	127.7	134.5	135.7
Gas and electric utilities	491,2,3	99.5	98.0	97.0	100.0	105.0	106.6	106.2	108.5	110.1	116.7	120.7
Electric utilities	491,3 pt.	93.8	93.0	95.3	100.0	104.9	107.7	110.1	113.4	115.2	120.6	127.7
Gas utilities	492,3 pt.	114.1	111.9	102.1	100.0	105.5	103.5	94.8	94.0	95.3	105.0	100.3
Scrap and waste materials	5093	89.1	93.4	97.7	100.0	95.4	86.0	98.6	98.9	101.7	109.4	106.6
Hardware stores	525	96.6	95.6	101.6	100.0	108.6	115.2	110.4	102.5	107.2	106.7	114.1
Department stores	531	90.4	92.6	97.4	100.0	99.2	96.9	94.2	98.2	101.2	105.0	108.5
Variety stores	533	141.9	129.2	106.7	100.0	101.9	124.5	151.3	154.3	167.7	170.4	155.2
Grocery stores	541	107.9	105.7	103.8	100.0	98.9	95.4	94.6	93.7	93.3	92.7	91.7
Retail bakeries	546	96.0	87.6	93.6	100.0	89.8	83.3	89.7	94.7	94.0	86.0	87.8
New and used car dealers	551	99.5	99.8	101.6	100.0	103.5	102.5	106.1	104.2	106.5	107.7	109.2
Auto and home supply stores	553	90.4	94.5	94.3	100.0	103.2	101.5	102.8	98.9	98.9	98.9	101.4
Gasoline service stations	554	87.0	93.5	101.8	100.0	103.0	105.1	102.6	104.3	109.7	112.4	115.0
Men's and boys' clothing stores	561	93.7	98.3	100.7	100.0	106.0	109.3	112.8	117.7	116.4	115.7	138.1
Women's clothing stores	562	98.0	99.8	107.0	100.0	97.5	99.1	100.8	101.9	110.7	116.2	115.9
Family clothing stores	565	106.2	103.1	103.3	100.0	102.4	105.5	104.9	106.9	112.3	111.6	116.7
Shoe stores	566	90.6	97.6	105.5	100.0	102.7	107.2	106.2	105.1	111.5	110.8	117.8
Furniture and homefurnishings stores	571	97.9	94.8	101.2	100.0	98.9	101.3	102.2	101.6	108.6	108.9	108.7
Household appliance stores	572	87.2	94.9	106.5	100.0	98.5	103.5	102.8	105.2	113.9	114.6	126.3
Radio, television, and computer stores	573	79.1	89.3	94.1	100.0	119.3	115.7	120.9	129.6	143.5	157.3	181.0
Eating and drinking places	58	98.9	96.2	99.3	100.0	102.8	102.2	104.0	103.1	102.4	103.1	103.8
Drug stores and proprietary stores	591	106.4	102.5	101.6	100.0	101.9	102.5	103.6	104.7	103.6	104.7	103.7
Liquor stores	592	93.6	101.9	93.8	100.0	98.2	101.1	105.2	105.9	108.4	100.5	96.7
Miscellaneous shopping goods stores	594	92.6	94.1	97.1	100.0	98.4	101.7	101.5	102.0	100.6	103.9	105.6
Commercial banks	602	89.6	94.3	96.2	100.0	103.4	102.2	108.6	112.3	117.2	129.9	....
Hotels and motels	701	101.6	101.2	98.9	100.0	97.6	95.0	96.0	99.0	107.6	106.5	110.0
Laundry, cleaning, and garment services	721	107.5	103.3	100.8	100.0	97.2	100.5	100.5	101.0	98.7	99.9	101.8
Beauty shops	723	98.5	96.1	96.9	100.0	95.1	99.6	96.8	94.8	99.7	95.9	100.0
Automotive repair shops	753	91.7	99.4	96.2	100.0	105.7	108.2	107.0	98.8	103.4	103.7	111.6

Part Five

Compensation of Employees

Compensation of Employees

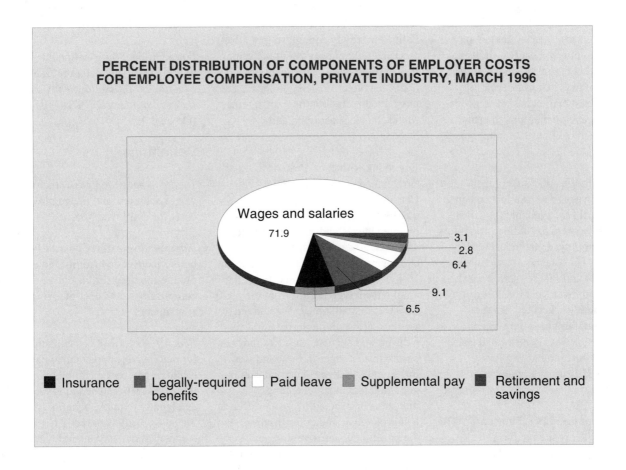

The pie chart above shows that only 72 percent of total compensation in private industry is for wages and salaries. The remainder consists of various voluntary and legally- required costs for providing benefits. Paid leave, health insurance, and social security payments each constitute over 20 percent of total benefits. While wage and salary costs in private industry rose 45 percent from 1984 to 1995, benefit costs rose 68 percent.

NOTES

Compensation of Employees—Employment Cost Index

Description of the Series

The Employment Cost Index (ECI) is a quarterly measure of the rate of change in compensation per hour worked and includes wages, salaries, and employer costs of employee benefits. It uses a fixed market basket of labor—similar in concept to the Consumer Price Index's fixed market basket of goods and services—to measure change over time in employer costs of employing labor.

Statistical series on total compensation costs, on wages and salaries, and on benefit costs are available for private nonfarm workers excluding proprietors, the self-employed, and household workers. The total compensation costs and wages and salaries series are also available for state and local government workers and for the civilian nonfarm economy, which consists of private industry and state and local government workers combined. Federal workers are excluded.

The ECI probability sample consists of about 4,400 private nonfarm establishments providing about 23,000 occupational observations and 1,000 state and local government establishments providing 6,000 occupational observations selected to represent total employment in each sector. On average, each reporting unit provides wage and compensation information on five well-specified occupations. The occupations are defined narrowly enough so that all workers in the job carry out the same task at roughly the same level of skill. Data are collected each quarter for the pay period including the 12th day of March, June, September, and December.

Beginning with June 1986 data, fixed employment weights from the 1980 Census of Population are used each quarter to calculate the civilian and private indexes and the index for state and local governments. 1990 employment counts were introduced in March 1995. (Prior to June 1986, the employment weights are from the 1970 Census of Population.) These fixed weights, also used to derive all of the industry and occupation series indexes, ensure that changes in these indexes reflect only changes in compensation, not employment shifts among industries or occupations with different levels of wages and compensation. For the bargaining status, region, and metropolitan/nonmetropolitan area series, however, employment data by industry and occupation are not available from the census. Instead, the 1980 employment weights are reallocated within these series each quarter based on the current sample. Therefore, these indexes are not strictly comparable to those for the aggregate, industry, and occupation series.

For additional information on methodology and data, see *BLS Bulletin 2466, Employment Cost Indexes and Levels, 1975-1995* (October 1995).

Definitions

Total compensation costs. Include wages, salaries, and the employer's costs for employee benefits.

Wages and salaries. Consist of earnings before payroll deductions, including production bonuses, incentive earnings, commissions, and cost-of-living adjustments.

Benefits. Include the cost to employers for paid leave, supplemental pay (including nonproduction bonuses), insurance, retirement and savings plans, and legally required benefits (such as Social Security, workers' compensation, and unemployment insurance).

Excluded from wages and salaries and employee benefit costs are such items as payment-in-kind, free room and board, and tips.

Employment Cost Index, Total Compensation, Civilian Workers, by Occupation and Industry, 1984-1995

(June 1989=100, not seasonally adjusted)

Series and year	Indexes				Percent change for 12 months ended December
	March	June	September	December	
CIVILIAN WORKERS					
1984	80.5	81.1	82.2	83.2	5.2
1985	84.3	84.9	86.2	86.8	4.3
1986	87.7	88.3	89.3	89.9	3.6
1987	90.7	91.3	92.3	93.1	3.6
1988	94.4	95.4	96.7	97.7	4.9
1989	98.9	100.0	101.6	102.6	5.0
1990	104.3	105.4	106.9	107.6	4.9
1991	109.1	110.2	111.5	112.2	4.3
1992	113.5	114.2	115.4	116.1	3.5
1993	117.5	118.3	119.5	120.2	3.5
1994	121.3	122.1	123.3	123.8	3.0
1995	124.8	125.6	126.6	127.4	2.9
WORKERS, BY OCCUPATIONAL GROUP					
White-collar occupations					
1984	78.8	79.6	80.8	81.8	5.5
1985	83.0	83.6	85.2	85.8	4.9
1986	86.8	87.5	88.7	89.2	4.0
1987	90.3	90.8	92.0	92.7	3.9
1988	94.0	95.0	96.4	97.6	5.3
1989	99.0	100.0	102.0	102.9	5.4
1990	104.6	105.8	107.5	108.3	5.2
1991	109.8	110.8	112.1	112.8	4.2
1992	113.9	114.6	115.8	116.6	3.4
1993	117.9	118.6	119.9	120.6	3.4
1994	121.8	122.6	123.9	124.4	3.2
1995	125.5	126.3	127.4	128.2	3.1
Professional specialty and technical					
1989	....	100.0	102.6	103.7	....
1990	105.5	106.3	108.7	109.8	5.9
1991	111.0	111.7	113.5	114.4	4.2
1992	115.4	116.2	118.2	119.1	4.1
1993	120.1	120.6	122.0	122.5	2.9
1994	123.7	124.2	125.7	126.2	3.0
1995	127.0	127.5	128.9	129.8	2.9
Executive, administrative, and managerial					
1989	....	100.0	101.2	101.9	....
1990	104.0	105.4	107.0	107.7	5.7
1991	109.4	110.6	111.8	112.5	4.5
1992	113.0	113.4	114.3	115.0	2.2
1993	116.9	117.5	118.6	119.4	3.8
1994	120.6	121.6	122.9	123.6	3.5
1995	125.2	125.7	126.7	127.7	3.3
Administrative support, including clerical					
1989	....	100.0	101.4	102.5	....
1990	104.4	105.4	106.8	107.8	5.2
1991	109.2	110.2	111.4	112.2	4.1
1992	113.9	114.6	115.9	116.8	4.1
1993	118.3	119.3	120.4	121.3	3.9
1994	122.6	123.5	124.6	125.2	3.2
1995	126.5	127.3	128.1	129.2	3.2
Blue-collar occupations					
1984	83.3	83.9	84.6	85.6	4.4
1985	86.5	87.1	88.0	88.4	3.3
1986	89.3	89.7	90.4	90.9	2.8
1987	91.4	92.1	92.9	93.8	3.2
1988	95.3	96.4	97.1	97.8	4.3
1989	98.8	100.0	101.1	102.0	4.3
1990	103.6	104.8	105.8	106.5	4.4
1991	108.0	109.2	110.3	111.1	4.3
1992	112.6	113.5	114.4	115.2	3.7
1993	116.7	117.8	118.8	119.4	3.6
1994	120.4	121.3	122.4	122.7	2.8
1995	123.6	124.5	125.2	125.9	2.6

COMPENSATION OF EMPLOYEES

Employment Cost Index, Total Compensation, Civilian Workers, by Occupation and Industry, 1984-1995—Continued

(June 1989=100, not seasonally adjusted)

Series and year	Indexes				Percent change for 12 months ended December
	March	June	September	December	
Service occupations					
1984	80.7	80.8	82.4	83.9	6.5
1985	84.5	84.7	86.6	87.2	3.9
1986	88.0	88.4	89.6	90.3	3.6
1987	91.3	91.6	92.5	93.1	3.1
1988	94.5	95.4	97.4	98.2	5.5
1989	99.2	100.0	101.7	102.8	4.7
1990	104.2	105.1	106.6	108.0	5.1
1991	109.4	110.4	112.3	113.1	4.7
1992	114.1	114.7	116.2	116.7	3.2
1993	117.9	118.7	119.9	120.5	3.3
1994	121.6	122.1	123.5	124.3	3.2
1995	125.0	125.8	126.7	127.5	2.6
WORKERS, BY INDUSTRY DIVISION					
Goods-producing					
1984	82.8	83.6	84.4	85.3	4.7
1985	86.6	87.1	87.8	88.2	3.4
1986	89.2	90.0	90.5	91.0	3.2
1987	91.5	92.1	92.9	93.8	3.1
1988	95.4	96.5	97.1	97.9	4.4
1989	98.9	100.0	101.1	102.1	4.3
1990	103.9	105.2	106.2	107.1	4.9
1991	108.6	109.9	111.0	111.9	4.5
1992	113.5	114.3	115.3	116.2	3.8
1993	118.0	119.1	120.0	120.6	3.8
1994	121.9	123.0	123.9	124.4	3.2
1995	125.3	126.0	126.5	127.4	2.4
Manufacturing					
1984	82.2	83.0	83.9	85.0	5.2
1985	86.3	86.8	87.5	87.8	3.3
1986	89.0	89.7	90.1	90.7	3.3
1987	91.1	91.6	92.5	93.4	3.0
1988	95.3	96.2	96.9	97.6	4.5
1989	98.9	100.0	101.1	102.0	4.5
1990	104.0	105.3	106.4	107.2	5.1
1991	108.6	110.0	111.2	112.2	4.7
1992	114.0	114.7	115.7	116.5	3.8
1993	118.6	119.7	120.6	121.3	4.1
1994	122.5	123.5	124.4	125.1	3.1
1995	126.2	126.9	127.3	128.4	2.6
Service-producing					
1984	79.1	79.9	81.0	82.1	5.5
1985	83.0	83.6	85.5	86.0	4.8
1986	86.9	87.4	88.7	89.3	3.8
1987	90.3	90.8	92.1	92.7	3.8
1988	93.9	94.9	96.5	97.6	5.3
1989	99.0	100.0	102.0	102.9	5.4
1990	104.4	105.5	107.2	108.0	5.0
1991	109.5	110.4	111.8	112.4	4.1
1992	113.5	114.2	115.4	116.2	3.4
1993	117.2	118.0	119.3	120.0	3.3
1994	121.0	121.7	123.1	123.6	3.0
1995	124.6	125.5	126.6	127.3	3.0
Services					
1984	76.6	76.9	79.0	80.3	6.8
1985	80.9	81.3	83.6	84.1	4.7
1986	85.1	85.5	87.3	88.0	4.6
1987	89.0	89.4	91.5	92.3	4.9
1988	93.7	94.3	96.7	97.9	6.1
1989	99.2	100.0	102.7	103.7	5.9
1990	105.5	106.6	109.0	110.2	6.3
1991	111.5	112.0	113.8	114.6	4.0
1992	115.5	116.3	118.2	119.2	4.0
1993	120.1	120.6	122.2	122.9	3.1
1994	123.8	124.2	125.8	126.4	2.8
1995	127.2	127.8	128.9	129.7	2.6

Employment Cost Index, Total Compensation, Civilian Workers, by Occupation and Industry, 1984-1995—Continued

(June 1989=100, not seasonally adjusted)

Series and year	Indexes				Percent change for 12 months ended December
	March	June	September	December	
Health services					
1985	82.0	82.4	83.8	84.0	....
1986	85.0	85.6	87.0	87.9	4.6
1987	89.0	89.6	90.7	91.8	4.4
1988	92.9	94.2	95.8	97.0	5.7
1989	98.9	100.0	102.2	103.9	7.1
1990	105.9	107.1	109.2	110.9	6.7
1991	112.6	113.2	115.0	116.1	4.7
1992	117.5	118.4	120.2	121.3	4.5
1993	122.3	123.2	124.4	125.4	3.4
1994	126.1	126.6	127.8	128.5	2.5
1995	129.4	130.2	131.1	132.1	2.8
Hospitals					
1986	....	85.0	86.3	87.3	....
1987	88.1	88.8	90.3	91.4	4.7
1988	92.6	93.9	95.6	96.9	6.0
1989	98.7	100.0	102.3	103.7	7.0
1990	105.6	106.7	109.1	110.9	6.9
1991	112.2	112.9	114.7	115.9	4.5
1992	117.3	118.1	119.8	121.0	4.4
1993	122.0	122.6	123.9	125.0	3.3
1994	125.9	126.4	127.5	128.4	2.7
1995	128.8	129.7	130.4	131.5	2.4
Educational services					
1989	99.5	100.0	104.1	104.8	....
1990	106.0	106.6	110.3	111.4	6.3
1991	112.3	112.4	114.9	115.4	3.6
1992	115.7	116.1	118.9	119.7	3.7
1993	120.1	120.2	122.6	122.9	2.7
1994	123.2	123.6	126.0	126.4	2.8
1995	126.9	127.4	129.8	130.4	3.2
Public administration					
1984	77.8	78.3	80.4	81.4	5.9
1985	82.4	82.5	85.0	85.4	4.9
1986	86.6	87.4	89.0	89.7	5.0
1987	91.3	91.6	92.7	93.8	4.6
1988	95.2	95.8	97.5	97.8	4.3
1989	99.2	100.0	102.5	103.2	5.5
1990	105.1	105.5	107.8	108.7	5.3
1991	110.8	110.9	112.2	112.6	3.6
1992	114.0	114.6	115.8	116.3	3.3
1993	117.6	118.0	119.3	120.0	3.2
1994	121.5	122.2	123.7	124.2	3.5
1995	125.4	126.1	127.4	128.5	3.5
Nonmanufacturing					
1984	79.8	80.4	81.5	82.5	5.2
1985	83.5	84.1	85.8	86.4	4.7
1986	87.2	87.8	89.0	89.6	3.7
1987	90.5	91.1	92.3	92.9	3.7
1988	94.1	95.2	96.6	97.7	5.2
1989	99.0	100.0	101.9	102.8	5.2
1990	104.3	105.5	107.0	107.8	4.9
1991	109.4	110.3	111.7	112.3	4.2
1992	113.3	114.1	115.3	116.0	3.3
1993	117.1	117.9	119.2	119.8	3.3
1994	120.9	121.7	123.0	123.4	3.0
1995	124.4	125.2	126.3	127.0	2.9

COMPENSATION OF EMPLOYEES

Employment Cost Index, Total Compensation, Private Industry Workers, by Occupation and Industry, 1984-1995

(June 1989=100, not seasonally adjusted)

Series and year	Indexes				Percent change for 12 months ended December
	March	June	September	December	
PRIVATE INDUSTRY WORKERS					
1984	81.5	82.2	82.9	84.0	4.9
1985	85.0	85.7	86.8	87.3	3.9
1986	88.2	88.9	89.5	90.1	3.2
1987	91.0	91.6	92.5	93.1	3.3
1988	94.5	95.7	96.6	97.6	4.8
1989	98.8	100.0	101.2	102.3	4.8
1990	103.9	105.2	106.2	107.0	4.6
1991	108.5	109.8	111.0	111.7	4.4
1992	113.1	113.9	114.8	115.6	3.5
1993	117.1	118.0	119.1	119.8	3.6
1994	121.0	122.0	123.0	123.5	3.1
1995	124.5	125.4	126.2	126.9	2.8
Private industry workers, excluding sales					
1984	81.7	82.5	83.3	84.3	5.1
1985	85.2	85.8	86.9	87.3	3.6
1986	88.3	88.9	89.6	90.2	3.3
1987	91.0	91.7	92.7	93.4	3.5
1988	94.9	95.9	96.9	97.7	4.6
1989	99.0	100.0	101.2	102.1	4.5
1990	103.9	105.1	106.3	107.1	4.9
1991	108.6	109.8	111.1	112.0	4.6
1992	113.3	114.1	115.1	115.9	3.5
1993	117.5	118.5	119.5	120.2	3.7
1994	121.4	122.3	123.4	123.9	3.1
1995	125.0	125.7	126.5	127.4	2.8
WORKERS BY OCCUPATIONAL GROUPS					
White-collar occupations					
1984	79.8	80.8	81.4	82.4	5.1
1985	83.7	84.6	85.7	86.4	4.9
1986	87.4	88.2	88.8	89.4	3.5
1987	90.6	91.2	92.1	92.7	3.7
1988	93.9	95.1	96.2	97.3	5.0
1989	98.9	100.0	101.4	102.4	5.2
1990	104.1	105.5	106.7	107.4	4.9
1991	109.0	110.3	111.4	112.2	4.5
1992	113.4	114.2	115.1	115.9	3.3
1993	117.4	118.3	119.4	120.2	3.7
1994	121.5	122.5	123.5	124.1	3.2
1995	125.3	126.2	127.0	127.9	3.1
White-collar occupations, excluding sales					
1984	80.1	81.0	81.9	82.9	5.6
1985	83.7	84.6	85.7	86.1	3.9
1986	87.3	88.1	88.7	89.4	3.8
1987	90.6	91.3	92.5	93.2	4.3
1988	94.5	95.5	96.7	97.5	4.6
1989	99.0	100.0	101.3	102.2	4.8
1990	104.2	105.4	106.9	107.7	5.4
1991	109.2	110.4	111.8	112.7	4.6
1992	113.8	114.6	115.8	116.6	3.5
1993	118.3	119.2	120.2	121.0	3.8
1994	122.4	123.3	124.4	125.1	3.4
1995	126.3	127.0	127.8	128.9	3.0
Professional specialty and technical					
1985	....	....	....	86.1	....
1986	87.1	87.8	88.6	89.3	3.7
1987	90.3	90.8	92.1	92.9	4.0
1988	94.3	95.4	96.9	97.5	5.0
1989	99.0	100.0	101.8	102.9	5.5
1990	104.9	105.8	107.5	108.7	5.6
1991	110.1	111.1	112.8	113.9	4.8
1992	115.3	116.4	118.0	119.0	4.5
1993	120.4	121.3	122.2	122.9	3.3
1994	124.6	125.3	126.3	126.8	3.2
1995	127.7	128.4	129.3	130.4	2.8

Employment Cost Index, Total Compensation, Private Industry Workers, by Occupation and Industry, 1984-1995—Continued

(June 1989=100, not seasonally adjusted)

Series and year	Indexes				Percent change for 12 months ended December
	March	June	September	December	
Executive, administrative, and managerial occupations					
1985	....	....	....	86.4	....
1986	87.8	88.7	89.2	89.9	4.1
1987	91.6	92.2	93.5	93.9	4.4
1988	94.7	95.7	96.6	97.8	4.2
1989	99.1	100.0	100.9	101.5	3.8
1990	103.7	105.3	106.6	107.2	5.6
1991	108.9	110.3	111.5	112.3	4.8
1992	112.7	113.1	113.9	114.5	2.0
1993	116.5	117.2	118.1	118.9	3.8
1994	120.3	121.3	122.6	123.3	3.7
1995	124.9	125.4	126.2	127.2	3.2
Sales occupations					
1986	87.6	88.6	89.1	89.1	....
1987	90.0	90.5	90.5	90.2	1.2
1988	91.4	93.6	94.1	96.3	6.8
1989	98.3	100.0	101.9	103.3	7.3
1990	103.6	105.6	105.9	106.0	2.6
1991	108.0	109.8	109.8	109.6	3.4
1992	111.6	112.2	111.8	112.6	2.7
1993	112.9	113.8	115.6	116.5	3.5
1994	117.2	118.8	119.2	119.6	2.7
1995	120.2	122.4	123.2	123.1	2.9
Administrative support, including clerical					
1985	....	....	....	85.9	....
1986	87.0	87.8	88.3	89.0	3.6
1987	90.0	90.8	91.8	92.6	4.0
1988	94.4	95.3	96.6	97.3	5.1
1989	98.9	100.0	101.2	102.3	5.1
1990	104.2	105.3	106.4	107.3	4.9
1991	108.6	109.9	111.0	111.9	4.3
1992	113.6	114.4	115.5	116.4	4.0
1993	118.1	119.2	120.3	121.2	4.1
1994	122.5	123.5	124.5	125.1	3.2
1995	126.5	127.3	128.1	129.2	3.3
Blue-collar occupations					
1984	83.6	84.2	84.9	85.8	4.3
1985	86.7	87.3	88.2	88.5	3.1
1986	89.4	89.8	90.5	90.9	2.7
1987	91.3	92.1	92.9	93.7	3.1
1988	95.4	96.4	97.1	97.9	4.5
1989	98.8	100.0	101.1	101.9	4.1
1990	103.5	104.7	105.6	106.4	4.4
1991	107.9	109.0	110.2	111.0	4.3
1992	112.5	113.4	114.3	115.0	3.6
1993	116.6	117.7	118.7	119.3	3.7
1994	120.3	121.2	122.3	122.6	2.8
1995	123.5	124.4	125.1	125.7	2.5
Precision production, craft, and repair occupations					
1985	....	....	....	89.0	....
1986	90.1	90.5	91.2	91.6	2.9
1987	92.0	92.7	93.7	94.4	3.1
1988	95.8	96.8	97.3	98.0	3.8
1989	98.7	100.0	101.2	102.0	4.1
1990	103.4	104.7	105.6	106.2	4.1
1991	108.0	109.2	110.5	111.0	4.5
1992	112.2	113.1	114.3	115.0	3.6
1993	116.6	117.6	118.7	118.9	3.4
1994	120.2	121.2	122.5	122.5	3.0
1995	123.4	124.4	125.4	125.7	2.6

Employment Cost Index, Total Compensation, Private Industry Workers, by Occupation and Industry, 1984-1995—Continued

(June 1989=100, not seasonally adjusted)

Series and year	Indexes				Percent change for 12 months ended December
	March	June	September	December	
Machine operators, assemblers, and inspectors					
1985	....	....	....	87.4	....
1986	88.3	88.7	89.2	89.8	2.7
1987	90.2	91.1	91.6	92.8	3.3
1988	94.7	95.8	96.5	97.6	5.2
1989	98.9	100.0	100.9	101.8	4.3
1990	103.7	105.0	105.9	106.9	5.0
1991	108.3	109.4	110.5	111.6	4.4
1992	113.9	114.6	115.0	115.8	3.8
1993	117.8	119.0	120.0	120.8	4.3
1994	121.3	122.2	122.9	123.4	2.2
1995	124.2	124.8	125.1	126.2	2.3
Transportation and material moving occupations					
1985	....	....	....	88.8	....
1986	89.3	89.9	90.9	91.2	2.7
1987	91.6	92.6	93.3	93.9	3.0
1988	95.3	97.0	97.9	98.2	4.6
1989	99.0	100.0	101.2	101.4	3.3
1990	103.1	104.3	104.9	105.5	4.0
1991	106.3	107.6	108.3	109.0	3.3
1992	110.4	111.4	112.5	113.0	3.7
1993	113.9	115.2	115.9	117.0	3.5
1994	118.5	119.1	120.3	120.6	3.1
1995	121.8	122.4	122.9	123.5	2.4
Handlers, equipment cleaners, helpers, and laborers					
1985	....	....	....	89.1	....
1986	89.6	89.9	90.5	91.0	2.1
1987	91.3	91.7	92.5	93.5	2.7
1988	95.5	96.2	97.0	97.7	4.5
1989	98.8	100.0	101.3	102.2	4.6
1990	103.6	104.7	105.7	106.7	4.4
1991	108.1	109.3	110.4	111.4	4.4
1992	112.6	113.4	114.6	115.3	3.5
1993	116.8	117.6	118.4	119.1	3.3
1994	120.2	121.4	122.7	122.9	3.2
1995	124.1	125.3	125.9	127.0	3.3
Service occupations					
1984	82.9	82.7	84.1	85.8	6.6
1985	86.2	86.3	87.9	88.4	3.0
1986	89.4	89.5	90.3	91.1	3.1
1987	91.9	92.3	92.8	93.3	2.4
1988	94.6	95.6	97.1	98.2	5.3
1989	99.2	100.0	101.1	102.5	4.4
1990	103.9	104.9	105.7	107.3	4.7
1991	108.3	109.9	111.5	112.4	4.8
1992	113.5	114.2	115.4	115.9	3.1
1993	117.2	118.0	118.9	119.5	3.1
1994	120.6	121.0	121.8	122.9	2.8
1995	123.4	124.0	124.7	125.3	2.0
Production and nonsupervisory occupations					
1984	81.8	82.5	83.1	84.2	4.7
1985	85.1	85.7	86.8	87.3	3.7
1986	88.1	88.7	89.4	89.8	2.9
1987	90.6	91.3	92.1	92.8	3.3
1988	94.3	95.5	96.6	97.5	5.1
1989	98.8	100.0	101.4	102.4	5.0
1990	103.8	105.1	106.0	106.9	4.4
1991	108.4	109.6	110.8	111.5	4.3
1992	113.0	113.8	114.8	115.5	3.6
1993	116.9	117.9	119.0	119.7	3.6
1994	120.7	121.6	122.6	123.1	2.8
1995	124.1	125.0	125.8	126.5	2.8

Employment Cost Index, Total Compensation, Private Industry Workers, by Occupation and Industry, 1984-1995—Continued

(June 1989=100, not seasonally adjusted)

Series and year	Indexes				Percent change for 12 months ended December
	March	June	September	December	
WORKERS, BY INDUSTRY DIVISION					
Goods-producing industries					
1984	82.9	83.7	84.4	85.4	4.7
1985	86.6	87.2	87.7	88.2	3.3
1986	89.2	90.0	90.6	91.0	3.2
1987	91.5	92.1	92.9	93.8	3.1
1988	95.5	96.5	97.1	97.9	4.4
1989	98.9	100.0	101.1	102.1	4.3
1990	103.9	105.2	106.2	107.0	4.8
1991	108.5	109.8	111.0	111.9	4.6
1992	113.5	114.3	115.3	116.1	3.8
1993	118.0	119.1	119.9	120.6	3.9
1994	121.8	123.0	123.9	124.3	3.1
1995	125.3	125.9	126.5	127.4	2.5
Goods-producing, excluding sales occupations					
1984	83.2	83.9	84.8	85.6	4.5
1985	86.6	87.2	87.9	88.3	3.2
1986	89.2	90.0	90.5	91.0	3.1
1987	91.5	92.1	92.9	93.8	3.1
1988	95.4	96.5	97.1	97.9	4.4
1989	98.9	100.0	101.1	102.2	4.4
1990	103.9	105.1	106.1	107.0	4.7
1991	108.4	109.8	110.9	111.8	4.5
1992	113.4	114.1	115.2	115.9	3.7
1993	117.8	118.8	119.6	120.1	3.6
1994	121.4	122.5	123.5	124.0	3.2
1995	124.9	125.6	126.1	127.1	2.5
Goods-producing, white-collar occupations					
1987		92.3	93.1	94.0	
1988	95.6	96.4	97.2	97.8	4.0
1989	99.0	100.0	101.2	101.9	4.2
1990	104.1	105.3	106.7	107.4	5.4
1991	108.8	110.1	111.2	112.3	4.6
1992	113.6	114.5	115.5	116.7	3.9
1993	118.6	119.6	120.5	121.1	3.8
1994	123.0	124.3	125.1	125.9	4.0
1995	127.2	127.6	128.1	129.0	2.5
Goods-producing, white-collar occupations, excluding sales occupations					
1987		92.2	93.0	93.9	
1988	95.4	96.4	97.1	97.7	4.0
1989	99.0	100.0	101.2	102.0	4.4
1990	103.9	105.2	106.4	107.1	5.0
1991	108.5	110.0	111.1	112.2	4.8
1992	113.2	113.9	115.1	116.2	3.6
1993	118.1	119.0	119.7	119.9	3.2
1994	121.9	123.2	124.1	125.0	4.3
1995	126.2	126.7	127.2	128.3	2.6
Goods-producing, blue-collar occupations					
1987		92.1	92.8	93.8	
1988	95.4	96.6	97.1	98.0	4.5
1989	98.9	100.0	101.1	102.3	4.4
1990	103.9	105.1	106.0	106.9	4.5
1991	108.4	109.7	110.8	111.6	4.4
1992	113.4	114.1	115.1	115.8	3.8
1993	117.6	118.7	119.6	120.2	3.8
1994	121.1	122.2	123.1	123.4	2.7
1995	124.1	124.9	125.5	126.4	2.4
Goods-producing, service occupations					
1987		91.4	92.2	93.0	
1988	95.0	95.7	96.2	97.0	4.3
1989	98.9	100.0	100.9	102.2	5.4
1990	104.0	104.4	105.3	106.4	4.1
1991	107.9	109.3	110.5	112.1	5.4
1992	113.8	115.5	116.9	117.5	4.8
1993	120.0	120.6	121.5	122.4	4.2
1994	123.5	123.8	126.5	126.3	3.2
1995	127.3	127.9	128.8	129.6	2.6

Employment Cost Index, Total Compensation, Private Industry Workers, by Occupation and Industry, 1984-1995—Continued

(June 1989=100, not seasonally adjusted)

Series and year	Indexes				Percent change for 12 months ended December
	March	June	September	December	
Contract construction					
1985	86.1	87.1	87.7	88.2	
1986	88.5	89.9	90.6	90.7	2.8
1987	91.5	92.7	93.4	94.0	3.6
1988	95.2	96.4	97.2	98.0	4.3
1989	99.0	100.0	101.2	102.4	4.5
1990	103.1	104.3	105.2	105.6	3.1
1991	107.4	108.5	109.3	109.9	4.1
1992	110.6	111.7	113.1	113.8	3.5
1993	114.9	116.0	116.8	116.5	2.4
1994	118.6	120.2	121.4	120.8	3.7
1995	121.1	122.0	123.1	123.4	2.2
Manufacturing					
1984	82.2	83.0	83.9	85.0	5.2
1985	86.3	86.8	87.5	87.8	3.3
1986	89.0	89.7	90.1	90.7	3.3
1987	91.1	91.6	92.5	93.4	3.0
1988	95.3	96.2	96.9	97.6	4.5
1989	98.9	100.0	101.1	102.0	4.5
1990	104.0	105.3	106.4	107.2	5.1
1991	108.6	110.0	111.2	112.2	4.7
1992	114.0	114.7	115.7	116.5	3.8
1993	118.6	119.7	120.6	121.3	4.1
1994	122.5	123.5	124.4	125.1	3.1
1995	126.2	126.9	127.3	128.4	2.6
Manufacturing, white-collar occupations					
1987		92.2	93.1	94.1	
1988	95.7	96.4	97.1	97.7	3.8
1989	99.0	100.0	101.1	101.9	4.3
1990	104.1	105.3	106.8	107.4	5.4
1991	108.8	110.2	111.3	112.4	4.7
1992	113.6	114.6	115.5	116.6	3.7
1993	118.7	119.7	120.5	121.3	4.0
1994	122.7	123.9	124.9	126.0	3.9
1995	127.4	128.0	128.7	129.5	2.8
Manufacturing, white-collar occupations, excluding sales occupations					
1987		92.1	93.0	93.9	
1988	95.5	96.3	97.1	97.7	4.0
1989	99.0	100.0	101.1	101.9	4.3
1990	104.0	105.1	106.4	107.0	5.0
1991	108.3	109.9	111.1	112.2	4.9
1992	113.0	113.8	115.0	115.9	3.3
1993	118.0	118.8	119.5	119.9	3.5
1994	121.3	122.5	123.6	124.9	4.2
1995	126.1	126.6	127.4	128.4	2.8
Manufacturing, blue-collar occupations					
1987		91.3	92.0	93.1	
1988	95.1	96.1	96.7	97.6	4.8
1989	98.8	100.0	101.1	102.1	4.6
1990	104.0	105.2	106.2	107.2	5.0
1991	108.5	109.8	111.1	112.0	4.5
1992	114.2	114.8	115.7	116.4	3.9
1993	118.5	119.6	120.5	121.3	4.2
1994	122.3	123.2	124.0	124.5	2.6
1995	125.3	126.0	126.3	127.5	2.4
Manufacturing, service occupations					
1987		91.2	92.0	93.0	
1988	95.0	95.9	96.4	97.3	4.6
1989	98.8	100.0	100.8	102.1	4.9
1990	104.1	104.5	105.1	106.3	4.1
1991	107.8	109.2	110.3	112.1	5.5
1992	113.9	115.4	117.0	117.6	4.9
1993	120.3	120.7	121.7	122.7	4.3
1994	123.8	124.1	127.0	127.0	3.5
1995	128.0	128.6	129.5	130.2	2.5

Employment Cost Index, Total Compensation, Private Industry Workers, by Occupation and Industry, 1984-1995—Continued

(June 1989=100, not seasonally adjusted)

Series and year	Indexes				Percent change for 12 months ended December
	March	June	September	December	
Durables					
1985	....	....	....	88.6	....
1986	89.6	90.1	90.6	91.1	2.8
1987	91.3	92.0	92.6	93.5	2.6
1988	95.6	96.5	97.0	97.7	4.5
1989	99.0	100.0	101.1	102.2	4.6
1990	104.0	105.1	106.3	107.2	4.9
1991	108.5	109.9	111.2	112.1	4.6
1992	114.1	114.8	115.8	116.7	4.1
1993	119.0	120.0	121.0	121.9	4.5
1994	122.9	123.8	125.1	125.8	3.2
1995	127.0	127.7	128.2	129.1	2.6
Non-durables					
1985	....	....	....	86.5	....
1986	87.7	88.9	89.4	90.0	4.0
1987	90.7	91.2	92.3	93.4	3.8
1988	94.8	95.6	96.5	97.5	4.4
1989	98.8	100.0	101.2	101.9	4.5
1990	104.1	105.5	106.6	107.4	5.4
1991	108.8	110.1	111.2	112.3	4.6
1992	113.8	114.7	115.4	116.3	3.6
1993	117.9	119.0	119.7	120.3	3.4
1994	121.7	122.8	123.2	123.8	2.9
1995	124.7	125.4	125.7	127.0	2.6
Service-producing industries					
1984	80.3	81.1	81.7	82.9	5.1
1985	83.7	84.5	86.1	86.6	4.5
1986	87.5	88.0	88.8	89.3	3.1
1987	90.5	91.2	92.1	92.6	3.7
1988	93.8	95.1	96.2	97.3	5.1
1989	98.8	100.0	101.3	102.3	5.1
1990	103.8	105.2	106.2	107.0	4.6
1991	108.5	109.8	111.0	111.6	4.3
1992	112.8	113.6	114.4	115.2	3.2
1993	116.4	117.3	118.5	119.3	3.6
1994	120.4	121.2	122.3	122.8	2.9
1995	123.9	124.9	125.8	126.5	3.0
Service-producing, excluding sales					
1984	80.5	81.3	82.0	83.2	5.4
1985	83.9	84.7	86.2	86.5	4.0
1986	87.5	88.0	88.8	89.5	3.5
1987	90.6	91.4	92.5	93.1	4.0
1988	94.3	95.4	96.7	97.5	4.7
1989	98.9	100.0	101.2	102.1	4.7
1990	103.9	105.1	106.4	107.3	5.1
1991	108.7	109.9	111.3	112.1	4.5
1992	113.2	114.0	115.1	115.9	3.4
1993	117.3	118.3	119.3	120.2	3.7
1994	121.4	122.1	123.3	123.8	3.0
1995	125.0	125.8	126.6	127.5	3.0
Service-producing, white-collar occupations					
1987	....	90.7	91.8	92.1	....
1988	93.4	94.7	95.9	97.2	5.5
1989	98.8	100.0	101.4	102.6	5.6
1990	104.2	105.5	106.7	107.4	4.7
1991	109.1	110.4	111.5	112.1	4.4
1992	113.4	114.1	114.9	115.7	3.2
1993	116.9	117.8	119.0	119.8	3.5
1994	121.0	121.9	122.9	123.4	3.0
1995	124.6	125.6	126.5	127.4	3.2

Employment Cost Index, Total Compensation, Private Industry Workers, by Occupation and Industry, 1984-1995—Continued

(June 1989=100, not seasonally adjusted)

Series and year	Indexes				Percent change for 12 months ended December
	March	June	September	December	
Service-producing, white-collar, excluding sales					
1987	....	90.9	92.3	92.9	....
1988	94.1	95.1	96.6	97.5	5.0
1989	99.0	100.0	101.4	102.3	4.9
1990	104.4	105.6	107.1	108.0	5.6
1991	109.5	110.6	112.1	113.0	4.6
1992	114.1	114.9	116.1	116.8	3.4
1993	118.4	119.3	120.4	121.4	3.9
1994	122.7	123.4	124.6	125.1	3.0
1995	126.4	127.1	128.0	129.1	3.2
Service-producing, blue-collar occupations					
1987	....	92.2	93.0	93.8	....
1988	95.2	96.2	97.1	97.5	3.9
1989	98.7	100.0	101.1	101.1	3.7
1990	102.6	103.9	104.8	105.4	4.3
1991	106.6	107.6	108.7	109.4	3.8
1992	110.4	111.6	112.4	113.2	3.5
1993	114.3	115.5	116.6	117.2	3.5
1994	118.4	119.1	120.6	120.7	3.0
1995	122.1	123.1	123.9	124.2	2.9
Service-producing, service occupations					
1987	....	92.4	92.9	93.4	....
1988	94.6	95.6	97.1	98.4	5.4
1989	99.3	100.0	101.1	102.5	4.2
1990	103.9	105.0	105.8	107.4	4.8
1991	108.4	109.9	111.6	112.5	4.7
1992	113.4	114.1	115.2	115.7	2.8
1993	116.8	117.7	118.6	119.1	2.9
1994	120.2	120.7	121.3	122.5	2.9
Transportation and public utilities					
1985	87.6	88.4	89.7	90.0	....
1986	91.2	91.4	91.9	92.0	2.2
1987	92.9	93.9	94.4	94.8	3.0
1988	95.8	96.8	97.5	97.5	2.8
1989	98.7	100.0	100.7	101.2	3.8
1990	103.0	103.3	104.2	105.1	3.9
1991	106.0	107.7	109.0	109.7	4.4
1992	111.1	111.9	112.9	113.5	3.5
1993	114.8	116.0	116.8	117.5	3.5
1994	119.2	119.8	121.4	122.1	3.9
1995	124.0	124.7	126.0	127.0	4.0
Transportation					
1985	87.5	88.3	89.5	89.5	....
1986	91.3	91.1	91.9	91.5	2.2
1987	92.4	93.7	93.8	94.0	2.7
1988	95.3	96.9	97.6	97.3	3.5
1989	98.8	100.0	100.5	100.8	3.6
1990	102.8	103.0	103.8	104.6	3.8
1991	105.2	106.8	107.8	108.6	3.8
1992	109.9	110.5	111.7	111.8	2.9
1993	112.8	114.1	114.8	115.7	3.5
1994	117.1	117.7	119.7	120.3	4.0
1995	122.3	123.0	124.7	125.7	4.5

Employment Cost Index, Total Compensation, Private Industry Workers, by Occupation and Industry, 1984-1995—Continued

(June 1989=100, not seasonally adjusted)

Series and year	Indexes				Percent change for 12 months ended December
	March	June	September	December	
Public utilities					
1985	87.9	88.6	90.1	90.9	....
1986	91.1	91.6	92.1	92.7	2.0
1987	93.5	94.3	95.2	95.7	3.2
1988	96.4	96.7	97.3	97.7	2.1
1989	98.8	100.0	101.0	101.7	4.1
1990	103.2	103.8	104.8	105.7	3.9
1991	107.0	108.8	110.4	111.2	5.2
1992	112.6	113.7	114.4	115.6	4.0
1993	117.4	118.3	119.2	119.9	3.7
1994	121.7	122.6	123.6	124.4	3.8
1995	126.1	126.8	127.5	128.5	3.3
Communications					
1987	....	....	95.6	96.3	....
1988	96.7	96.9	97.5	97.5	1.2
1989	98.5	100.0	101.0	101.6	4.2
1990	103.1	103.1	104.2	105.2	3.5
1991	106.0	108.0	109.9	110.7	5.2
1992	111.8	112.7	113.4	114.7	3.6
1993	116.5	117.5	118.5	119.2	3.9
1994	121.0	122.1	122.9	124.0	4.0
1995	126.3	126.6	127.4	128.3	3.5
Electric, gas, and sanitary services					
1987	....	....	....	95.0	....
1988	96.0	96.7	97.1	98.0	3.2
1989	99.2	100.0	101.0	101.7	3.8
1990	103.2	104.6	105.5	106.2	4.4
1991	108.3	109.8	111.0	111.7	5.2
1992	113.7	115.0	115.9	116.7	4.5
1993	118.6	119.4	120.2	120.8	3.5
1994	122.7	123.2	124.4	124.8	3.3
1995	125.9	127.0	127.7	128.7	3.1
Wholesale and retail trade					
1985	84.7	86.1	87.2	87.8	....
1986	88.3	89.1	89.6	90.0	2.5
1987	90.7	92.1	92.6	92.8	3.1
1988	94.0	95.8	96.8	97.6	5.2
1989	98.9	100.0	101.6	102.6	5.1
1990	103.5	105.0	105.6	106.2	3.5
1991	107.4	109.2	110.3	110.7	4.2
1992	111.4	112.5	113.0	113.7	2.7
1993	114.7	115.9	116.4	117.1	3.0
1994	117.6	119.4	120.5	120.6	3.0
1995	121.7	122.8	123.8	124.2	3.0
Wholesale and retail trade, excluding sales					
1985	85.4	86.7	87.7	88.1	....
1986	88.6	89.4	89.9	90.7	3.0
1987	91.5	92.6	93.3	93.8	3.4
1988	94.9	96.2	97.3	98.2	4.7
1989	99.2	100.0	101.3	102.0	3.9
1990	103.0	104.5	105.4	106.1	4.0
1991	107.7	109.1	110.1	110.8	4.4
1992	111.5	112.7	113.5	114.1	3.0
1993	115.4	116.2	117.0	118.0	3.4
1994	118.6	119.8	120.9	120.9	2.5
1995	122.4	123.1	124.1	125.2	3.6

Employment Cost Index, Total Compensation, Private Industry Workers, by Occupation and Industry, 1984-1995—Continued

(June 1989=100, not seasonally adjusted)

Series and year	Indexes				Percent change for 12 months ended December
	March	June	September	December	
Wholesale trade					
1986	86.4	87.3	87.8	88.7	....
1987	89.7	91.1	91.6	92.2	3.9
1988	93.0	94.7	95.6	96.1	4.2
1989	98.5	100.0	102.6	104.5	8.7
1990	104.8	105.4	105.8	106.5	1.9
1991	107.8	109.6	110.7	111.1	4.3
1992	112.5	113.5	113.2	114.4	3.0
1993	115.3	116.4	116.6	117.8	3.0
1994	117.9	119.7	120.6	121.5	3.1
1995	123.2	124.8	126.1	126.8	4.4
Wholesale trade, excluding sales					
1986	88.3	89.5	89.9	90.8	....
1987	91.7	92.3	93.4	94.1	3.6
1988	95.2	96.2	97.2	97.7	3.8
1989	98.9	100.0	101.8	102.6	5.0
1990	103.7	105.0	105.4	106.2	3.5
1991	108.2	109.6	110.3	111.2	4.7
1992	112.5	113.5	114.1	114.9	3.3
1993	116.0	116.8	117.6	118.7	3.3
1994	119.3	120.3	121.3	122.0	2.8
1995	124.4	125.1	126.2	127.3	4.3
Retail trade					
1985	85.5	86.7	88.1	88.8	....
1986	89.2	89.9	90.5	90.8	2.3
1987	91.3	92.5	93.0	93.0	2.4
1988	94.5	96.3	97.3	98.4	5.8
1989	99.1	100.0	101.1	101.6	3.3
1990	103.0	104.8	105.5	106.0	4.3
1991	107.3	109.0	110.1	110.5	4.2
1992	110.8	112.1	112.9	113.4	2.6
1993	114.5	115.6	116.2	116.8	3.0
1994	117.5	119.2	120.4	120.1	2.8
1995	120.9	121.8	122.6	122.8	2.2
Food stores					
1987	....	....	94.5	95.5	....
1988	96.3	96.8	97.1	98.2	2.8
1989	99.8	100.0	100.8	101.7	3.6
1990	103.2	104.6	105.7	106.4	4.6
1991	107.5	109.3	110.3	111.7	5.0
1992	112.6	113.6	114.2	115.1	3.0
1993	115.9	117.2	117.1	118.3	2.8
1994	119.6	120.6	120.3	120.0	1.4
1995	120.8	120.7	121.8	122.5	2.1
General merchandise stores					
1988	....	97.2	98.5	99.6	....
1989	100.5	100.0	100.4	101.5	1.9
1990	102.6	105.7	105.9	106.9	5.3
1991	108.3	110.1	111.2	111.1	3.9
1992	111.7	112.9	113.3	113.3	2.0
1993	114.1	114.7	115.5	116.3	2.6
1994	115.3	118.0	118.7	119.3	2.6
1995	120.1	120.7	121.0	121.7	2.0

Employment Cost Index, Total Compensation, Private Industry Workers, by Occupation and Industry, 1984-1995—Continued

(June 1989=100, not seasonally adjusted)

Series and year	Indexes				Percent change for 12 months ended December
	March	June	September	December	
Finance, insurance, and real estate					
1985	83.1	83.0	84.6	85.9	....
1986	86.7	87.4	87.9	88.6	3.1
1987	90.9	90.0	90.2	90.4	2.0
1988	91.5	92.8	92.9	96.2	6.4
1989	98.3	100.0	100.4	101.4	5.4
1990	102.6	104.4	105.4	105.5	4.0
1991	108.3	109.5	109.7	110.0	4.3
1992	111.7	110.8	111.1	111.3	1.2
1993	112.6	113.1	115.7	116.4	4.6
1994	117.7	117.7	118.5	118.9	2.1
1995	120.2	121.8	122.7	123.5	3.9
Banking, savings and loan, and other credit agencies					
1986	....	....	....	87.5	....
1987	89.8	90.7	91.4	92.3	5.5
1988	95.3	96.0	97.0	97.8	6.0
1989	98.8	100.0	100.6	100.7	3.0
1990	102.1	104.1	104.4	105.8	5.1
1991	107.4	107.0	107.5	107.4	1.5
1992	110.2	110.0	111.0	111.4	3.7
1993	114.6	116.0	116.9	117.8	5.7
1994	118.7	119.4	120.8	120.5	2.3
1995	123.5	124.1	124.8	125.4	4.1
Insurance carriers, agents, brokers, and services					
1987	....	89.6	90.3	91.9	....
1988	92.6	95.0	95.8	97.0	5.5
1989	98.3	100.0	99.9	101.0	4.1
1990	103.2	105.2	106.5	106.0	5.0
1991	107.4	109.5	109.5	110.7	4.4
1992	113.2	114.7	114.9	115.2	4.1
1993	114.3	116.1	117.4	119.7	3.9
1994	119.9	120.5	121.5	122.3	2.2
1995	123.5	124.6	124.9	126.0	3.0
Insurance, excluding sales occupations					
1987	....	90.9	91.9	92.3	....
1988	93.8	95.3	96.5	97.3	5.4
1989	98.6	100.0	101.0	101.8	4.6
1990	104.5	106.1	106.8	107.6	5.7
1991	108.7	110.3	111.4	112.5	4.6
1992	113.9	115.7	116.1	117.2	4.2
1993	118.6	120.6	121.8	122.7	4.7
1994	124.4	125.0	126.0	126.5	3.1
1995	127.6	129.0	129.6	130.3	3.0
Service industries					
1985	81.3	82.0	83.8	84.1	....
1986	85.3	85.8	86.8	87.7	4.3
1987	89.0	89.5	91.3	92.2	5.1
1988	93.6	94.5	96.4	97.5	5.7
1989	99.0	100.0	101.8	102.9	5.5
1990	105.0	106.5	108.1	109.3	6.2
1991	110.8	111.5	113.1	114.0	4.3
1992	115.3	116.4	117.8	118.9	4.3
1993	120.1	120.9	122.3	123.1	3.5
1994	124.4	124.9	125.9	126.6	2.8
1995	127.5	128.2	128.9	129.7	2.4

Employment Cost Index, Total Compensation, Private Industry Workers, by Occupation and Industry, 1984-1995—Continued

(June 1989=100, not seasonally adjusted)

Series and year	Indexes				Percent change for 12 months ended December
	March	June	September	December	
Business services					
1986	....	....	....	87.2	....
1987	88.5	89.5	91.7	92.5	6.1
1988	93.8	94.9	96.2	97.2	5.1
1989	98.1	100.0	100.7	101.3	4.2
1990	103.6	105.3	106.3	107.4	6.0
1991	110.3	110.4	110.0	111.1	3.4
1992	112.5	113.6	115.2	115.9	4.3
1993	116.5	117.4	118.1	118.6	2.3
1994	121.3	122.1	122.4	123.0	3.7
1995	124.5	125.3	125.7	126.5	2.8
Health services					
1985	81.9	82.5	83.4	83.7	....
1986	84.7	85.2	86.6	87.7	4.8
1987	88.8	89.4	90.4	91.5	4.3
1988	92.6	94.1	95.6	97.0	6.0
1989	98.9	100.0	101.9	103.7	6.9
1990	105.8	107.1	109.0	110.8	6.8
1991	112.6	113.5	115.3	116.5	5.1
1992	117.9	118.9	120.6	121.8	4.5
1993	123.0	124.0	125.0	126.0	3.4
1994	126.7	127.1	127.9	128.7	2.1
1995	129.7	130.3	131.3	132.3	2.8
Hospitals					
1986	....	84.5	85.8	86.8	....
1987	87.8	88.3	89.9	91.0	4.8
1988	92.2	93.6	95.2	96.6	6.2
1989	98.8	100.0	101.9	103.5	7.1
1990	105.4	106.6	108.9	110.7	7.0
1991	112.2	113.2	114.9	116.1	4.9
1992	117.7	118.5	120.2	121.6	4.7
1993	122.7	123.4	124.5	125.6	3.3
1994	126.7	127.1	127.7	128.6	2.4
1995	128.9	129.7	130.3	131.4	2.2
Educational services					
1988	....	....	....	98.3	....
1989	99.1	100.0	103.9	104.2	6.0
1990	105.4	105.9	110.2	111.4	6.9
1991	111.9	111.5	114.9	115.7	3.9
1992	115.8	116.3	119.3	120.0	3.7
1993	120.5	120.6	123.8	124.1	3.4
1994	124.5	125.4	128.2	128.4	3.5
1995	128.8	130.3	133.2	134.0	4.4
Colleges and universities					
1988	....	....	....	98.2	....
1989	99.0	100.0	103.3	103.8	5.7
1990	105.2	105.7	109.8	110.6	6.6
1991	111.3	112.0	115.5	116.3	5.2
1992	116.8	117.4	120.3	120.8	3.9
1993	121.5	121.5	125.0	125.3	3.7
1994	125.7	126.0	128.5	128.8	2.8
1995	129.3	131.3	134.6	135.7	5.4

Employment Cost Index, Total Compensation, Private Industry Workers, by Occupation and Industry, 1984-1995—Continued

(June 1989=100, not seasonally adjusted)

Series and year	Indexes				Percent change for 12 months ended December
	March	June	September	December	
Nonmanufacturing, total					
1984	81.0	81.8	82.4	83.4	4.8
1985	84.3	85.1	86.4	87.0	4.3
1986	87.9	88.5	89.2	89.7	3.1
1987	90.9	91.5	92.4	92.9	3.6
1988	94.1	95.4	96.5	97.5	5.0
1989	98.8	100.0	101.3	102.3	4.9
1990	103.8	105.1	106.2	106.9	4.5
1991	108.5	109.7	110.9	111.5	4.3
1992	112.7	113.5	114.4	115.1	3.2
1993	116.3	117.2	118.4	119.0	3.4
1994	120.3	121.2	122.3	122.6	3.0
1995	123.7	124.6	125.5	126.2	2.9
Nonmanufacturing, white-collar occupations					
1987		90.8	91.8	92.2	
1988	93.4	94.8	95.9	97.2	5.4
1989	98.8	100.0	101.4	102.6	5.6
1990	104.1	105.5	106.7	107.4	4.7
1991	109.1	110.4	111.5	112.1	4.4
1992	113.4	114.1	114.9	115.7	3.2
1993	117.0	117.9	119.0	119.9	3.6
1994	121.1	122.1	123.1	123.5	3.0
1995	124.7	125.6	126.5	127.3	3.1
Nonmanufacturing, white-collar occupations, excluding sales occupations					
1987		91.0	92.3	92.9	
1988	94.1	95.3	96.6	97.5	5.0
1989	99.0	100.0	101.4	102.3	4.9
1990	104.3	105.6	107.0	108.0	5.6
1991	109.5	110.6	112.1	112.9	4.5
1992	114.1	114.9	116.0	116.9	3.5
1993	118.5	119.4	120.4	121.4	3.8
1994	122.8	123.6	124.7	125.1	3.0
1995	126.4	127.1	128.0	129.0	3.1
Nonmanufacturing, blue-collar occupations					
1987		92.9	93.7	94.5	
1988	95.7	96.8	97.6	98.1	3.8
1989	98.8	100.0	101.1	101.7	3.7
1990	102.9	104.1	105.0	105.6	3.8
1991	107.2	108.2	109.2	109.8	4.0
1992	110.7	111.8	112.8	113.4	3.3
1993	114.6	115.6	116.6	117.1	3.3
1994	118.2	119.1	120.5	120.5	2.9
1995	121.5	122.5	123.5	123.8	2.7
Nonmanufacturing, service occupations					
1987		92.4	92.8	93.3	
1988	94.6	95.6	97.1	98.3	5.4
1989	99.2	100.0	101.0	102.4	4.2
1990	103.9	105.0	105.8	107.4	4.9
1991	108.4	109.9	111.7	112.5	4.7
1992	113.4	114.1	115.2	115.7	2.8
1993	116.8	117.7	118.6	119.1	2.9
1994	120.2	120.7	121.3	122.4	2.8
1995	123.0	123.5	124.2	124.8	2.0

Employment Cost Index, Total Compensation, State and Local Government, by Occupation and Industry, 1984-1995

(June 1989=100, not seasonally adjusted)

Series and year	Indexes				Percent change for 12 months ended December
	March	June	September	December	
STATE AND LOCAL GOVERNMENT WORKERS, TOTAL					
1984	76.2	76.6	79.3	80.1	6.7
1985	81.0	81.2	84.0	84.6	5.6
1986	85.5	86.0	88.4	89.0	5.2
1987	89.8	90.0	92.1	93.0	4.5
1988	94.2	94.5	97.1	98.2	5.6
1989	99.4	100.0	103.3	104.3	6.2
1990	105.8	106.5	109.4	110.4	5.8
1991	111.8	112.0	113.9	114.4	3.6
1992	115.2	115.7	117.9	118.6	3.7
1993	119.3	119.6	121.4	121.9	2.8
1994	122.6	123.1	125.0	125.6	3.0
1995	126.4	126.9	128.7	129.4	3.0
WORKERS, BY OCCUPATIONAL GROUP					
White-collar occupations					
1984	75.6	75.9	78.8	79.6	6.8
1985	80.5	80.7	83.6	84.2	5.8
1986	85.1	85.4	88.1	88.7	5.3
1987	89.4	89.6	91.9	92.8	4.6
1988	94.0	94.3	97.0	98.3	5.9
1989	99.5	100.0	103.6	104.6	6.4
1990	106.1	106.7	109.9	110.9	6.0
1991	112.2	112.3	114.2	114.6	3.3
1992	115.4	115.8	118.1	118.9	3.8
1993	119.5	119.6	121.5	121.9	2.5
1994	122.6	122.9	124.9	125.5	3.0
1995	126.2	126.6	128.6	129.3	3.0
Professional specialty and technical					
1989	....	100.0	103.8	104.7	....
1990	106.4	107.0	110.3	111.2	6.2
1991	112.3	112.4	114.5	115.0	3.4
1992	115.5	116.0	118.5	119.2	3.7
1993	119.6	119.7	121.7	122.0	2.3
1994	122.5	122.7	125.0	125.5	2.9
1995	126.0	126.3	128.4	129.0	2.8
Executive, administrative, and managerial					
1989	....	100.0	103.1	104.1	....
1990	105.7	106.4	109.3	110.1	5.8
1991	112.2	112.0	113.3	113.7	3.3
1992	115.0	115.2	116.8	117.8	3.6
1993	119.0	119.2	121.0	121.6	3.2
1994	122.8	123.4	124.7	125.3	3.0
1995	126.9	127.4	129.1	130.3	4.0
Administrative support, including clerical					
1989	....	100.0	102.9	103.9	....
1990	105.4	106.0	108.7	110.2	6.1
1991	111.8	111.7	113.5	114.0	3.4
1992	115.4	115.7	117.5	118.5	3.9
1993	119.2	119.6	121.0	121.6	2.6
1994	122.7	123.3	124.9	125.6	3.3
1995	126.3	126.9	128.4	129.2	2.9
Blue-collar occupations					
1984	79.7	79.9	81.7	82.3	5.6
1985	83.7	84.0	86.2	86.7	5.3
1986	88.0	89.1	90.5	91.2	5.2
1987	92.0	92.4	93.7	94.3	3.4
1988	95.4	95.4	97.0	97.5	3.4
1989	99.3	100.0	102.1	103.7	6.4
1990	105.5	106.3	108.2	108.7	4.8
1991	110.4	110.9	112.4	112.9	3.9
1992	114.2	115.3	116.9	117.8	4.3
1993	118.3	118.7	120.5	121.4	3.1
1994	122.3	122.7	124.2	124.7	2.7
1995	125.4	126.3	127.2	128.1	2.7

Employment Cost Index, Total Compensation, State and Local Government, by Occupation and Industry, 1984-1995—Continued

(June 1989=100, not seasonally adjusted)

Series and year	Indexes				Percent change for 12 months ended December
	March	June	September	December	
Service occupations					
1984	77.0	77.5	79.8	80.8	6.2
1985	81.8	82.0	84.5	85.3	5.6
1986	86.1	86.9	88.4	89.1	4.5
1987	90.2	90.7	92.2	92.9	4.3
1988	94.4	95.1	97.9	98.2	5.7
1989	99.2	100.0	102.8	103.6	5.5
1990	104.8	105.3	108.1	109.2	5.4
1991	111.0	111.3	113.4	114.0	4.4
1992	115.0	115.6	117.4	118.0	3.5
1993	119.1	119.7	121.4	122.1	3.5
1994	123.1	123.9	126.0	126.6	3.7
1995	127.6	128.8	130.1	131.1	3.6
WORKERS, BY INDUSTRY DIVISION					
Service industries					
1984	75.2	75.5	78.5	79.3	7.0
1985	80.2	80.5	83.3	84.0	5.9
1986	84.8	85.1	87.9	88.6	5.5
1987	89.0	89.2	91.7	92.5	4.4
1988	93.8	94.0	97.0	98.5	6.5
1989	99.5	100.0	103.8	104.7	6.3
1990	106.1	106.8	110.2	111.3	6.3
1991	112.4	112.6	114.8	115.3	3.6
1992	115.8	116.2	118.8	119.6	3.7
1993	120.0	120.2	122.2	122.6	2.5
1994	123.1	123.4	125.6	126.1	2.9
1995	126.7	127.1	129.2	129.8	2.9
Services, excluding schools					
1984	78.4	79.2	80.6	81.4	5.3
1985	82.6	82.9	84.5	85.2	4.7
1986	86.2	86.9	87.8	88.9	4.3
1987	89.8	90.3	91.4	92.2	3.7
1988	94.7	94.8	96.5	97.8	6.1
1989	99.1	100.0	102.5	103.2	5.5
1990	105.4	106.4	108.8	110.2	6.8
1991	112.2	111.7	113.7	114.4	3.8
1992	115.1	115.6	117.5	118.6	3.7
1993	119.6	120.0	121.4	121.9	2.8
1994	122.8	123.3	124.9	125.6	3.0
1995	126.4	127.7	128.9	129.3	2.9
Health services					
1985	82.5	82.6	84.8	85.3	....
1986	86.0	86.8	88.1	88.8	4.1
1987	89.5	90.1	92.0	93.0	4.7
1988	94.0	94.4	96.5	97.3	4.6
1989	98.8	100.0	103.1	104.2	7.1
1990	106.2	106.9	109.9	111.1	6.6
1991	112.6	112.2	113.9	114.9	3.4
1992	115.9	116.8	118.6	119.4	3.9
1993	120.2	120.7	122.2	123.1	3.1
1994	124.2	125.2	127.2	127.7	3.7
1995	128.4	129.8	131.0	131.5	3.0
Hospitals					
1988	94.0	94.8	97.0	97.6	....
1989	98.6	100.0	103.2	104.5	7.1
1990	106.0	107.0	109.8	111.4	6.6
1991	112.2	112.1	114.1	115.2	3.4
1992	115.9	116.7	118.6	119.4	3.6
1993	120.0	120.4	122.0	123.3	3.3
1994	123.7	124.5	127.0	127.7	3.6
1995	128.4	129.9	131.1	131.7	3.1

Employment Cost Index, Total Compensation, State and Local Government, by Occupation and Industry, 1984-1995—Continued

(June 1989=100, not seasonally adjusted)

Series and year	Indexes				Percent change for 12 months ended December
	March	June	September	December	
Educational services					
1989	99.5	100.0	104.1	104.9	....
1990	106.2	106.8	110.3	111.4	6.2
1991	112.4	112.6	114.9	115.3	3.5
1992	115.7	116.1	118.9	119.7	3.8
1993	120.0	120.1	122.3	122.7	2.5
1994	122.9	123.1	125.5	126.0	2.7
1995	126.5	126.8	129.0	129.6	2.9
Schools					
1984	74.2	74.3	77.8	78.7	7.7
1985	79.5	79.7	82.9	83.6	6.2
1986	84.3	84.4	88.0	88.4	5.7
1987	88.7	88.9	91.8	92.7	4.9
1988	93.4	93.7	97.2	98.7	6.5
1989	99.6	100.0	104.4	105.3	6.7
1990	106.4	106.9	110.6	111.6	6.0
1991	112.5	112.9	115.2	115.6	3.6
1992	116.0	116.4	119.2	119.9	3.7
1993	120.2	120.3	122.5	122.9	2.5
1994	123.2	123.4	125.9	126.3	2.8
1995	126.8	127.1	129.4	129.9	2.9
Elementary and secondary schools					
1984	73.8	74.0	77.8	78.6	7.8
1985	79.1	79.2	82.9	83.6	6.4
1986	84.2	84.3	87.9	88.5	5.9
1987	88.6	88.7	92.1	92.9	5.0
1988	93.5	93.8	97.4	99.1	6.7
1989	99.6	100.0	104.6	105.5	6.5
1990	106.5	107.1	111.1	112.1	6.3
1991	112.9	113.0	115.7	116.2	3.7
1992	116.6	117.1	119.9	120.7	3.9
1993	120.7	120.8	123.0	123.6	2.4
1994	123.7	123.8	126.3	126.5	2.3
1995	127.1	127.4	129.8	130.3	3.0
Colleges and universities					
1989	99.6	100.0	103.4	104.7	....
1990	106.1	106.3	109.2	110.2	5.3
1991	111.3	112.5	113.4	113.5	3.0
1992	114.0	114.1	116.9	117.2	3.3
1993	118.4	118.5	120.8	120.7	3.0
1994	121.5	122.0	124.5	125.5	4.0
1995	126.0	126.1	128.0	129.0	2.8
Public administration					
1984	77.8	78.3	80.4	81.4	5.9
1985	82.4	82.5	85.0	85.4	4.9
1986	86.6	87.4	89.0	89.7	5.0
1987	91.3	91.6	92.7	93.8	4.6
1988	95.2	95.8	97.5	97.8	4.3
1989	99.2	100.0	102.5	103.2	5.5
1990	105.1	105.5	107.8	108.7	5.3
1991	110.8	110.9	112.2	112.6	3.6
1992	114.0	114.6	115.8	116.3	3.3
1993	117.6	118.0	119.3	120.0	3.2
1994	121.5	122.2	123.7	124.2	3.5
1995	125.4	126.1	127.4	128.5	3.5

Employment Cost Index, Wages and Salaries, Civilian Workers, by Occupation and Industry, 1984-1995

(June 1989=100, not seasonally adjusted)

Series and year	Indexes				Percent change for 12 months ended December
	March	June	September	December	
CIVILIAN WORKERS					
1984	81.5	82.2	83.2	84.2	4.5
1985	85.1	85.9	87.3	87.8	4.3
1986	88.7	89.4	90.4	90.9	3.5
1987	91.8	92.3	93.5	94.1	3.5
1988	95.0	95.9	97.2	98.1	4.3
1989	99.2	100.0	101.6	102.4	4.4
1990	103.6	104.7	106.0	106.8	4.3
1991	108.0	108.9	110.0	110.6	3.6
1992	111.5	112.1	113.0	113.6	2.7
1993	114.5	115.2	116.4	117.1	3.1
1994	117.8	118.6	119.8	120.4	2.8
1995	121.3	122.2	123.2	123.9	2.9
Civilian workers, excluding sales					
1984	81.7	82.3	83.5	84.4	4.7
1985	85.2	85.9	87.4	87.8	4.0
1986	88.8	89.3	90.4	91.0	3.6
1987	91.9	92.4	93.7	94.4	3.7
1988	95.2	96.1	97.3	98.2	4.0
1989	99.2	100.0	101.4	102.3	4.2
1990	103.6	104.6	106.1	106.8	4.4
1991	108.0	108.9	110.1	110.8	3.7
1992	111.6	112.2	113.2	113.9	2.8
1993	114.8	115.5	116.6	117.2	2.9
1994	118.0	118.8	120.1	120.7	3.0
1995	121.7	122.4	123.4	124.2	2.9
WORKERS, BY OCCUPATIONAL GROUP					
White-collar occupations					
1984	79.6	80.4	81.6	82.4	4.7
1985	83.6	84.4	86.0	86.6	5.1
1986	87.6	88.4	89.5	90.1	4.0
1987	91.2	91.7	93.1	93.6	3.9
1988	94.5	95.5	96.9	98.0	4.7
1989	99.2	100.0	101.9	102.8	4.9
1990	104.1	105.2	106.8	107.4	4.5
1991	108.7	109.6	110.8	111.3	3.6
1992	112.2	112.8	113.7	114.5	2.9
1993	115.4	116.0	117.4	118.1	3.1
1994	118.8	119.7	120.8	121.5	2.9
1995	122.4	123.1	124.3	125.1	3.0
White-collar occupations, excluding sales					
1984	79.7	80.3	81.8	82.7	5.4
1985	83.5	84.3	85.9	86.4	4.5
1986	87.5	88.2	89.4	90.1	4.3
1987	91.2	91.7	93.3	94.0	4.3
1988	94.9	95.6	97.2	98.2	4.5
1989	99.3	100.0	101.8	102.6	4.5
1990	104.2	105.1	107.0	107.8	5.1
1991	109.0	109.8	111.2	111.9	3.8
1992	112.6	113.2	114.4	115.1	2.9
1993	116.2	116.8	118.0	118.7	3.1
1994	119.5	120.2	121.5	122.2	2.9
1995	123.2	123.8	125.0	125.9	3.0
Professional specialty and technical					
1989		100.0	102.5	103.3	
1990	104.8	105.5	107.9	108.8	5.3
1991	109.9	110.4	112.3	113.0	3.9
1992	113.6	114.4	116.0	116.7	3.3
1993	117.5	118.0	119.5	120.0	2.8
1994	120.7	121.3	122.8	123.5	2.9
1995	124.2	124.7	126.1	127.0	2.8
Executive, administrative, and managerial					
1989		100.0	101.1	101.8	
1990	103.6	105.0	106.5	107.2	5.3
1991	108.5	109.6	110.8	111.5	4.0
1992	111.9	112.2	112.8	113.5	1.8
1993	115.0	115.5	116.5	117.3	3.3
1994	118.1	119.0	120.2	120.8	3.0
1995	122.2	122.8	123.8	124.9	3.4

COMPENSATION OF EMPLOYEES

Employment Cost Index, Wages and Salaries, Civilian Workers, by Occupation and Industry, 1984-1995—Continued

(June 1989=100, not seasonally adjusted)

Series and year	Indexes				Percent change for 12 months ended December
	March	June	September	December	
Administrative support, including clerical					
1989	....	100.0	101.4	102.4	....
1990	103.7	104.7	105.9	106.7	4.2
1991	107.9	108.8	109.9	110.6	3.7
1992	111.8	112.5	113.4	114.2	3.3
1993	115.3	116.1	117.1	118.0	3.3
1994	118.9	119.8	120.9	121.6	3.1
1995	122.8	123.4	124.3	125.3	3.0
Blue-collar occupations					
1984	84.8	85.4	86.0	86.9	3.7
1985	87.7	88.6	89.7	89.9	3.5
1986	90.7	91.2	91.9	92.4	2.8
1987	92.8	93.5	94.3	95.1	2.9
1988	95.9	96.8	97.4	98.1	3.2
1989	99.0	100.0	101.0	101.7	3.7
1990	102.8	103.9	104.7	105.4	3.6
1991	106.6	107.4	108.2	108.9	3.3
1992	109.8	110.6	111.3	111.9	2.8
1993	112.7	113.4	114.4	115.0	2.8
1994	115.8	116.7	117.8	118.2	2.8
1995	119.2	120.3	121.1	121.5	2.8
Service occupations					
1984	82.9	82.7	84.5	85.8	5.8
1985	86.2	86.5	88.4	88.8	3.5
1986	89.6	89.8	91.0	91.7	3.3
1987	92.7	93.0	93.9	94.3	2.8
1988	95.3	96.2	97.9	98.7	4.7
1989	99.4	100.0	101.4	102.5	3.9
1990	103.4	104.2	105.6	106.8	4.2
1991	107.8	108.9	110.6	111.3	4.2
1992	111.9	112.4	113.4	113.8	2.2
1993	114.5	115.2	116.1	116.6	2.5
1994	117.5	118.1	119.4	120.4	3.3
1995	121.2	121.8	122.8	123.4	2.5
WORKERS, BY INDUSTRY DIVISION					
Goods-producing industries					
1984	84.0	84.6	85.4	86.3	3.9
1985	87.4	88.2	89.0	89.4	3.6
1986	90.3	91.2	91.7	92.2	3.1
1987	92.8	93.3	94.3	95.1	3.1
1988	96.0	96.9	97.4	98.1	3.2
1989	99.0	100.0	100.9	101.9	3.9
1990	103.1	104.2	105.1	105.8	3.8
1991	107.0	108.0	108.8	109.7	3.7
1992	110.7	111.4	112.2	112.9	2.9
1993	113.8	114.6	115.4	116.2	2.9
1994	117.0	118.0	119.0	119.6	2.9
1995	120.5	121.4	122.1	122.8	2.7
Manufacturing					
1984	83.4	84.1	85.0	86.1	4.4
1985	87.2	88.1	88.8	89.2	3.6
1986	90.3	91.1	91.6	92.1	3.3
1987	92.7	93.3	94.2	95.2	3.4
1988	96.0	96.8	97.3	98.1	3.0
1989	99.0	100.0	100.9	101.9	3.9
1990	103.3	104.5	105.4	106.2	4.2
1991	107.4	108.4	109.3	110.3	3.9
1992	111.5	112.2	112.9	113.7	3.1
1993	114.7	115.5	116.3	117.3	3.2
1994	118.0	119.0	120.0	120.8	3.0
1995	121.9	122.9	123.5	124.3	2.9
Service-producing industries					
1984	80.3	80.9	82.0	83.0	4.8
1985	83.9	84.6	86.5	87.0	4.8
1986	87.9	88.4	89.7	90.2	3.7
1987	91.3	91.8	93.1	93.6	3.8
1988	94.5	95.4	97.0	98.0	4.7
1989	99.2	100.0	101.8	102.7	4.8
1990	103.8	104.9	106.5	107.2	4.4
1991	108.4	109.3	110.6	111.0	3.5
1992	111.8	112.4	113.3	114.0	2.7
1993	114.8	115.5	116.8	117.5	3.1
1994	118.2	118.9	120.2	120.7	2.7
1995	121.7	122.5	123.7	124.4	3.1

Employment Cost Index, Wages and Salaries, Civilian Workers, by Occupation and Industry, 1984-1995—Continued

(June 1989=100, not seasonally adjusted)

Series and year	Indexes				Percent change for 12 months ended December
	March	June	September	December	
Services					
1984	77.8	78.2	80.3	81.4	6.3
1985	81.9	82.4	84.7	85.1	4.5
1986	86.1	86.5	88.3	89.1	4.7
1987	90.1	90.5	92.7	93.6	5.1
1988	94.4	94.9	97.2	98.3	5.0
1989	99.4	100.0	102.5	103.3	5.1
1990	104.8	105.9	108.1	109.2	5.7
1991	110.2	110.7	112.4	113.0	3.5
1992	113.7	114.3	115.9	116.7	3.3
1993	117.4	117.8	119.5	120.0	2.8
1994	120.9	121.3	122.8	123.5	2.9
1995	124.4	124.8	126.2	126.9	2.8
Health services					
1985	82.3	82.9	84.0	84.2	....
1986	85.1	85.7	87.2	88.2	4.8
1987	89.4	90.0	91.3	92.3	4.6
1988	92.9	94.4	96.1	97.4	5.5
1989	99.0	100.0	102.0	103.5	6.3
1990	105.3	106.2	108.3	109.7	6.0
1991	111.1	111.8	113.4	114.5	4.4
1992	115.4	116.2	117.7	118.6	3.6
1993	119.5	120.3	121.4	122.2	3.0
1994	122.8	123.4	124.4	125.4	2.6
1995	126.1	126.6	127.5	128.4	2.4
Hospitals					
1986	....	85.3	86.6	87.6	....
1987	88.7	89.3	90.9	92.0	5.0
1988	92.9	94.3	96.0	97.3	5.8
1989	98.9	100.0	102.2	103.5	6.4
1990	105.0	106.0	108.3	109.8	6.1
1991	110.8	111.5	113.1	114.3	4.1
1992	115.2	115.7	117.1	118.0	3.2
1993	118.9	119.5	120.7	121.7	3.1
1994	122.4	123.0	124.0	124.9	2.6
1995	125.5	126.0	126.8	127.8	2.3
Educational services					
1989	99.5	100.0	103.8	104.4	....
1990	105.4	105.8	109.6	110.4	5.7
1991	111.1	111.1	113.6	114.0	3.3
1992	114.1	114.4	116.9	117.5	3.1
1993	117.9	118.0	120.4	120.7	2.7
1994	121.0	121.3	123.8	124.3	3.0
1995	125.0	125.1	127.8	128.5	3.4
Public administration					
1984	79.3	79.9	81.9	82.8	5.2
1985	83.7	83.8	86.6	87.0	5.1
1986	88.1	88.7	90.6	91.0	4.6
1987	92.6	92.9	93.9	94.7	4.1
1988	95.8	96.4	98.1	98.4	3.9
1989	99.4	100.0	102.1	102.8	4.5
1990	104.3	104.6	106.5	107.3	4.4
1991	109.1	109.5	110.6	110.9	3.4
1992	111.9	112.4	113.1	113.6	2.4
1993	114.4	114.9	115.9	116.6	2.6
1994	117.9	118.5	119.9	120.6	3.4
1995	121.9	122.3	123.2	124.2	3.0
Nonmanufacturing					
1984	80.9	81.4	82.5	83.4	4.4
1985	84.3	85.0	86.8	87.3	4.7
1986	88.2	88.7	89.9	90.5	3.7
1987	91.5	92.0	93.3	93.7	3.5
1988	94.6	95.6	97.1	98.0	4.6
1989	99.2	100.0	101.8	102.6	4.7
1990	103.7	104.8	106.2	106.9	4.2
1991	108.1	109.0	110.2	110.7	3.6
1992	111.5	112.0	113.0	113.6	2.6
1993	114.4	115.1	116.4	117.0	3.0
1994	117.7	118.5	119.7	120.2	2.7
1995	121.1	121.9	123.1	123.8	3.0

COMPENSATION OF EMPLOYEES

Employment Cost Index, Wages and Salaries, Private Industry Workers, by Occupation and Industry, 1984-1995

(June 1989=100, not seasonally adjusted)

Series and year	Indexes				Percent change for 12 months ended December
	March	June	September	December	
PRIVATE INDUSTRY WORKERS					
1984	82.4	83.1	83.8	84.8	4.2
1985	85.8	86.7	87.8	88.3	4.1
1986	89.2	89.9	90.6	91.1	3.2
1987	92.0	92.6	93.5	94.1	3.3
1988	95.0	96.1	97.0	98.0	4.1
1989	99.0	100.0	101.2	102.0	4.1
1990	103.2	104.5	105.4	106.1	4.0
1991	107.3	108.4	109.3	110.0	3.7
1992	110.9	111.6	112.2	112.9	2.6
1993	113.9	114.6	115.7	116.4	3.1
1994	117.2	118.1	119.1	119.7	2.8
1995	120.6	121.5	122.4	123.1	2.8
Private industry workers, excluding sales					
1984	82.7	83.4	84.2	85.3	4.7
1985	86.0	86.9	88.1	88.4	3.6
1986	89.3	90.0	90.6	91.2	3.2
1987	92.1	92.7	93.8	94.5	3.6
1988	95.4	96.3	97.3	98.0	3.7
1989	99.1	100.0	101.1	101.9	4.0
1990	103.2	104.4	105.4	106.2	4.2
1991	107.4	108.4	109.4	110.2	3.8
1992	111.1	111.8	112.5	113.2	2.7
1993	114.2	115.0	115.9	116.6	3.0
1994	117.5	118.3	119.4	120.0	2.9
1995	121.0	121.8	122.6	123.4	2.8
WORKERS, BY OCCUPATIONAL GROUPS					
White-collar occupations					
1984	80.4	81.4	82.1	83.0	4.3
1985	84.2	85.2	86.4	87.1	4.9
1986	88.0	89.0	89.6	90.1	3.4
1987	91.4	91.9	93.0	93.4	3.7
1988	94.4	95.6	96.7	97.8	4.7
1989	99.0	100.0	101.4	102.4	4.7
1990	103.6	104.9	106.0	106.6	4.1
1991	107.9	109.1	110.1	110.7	3.8
1992	111.7	112.3	112.9	113.7	2.7
1993	114.7	115.5	116.7	117.5	3.3
1994	118.3	119.3	120.2	120.8	2.8
1995	121.7	122.7	123.6	124.4	3.0
White-collar occupations, excluding sales					
1984	80.7	81.5	82.5	83.5	5.0
1985	84.3	85.3	86.4	86.8	4.0
1986	88.0	88.9	89.5	90.1	3.8
1987	91.4	92.0	93.4	94.0	4.3
1988	95.0	95.9	97.1	98.0	4.3
1989	99.2	100.0	101.2	102.1	4.2
1990	103.7	104.8	106.2	106.9	4.7
1991	108.2	109.2	110.5	111.3	4.1
1992	112.1	112.8	113.7	114.4	2.8
1993	115.7	116.4	117.4	118.2	3.3
1994	119.0	119.9	121.0	121.7	3.0
1995	122.8	123.4	124.3	125.4	3.0
Professional specialty and technical					
1984	80.3	81.4	82.3	83.7	5.7
1985	84.0	84.6	86.3	86.5	3.3
1986	87.2	88.1	89.0	89.7	3.7
1987	91.0	91.5	92.8	93.8	4.6
1988	94.7	95.9	97.4	97.9	4.4
1989	99.3	100.0	101.6	102.5	4.7
1990	104.1	104.8	106.5	107.5	4.9
1991	108.6	109.5	111.1	112.0	4.2
1992	113.0	114.0	115.3	116.0	3.6
1993	117.1	117.9	118.9	119.5	3.0
1994	120.4	121.3	122.2	123.0	2.9
1995	123.7	124.4	125.3	126.4	2.8

Employment Cost Index, Wages and Salaries, Private Industry Workers, by Occupation and Industry, 1984-1995—Continued

(June 1989=100, not seasonally adjusted)

Series and year	Indexes				Percent change for 12 months ended December
	March	June	September	December	
Executive, administrative, and managerial occupations					
1984	80.1	80.9	82.1	83.0	5.7
1985	84.0	85.9	86.7	87.2	5.1
1986	88.6	89.7	89.9	90.6	3.9
1987	92.1	92.6	94.1	94.5	4.3
1988	95.0	95.9	96.7	98.0	3.7
1989	99.3	100.0	100.8	101.5	3.6
1990	103.3	104.9	106.2	106.9	5.3
1991	108.2	109.4	110.6	111.4	4.2
1992	111.6	112.0	112.5	113.2	1.6
1993	114.7	115.3	116.2	117.0	3.4
1994	117.8	118.8	120.0	120.5	3.0
1995	121.9	122.5	123.4	124.5	3.3
Sales occupations					
1984	79.5	80.7	79.7	80.5	0.4
1985	83.9	84.6	86.0	88.3	9.7
1986	88.2	89.6	90.3	90.1	2.0
1987	91.3	91.6	91.6	90.9	0.9
1988	91.9	94.3	94.8	96.9	6.6
1989	98.6	100.0	102.1	103.7	7.0
1990	103.3	105.3	105.4	105.2	1.4
1991	106.8	108.5	108.2	107.9	2.6
1992	109.7	110.1	109.7	110.7	2.6
1993	110.5	111.6	113.8	114.7	3.6
1994	114.8	116.2	116.5	116.7	1.7
1995	116.9	119.3	120.5	120.2	3.0
Administrative support, including clerical					
1984	81.3	81.9	82.8	83.4	3.9
1985	84.6	85.2	86.2	86.8	4.1
1986	87.9	88.7	89.3	90.0	3.7
1987	91.1	91.9	93.0	93.7	4.1
1988	95.1	95.8	97.2	97.8	4.4
1989	99.1	100.0	101.1	102.2	4.5
1990	103.6	104.7	105.7	106.4	4.1
1991	107.6	108.6	109.6	110.4	3.8
1992	111.6	112.4	113.2	114.0	3.3
1993	115.2	116.1	117.1	118.0	3.5
1994	119.0	119.9	120.9	121.6	3.1
1995	122.9	123.5	124.3	125.3	3.0
Blue-collar occupations					
1984	85.0	85.6	86.2	87.1	3.6
1985	88.0	88.8	89.9	90.1	3.4
1986	90.9	91.4	91.9	92.4	2.6
1987	92.8	93.5	94.3	95.2	3.0
1988	95.9	96.8	97.4	98.2	3.2
1989	99.0	100.0	101.0	101.6	3.5
1990	102.7	103.8	104.6	105.2	3.5
1991	106.4	107.3	108.0	108.8	3.4
1992	109.7	110.4	111.1	111.6	2.6
1993	112.5	113.2	114.1	114.8	2.9
1994	115.6	116.5	117.5	118.0	2.8
1995	119.0	120.1	120.8	121.3	2.8
Precision production, craft, and repair occupations					
1984	84.5	85.1	85.6	86.6	3.5
1985	87.7	88.5	89.8	89.8	3.7
1986	90.9	91.2	91.9	92.5	3.0
1987	92.8	93.5	94.5	95.1	2.8
1988	95.9	96.8	97.2	97.9	2.9
1989	98.8	100.0	101.0	101.6	3.8
1990	102.5	103.6	104.4	104.9	3.2
1991	106.3	107.0	107.8	108.4	3.3
1992	109.3	110.1	111.0	111.5	2.9
1993	112.4	113.2	114.2	114.7	2.9
1994	115.5	116.5	117.8	117.9	2.8
1995	118.8	119.9	121.0	121.1	2.7

Employment Cost Index, Wages and Salaries, Private Industry Workers, by Occupation and Industry, 1984-1995—Continued

(June 1989=100, not seasonally adjusted)

Series and year	Indexes				Percent change for 12 months ended December
	March	June	September	December	
Machine operators, assemblers, and inspectors					
1984	84.5	85.2	85.8	86.8	3.8
1985	87.5	88.4	89.1	89.5	3.1
1986	90.2	90.9	91.3	91.9	2.7
1987	92.3	93.2	93.8	95.1	3.5
1988	95.6	96.5	97.1	98.1	3.2
1989	99.0	100.0	100.6	101.6	3.6
1990	103.0	104.2	104.9	105.8	4.1
1991	107.1	108.0	108.7	109.8	3.8
1992	110.9	111.6	111.7	112.4	2.4
1993	113.2	113.8	114.7	115.6	2.8
1994	116.2	117.2	118.0	118.8	2.8
1995	119.6	120.9	121.4	122.3	2.9
Transportation and material moving occupations					
1984	86.8	87.6	88.1	88.6	3.5
1985	89.0	89.9	91.5	91.5	3.3
1986	91.7	92.4	93.1	93.3	2.0
1987	93.6	94.4	95.0	95.5	2.4
1988	96.1	97.4	98.4	98.6	3.2
1989	99.3	100.0	101.2	101.2	2.6
1990	102.0	103.1	103.6	104.1	2.9
1991	104.5	105.6	106.1	106.7	2.5
1992	107.4	108.3	109.3	109.7	2.8
1993	110.0	111.2	111.7	112.6	2.6
1994	113.5	114.0	115.2	115.6	2.7
1995	117.0	117.8	118.5	118.6	2.6
Handlers, equipment cleaners, helpers, and laborers					
1984	85.8	86.7	87.2	88.1	3.4
1985	88.7	90.0	90.1	91.0	3.3
1986	91.2	91.4	91.9	92.2	1.3
1987	92.6	93.2	94.0	95.0	3.0
1988	96.3	96.9	97.6	98.3	3.5
1989	99.1	100.0	101.1	102.0	3.8
1990	103.0	104.4	105.3	106.2	4.1
1991	107.3	108.5	109.2	109.9	3.5
1992	110.6	111.3	112.1	112.6	2.5
1993	113.6	114.3	114.9	115.7	2.8
1994	116.6	117.3	117.9	118.9	2.8
1995	120.1	121.2	121.5	122.8	3.3
Service occupations					
1984	85.0	84.7	86.0	87.8	6.2
1985	87.9	88.3	89.6	89.9	2.4
1986	90.8	90.8	91.5	92.3	2.7
1987	93.3	93.6	94.1	94.5	2.4
1988	95.5	96.4	97.7	98.7	4.4
1989	99.4	100.0	100.9	102.3	3.6
1990	103.1	104.2	104.9	106.4	4.0
1991	106.9	108.3	109.8	110.6	3.9
1992	111.2	111.6	112.5	112.9	2.1
1993	113.5	114.1	114.9	115.3	2.1
1994	116.3	116.8	117.6	118.8	3.0
1995	119.4	120.0	120.8	121.4	2.2
Production and nonsupervisory occupations					
1984	82.9	83.6	84.1	85.2	3.9
1985	86.0	86.8	88.1	88.6	4.0
1986	89.3	89.9	90.5	91.0	2.7
1987	91.9	92.5	93.4	93.9	3.2
1988	94.8	96.0	97.0	97.9	4.3
1989	99.0	100.0	101.3	102.2	4.4
1990	103.2	104.3	105.2	105.9	3.6
1991	107.0	108.1	109.0	109.6	3.5
1992	110.6	111.3	112.0	112.6	2.7
1993	113.4	114.2	115.3	115.9	2.9
1994	116.6	117.5	118.5	119.1	2.8
1995	119.9	121.0	121.8	122.4	2.8

Employment Cost Index, Wages and Salaries, Private Industry Workers, by Occupation and Industry, 1984-1995—Continued

(June 1989=100, not seasonally adjusted)

Series and year	Indexes				Percent change for 12 months ended December
	March	June	September	December	
WORKERS, BY INDUSTRY DIVISION					
Goods-producing industries					
1984	84.1	84.7	85.5	86.4	3.8
1985	87.5	88.4	89.0	89.4	3.5
1986	90.4	91.3	91.8	92.3	3.2
1987	92.8	93.4	94.3	95.2	3.1
1988	96.1	96.9	97.5	98.2	3.2
1989	99.1	100.0	101.0	102.0	3.9
1990	103.1	104.2	105.1	105.8	3.7
1991	107.0	108.0	108.7	109.7	3.7
1992	110.7	111.4	112.1	112.8	2.8
1993	113.8	114.5	115.3	116.1	2.9
1994	116.9	118.0	118.9	119.6	3.0
1995	120.4	121.4	122.1	122.8	2.7
Goods-producing, excluding sales occupations					
1984	84.3	84.9	85.7	86.5	3.8
1985	87.5	88.4	89.1	89.5	3.5
1986	90.4	91.2	91.8	92.2	3.0
1987	92.9	93.4	94.3	95.2	3.3
1988	95.9	96.9	97.4	98.2	3.2
1989	99.1	100.0	101.0	102.0	3.9
1990	103.0	104.2	105.0	105.7	3.6
1991	106.9	107.9	108.7	109.7	3.8
1992	110.5	111.2	112.0	112.6	2.6
1993	113.5	114.2	114.9	115.6	2.7
1994	116.4	117.4	118.4	119.1	3.0
1995	119.9	120.9	121.6	122.3	2.7
Goods-producing, white-collar occupations					
1987		92.9	94.0	94.9	
1988	96.2	96.9	97.6	98.3	3.6
1989	99.2	100.0	101.0	101.9	3.7
1990	103.5	104.6	105.7	106.3	4.3
1991	107.4	108.5	109.5	110.4	3.9
1992	111.7	112.5	113.2	114.2	3.4
1993	115.4	116.4	117.3	118.2	3.5
1994	119.1	120.3	121.1	122.0	3.2
1995	123.0	123.8	124.4	125.1	2.5
Goods-producing, white-collar occupations, excluding sales occupations					
1987		92.9	93.9	94.8	
1988	96.0	96.9	97.6	98.2	3.6
1989	99.2	100.0	101.0	102.0	3.9
1990	103.3	104.4	105.6	106.2	4.1
1991	107.2	108.5	109.5	110.5	4.0
1992	111.3	112.0	112.9	113.7	2.9
1993	114.9	115.6	116.4	116.8	2.7
1994	117.7	118.8	119.8	120.8	3.4
1995	121.8	122.5	123.2	124.1	2.7
Goods-producing, blue-collar occupations					
1987		93.6	94.4	95.3	
1988	95.9	96.9	97.3	98.1	2.9
1989	99.0	100.0	101.0	101.9	3.9
1990	102.9	104.1	104.7	105.5	3.5
1991	106.8	107.6	108.3	109.2	3.5
1992	110.1	110.7	111.4	111.9	2.5
1993	112.8	113.4	114.1	114.9	2.7
1994	115.6	116.6	117.5	118.1	2.8
1995	118.8	119.9	120.7	121.4	2.8
Goods-producing, service occupations					
1987		94.0	95.0	96.1	
1988	96.4	96.8	96.9	97.8	1.8
1989	99.0	100.0	100.7	101.9	4.2
1990	102.7	103.0	104.3	105.0	3.0
1991	106.0	106.7	107.8	109.4	4.2
1992	110.1	111.0	112.2	113.1	3.4
1993	113.9	114.4	115.7	116.9	3.4
1994	116.4	117.7	120.1	119.7	2.4
1995	120.6	121.9	122.8	123.5	3.2

COMPENSATION OF EMPLOYEES

Employment Cost Index, Wages and Salaries, Private Industry Workers, by Occupation and Industry, 1984-1995—Continued

(June 1989=100, not seasonally adjusted)

Series and year	Indexes				Percent change for 12 months ended December
	March	June	September	December	
Contract construction					
1984	86.1	86.6	86.9	86.9	1.3
1985	87.8	88.6	89.1	89.6	3.1
1986	89.9	91.0	91.6	91.8	2.5
1987	92.5	93.2	94.1	94.8	3.3
1988	95.7	97.0	97.7	98.3	3.7
1989	99.1	100.0	101.1	101.7	3.5
1990	102.0	102.9	103.5	103.7	2.0
1991	105.1	105.9	106.3	106.8	3.0
1992	107.2	107.9	108.7	108.9	2.0
1993	109.5	110.4	111.3	111.1	2.0
1994	112.2	113.6	114.6	114.7	3.2
1995	114.8	115.7	116.8	117.2	2.2
Manufacturing					
1984	83.4	84.1	85.0	86.1	4.4
1985	87.2	88.1	88.8	89.2	3.6
1986	90.3	91.1	91.6	92.1	3.3
1987	92.7	93.3	94.2	95.2	3.4
1988	96.0	96.8	97.3	98.1	3.0
1989	99.0	100.0	100.9	101.9	3.9
1990	103.3	104.5	105.4	106.2	4.2
1991	107.4	108.4	109.3	110.3	3.9
1992	111.5	112.2	112.9	113.7	3.1
1993	114.7	115.5	116.3	117.3	3.2
1994	118.0	119.0	120.0	120.8	3.0
1995	121.9	122.9	123.5	124.3	2.9
Manufacturing, white-collar occupations					
1987	....	93.0	94.0	95.0	....
1988	96.2	96.9	97.5	98.2	3.4
1989	99.2	100.0	100.9	101.8	3.7
1990	103.7	104.7	105.9	106.4	4.5
1991	107.6	108.8	109.8	110.7	4.0
1992	111.9	112.9	113.6	114.6	3.5
1993	116.0	116.9	117.7	118.8	3.7
1994	119.5	120.6	121.7	122.7	3.3
1995	123.9	124.7	125.3	125.9	2.6
Manufacturing, white-collar occupations, excluding sales occupations					
1987	....	92.9	93.9	94.8	....
1988	96.0	96.8	97.4	98.0	3.4
1989	99.1	100.0	100.9	101.9	4.0
1990	103.4	104.4	105.6	106.2	4.2
1991	107.2	108.6	109.7	110.7	4.2
1992	111.4	112.2	113.0	114.0	3.0
1993	115.3	115.9	116.7	117.2	2.8
1994	118.0	119.1	120.2	121.4	3.6
1995	122.4	123.2	123.9	124.7	2.7
Manufacturing, blue-collar occupations					
1987	....	93.5	94.4	95.4	....
1988	96.0	96.8	97.2	98.1	2.8
1989	98.9	100.0	100.9	102.0	4.0
1990	103.1	104.4	105.1	106.1	4.0
1991	107.3	108.2	109.0	110.0	3.7
1992	111.1	111.7	112.4	113.1	2.8
1993	113.9	114.5	115.2	116.2	2.7
1994	116.9	117.8	118.7	119.5	2.8
1995	120.4	121.6	122.2	123.1	3.0
Manufacturing, service occupations					
1987	....	94.0	95.0	96.2	....
1988	96.4	97.0	97.2	98.1	2.0
1989	98.9	100.0	100.7	102.0	4.0
1990	102.9	103.2	104.1	104.9	2.8
1991	105.8	106.5	107.7	109.3	4.2
1992	110.1	111.0	112.3	113.4	3.8
1993	114.3	114.5	116.0	117.3	3.4
1994	116.8	118.2	120.6	120.6	2.8
1995	121.5	122.8	123.7	124.3	3.1

Employment Cost Index, Wages and Salaries, Private Industry Workers, by Occupation and Industry, 1984-1995—Continued

(June 1989=100, not seasonally adjusted)

Series and year	Indexes				Percent change for 12 months ended December
	March	June	September	December	
Durables					
1984	84.3	84.9	85.7	86.7	4.1
1985	87.8	88.9	89.4	89.9	3.7
1986	90.9	91.6	92.1	92.6	3.0
1987	93.0	93.7	94.5	95.5	3.1
1988	96.2	96.9	97.4	98.0	2.6
1989	99.0	100.0	100.7	101.9	4.0
1990	103.2	104.3	105.3	106.1	4.1
1991	107.3	108.3	109.2	110.2	3.9
1992	111.2	111.8	112.7	113.4	2.9
1993	114.4	115.1	115.9	117.2	3.4
1994	117.8	118.7	119.8	120.8	3.1
1995	121.9	122.9	123.6	124.2	2.8
Non-durables					
1984	81.8	82.7	83.8	84.9	4.9
1985	85.9	86.6	87.6	88.0	3.7
1986	89.1	90.3	90.7	91.3	3.8
1987	92.2	92.5	93.8	94.7	3.7
1988	95.8	96.5	97.2	98.2	3.7
1989	99.0	100.0	101.1	101.8	3.7
1990	103.6	104.8	105.7	106.3	4.4
1991	107.6	108.6	109.4	110.6	4.0
1992	111.8	112.8	113.2	114.3	3.3
1993	115.5	116.3	116.9	117.5	2.8
1994	118.3	119.5	120.3	120.8	2.8
1995	121.9	122.9	123.3	124.4	3.0
Service-producing industries					
1984	81.3	82.1	82.7	83.7	4.4
1985	84.6	85.6	87.1	87.7	4.8
1986	88.5	89.1	89.8	90.3	3.0
1987	91.5	92.1	93.1	93.4	3.4
1988	94.3	95.5	96.7	97.8	4.7
1989	99.1	100.0	101.4	102.2	4.5
1990	103.3	104.6	105.7	106.3	4.0
1991	107.5	108.7	109.7	110.2	3.7
1992	111.1	111.7	112.3	113.0	2.5
1993	113.9	114.7	115.9	116.6	3.2
1994	117.3	118.2	119.2	119.7	2.7
1995	120.7	121.6	122.6	123.3	3.0
Service-producing, excluding sales					
1984	81.6	82.2	83.1	84.3	5.1
1985	84.8	85.8	87.3	87.5	3.8
1986	88.5	89.0	89.7	90.4	3.3
1987	91.5	92.2	93.5	94.0	4.0
1988	94.9	95.8	97.1	98.0	4.3
1989	99.2	100.0	101.2	101.8	3.9
1990	103.4	104.5	105.8	106.6	4.7
1991	107.7	108.7	110.0	110.7	3.8
1992	111.5	112.2	113.0	113.7	2.7
1993	114.8	115.6	116.6	117.4	3.3
1994	118.3	119.0	120.2	120.7	2.8
1995	121.8	122.5	123.4	124.3	3.0
Service-producing, white-collar occupations					
1987	....	91.6	92.6	92.9	....
1988	93.7	95.1	96.3	97.5	5.0
1989	99.0	100.0	101.5	102.5	5.1
1990	103.6	105.0	106.1	106.8	4.2
1991	108.1	109.3	110.3	110.7	3.7
1992	111.7	112.2	112.8	113.6	2.6
1993	114.5	115.2	116.5	117.3	3.3
1994	118.0	118.9	119.9	120.4	2.6
1995	121.3	122.3	123.2	124.1	3.1

Employment Cost Index, Wages and Salaries, Private Industry Workers, by Occupation and Industry, 1984-1995—Continued

(June 1989=100, not seasonally adjusted)

Series and year	Indexes				Percent change for 12 months ended December
	March	June	September	December	
Service-producing, white-collar, excluding sales					
1987	....	91.7	93.1	93.7	....
1988	94.5	95.5	96.9	97.9	4.5
1989	99.2	100.0	101.3	102.1	4.3
1990	103.8	105.0	106.4	107.2	5.0
1991	108.5	109.5	110.9	111.6	4.1
1992	112.4	113.1	114.0	114.7	2.8
1993	116.0	116.8	117.8	118.7	3.5
1994	119.6	120.4	121.5	122.1	2.9
1995	123.2	123.8	124.7	125.8	3.0
Service-producing, blue-collar occupations					
1987	....	93.2	94.1	94.8	....
1988	95.9	96.7	97.5	98.0	3.4
1989	99.0	100.0	100.9	100.9	3.0
1990	102.1	103.3	104.2	104.7	3.8
1991	105.6	106.5	107.3	107.8	3.0
1992	108.7	109.7	110.3	111.0	3.0
1993	111.9	112.9	114.1	114.6	3.2
1994	115.5	116.2	117.5	117.6	2.6
1995	119.2	120.3	121.1	121.1	3.0
Service-producing, service occupations					
1987	....	93.6	94.1	94.4	....
1988	95.3	96.3	97.7	98.8	4.7
1989	99.4	100.0	100.8	102.3	3.5
1990	103.2	104.3	105.0	106.5	4.1
1991	107.0	108.4	110.0	110.7	3.9
1992	111.3	111.7	112.6	112.9	2.0
1993	113.5	114.1	114.9	115.2	2.0
1994	116.3	116.7	117.3	118.7	3.0
1995	119.3	119.8	120.7	121.3	2.2
Transportation and public utilities					
1984	87.6	88.2	88.6	89.2	3.4
1985	89.9	90.8	92.2	92.5	3.7
1986	93.3	93.6	94.1	94.2	1.8
1987	94.7	95.6	96.1	96.2	2.1
1988	97.0	97.9	98.7	98.6	2.5
1989	99.5	100.0	100.7	101.2	2.6
1990	102.6	103.2	104.1	104.6	3.4
1991	105.4	106.6	107.7	108.4	3.6
1992	109.7	110.6	111.2	111.8	3.1
1993	112.9	114.0	114.7	115.4	3.2
1994	116.4	117.2	118.9	119.6	3.6
1995	121.2	122.0	122.9	123.7	3.4
Transportation					
1985	91.2	92.2	93.6	93.5	....
1986	94.5	94.5	95.0	94.7	1.3
1987	94.9	96.1	96.5	96.3	1.7
1988	97.1	98.2	99.0	98.7	2.5
1989	99.4	100.0	100.6	100.7	2.0
1990	102.3	102.3	103.3	103.5	2.8
1991	104.3	105.5	106.6	107.0	3.4
1992	108.3	109.2	109.8	109.9	2.7
1993	110.8	112.0	112.6	113.4	3.2
1994	114.2	114.8	116.7	117.5	3.6
1995	119.0	119.8	121.0	121.6	3.5

Employment Cost Index, Wages and Salaries, Private Industry Workers, by Occupation and Industry, 1984-1995—Continued

(June 1989=100, not seasonally adjusted)

Series and year	Indexes				Percent change for 12 months ended December
	March	June	September	December	
Public utilities					
1985	88.4	89.0	90.6	91.5	....
1986	92.0	92.7	93.1	93.8	2.5
1987	94.4	95.1	95.7	96.2	2.6
1988	97.0	97.6	98.3	98.7	2.6
1989	99.5	100.0	101.1	101.8	3.1
1990	103.0	104.1	105.0	106.0	4.1
1991	106.9	108.0	109.0	110.0	3.8
1992	111.4	112.4	113.0	114.1	3.7
1993	115.4	116.4	117.2	117.9	3.3
1994	119.1	120.1	121.4	122.3	3.7
1995	123.9	124.5	125.2	126.1	3.1
Communications					
1987	....	....	96.4	97.1	....
1988	97.6	98.1	98.9	99.0	2.0
1989	99.9	100.0	101.1	101.8	2.8
1990	103.1	104.1	105.0	106.1	4.2
1991	106.5	107.6	108.5	109.6	3.3
1992	110.8	111.7	112.2	113.5	3.6
1993	114.7	115.6	116.5	117.1	3.2
1994	118.4	119.5	121.0	122.1	4.3
1995	124.3	124.6	125.3	126.2	3.4
Electric, gas, and sanitary services					
1987	....	....	....	94.9	....
1988	96.1	96.9	97.3	98.2	3.5
1989	99.0	100.0	101.0	101.7	3.6
1990	103.0	104.2	105.0	105.7	3.9
1991	107.3	108.6	109.5	110.5	4.5
1992	112.2	113.3	114.2	114.8	3.9
1993	116.3	117.4	118.2	118.8	3.5
1994	119.9	120.9	121.9	122.4	3.0
1995	123.4	124.4	125.2	125.9	2.9
Wholesale and retail trade					
1984	81.7	82.9	83.3	84.4	5.1
1985	84.9	86.6	87.7	88.4	4.7
1986	89.0	89.9	90.4	90.7	2.6
1987	91.4	92.9	93.4	93.4	3.0
1988	94.3	96.2	97.2	97.9	4.8
1989	99.1	100.0	101.6	102.7	4.9
1990	103.3	104.6	105.1	105.6	2.8
1991	106.6	108.4	109.4	109.6	3.8
1992	109.9	111.2	111.5	112.3	2.5
1993	113.0	114.2	114.7	115.4	2.8
1994	115.5	117.4	118.3	118.4	2.6
1995	119.4	120.6	121.6	122.1	3.1
Wholesale and retail trade, excluding sales					
1984	82.5	83.5	84.1	85.2	5.1
1985	85.8	87.4	88.5	88.7	4.1
1986	89.4	90.2	90.6	91.4	3.0
1987	92.2	93.2	94.1	94.5	3.4
1988	95.3	96.6	97.5	98.4	4.1
1989	99.4	100.0	101.1	101.9	3.6
1990	102.6	104.2	104.9	105.5	3.5
1991	106.8	108.3	109.2	109.6	3.9
1992	110.1	111.4	112.1	112.6	2.7
1993	113.6	114.4	115.2	116.1	3.1
1994	116.5	117.8	118.7	118.8	2.3
1995	120.2	120.9	121.9	123.2	3.7

COMPENSATION OF EMPLOYEES

Employment Cost Index, Wages and Salaries, Private Industry Workers, by Occupation and Industry, 1984-1995—Continued

(June 1989=100, not seasonally adjusted)

Series and year	Indexes				Percent change for 12 months ended December
	March	June	September	December	
Wholesale trade					
1984	79.3	80.5	81.0	82.5	5.5
1985	83.0	85.1	85.7	86.1	4.4
1986	87.0	88.1	88.5	89.3	3.7
1987	90.5	92.1	92.5	93.0	4.1
1988	93.3	95.1	96.1	96.4	3.7
1989	99.0	100.0	102.8	105.2	9.1
1990	104.6	105.2	105.5	106.2	1.0
1991	107.3	109.2	110.4	110.3	3.9
1992	111.4	112.5	111.9	113.5	2.9
1993	113.9	115.1	115.1	116.4	2.6
1994	116.2	118.3	118.9	119.9	3.0
1995	120.9	122.7	123.9	125.1	4.3
Wholesale trade, excluding sales					
1984	82.9	83.5	84.5	85.8	5.1
1985	86.5	87.8	88.7	88.9	3.6
1986	89.4	90.6	91.0	91.8	3.3
1987	92.7	93.3	94.4	95.2	3.7
1988	95.7	96.7	97.7	98.3	3.3
1989	99.2	100.0	101.7	102.5	4.3
1990	103.2	104.7	105.2	105.9	3.3
1991	107.9	109.2	109.8	110.5	4.3
1992	111.5	112.7	113.3	114.1	3.3
1993	114.7	115.5	116.3	117.5	3.0
1994	117.8	118.8	119.6	120.2	2.3
1995	122.2	122.9	123.7	125.6	4.5
Retail trade					
1984	82.8	83.9	84.3	85.3	5.2
1985	85.8	87.2	88.6	89.4	4.8
1986	89.9	90.8	91.3	91.3	2.1
1987	91.9	93.3	93.8	93.7	2.6
1988	94.8	96.6	97.7	98.5	5.1
1989	99.1	100.0	101.0	101.6	3.1
1990	102.7	104.4	105.0	105.3	3.6
1991	106.2	108.0	109.0	109.2	3.7
1992	109.3	110.6	111.3	111.8	2.4
1993	112.6	113.8	114.5	115.0	2.9
1994	115.2	117.0	118.0	117.8	2.4
1995	118.7	119.6	120.5	120.6	2.4
Food stores					
1987	.....	.....	95.8	96.7	.....
1988	97.3	97.8	98.2	99.0	2.4
1989	100.0	100.0	100.4	101.7	2.7
1990	102.8	104.3	105.1	105.8	4.0
1991	106.9	108.7	109.4	110.4	4.3
1992	110.9	112.3	112.9	113.7	3.0
1993	114.6	115.4	114.9	115.9	1.9
1994	117.0	117.8	117.4	117.3	1.2
1995	117.8	117.6	118.6	119.0	1.4
General merchandise stores					
1988	.....	95.6	97.0	98.2	.....
1989	99.2	100.0	100.3	101.4	3.3
1990	102.4	105.2	105.6	106.5	5.0
1991	107.8	110.0	110.9	110.6	3.8
1992	111.1	111.7	111.7	111.8	1.1
1993	112.4	113.4	114.5	115.0	2.9
1994	114.0	116.4	116.5	117.5	2.2
1995	117.9	118.6	119.0	120.0	2.1

Employment Cost Index, Wages and Salaries, Private Industry Workers, by Occupation and Industry, 1984-1995—Continued

(June 1989=100, not seasonally adjusted)

Series and year	Indexes				Percent change for 12 months ended December
	March	June	September	December	
Finance, insurance, and real estate					
1984	80.0	80.5	79.4	79.8	-0.9
1985	84.0	83.8	85.5	87.1	9.1
1986	87.2	88.2	88.8	89.5	2.8
1987	91.9	90.6	90.8	90.6	1.2
1988	91.5	92.9	92.9	96.3	6.3
1989	98.3	100.0	100.6	101.3	5.2
1990	101.8	103.5	104.9	104.8	3.5
1991	107.0	108.1	108.0	108.4	3.4
1992	109.5	108.2	108.2	108.3	-0.1
1993	109.3	109.3	112.3	112.9	4.2
1994	113.7	113.2	113.8	114.2	1.2
1995	115.0	117.0	118.0	118.8	4.0
Banking, savings and loan, and other credit agencies					
1986	....	....	....	87.7	....
1987	89.8	90.9	91.7	92.4	5.4
1988	95.2	96.0	97.0	97.8	5.8
1989	98.8	100.0	101.1	100.9	3.2
1990	101.6	103.6	103.9	105.4	4.5
1991	106.6	105.9	106.4	106.3	0.9
1992	108.2	107.7	108.6	109.0	2.5
1993	112.1	112.9	113.7	114.5	5.0
1994	114.7	115.0	116.5	116.2	1.5
1995	119.2	119.7	120.4	121.2	4.3
Insurance carriers, agents, brokers, and services					
1987	....	90.0	90.8	92.4	....
1988	93.1	95.4	96.2	97.4	5.4
1989	98.5	100.0	99.6	100.8	3.5
1990	102.3	104.1	105.8	105.1	4.3
1991	105.7	107.8	107.5	108.6	3.3
1992	111.2	112.7	112.7	112.7	3.8
1993	111.2	112.9	113.9	116.6	3.5
1994	116.0	116.8	117.7	118.6	1.7
1995	119.8	120.8	121.1	122.2	3.0
Service industries, total					
1984	78.7	79.0	80.5	82.1	6.3
1985	82.3	83.0	84.9	85.0	3.5
1986	86.3	86.8	87.6	88.4	4.0
1987	89.9	90.5	92.5	93.2	5.4
1988	94.2	94.9	96.9	97.8	4.9
1989	99.1	100.0	101.6	102.5	4.8
1990	104.2	105.7	107.1	108.3	5.7
1991	109.5	110.0	111.5	112.2	3.6
1992	113.2	114.0	115.2	116.1	3.5
1993	117.0	117.6	118.9	119.6	3.0
1994	120.8	121.3	122.2	123.0	2.8
1995	123.9	124.4	125.3	126.1	2.5

Employment Cost Index, Wages and Salaries, Private Industry Workers, by Occupation and Industry, 1984-1995—Continued

(June 1989=100, not seasonally adjusted)

Series and year	Indexes				Percent change for 12 months ended December
	March	June	September	December	
Business services					
1986				87.6	
1987	89.1	90.2	92.8	93.5	6.7
1988	94.3	95.1	96.5	97.4	4.2
1989	98.4	100.0	100.9	101.2	3.9
1990	103.0	105.1	105.7	107.4	6.1
1991	109.6	109.5	108.9	110.0	2.4
1992	111.0	111.7	113.3	113.9	3.5
1993	114.2	114.6	115.3	115.7	1.6
1994	118.8	119.4	119.9	120.4	4.1
1995	122.1	122.9	123.6	124.3	3.2
Health services					
1985	82.1	82.8	83.6	83.8	
1986	84.8	85.4	86.8	88.0	5.0
1987	89.2	89.8	91.1	92.1	4.7
1988	92.7	94.4	96.0	97.3	5.6
1989	99.1	100.0	101.9	103.5	6.4
1990	105.3	106.3	108.1	109.7	6.0
1991	111.1	111.9	113.5	114.6	4.5
1992	115.6	116.3	117.9	118.9	3.8
1993	119.8	120.7	121.7	122.6	3.1
1994	123.1	123.5	124.3	125.4	2.3
1995	126.2	126.7	127.5	128.4	2.4
Hospitals					
1986		84.7	85.8	87.1	5.0
1987	88.2	88.8	90.4	91.5	4.7
1988	92.5	94.0	95.6	96.9	5.6
1989	98.9	100.0	101.9	103.3	6.4
1990	105.0	106.0	108.2	109.8	6.0
1991	110.8	111.6	113.2	114.4	4.5
1992	115.4	115.9	117.3	118.3	3.8
1993	119.3	119.9	121.0	122.0	3.1
1994	122.8	123.3	123.9	124.8	2.3
1995	125.4	125.9	126.6	127.7	2.4
Educational services					
1988				98.8	
1989	99.1	100.0	103.7	103.9	5.2
1990	104.7	105.0	109.2	110.2	6.1
1991	110.3	109.7	113.0	113.7	3.2
1992	113.4	113.6	116.5	117.1	3.0
1993	117.5	117.4	120.7	120.9	3.2
1994	121.2	122.2	124.9	125.1	3.5
1995	125.6	125.9	128.6	129.3	3.4
Colleges and universities					
1988				98.7	
1989	99.1	100.0	103.3	103.7	5.1
1990	104.4	104.8	108.7	109.3	5.4
1991	109.6	110.2	113.7	114.2	4.5
1992	114.2	114.5	117.3	117.6	3.0
1993	118.0	117.7	121.3	121.6	3.4
1994	122.0	122.2	124.5	124.9	2.7
1995	125.5	125.9	129.0	130.1	4.2

Employment Cost Index, Wages and Salaries, Private Industry Workers, by Occupation and Industry, 1984-1995—Continued

(June 1989=100, not seasonally adjusted)

Series and year	Indexes				Percent change for 12 months ended December
	March	June	September	December	
Nonmanufacturing, total					
1984	82.0	82.7	83.3	84.2	4.0
1985	85.2	86.1	87.5	88.0	4.5
1986	88.7	89.4	90.1	90.6	3.0
1987	91.7	92.3	93.3	93.7	3.4
1988	94.5	95.8	96.9	97.8	4.4
1989	99.1	100.0	101.4	102.2	4.5
1990	103.2	104.5	105.4	106.1	3.8
1991	107.3	108.4	109.3	109.8	3.5
1992	110.7	111.3	111.9	112.6	2.6
1993	113.4	114.2	115.4	116.0	3.0
1994	116.8	117.7	118.7	119.1	2.7
1995	120.0	120.9	121.9	122.5	2.9
Nonmanufacturing, white-collar occupations					
1987		91.7	92.7	93.0	
1988	93.8	95.2	96.4	97.6	4.9
1989	99.1	100.0	101.5	102.5	5.0
1990	103.6	105.0	106.1	106.7	4.1
1991	108.0	109.2	110.2	110.6	3.7
1992	111.6	112.1	112.8	113.5	2.6
1993	114.4	115.2	116.4	117.2	3.3
1994	117.9	118.9	119.7	120.2	2.6
1995	121.1	122.1	123.1	123.9	3.1
Nonmanufacturing, white-collar occupations, excluding sales occupations					
1987		91.7	93.1	93.7	
1988	94.5	95.6	97.0	97.9	4.5
1989	99.2	100.0	101.3	102.0	4.2
1990	103.8	105.0	106.3	107.2	5.1
1991	108.5	109.4	110.7	111.5	4.0
1992	112.3	113.0	113.9	114.6	2.8
1993	115.8	116.6	117.6	118.5	3.4
1994	119.4	120.2	121.3	121.8	2.8
1995	122.9	123.5	124.4	125.5	3.0
Nonmanufacturing, blue-collar occupations					
1987		93.5	94.3	95.0	
1988	95.9	96.9	97.7	98.1	3.3
1989	99.0	100.0	101.0	101.3	3.3
1990	102.2	103.2	104.0	104.3	3.0
1991	105.5	106.3	107.1	107.5	3.1
1992	108.2	109.1	109.7	110.2	2.5
1993	111.1	111.9	113.0	113.4	2.9
1994	114.2	115.1	116.4	116.4	2.6
1995	117.5	118.5	119.4	119.5	2.7
Nonmanufacturing, service occupations					
1987		93.6	94.1	94.4	
1988	95.4	96.3	97.7	98.8	4.7
1989	99.4	100.0	100.8	102.3	3.5
1990	103.2	104.3	105.0	106.5	4.1
1991	107.1	108.4	110.0	110.7	3.9
1992	111.3	111.7	112.6	112.9	2.0
1993	113.4	114.1	114.8	115.1	1.9
1994	116.3	116.7	117.3	118.6	3.0
1995	119.2	119.8	120.6	121.2	2.2

COMPENSATION OF EMPLOYEES

Employment Cost Index, Wages and Salaries, State and Local Government, by Occupation and Industry, 1984-1995

(June 1989=100, not seasonally adjusted)

Series and year	Indexes				Percent change for 12 months ended December
	March	June	September	December	
STATE AND LOCAL GOVERNMENT WORKERS, TOTAL					
1984	77.7	77.9	80.5	81.2	6.0
1985	82.0	82.2	85.1	85.7	5.5
1986	86.5	86.8	89.7	90.3	5.4
1987	91.0	91.2	93.3	94.1	4.2
1988	95.0	95.2	97.7	98.7	4.9
1989	99.5	100.0	103.1	103.9	5.3
1990	105.1	105.7	108.6	109.4	5.3
1991	110.6	110.9	112.8	113.2	3.5
1992	113.8	114.2	115.9	116.6	3.0
1993	117.2	117.4	119.3	119.7	2.7
1994	120.4	120.7	122.8	123.4	3.1
1995	124.3	124.6	126.6	127.3	3.2
WORKERS, BY OCCUPATIONAL GROUP					
White-collar occupations					
1984	77.0	77.2	80.1	80.7	6.2
1985	81.5	81.7	84.6	85.3	5.7
1986	86.1	86.3	89.4	90.0	5.5
1987	90.7	90.8	93.1	94.1	4.6
1988	94.8	95.0	97.6	98.8	5.0
1989	99.6	100.0	103.4	104.2	5.5
1990	105.5	106.0	109.2	109.9	5.5
1991	111.0	111.2	113.1	113.5	3.3
1992	114.0	114.3	116.2	116.9	3.0
1993	117.5	117.6	119.6	119.9	2.6
1994	120.6	120.9	122.9	123.6	3.1
1995	124.4	124.6	126.8	127.5	3.2
Professional specialty and technical					
1989	....	100.0	103.7	104.4	....
1990	105.8	106.3	109.8	110.6	5.9
1991	111.5	111.7	113.8	114.2	3.3
1992	114.5	114.8	117.0	117.6	3.0
1993	118.1	118.2	120.4	120.7	2.6
1994	121.1	121.3	123.6	124.2	2.9
1995	124.8	125.0	127.4	128.0	3.1
Executive, administrative, and managerial					
1989	....	100.0	102.8	103.7	....
1990	104.9	105.7	108.4	108.9	5.0
1991	110.6	110.7	112.0	112.3	3.1
1992	113.3	113.5	114.7	115.5	2.8
1993	116.5	116.6	118.2	118.8	2.9
1994	119.8	120.3	121.6	122.4	3.0
1995	124.1	124.3	126.0	127.2	3.9
Administrative support, including clerical					
1989	....	100.0	102.4	103.0	....
1990	104.4	104.8	107.2	107.9	4.8
1991	109.4	109.7	111.4	111.8	3.6
1992	112.7	112.9	114.1	114.9	2.8
1993	115.4	115.9	117.2	117.8	2.5
1994	118.9	119.4	120.9	121.7	3.3
1995	122.5	122.9	124.4	125.1	2.8
Blue-collar occupations					
1984	81.1	81.5	83.0	83.4	4.8
1985	84.6	84.8	87.1	87.5	4.9
1986	88.8	89.9	91.6	92.0	5.1
1987	92.8	93.3	94.7	95.1	3.4
1988	96.1	96.1	97.8	98.2	3.3
1989	99.5	100.0	101.9	103.3	5.2
1990	104.3	105.3	107.2	107.7	4.3
1991	109.1	110.0	111.1	111.6	3.6
1992	112.5	113.7	115.0	115.6	3.6
1993	116.2	116.5	118.4	119.0	2.9
1994	119.7	120.1	121.8	122.5	2.9
1995	123.1	123.8	124.8	125.7	2.6
Service occupations					
1984	78.9	79.3	81.5	82.2	5.2
1985	83.2	83.2	86.1	86.9	5.7
1986	87.6	88.0	90.0	90.6	4.3
1987	91.7	92.1	93.5	93.9	3.6
1988	95.1	95.9	98.4	98.7	5.1
1989	99.3	100.0	102.4	102.9	4.3
1990	103.9	104.2	106.7	107.6	4.6
1991	109.3	110.1	112.0	112.7	4.7
1992	113.2	113.7	114.9	115.5	2.5
1993	116.3	117.1	118.3	118.9	2.9
1994	119.7	120.4	122.7	123.3	3.7
1995	124.6	125.2	126.6	127.3	3.2
WORKERS, BY INDUSTRY DIVISION					
Service industries					
1984	76.7	76.9	79.8	80.4	6.2
1985	81.2	81.4	84.4	85.1	5.8
1986	85.9	86.1	89.2	90.0	5.8
1987	90.3	90.5	93.0	93.8	4.2
1988	94.6	94.9	97.7	98.9	5.4
1989	99.6	100.0	103.6	104.3	5.5
1990	105.5	106.0	109.5	110.3	5.8
1991	111.3	111.5	113.7	114.1	3.4
1992	114.4	114.7	116.9	117.5	3.0
1993	118.1	118.2	120.3	120.6	2.6
1994	121.1	121.3	123.6	124.2	3.0
1995	124.9	125.1	127.6	128.2	3.2

Employment Cost Index, Wages and Salaries, State and Local Government, by Occupation and Industry, 1984-1995—Continued

(June 1989=100, not seasonally adjusted)

Series and year	Indexes				Percent change for 12 months ended December
	March	June	September	December	
Services, excluding schools					
1984	80.5	81.3	82.6	83.1	4.4
1985	84.3	84.5	85.9	86.4	4.0
1986	87.4	88.0	89.6	90.6	4.9
1987	91.5	92.0	93.2	93.9	3.6
1988	95.4	95.5	97.3	98.2	4.6
1989	99.1	100.0	102.5	103.0	4.9
1990	105.4	106.4	108.8	109.6	6.4
1991	111.4	111.4	113.5	114.2	4.2
1992	114.8	115.2	116.4	117.4	2.8
1993	118.4	118.7	120.1	120.4	2.6
1994	121.3	121.9	123.2	124.0	3.0
1995	125.0	125.5	126.9	127.3	2.7
Health services					
1985	83.3	83.3	85.5	85.8	....
1986	86.3	86.9	88.8	89.3	4.1
1987	89.9	90.5	92.3	93.2	4.4
1988	93.8	94.4	96.7	97.7	4.8
1989	98.9	100.0	102.7	103.7	6.1
1990	105.5	106.1	108.9	109.7	5.8
1991	111.1	111.7	113.0	114.0	3.9
1992	114.9	115.7	116.7	117.4	3.0
1993	118.1	118.8	120.4	121.0	3.1
1994	121.9	122.9	124.7	125.3	3.6
1995	126.0	126.6	127.9	128.5	2.6
Hospitals					
1988	94.0	94.8	97.0	97.9	....
1989	98.7	100.0	102.9	103.8	6.0
1990	105.0	105.9	108.6	109.8	5.8
1991	110.7	111.3	112.9	114.1	3.9
1992	114.5	115.2	116.5	117.1	2.6
1993	117.6	118.2	119.9	120.7	3.1
1994	121.2	122.0	124.2	125.1	3.6
1995	125.8	126.3	127.6	128.3	2.6
Educational services					
1989	99.6	100.0	103.8	104.5	....
1990	105.5	106.0	109.7	110.5	5.7
1991	111.3	111.5	113.8	114.1	3.3
1992	114.3	114.6	116.9	117.6	3.1
1993	118.0	118.1	120.3	120.6	2.6
1994	120.9	121.1	123.6	124.2	3.0
1995	124.8	124.9	127.7	128.3	3.3
Schools					
1984	75.6	75.6	79.0	79.6	6.7
1985	80.3	80.5	84.0	84.7	6.4
1986	85.3	85.5	89.1	89.7	5.9
1987	90.0	90.0	92.9	93.9	4.7
1988	94.4	94.6	97.7	99.1	5.5
1989	99.7	100.0	104.0	104.7	5.7
1990	105.5	105.9	109.7	110.5	5.5
1991	111.2	111.5	113.7	114.0	3.2
1992	114.3	114.6	117.0	117.5	3.1
1993	117.9	118.0	120.3	120.7	2.7
1994	121.0	121.2	123.8	124.3	3.0
1995	125.0	125.1	127.8	128.4	3.3
Elementary and secondary schools					
1984	75.3	75.3	79.2	79.7	7.0
1985	80.1	80.3	84.2	84.8	6.4
1986	85.4	85.4	89.2	89.7	5.8
1987	89.7	89.8	93.1	93.9	4.7
1988	94.3	94.5	97.8	99.3	5.8
1989	99.7	100.0	104.2	104.9	5.6
1990	105.5	105.9	110.1	110.9	5.7
1991	111.6	111.7	114.3	114.7	3.4
1992	114.9	115.3	117.9	118.5	3.3
1993	118.7	118.8	121.1	121.6	2.6
1994	121.7	121.8	124.5	124.9	2.7
1995	125.5	125.8	128.7	129.2	3.4
Colleges and universities					
1989	99.6	100.0	102.9	104.1	....
1990	105.6	105.9	108.4	109.2	4.9
1991	110.2	111.0	112.0	112.0	2.6
1992	112.3	112.3	114.1	114.3	2.1
1993	115.5	115.6	117.8	117.7	3.0
1994	118.6	119.2	121.5	122.5	4.1
1995	123.2	122.9	125.0	126.0	2.9
Public administration					
1984	79.3	79.9	81.9	82.8	5.2
1985	83.7	83.8	86.6	87.0	5.1
1986	88.1	88.7	90.6	91.0	4.6
1987	92.6	92.9	93.9	94.7	4.1
1988	95.8	96.4	98.1	98.4	3.9
1989	99.4	100.0	102.1	102.8	4.5
1990	104.3	104.6	106.5	107.3	4.4
1991	109.1	109.5	110.6	110.9	3.4
1992	111.9	112.4	113.1	113.6	2.4
1993	114.4	114.9	115.9	116.6	2.6
1994	117.9	118.5	119.9	120.6	3.4
1995	121.9	122.3	123.2	124.2	3.0

COMPENSATION OF EMPLOYEES

Employment Cost Index, Benefit Costs, by Occupation and Industry, and Bargaining Status, 1984-1995

(June 1989=100, not seasonally adjusted)

Series and year	Indexes				Percent change for 12 months ended December
	March	June	September	December	
CIVILIAN WORKERS					
1984	77.8	78.6	79.8	80.9	6.9
1985	82.3	82.4	83.6	84.1	4.0
1986	85.3	85.7	86.6	87.3	3.8
1987	88.0	88.6	89.6	90.5	3.7
1988	93.2	94.3	95.7	96.8	7.0
1989	98.6	100.0	101.9	103.2	6.6
1990	105.9	107.2	108.9	110.1	6.7
1991	112.2	113.6	115.4	116.3	5.6
1992	118.6	119.6	121.4	122.5	5.3
1993	125.0	126.2	127.4	128.1	4.6
1994	130.1	131.0	132.3	132.5	3.4
1995	133.8	134.5	135.2	136.2	2.8
PRIVATE INDUSTRY WORKERS					
1984	78.9	79.9	80.6	81.7	6.5
1985	83.1	83.2	84.2	84.6	3.5
1986	85.8	86.1	87.0	87.5	3.4
1987	88.2	89.0	89.6	90.5	3.4
1988	93.4	94.7	95.7	96.7	6.9
1989	98.4	100.0	101.4	102.6	6.1
1990	105.5	106.9	108.3	109.4	6.6
1991	111.6	113.5	115.2	116.2	6.2
1992	118.6	119.7	121.2	122.2	5.2
1993	125.2	126.7	127.7	128.3	5.0
1994	130.7	131.7	132.8	133.0	3.7
1995	134.5	135.1	135.6	136.6	2.7
White-collar occupations					
1984	77.8	79.0	79.7	80.9	7.2
1985	82.3	82.7	83.8	84.3	4.2
1986	85.5	86.0	86.6	87.3	3.6
1987	88.2	88.9	89.7	90.5	3.7
1988	92.8	94.0	95.0	96.2	6.3
1989	98.3	100.0	101.4	102.6	6.7
1990	105.6	107.1	108.6	109.7	6.9
1991	112.1	113.8	115.3	116.4	6.1
1992	118.4	119.4	121.0	122.0	4.8
1993	124.7	125.9	126.8	127.6	4.6
1994	130.5	131.6	132.8	133.3	4.5
1995	135.2	136.0	136.6	137.5	3.2
Blue-collar occupations					
1984	80.5	81.2	81.9	83.0	5.9
1985	84.1	84.1	84.7	85.1	2.5
1986	86.3	86.5	87.4	87.7	3.1
1987	88.2	89.1	89.8	90.7	3.4
1988	94.2	95.7	96.5	97.4	7.4
1989	98.6	100.0	101.4	102.6	5.3
1990	105.2	106.6	107.9	109.0	6.2
1991	111.0	112.8	114.9	115.7	6.1
1992	118.7	119.7	121.2	122.2	5.6
1993	125.5	127.3	128.4	128.9	5.5
1994	130.5	131.5	132.7	132.5	2.8
1995	133.3	133.6	134.1	135.2	2.0
Service occupations					
1985	....	....	82.7	84.0	....
1986	84.9	85.4	86.6	87.6	4.3
1987	88.2	88.4	88.7	89.7	2.4
1988	92.1	93.4	95.1	96.8	7.9
1989	98.7	100.0	101.6	103.0	6.4
1990	106.0	107.0	108.1	109.9	6.7
1991	112.3	114.5	116.5	117.8	7.2
1992	120.0	121.6	123.7	124.6	5.8
1993	127.7	129.3	130.5	131.5	5.5
1994	132.9	133.1	134.2	134.7	2.4
1995	135.0	135.6	135.7	136.5	1.3
Goods-producing industries					
1984	80.4	81.3	82.1	83.2	6.3
1985	84.9	84.7	85.2	85.7	3.0
1986	86.8	87.4	87.9	88.3	3.0
1987	88.7	89.4	90.0	90.9	2.9
1988	94.4	95.7	96.5	97.3	7.0
1989	98.7	100.0	101.5	102.6	5.4
1990	105.7	107.2	108.7	109.9	7.1
1991	111.9	113.9	115.8	116.7	6.2
1992	119.7	120.6	122.3	123.4	5.7
1993	127.3	129.0	130.0	130.3	5.6
1994	132.7	133.9	134.8	134.8	3.5
1995	135.9	135.9	136.2	137.5	2.0
Manufacturing					
1984	79.6	80.6	81.5	82.7	6.7
1985	84.6	84.2	84.6	85.0	2.8
1986	86.3	86.6	87.0	87.5	2.9
1987	87.5	88.2	88.8	89.8	2.6
1988	93.7	94.9	95.8	96.6	7.6
1989	98.8	100.0	101.6	102.3	5.9
1990	105.5	106.9	108.4	109.5	7.0
1991	111.2	113.3	115.3	116.1	6.0
1992	119.3	120.1	121.5	122.6	5.6
1993	126.8	128.6	129.7	130.0	6.0
1994	132.0	133.0	133.9	134.3	3.3
1995	135.4	135.2	135.5	137.0	2.0

Employment Cost Index, Benefit Costs, by Occupation and Industry, and Bargaining Status, 1984-95—Continued

(June 1989=100, not seasonally adjusted)

Series and year	Indexes				Percent change for 12 months ended December
	March	June	September	December	
Service-producing industries					
1984	77.6	78.6	79.2	80.4	6.9
1985	81.4	81.9	83.2	83.6	4.0
1986	84.9	85.1	86.1	86.8	3.8
1987	87.8	88.6	89.4	90.2	3.9
1988	92.5	93.8	94.9	96.1	6.5
1989	98.2	100.0	101.4	102.6	6.8
1990	105.3	106.6	107.9	109.0	6.2
1991	111.4	113.0	114.6	115.7	6.1
1992	117.7	118.8	120.4	121.2	4.8
1993	123.4	124.6	125.7	126.7	4.5
1994	128.9	129.7	131.2	131.5	3.8
1995	133.2	134.1	134.8	135.6	3.1
Nonmanufacturing					
1984	78.5	79.4	80.0	81.1	6.4
1985	82.0	82.6	83.9	84.4	4.1
1986	85.5	85.9	86.9	87.5	3.7
1987	88.7	89.5	90.3	91.0	4.0
1988	93.2	94.5	95.5	96.8	6.4
1989	98.2	100.0	101.4	102.8	6.2
1990	105.4	106.9	108.2	109.3	6.3
1991	111.9	113.5	115.1	116.2	6.3
1992	118.2	119.4	121.0	122.0	5.0
1993	124.2	125.5	126.5	127.4	4.4
1994	129.9	130.8	132.2	132.3	3.8
1995	133.9	134.7	135.4	136.2	2.9
Union workers					
1984	82.1	83.0	83.9	84.9	6.0
1985	85.7	85.3	85.8	86.4	1.8
1986	87.6	87.6	88.0	88.3	2.2
1987	89.0	89.7	90.2	91.1	3.2
1988	94.9	96.1	96.9	97.5	7.0
1989	98.6	100.0	101.3	102.1	4.7
1990	104.6	105.6	106.7	108.2	6.0
1991	110.1	112.1	113.9	115.2	6.5
1992	119.2	120.0	121.7	122.5	6.3
1993	126.6	128.5	129.7	130.6	6.6
1994	131.9	132.9	133.3	133.7	2.4
1995	134.8	135.5	136.6	138.0	3.2
Nonunion workers					
1984	77.3	78.2	78.9	80.1	6.9
1985	81.7	82.2	83.4	83.8	4.6
1986	85.0	85.5	86.5	87.1	3.9
1987	88.0	88.7	89.5	90.3	3.7
1988	92.6	94.0	95.1	96.3	6.6
1989	98.4	100.0	101.5	102.9	6.9
1990	105.8	107.4	108.9	109.9	6.8
1991	112.3	114.0	115.7	116.6	6.1
1992	118.4	119.5	121.0	122.1	4.7
1993	124.6	125.9	126.9	127.4	4.3
1994	130.1	131.1	132.6	132.7	4.2
1995	134.2	134.8	135.2	135.1	1.8
STATE AND LOCAL GOVERNMENT WORKERS					
1989	....	100.0	103.9	105.3	....
1990	107.5	108.3	111.3	112.7	7.0
1991	114.6	114.4	116.4	117.1	3.9
1992	118.5	119.3	122.3	123.4	5.4
1993	124.2	124.5	126.2	127.0	2.9
1994	127.9	128.5	130.3	130.5	2.8
1995	131.1	132.2	133.6	134.4	3.0

COMPENSATION OF EMPLOYEES

Employment Cost Index, Total Compensation, Private Industry, by Bargaining Status and Industry, 1984-1995

(June 1989=100, not seasonally adjusted)

Series and year	Indexes				Percent change for 12 months ended December
	March	June	September	December	
UNION WORKERS, TOTAL					
1984	85.5	86.3	86.9	87.8	4.3
1985	88.4	88.9	89.7	90.1	2.6
1986	91.0	91.2	91.7	92.0	2.1
1987	92.5	93.0	93.6	94.5	2.7
1988	96.1	97.0	97.7	98.2	3.9
1989	99.0	100.0	100.9	101.8	3.7
1990	103.3	104.1	105.1	106.2	4.3
1991	107.5	108.8	110.1	111.1	4.6
1992	113.1	114.0	115.2	115.9	4.3
1993	117.8	119.1	120.0	120.9	4.3
1994	121.9	123.0	123.8	124.2	2.7
1995	125.1	125.8	126.8	127.9	3.0
Union blue-collar workers					
1987		92.7	93.2	94.2	
1988	96.1	97.0	97.6	98.3	4.4
1989	98.9	100.0	100.9	101.7	3.5
1990	103.0	104.1	104.8	105.9	4.1
1991	107.4	108.6	109.7	110.7	4.5
1992	112.9	113.8	114.8	115.5	4.3
1993	117.4	118.7	119.7	120.6	4.4
1994	121.2	122.4	123.1	123.4	2.3
1995	124.0	124.8	125.7	126.5	2.5
Union workers, goods-producing industries					
1984	85.5	86.4	87.1	88.2	4.9
1985	88.7	88.9	89.4	89.8	1.8
1986	90.7	90.9	91.3	91.5	1.9
1987	91.8	92.3	92.9	94.2	3.0
1988	96.2	97.1	97.7	98.4	4.5
1989	98.9	100.0	100.9	101.9	3.6
1990	103.3	104.5	105.1	106.3	4.3
1991	107.9	109.2	110.3	111.3	4.7
1992	114.0	114.6	115.7	116.4	4.6
1993	118.7	120.0	121.0	121.9	4.7
1994	122.5	123.8	124.4	124.7	2.3
1995	125.2	125.9	126.7	127.5	2.2
Union workers, service-producing industries					
1984	85.4	85.9	86.5	87.3	3.6
1985	88.0	89.0	90.0	90.5	3.7
1986	91.5	91.7	92.3	92.7	2.4
1987	93.4	94.0	94.4	95.0	2.5
1988	95.9	96.9	97.6	97.9	3.1
1989	99.1	100.0	100.8	101.7	3.9
1990	103.2	103.6	104.9	106.0	4.2
1991	107.1	108.3	109.8	110.9	4.6
1992	111.9	113.2	114.6	115.2	3.9
1993	116.7	117.7	118.6	119.6	3.8
1994	121.0	121.8	122.9	123.6	3.3
1995	124.8	125.6	126.8	128.2	3.7
Union workers, manufacturing					
1984	84.4	85.3	86.1	87.2	5.2
1985	87.9	87.9	88.5	88.8	1.8
1986	89.9	89.8	90.2	90.5	1.9
1987	90.6	91.1	91.6	93.1	2.9
1988	95.5	96.4	97.0	97.8	5.0
1989	99.0	100.0	100.8	102.0	4.3
1990	103.6	104.7	105.3	106.6	4.5
1991	108.1	109.5	110.6	111.7	4.8
1992	114.8	115.2	116.1	116.9	4.7
1993	119.8	121.1	121.9	123.0	5.2
1994	123.6	124.8	125.3	125.8	2.3
1995	126.3	126.6	127.1	128.2	1.9
Union workers, manufacturing, blue-collar occupations					
1987		90.9	91.5	93.0	
1988	95.5	96.4	96.9	97.8	5.2
1989	99.0	100.0	100.9	101.9	4.2
1990	103.5	104.6	105.1	106.5	4.5
1991	108.1	109.4	110.6	111.6	4.8
1992	114.7	115.1	116.0	116.8	4.7
1993	119.6	121.0	121.8	122.9	5.2
1994	123.5	124.6	125.1	125.6	2.2
1995	126.1	126.4	126.8	127.9	1.8
Union workers, nonmanufacturing					
1984	86.5	87.1	87.7	88.3	3.4
1985	88.9	89.8	90.6	91.2	3.3
1986	92.0	92.5	93.0	93.3	2.3
1987	94.0	94.7	95.2	95.8	2.7
1988	96.6	97.5	98.3	98.5	2.8
1989	98.9	100.0	100.8	101.6	3.1
1990	103.0	103.7	104.9	105.9	4.2
1991	107.1	108.3	109.7	110.6	4.4
1992	111.8	113.1	114.5	115.1	4.1
1993	116.3	117.4	118.5	119.3	3.6
1994	120.5	121.5	122.6	123.0	3.1
1995	124.0	125.0	126.2	127.4	3.6

Employment Cost Index, Total Compensation, Private Industry, by Bargaining Status and Industry, 1984-1995—Continued

(June 1989=100, not seasonally adjusted)

Series and year	Indexes				Percent change for 12 months ended December
	March	June	September	December	
NONUNION WORKERS, TOTAL					
1984	79.9	80.7	81.4	82.5	5.1
1985	83.8	84.6	85.8	86.3	4.6
1986	87.3	88.2	88.8	89.4	3.6
1987	90.5	91.1	92.1	92.7	3.7
1988	94.0	95.3	96.3	97.4	5.1
1989	98.8	100.0	101.4	102.4	5.1
1990	104.1	105.5	106.6	107.3	4.8
1991	108.8	110.1	111.2	111.9	4.3
1992	113.1	113.8	114.7	115.5	3.2
1993	116.8	117.7	118.8	119.5	3.5
1994	120.7	121.7	122.7	123.2	3.1
1995	124.3	125.2	126.0	126.7	2.8
Nonunion blue-collar workers					
1987	....	91.6	92.6	93.3	....
1988	94.6	96.0	96.6	97.5	4.5
1989	98.7	100.0	101.3	102.1	4.7
1990	103.9	105.3	106.3	106.8	4.6
1991	108.3	109.4	110.6	111.2	4.1
1992	112.2	113.0	113.9	114.6	3.1
1993	115.9	116.9	117.8	118.2	3.1
1994	119.6	120.4	121.7	121.9	3.1
1995	123.0	123.9	124.5	125.1	2.6
Nonunion workers, goods-producing industries					
1984	81.1	81.8	82.7	83.5	4.4
1985	85.5	86.2	86.9	87.4	4.7
1986	88.5	89.5	90.2	90.8	3.9
1987	91.3	92.0	92.9	93.6	3.1
1988	95.1	96.2	96.9	97.7	4.4
1989	98.9	100.0	101.3	102.3	4.7
1990	104.2	105.5	106.7	107.4	5.0
1991	108.8	110.1	111.3	112.2	4.5
1992	113.3	114.1	115.1	116.0	3.4
1993	117.7	118.6	119.4	119.9	3.4
1994	121.5	122.6	123.6	124.1	3.5
1995	125.2	125.9	126.4	127.3	2.6
Nonunion workers, service-producing industries					
1984	79.1	80.1	80.7	81.9	5.7
1985	82.9	83.6	85.2	85.7	4.6
1986	86.6	87.3	88.0	88.6	3.4
1987	89.9	90.6	91.6	92.1	4.0
1988	93.4	94.7	95.9	97.2	5.5
1989	98.7	100.0	101.5	102.4	5.3
1990	103.9	105.5	106.5	107.2	4.7
1991	108.8	110.1	111.2	111.8	4.3
1992	113.0	113.7	114.4	115.2	3.0
1993	116.3	117.2	118.4	119.2	3.5
1994	120.3	121.1	122.2	122.7	2.9
1995	123.8	124.8	125.6	126.2	2.9
Nonunion workers, manufacturing					
1984	80.5	81.4	82.4	83.4	5.0
1985	85.4	86.2	86.8	87.2	4.6
1986	88.5	89.6	90.1	90.7	4.0
1987	91.3	92.0	93.0	93.6	3.2
1988	95.2	96.1	96.8	97.6	4.3
1989	98.8	100.0	101.2	102.1	4.6
1990	104.2	105.5	106.9	107.6	5.4
1991	108.8	110.2	111.5	112.4	4.5
1992	113.6	114.5	115.5	116.4	3.6
1993	118.1	119.0	120.0	120.6	3.6
1994	122.0	122.9	124.0	124.8	3.5
1995	126.1	126.9	127.3	128.3	2.8
Nonunion workers, manufacturing, blue-collar occupations					
1987	....	91.8	92.8	93.2	....
1988	94.6	95.7	96.4	97.4	4.5
1989	98.7	100.0	101.4	102.4	5.1
1990	104.4	105.9	107.2	107.9	5.4
1991	109.0	110.3	111.7	112.5	4.3
1992	113.8	114.6	115.5	116.2	3.3
1993	117.5	118.4	119.4	119.9	3.2
1994	121.2	121.9	123.0	123.5	3.0
1995	124.5	125.5	125.7	127.0	2.8
Nonunion workers, nonmanufacturing					
1984	79.5	80.3	81.0	82.1	5.1
1985	83.1	83.9	85.4	85.9	4.6
1986	86.9	87.5	88.3	88.9	3.5
1987	90.1	90.7	91.8	92.2	3.7
1988	93.5	94.9	96.0	97.3	5.5
1989	98.8	100.0	101.4	102.4	5.2
1990	104.0	105.4	106.5	107.2	4.7
1991	108.8	110.1	111.2	111.7	4.2
1992	112.9	113.5	114.3	115.1	3.0
1993	116.3	117.2	118.3	119.0	3.4
1994	120.2	121.1	122.2	122.5	2.9
1995	123.6	124.5	125.3	125.7	2.6

COMPENSATION OF EMPLOYEES

Employment Cost Index, Wages and Salaries, Private Industry, by Bargaining Status and Industry, 1984-1995

(June 1989=100, not seasonally adjusted)

Series and year	Indexes				Percent change for 12 months ended December
	March	June	September	December	
UNION WORKERS, TOTAL					
1984	87.2	87.9	88.5	89.3	3.5
1985	89.9	90.8	91.7	92.1	3.1
1986	92.8	93.1	93.7	93.9	2.0
1987	94.3	94.8	95.3	96.4	2.7
1988	96.8	97.5	98.2	98.5	2.2
1989	99.2	100.0	100.6	101.6	3.1
1990	102.6	103.3	104.2	105.1	3.4
1991	106.2	107.1	108.0	108.9	3.6
1992	109.8	110.8	111.7	112.3	3.1
1993	113.1	113.9	114.8	115.7	3.0
1994	116.5	117.6	118.6	119.1	2.9
1995	119.8	120.6	121.5	122.2	2.6
Union blue-collar workers					
1987	....	94.5	95.0	96.2	....
1988	96.5	97.2	97.8	98.4	2.3
1989	99.1	100.0	100.7	101.5	3.2
1990	102.2	103.2	103.8	104.8	3.3
1991	105.8	106.7	107.3	108.2	3.2
1992	109.1	109.9	110.8	111.3	2.9
1993	112.0	112.8	113.7	114.5	2.9
1994	115.1	116.2	117.3	117.6	2.7
1995	118.2	119.1	120.0	120.4	2.4
Union workers, goods-producing industries					
1984	87.0	87.9	88.5	89.4	3.7
1985	90.0	90.9	91.6	92.0	2.9
1986	92.5	93.0	93.3	93.6	1.7
1987	93.7	94.3	94.8	96.3	2.9
1988	96.5	97.2	97.8	98.4	2.2
1989	99.0	100.0	100.6	101.6	3.3
1990	102.3	103.5	104.0	105.0	3.3
1991	106.2	107.1	107.7	108.7	3.5
1992	109.6	110.2	111.1	111.7	2.8
1993	112.2	113.0	113.8	114.8	2.8
1994	115.4	116.7	117.5	117.9	2.7
1995	118.4	119.3	120.2	120.5	2.2
Union workers, service-producing industries					
1984	87.7	88.1	88.5	89.2	2.9
1985	89.7	90.8	91.8	92.3	3.5
1986	93.2	93.4	94.3	94.6	2.5
1987	95.2	95.5	96.0	96.5	2.0
1988	97.1	97.8	98.8	98.8	2.4
1989	99.6	100.0	100.7	101.7	2.9
1990	102.9	103.1	104.4	105.2	3.4
1991	106.1	107.0	108.4	109.2	3.8
1992	110.1	111.5	112.5	113.1	3.6
1993	114.2	115.1	116.0	116.8	3.3
1994	118.0	118.7	120.1	120.6	3.3
1995	121.6	122.3	123.2	124.3	3.1
Union workers, manufacturing					
1984	86.4	87.1	87.9	88.9	4.1
1985	89.6	90.6	91.4	91.7	3.1
1986	92.4	92.7	93.0	93.4	1.9
1987	93.5	93.9	94.5	96.2	3.0
1988	96.4	97.0	97.5	98.3	2.2
1989	99.0	100.0	100.5	101.7	3.5
1990	102.6	103.8	104.3	105.5	3.7
1991	106.7	107.5	108.3	109.4	3.7
1992	110.4	110.9	111.7	112.5	2.8
1993	113.2	113.9	114.6	115.9	3.0
1994	116.6	117.8	118.5	119.2	2.8
1995	119.8	120.5	121.3	121.9	2.3
Union workers, manufacturing, blue-collar occupations					
1987	....	93.8	94.4	96.2	....
1988	96.4	97.0	97.5	98.3	2.2
1989	99.0	100.0	100.6	101.8	3.6
1990	102.6	103.8	104.2	105.4	3.5
1991	106.6	107.5	108.2	109.3	3.7
1992	110.3	110.8	111.6	112.4	2.8
1993	113.1	113.8	114.4	115.7	2.9
1994	116.4	117.6	118.3	118.9	2.8
1995	119.5	120.2	121.0	121.6	2.3
Union workers, nonmanufacturing					
1984	88.2	88.6	89.1	89.6	2.6
1985	90.2	91.1	92.0	92.4	3.1
1986	93.2	93.5	94.3	94.5	2.3
1987	95.1	95.5	96.0	96.5	2.1
1988	97.0	97.9	98.8	98.8	2.4
1989	99.4	100.0	100.7	101.5	2.7
1990	102.5	103.0	104.1	104.8	3.3
1991	105.8	106.7	107.9	108.6	3.6
1992	109.4	110.7	111.7	112.2	3.3
1993	113.0	113.9	114.9	115.5	2.9
1994	116.4	117.3	118.6	119.0	3.0
1995	119.8	120.6	121.6	122.3	2.8

Employment Cost Index, Wages and Salaries, Private Industry, by Bargaining Status and Industry, 1984-1995—Continued

(June 1989=100, not seasonally adjusted)

Series and year	Indexes				Percent change for 12 months ended December
	March	June	September	December	
NONUNION WORKERS, TOTAL					
1984	80.8	81.6	82.3	83.4	4.5
1985	84.6	85.5	86.7	87.2	4.6
1986	88.2	89.0	89.6	90.2	3.4
1987	91.3	92.0	93.0	93.5	3.7
1988	94.5	95.6	96.6	97.7	4.5
1989	99.0	100.0	101.3	102.1	4.5
1990	103.4	104.8	105.8	106.4	4.2
1991	107.6	108.7	109.7	110.3	3.7
1992	111.2	111.8	112.4	113.1	2.5
1993	114.1	114.8	115.9	116.6	3.1
1994	117.4	118.3	119.2	119.8	2.7
1995	120.8	121.8	122.6	123.3	2.9
Nonunion blue-collar workers					
1987	....	92.6	93.7	94.2	....
1988	95.3	96.4	97.0	97.8	3.8
1989	98.8	100.0	101.2	101.7	4.0
1990	103.0	104.3	105.1	105.5	3.7
1991	106.8	107.7	108.5	109.2	3.5
1992	110.1	110.8	111.3	111.9	2.5
1993	112.8	113.6	114.4	115.0	2.8
1994	115.9	116.7	117.7	118.3	2.9
1995	119.5	120.7	121.4	121.9	3.0
Nonunion workers, goods-producing industries					
1984	82.3	82.9	83.8	84.7	3.9
1985	86.2	87.0	87.7	88.2	4.1
1986	89.2	90.4	91.0	91.6	3.9
1987	92.3	92.9	94.0	94.7	3.4
1988	95.8	96.8	97.3	98.1	3.6
1989	99.1	100.0	101.1	102.1	4.1
1990	103.5	104.5	105.5	106.1	3.9
1991	107.3	108.3	109.2	110.1	3.8
1992	111.2	111.9	112.6	113.3	2.9
1993	114.4	115.2	116.0	116.7	3.0
1994	117.6	118.6	119.5	120.3	3.1
1995	121.3	122.2	122.9	123.7	2.8
Nonunion workers, service-producing					
1984	80.0	80.8	81.5	82.6	4.8
1985	83.6	84.5	86.2	86.8	5.1
1986	87.6	88.2	88.9	89.5	3.1
1987	90.8	91.4	92.5	92.9	3.8
1988	93.8	95.1	96.3	97.6	5.1
1989	98.9	100.0	101.4	102.2	4.7
1990	103.4	104.9	105.9	106.5	4.2
1991	107.8	108.9	109.9	110.4	3.7
1992	111.2	111.7	112.3	113.0	2.4
1993	113.8	114.6	115.9	116.6	3.2
1994	117.2	118.1	119.0	119.5	2.5
1995	120.5	121.5	122.4	123.1	3.0
Nonunion workers, manufacturing					
1984	81.6	82.4	83.4	84.5	4.6
1985	85.9	86.8	87.5	88.0	4.1
1986	89.2	90.3	90.9	91.6	4.1
1987	92.4	93.0	94.1	94.7	3.4
1988	95.8	96.7	97.2	98.0	3.5
1989	98.9	100.0	101.0	102.0	4.1
1990	103.6	104.8	105.9	106.5	4.4
1991	107.7	108.8	109.7	110.7	3.9
1992	111.9	112.7	113.4	114.2	3.2
1993	115.4	116.1	117.0	117.9	3.2
1994	118.6	119.5	120.5	121.5	3.1
1995	122.7	123.8	124.3	125.1	3.0
Nonunion workers, manufacturing, blue-collar occupations					
1987	....	93.1	94.2	94.4	....
1988	95.4	96.3	96.8	97.8	3.6
1989	98.7	100.0	101.2	102.2	4.5
1990	103.6	105.0	106.0	106.7	4.4
1991	107.9	108.8	109.7	110.7	3.7
1992	111.9	112.5	113.1	113.7	2.7
1993	114.6	115.2	116.0	116.7	2.6
1994	117.5	118.1	119.1	120.0	2.8
1995	121.2	122.6	123.1	124.2	3.5
Nonunion workers, nonmanufacturing					
1984	80.5	81.2	81.9	82.9	4.4
1985	84.0	84.9	86.5	87.0	4.9
1986	87.8	88.5	89.1	89.7	3.1
1987	90.9	91.6	92.7	93.0	3.7
1988	94.0	95.3	96.4	97.7	5.1
1989	99.0	100.0	101.4	102.3	4.7
1990	103.3	104.8	105.7	106.3	3.9
1991	107.6	108.7	109.6	110.1	3.6
1992	110.9	111.4	112.0	112.7	2.4
1993	113.5	114.3	115.5	116.1	3.0
1994	116.9	117.8	118.7	119.1	2.6
1995	120.0	121.0	121.9	122.6	2.9

COMPENSATION OF EMPLOYEES

Employer Compensation Costs per Hour Worked and Percent of Total Compensation, Private Industry, March 1996

Compensation component	All workers in private industry		Goods-producing industries[1]		Service-producing industries[2]		Manufacturing industries		Nonmanufacturing industries	
	Cost	Percent	Cost	Percent	Cost	Percent	Cost	Percent	Cost	Percent
Total compensation	$ 17.49	100.0	$ 21.27	100.0	$ 16.28	100.0	$ 20.99	100.0	$ 16.69	100.0
Wages and salaries	12.58	71.9	14.38	67.6	12.01	73.7	14.13	67.3	12.23	73.3
Total benefits	4.91	28.1	6.89	32.4	4.27	26.3	6.86	32.7	4.46	26.7
Paid leave	1.12	6.4	1.43	6.7	1.02	6.2	1.60	7.6	1.00	6.0
Vacation pay	0.55	3.2	0.76	3.6	0.49	3.0	0.83	4.0	0.49	2.9
Holiday pay	0.38	2.2	0.51	2.4	0.34	2.1	0.58	2.8	0.33	2.0
Sick leave	0.14	0.8	0.11	0.5	0.15	0.9	0.12	0.6	0.14	0.8
Other leave pay	0.05	0.3	0.05	0.2	0.05	0.3	0.06	0.3	0.05	0.3
Supplemental pay	0.49	2.8	0.85	4.0	0.38	2.3	0.88	4.2	0.40	2.4
Premium pay	0.20	1.1	0.42	2.0	0.13	0.8	0.42	2.0	0.15	0.9
Nonproduction bonuses	0.24	1.4	0.36	1.7	0.20	1.2	0.37	1.8	0.21	1.3
Shift pay	0.06	0.3	0.07	0.3	0.05	0.3	0.09	0.4	0.05	0.3
Insurance	1.14	6.5	1.67	7.8	0.97	5.9	1.72	8.2	1.00	6.0
Life insurance	0.04	0.3	0.06	0.3	0.04	0.2	0.06	0.3	0.04	0.2
Health insurance	1.04	5.9	1.52	7.2	0.88	5.4	1.56	7.5	0.92	5.5
Sickness and accident insurance	0.03	0.2	0.06	0.3	0.03	0.2	0.07	0.3	0.03	0.2
Long-term disability insurance	0.02	0.1	0.02	0.1	0.02	0.1	0.02	0.1	0.02	0.1
Retirement and savings	0.55	3.1	0.80	3.7	0.47	2.9	0.71	3.4	0.51	3.0
Defined benefit pension	0.30	1.7	0.48	2.3	0.24	1.5	0.42	2.0	0.27	1.6
Defined contribution pension	0.25	1.4	0.32	1.5	0.23	1.4	0.29	1.4	0.24	1.4
Legally required benefits	1.59	9.1	2.08	9.8	1.44	8.8	1.86	8.9	1.53	9.2
Social Security	1.05	6.0	1.22	5.8	0.99	6.1	1.22	5.8	1.01	6.0
OASDI[3]	0.84	4.8	0.99	4.6	0.79	4.9	0.98	4.7	0.81	4.8
Medicare	0.21	1.2	0.24	1.1	0.20	1.2	0.24	1.1	0.20	1.2
Federal unemployment insurance	0.03	0.2	0.03	0.1	0.03	0.2	0.03	0.1	0.03	0.2
State unemployment insurance	0.12	0.7	0.16	0.7	0.11	0.6	0.13	0.6	0.11	0.7
Workers' compensation	0.40	2.3	0.67	3.2	0.31	1.9	0.48	2.3	0.38	2.3
Other benefits[4]	0.03	0.2	0.07	0.3	5	5	0.08	0.4	5	5

1. Including mining, construction, and manufacturing.
2. Includes transportation, communication, and public utilities; wholesale and retail trade; finance, insurance, and real estate; and service industries.
3. OASDI is the abbreviation for Old-Age, Survivors, and Disability Insurance. The total employer's cost for Social Security is comprised of an OASDI portion and a medicare portion.
4. Includes severance pay and supplemental unemployment benefits.
5. Cost per hour worked is $0.01 or less.

NOTES

Compensation of Employees—Employee Benefits Survey

Description of the Series

Employee benefits data are obtained from an annual survey of the incidence and provisions of selected benefits provided by employers. The survey collects data from a sample of approximately 6,000 private sector and state and local government establishments. The data are presented as a percentage of employees who participate in a certain benefit, or as an average benefit provision (for example, the average number of paid holidays provided to employees per year).

The survey covers paid leave benefits such as lunch and rest periods, holidays and vacations, and personal, funeral, jury duty, military, parental, and sick leave; sickness and accident, long-term disability, and life insurance; medical, dental, and vision care plans; defined benefit and defined contribution plans; flexible benefits plans; reimbursement accounts; and unpaid parental leave.

Definitions

Employer-provided benefits are benefits that are financed either wholly or partly by the employer. They may be sponsored by a union or other third party, as long as there is some employer financing. However, some benefits that are fully paid for by the employee but the premiums for which are available at group rates are also included.

Participants are workers who are covered by a benefit, whether or not they use that benefit. If the benefit plan is financed wholly by employers and requires employees to complete a

minimum length of service for eligibility, the workers are considered participants whether or not they have met the requirement. If workers are required to contribute towards the cost of a plan, they are considered participants only if they elect the plan and agree to make the required contributions.

Defined benefit pension plans use pre-determined formulas to calculate a retirement benefit, and obligate the employer to provide those benefits. Benefits are generally based on salary, years of service, or both.

Defined contribution plans generally specify the level of employer and employee contributions to a plan, but not the formula for determining eventual benefits. Instead, individual accounts are set up for participants, and benefits are based on amounts credited to these accounts.

Tax-deferred savings plans are a type of defined contribution plan that allow participants to contribute a portion of their salary to an employer-sponsored plan and defer income taxes until withdrawal.

Flexible benefit plans allow employees to choose among several benefits, such as life insurance, medical care, and vacation days, and among several levels of care within a given benefit.

Notes on the Data

Surveys of employees in medium and large establishments conducted over the 1979-1986 period included

establishments that employed at least 50, 100, or 250 workers, depending on the industry; most service industries were excluded. The survey conducted in 1987 covered only state and local governments with 50 or more employees. The surveys conducted in 1988 and 1989 included medium and large establishments with 100 workers or more in all private industries. All surveys conducted over the 1979-1989 period excluded establishments in Alaska and Hawaii, as well as part-time employees.

Since 1990, surveys of state and local governments and small establishments have been conducted in even-numbered years and surveys of medium and large establishments have been conducted in odd-numbered years. The small establishment survey includes all private nonfarm establishments with fewer than 100 workers, while the state and local government survey includes all governments, regardless of the number of workers. All three surveys include full- and part-time workers, and workers in all 50 states and the District of Columbia.

Further information on methodology is available in *BLS Bulletin 2456, Employee Benefits in Medium and Large Private Establishments* (November 1994), *Bulletin 2475, Employee Benefits for Small Private Establishments* (April 1996), and *Bulletin 2477, Employee Benefits for State and Local Governments* (May 1996).

COMPENSATION OF EMPLOYEES

Percent of Full-time Employees Participating in Employer-provided Benefit Plans, Medium and Large Private Establishments, Selected Years, 1980-1993

Benefit plans	1980	1981	1982	1983	1984	1985	1986	1988	1989	1991	1993
TIME-OFF PLANS											
Participants with:											
Paid lunch time	10	10	9	11	9	10	10	11	10	8	9
Average minutes per day	.....	.....	25	25	26	27	27	29	26	30	29
Paid rest time	75	75	76	74	73	72	72	72	71	67	68
Average minutes per day	.....	.....	25	25	26	26	26	26	26	26	26
Paid funeral leave	.....	.....	.....	.....	.....	88	88	85	84	80	83
Average days per occurrence	.....	.....	.....	.....	.....	3.2	3.2	3.2	3.3	3.3	3.0
Paid holidays	99	99	99	99	99	98	99	96	97	92	91
Average days per year	10.1	10.2	10.0	9.8	9.8	10.1	10.0	9.4	9.2	10.2	10.2
Paid personal leave	20	23	24	25	23	26	25	24	22	21	21
Average days per year	.....	.....	3.8	3.7	3.6	3.7	3.7	3.3	3.1	3.3	3.1
Paid vacations	100	99	99	100	99	99	100	98	97	96	97
Paid sick leave	62	65	67	67	67	67	70	69	68	67	65
Unpaid maternity leave	.....	.....	.....	.....	.....	.....	.....	33	37	37	60
Unpaid paternity leave	.....	.....	.....	.....	.....	.....	.....	16	18	26	53
INSURANCE PLANS											
Participants in medical care plans	97	97	97	96	97	96	95	90	92	83	82
Participants with coverage for:											
Home health care	.....	.....	.....	37	46	56	66	76	75	81	86
Extended care facilities	58	60	62	58	62	67	70	79	80	80	82
Mental health care	98	99	99	99	99	99	99	98	97	98	98
Alcohol abuse treatment	.....	.....	50	53	61.0	68	70	80	97	97	98
Drug abuse treatment	.....	.....	37	43	52	61	66	74	96	96	98
Participants with employee contribution required for:											
Self coverage	26	27	27	33	36	36	43	44	47	51	61
Average monthly contribution	.....	.....	.....	$10.13	$11.93	$12.05	$12.80	$19.29	$25.31	$26.60	.....
Family coverage	46	49	51	54	58	56	63	64	66	69	76
Average monthly contribution	.....	.....	.....	$32.51	$35.93	$38.33	$41.40	$60.07	$72.10	$96.97	$107.42
Medical care in HMOs	.....	.....	.....	.....	.....	.....	.....	19.0	17.0	17.0	23.0
Medical care in PPOs	.....	.....	.....	.....	.....	.....	.....	7.0	10.0	16.0	26.0
Medical care in fee-for-service	.....	.....	.....	.....	.....	.....	.....	74.0	74.0	67.0	50.0
Participants in life insurance plans	96	96	96	96	96	96	96	92	94	94	91
Participants with:											
Survivor income benefits	.....	.....	.....	.....	.....	12	10	7	7	6	5
Retiree protection available	.....	64	64	66	64	62	59	49	42	44	41
Participants in long-term disability insurance plans	40	41	43	45	47	48	48	42	45	40	41
RETIREMENT PLANS											
Participants in defined benefit pension plans	84	84	84	82	82	80	76	63	63	59	56
Participants with:											
Normal retirement prior to age 65	55	56	58	64	63	67	64	59	62	55	52
Early retirement available	98	98	97	97	97	97	98	98	97	98	95
Ad hoc pension increase in last five years	.....	.....	51	47	41	35	26	22	7	6	
Terminal earnings formula	53	50	52	54	54	57	57	55	64	56	61
Benefit coordinated with Social Security	45	43	45	55	56	61	62	62	63	54	48
Participants in defined contribution plans	.....	.....	.....	.....	.....	53	60	45	48	48	49
Participants in plans with tax-deferred savings arrangement	.....	.....	.....	.....	.....	26	33	36	41	44	.....
OTHER BENEFITS											
Employees eligible for:											
Flexible benefits plans	.....	.....	.....	.....	.....	.....	2	5	9	10	12
Reimbursement accounts	.....	.....	.....	.....	.....	.....	5	12	23	36	52

Percent of Full-time Employees Participating in Employer-provided Benefit Programs, Small Private Establishments and State and Local Governments, Selected Years, 1987-1994

Benefit plans	Small private establishments			State and local governments			
	1990	1992	1994	1987	1990	1992	1994
TIME-OFF PLANS							
Participants with							
Paid lunch time	8	9	....	17	11	10	....
Average minutes per day	37	37	....	34	36	34	....
Paid rest time	48	49	....	58	56	53	....
Average minutes per day	27	26	....	29	29	29	....
Paid funeral leave	47	50	50	56	63	65	62
Average days per year	2.9	3	3.1	3.7	3.7	3.7	3.7
Paid holidays	84	82	82	81	74	75	73
Average days per year	7.6	7.7	7.5	10.9	11.4	11.4	11.5
Paid personal leave	11	12	13	38	39	38	38
Average days per year	2.8	2.6	2.6	2.7	2.9	2.9	3
Paid vacations	88	88	88	72	67	67	66
Paid sick leave	47	53	80	97	95	95	94
Unpaid maternity leave	17	18	....	57	51	59	....
Unpaid paternity leave	8	8	....	30	33	44	....
INSURANCE PLANS	....	....	47	....	....	....	93
Participants in medical care plans	69	71	66	93	93	90	87
Participants with coverage for:							
Home health care	79	80	....	76	82	87	84
Extended care facilities	83	84	....	78	79	84	81
Mental health care	98	98	....	98	99	99	99
Alcohol abuse treatment	97	95	....	87	99	99	99
Drug abuse treatment	94	94	....	86	98	99	98
Participants with employee contribution required for:							
Self coverage	42	47	52	35	38	43	47
Average monthly contribution	$25.13	$36.51	$40.97	$15.74	$25.53	$28.97	$30.20
Family coverage	67	73	75	71	65	72	71
Average monthly contribution	$109.34	$150.54	$159.63	$71.89	$117.59	$139.23	$149.70
Medical care in HMOs	14	14	....	24	22	27	....
Medical care in PPOs	13	18	....	7	17	29	....
Medical care in fee-for-service	74	68	....	67	61	43	....
Participants in life insurance plans	64	64	61	85	88	89	87
Participants with:							
Accidental death and dismemberment insurance	....	....	....	....	....	....	....
Survivor income benefits	....	....	....	....	....	....	....
Retiree protection available	19	25	20	55	45	46	46
Participants in long-term disability insurance plans	19	23	20	31	27	28	30
Participants in sickness and accident insurance plans	26	26	26	14	21	22	21
RETIREMENT PLANS							
Participants in defined benefit pension plans	20	22	15	93	90	87	91
Participants with:							
Normal retirement prior to age 65	54	50	....	92	89	92	92
Early retirement available	95	95	....	90	88	89	87
Ad hoc pension increase in last five years	7	4	....	33	16	10	13
Terminal earnings formula	58	54	....	100	100	100	99
Benefit coordinated with Social Security	49	46	....	18	8	10	4
Participants in defined contribution plans	31	33	34	9	9	9	9
Participants in plans with tax-deferred savings arrangements	17	24	23	28	45	45	24
OTHER BENEFITS							
Employees eligible for:							
Flexible benefits plans	1	2	3	5	5	5	5
Reimbursement accounts	8	14	19	5	31	50	64

Percent of Full-time Employees Participating in Employer-provided Benefit Programs, Small Private Establishments and State and Local Governments, by Class of Employee, 1994

Benefit plans	Small private establishments				State and local governments			
	All employees	Profes-sional, tech-nical, and related employees	Clerical and sales employees	Blue-collar and service employees	All employees	White-collar employees, except teachers	Teachers	Blue-collar and service employees
PAID TIME OFF								
Holidays	82	91	89	75	73	86	33	91
Vacations	88	92	93	83	66	84	9	91
Personal leave	13	21	17	7	38	30	58	31
Funeral leave	50	58	55	45	62	59	58	70
Jury duty leave	58	74	66	48	94	94	94	93
Military leave	17	23	19	13	75	80	61	82
Sick leave	50	69	61	36	94	93	96	94
Family leave	2	5	2	1	4	4	3	6
UNPAID TIME OFF								
Family leave	47	53	50	43	93	93	96	90
INSURANCE								
Sickness and accident insurance	26	27	27	25	21	24	11	26
Long-term disability insurance	20	36	27	10	30	31	37	23
Medical care	66	80	70	57	87	89	84	86
Dental care	28	40	31	22	62	62	59	66
Life Insurance	61	73	68	52	87	87	85	87
RETIREMENT								
All retirement	42	53	47	35	96	96	97	95
Defined benefit pension	15	16	16	15	91	90	93	91
Defined contribution	34	45	39	26	9	10	7	9
Types of plans:.								
Savings and thrift	17	23	20	13	2	3	1	2
Deferred profit sharing	13	16	17	10	....	....	....	....
Employee stock ownership	1	2	1	1	....	....	....	....
Money purchase pension	5	9	5	4	7	7	5	7
Simplified employee pension	1	1	1	1	....	....	....	....
401(k) plans with employer contribution	20	28	23	15	7	8	5	8
OTHER BENEFITS								
Flexible benefits plans	3	2	5	2	5	5	7	3
Reimbursement accounts	19	28	23	13	64	68	59	61
Child care	1	2	1	1	9	11	5	9

Part Six

Prices and Living Conditions

Prices and Living Conditions

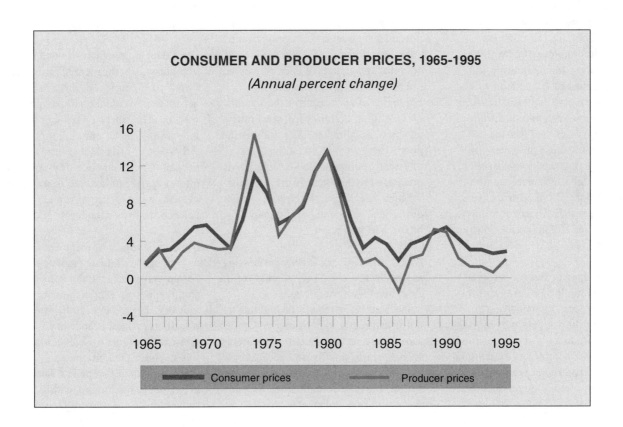

CONSUMER AND PRODUCER PRICES, 1965-1995

(Annual percent change)

Consumer prices   Producer prices

he United States has experienced two periods of severe inflation since 1967, both precipitated in part by large increases in world oil prices. According to the Consumer and Producer Prices graph, the annual consumer price increase peaked at 11 percent in 1974, while the increase in producer prices of finished goods reached 15.4 percent. Following the second round of oil price increases in 1980, both consumer prices and producer prices of finished goods rose more than 13 percent.

Inflation had eased by 1986, when consumer prices rose only 1.9 percent and producer prices of finished goods actually declined more than 1 percent. The rate of price increase then climbed gradually, reaching the 5 percent range by 1990. From 1990 to 1993, the inflation rate declined fairly steadily while the rate of consumer price increase remained at 3 percent less during 1994 and 1995.

NOTES
Prices and Living Conditions—Producer Price Index

The *Producer Price Index* (PPI) measures average changes in prices received by domestic producers of goods and services. Most of the information used in calculating the indexes is obtained through the systematic sampling of nearly every industry in the manufacturing and mining sectors of the economy. The PPI program also includes data from other sectors—agriculture, fishing, forestry, services, and gas and electricity. Because producer price indexes are designed to measure only the change in prices received for the output of domestic industries, *imports are not included.* The sample currently contains over 100,000 price quotations per month.

There are three primary systems of indexes within the PPI program: (1) stage-of-processing indexes; (2) indexes for the net output of industries and their products; and (3) commodity indexes. The commodity-based *stage-of-processing* structure organizes products by class of buyer and degree of fabrication. The entire output of various industries is sampled to derive price indexes for the net output of industries and their products. The commodity structure organizes products by similarity of end-use or material composition.

Within the commodity stage-of-processing system, finished goods are commodities that will not undergo further processing and are ready for sale to the final demand user, either an individual consumer or a business firm. Consumer foods include unprocessed foods, such as eggs and fresh vegetables, as well as processed foods, such as bakery products and meats. Other finished consumer goods include durable goods, such as automobiles, household furniture, and appliances; and nondurable goods, such as apparel and home heating oil. Capital

equipment includes producer durable goods such as heavy motor trucks, tractors, and machine tools.

The stage-of-processing category for intermediate materials, supplies, and components consists partly of commodities that have been processed but require further processing. Examples of such semifinished goods include flour, cotton, yarn, steel mill products, and lumber. The intermediate goods category also encompasses physically complete nondurable goods purchased by business firms as inputs for their operations. Examples include diesel fuel, belts and belting, paper boxes, and fertilizers.

Crude materials for further processing are products entering the market for the first time that have not been manufactured or fabricated and that are not sold directly to consumers. Crude foodstuffs and feedstuffs include items such as grains and livestock. Examples of crude nonfood materials include raw cotton, crude petroleum, coal, hides and skins, and iron and steel scrap.

Producer price indexes for the net output of industries and their products are grouped according to the Standard Industrial Classification (SIC) and the Census product code extensions of the SIC. Industry price indexes are compatible with other economic time series organized by SIC codes, such as data on employment, wages, and productivity.

Producer price indexes are based on selling prices reported by establishments of all sizes selected by probability sampling, with the probability of selection proportionate to size. Individual items and transaction terms from these firms are also chosen by probability proportionate to size. BLS strongly encourages cooperating companies to supply actual transaction

prices at the time of shipment to minimize the use of list prices. Prices are normally reported monthly by mail questionnaire for the Tuesday of the week containing the 13th.

Price data are always provided on a voluntary and confidential basis; only sworn BLS employees are allowed access to individual company price reports. The Bureau publishes price indexes instead of unit dollar prices. All producer price indexes are routinely subject to revision once, four months after original publication, to reflect the availability of late reports and corrections by respondents.

Net output values of shipments are used as weights for industry indexes. Net output values refer to the value of shipments from establishments in one industry shipped to establishments classified in another industry. However, *weights for commodity price indexes* are based on gross shipment values, including shipment values between establishments within the same industry. As a result, commodity aggregate indexes such as the *all commodities index* are affected by the multiple counting of price change at successive stages of processing, which can lead to exaggerated or misleading signals about inflation. Stage-of-processing indexes partially correct this defect, but industry indexes consistently correct this weakness at all levels of aggregation. Therefore, industry and stage-of-processing indexes are more appropriate than commodity aggregate indexes for economic analysis of general price trends.

Weights for most traditional commodity groupings of the PPI, as well as all indexes calculated from traditional commodity groupings (such as stage-of-processing indexes), currently reflect 1992 values of shipments as reported in the Census of Manufactures and other sources. Major industry group indexes, which are based on the SIC system, are currently calculated using 1992 net output weights.

Additional information is published monthly in the *Producer Price Index Detailed Report*.

PRICES AND LIVING CONDITIONS

Producer Price Indexes by Stage of Processing, 1947-1995

(1982=100)

Year	Crude materials for further processing				Intermediate materials, supplies, and components						Finished goods		
	Total	Food-stuffs and feedstuffs	Nonfood materials, except fuel	Fuel	Total	Materials and components for construction	Materials and components for manufacturing	Processed fuels and lubricants	Containers	Supplies	Total	Consumer goods	Capital equipment
1947	31.7	45.1	24.0	7.5	23.3	22.5	24.9	14.4	23.4	28.5	26.4	28.6	19.8
1948	34.7	48.8	26.7	8.9	25.2	24.9	26.8	16.4	24.4	29.8	28.5	30.8	21.6
1949	30.1	40.5	24.3	8.8	24.2	24.9	25.7	14.9	24.5	28.0	27.7	29.4	22.7
1950	32.7	43.4	27.8	8.8	25.3	26.2	26.9	15.2	25.2	29.0	28.2	29.9	23.2
1951	37.6	50.2	32.0	9.0	28.4	28.7	30.5	15.9	29.6	32.6	30.8	32.7	25.5
1952	34.5	47.3	27.8	9.0	27.5	28.5	29.3	15.7	28.0	32.6	30.6	32.3	25.9
1953	31.9	42.3	26.6	9.3	27.7	29.0	29.7	15.8	28.0	31.0	30.3	31.7	26.3
1954	31.6	42.3	26.1	8.9	27.9	29.1	29.8	15.8	28.5	31.7	30.4	31.7	26.7
1955	30.4	38.4	27.5	8.9	28.4	30.3	30.5	15.8	28.9	31.2	30.5	31.5	27.4
1956	30.6	37.6	28.6	9.5	29.6	31.8	32.0	16.3	31.0	32.0	31.3	32.0	29.5
1957	31.2	39.2	28.2	10.1	30.3	32.0	32.7	17.2	32.4	32.3	32.5	32.9	31.3
1958	31.9	41.6	27.1	10.2	30.4	32.0	32.8	16.2	33.2	33.1	33.2	33.6	32.1
1959	31.1	38.8	28.1	10.4	30.8	32.9	33.3	16.2	33.0	33.5	33.1	33.3	32.7
1960	30.4	38.4	26.9	10.5	30.8	32.7	33.3	16.6	33.4	33.3	33.4	33.6	32.8
1961	30.2	37.9	27.2	10.5	30.6	32.2	32.9	16.8	33.2	33.7	33.4	33.6	32.9
1962	30.5	38.6	27.1	10.4	30.6	32.1	32.7	16.7	33.6	34.5	33.5	33.7	33.0
1963	29.9	37.5	26.7	10.5	30.7	32.2	32.7	16.6	33.2	35.0	33.4	33.5	33.1
1964	29.6	36.6	27.2	10.5	30.8	32.5	33.1	16.2	32.9	34.7	33.5	33.6	33.4
1965	31.1	39.2	27.7	10.6	31.2	32.8	33.6	16.5	33.5	35.0	34.1	34.2	33.8
1966	33.1	42.7	28.3	10.9	32.0	33.6	34.3	16.8	34.5	36.5	35.2	35.4	34.6
1967	31.3	40.3	26.5	11.3	32.2	34.0	34.5	16.9	35.0	36.8	35.6	35.6	35.8
1968	31.8	40.9	27.1	11.5	33.0	35.7	35.3	16.5	35.9	37.1	36.6	36.5	37.0
1969	33.9	44.1	28.4	12.0	34.1	37.7	36.5	16.6	37.2	37.8	38.0	37.9	38.3
1970	35.2	45.2	29.1	13.8	35.4	38.3	38.0	17.7	39.0	39.7	39.3	39.1	40.1
1971	36.0	46.1	29.4	15.7	36.8	40.8	38.9	19.5	40.8	40.8	40.5	40.2	41.7
1972	39.9	51.5	32.3	16.8	38.2	43.0	40.4	20.1	42.7	42.5	41.8	41.5	42.8
1973	54.5	72.6	42.9	18.6	42.4	46.5	44.1	22.2	45.2	51.7	45.6	46.0	44.2
1974	61.4	76.4	54.5	24.8	52.5	55.0	56.0	33.6	53.3	56.8	52.6	53.1	50.5
1975	61.6	77.4	50.0	30.6	58.0	60.1	61.7	39.4	60.0	61.8	58.2	58.2	58.2
1976	63.4	76.8	54.9	34.5	60.9	64.1	64.0	42.3	63.1	65.8	60.8	60.4	62.1
1977	65.5	77.5	56.3	42.0	64.9	69.3	67.4	47.7	65.9	69.3	64.7	64.3	66.1
1978	73.4	87.3	61.9	48.2	69.5	76.5	72.0	49.9	71.0	72.9	69.8	69.4	71.3
1979	85.9	100.0	75.5	57.3	78.4	84.2	80.9	61.6	79.4	80.2	77.6	77.5	77.5
1980	95.3	104.6	91.8	69.4	90.3	91.3	91.7	85.0	89.1	89.9	88.0	88.6	85.8
1981	103.0	103.9	109.8	84.8	98.6	97.9	98.7	100.6	96.7	96.9	96.1	96.6	94.6
1982	100.0	100.0	100.0	100.0	100.0	100.0	100.0	100.0	100.0	100.0	100.0	100.0	100.0
1983	101.3	101.8	98.8	105.1	100.6	102.8	101.2	95.4	100.4	101.8	101.6	101.3	102.8
1984	103.5	104.7	101.0	105.1	103.1	105.6	104.1	95.7	105.9	104.1	103.7	103.3	105.2
1985	95.8	94.8	94.3	102.7	102.7	107.3	103.3	92.8	109.0	104.4	104.7	103.8	107.5
1986	87.7	93.2	76.0	92.2	99.1	108.1	102.2	72.7	110.3	105.6	103.2	101.4	109.7
1987	93.7	96.2	88.5	84.1	101.5	109.8	105.3	73.3	114.5	107.7	105.4	103.6	111.7
1988	96.0	106.1	85.9	82.1	107.1	116.1	113.2	71.2	120.1	113.7	108.0	106.2	114.3
1989	103.1	111.2	95.8	85.3	112.0	121.3	118.1	76.4	125.4	118.1	113.6	112.1	118.8
1990	108.9	113.1	107.3	84.8	114.5	122.9	118.7	85.9	127.7	119.4	119.2	118.2	122.9
1991	101.2	105.5	97.5	82.9	114.4	124.5	118.1	85.3	128.1	121.4	121.7	120.5	126.7
1992	100.4	105.1	94.2	84.0	114.7	126.5	117.9	84.5	127.7	122.7	123.2	121.7	129.1
1993	102.4	108.4	94.1	87.1	116.2	132.0	118.9	84.7	126.4	125.0	124.7	123.0	131.4
1994	101.8	106.5	97.0	82.4	118.5	136.6	122.1	83.1	129.7	127.0	125.5	123.3	134.1
1995	102.7	105.8	105.8	72.1	124.9	142.1	130.4	84.2	148.8	132.1	127.9	125.6	136.7

Producer Price Indexes by Commodity Group, 1913-1995

(1982=100)

Year	All commodities	Industrial commodities	Farm products 01	Processed foods and feeds 02	Textile products and apparel 03	Hides, leather, and related products 04	Fuels and related products and power 05	Chemicals and related products 06
1913	12.0	11.9	18.0					
1914	11.8	11.3	17.9					
1915	12.0	11.6	18.0					
1916	14.7	15.0	21.3					
1917	20.2	19.5	32.6					
1918	22.6	21.1	37.4					
1919	23.9	22.0	39.8					
1920	26.6	27.4	38.0					
1921	16.8	17.8	22.3					
1922	16.7	17.4	23.7					
1923	17.3	17.8	24.9					
1924	16.9	17.0	25.2					
1925	17.8	17.5	27.7					
1926	17.2	17.0	25.3			17.1	10.3	
1927	16.5	16.0	25.1			18.4	9.1	
1928	16.7	15.8	26.7			20.7	8.7	
1929	16.4	15.6	26.4			18.6	8.6	
1930	14.9	14.5	22.4			17.1	8.1	
1931	12.6	12.8	16.4			14.7	7.0	
1932	11.2	11.9	12.2			12.5	7.3	
1933	11.4	12.1	13.0			13.8	6.9	16.2
1934	12.9	13.3	16.5			14.8	7.6	17.0
1935	13.8	13.3	19.8			15.3	7.6	17.7
1936	13.9	13.5	20.4			16.3	7.9	17.8
1937	14.9	14.5	21.8			17.9	8.0	18.6
1938	13.5	13.9	17.3			15.8	7.9	17.7
1939	13.3	13.9	16.5			16.3	7.5	17.6
1940	13.5	14.1	17.1			17.2	7.4	17.9
1941	15.1	15.1	20.8			18.4	7.9	19.5
1942	17.0	16.2	26.7			20.1	8.1	21.7
1943	17.8	16.5	30.9			20.1	8.3	21.9
1944	17.9	16.7	31.2			19.9	8.6	22.2
1945	18.2	17.0	32.4			20.1	8.7	22.3
1946	20.8	18.6	37.5			23.3	9.3	24.1
1947	25.6	22.7	45.1	33.0	50.6	31.7	11.1	32.1
1948	27.7	24.6	48.5	35.3	52.8	32.1	13.1	32.8
1949	26.3	24.1	41.9	32.1	48.3	30.4	12.4	30.0
1950	27.3	25.0	44.0	33.2	50.2	32.9	12.6	30.4
1951	30.4	27.6	51.2	36.9	56.0	37.7	13.0	34.8
1952	29.6	26.9	48.4	36.4	50.5	30.5	13.0	33.0
1953	29.2	27.2	43.8	34.8	49.3	31.0	13.4	33.4
1954	29.3	27.2	43.2	35.4	48.2	29.5	13.2	33.8
1955	29.3	27.8	40.5	33.8	48.2	29.4	13.2	33.7
1956	30.3	29.1	40.0	33.8	48.2	31.2	13.6	33.9
1957	31.2	29.9	41.1	34.8	48.3	31.2	14.3	34.6
1958	31.6	30.0	42.9	36.5	47.4	31.6	13.7	34.9
1959	31.7	30.5	40.2	35.6	48.1	35.9	13.7	34.8
1960	31.7	30.5	40.1	35.6	48.6	34.6	13.9	34.8
1961	31.6	30.4	39.7	36.2	47.8	34.9	14.0	34.5
1962	31.7	30.4	40.4	36.5	48.2	35.3	14.0	33.9
1963	31.6	30.3	39.6	36.8	48.2	34.3	13.9	33.5
1964	31.6	30.5	39.0	36.7	48.5	34.4	13.5	33.6
1965	32.3	30.9	40.7	38.0	48.8	35.9	13.8	33.9
1966	33.3	31.5	43.7	40.2	48.9	39.4	14.1	34.0
1967	33.4	32.0	41.3	39.8	48.9	38.1	14.4	34.2
1968	34.2	32.8	42.3	40.6	50.7	39.3	14.3	34.1
1969	35.6	33.9	45.0	42.7	51.8	41.5	14.6	34.2
1970	36.9	35.2	45.8	44.6	52.4	42.0	15.3	35.0
1971	38.1	36.5	46.6	45.5	53.3	43.4	16.6	35.6
1972	39.8	37.8	51.6	48.0	55.5	50.0	17.1	35.6
1973	45.0	40.3	72.7	58.9	60.5	54.5	19.4	37.6
1974	53.5	49.2	77.4	68.0	68.0	55.2	30.1	50.2
1975	58.4	54.9	77.0	72.6	67.4	56.5	35.4	62.0
1976	61.1	58.4	78.8	70.8	72.4	63.9	38.3	64.0
1977	64.9	62.5	79.4	74.0	75.3	68.3	43.6	65.9
1978	69.9	67.0	87.7	80.6	78.1	76.1	46.5	68.0
1979	78.7	75.7	99.6	88.5	82.5	96.1	58.9	76.0
1980	89.8	88.0	102.9	95.9	89.7	94.7	82.8	89.0
1981	98.0	97.4	105.2	98.9	97.6	99.3	100.2	98.4
1982	100.0	100.0	100.0	100.0	100.0	100.0	100.0	100.0
1983	101.3	101.1	102.4	101.8	100.3	103.2	95.9	100.3
1984	103.7	103.3	105.5	105.4	102.7	109.0	94.8	102.9
1985	103.2	103.7	95.1	103.5	102.9	108.9	91.4	103.7
1986	100.2	100.0	92.9	105.4	103.2	113.0	69.8	102.6
1987	102.8	102.6	95.5	107.9	105.1	120.4	70.2	106.4
1988	106.9	106.3	104.9	112.7	109.2	131.4	66.7	116.3
1989	112.2	111.6	110.9	117.8	112.3	136.3	72.9	123.0
1990	116.3	115.8	112.2	121.9	115.0	141.7	82.3	123.6
1991	116.5	116.5	105.7	121.9	116.3	138.9	81.2	125.6
1992	117.2	117.4	103.6	122.1	117.8	140.4	80.4	125.9
1993	118.9	119.0	107.1	124.0	118.0	143.7	80.0	128.2
1994	120.4	120.7	106.3	125.5	118.3	148.5	77.8	132.1
1995	124.7	125.5	107.4	127.0	120.8	153.7	78.0	142.5

Producer Price Indexes by Commodity Group, 1913-1995—Continued

(1982=100)

Year	Rubber and plastic products	Lumber and wood products	Pulp, paper, and allied products	Metals and metal products	Machinery and equipment	Furniture and household durables	Nonmetallic mineral products	Transportation equipment	Miscellaneous products
	07	08	09	10	11	12	13	14	15
1913									
1914									
1915									
1916									
1917									
1918									
1919									
1920									
1921									
1922									
1923									
1924									
1925									
1926	47.1	9.3		13.7		28.6	16.4		
1927	35.7	8.8		12.9		27.9	15.7		
1928	28.3	8.5		12.9		27.2	16.2		
1929	24.6	8.8		13.3		27.0	16.0		
1930	21.5	8.0		12.0		26.5	15.9		
1931	18.3	6.5		10.8		24.4	14.9		
1932	15.9	5.6		9.9		21.5	13.9		
1933	16.7	6.7		10.2		21.6	14.7		
1934	19.5	7.8		11.2		23.4	15.7		
1935	19.6	7.5		11.2		23.2	15.7		
1936	21.1	7.9		11.4		23.6	15.8		
1937	24.9	9.3		13.1		26.1	16.1		
1938	24.4	8.5		12.6		25.5	15.6		
1939	25.4	8.7		12.5	14.8	25.4	15.3		
1940	23.7	9.6		12.5	14.9	26.0	15.3		
1941	25.5	11.5		12.8	15.1	27.6	15.7		
1942	29.7	12.5		13.0	15.4	29.9	16.3		
1943	30.5	13.2		12.9	15.2	29.7	16.4		
1944	30.1	14.3		12.9	15.1	30.5	16.7		
1945	29.2	14.5		13.1	15.1	30.5	17.4		
1946	29.3	16.6		14.7	16.6	32.4	18.5		
1947	29.2	25.8	25.1	18.2	19.3	37.2	20.7		26.6
1948	30.2	29.5	26.2	20.7	20.9	39.4	22.4		27.7
1949	29.2	27.3	25.1	20.9	21.9	40.1	23.0		28.2
1950	35.6	31.4	25.7	22.0	22.6	40.9	23.5		28.6
1951	43.7	34.1	30.5	24.5	25.3	44.4	25.0		30.3
1952	39.6	33.2	29.7	24.5	25.3	43.5	25.0		30.2
1953	36.9	33.1	29.6	25.3	25.9	44.4	26.0		31.0
1954	37.5	32.5	29.6	25.5	26.3	44.9	26.6		31.3
1955	42.4	34.1	30.4	27.2	27.2	45.1	27.3		31.3
1956	43.0	34.6	32.4	29.6	29.3	46.3	28.5		31.7
1957	42.8	32.8	33.0	30.2	31.4	47.5	29.6		32.6
1958	42.8	32.5	33.4	30.0	32.1	47.9	29.9		33.3
1959	42.6	34.7	33.7	30.6	32.8	48.0	30.3		33.4
1960	42.7	33.5	34.0	30.6	33.0	47.8	30.4		33.6
1961	41.1	32.0	33.0	30.5	33.0	47.5	30.5		33.7
1962	39.9	32.2	33.4	30.2	33.0	47.2	30.5		33.9
1963	40.1	32.8	33.1	30.3	33.1	46.9	30.3		34.2
1964	39.6	33.5	33.0	31.1	33.3	47.1	30.4		34.4
1965	39.7	33.7	33.3	32.0	33.7	46.8	30.4		34.7
1966	40.5	35.2	34.2	32.8	34.7	47.4	30.7		35.3
1967	41.4	35.1	34.6	33.2	35.9	48.3	31.2		36.2
1968	42.8	39.8	35.0	34.0	37.0	49.7	32.4		37.0
1969	43.6	44.0	36.0	36.0	38.2	50.7	33.6	40.4	38.1
1970	44.9	39.9	37.5	38.7	40.0	51.9	35.3	41.9	39.8
1971	45.2	44.7	38.1	39.4	41.4	53.1	38.2	44.2	40.8
1972	45.3	50.7	39.3	40.9	42.3	53.8	39.4	45.5	41.5
1973	46.6	62.2	42.3	44.0	43.7	55.7	40.7	46.1	43.3
1974	56.4	64.5	52.5	57.0	50.0	61.8	47.8	50.3	48.1
1975	62.2	62.1	59.0	61.5	57.9	67.5	54.4	56.7	53.4
1976	66.0	72.2	62.1	65.0	61.3	70.3	58.2	60.5	55.6
1977	69.4	83.0	64.6	69.3	65.2	73.2	62.6	64.6	59.4
1978	72.4	96.9	67.7	75.3	70.3	77.5	69.6	69.5	66.7
1979	80.5	105.5	75.9	86.0	76.7	82.8	77.6	75.3	75.5
1980	90.1	101.5	86.3	95.0	86.0	90.7	88.4	82.9	93.6
1981	96.4	102.8	94.8	99.6	94.4	95.9	96.7	94.3	96.1
1982	100.0	100.0	100.0	100.0	100.0	100.0	100.0	100.0	100.0
1983	100.8	107.9	103.3	101.8	102.7	103.4	101.6	102.8	104.8
1984	102.3	108.0	110.3	104.8	105.1	105.7	105.4	105.2	107.0
1985	101.9	106.6	113.3	104.4	107.2	107.1	108.6	107.9	109.4
1986	101.9	107.2	116.1	103.2	108.8	108.2	110.0	110.5	111.6
1987	103.0	112.8	121.8	107.1	110.4	109.9	110.0	112.5	114.9
1988	109.3	118.9	130.4	118.7	113.2	113.1	111.2	114.3	120.2
1989	112.6	126.7	137.8	124.1	117.4	116.9	112.6	117.7	126.5
1990	113.6	129.7	141.2	122.9	120.7	119.2	114.7	121.5	134.2
1991	115.1	132.1	142.9	120.2	123.0	121.2	117.2	126.4	140.8
1992	115.1	146.6	145.2	119.2	123.4	122.2	117.3	130.4	145.3
1993	116.0	174.0	147.3	119.2	124.0	123.7	120.0	133.7	145.4
1994	117.6	180.0	152.5	124.8	125.1	126.1	124.2	137.2	141.9
1995	124.3	178.1	172.2	134.5	126.6	128.2	129.0	139.7	145.4

Producer Price Indexes for the Net Output of Selected Industries, 1984-1995

(December 1984=100, unless otherwise indicated)

Industry	1984	1985	1986	1987	1988	1989	1990	1991	1992	1993	1994	1995
MINING INDUSTRIES												
Metal mining			91.2	100.1	100.7	100.3	93.4	82.2	76.6	69.7	81.4	101.4
Iron ores		96.5	90.0	81.8	80.9	82.2	82.7	82.8	82.1	82.1	91.0	
Copper ores						129.5	112.8	99.5	96.6	79.1	106.9	157.1
Lead and zinc ores										82.2	93.5	103.1
Gold and silver ores			76.7	96.0	96.1	82.9	81.2	71.3	68.0	69.1	75.9	77.1
Metal mining services			100.1	100.6	102.5	107.2	108.6	108.7	108.8	111.2	111.3	111.4
Miscellaneous metal ores			98.5	100.7	87.9	57.9	58.0	49.2	33.9	32.6	32.9	33.6
Coal mining (12/85=100)			99.5	96.0	94.6	94.3	96.5	96.3	94.0	93.3	93.2	91.6
Bituminous coal and lignite											99.1	97.3
Anthracite mining											99.4	98.2
Coal mining services										96.1	98.0	98.3
Oil and gas extraction (12/85=100)			76.9	74.3	68.5	75.7	82.7	77.9	76.5	76.2	71.1	66.6
Mining and quarrying of nonmetallic minerals, except fuels		102.8	104.2	105.1	108.0	111.2	113.7	116.3	117.5	118.8	120.5	123.8
MANUFACTURING INDUSTRIES												
Food and kindred products		99.0	100.3	102.6	107.1	112.2	116.2	116.5	116.9	118.7	120.1	121.7
Meat products		96.0	97.9	101.7	103.9	110.0	118.1	114.8	110.0	113.6	110.7	109.3
Dairy products		98.0	97.5	99.4	100.1	108.0	113.5	111.0	113.7	114.1	115.6	115.8
Canned and preserved fruits and vegetables		101.5	100.7	104.1	108.9	114.5	119.5	119.5	121.5	121.2	123.7	125.5
Grain mill products			96.8	97.8	111.3	116.4	114.5	115.9	119.1	120.5	124.9	125.9
Bakery products		102.6	105.1	107.3	115.2	123.5	128.7	133.7	139.1	142.7	145.3	149.6
Sugar and confectionery products		99.1	102.4	104.7	106.0	110.2	112.5	117.4	117.0	118.7	120.4	123.3
Fats and oils		94.1	85.5	89.4	109.4	104.6	98.8	93.3	93.1	100.4	105.0	103
Beverages		100.7	102.8	104.1	105.8	109.0	112.0	116.4	117.9	118.5	118.8	123.1
Miscellaneous food preparations and kindred products			109.6	108.7	110.2	114.2	116.7	118.4	117.7	118.3	125.4	131.1
Tobacco manufactures		106.6	115.5	126.5	141.8	161.4	183.2	207.5	230.2	218.0	187.8	193.2
Cigarettes	102.3	110.7	120.9	133.5	150.8	173.1	197.6	225.0	250.5	235.2	198.9	204.3
Cigars	104.4	110.3	111.5	116.0	121.2	130.5	141.4	150.0	159.1	166.4	172.9	186.5
Chewing and smoking tobacco and snuff	110.9	120.7	131.7	137.4	145.5	154.1	166.2	182.3	199.2	214.2	229.5	243.6
Tobacco stemming and redrying		98.0	96.0	95.5	97.7	98.9	103.9	107.6	107.5	108.7	109.4	112.2
Textile mill products		99.7	100.3	102.6	106.8	109.3	111.6	112.5	113.6	113.6	113.6	116.5
Cotton broadwoven fabric	103.0	99.5	99.0	101.9	107.6	107.2	109.3	109.6	112.8	112.2	113.5	118.6
Synthetic fiber and silk broadwoven fabric	103.1	101.2	100.9	103.7	110.1	112.3	115.6	115.2	115.9	114.6	109.9	112.4
Wool weaving and finishing			99.2	101.1	109.8	119.4	118.5	116.3	114.7	113.8	113.3	113.5
Narrow fabric mills		100.3	100.7	101.3	103.1	108.1	111.7	113.2	114.6	115.6	116.8	119.7
Knitting mills		100.6	101.3	103.3	105.5	107.4	109.9	110.9	112.8	113.3	113.0	115.7
Dyeing and finishing textiles, except woolen fabrics and knit goods		101.3	102.4	107.2	111.6	114.8	117.0	119.9	122.6	125.1	125.5	127.8
Floor covering mills			100.8	102.5	105.8	107.6	108.9	109.7	109.4	108.7	110.0	111.6
Yarn and thread mills		99.4	99.7	101.9	104.9	106.4	109.7	110.7	109.9	107.0	107.4	112.1
Miscellaneous textile goods			99.8	100.9	106.6	112.4	115.0	117.0	116.3	116.5	118.1	122.9
Apparel and other finished products made from fabrics and other similar materials		101.1	102.3	103.9	107.2	110.2	113.3	116.0	118.0	119.2	119.7	120.6
Mens' and boys' suits and coats	116.8	119.9	121.6	125.2	131.6	140.3	145.7	149.2	151.8	151.9	154.0	155.8
Mens', youths', and boys' furnishings, work clothes, and allied garments		100.8	101.6	103.1	106.9	110.1	113.0	116.2	119.7	121.9	122.7	124.0
Womens', misses', and juniors' outerwear		101.3	102.7	104.5	107.7	110.8	114.0	116.7	117.5	117.8	117.0	116.2
Womens', misses', childrens', and infants' undergarments		102.3	103.2	104.6	107.3	109.4	111.2	112.9	115.3	116.8	118.3	118.9
Hats, caps and millinery		102.0	102.4	104.9	109.8	115.1	118.2	122.9	126.0	129.5	130.8	
Girls', childrens', and infants' outerwear		100.0	100.4	101.7	103.4	106.3	110.7	113.1	114.6	115.8	115.4	118.1
Fur goods	100.1	101.8	101.3	120.1	115.9	104.9	98.7	100.5	102.6	101.4	107.5	103.8
Miscellaneous apparel and accessories			100.5	102.9	106.9	110.8	115.2	117.6	119.3	120.6	120.8	123.2
Miscellaneous fabricated textile products			102.8	102.7	105.6	107.9	110.8	113.4	115.1	116.6	117.7	119.6
Lumber and wood products, except furniture		100.3	101.5	105.3	109.2	115.3	117.0	119.4	129.7	148.3	154.4	154.1
Logging camps and logging contractors	95.8	94.8	93.1	100.4	112.8	128.0	135.6	135.0	151.3	186.4	192.6	194.3
Sawmills and planing mills		99.7	100.7	106.7	110.2	114.6	113.7	115.3	131.3	161.8	165.2	154.8
Millwork, veneer, plywood, and structural wood meters		99.9	101.7	105.3	107.5	114.1	115.4	118.3	128.4	142.8	148.7	150.5
Wood containers			100.4	101.3	103.8	109.7	113.9	115.8	123.5	141.7	147.5	148.6
Wood buildings and mobile homes		100.6	102.1	103.6	107.9	112.1	115.5	118.9	121.5	129.5	139.8	147.8
Miscellaneous wood products		101.2	102.1	104.7	108.6	113.3	114.9	118.0	123.4	132.8	140.9	144.9
Furniture and fixtures		101.9	103.9	106.4	111.4	115.6	119.1	121.6	122.9	125.4	129.7	133.3
Household furniture		101.6	103.3	105.9	110.1	114.0	117.2	119.9	121.6	124.8	128.7	132.2
Office furniture			105.5	108.1	115.0	119.0	123.4	125.8	125.3	127.3	132.9	137.5
Public building and related furniture		102.6	105.5	108.2	111.9	115.9	118.4	119.4	120.9	123.5	128.4	130.0
Partitions, shelving, lockers, and office and store fixtures		103.3	106.3	108.8	113.7	117.5	120.9	123.1	124.7	126.9	131.9	135.3
Miscellaneous furniture and fixtures			101.0	102.9	109.5	116.3	120.6	123.4	125.5	125.6	127.3	130.4
Paper and allied products		98.8	99.5	104.9	113.7	120.8	121.9	121.1	121.2	120.2	123.7	146.7
Pulp mills	112.0	100.9	103.0	117.0	141.7	161.3	153.8	121.8	118.5	105.8	116.5	182.4
Paper mill products, except building paper	110.0	109.5	110.3	115.5	127.4	134.6	134.0	131.0	126.6	126.6	128.6	164.8
Paperboard mills	116.3	112.0	113.0	126.2	141.6	149.9	146.0	140.7	142.6	138.3	152.6	203.1
Paperboard containers and boxes		98.4	97.3	104.3	111.7	117.2	117.7	116.6	118.5	118.0	123.7	148.5
Converted paper and paperboard products, except containers and boxes											100.7	110.1
Printing, publishing and allied industries		103.6	107.8	112.2	118.2	124.7	130.5	136.4	140.8	145.6	149.7	159.0
Newspaper publishing	153.8	164.0	172.3	181.7	193.9	206.9	220.4	235.7	248.7	259.5	269.5	286.7
Periodical publishing	147.8	157.9	167.0	173.8	183.8	194.0	205.7	217.8	227.9	233.3	239.1	246.3
Books			102.6	107.5	111.9	117.7	125.3	132.3	138.7	143.7	153.4	162.3
Miscellaneous publishing		104.1	109.0	116.4	123.1	128.2	133.8	142.0	148.3	154.6	160.6	167.1
Commercial printing		102.5	104.6	107.1	110.7	115.7	118.7	120.8	121.9	124.9	126.3	133.4
Blankbooks, looseleaf binders, and bookbinding and related work			103.5	107.2	111.9	119.6	124.8	132.3	135.4	139.0	142.9	150.1
Service industries for the printing trade			101.4	103.4	106.1	108.4	109.3	110.7	112.3	113.5	114.1	115.2
Manifold business forms	104.0	106.2	108.3	112.1	120.3	124.9	124.6	123.9	121.0	128.6	134.0	163.9
Greeting card publishing		100.2	102.8	108.4	114.4	120.3	125.3	131.3	139.4	145.7	156.5	

Producer Price Indexes for the Net Output of Selected Industries, 1984-1995—Continued

(December 1984=100, unless otherwise indicated)

Industry	1984	1985	1986	1987	1988	1989	1990	1991	1992	1993	1994	1995
Chemicals and allied products		100.7	100.5	103.6	113.0	119.6	121.0	124.4	125.8	127.2	130.0	143.4
Industrial inorganic chemicals		100.0	100.6	101.4	104.0	115.1	116.6	117.5	116.5	115.0	115.4	126.3
Plastic materials and synthetics, except glass fibers		99.0	96.2	99.6	114.7	118.0	114.9	113.2	110.0	110.6	113.8	127.8
Drugs		105.1	112.2	119.6	128.1	137.9	146.7	156.2	165.7	172.4	174.8	178.7
Soaps, detergents and other cleaning preparations; perfumes, cosmetics, and other toilet preparations		102.5	104.2	105.5	109.6	114.1	115.8	118.1	120.6	122.8	123.0	125.0
Paint and allied products	102.9	104.9	106.2	107.2	111.7	119.5	125.0	130.3	132.3	133.5	136.0	143.1
Industrial organic chemicals		99.0	94.6	98.4	114.2	122.3	120.2	123.3	123.1	122.7	125.9	158.1
Agricultural chemicals		99.6	96.6	97.8	106.9	109.4	108.2	111.9	110.0	109.7	119.6	129.7
Miscellaneous chemical products			98.9	99.8	106.8	114.2	117.4	122.1	123.7	127.2	131.2	137.1
Petroleum refining and related products			66.6	70.5	67.7	75.7	91.4	83.1	80.3	77.6	74.8	77.2
Petroleum refining	102.7	98.3	64.3	68.6	65.4	73.6	90.1	80.9	78.3	75.2	72.2	74.5
Paving and roofing materials		100.5	96.0	92.5	94.1	93.5	94.3	96.1	94.0	95.0	94.9	98.1
Miscellaneous products of petroleum and coal		100.3	99.9	98.6	104.3	114.4	123.6	131.1	128.4	129.9	130.6	136.3
Rubber and miscellaneous plastic products		100.0	100.3	100.9	106.7	110.2	111.3	113.7	114.2	115.4	117.1	123.3
Tires and inner tubes	98.2	96.8	95.6	95.1	99.5	102.9	103.0	105.0	106.0	106.2	106.4	108.5
Rubber and plastic footwear	103.7	99.9	108.7	111.7	114.6	120.2	121.5	122.0	122.8	124.1	125.5	126.9
Miscellaneous plastic products											101.9	108.3
Leather and leather products		101.3	103.0	106.6	113.4	118.0	122.6	124.8	127.0	129.0	130.6	134.1
Leather tanning and finishing	115.8	111.9	119.9	137.5	158.7	161.6	168.0	158.9	156.1	160.9	171.9	183.9
Boot and shoe cut stock and findings		99.5	103.1	107.9	114.6	116.7	119.6	122.3	123.3	124.4	125.0	129.6
Footwear, except rubber		101.4	103.4	106.3	112.1	117.5	122.2	125.2	128.1	130.3	131.6	135.3
Leather gloves and mittens			100.2	101.6	108.1	112.0	117.6	118.6	120.1	120.7	125.8	131.5
Luggage		101.0	97.3	98.7	104.1	109.0	113.4	116.2	118.8	119.9	120.3	120.3
Handbags and other personal leather goods		102.6	104.1	105.8	111.6	114.2	118.1	121.3	122.4	123.5	121.5	122.8
Leather goods, n.e.c.			101.2	105.7	113.5	117.7	122.1	123.7	123.4	125.1	127.2	131.7
Stone, clay, glass, and concrete products		102.1	103.8	104.5	105.8	107.9	110.0	112.3	112.8	115.4	119.6	124.3
Flat glass	109.2	106.1	109.1	113.6	115.1	112.8	109.2	105.4	104.9	106.1	113.0	116.6
Glass and glassware, pressed or blown		102.3	105.8	107.2	107.6	110.5	113.8	117.4	118.4	119.7	121.8	125.0
Products of purchased glass	102.2	105.8	108.2	110.0	113.4	116.7	117.6	118.8	120.4	122.1	123.7	126.8
Hydraulic cement	103.0	105.0	103.1	100.9	101.2	101.1	102.7	105.8	105.4	111.0	118.7	127.2
Structural clay products			104.3	106.0	109.6	111.8	114.2	115.6	117.1	119.7	121.9	124.4
Pottery and related products			103.0	104.4	109.2	113.1	117.0	119.6	120.6	122.7	125.2	129.3
Concrete, gypsum, and plaster products		102.5	104.1	103.6	103.3	104.4	106.1	108.0	108.6	111.7	117.7	123.5
Cut stone and stone products		100.6	105.9	109.8	116.2	120.1	122.7	128.0	129.3	130.7	131.7	134.0
Abrasives, asbestos, and miscellaneous nonmetallic mineral products			102.1	103.1	105.7	109.1	111.5	114.2	113.3	116.0	119.2	123.6
Primary metal industries		99.4	97.0	101.0	113.0	118.8	116.5	113.1	111.7	111.4	117.0	128.2
Blast furnaces, steelworks, and rolling and finishing mills		99.5	95.1	97.5	105.1	108.5	106.5	104.5	102.4	104.3	109.1	114.9
Iron and steel foundries		100.8	100.8	101.2	104.9	108.3	111.5	113.2	114.6	115.8	118.3	124.0
Primary smelting and refining of nonferrous metals	91.4	86.2	86.8	100.5	127.2	134.6	123.4	103.6	98.4	90.3	106.7	134.2
Secondary nonferrous metals	83.6	72.7	73.0	84.5	100.6	101.4	97.0	84.7	81.8	77.2	90.2	102.1
Rolling, drawing, and extruding of nonferrous metals		98.7	98.1	104.7	127.8	138.4	132.7	127.5	126.2	122.8	129.4	151.0
Nonferrous foundries (castings)		100.1	101.3	103.2	112.0	119.5	121.1	120.9	121.7	122.7	125.7	132.8
Miscellaneous primary metal products			101.9	105.2	112.2	116.1	115.9	116.1	116.3	115.9	119.0	124.4
Fabricated metal products, except machinery and transportation equipment		100.6	101.0	102.1	107.4	112.6	115.1	116.6	117.2	118.2	120.3	124.8
Metal cans and shipping containers		100.0	100.0	100.4	101.5	103.8	105.9	107.2	106.3	103.1	101.7	109.4
Cutlery, hand tools, and general hardware			101.6	102.3	106.1	111.7	116.5	120.7	123.2	125.7	127.9	131.3
Heating equipment, except electric and warm air, and plumbing fixtures		101.1	104.1	108.3	114.7	121.7	127.2	131.7	135.3	138.0	140.8	147.6
Fabricated structural metal products		100.6	100.6	102.5	110.7	116.3	117.9	118.1	117.7	118.8	122.6	129.6
Screw machines products, and bolts, nuts, rivets, screws and washers		99.9	99.8	101.1	104.7	109.9	113.3	114.9	115.4	116.3	117.6	120.0
Metal forgings and stampings		99.9	98.8	99.0	102.4	107.1	109.4	109.5	109.7	109.8	110.5	111.9
Coating, engraving, and allied services		102.3	105.0	106.7	110.7	116.0	117.9	119.3	120.1	121.8	123.5	125.8
Ordnance and accessories, except vehicles and guided missiles			105.1	105.5	108.2	111.2	112.6	116.4	120.2	124.3	125.5	127.6
Miscellaneous fabricated metal products		101.1	102.2	103.9	110.8	117.2	120.5	122.9	124.1	125.8	128.7	133.4
Machinery, except electrical		101.0	102.0	103.2	106.4	110.7	113.9	116.4	116.7	116.8	117.5	119
Engines and turbines		100.7	101.8	102.7	105.0	109.8	116.5	121.4	123.8	125.8	128.3	130.8
Farm and garden machinery and equipment		99.9	100.4	100.8	102.9	107.6	111.1	114.3	116.9	118.7	120.9	123.4
Construction, mining, and materials handling machinery and equipment		101.2	101.8	102.6	105.9	109.8	113.5	117.5	120.1	122.9	125.0	128.1
Metalworking machinery and equipment		101.0	102.8	104.2								
Special industry machinery, except metalworking machinery		102.3	105.2	108.5	112.6	117.5	121.6	125.6	128.4	132.1	134.2	137.3
General industrial machinery and equipment		101.5	102.9	104.1			119.6	124.3	127.4	130.6	133.4	137.8
Office, computing, and accounting machines												70.5
Refrigeration and service industry machinery		101.7	103.1	104.2	107.8	112.4	116.0	117.6	119.4	120.9	122.3	125.3
Miscellaneous machinery, except electrical		100.7	101.5	102.6	104.6	109.3	112.3	113.4	113.9	116.1	118.8	121.9
Electrical and electronic machinery, equipment, and supplies			102.1	103.3	104.6	107.1	108.9	110.1	110.8	112.0	112.7	113.3
Electric transmission and distribution equipment			101.1	103.1	105.8	113.2	118.7	122.0	122.8	123.4	125.8	129.5
Electrical industrial apparatus			103.5	104.5	108.5	113.5	117.5	120.7	122.9	125.7	127.1	130.1
Household appliances		100.5	100.0	99.7	100.4	102.9	105.2	106.0	106.8	108.1	108.7	108.8
Electric lighting and wiring equipment		101.1	103.4	105.0	108.3	113.4	116.3	118.6	119.8	122.1	123.2	126.6
Radio and television receiving equipment, except communication types		99.6	100.5	99.6	97.5	96.9	94.5	95.2	94.2	92.6	92.4	91.5
Communication equipment			101.9	103.5	103.9	105.8	107.5	108.5	109.7	111.7	113.3	113.9
Electronic components and accessories		100.5	102.5	102.6	104.0	105.1	104.9	104.9	104.6	105.3	104.8	102.5
Miscellaneous electrical machinery, equipment and supplies			100.9	103.2	105.4	107.8	109.8	110.6	110.9	110.4	110.7	111.9
Transportation equipment			104.4	105.9	107.8	112.1	115.6	119.8	123.0	126.3	130.1	132.2
Motor vehicles and motor vehicle equipment		101.4	104.5	106.4	107.7	110.7	113.0	117.4	120.5	123.8	127.5	129.1
Aircraft and parts			102.8	102.8	105.5	112.1	117.7	122.3	126.6	130.1	134.0	137.3
Ship and boat building and repairing			105.9	108.5	111.0	116.0	120.1	122.7	125.7	129.9	133.0	135.0
Railroad equipment		101.8	102.1	101.9	103.7	110.0	114.2	117.3	118.7	119.8	122.6	127.6
Motorcycles, bicycles, and parts		99.1	99.5	101.1	104.3	107.8	109.9	111.8	114.4	116.9	119.0	122.2
Miscellaneous transportation equipment			103.7	104.8	106.2	110.4	112.5	114.1	115.2	117.1	118.1	120.3

Producer Price Indexes for the Net Output of Selected Industries, 1984-1995—Continued

(December 1984=100, unless otherwise indicated)

Industry	1984	1985	1986	1987	1988	1989	1990	1991	1992	1993	1994	1995
Measuring and controlling instruments: photographic, medical, optical goods; watches, clocks	....	100.7	102.4	105.1	107.0	110.8	114.6	116.8	118.7	120.8	122.1	124.0
Engineering and scientific instruments	....	....	101.2	104.5	108.1	112.7	116.9	120.5	121.4	123.0	124.6	127.4
Measuring and controlling instruments	....	....	101.1	103.8	106.0	107.9	111.7	116.3	120.1	123.3	126.1	127.9	129.9
Surgical, medical, and dental instruments and supplies	....	....	101.1	104.2	109.0	111.5	115.9	120.7	124.1	127.9	131.9	133.4	134.1
Opthalmic goods	104.4	105.5	108.1	110.2	112.1	115.1	117.0	117.6	121.0	123.4	124.9	126.4
Photographic equipment and supplies	100.9	101.5	102.1	104.2	105.3	109.3	112.2	111.9	112.1	112.1	111.7	113.8
Watches, clocks, and watchcases	101.8	101.9	101.8	104.2	105.3	108.2	110.5	113.6	114.7	115.9	116.6	118.9
Miscellaneous manufacturing industries (12/85=100)	....	....	101.4	103.8	107.5	111.8	114.9	117.5	119.6	121.5	123.3	125.9
Jewelry, silverware, and plated ware	....	....	102.1	108.1	112.5	115.3	119.3	121.0	121.6	123.5	124.7	126.3
Musical instruments	103.4	101.5	103.5	106.4	110.4	115.7	119.5	123.7	128.3	134.4	140.2	147.5
Toys, amusements, and sporting and athletic goods	....	....	101.6	102.5	105.9	110.6	113.0	115.3	117.3	117.9	119.2	120.7
Pens, pencils, and other office and artist's materials	....	....	100.9	102.9	106.3	110.4	114.3	118.0	120.8	121.4	123.2	127.4
Costume jewelry, costume novelties, buttons, and other miscellaneous notions	....	....	100.2	100.7	103.1	107.7	111.0	113.8	116.0	117.1	117.9	119.1
Miscellaneous manufacturing industries	....	....	101.2	103.1	106.9	111.4	114.4	117.3	119.6	122.8	125.1	128.5
SERVICE INDUSTRIES												
Motor freight transportation and warehousing (6/93=100)	....	....	....	....	....	....	....	....	....	....	101.9	104.5
Trucking and courier services, except air	....	....	....	....	....	....	....	....	....	....	101.9	104.5
Public warehousing and storage	....	....	....	....	....	....	....	....	....	....	101.3	103.0
U.S. Postal Service (6/89=100)	79.3	85.3	86.5	86.5	96.6	100.0	100.0	117.9	119.8	119.8	119.8	132.2
Water transportation (12/92=100)	....	....	....	....	....	....	....	....	....	99.7	100.0	103.0
Transporation by air (12/92=100)	....	....	....	....	....	....	....	....	....	105.6	108.5	113.7
Transportation by air, scheduled and air courier services ..	....	....	....	....	....	....	110.2	121.2	114.2	125.4	129.1	135.9
Pipelines, except natural gas (12/86=100)	....	....	....	97.9	94.8	94.4	95.8	96.1	96.4	96.6	102.6	110.8

NOTES
Prices and Living Conditions—Consumer Price Index

The *Consumer Price Index* (CPI) measures the average change in prices of goods and services that urban consumers purchase for day-to-day living. The weights used in calculating the index, which remain fixed for relatively long periods, are based on actual expenditures reported in the Consumer Expenditure Surveys. The quantities and qualities of the sample items in the market basket remain essentially the same between consecutive pricing periods, so that the index measures only the effect of price change on the cost of living. The index does not measure changes in the total amount families spend for living. Geographic area indexes measure price changes over time in individual areas, not relative differences in prices or living costs between areas.

The index for the years 1913 to 1935 used a study of 1917-1919 spending by households of wage earners and clerical workers as the basis for its weights. Since then, there have been six updatings, bringing the market basket of goods and services up to date, revising the weights, and improving the sampling methods. In the past 20 years, several major changes have been introduced into the CPI.

The 1978 revision of the CPI updated the CPI for Urban Wage Earners and Clerical Workers (CPI-W), and introduced a new index for All Urban Consumers (CPI-U), which includes salaried workers, the self-employed, the retired, and the unemployed, as well as wage earners and clerical workers. The CPI-W represents the spending patterns of 32 percent of the population; the CPI-U, 80 percent. For years before 1978, changes in the CPI-U are based on changes in the CPI-W. The 1978 revision also instituted sampling for all levels of the index down to the selection of items within each retail outlet.

Starting with the index for January 1983, BLS changed the way the CPI-U measures homeowners' costs; the CPI-W made the same change starting in January 1985. The change converted the homeownership component from an asset approach, which included both the investment and consumption aspects of homeownership, to a flow-of-services approach, that measures only the cost of shelter services consumed by homeowners. The new approach uses a rental equivalence method to calculate homeowner shelter costs by estimating the implicit rent owners would have to pay to rent the homes they live in. The old method calculated homeowner costs as home purchase, mortgage interest costs, property taxes, property insurance, and maintenance and repair.

The 1987 major revision of both the CPI-U and the CPI-W introduced weights based upon data from the 1982, 1983, and 1984 Consumer Expenditure Surveys. The next CPI revision will go into effect with the index for January 1998, using expenditure data from the 1993-1995 Consumer Expenditure Surveys and population data from the 1990 Decennial Census.

Within each of 44 CPI areas (32 large metropolitan areas and 12 region-size classes) the CPI selected 85 pricing areas. Within each pricing area the CPI samples retail outlets and items within 207 broad item categories called item strata. BLS resamples the outlets and items in the pricing areas on a 5-year rotating basis. Before rotating the sample in a pricing area, the Bureau of the Census conducts a Point-of-Purchase Survey for BLS. This survey determines location of the retail outlets where consumers buy goods and services in various categories; it also determines how much they spend on each category in each reported outlet. BLS then draws outlet samples from the Point-of-Purchase Survey

information. BLS field agents visit the selected retail outlets and sample within the item categories using checklists, which exhaustively define these categories of goods and services. The original selection of the specific items to be priced in a specific retail store is generally done by a data collector using the checklist in systematic stages that take into account sales information provided by the respondent in each stage. Outlets may be located outside of their pricing area to represent out-of-town purchases.

After the initial selection, the same item (or a close substitute) is priced from period to period so that, as far as possible, differences in reported prices are measures of price change only. All taxes directly associated with the purchase or continued use of the items priced are included in the indexes. Foods, fuels, rents, and a few other items are priced monthly in all areas. Prices of most other commodities and services are obtained monthly in the five largest areas and bimonthly in the remaining areas. Half of the bimonthly prices are collected in the odd months and half in the even months. Between scheduled survey dates, prices are held at the level of their last pricing. BLS agents also collect data for a sample of rental units drawn from the Decennial Census of Population and Housing. This sample is heavily augmented with renter-occupied housing units in areas where there are many owner-occupied units. This survey is the basis for the Rent and Owners' equivalent rent components of the CPI.

BLS calculates basic indexes (elementary aggregates) for the 207 item strata in each of the 44 index areas. Basic indexes are combined with weights based on the 1982-1984 Consumer Expenditure Surveys and the Census of Population.

BLS publishes CPI indexes for a variety of commodities and services, by region, by size of city, for cross-classifications of regions and population size classes, and for 29 metropolitan areas.

The purchasing power of the consumer dollar for any given date is calculated as the reciprocal of the index for that date, expressed in dollars, with the dollar's value in 1982-1984 equal to $1.00. It shows changes in the value of the dollar resulting from changes in prices of consumer goods and services. The purchasing power of the dollar with reference to other bases can be calculated by dividing the index for the desired base date by the index for the current date and expressing the result in dollars.

The relative importance figures are percentage distributions of the cost or value weights used in the index calculation. At the time of their introduction, after a major weight revision, the cost weights represent average expenditures for specific classes of goods and services by consumers. However, in the subsequent pricing periods, the value weights and the corresponding relative importance figures change as prices change differentially (i.e., the relative importance increases for an item or group having a greater than average price increase and decreases for one having a less than average price increase.) Since the index measures only price change, the cost weights eventually become unrepresentative of actual expenditures and must be revised on the basis of new surveys of consumer expenditures.

A detailed description of the CPI before 1978 is contained in *The Consumer Price Index: History and Techniques*, *BLS Bulletin 1517* (1966). For further information about the revised CPI, see *The Consumer Price Index: Concepts and Content Over the Years*, and *BLS Report 517* (1977). The *Consumer Price Index Detailed Report* is published monthly and contains occasional articles.

Consumer Price Indexes, All Urban Consumers, Major Groups, 1967-1995

(1982-1984=100)

Year	Food and beverages	Housing	Apparel and upkeep	Transportation	Medical care	Entertainment	Other goods and services
1967	35.0	30.8	51.0	33.3	28.2	40.7	35.1
1968	36.2	32.0	53.7	34.3	29.9	43.0	36.9
1969	38.1	34.0	56.8	35.7	31.9	45.2	38.7
1970	40.1	36.4	59.2	37.5	34.0	47.5	40.9
1971	41.4	38.0	61.1	39.5	36.1	50.0	42.9
1972	43.1	39.4	62.3	39.9	37.3	51.5	44.7
1973	48.8	41.2	64.6	41.2	38.8	52.9	46.4
1974	55.5	45.8	69.4	45.8	42.4	56.9	49.8
1975	60.2	50.7	72.5	50.1	47.5	62.0	53.9
1976	62.1	53.8	75.2	55.1	52.0	65.1	57.0
1977	65.8	57.4	78.6	59.0	57.0	68.3	60.4
1978	72.2	62.4	81.4	61.7	61.8	71.9	64.3
1979	79.9	70.1	84.9	70.5	67.5	76.7	68.9
1980	86.7	81.1	90.9	83.1	74.9	83.6	75.2
1981	93.5	90.4	95.3	93.2	82.9	90.1	82.6
1982	97.3	96.9	97.8	97.0	92.5	96.0	91.1
1983	99.5	99.5	100.2	99.3	100.6	100.1	101.1
1984	103.2	103.6	102.1	103.7	106.8	103.8	107.9
1985	105.6	107.7	105.0	106.4	113.5	107.9	114.5
1986	109.1	110.9	105.9	102.3	122.0	111.6	121.4
1987	113.5	114.2	110.6	105.4	130.1	115.3	128.5
1988	118.2	118.5	115.4	108.7	138.6	120.3	137.0
1989	124.9	123.0	118.6	114.1	149.3	126.5	147.7
1990	132.1	128.5	124.1	120.5	162.8	132.4	159.0
1991	136.8	133.6	128.7	123.8	177.0	138.4	171.6
1992	138.7	137.5	131.9	126.5	190.1	142.3	183.3
1993	141.6	141.2	133.7	130.4	201.4	145.8	192.9
1994	144.9	144.8	133.4	134.3	211.0	150.1	198.5
1995	148.9	148.5	132.0	139.1	220.5	153.9	206.9

Consumer Price Indexes, Urban Wage Earners and Clerical Workers, Major Groups, 1967-1995

(1982-1984=100)

Year	Food and beverages	Housing	Apparel and upkeep	Transportation	Medical care	Entertainment	Other goods and services
1967	35.0	31.1	51.2	33.1	28.3	41.3	35.4
1968	36.2	32.3	54.0	34.1	30.0	43.7	37.2
1969	38.0	34.3	57.1	35.5	32.1	45.9	39.1
1970	40.1	36.7	59.5	37.3	34.1	48.2	41.3
1971	41.3	38.3	61.4	39.2	36.3	50.8	43.3
1972	43.1	39.8	62.7	39.7	37.5	52.3	45.1
1973	48.8	41.5	65.0	41.0	39.0	53.7	46.9
1974	55.5	46.2	69.8	45.5	42.6	57.8	50.2
1975	60.2	51.1	72.9	49.8	47.7	62.9	54.4
1976	62.0	54.2	75.6	54.7	52.3	66.0	57.6
1977	65.7	57.9	79.0	58.6	57.3	69.3	60.9
1978	72.1	62.9	81.7	61.5	62.1	72.8	64.8
1979	79.9	70.7	85.2	70.4	68.0	77.6	69.4
1980	86.9	81.7	90.9	82.9	75.6	84.2	75.6
1981	93.6	91.1	95.6	93.0	83.5	90.5	82.5
1982	97.3	97.7	97.8	97.0	92.5	96.0	90.9
1983	99.5	100.0	100.2	99.2	100.5	100.2	101.3
1984	103.2	102.2	102.0	103.8	106.9	103.8	107.9
1985	105.5	106.6	105.0	106.4	113.6	107.5	114.2
1986	108.9	109.7	105.8	101.7	122.0	111.0	120.9
1987	113.3	112.8	110.4	105.1	130.2	114.8	127.8
1988	117.9	116.8	114.9	108.3	139.0	119.7	136.5
1989	124.6	121.2	117.9	113.9	149.6	125.8	147.4
1990	131.8	126.4	123.1	120.1	162.7	131.4	158.9
1991	136.5	131.2	127.4	123.1	176.5	136.9	171.7
1992	138.3	135.0	130.7	125.8	189.6	140.8	183.3
1993	141.2	138.5	132.4	129.4	200.9	144.1	192.2
1994	144.4	142.0	132.2	133.4	210.4	148.2	196.4
1995	148.3	145.4	130.9	138.8	219.8	151.8	204.2

Consumer Price Indexes, All Urban Consumers, Commodity, Service, and Special Groups, 1967-1995

(1982-1984=100, except as noted)

Year	Commod-ities	Food and beverages	Commod-ities less food and beverages	Apparel commod-ities	Nondurables less food	Nondurables less food and apparel	Nondurables	Services	Household services less rent of shelter[1]	Transpor-tation services	Medical care services	Other services
1967	36.8	35.0	38.3	54.3	37.6	32.6	35.7	28.8	....	32.6	26.0	36.0
1968	38.1	36.2	39.7	57.3	39.1	33.7	37.1	30.3	....	33.9	27.9	38.1
1969	39.9	38.1	41.4	60.8	40.9	34.9	38.9	32.4	....	36.3	30.2	40.0
1970	41.7	40.1	43.1	63.3	42.5	36.3	40.8	35.0	....	40.2	32.3	42.2
1971	43.2	41.4	44.7	65.2	44.0	37.6	42.1	37.0	....	43.4	34.7	44.4
1972	44.5	43.1	45.8	66.6	45.0	38.6	43.5	38.4	....	44.4	35.9	45.6
1973	47.8	48.8	47.3	69.0	46.9	40.3	47.5	40.1	....	44.7	37.5	47.7
1974	53.5	55.5	52.4	73.9	52.9	46.9	54.0	43.8	....	46.3	41.4	51.3
1975	58.2	60.2	57.3	76.7	57.0	51.5	58.3	48.0	....	49.8	46.6	55.1
1976	60.7	62.1	60.2	79.2	59.5	54.1	60.5	52.0	....	56.9	51.3	58.4
1977	64.2	65.8	63.6	82.3	62.5	57.2	64.0	56.0	....	61.5	56.4	62.1
1978	68.8	72.2	67.3	84.5	65.5	60.4	68.6	60.8	....	64.4	61.2	66.4
1979	76.6	79.9	75.2	87.5	74.6	71.2	77.2	67.5	....	69.5	67.2	71.9
1980	86.0	86.7	85.7	92.9	88.4	87.1	87.6	77.9	....	79.2	74.8	78.7
1981	93.2	93.5	93.1	96.5	96.7	96.8	95.2	88.1	....	88.6	82.8	86.1
1982	97.0	97.3	96.9	98.3	98.3	98.2	97.8	96.0	....	96.1	92.6	93.5
1983	99.8	99.5	100.0	100.2	100.0	100.0	99.7	99.4	103.4	99.1	100.7	100.0
1984	103.2	103.2	103.1	101.5	101.7	101.8	102.5	104.6	108.1	104.8	106.7	106.5
1985	105.4	105.6	105.2	104.0	104.1	104.1	104.8	109.9	111.2	110.0	113.2	113.0
1986	104.4	109.1	101.4	104.2	98.5	96.9	103.5	115.4	112.8	116.3	121.9	119.4
1987	107.7	113.5	104.0	108.9	101.8	100.3	107.5	120.2	113.1	121.9	130.0	125.7
1988	111.5	118.2	107.3	113.7	105.8	104.0	111.8	125.7	115.3	128.0	138.3	132.6
1989	116.7	124.9	111.6	116.7	111.7	111.3	118.2	131.9	118.7	135.6	148.9	140.9
1990	122.8	132.1	117.0	122.0	119.9	120.9	126.0	139.2	121.7	144.2	162.7	150.2
1991	126.6	136.8	120.4	126.4	124.5	125.7	130.3	146.3	126.7	151.2	177.1	159.8
1992	129.1	138.7	123.2	129.4	127.6	128.9	132.8	152.0	130.2	155.7	190.5	168.5
1993	131.5	141.6	125.3	131.0	129.3	130.7	135.1	157.9	134.2	162.9	202.9	177.0
1994	133.8	144.9	126.9	130.4	129.7	131.6	136.8	163.1	136.3	168.6	213.4	185.4
1995	136.4	148.9	128.9	128.7	130.9	134.1	139.3	168.7	138.3	175.9	224.2	193.3

1. December 1982=100.

Consumer Price Indexes, All Urban Consumers, Commodity, Service, and Special Groups, 1967-1995—Continued

(1982-1984=100)

Year	Services less medical care	All items less food	All items less shelter	All items less medical care	Energy	All items less energy	All items less food and energy	Commodities less food and energy	Energy commodities	Services less energy	Gas (piped) and electricity
1967	29.3	33.4	35.2	33.7	23.8	34.4	34.7	41.3	23.9	29.3	23.7
1968	30.8	34.9	36.7	35.1	24.2	35.9	36.3	42.9	24.4	30.9	23.9
1969	32.9	36.8	38.4	37.0	24.8	38.0	38.4	44.7	25.2	33.2	24.3
1970	35.6	39.0	40.3	39.2	25.5	40.3	40.8	46.7	25.6	36.0	25.4
1971	37.5	40.8	42.0	40.8	26.5	42.0	42.7	48.5	26.1	38.0	27.1
1972	38.9	42.0	43.3	42.1	27.2	43.4	44.0	49.7	26.4	39.4	28.5
1973	40.6	43.7	46.2	44.8	29.4	46.1	45.6	51.1	29.1	41.1	29.9
1974	44.3	48.0	51.4	49.8	38.1	50.6	49.4	55.0	40.4	44.8	34.5
1975	48.3	52.5	56.0	54.3	42.1	55.1	53.9	60.1	43.4	48.8	40.1
1976	52.2	56.0	59.3	57.2	45.1	58.2	57.4	63.2	45.4	52.7	44.7
1977	55.9	59.6	63.1	60.8	49.4	61.9	61.0	66.5	48.7	56.5	50.5
1978	60.7	63.9	67.4	65.4	52.5	66.7	65.5	70.5	51.0	61.3	55.0
1979	67.5	71.2	74.2	72.9	65.7	73.4	71.9	76.4	68.7	68.2	61.0
1980	78.2	81.5	82.9	82.8	86.0	81.9	80.8	83.5	95.2	78.5	71.4
1981	88.7	90.4	91.0	91.4	97.7	90.1	89.2	90.0	107.6	88.7	81.9
1982	96.4	96.3	96.2	96.8	99.2	96.1	95.8	95.3	102.9	96.3	93.2
1983	99.2	99.7	99.8	99.6	99.9	99.6	99.6	100.2	99.0	99.2	101.5
1984	104.4	104.0	103.9	103.7	100.9	104.3	104.6	104.4	98.1	104.5	105.4
1985	109.6	108.0	107.0	107.2	101.6	108.4	109.1	107.1	98.2	110.2	107.1
1986	114.6	109.8	108.0	108.8	88.2	112.6	113.5	108.6	77.2	116.5	105.7
1987	119.1	113.6	111.6	112.6	88.6	117.2	118.2	111.8	80.2	122.0	103.8
1988	124.3	118.3	115.9	117.0	89.3	122.3	123.4	115.8	80.8	127.9	104.6
1989	130.1	123.7	121.6	122.4	94.3	128.1	129.0	119.6	87.9	134.4	107.5
1990	136.8	130.3	128.2	128.8	102.1	134.7	135.5	123.6	101.2	142.3	109.3
1991	143.3	136.1	133.5	133.8	102.5	140.9	142.1	128.8	99.1	149.8	112.6
1992	148.4	140.8	137.3	137.5	103.0	145.4	147.3	132.5	98.3	155.9	114.8
1993	153.6	145.1	141.4	141.2	104.2	150.0	152.2	135.2	97.3	161.9	118.5
1994	158.4	149.0	144.8	144.7	104.6	154.1	156.5	137.1	97.6	167.6	119.2
1995	163.5	153.1	148.6	148.6	105.2	158.7	161.2	139.3	98.8	173.7	119.2

PRICES AND LIVING CONDITIONS

Consumer Price Indexes, Urban Wage and Clerical Workers, Commodity, Service, and Special Groups, 1967-1995

(1982-1984=100, except as noted)

Year	Commod-ities	Food and beverages	Commod-ities less food and beverages	Apparel commod-ities	Nondurables less food	Nondurables less food and apparel	Nondurables	Services	Household services less rent of shelter[1]	Transpor-tation services	Medical care services	Other services
1967	36.7	35.0	38.2	54.4	37.3	32.5	35.6	29.0	....	33.0	26.2	36.3
1968	38.1	36.2	39.6	57.5	38.8	33.6	37.0	30.5	....	34.3	28.1	38.4
1969	39.8	38.0	41.3	60.9	40.6	34.8	38.8	32.6	....	36.7	30.4	40.3
1970	41.7	40.1	43.0	63.4	42.2	36.1	40.6	35.3	....	40.6	32.5	42.6
1971	43.1	41.3	44.6	65.3	43.6	37.4	41.9	37.2	....	43.8	34.9	44.8
1972	44.4	43.1	45.6	66.8	44.7	38.4	43.4	38.6	....	44.8	36.2	46.0
1973	47.7	48.8	47.2	69.2	46.6	40.1	47.3	40.3	....	45.1	37.8	48.1
1974	53.4	55.5	52.2	74.0	52.6	46.7	53.8	44.1	....	46.8	41.7	51.8
1975	58.1	60.2	57.1	76.8	56.6	51.3	58.1	48.3	....	50.3	46.9	55.6
1976	60.6	62.0	60.0	79.3	59.0	53.8	60.3	52.3	....	57.5	51.6	58.9
1977	64.1	65.7	63.4	82.5	62.1	56.9	63.7	56.3	....	62.1	56.8	62.6
1978	68.6	72.1	67.0	84.7	65.1	60.1	68.4	61.1	....	65.2	61.6	67.1
1979	76.6	79.9	75.0	87.7	74.5	71.2	77.2	68.0	....	70.3	67.7	72.7
1980	85.9	86.9	85.5	92.8	88.5	87.4	87.8	78.5	....	79.8	75.7	79.6
1981	93.3	93.6	93.1	96.7	97.0	97.0	95.4	88.8	....	89.2	83.4	86.5
1982	96.9	97.3	96.7	98.3	98.2	98.2	97.8	96.8	....	96.5	92.6	93.7
1983	100.2	99.5	100.5	100.2	100.1	100.0	99.8	99.4	....	98.9	100.6	100.0
1984	102.9	103.2	102.8	101.5	101.7	101.7	102.4	103.8	....	104.6	106.8	106.3
1985	105.1	105.5	104.9	104.1	104.1	104.0	104.7	109.4	102.6	109.5	113.3	112.6
1986	103.9	108.9	100.8	104.2	98.0	96.4	103.3	114.7	103.9	115.4	122.0	118.7
1987	107.3	113.3	103.6	108.8	101.4	100.0	107.2	119.4	104.0	120.8	130.3	124.7
1988	111.0	117.9	106.8	113.4	105.3	103.7	111.5	124.7	105.9	127.1	139.0	131.4
1989	116.3	124.6	111.2	116.1	111.3	111.2	118.0	130.8	109.1	134.8	149.6	139.6
1990	122.4	131.8	116.6	121.2	119.7	121.1	125.9	137.7	111.9	142.7	162.8	148.7
1991	126.2	136.5	119.8	125.2	124.2	125.9	130.1	144.6	116.6	149.8	176.7	157.8
1992	128.7	138.3	122.7	128.3	127.4	129.0	132.5	150.0	119.7	154.3	190.3	166.1
1993	131.2	141.2	125.0	129.8	128.9	130.7	134.7	155.5	123.5	160.0	202.7	174.1
1994	133.4	144.4	126.6	129.4	129.2	131.2	136.4	160.6	125.4	165.7	213.0	182.4
1995	136.4	148.3	129.0	127.7	130.4	133.7	139.0	166.0	127.0	173.6	223.8	190.1

1. December 1984=100.

Consumer Price Indexes, Urban Wage Earners and Clerical Workers, Commodity, Service, and Special Groups, 1967-1995—Continued

(1982-1984=100)

Year	Services less medical care	All items less food	All items less shelter	All items less medical care	Energy	All items less energy	All items less food and energy	Commodities less food and energy	Energy commodities	Services less energy	Gas (piped) and electricity
1967	29.5	33.6	35.2	33.9	23.8	34.7	35.1	41.4	23.9	29.5	23.7
1968	31.0	35.1	36.7	35.3	24.1	36.3	36.7	43.0	24.4	31.2	23.9
1969	33.1	37.0	38.4	37.2	24.8	38.3	38.8	44.9	25.1	33.5	24.4
1970	35.8	39.2	40.3	39.4	25.5	40.6	41.2	46.9	25.6	36.2	25.4
1971	37.7	41.0	42.0	41.0	26.5	42.4	43.2	48.7	26.1	38.3	27.2
1972	39.1	42.3	43.3	42.4	27.2	43.8	44.5	49.9	26.4	39.7	28.6
1973	40.8	43.9	46.2	45.1	29.4	46.5	46.0	51.3	29.1	41.4	30.0
1974	44.6	48.3	51.4	50.1	38.0	51.0	49.8	55.2	40.3	45.1	34.6
1975	48.6	52.8	56.0	54.6	42.0	55.6	54.4	60.4	43.3	49.2	40.2
1976	52.5	56.3	59.3	57.5	45.0	58.8	58.0	63.5	45.3	53.1	44.8
1977	56.3	59.9	63.1	61.1	49.3	62.4	61.6	66.7	48.6	57.0	50.6
1978	61.1	64.2	67.4	65.8	52.4	67.3	66.1	70.7	50.9	61.8	55.2
1979	68.0	71.6	74.4	73.3	66.1	74.0	72.5	76.5	68.9	68.7	61.1
1980	78.9	82.0	83.2	83.3	86.8	82.4	81.3	83.3	95.3	79.3	71.4
1981	89.4	91.0	91.3	91.8	98.4	90.5	89.7	89.9	107.6	89.6	81.8
1982	97.3	96.8	96.3	97.1	99.4	96.6	96.4	95.4	102.8	97.3	93.1
1983	99.2	99.9	99.8	99.8	99.9	99.8	99.9	100.8	99.0	99.1	101.5
1984	103.5	103.3	103.9	103.1	100.7	103.6	103.7	103.8	98.1	103.6	105.3
1985	108.9	107.3	106.8	106.6	101.4	107.6	108.2	106.4	98.2	109.6	107.1
1986	113.9	108.5	107.4	107.8	87.4	111.5	112.3	107.6	77.2	115.8	105.7
1987	118.2	112.2	111.0	111.5	88.0	116.0	116.8	110.8	80.3	121.2	103.6
1988	123.3	116.7	115.2	115.8	88.6	121.0	121.9	114.7	80.9	127.0	104.4
1989	129.0	122.0	120.9	121.2	93.9	126.7	127.3	118.6	88.2	133.4	107.3
1990	135.4	128.3	127.3	127.4	102.0	133.0	133.3	122.3	101.4	141.0	108.9
1991	141.7	133.8	132.3	132.2	102.2	138.9	139.6	127.3	99.4	148.2	112.1
1992	146.5	138.2	135.9	135.7	102.6	143.2	144.7	131.2	98.5	154.0	114.3
1993	151.4	142.3	139.7	139.2	103.6	147.5	149.3	134.3	97.5	159.7	118.0
1994	156.1	145.9	143.0	142.6	104.1	151.5	153.5	136.2	97.8	165.3	118.7
1995	161.1	150.0	146.8	146.4	104.7	156.1	158.2	138.9	99.1	171.3	118.4

Consumer Price Indexes, Selected Groups, and Purchasing Power of the Consumer Dollar, 1913-1995

(1982-1984=100, except as noted)

Year	All urban consumers					Urban wage earners and clerical workers				
	All items	Food	Renters' costs	Apparel and upkeep	Purchasing power of consumer dollar	All items	Food	Renters' costs	Apparel and upkeep	Purchasing power of consumer dollar
1913	9.9	10.0		14.9	1 007.7	10.0	10.0		15.0	1 002.3
1914	10.0	10.2		15.0	994.2	10.1	10.2		15.1	988.9
1915	10.1	10.0		15.3	984.3	10.2	10.0		15.4	979.1
1916	10.9	11.3		16.8	915.2	11.0	11.3		16.9	910.3
1917	12.8	14.5		20.2	779.3	12.9	14.5		20.3	775.2
1918	15.1	16.7		27.3	663.5	15.1	16.7		27.5	660.0
1919	17.3	18.6		36.2	577.9	17.4	18.6		36.4	574.8
1920	20.0	21.0		43.1	498.9	20.1	21.0		43.3	496.3
1921	17.9	15.9		33.2	558.5	18.0	15.9		33.4	555.5
1922	16.8	14.9		27.0	596.2	16.9	14.9		27.2	593.0
1923	17.1	15.4		27.1	585.7	17.2	15.4		27.2	582.6
1924	17.1	15.2		26.8	584.5	17.2	15.2		26.9	581.4
1925	17.5	16.5		26.3	570.1	17.6	16.5		26.4	567.1
1926	17.7	17.0		25.9	564.7	17.8	17.0		26.0	561.7
1927	17.4	16.4		25.3	575.5	17.5	16.4		25.5	572.5
1928	17.1	16.3		25.0	583.3	17.2	16.3		25.1	580.2
1929	17.1	16.5		24.7	583.3	17.2	16.5		24.8	580.2
1930	16.7	15.6		24.2	598.6	16.8	15.6		24.3	595.4
1931	15.2	12.9		22.0	656.3	15.3	12.9		22.1	652.8
1932	13.7	10.7		19.5	731.7	13.7	10.7		19.6	727.9
1933	13.0	10.4		18.8	771.2	13.0	10.4		18.9	767.2
1934	13.4	11.6		20.6	746.4	13.5	11.6		20.7	742.4
1935	13.7	12.4		20.8	728.1	13.8	12.4		20.9	724.3
1936	13.9	12.6		21.0	721.3	13.9	12.6		21.1	717.4
1937	14.4	13.1		22.0	696.1	14.4	13.1		22.1	692.4
1938	14.1	12.1		21.9	709.3	14.2	12.1		22.0	705.5
1939	13.9	11.8		21.6	719.5	14.0	11.8		21.7	715.7
1940	14.0	12.0		21.8	712.6	14.1	12.0		21.9	708.8
1941	14.7	13.1		22.8	678.8	14.8	13.1		23.0	675.2
1942	16.3	15.4		26.7	613.2	16.4	15.4		26.8	610.0
1943	17.3	17.1		27.8	577.9	17.4	17.1		28.0	574.8
1944	17.6	16.9		29.8	568.0	17.7	16.9		30.0	565.0
1945	18.0	17.3		31.4	555.2	18.1	17.3		31.5	552.2
1946	19.5	19.8		34.4	511.5	19.6	19.8		34.6	508.8
1947	22.3	24.1		39.9	447.4	22.5	24.1		40.1	445.1
1948	24.1	26.1		42.5	415.1	24.2	26.1		42.7	412.9
1949	23.8	25.0		40.8	419.3	24.0	25.0		41.0	417.1
1950	24.1	25.4		40.3	415.1	24.2	25.4		40.5	412.9
1951	26.0	28.2		43.9	384.6	26.1	28.2		44.1	382.5
1952	26.5	28.7		43.5	376.5	26.7	28.7		43.7	374.5
1953	26.7	28.3		43.1	373.5	26.9	28.3		43.3	371.5
1954	26.9	28.2		43.1	371.7	27.0	28.2		43.3	369.7
1955	26.8	27.8		42.9	373.2	26.9	27.8		43.1	371.2
1956	27.2	28.0		43.7	367.8	27.3	28.0		44.0	365.9
1957	28.1	28.9		44.5	354.9	28.3	28.9		44.7	353.1
1958	28.9	30.2		44.6	345.7	29.1	30.2		44.8	343.8
1959	29.1	29.7		45.0	342.7	29.3	29.7		45.2	340.9
1960	29.6	30.0		45.7	337.3	29.8	30.0		45.9	335.5
1961	29.9	30.4		46.1	334.0	30.1	30.4		46.3	332.2
1962	30.2	30.6		46.3	330.4	30.4	30.6		46.6	328.7
1963	30.6	31.1		46.9	326.5	30.8	31.1		47.1	324.8
1964	31.0	31.5		47.3	322.0	31.2	31.5		47.5	320.3
1965	31.5	32.2		47.8	316.6	31.7	32.2		48.0	315.0
1966	32.4	33.8		49.0	308.0	32.6	33.8		49.2	306.3
1967	33.4	34.1		51.0	299.3	33.6	34.1		51.2	297.7
1968	34.8	35.3		53.7	287.3	35.0	35.3		54.0	285.8
1969	36.7	37.1		56.8	272.6	36.9	37.1		57.1	271.2
1970	38.8	39.2		59.2	257.4	39.0	39.2		59.5	256.0
1971	40.5	40.4		61.1	246.6	40.7	40.3		61.4	245.3
1972	41.8	42.1		62.3	239.1	42.1	42.1		62.7	237.9
1973	44.4	48.2		64.6	225.1	44.7	48.2		65.0	223.9
1974	49.3	55.1		69.4	202.9	49.6	55.1		69.8	201.8

Consumer Price Indexes, Selected Groups, and Purchasing Power of the Consumer Dollar, 1913-1995—Continued

(1982-1984=100, except as noted)

Year	All urban consumers					Urban wage earners and clerical workers				
	All items	Food	Renters' costs[1]	Apparel and upkeep	Purchasing power of consumer dollar	All items	Food	Renters' costs[2]	Apparel and upkeep	Purchasing power of consumer dollar
1975	53.8	59.8	....	72.5	185.9	54.1	59.8	....	72.9	184.9
1976	56.9	61.6	....	75.2	175.7	57.2	61.6	....	75.6	174.7
1977	60.6	65.5	....	78.6	164.9	60.9	65.5	....	79.0	164.0
1978	65.2	72.0	....	81.4	153.2	65.6	72.0	....	81.7	152.4
1979	72.6	79.9	....	84.9	138.0	73.1	80.0	....	85.2	136.9
1980	82.4	86.8	....	90.9	121.5	82.9	87.0	....	90.9	120.6
1981	90.9	93.6	....	95.3	109.8	91.4	93.7	....	95.6	109.6
1982	96.5	97.4	....	97.8	103.5	96.9	97.4	....	97.8	103.3
1983	99.6	99.4	103.0	100.2	100.3	99.8	99.4	....	100.2	100.0
1984	103.9	103.2	108.6	102.1	96.1	103.3	103.2	....	102.0	96.8
1985	107.6	105.6	115.4	105.0	92.8	106.9	105.4	103.6	105.0	93.5
1986	109.6	109.0	121.9	105.9	91.3	108.6	108.8	109.5	105.8	92.0
1987	113.6	113.5	128.1	110.6	88.0	112.5	113.3	114.6	110.4	89.0
1988	118.3	118.2	133.6	115.4	84.6	117.0	117.9	119.2	114.9	85.5
1989	124.0	125.1	138.9	118.6	80.7	122.6	124.8	123.9	117.9	81.6
1990	130.7	132.4	146.7	124.1	76.6	129.0	132.1	130.1	123.1	77.5
1991	136.2	136.3	155.6	128.7	73.4	134.3	136.0	136.9	127.4	74.5
1992	140.3	137.9	160.9	131.9	71.3	138.2	137.5	141.3	130.7	72.4
1993	144.5	140.9	165.0	133.7	69.2	142.1	140.5	144.7	132.4	70.4
1994	148.2	144.3	169.4	133.4	67.5	145.6	143.9	148.5	132.2	68.7
1995	152.4	148.4	174.3	132.0	65.6	149.8	147.9	152.5	130.9	66.8

1. December 1982=100.
2. December 1984=100.

Relative Importance of Components in the Consumer Price Index, December 1995 and Dates of Major Weight Revisions

(Percent of all items)

Index and year	All items	Food and beverages	Housing	Apparel and upkeep	Transpor-tation	Medical care	Entertain-ment	Other goods and services
ALL URBAN CONSUMERS (CPI-U)								
December 1977	100.0	18.8	43.9	5.8	18.0	5.0	4.1	4.4
December 1982[1]	100.0	20.1	37.7	5.2	21.8	6.0	4.2	5.0
December 1995	100.0	17.3	41.3	5.5	17.0	7.4	4.4	7.1
URBAN WAGE EARNERS AND CLERICAL WORKERS (CPI-W)								
1935-1939	100.0	35.4	33.7[3]	11.0[4]	8.1	4.1	2.8	4.9
December 1952[2]	100.0	32.2	33.5	9.4	11.3	4.8	4.0	4.8
December 1963	100.0	25.2	34.9	10.6[5]	14.0	5.7	3.9	5.7
December 1977	100.0	20.5	40.7	5.8	20.2	4.5	3.9	4.4
December 1984[1]	100.0	21.3	34.9	5.0	24.1	5.6	3.9	5.2
December 1995	100.0	19.3	38.9	5.5	19.0	6.3	4.0	7.0

1. Reflects change in relative weights associated with the conceptual change in the treatment of homeownership, but still reflects the expenditure pattern introduced in December 1977. The change in relative weighting was introduced in the CPI-U in December 1982 and in the CPI-W in December 1984.
2. Includes home purchase, previously excluded from index coverage.
3. Includes radios, transferred to 'Reading and recreation' as of January 1950. 'Reading and recreation' retitled 'Entertainment' as of December 1977.
4. Included Laundry and drycleaning, transferred to 'Housing' in December 1952.
5. Includes drycleaning and one-half the weight of laundry service included in 'Housing' in December 1952.

Consumer Price Indexes for All Urban Consumers, All Items, Selected Areas, Selected Years, 1945-1995

(1982-1984=100)

Area	1945	1950	1955	1960	1965	1970	1975	1980	1981	1982	1983	1984
NORTHEAST												
New York	18.9	24.6	27.1	30.2	32.6	41.2	57.6	82.1	90.1	95.3	99.8	104.8
Philadelphia	18.5	24.7	27.9	30.6	32.8	40.8	56.8	83.6	92.1	96.6	99.4	104.1
Boston	17.9	23.9	26.4	29.8	32.5	40.2	55.8	82.6	91.8	95.5	99.8	104.7
Pittsburgh	17.6	23.7	26.3	29.7	31.4	38.1	52.4	81.0	89.3	94.4	101.1	104.5
Buffalo	....	....	....	....	33.4	41.2	57.4	83.5	91.3	94.7	100.9	104.4
NORTH CENTRAL												
Chicago	17.5	24.2	27.5	30.4	31.7	38.9	52.8	82.2	90.0	96.2	100.0	103.8
Detroit	18.3	24.6	27.7	29.7	31.2	39.5	53.9	85.3	93.2	97.0	99.8	103.2
St. Louis	17.6	23.9	27.0	29.5	31.7	38.8	52.6	82.5	90.1	96.6	100.1	103.3
Cleveland	17.2	22.8	25.7	28.3	29.6	37.2	50.2	78.9	87.2	94.0	101.2	104.8
Minneapolis-St. Paul	16.7	22.9	25.9	28.3	30.1	37.4	51.2	78.9	88.6	97.4	99.5	103.1
Milwaukee	17.3	23.9	27.1	29.2	31.0	37.5	50.8	81.4	90.7	95.9	100.2	103.8
Cincinnati	17.8	23.9	26.6	29.1	30.5	37.4	51.8	82.1	87.9	94.9	100.8	104.3
Kansas City	18.1	23.7	26.5	29.3	32.2	39.0	53.2	83.6	90.5	95.0	100.5	104.5
SOUTH												
Washington	18.9	24.9	27.4	29.7	31.9	39.8	54.7	82.9	90.5	95.5	99.8	104.6
Dallas-Fort Worth	....	....	....	....	29.9	37.6	50.4	81.5	90.8	96.0	99.7	104.3
Baltimore	17.8	23.9	26.7	29.8	31.6	39.1	55.2	83.7	91.5	95.6	99.9	104.5
Houston	16.6	23.4	25.7	27.8	29.6	36.4	51.4	82.7	91.0	97.3	100.0	102.7
Atlanta	17.9	24.1	27.1	29.6	31.2	38.6	53.6	80.3	90.2	96.0	99.9	104.1
Miami	....	....	....	....	....	....	....	81.1	90.5	96.7	99.9	103.5
WEST												
L.A.-Long Beach	18.1	23.7	26.7	30.0	32.4	38.7	53.3	83.7	91.9	97.3	99.1	103.6
San Francisco-Oakland	16.8	22.0	24.9	28.6	30.8	37.7	51.8	80.4	90.8	97.6	98.4	104.0
Seattle-Everett	17.3	23.1	25.9	28.8	31.0	37.4	51.1	82.7	91.8	97.7	99.3	103.0
San Diego	....	....	....	....	28.2	34.1	47.6	79.4	90.1	96.2	99.0	104.8
Portland	18.2	24.3	26.8	29.8	32.3	38.7	53.5	87.2	95.0	98.0	99.1	102.8
Honolulu	....	....	....	....	34.4	41.5	56.3	83.0	91.7	97.2	99.3	103.5
Anchorage	....	....	....	....	35.3	41.1	57.1	85.5	92.4	97.4	99.2	103.3
Denver	....	....	....	....	28.8	34.5	48.4	78.4	87.2	95.1	100.5	104.3

Area	1985	1986	1987	1988	1989	1990	1991	1992	1993	1994	1995
NORTHEAST											
New York	108.7	112.3	118.0	123.7	130.6	138.5	144.8	150.0	154.5	158.2	162.2
Philadelphia	108.8	111.5	116.8	122.4	128.3	135.8	142.2	146.6	150.2	154.6	158.7
Boston	109.4	112.2	117.1	124.2	131.3	138.9	145.0	148.6	152.9	154.9	158.6
Pittsburgh	106.9	108.2	111.4	114.9	120.1	126.2	131.3	136.0	139.9	144.6	149.2
Buffalo	108.6	109.6	113.0	117.4	121.6	127.7	133.4	137.9	142.7	146.8	151.5
NORTH CENTRAL											
Chicago	107.7	110.0	114.5	119.0	125.0	131.7	137.0	141.1	145.4	148.6	153.3
Detroit	106.8	108.3	111.7	116.1	122.3	128.6	133.1	135.9	139.6	144.0	148.6
St. Louis	107.1	108.6	112.2	115.7	121.8	128.1	132.1	134.7	137.5	141.3	145.2
Cleveland	107.8	109.4	112.7	116.7	122.7	129.0	134.2	136.8	140.3	144.4	147.9
Minneapolis-St. Paul	107.0	108.4	111.6	117.2	122.0	127.0	130.4	135.0	139.2	143.6	147.0
Milwaukee	107.0	107.4	111.5	115.9	120.8	126.2	132.2	137.1	142.1	147.0	151.0
Cincinnati	106.6	107.6	111.9	116.1	120.9	126.5	131.4	134.1	137.8	142.4	146.2
Kansas City	107.7	108.7	113.1	117.4	121.6	126.0	131.2	134.3	138.1	141.3	145.3
SOUTH											
Washington	109.0	112.2	116.2	121.0	128.0	135.6	141.2	144.7	149.3	152.2	155.3
Dallas-Fort Worth	108.2	109.9	112.9	116.1	119.5	125.1	130.8	133.9	137.3	141.2	144.9
Baltimore	108.2	110.9	114.2	119.3	124.5	130.8	136.4	140.1	143.1	146.9	150.7
Houston	104.9	103.9	106.5	109.5	114.1	120.6	125.1	129.1	133.4	137.9	139.8
Atlanta	108.9	112.2	116.5	120.4	126.1	131.7	135.9	138.5	143.4	146.7	150.9
Miami	106.5	107.9	111.8	116.8	121.5	128.0	132.3	134.5	139.1	143.6	148.9
WEST											
L.A.-Long Beach	108.4	111.9	116.7	122.1	128.3	135.9	141.4	146.5	150.3	152.3	154.6
San Francisco-Oakland	108.4	111.6	115.4	120.5	126.4	132.1	137.9	142.5	146.3	148.7	151.6
Seattle-Everett	105.6	106.7	109.2	112.8	118.1	126.8	134.1	139.0	142.9	147.8	152.3
San Diego	110.4	113.5	117.5	123.4	130.6	138.4	143.4	147.4	150.6	154.5	156.8
Portland	106.7	108.2	110.9	114.7	120.4	127.4	133.9	139.8	144.7	148.9	153.2
Honolulu	106.8	109.4	114.9	121.7	128.7	138.1	148.0	155.1	160.1	164.5	168.1
Anchorage	105.8	107.8	108.2	108.6	111.7	118.6	124.0	128.2	132.2	135.0	138.9
Denver	107.1	107.9	110.8	113.7	115.8	120.9	125.6	130.3	135.8	141.8	147.9

NOTES

Prices and Living Conditions—Export and Import Price Indexes

United States export and import price indexes cover transactions in nonmilitary goods between the United States and the rest of the world. The export price indexes provide a measure of price change for U.S. products sold to other countries, and the import price indexes provide a measure of price change for goods purchased from other countries by U.S. residents.

Prices used in constructing the indexes are initially collected through personal visits by BLS field representatives; thereafter, the prices are generally collected each month by mail questionnaire or telephone. To the extent possible, products are priced at the U.S. border for exports and at both the foreign border and the U.S. border for imports. For a given product, however, only one price basis series is used in constructing the index. For most products, prices represent the actual transaction completed nearest the first of the month. Indexes published here are based on the Standard International Trade Classification System (SITC), a United Nations product classification system. The SITC is especially useful for international comparisons.

Prices are collected according to the specification method. The specifications for each product include detailed descriptions of the physical and functional characteristics of the product. The terms of transaction include information on the number of units bought or sold, discount, credit terms, packaging, class of buyer or seller, etc. When there are changes in either the specifications or terms of transaction of a product, the dollar value of each change is deleted from the total price changes in order to obtain the "pure changes." Once this value is determined, a linking procedure is employed which allows for continued repricing of the item.

At the elementary level, the price changes for all items within a given weight are averaged together using equal weights to construct what is referred to as a classification group. Classification groups are then averaged together using their relative importances to construct publication strata. Beginning with the release of data for January 1997, the values assigned to each classification group are essentially based on the relative importance of a given company's trade in a given product area. (Prior to 1987, the relative importance of each weight group was based on the entire value of trade in a given product area.) Successively higher levels of publication strata are then averaged together using relative importances based on 1995 U.S. trade values.

BLS publishes indexes for selected categories of internationally traded services calculated on an international basis.

U.S. Export Price Indexes, by Standard International Trade Classifications, 1984-95

(1990=100, unless otherwise indicated)

Category	1984				1985				1986			
	March	June	September	December	March	June	September	December	March	June	September	December
Food and live animals	108.0	111.5	105.2	98.1	97.2	96.3	93.2	96.5	93.2	93.0	82.4	86.3
Meat and meat preparations	81.4	81.3	78.9	78.0	77.9	78.6	79.3	82.4	81.5	83.7	88.5	91.1
Cereals and cereal preparations	124.2	129.9	122.4	112.4	111.9	109.3	100.0	105.4	97.9	95.0	70.7	77.3
Vegetables, fruits, and nuts, prepared, fresh or dry	83.3	91.0	90.0	82.2	85.8	88.6	92.8	87.0	85.8	88.6	92.8	87.0
Crude materials, inedible, except fuels	86.0	90.5	80.5	77.5	74.6	74.4	72.0	71.8	74.2	74.8	72.9	74.9
Hides, skins, and furskins, raw	72.2	76.7	76.2	66.2	59.6	63.3	65.5	71.4	70.6	76.0	70.3	75.2
Oilseeds and oleaginous fruits	122.1	135.6	103.9	97.2	92.4	92.8	83.5	83.3	87.2	86.4	85.8	83.8
Crude rubber (including synthetic and reclaimed)	83.9	86.0	84.5	84.4	85.8	85.6	86.3	85.5	85.5	85.7	85.4	84.9
Cork and wood	58.5	57.7	55.3	55.9	57.8	56.2	55.8	58.0	57.8	57.6	58.6	61.5
Pulp and waste paper	67.5	73.3	72.5	68.5	60.7	57.6	55.9	55.6	59.9	66.9	74.1	74.4
Textile fibers and their waste	95.3	99.4	86.5	84.4	81.2	85.3	83.8	79.5	82.6	80.8	60.2	74.9
Crude fertilizers and crude minerals	88.6	89.2	98.5	98.6	100.0	100.8	101.2	99.6	100.4	98.8	98.4	97.2
Metalliferous ores and metal scrap	83.5	82.1	77.6	77.0	74.8	70.7	68.2	66.4	70.2	68.6	70.3	67.8
Mineral fuels, lubricants, and related products	103.7	104.3	104.3	104.3	104.5	104.6	102.3	99.6	85.9	78.9	79.6	79.9
Coal, coke, and briquettes				105.1	104.6	103.1	101.5	101.4	97.3	96.5	96.0	94.5
Petroleum, petroleum products, and related materials												
Animal and vegetable oils, fats, and waxes	112.5	142.6	126.3	128.2	123.0	123.5	99.4	89.8	80.9	73.7	67.7	78.2
Chemicals and related products, n.e.s.	87.9	86.5	85.2	84.7	84.4	84.5	84.5	84.0	84.2	82.7	80.8	80.3
Medicinal and pharmaceutical products												90.8
Essential oils; polishing and cleaning preparations				78.5	78.5	78.7	79.5	79.2	80.6	83.1	82.5	82.3
Plastics in primary forms (12/92=100)												
Plastics in nonprimary forms (12/92=100)												
Chemical materials and products, n.e.s.	84.1	84.3	84.1	86.4	86.7	86.7	86.8	87.0	87.4	88.4	84.7	84.4
Manufactured goods classified chiefly by materials	82.2	82.4	83.0	81.7	81.4	81.3	81.0	81.0	82.2	83.2	84.3	84.6
Rubber manufactures, n.e.s.	84.9	85.3	86.1	85.9	86.9	86.6	86.0	86.2	87.0	86.5	86.9	87.3
Paper, paperboard, and articles of paper, pulp, and paperboard	75.6	77.9	80.6	80.3	78.3	76.7	75.8	74.8	76.8	80.0	83.4	84.6
Nonmetallic mineral manufactures, n.e.s.							78.5	78.7	79.4	80.4	82.2	84.8
Nonferrous metals	85.5	84.3	82.1	74.9	75.4	77.1	75.1	74.7	78.8	77.9	79.6	77.5
Machinery and transport equipment	88.1	88.7	89.1	90.0	90.3	90.7	90.8	90.9	91.3	91.4	91.6	92.2
Power generating machinery and equipment	80.1	79.4	81.3	84.7	83.9	85.2	85.2	86.3	87.1	87.2	87.3	88.3
Machinery specialized for particular industries	85.7	86.0	86.5	86.4	87.2	87.7	87.9	88.0	88.2	88.0	88.0	88.2
General industrial machines and parts, n.e.a., and machine parts	81.9	82.1	82.2	82.7	83.7	84.4	84.7	84.8	85.1	85.7	86.5	87.2
Computer equipment and office machines	108.6	108.7	106.9	108.6	107.6	105.9	105.8	105.2	106.0	105.0	104.8	104.2
Telecommunications and sound recording and reproducing apparatus	90.2	89.8	91.2	91.1	90.3	89.6	89.9	90.1	89.2	89.0	89.7	91.1
Electrical machinery and equipment	89.5	91.5	92.5	93.1	93.2	93.8	93.0	92.0	92.5	92.3	92.7	93.2
Road vehicles	86.9	87.6	87.4	88.0	88.8	89.8	89.8	90.6	90.6	91.3	91.5	92.7
Professional, scientific, and controlling instruments and apparatus	76.7	76.8	78.5	76.7	77.9	79.5	79.5	79.6	80.7	81.6	81.5	81.9

Category	1987				1988				1989			
	March	June	September	December	March	June	September	December	March	June	September	December
Food and live animals	83.6	86.1	83.1	90.6	91.2	99.1	113.8	109.5	112.6	110.6	105.8	103.7
Meat and meat preparations	91.5	96.4	94.5	92.9	97.7	104.3	109.0	103.7	105.8	102.0	95.0	93.1
Cereals and cereal preparations	72.9	75.7	72.3	82.6	85.2	93.0	115.7	108.8	115.6	113.5	108.3	107.8
Vegetables, fruits, and nuts, prepared, fresh or dry	102.1	99.5	89.5	89.0	86.3	92.4	97.3	97.6	96.3	100.6	100.8	97.6
Crude materials, inedible, except fuels	77.4	83.8	86.9	91.7	95.2	102.4	103.1	99.4	104.4	104.7	101.8	100.0
Hides, skins, and furskins, raw	85.7	97.1	95.9	102.0	111.3	108.3	101.8	88.9	95.3	97.4	101.5	102.6
Oilseeds and oleaginous fruits	79.5	89.5	83.7	96.4	101.8	125.8	136.2	119.5	122.6	114.3	98.2	96.4
Crude rubber (including synthetic and reclaimed)	85.7	86.7	88.2	90.4	89.6	91.0	93.6	94.3	95.3	98.3	100.9	100.7
Cork and wood	63.4	66.2	80.7	83.1	85.5	85.2	85.5	84.6	89.6	97.2	101.2	100.8
Pulp and waste paper	82.9	86.1	87.9	92.1	98.4	103.2	104.4	104.6	110.8	111.2	111.1	111.4
Textile fibers and their waste	80.6	92.7	96.1	92.0	88.7	90.6	83.1	85.4	88.0	95.3	96.8	95.9
Crude fertilizers and crude minerals	94.7	94.4	91.9	92.0	93.2	94.6	95.2	95.1	99.2	99.6	99.7	98.1
Metalliferous ores and metal scrap	69.2	75.0	82.2	88.1	92.3	102.3	101.5	105.3	114.5	110.1	105.4	97.0
Mineral fuels, lubricants, and related products	83.5	85.0	86.9	84.8	81.5	84.4	81.7	81.6	84.0	88.4	90.3	93.6
Coal, coke, and briquettes	95.1	90.5	93.4	92.2	93.0	94.5	95.3	95.9	96.2	96.8	98.2	98.9
Petroleum, petroleum products, and related materials				77.2	70.1	75.1	68.9	68.2	73.0	81.4	83.9	89.9
Animal and vegetable oils, fats, and waxes	80.5	85.8	85.5	88.9	100.9	105.9	110.6	99.6	98.4	95.1	91.2	94.5
Chemicals and related products, n.e.s.	84.0	90.0	90.9	95.2	99.5	102.6	105.4	105.9	105.9	102.9	99.3	97.2
Medicinal and pharmaceutical products	91.7	92.0	92.8	95.6	99.2	96.5	96.2	97.6	98.9	98.8	99.3	98.5
Essential oils; polishing and cleaning preparations	83.3	83.5	84.7	85.6	87.8	89.7	94.9	96.7	99.0	98.5	96.7	97.1
Plastics in primary forms (12/92=100)												
Plastics in nonprimary forms (12/92=100)												
Chemical materials & products, n.e.s.	84.7	84.8	84.3	85.3	87.1	88.3	90.4	91.5	94.1	95.0	95.1	95.7
Manufactured goods classified chiefly by materials	86.4	87.6	89.6	90.3	92.9	95.5	97.1	97.9	99.5	99.9	99.6	99.5
Rubber manufactures, n.e.s.	88.2	88.6	89.8	90.0	91.0	94.0	94.6	95.4	97.7	97.6	98.1	98.6
Paper, paperboard, and articles of paper, pulp, and paperboard	87.6	89.4	91.8	93.5	96.4	98.6	99.5	100.2	101.2	102.1	101.5	100.0
Nonmetallic mineral manufactures, n.e.s.	83.8	85.3	86.7	87.4	89.0	89.6	90.8	91.7	94.5	96.1	97.3	98.0
Nonferrous metals	80.6	85.4	93.0	94.0	101.3	108.4	112.7	113.3	114.6	110.2	106.1	102.7
Machinery and transport equipment	92.2	92.3	92.6	92.9	93.6	94.3	95.1	95.9	96.7	97.2	97.9	98.5
Power generating machinery and equipment	89.1	88.3	89.3	89.6	91.1	92.3	92.4	93.1	95.2	96.0	97.5	97.6
Machinery specialized for particular industries	87.7	87.7	88.1	88.5	89.6	90.8	91.8	92.9	94.1	95.4	96.3	97.7
General industrial machines and parts, n.e.a., and machine parts	88.0	88.2	88.3	88.9	90.0	91.2	92.3	93.1	95.1	95.6	96.4	97.3
Computer equipment and office machines	101.9	101.9	101.5	101.3	101.6	101.5	102.7	102.3	101.7	100.6	100.6	100.5
Telecommunications and sound recording and reproducing apparatus	91.7	91.3	91.2	91.7	92.5	94.1	93.7	94.6	96.0	96.8	97.8	98.5
Electrical machinery and equipment	94.6	95.0	95.3	94.7	95.8	96.1	97.9	98.3	98.7	99.0	99.5	99.4
Road vehicles	92.6	92.9	93.1	93.9	93.8	94.1	94.6	95.9	96.2	96.8	97.6	98.7
Professional, scientific, and controlling instruments and apparatus	82.6	83.5	84.1	84.7	87.0	87.9	89.0	90.1	91.4	93.5	94.6	96.0

U.S. Export Price Indexes, by Standard International Trade Classifications, 1984-1995—Continued

(1990=100, unless otherwise indicated)

Category	1990				1991				1992			
	March	June	September	December	March	June	September	December	March	June	September	December
Food and live animals	102.9	104.3	97.9	94.9	98.1	100.7	99.8	102.1	106.1	102.8	100.5	99.9
Meat and meat preparations	100.2	98.5	98.9	102.4	102.9	101.9	103.1	100.2	104.8	106.1	104.6	106.7
Cereals and cereal preparations	104.9	108.6	96.5	89.9	92.6	96.8	96.8	102.7	109.4	104.8	99.0	98.1
Vegetables, fruits, and nuts, prepared, fresh or dry	101.3	102.0	98.7	98.0	113.8	121.5	113.2	104.7	106.1	100.0	100.7	102.9
Crude materials, inedible, except fuels	100.2	100.5	100.9	98.5	98.3	95.4	91.7	89.6	91.0	93.4	94.0	93.6
Hides, skins, and furskins, raw	105.0	105.2	97.4	92.4	84.1	81.5	71.7	80.4	78.8	80.8	82.8	86.8
Oilseeds and oleaginous fruits	96.4	97.1	103.3	103.2	103.9	99.4	97.8	93.6	95.2	98.4	92.2	92.2
Crude rubber (including synthetic and reclaimed)	98.7	99.1	99.9	102.4	105.2	103.2	105.3	103.6	101.8	101.0	102.6	102.5
Cork and wood	102.9	102.1	99.1	96.0	97.6	97.9	99.2	99.0	105.3	110.1	119.9	125.0
Pulp and waste paper	107.3	100.2	96.6	96.0	93.2	86.6	78.9	78.5	79.5	82.6	84.2	79.2
Textile fibers and their waste	96.5	102.6	100.7	100.1	104.5	107.0	97.7	89.1	85.1	86.0	82.2	81.7
Crude fertilizers and crude minerals	99.1	100.1	100.4	100.5	101.4	101.1	98.6	98.8	99.7	99.7	99.5	95.6
Metalliferous ores and metal scrap	97.0	99.9	105.6	97.6	96.4	89.1	87.1	82.3	85.8	85.1	85.8	82.1
Mineral fuels, lubricants, and related products	93.3	91.1	106.1	109.4	93.7	89.9	89.8	90.9	83.0	86.5	87.6	86.2
Coal, coke, and briquettes	98.7	100.1	100.5	100.6	100.3	98.6	98.7	98.7	97.6	96.9	96.2	96.8
Petroleum, petroleum products, and related materials	87.7	83.9	112.7	115.7	86.6	80.1	80.2	81.8	69.2	77.2	79.7	76.2
Animal and vegetable oils, fats, and waxes	97.0	103.0	98.9	101.2	97.6	93.8	94.5	91.8	91.6	94.9	95.3	99.0
Chemicals and related products, n.e.s.	97.4	97.4	100.5	104.7	103.5	99.7	98.0	97.3	97.1	97.4	97.1	95.9
Medicinal and pharmaceutical products	99.5	99.8	100.1	100.6	100.4	100.5	102.2	102.3	103.5	104.1	104.1	104.3
Essential oils; polishing and cleaning preparations	98.8	100.1	100.4	100.7	100.9	101.0	101.7	101.3	103.0	103.7	102.6	102.5
Plastics in primary forms (12/92=100)	....	....	....	....	....	....	....	....	....	....	....	100.0
Plastics in nonprimary forms (12/92=100)	....	....	....	....	....	....	....	....	....	....	....	100.0
Chemical materials and products, n.e.s.	98.0	98.7	100.6	102.8	104.8	103.4	102.4	102.2	102.9	102.9	103.4	103.5
Manufactured goods classified chiefly by materials	99.7	99.8	100.3	100.2	100.4	100.1	99.8	99.7	100.4	100.1	99.8	99.7
Rubber manufactures, n.e.s.	98.8	98.9	99.9	102.4	104.2	105.0	105.3	105.8	105.5	105.6	106.3	106.6
Paper, paperboard, and articles of paper, pulp and paperboard	99.9	99.5	100.2	100.4	99.9	99.5	98.6	98.9	98.6	98.4	97.9	97.3
Nonmetallic mineral manufactures, n.e.s.	100.2	99.6	99.6	100.6	101.2	101.2	101.2	102.1	102.4	103.5	103.7	103.8
Nonferrous metals	99.2	100.2	102.7	97.8	93.3	88.1	87.5	85.1	86.8	87.9	88.0	85.1
Machinery and transport equipment	99.3	99.8	100.2	100.7	102.2	102.9	103.4	103.7	104.1	104.4	104.6	104.6
Power generating machinery and equipment	99.0	99.8	100.2	100.9	103.5	104.7	105.5	106.1	107.6	109.6	109.4	109.7
Machinery specialized for particular industries	99.2	99.3	100.1	101.4	102.4	103.3	103.4	103.9	104.8	105.5	106.1	106.8
General industrial machines and parts, n.e.a., and machine parts	98.9	99.7	100.4	100.9	103.1	103.7	104.5	104.5	106.0	106.1	106.6	107.2
Computer equipment and office machines	100.5	100.3	100.2	99.0	99.2	98.4	97.2	96.1	95.5	94.7	94.0	91.9
Telecommunications and sound recording and reproducing apparatus	98.2	100.1	100.6	101.1	103.6	106.4	107.9	108.8	107.4	108.3	108.7	108.8
Electrical machinery and equipment	100.3	99.9	99.7	100.0	100.1	100.6	102.4	103.1	104.3	103.6	104.1	104.0
Road vehicles	99.1	99.6	100.1	101.2	102.1	102.4	102.7	103.4	103.5	104.0	104.2	104.7
Professional, scientific, and controlling instruments and apparatus	97.1	98.7	101.0	103.2	104.4	105.8	106.0	107.0	108.1	108.6	108.4	108.6

Category	1993				1994				1995			
	March	June	September	December	March	June	September	December	March	June	September	December
Food and live animals	99.5	97.8	102.2	107.8	108.5	103.9	102.4	106.7	108.2	114.1	123.7	128.8
Meat and meat preparations	108.6	111.6	106.9	107.1	110.5	107.3	107.7	109.0	112.4	115.8	120.3	122.7
Cereals and cereal preparations	96.8	90.9	96.0	111.2	112.0	101.8	96.1	103.9	103.1	114.4	128.5	144.2
Vegetables, fruits, and nuts, prepared, fresh, or dry	103.6	103.0	118.0	114.3	112.1	109.6	109.6	113.3	116.8	117.4	134.2	121.6
Crude materials, inedible, except fuels	97.1	99.6	98.0	98.7	104.7	108.1	108.9	116.8	127.4	130.3	123.7	120.5
Hides, skins, and furskins, raw	82.1	79.2	82.9	86.0	91.3	94.4	103.9	110.4	109.6	103.5	90.0	91.2
Oilseeds and oleaginous fruits	95.8	97.9	108.8	112.0	112.3	112.9	96.2	91.9	93.7	96.7	103.0	113.8
Crude rubber (including synthetic and reclaimed)	99.1	99.2	97.6	93.6	92.9	96.1	99.3	104.7	115.9	118.0	117.5	112.2
Cork and wood	146.8	161.4	148.7	146.8	153.0	149.4	149.1	151.5	157.3	156.8	148.7	149.5
Pulp and waste paper	71.6	70.2	66.7	67.3	76.2	94.6	105.0	126.8	156.0	172.7	157.5	133.5
Textile fibers and their waste	84.9	83.5	81.1	83.0	98.4	105.0	101.8	110.5	132.5	134.0	122.6	123.5
Crude fertilizers and crude minerals	94.9	95.0	97.2	97.3	95.4	95.6	96.2	96.4	98.4	97.7	98.6	98.0
Metalliferous ores and metal scrap	82.9	83.9	83.9	85.2	90.6	91.2	100.2	116.5	124.9	124.7	117.9	109.8
Mineral fuels, lubricants, and related products	87.4	88.0	85.6	81.8	83.7	87.4	87.6	89.3	88.9	92.9	91.4	92.8
Coal, coke, and briquettes	95.2	93.9	93.9	94.0	95.2	93.9	93.3	94.1	94.7	97.3	98.5	98.6
Petroleum, petroleum products, and related products	78.1	80.7	76.8	70.4	73.1	80.3	81.1	82.8	81.9	87.0	83.7	86.4
Animal and vegetable oils, fats, and waxes	97.7	98.4	100.9	105.6	110.0	110.0	116.2	132.1	122.0	114.8	115.5	117.4
Chemicals and related products, n.e.s.	96.0	96.1	95.3	95.4	96.4	99.0	103.8	109.2	115.4	116.8	112.4	109.9
Medicinal and pharmaceutical products	105.7	107.0	107.4	108.2	108.8	108.4	107.9	107.5	108.3	109.3	109.3	108.7
Essential oils; polishing and cleaning preparations	103.8	103.6	104.3	104.9	106.4	109.2	109.7	109.4	110.4	110.4	110.9	112.0
Plastics in primary forms (12/92=100)	99.9	102.2	101.4	100.5	101.7	106.5	121.5	134.0	141.9	140.3	126.5	119.8
Plastics in nonprimary forms (12/92=100)	99.7	96.8	97.6	97.5	98.3	99.5	101.4	104.8	106.5	109.5	109.8	109.0
Chemical materials and products, n.e.s.	105.0	105.7	105.8	105.7	108.2	108.7	109.0	110.9	113.3	115.0	115.9	115.7
Manufactured goods classified chiefly by materials	101.7	100.7	101.3	100.8	103.0	104.4	106.6	110.9	113.9	115.8	115.7	114.3
Rubber manufactures, n.e.s.	107.8	108.5	108.9	108.7	108.9	109.2	110.2	110.5	115.8	116.3	118.0	119.5
Paper, paperboard, and articles of paper, pulp and paperboard	96.0	93.9	92.9	93.1	93.8	96.2	101.8	111.0	118.5	126.8	125.1	119.6
Nonmetallic mineral manufactures, n.e.s.	104.0	105.4	106.7	105.8	106.9	107.3	107.6	108.6	109.3	109.4	109.5	110.5
Nonferrous metals	85.6	81.3	83.2	79.0	87.8	92.5	98.7	111.4	115.2	113.0	113.9	107.9
Machinery and transport equipment	104.3	104.5	104.2	104.4	104.4	104.1	103.7	103.7	104.2	104.8	105.0	105.2
Power generating machinery and equipment	110.6	110.7	111.1	111.8	112.6	112.8	113.7	114.6	114.5	114.8	115.1	117.1
Machinery specialized for particular industries	107.5	108.0	108.6	109.2	109.3	109.8	109.9	109.9	111.6	112.8	113.8	114.3
General industrial machines and parts, n.e.a., and machine parts	107.8	108.3	109.0	109.5	109.9	110.1	110.5	110.5	111.8	111.2	112.6	112.3
Computer equipment and office machines	88.8	87.7	85.9	84.6	82.5	81.0	78.8	78.1	76.9	76.6	75.2	74.2
Telecommunications and sound recording and reproducing apparatus	108.0	109.4	108.7	108.6	107.5	107.3	106.8	106.4	106.4	106.7	106.2	105.3
Electrical machinery and equipment	103.0	103.5	102.8	103.5	103.6	103.2	101.8	101.5	102.2	104.0	104.2	103.6
Road vehicles	105.1	105.2	105.2	105.5	106.2	106.3	106.6	107.3	107.8	107.9	108.1	109.1
Professional, scientific, and controlling instruments and apparatus	109.5	110.1	110.9	110.8	111.4	111.6	112.5	112.6	113.2	113.7	113.8	113.9

U.S. Import Price Indexes, by Standard International Trade Classifications, 1984-1995

(1990=100, unless otherwise indicated)

Category	1984				1985				1986			
	March	June	September	December	March	June	September	December	March	June	September	December
Food and live animals	91.0	91.9	90.6	87.1	87.5	87.2	84.7	93.3	100.2	94.6	98.8	96.2
Meat and meat preparations	78.8	79.1	80.0	78.2	75.4	68.8	70.6	78.2	72.3	70.3	76.4	80.0
Fish and crustaceans, mollusks, and other aquatic invertebrates	77.2	78.1	78.1	77.9	77.6	75.5	76.1	77.3	82.0	84.6	87.4	91.3
Cereals and cereal preparations	64.8	64.0	63.1	63.1	62.6	63.2	65.6	68.9	71.8	73.2	76.7	77.3
Vegetables and fruit, prepared, fresh, or dried	84.6	84.4	84.2	72.9	77.4	81.0	72.4	83.8	76.7	78.6	83.4	82.0
Sugars, sugar preparations, and honey	84.7	87.0	86.1	85.7	84.4	87.4	87.3	82.6	91.2	89.4	90.7	91.0
Coffee, tea, cocoa, spices, and manufactures thereof	155.8	158.4	153.0	148.2	146.0	145.1	141.8	166.9	215.5	175.8	182.1	157.4
Beverages and tobacco	75.9	76.3	76.7	76.4	76.4	77.1	77.8	79.6	80.4	81.8	80.7	83.0
Beverages	74.9	75.4	75.3	75.0	75.6	75.9	76.9	78.4	80.0	81.4	82.4	84.0
Crude materials, inedible, except fuels	84.3	83.8	82.2	80.8	78.3	77.8	76.3	77.0	79.9	82.3	84.7	84.4
Crude rubber (including synthetic and reclaimed)	125.6	117.7	113.9	105.2	100.8	98.3	93.4	96.9	102.0	96.9	95.1	95.8
Cork and wood	98.6	88.8	85.6	89.4	87.3	93.4	88.6	86.5	90.5	92.8	95.7	93.2
Pulp and waste paper	62.1	68.1	68.2	66.0	59.6	56.9	54.3	53.6	52.8	56.3	60.6	65.6
Crude fertilizers	101.9	98.0	99.8	100.4	100.9	102.8	102.4	102.4	101.6	101.1	100.5	100.7
Metalliferous ores and metal scrap	69.9	71.8	69.9	66.8	64.7	59.9	61.4	64.7	70.3	76.3	78.2	74.2
Crude animal and vegetable materials, n.e.s.	80.4	81.0	81.3	85.6	86.7	83.9	87.4	96.0	98.6	98.5	99.5	99.1
Mineral fuels, lubricants, and related products	125.2	124.8	123.2	120.8	117.9	114.5	113.1	113.7	69.9	59.1	59.9	64.1
Petroleum, petroleum products, and related materials	120.9	120.8	119.3	116.8	116.0	112.1	110.5	112.0	65.8	55.2	56.3	62.0
Gas, natural and manufactured	....	....	....	....	....	....	....	....	....	....	....	....
Electrical energy	....	....	....	....	....	....	....	....	....	....	57.2	72.9
Animal and vegetable oils, fats, and waxes	151.6	183.1	160.6	148.4	125.0	115.5	93.9	85.7	71.8	70.1	64.3	87.6
Chemicals and related products, n.e.s.	87.6	87.1	85.6	84.1	83.5	83.7	83.5	82.7	83.6	83.1	83.2	82.5
Inorganic chemicals	130.2	127.2	125.1	123.4	119.8	118.8	114.0	112.6	112.0	112.0	112.6	110.0
Dyeing, tanning, and coloring materials	....	....	....	....	....	....	....	....	....	....	....	....
Medicinal and pharmaceutical products	66.8	65.8	64.4	63.2	62.8	64.5	65.4	66.6	71.0	72.1	75.1	73.7
Essential oils; polishing and cleaning preparations	72.4	74.6	73.7	73.7	72.0	76.0	76.7	74.3	76.3	79.5	79.5	79.9
Fertilizers	87.0	88.5	85.7	80.8	83.3	75.3	73.6	70.5	69.2	70.4	68.0	68.1
Plastic in primary forms (12/92=100)	....	....	....	....	....	....	....	....	....	....	....	....
Plastic in nonprimary forms (12/92=100)	....	....	....	....	....	....	....	....	....	....	....	....
Chemical materials and products, n.e.s.	....	....	70.9	69.1	68.9	68.1	70.0	71.4	75.7	76.6	77.5	78.4
Manufactured goods classified chiefly by material	75.7	76.8	75.5	75.2	73.5	73.1	73.9	74.3	75.3	76.3	78.0	78.6
Rubber manufactures, n.e.s.	88.8	88.2	87.4	88.0	86.5	85.9	86.1	86.8	86.5	87.3	88.0	87.9
Paper, paperboard, and articles of paper pulp, paper, or paperboard	77.9	79.2	82.2	82.9	83.0	82.7	83.0	82.5	83.2	83.4	83.6	86.8
Nonmetallic mineral manufactures, n.e.s.	66.9	66.2	62.2	63.4	61.6	60.1	62.9	65.2	66.8	69.0	72.8	73.6
Nonferrous metals	80.2	81.3	76.1	73.7	69.1	69.0	69.8	67.5	67.5	68.1	71.1	69.9
Manufactures of metals, n.e.s.	73.3	73.8	73.1	73.1	72.2	72.9	73.4	75.3	77.0	79.2	79.1	79.6
Machinery and transport equipment	76.2	76.3	75.2	75.4	74.4	75.1	75.8	78.3	81.2	83.7	85.7	86.8
Machinery specialized for particular industries	61.6	61.3	60.6	60.1	58.9	59.1	62.5	64.6	69.3	71.6	75.2	75.3
General industrial machinery and equipment, n.e.s., and machinery parts	64.5	65.0	63.6	62.9	61.2	62.6	64.6	67.2	71.0	74.2	76.6	77.2
Computer equipment and office machines	92.4	91.3	88.9	87.1	85.0	85.0	86.2	89.1	90.5	94.2	94.9	94.0
Telecommunications and sound recording and reproducing apparatus	96.0	96.6	95.3	93.0	92.1	90.1	88.3	89.3	92.5	95.7	98.2	98.0
Electrical machinery and equipment	85.5	82.8	79.0	78.5	75.9	77.4	76.7	79.0	79.6	82.2	84.0	84.8
Road vehicles	72.9	73.8	73.4	74.4	74.6	75.1	75.6	78.7	82.0	84.2	85.8	88.2
Footwear	71.3	73.4	72.1	74.3	70.4	70.6	72.6	74.2	77.1	77.7	79.6	80.8
Photo apparatus, equipment, supplies, and optic goods, n.e.s.	72.8	75.4	74.1	74.2	72.2	73.5	74.6	77.1	82.2	84.6	87.7	88.5

U.S. Import Price Indexes, by Standard International Trade Classifications, 1984-1995—Continued

(1990=100, unless otherwise indicated)

Category	1987 March	June	September	December	1988 March	June	September	December	1989 March	June	September	December
Food and live animals	92.7	95.5	96.2	99.2	100.6	100.5	99.4	100.8	100.6	98.2	93.5	95.4
Fish and crustaceans, mollusks, and other aquatic invertebrates	93.4	96.5	99.9	100.4	101.6	99.1	96.5	97.1	97.3	94.1	93.2	93.6
Cereals and cereal preparations	79.6	82.1	81.2	85.0	88.3	91.0	89.1	92.5	91.3	91.2	92.2	93.0
Vegetables and fruit, prepared, fresh or dried	80.2	86.6	86.5	91.3	90.7	94.6	97.3	100.4	97.1	96.9	93.6	100.8
Sugars, sugar preparations, and honey	91.8	93.6	93.1	91.4	93.7	94.0	95.8	94.7	93.8	95.5	97.7	99.9
Coffee, tea, cocoa, spices, and manufactures thereof	134.9	130.4	127.6	135.8	141.5	140.0	131.0	135.8	136.8	128.0	93.6	85.9
Beverages and tobacco	83.8	87.7	87.2	88.2	90.2	90.3	89.6	90.3	90.9	91.1	93.8	95.1
Beverages	86.0	87.6	88.0	89.1	91.0	92.0	91.2	92.0	92.6	92.6	94.2	95.2
Crude materials, inedible, except fuels	89.0	89.9	93.1	94.4	100.0	106.6	104.7	110.8	113.1	111.6	106.2	105.3
Crude rubber (including synthetic and reclaimed)	95.8	101.0	107.8	116.9	118.5	147.1	129.8	118.2	119.8	100.6	95.7	95.9
Cork and wood	101.0	98.0	104.4	96.8	100.0	99.1	97.6	95.9	99.7	100.0	101.0	99.3
Pulp and waste paper	71.3	74.1	74.9	79.1	84.7	90.1	95.2	98.0	103.6	106.6	106.6	106.3
Crude fertilizers	100.3	101.7	101.3	102.0	102.6	103.1	99.2	102.3	105.5	106.9	103.4	100.1
Metalliferous ores and metal scrap	77.0	78.1	80.7	86.5	94.8	105.1	108.0	128.8	128.1	133.1	115.0	110.7
Crude animal and vegetable materials, n.e.s.	100.0	96.5	95.2	104.7	120.2	131.2	108.0	123.5	122.6	97.6	96.1	113.0
Mineral fuels, lubricants, and related products	77.4	85.1	85.3	77.1	69.5	72.8	66.3	64.7	76.6	84.2	79.0	85.0
Petroleum, petroleum products, and related materials	76.0	83.9	84.7	76.4	68.1	71.7	65.0	63.2	75.8	83.8	78.3	84.3
Gas, natural and manufactured								86.7	89.1	88.5	87.3	95.2
Electrical energy	79.1	78.2	75.3	66.3	87.0	67.4	92.0	80.8	110.9	78.4	113.7	98.0
Animal and vegetable oils, fats, and waxes	87.1	92.4	101.3	107.2	111.8	116.8	119.8	118.0	118.2	123.3	112.1	105.8
Chemicals and related products, n.e.s.	85.5	87.3	88.0	91.7	95.2	97.0	99.3	101.8	103.0	100.4	98.1	99.1
Inorganic chemicals	105.3	104.4	104.4	104.8	107.0	107.3	108.1	111.8	108.3	100.7	99.6	100.1
Dyeing, tanning, and coloring materials												
Medicinal and pharmaceutical products	77.9	80.0	80.6	81.9	87.7	91.0	94.3	94.9	100.4	99.5	96.8	97.1
Essential oils; polishing and cleaning preparations	87.9	88.0	89.1	92.0	94.0	94.3	95.3	97.5	97.4	97.4	95.1	101.1
Fertilizers	70.3	71.6	82.7	101.1	101.2	103.2	103.3	105.9	108.6	107.5	100.2	98.8
Plastics in primary forms (12/92=100)												
Plastics in nonprimary forms (12/92=100)												
Chemical materials and products, n.e.s.	80.1	81.9	83.9	86.9	96.5	103.3	106.8	108.9	107.7	105.5	104.5	105.0
Manufactured goods classified chiefly by material	80.1	82.9	85.7	88.3	91.7	97.4	97.5	99.5	101.2	100.3	99.7	98.7
Rubber manufactures, n.e.s.	90.0	90.3	89.1	90.3	91.5	93.0	94.2	95.9	96.4	96.9	98.1	98.4
Paper, paperboard, and articles of paper pulp, paper, or paperboard	86.7	86.8	91.3	93.0	97.0	98.0	98.9	99.3	99.8	100.0	99.1	98.4
Nonmetallic mineral manufactures, n.e.s.	75.3	79.2	81.4	83.3	85.8	89.0	87.2	88.6	92.1	93.4	94.7	95.6
Nonferrous metals	70.5	77.4	83.2	86.6	91.3	109.9	109.4	116.4	118.9	109.2	103.7	99.2
Manufactures of metals, n.e.s.	82.3	82.8	84.2	86.6	89.0	93.2	93.7	96.0	97.3	97.4	97.8	98.3
Machinery and transport equipment	89.2	91.0	91.0	93.4	95.1	96.6	96.2	98.6	98.7	98.1	97.9	98.8
Machinery specialized for particular industries	79.9	83.4	82.3	87.0	90.0	91.8	88.0	92.4	91.4	89.3	89.3	90.8
General industrial machinery and equipment, n.e.s., and machinery parts	81.7	83.5	83.1	87.5	89.7	91.8	89.2	92.1	92.4	91.3	91.8	92.9
Computer equipment and office machines	94.9	98.4	99.1	102.1	102.0	103.1	102.5	102.4	103.2	103.0	101.1	101.7
Telecommunications and sound recording and reproducing apparatus	99.4	99.2	99.1	100.8	101.5	102.3	102.5	103.9	104.0	104.1	103.5	102.4
Electrical machinery and equipment	86.8	89.5	88.9	91.3	94.4	95.9	97.3	99.9	100.8	100.1	99.4	99.6
Road vehicles	90.1	91.5	91.6	93.1	95.3	97.0	96.6	99.4	99.2	98.5	98.4	100.2
Footwear	82.6	86.2	85.6	89.5	90.2	93.3	92.1	92.9	91.5	92.0	92.6	94.2
Photo apparatus, equipment, supplies, and optic goods, n.e.s.	91.9	93.7	90.7	94.7	96.1	96.1	93.2	97.1	96.8	95.1	93.9	95.7

U.S. Import Price Indexes, by Standard International Trade Classifications, 1984-1995—Continued

(1990=100, unless otherwise indicated)

Category	1990				1991				1992			
	March	June	September	December	March	June	September	December	March	June	September	December
Food and live animals	98.4	98.6	100.5	102.5	102.5	102.4	101.3	102.3	104.3	97.9	98.6	99.8
Meat and meat preparations	95.5	100.0	102.8	101.7	102.1	105.6	101.0	97.9	96.9	94.9	94.2	92.5
Fish and crustaceans, mollusks, and other aquatic invertebrates	96.5	96.7	101.6	105.2	108.8	107.6	106.6	106.7	107.8	107.9	109.6	106.8
Cereals and cereal preparations	96.6	98.7	101.3	103.3	102.6	96.4	96.1	100.5	99.7	99.3	105.5	100.8
Vegetables, fruits, and nuts, prepared, fresh or dried	103.3	99.0	94.6	103.1	100.5	104.1	104.6	108.9	122.6	102.3	101.9	104.3
Sugars, sugar preparations, and honey	99.3	99.7	99.9	101.2	97.4	96.7	96.9	96.9	96.7	95.3	95.8	92.8
Coffee, tea, cocoa, spices, and manufactures thereof	97.7	99.4	104.3	98.6	98.7	93.2	92.6	92.9	84.8	77.3	77.0	90.6
Beverages and tobacco	96.9	99.2	100.6	103.3	109.2	110.8	110.6	111.9	113.0	113.4	114.5	113.1
Beverages	97.3	99.3	100.8	102.6	109.0	110.3	109.8	111.1	112.1	112.5	114.0	112.2
Crude materials, inedible, except fuels	103.0	101.9	99.3	95.9	95.2	95.9	92.2	91.9	95.4	95.8	97.4	96.8
Crude rubber (including synthetic and reclaimed)	98.3	101.2	101.4	99.1	100.8	98.4	97.2	96.9	99.0	100.8	102.5	102.9
Cork and wood	101.4	102.4	101.6	94.6	96.5	107.7	102.2	104.4	115.6	116.8	118.3	121.4
Pulp and waste paper	104.8	102.8	99.2	93.1	85.6	79.2	71.1	69.3	71.6	74.4	77.7	74.0
Crude fertilizers	98.9	99.6	100.6	100.9	101.7	100.9	96.6	91.8	89.8	89.0	89.2	84.7
Metalliferous ores and metal scrap	105.4	100.8	97.5	96.3	96.3	93.6	93.8	93.1	92.9	91.1	92.3	90.5
Crude animal and vegetable materials, n.e.s.	99.1	103.9	95.3	101.7	106.9	103.7	102.8	106.5	107.9	107.2	108.8	113.2
Mineral fuels, lubricants, and related products	86.0	73.1	116.6	124.2	87.9	83.2	85.0	84.6	75.9	86.7	87.3	80.2
Petroleum, petroleum products, and related materials	84.9	72.0	118.1	125.0	87.1	82.8	84.8	84.3	75.5	86.7	87.0	79.2
Gas, natural and manufactured	103.9	89.4	94.0	112.7	100.2	88.1	87.0	94.1	81.0	83.7	90.2	94.7
Electrical energy	113.1	86.6	85.1	88.6	93.8	84.8	91.7	97.2	91.4	104.8	96.8	94.3
Animal and vegetable oils, fats, and waxes	103.3	100.6	95.4	100.7	102.8	102.2	109.0	126.6	138.3	134.9	128.5	125.3
Chemicals and related products, n.e.s.	99.1	98.5	99.8	102.7	102.4	100.7	100.3	100.5	101.2	101.7	102.5	102.1
Inorganic chemicals	98.1	98.5	99.8	103.5	104.4	103.1	100.9	97.6	98.2	96.8	96.4	101.8
Dyeing, tanning, and coloring materials	....	....	....	....	....	....	....	....	....	....	....	....
Medicinal and pharmaceutical products	98.7	98.9	100.0	102.5	102.0	100.2	102.0	106.0	107.0	107.4	110.5	110.1
Essential oils; polishing and cleaning preparations	98.1	99.3	99.9	102.6	101.3	101.1	104.1	103.3	105.7	106.9	107.2	107.1
Fertilizers	97.9	97.7	100.9	103.5	108.6	108.2	107.8	104.9	102.6	105.7	103.8	101.9
Plastics in primary forms (12/92=100)	....	....	....	....	....	....	....	....	....	....	....	100.0
Plastics in nonprimary forms (12/92=100)	....	....	....	....	....	....	....	....	....	....	....	100.0
Chemical materials and products, n.e.s.	104.5	100.0	98.5	97.0	96.4	94.7	95.0	96.9	101.1	104.5	108.6	107.6
Manufactured goods classified chiefly by material	98.6	99.5	101.5	100.5	101.0	99.2	98.4	98.6	99.1	99.4	100.1	98.4
Rubber manufactures, n.e.s.	99.4	99.8	99.8	101.1	100.8	100.6	100.2	101.2	102.1	102.0	103.4	103.2
Paper, paperboard, and articles of paper pulp, paper or paperboard	97.3	100.4	100.9	101.4	103.6	101.0	99.2	98.7	95.6	94.1	94.8	94.7
Nonmetallic mineral manufactures, n.e.s.	98.4	99.8	100.3	101.4	103.2	103.3	103.5	104.4	104.7	105.5	106.5	106.1
Nonferrous metals	94.8	98.7	108.5	98.0	96.2	89.0	85.5	83.0	86.4	88.6	88.7	82.1
Manufactures of metals, n.e.s.	99.7	98.9	100.3	101.1	101.9	101.2	100.6	102.0	102.9	103.0	104.9	103.1
Machinery and transport equipment	99.5	98.7	99.7	102.0	103.2	101.6	101.7	103.2	103.5	103.5	104.7	103.9
Machinery specialized for particular industries	96.4	97.3	101.0	105.2	106.8	101.7	101.4	104.4	105.3	105.4	110.7	106.6
General industrial machinery and equipment, n.e.s., and machinery parts	96.5	97.7	101.4	104.4	105.4	101.5	101.7	104.6	104.8	104.9	108.0	105.9
Computer equipment and office machines	101.0	99.8	99.0	100.2	99.2	97.3	96.2	96.4	96.6	95.7	96.0	95.1
Telecommunications and sound recording and reproducing apparatus	101.5	100.2	98.8	99.5	98.4	97.8	97.2	97.6	97.2	97.1	97.2	97.4
Electrical machinery and equipment	100.3	98.7	99.9	101.0	102.4	100.6	100.0	101.5	101.3	102.1	103.1	101.6
Road vehicles	99.7	98.4	99.4	102.5	104.5	103.5	104.1	105.6	105.8	105.6	106.3	106.5
Footwear	97.6	99.0	100.8	102.6	102.8	100.9	100.6	101.4	101.9	102.6	104.1	101.3
Photographic apparatus, equipment, supplies, and optic goods, n.e.s.	97.7	98.0	101.2	103.1	103.4	100.1	100.5	102.9	103.6	102.9	106.5	104.8

U.S. Import Price Indexes, by Standard International Trade Classifications, 1984-1995—Continued

(1990=100, unless otherwise indicated)

Category	1993				1994				1995			
	March	June	September	December	March	June	September	December	March	June	September	December
Food and live animals	97.6	101.1	102.3	102.1	103.1	109.0	118.8	118.7	120.6	116.3	114.3	112.2
Meat and meat preparations	95.8	99.3	97.9	94.0	96.5	91.0	91.9	91.7	88.6	85.2	82.2	84.2
Fish and crustaceans, mollusks, and other aquatic invertebrates	107.6	107.9	109.1	114.1	116.6	121.2	123.5	127.9	127.7	126.1	121.7	118.0
Cereals and cereal preparations	100.9	102.9	98.5	99.8	99.5	102.0	100.5	101.9	102.2	101.4	104.8	108.3
Vegetables and fruit, prepared, fresh or dried	97.2	109.9	106.5	101.7	100.2	102.5	100.1	112.6	114.4	111.1	114.9	121.1
Sugars, sugar preparations, and honey	94.1	95.1	96.5	96.4	96.9	98.2	96.8	97.2	98.1	103.9	101.8	102.2
Coffee, tea, cocoa, spices, and manufactures thereof	84.7	81.2	98.2	101.6	103.1	137.1	202.2	172.3	183.7	166.2	156.3	133.8
Beverages and tobacco	112.5	112.6	111.8	112.7	112.3	113.2	113.4	113.5	114.4	114.9	115.9	117.6
Beverages	112.2	112.9	112.0	112.4	112.3	112.8	113.5	113.6	114.5	114.8	115.5	115.8
Crude materials, inedible, except fuels	104.0	95.3	96.9	102.3	105.3	106.7	108.5	114.6	121.3	123.5	128.1	125.2
Crude rubber (including synthetic and reclaimed)	106.1	102.9	99.1	98.0	103.4	106.3	121.0	143.8	165.6	156.8	147.6	155.1
Cork and wood	162.5	130.3	141.9	170.2	166.9	159.9	155.4	149.6	143.3	131.0	145.4	135.8
Pulp and waste paper	65.5	63.7	60.4	58.4	61.6	70.1	80.1	90.7	104.7	116.0	118.9	122.1
Crude fertilizers	82.7	82.5	83.0	84.0	81.2	82.3	82.3	86.6	90.2	100.7	99.5	99.4
Metalliferous ores and metal scrap	89.5	88.3	87.1	83.2	90.2	89.6	92.3	97.2	106.6	106.4	109.7	108.3
Crude animal and vegetable materials, n.e.s.	112.9	106.1	109.2	115.4	120.7	131.2	118.3	139.2	140.1	163.8	170.5	153.1
Mineral fuels, lubricants, and related products	82.2	79.9	73.5	63.8	64.4	76.3	73.5	75.3	79.1	82.7	77.0	79.2
Petroleum, petroleum products, and related materials	81.6	79.2	72.3	61.8	62.7	75.7	72.6	74.5	79.0	82.7	76.8	79.1
Gas, natural and manufactured	89.4	90.3	91.7	94.1	90.7	83.7	87.4	88.3	79.5	80.3	76.8	80.0
Electrical energy	95.6	91.0	87.5	85.8	89.3	83.7	88.8	83.5	78.0	78.8	78.4	75.6
Animal and vegetable oils, fats, and waxes	119.8	117.8	117.3	120.0	123.3	135.1	140.0	155.0	152.4	159.3	171.0	176.8
Chemicals and related products, n.e.s.	102.1	102.8	102.1	101.3	101.2	102.6	105.7	108.8	110.8	112.3	112.0	111.9
Inorganic chemicals	102.0	100.7	100.5	100.2	99.6	100.7	102.7	107.6	113.1	114.3	114.0	113.3
Dyeing, tanning, and coloring materials	99.2	101.0	100.0	99.9	101.0	101.5	102.5	102.9	106.4	108.0	108.6	109.7
Medicinal and pharmaceutical products	111.5	117.5	115.7	116.6	117.4	117.5	119.7	120.5	121.6	128.0	127.6	129.5
Essential oils; polishing and cleaning preparations	109.4	110.8	108.7	109.9	108.0	108.4	110.5	113.4	116.8	123.4	124.4	125.2
Fertilizers	102.4	101.4	102.4	100.5	102.7	104.0	102.1	107.2	112.0	111.0	109.1	113.0
Plastics in primary forms (12/92=100)	101.0	99.0	99.7	99.7	100.9	101.2	101.6	102.9	106.8	109.7	108.6	111.5
Plastics in nonprimary forms (12/92=100)	99.3	99.5	98.7	97.5	95.3	98.3	102.8	107.1	115.5	118.0	113.4	106.9
Chemical materials and products, n.e.s.	106.2	105.4	103.4	101.7	102.7	101.7	105.2	103.7	103.8	106.2	109.3	112.1
Manufactured goods classified chiefly by material	98.9	99.3	98.7	97.8	99.3	101.0	103.0	106.4	109.1	111.8	114.3	113.6
Rubber manufactures, n.e.s.	104.0	103.8	103.1	103.2	101.6	102.4	101.5	102.3	102.8	105.0	106.3	106.6
Paper, paperboard, and articles of paper pulp, paper, or paperboard	96.2	96.7	95.4	94.2	94.0	95.6	99.4	105.2	114.4	125.1	135.5	136.7
Nonmetallic mineral manufactures, n.e.s.	106.8	108.0	107.8	107.9	107.8	108.5	109.8	110.5	110.8	111.4	111.8	112.1
Nonferrous metals	80.0	76.6	75.9	72.3	80.3	85.2	91.0	103.1	105.9	103.8	106.1	102.2
Manufactures of metals, n.e.s.	103.4	104.5	104.3	103.9	103.9	104.6	106.0	106.4	108.4	110.8	110.8	111.5
Machinery and transport equipment	103.9	105.0	105.5	106.2	106.4	106.8	107.4	108.0	108.5	110.1	109.8	109.7
Machinery specialized for particular industries	106.0	107.5	107.1	107.3	108.3	109.7	111.5	112.5	114.0	117.0	116.0	118.0
General industrial machinery and equipment, n.e.s., and machinery parts	105.3	107.0	107.0	107.8	108.4	109.0	110.3	111.6	113.0	116.6	116.8	117.6
Computer equipment and office machines	93.7	91.9	90.6	89.5	88.3	87.1	86.0	84.8	84.0	84.1	83.5	82.2
Telecommunications and sound recording and reproducing apparatus	97.1	98.0	99.0	98.2	97.4	97.4	97.5	97.7	97.6	98.7	98.6	97.7
Electrical machinery and equipment	102.1	103.9	105.9	105.4	105.6	106.1	106.6	106.5	106.9	109.0	107.0	106.1
Road vehicles	106.9	108.4	109.0	111.4	111.9	112.7	113.5	115.1	115.8	116.7	117.4	117.7
Footwear	100.6	101.2	100.4	100.1	99.6	100.2	101.0	101.1	101.1	101.9	102.2	102.8
Photo apparatus, equipment, supplies, and optic goods, n.e.s.	104.8	106.9	107.9	108.7	108.5	109.1	110.8	110.6	111.0	115.3	114.7	114.7

NOTES
Prices and Living Conditions—Consumer Expenditure Survey

The buying habits of American consumers change over time as a result of changes in relative prices, real income, family size and composition, and other determinants of people's tastes and preferences. The introduction into the marketplace of new products and the emergence of new concepts in retailing also influence consumer buying habits. As the only national survey that can relate family expenditures to demographic characteristics, data from the Consumer Expenditure Survey (CEX) are of great importance to researchers. The survey data are also used to revise the Consumer Price Index market baskets and item samples.

Definitions

The terms *family*, *household*, and *consumer unit* are used interchangeably in descriptions of the CEX. A consumer unit comprises either (1) all members of a particular household who are related by blood, marriage, adoption, or other legal arrangement; (2) a person living alone or sharing a household with others or living as a roomer in a private home or lodging house or in permanent living quarters in a hotel or motel, but who is financially independent; or (3) two or more persons living together who pool their income to make joint expenditure decisions. Financial independence is determined by the three major expense categories: housing, food, and other living expenses. To be considered financially independent, at least two of the three major expense categories have to be provided by the respondent.

The *householder* or *reference person* is the first member of the consumer unit mentioned by the respondent as owner or renter of the premises at the time of the initial interview.

Description of the Survey

The Bureau of Labor Statistics (BLS) historically has conducted surveys of consumer expenditures at intervals of approximately 10 years. The last such survey was conducted in 1972-1973. In late 1979, in a significant departure from previous surveys, BLS initiated a survey to be conducted on a continuous basis, with rotating panels of respondents. The regular flow of data that results from this design substantially enhances the usefulness of the survey by providing more timely information on consumption patterns of different kinds of consumer units.

The current CEX is similar to its 1972-1973 predecessor in that it consists of two separate components, each with its own questionnaire and sample: (1) an interview panel survey in which each of about 5,000 consumer units in the sample is visited by an interviewer every three months over a 12-month period, and (2) a diary, or recordkeeping survey, completed by 5,000 other consumer units for two consecutive 1-week periods. The Bureau of the Census, under contract to BLS, collects the data for both components of the survey.

The Interview Survey is designed to collect data on the types of expenditures that respondents can be expected to recall for a period of three months or longer. These include relatively large expenditures such as those for property, travel, automobiles, and major appliances, and expenditures that occur on a regular basis such as rent, utilities, insurance premiums, and clothing. The interview also obtains "global estimates" of food expenditures both for food at home and food away from home. For food-at-home expenditures, respondents are asked to estimate the usual monthly expenditure at the grocery store, and how much of

the expenditure was for nonfood items. Nonfood items are then subtracted from the total expenditure. Convenience and specialty stores are also included in the food-at-home estimates. The Interview Survey collects approximately 95 percent of total expenditures. Excluded from the Interview Survey are nonprescription drugs, household supplies, and personal care supplies.

The Diary Survey is designed to collect expenditures on frequently purchased items which are more difficult to recall over longer periods of time. Respondents keep detailed records of expenses for food and beverages at home and in eating places away from home. Expenditures for tobacco, drugs, including nonprescription drugs, and personal care supplies and services are also collected in the diary.

Participants in both surveys record dollar amounts for goods and services purchased during the reporting period whether or not payment is made at the time of purchase. Excluded from both surveys are business-related expenditures as well as expenditures for which the family is reimbursed. At the initial interview for each survey, information is collected on demographic and family characteristics.

The tables present integrated data from the Diary and Interview Surveys, providing a complete accounting of consumer expenditures and income, which neither survey component alone is designed to do. Data on some expenditure items are collected only in either the Diary or the Interview Survey. For example, the Diary does not collect data for expenditures on overnight travel, or information on reimbursements, as the Interview Survey does. Examples of expenditures for which any reimbursements (e.g., from insurance) are netted out include those for medical care, auto repair, and construction, repairs, alterations, and maintenance of property.

For items unique to one or the other survey, the choice of which survey to use as the source of data is obvious. However, there is considerable overlap in coverage between the surveys. Because of this, integrating the data presents a problem in determining the appropriate survey component. When data are available from both survey sources, the more reliable of the two is selected as determined by statistical methods. As a result, some items are selected from the Interview Survey and others from the Diary Survey.

Description of Tabular Data

The data cover the calendar year 1994. Income values from the survey are derived from "complete income reporters" only. Complete income reporters are defined as consumer units that provide values for at least one of the major sources of their income, such as wages and salaries, self-employment income, and Social Security income.

Some consumer units are defined as complete income reporters even though they may not have provided a full accounting of all income from all sources.

Consumer units are classified by quintiles of income before taxes, age of reference person, size of consumer unit, region, composition of consumer unit, number of earners in consumer unit, housing tenure, race, type of area (urban or rural), and occupation.

Notes on the Data

In interpreting the expenditure data, several factors should be considered. First, expenditures are averages for consumer units with the specified characteristics, regardless of whether a particular unit incurred an expense for that specific item or service during the recordkeeping period. Also, an individual consumer unit may have spent substantially more or substantially less than the average. The less frequently an item or service is purchased, the greater the difference between the average for all consumer

units and the average of those purchasing. Income, age of family members, taste, personal preferences, and geographic location are among the factors which influence expenditures and should be considered when relating averages to individual circumstances.

Expenditures reported are the direct out-of-pocket expenditures of consumer units. Indirect expenditures may be significant for some expenditure categories, for example, utilities. Rental contracts may include some or all utilities, and renters with such contracts would record little or no direct expense for utilities. Therefore, caution should be exercised in making comparisons of expenditures for utilities by consumers of various income classes and types of housing.

Descriptions of sampling and estimation methodology and additional data are published every two years in Bulletins. The most recent Bulletin is *BLS Bulletin 2462*, which covers 1992-1993.

Consumer Expenditures, Averages by Income Before Taxes, 1994

Item	All consumer units	Complete reporting of income									
		Complete reporting of income	Less than 5,000	5,000 to 9,999	10,000 to 14,999	15,000 to 19,999	20,000 to 29,999	30,000 to 39,999	40,000 to 49,999	50,000 to 69,999	70,000 and over
Number of consumer units (Thousands)	102 210	85 994	4 061	10 516	9 780	7 851	13 975	10 922	8 280	10 510	10 099
Income before taxes (Dollars)	36 838	36 838	2 390	7 502	12 340	17 229	24 721	34 402	44 388	58 417	110 955
Age of reference person	47.6	47.7	42.2	55.0	52.8	50.3	46.3	44.3	45.0	44.3	46.5
Average number in consumer unit											
Persons	2.5	2.5	1.8	1.8	2.1	2.3	2.5	2.8	2.9	3.1	3.1
Children under 18	0.7	0.7	0.5	0.5	0.6	0.6	0.7	0.8	0.9	0.9	0.8
Persons 65 and over	0.3	0.3	0.2	0.5	0.5	0.5	0.4	0.2	0.2	0.1	0.1
Earners	1.3	1.3	0.8	0.5	0.7	1.0	1.3	1.6	1.8	2.0	2.0
Vehicles	1.9	2.0	0.9	0.9	1.3	1.6	1.9	2.2	2.6	2.7	2.8
Percent homeowners	63	63	34	41	51	53	58	66	75	82	89
With mortgage	37	37	15	8	14	17	31	44	53	65	72
Without mortgage	26	26	19	33	37	35	27	23	21	18	17
Average annual expenditures (Dollars)	31 751	32 763	15 201	13 060	17 800	22 139	27 042	32 475	40 300	48 177	69 506
Food	4 411	4 527	2 579	2 347	3 042	3 526	3 932	4 655	5 387	6 409	7 985
Food at home	2 712	2 764	1 703	1 790	2 220	2 437	2 598	2 834	3 176	3 582	4 023
Cereals and bakery products	429	439	249	271	345	410	396	437	525	578	663
Meats, poultry, fish, and eggs	732	729	495	527	622	677	722	768	790	864	969
Dairy products	289	298	183	209	247	256	275	300	331	390	433
Fruits and vegetables	437	446	295	274	370	380	409	451	494	586	685
Other food at home	825	852	481	509	635	714	797	878	1 036	1 164	1 273
Food away from home	1 698	1 763	876	557	822	1 089	1 334	1 821	2 212	2 827	3 962
Alcoholic beverages	278	297	215	105	135	216	287	347	327	460	532
Housing	10 106	10 189	5 294	4 864	6 445	7 238	8 490	10 052	11 885	13 977	20 862
Shelter	5 686	5 696	3 027	2 606	3 488	4 021	4 727	5 652	6 543	7 816	11 912
Owned dwellings	3 492	3 464	1 148	819	1 342	1 662	2 210	3 264	4 261	5 898	9 371
Rented dwellings	1 799	1 829	1 639	1 693	2 000	2 116	2 233	2 138	1 858	1 385	1 199
Other lodging	395	403	239	94	146	243	284	250	424	534	1 342
Utilities, fuels, and public services	2 189	2 170	1 351	1 405	1 744	1 928	2 037	2 226	2 458	2 663	3 275
Household operations	490	500	174	180	232	279	375	405	545	685	1 441
Housekeeping supplies	393	424	256	215	284	291	379	431	517	641	728
Household furnishings and equipment ...	1 348	1 399	487	458	697	719	972	1 338	1 823	2 172	3 507
Apparel and services	1 644	1 688	845	599	790	1 080	1 465	1 673	1 891	2 463	3 944
Transportation	6 044	6 076	2 515	1 845	2 758	4 313	5 598	6 011	8 886	9 176	11 705
Vehicle purchases (Net outlay)	2 725	2 703	1 017	662	987	1 919	2 679	2 560	4 611	4 125	4 921
Gasoline and motor oil	986	990	504	458	606	749	949	1 123	1 276	1 369	1 582
Other vehicle expenses	1 953	1 989	783	596	967	1 353	1 715	2 014	2 607	3 141	4 067
Public transportation	381	393	211	129	198	292	255	315	392	541	1 134
Health care	1 755	1 768	903	1 186	1 484	1 666	1 579	1 762	2 008	2 210	2 694
Health insurance	815	818	365	595	790	848	768	791	934	946	1 109
Medical services	571	567	325	268	361	421	452	603	662	828	1 062
Drugs	286	294	169	283	284	321	281	284	301	315	353
Medical supplies	83	88	44	40	50	76	77	84	110	121	170
Entertainment	1 567	1 619	767	552	726	943	1 292	1 565	1 915	2 544	3 781
Personal care products and services	397	415	228	192	256	286	349	454	492	663	725
Reading	165	171	63	65	103	117	140	177	213	253	351
Education	460	469	632	256	254	293	238	292	482	614	1 327
Tobacco products and smoking supplies ...	259	262	184	172	222	251	281	341	295	317	237
Miscellaneous	749	811	417	356	500	638	633	890	999	1 179	1 510
Cash contributions	960	1 067	324	224	396	456	772	1 050	1 005	1 648	3 240
Personal insurance and pensions	2 957	3 404	235	297	687	1 116	1 986	3 207	4 514	6 264	10 612
Life and other personal insurance	398	413	99	120	213	249	293	350	503	632	1 101
Pensions and Social Security	2 559	2 991	136	176	474	867	1 693	2 856	4 011	5 633	9 511

Consumer Expenditures, Averages by Quintiles of Income Before Taxes, 1994

Item	All consumer units	Complete reporting of income						Incomplete reporting of income
		Total complete reporting	Lowest 20 percent	Second 20 percent	Third 20 percent	Fourth 20 percent	Highest 20 percent	
Number of consumer units (Thousands)	102 210	85 994	17 147	17 222	17 186	17 193	17 246	16 216
Income before taxes (Dollars)	36 838	36 838	6 748	15 906	27 511	43 421	90 390	0
Age of reference person	47.6	47.7	51.8	51.1	45.1	44.7	45.7	47.4
Average number in consumer unit								
Persons	2.5	2.5	1.8	2.3	2.5	2.9	3.1	2.6
Children under 18	0.7	0.7	0.5	0.6	0.7	0.9	0.9	0.7
Persons 65 and over	0.3	0.3	0.4	0.5	0.3	0.2	0.1	0.3
Earners	1.3	1.3	0.6	0.9	1.3	1.7	2.0	1.3
Vehicles	1.9	2.0	0.9	1.5	2.0	2.5	2.8	1.8
Percent homeowners	63	63	41	53	59	74	87	65
With mortgage	37	37	11	17	34	53	70	36
Without mortgage	26	26	30	36	25	22	17	30
Average annual expenditures (Dollars)	31 751	32 763	14 066	20 821	28 712	39 127	60 978	26 859
Food	4 411	4 527	2 488	3 347	4 091	5 348	7 353	3 987
Food at home	2 712	2 764	1 833	2 328	2 659	3 146	3 851	2 526
Cereals and bakery products	429	439	273	385	400	506	632	391
Meats, poultry, fish, and eggs	732	729	543	638	740	803	921	745
Dairy products	289	298	211	251	277	333	417	258
Fruits and vegetables	437	446	299	369	420	494	648	403
Other food at home	825	852	508	684	823	1 011	1 233	728
Food away from home	1 698	1 763	654	1 019	1 432	2 202	3 502	1 462
Alcoholic beverages	278	297	135	177	320	354	497	211
Housing	10 106	10 189	5 198	7 022	8 935	11 593	18 166	9 765
Shelter	5 686	5 696	2 848	3 870	5 012	6 442	10 288	5 635
Owned dwellings	3 492	3 464	988	1 574	2 490	4 265	7 984	3 638
Rented dwellings	1 799	1 829	1 723	2 094	2 247	1 800	1 279	1 645
Other lodging	395	403	136	203	274	377	1 024	352
Utilities, fuels, and public services	2 189	2 170	1 441	1 856	2 080	2 421	3 050	2 285
Household operations	490	500	185	272	380	518	1 142	431
Housekeeping supplies	393	424	231	300	382	528	679	285
Household furnishings and equipment	1 348	1 399	494	724	1 082	1 684	3 008	1 128
Apparel and services	1 644	1 688	680	995	1 490	1 905	3 367	1 465
Transportation	6 044	6 076	2 046	3 870	5 710	8 053	10 677	5 879
Vehicle purchases (Net outlay)	2 725	2 703	726	1 673	2 652	3 938	4 517	2 839
Gasoline and motor oil	986	990	484	703	1 007	1 258	1 496	964
Other vehicle expenses	1 953	1 989	690	1 218	1 799	2 473	3 758	1 760
Public transportation	381	393	147	275	252	384	907	315
Health care	1 755	1 768	1 114	1 607	1 653	2 008	2 455	1 702
Health insurance	815	818	564	816	771	895	1 044	796
Medical services	571	567	266	417	509	710	933	591
Drugs	286	294	243	309	294	292	333	255
Medical supplies	83	88	40	65	80	111	144	59
Entertainment	1 567	1 619	618	892	1 401	1 881	3 297	1 309
Personal care products and services	397	415	204	285	374	524	686	333
Reading	165	171	68	118	145	209	315	130
Education	460	469	373	248	253	402	1 069	414
Tobacco products and smoking supplies	259	262	179	249	293	321	267	242
Miscellaneous	749	811	374	575	757	947	1 398	439
Cash contributions	960	1 067	274	431	913	1 274	2 436	396
Personal insurance and pensions	2 957	3 404	315	1 006	2 376	4 306	8 995	587
Life and other personal insurance	398	413	120	238	320	459	929	314
Pensions and Social Security	2 559	2 991	195	768	2 056	3 848	8 066	273

Consumer Expenditures, Averages by Age of Reference Person, 1994

Item	All consumer units	Under 25 years	25 to 34 years	35 to 44 years	45 to 54 years	55 to 64 years	65 years and over	65 to 74 years	75 years and over
Number of consumer units (Thousands)	102 210	7 453	20 606	22 825	17 812	12 015	21 500	12 038	9 463
Income before taxes (Dollars)	36 838	16 407	34 051	46 217	49 627	41 884	23 835	26 266	20 736
Age of reference person	47.6	21.7	29.9	39.3	49.2	59.4	74.7	69.5	81.3
Average number in consumer unit									
Persons	2.5	2.0	2.8	3.2	2.8	2.2	1.7	1.8	1.5
Children under 18	0.7	0.5	1.1	1.4	0.6	0.2	0.1	0.1	0.0
Persons 65 and over	0.3	0.0	0.0	0.0	0.0	0.1	1.3	1.4	1.3
Earners	1.3	1.3	1.4	1.7	1.8	1.3	0.4	0.6	0.2
Vehicles	1.9	1.2	1.8	2.2	2.6	2.1	1.4	1.6	1.1
Percent homeowner	63	12	41	66	77	79	79	81	76
With mortgage	37	8	34	56	55	37	13	19	6
Without mortgage	26	4	7	10	22	42	66	62	71
Average annual expenditures (Dollars)	31 751	18 418	30 466	37 588	41 444	33 702	22 557	25 093	19 306
Food	4 411	2 793	4 159	5 367	5 614	4 549	3 251	3 543	2 871
Food at home	2 712	1 617	2 454	3 336	3 319	2 733	2 245	2 346	2 112
Cereals and bakery products	429	250	387	536	512	414	368	385	346
Meats, poultry, fish, and eggs	732	429	650	919	936	773	555	596	500
Dairy products	289	180	261	360	338	272	253	257	248
Fruits and vegetables	437	238	384	507	522	448	416	415	417
Other food at home	825	519	771	1 014	1 012	826	652	692	600
Food away from home	1 698	1 177	1 706	2 031	2 295	1 816	1 006	1 196	759
Alcoholic beverages	278	247	347	296	292	338	164	231	77
Housing	10 106	5 594	10 065	12 274	12 457	10 222	7 445	8 017	6 712
Shelter	5 686	3 481	5 972	7 173	7 024	5 253	3 733	3 951	3 456
Owned dwellings	3 492	473	2 709	4 963	5 069	3 691	2 307	2 624	1 905
Rented dwellings	1 799	2 840	3 074	1 841	1 318	1 007	1 013	838	1 236
Other lodging	395	168	188	368	636	555	412	488	315
Utilities, fuels, and public services	2 189	1 210	1 948	2 428	2 603	2 417	2 033	2 165	1 866
Household operations	490	188	568	673	416	404	435	385	500
Housekeeping supplies	393	171	340	435	464	453	396	440	338
Household furnishings and equipment	1 348	544	1 237	1 565	1 950	1 696	847	1 076	552
Apparel and services	1 644	1 107	1 748	2 054	2 262	1 586	873	1 056	635
Transportation	6 044	4 409	6 523	6 796	7 893	6 504	3 572	4 205	2 766
Vehicle purchases (Net outlay)	2 725	2 330	3 347	2 984	3 387	2 909	1 338	1 536	1 087
Gasoline and motor oil	986	670	982	1 193	1 295	1 005	614	765	421
Other vehicle expenses	1 953	1 201	1 931	2 248	2 720	2 113	1 202	1 449	888
Public transportation	381	208	264	372	492	477	418	455	370
Health care	1 755	505	1 086	1 616	1 855	2 144	2 678	2 592	2 787
Health insurance	815	186	479	689	772	895	1 479	1 467	1 496
Medical services	571	218	407	627	673	791	583	539	639
Drugs	286	71	138	213	291	349	541	504	588
Medical supplies	83	31	61	86	119	110	75	82	65
Entertainment	1 567	1 018	1 519	2 025	2 104	1 565	879	1 055	656
Personal care products and services	397	234	396	457	507	393	311	331	285
Reading	165	65	136	184	204	202	153	169	133
Education	460	812	368	483	882	351	114	178	33
Tobacco products and smoking supplies	259	217	270	319	327	302	117	152	73
Miscellaneous	749	255	620	908	1 071	814	573	640	488
Cash contributions	960	96	381	788	1 436	1 292	1 419	1 567	1 230
Personal insurance and pensions	2 957	1 067	2 847	4 022	4 539	3 440	1 007	1 359	559
Life and other personal insurance	398	62	232	439	590	554	382	523	203
Pensions and Social Security	2 559	1 005	2 616	3 583	3 949	2 886	624	836	356

Consumer Expenditures, Averages by Size of Consumer Unit, 1994

Item	All consumer units	One person	Two or more persons	Two persons	Three persons	Four persons	Five or more persons
Number of consumer units (Thousands)	102 210	29 097	73 113	32 012	15 863	14 718	10 520
Income before taxes (Dollars)	36 838	21 347	43 187	40 384	43 371	47 432	45 330
Age of reference person	47.6	51.3	46.2	52.5	43.1	39.4	41
Average number in consumer unit							
Persons	2.5	1.0	3.1	2.0	3.0	4.0	5.6
Children under 18	0.7	0.0	1.0	0.1	0.8	1.7	2.9
Persons 65 and over	0.3	0.3	0.3	0.5	0.2	0.1	0.1
Earners	1.3	0.6	1.6	1.2	1.7	2.0	2.2
Vehicles	1.9	1.0	2.3	2.1	2.3	2.5	2.4
Percent homeowners	63	45	70	72	66	72	68
With mortgage	37	17	44	34	46	58	54
Without mortgage	26	28	26	38	20	13	15
Average annual expenditures (Dollars)	31 751	19 345	36 686	33 088	36 750	41 514	40 732
Food	4 411	2 464	5 184	4 324	5 135	6 063	6 614
Food at home	2 712	1 386	3 239	2 549	3 212	3 797	4 579
Cereals and bakery products	429	220	512	394	509	602	743
Meats, poultry, fish, and eggs	732	348	885	675	872	1 039	1 324
Dairy products	289	151	344	267	339	407	495
Fruits and vegetables	437	252	510	425	507	579	676
Other food at home	825	415	989	789	985	1 170	1 341
Food away from home	1 698	1 079	1 945	1 776	1 923	2 266	2 036
Alcoholic beverages	278	255	287	328	267	273	212
Housing	10 106	6 650	11 482	10 332	11 438	13 177	12 669
Shelter	5 686	4 089	6 322	5 729	6 193	7 241	7 037
Owned dwellings	3 492	1 691	4 208	3 636	3 997	5 224	4 848
Rented dwellings	1 799	2 179	1 648	1 532	1 804	1 603	1 831
Other lodging	395	219	465	561	392	415	358
Utilities, fuels, and public services	2 189	1 404	2 501	2 283	2 489	2 731	2 856
Household operations	490	225	596	411	629	865	730
Housekeeping supplies	393	209	467	432	486	472	533
Household furnishings and equipment	1 348	722	1 597	1 477	1 641	1 869	1 513
Apparel and services	1 644	876	1 949	1 519	2 124	2 338	2 436
Transportation	6 044	3 374	7 107	6 361	7 452	7 961	7 660
Vehicle purchases (Net outlay)	2 725	1 454	3 230	2 742	3 653	3 723	3 390
Gasoline and motor oil	986	526	1 169	1 029	1 159	1 347	1 360
Other vehicle expenses	1 953	1 119	2 284	2 090	2 301	2 531	2 506
Public transportation	381	275	423	500	340	360	404
Health care	1 755	1 178	1 984	2 171	1 801	1 865	1 859
Health insurance	815	546	922	1 056	806	848	793
Medical services	571	363	654	635	619	670	742
Drugs	286	225	310	380	269	254	238
Medical supplies	83	44	98	100	107	94	87
Entertainment	1 567	945	1 814	1 623	1 757	2 128	2 042
Personal care products and services	397	231	462	408	491	507	519
Reading	165	127	180	191	161	186	168
Education	460	284	530	385	572	698	671
Tobacco products and smoking supplies	259	159	298	263	325	312	346
Miscellaneous	749	558	824	787	757	959	852
Cash contributions	960	737	1 049	1 256	881	871	924
Personal insurance and pensions	2 957	1 507	3 534	3 139	3 587	4 177	3 760
Life and other personal insurance	398	159	493	485	470	528	501
Pensions and Social Security	2 559	1 348	3 042	2 654	3 117	3 648	3 259

Consumer Expenditures, Averages by Composition of Consumer Unit, 1994

Item	All consumer units	Total	Husband and wife consumer units						One parent, at least one child under 18 years	Single person and other consumer units
			Husband and wife only	Husband and wife with children				Other husband and wife consumer units		
				Total	Oldest child under 6 years	Oldest child 6 to 17 years	Oldest child 18 years or over			
Number of consumer units (Thousands)	102 210	53 578	22 017	27 572	5 529	14 965	7 079	3 989	7 065	41 567
Income before taxes (Dollars)	36 838	48 919	45 100	52 005	45 202	51 947	58 006	48 311	19 069	24 401
Age of reference person	47.6	47.5	56.0	40.7	31.2	39.2	51.2	47.5	35.7	49.9
Average number in consumer unit										
Persons	2.5	3.2	2.0	4.0	3.5	4.2	3.8	5.0	2.9	1.6
Children under 18	0.7	1.0	0.0	1.6	1.5	2.2	0.5	1.7	1.8	0.2
Persons 65 and over	0.3	0.3	0.7	0.0	0.0	0.0	0.2	0.5	0.0	0.3
Earners	1.3	1.7	1.2	2.0	1.6	1.9	2.7	2.3	0.9	0.9
Vehicles	1.9	2.6	2.3	2.7	2.2	2.5	3.4	2.9	1.0	1.3
Percent homeowners	63	79	82	77	62	77	88	78	31	48
With mortgage	37	52	38	62	55	66	58	56	23	20
Without mortgage	26	28	44	15	8	11	30	22	9	28
Average annual expenditures (Dollars)	31 751	40 731	36 198	44 088	38 560	44 145	48 489	42 386	21 671	21 861
Food	4 411	5 614	4 650	6 276	4 880	6 558	6 921	6 229	3 599	2 986
Food at home	2 712	3 432	2 689	3 895	3 282	4 015	4 205	4 311	2 626	1 800
Cereals and bakery products	429	550	422	636	534	665	672	646	409	276
Meats, poultry, fish, and eggs	732	909	700	1 026	808	1 072	1 131	1 262	802	496
Dairy products	289	367	280	423	346	446	448	454	268	192
Fruits and vegetables	437	548	458	603	511	616	662	666	374	302
Other food at home	825	1 058	829	1 206	1 084	1 216	1 293	1 284	772	535
Food away from home	1 698	2 182	1 961	2 382	1 597	2 543	2 716	1 918	973	1 186
Alcoholic beverages	278	307	343	288	267	264	354	229	89	269
Housing	10 106	12 551	11 087	13 658	13 114	14 231	12 902	12 984	8 178	7 274
Shelter	5 686	6 877	6 048	7 531	7 315	7 951	6 815	6 935	4 675	4 323
Owned dwellings	3 492	4 999	4 250	5 605	4 818	6 047	5 283	4 948	1 763	1 843
Rented dwellings	1 799	1 312	1 091	1 453	2 300	1 444	810	1 556	2 810	2 256
Other lodging	395	567	707	474	198	459	722	431	102	224
Utilities, fuels, and public services	2 189	2 632	2 391	2 773	2 364	2 750	3 143	2 983	1 942	1 659
Household operations	490	653	414	863	1 504	885	317	521	628	257
Housekeeping supplies	393	522	487	542	478	550	584	576	244	250
Household furnishings and equipment	1 348	1 866	1 746	1 948	1 453	2 096	2 044	1 969	689	786
Apparel and services	1 644	2 117	1 639	2 427	2 071	2 485	2 597	2 576	1 624	1 042
Transportation	6 044	7 993	6 929	8 770	8 382	7 765	11 188	8 475	3 246	4 005
Vehicle purchases (Net outlay)	2 725	3 662	2 975	4 166	4 634	3 464	5 284	3 972	1 395	1 742
Gasoline and motor oil	986	1 292	1 105	1 419	1 176	1 342	1 773	1 437	619	654
Other vehicle expenses	1 953	2 562	2 264	2 779	2 313	2 555	3 605	2 695	1 048	1 318
Public transportation	381	477	584	406	260	404	526	370	184	291
Health care	1 755	2 274	2 555	2 049	1 775	2 008	2 347	2 281	884	1 233
Health insurance	815	1 060	1 247	895	772	870	1 044	1 166	391	571
Medical services	571	747	740	773	762	783	758	608	351	382
Drugs	286	354	451	275	180	249	401	371	97	229
Medical supplies	83	113	117	107	61	106	144	136	45	51
Entertainment	1 567	2 039	1 786	2 272	1 657	2 475	2 338	1 816	1 057	1 045
Personal care products and services	397	504	451	530	428	540	595	627	316	272
Reading	165	203	212	200	158	207	216	169	84	130
Education	460	600	392	787	203	715	1 407	448	299	307
Tobacco products and smoking supplies	259	290	232	316	266	287	415	424	219	225
Miscellaneous	749	869	785	916	689	951	1 014	1 018	535	629
Cash contributions	960	1 262	1 577	993	608	960	1 364	1 376	216	698
Personal insurance and pensions	2 957	4 111	3 561	4 605	4 061	4 699	4 832	3 735	1 326	1 747
Life and other personal insurance	398	590	599	584	440	582	702	587	189	185
Pensions and Social Security	2 559	3 521	2 962	4 021	3 621	4 117	4 130	3 149	1 137	1 562

Consumer Expenditures, Averages by Number of Earners, 1994

Item	All consumer units	Single consumers		Consumer units of two or more persons			
		No earner	One earner	No earner	One earner	Two earners	Three or more earners
Number of consumer units (Thousands)	102 210	11 432	17 665	10 612	19 886	33 584	9 031
Income before taxes (Dollars)	36 838	11 403	27 485	20 239	33 505	52 191	57 726
Age of reference person	47.6	69.9	39.4	61.3	46.4	41.3	46.2
Average number in consumer unit							
Persons	2.5	1.0	1.0	2.5	3.0	3.1	4.3
Children under 18	0.7	0.0	0.0	0.6	1.1	1.0	1.2
Persons 65 and over	0.3	0.8	0.1	1.1	0.3	0.1	0.1
Earners	1.3	0.0	1.0	0.0	1.0	2.0	3.3
Vehicles	1.9	0.7	1.2	1.6	1.8	2.5	3.4
Percent homeowners	63	59	36	68	62	73	82
With mortgage	37	8	24	13	35	55	62
Without mortgage	26	52	12	56	27	17	20
Average annual expenditures (Dollars)	31 751	14 219	22 644	22 887	31 518	40 616	49 044
Food	4 411	2 138	2 670	3 882	4 621	5 398	6 864
Food at home	2 712	1 528	1 297	2 690	3 202	3 165	4 131
Cereals and bakery products	429	236	210	443	504	501	634
Meats, poultry, fish, and eggs	732	399	317	709	917	840	1 164
Dairy products	289	183	131	285	338	338	436
Fruits and vegetables	437	304	219	441	517	489	640
Other food at home	825	407	420	813	926	997	1 257
Food away from home	1 698	611	1 373	1 191	1 419	2 233	2 732
Alcoholic beverages	278	96	354	197	231	331	332
Housing	10 106	5 455	7 423	7 655	10 572	12 665	13 467
Shelter	5 686	2 961	4 819	3 695	5 973	7 094	7 305
Owned dwellings	3 492	1 342	1 917	2 004	3 559	4 952	5 462
Rented dwellings	1 799	1 446	2 653	1 302	1 981	1 659	1 283
Other lodging	395	173	248	389	433	483	559
Utilities, fuels, and public services	2 189	1 427	1 389	2 125	2 405	2 512	3 112
Household operations	490	306	173	359	583	724	421
Housekeeping supplies	393	236	193	461	427	468	538
Household furnishings and equipment	1 348	525	849	1 016	1 185	1 867	2 092
Apparel and services	1 644	460	1 139	1 036	1 834	2 061	2 763
Transportation	6 044	1 889	4 333	3 470	5 600	8 034	11 220
Vehicle purchases (Net outlay)	2 725	766	1 899	1 188	2 484	3 732	5 410
Gasoline and motor oil	986	294	677	686	957	1 285	1 771
Other vehicle expenses	1 953	618	1 441	1 199	1 757	2 599	3 518
Public transportation	381	211	316	397	401	418	520
Health care	1 755	1 713	832	2 478	1 850	1 861	2 154
Health insurance	815	884	327	1 332	847	824	973
Medical services	571	435	316	505	634	689	740
Drugs	286	348	146	552	291	243	313
Medical supplies	83	45	44	89	78	105	127
Entertainment	1 567	513	1 224	1 005	1 486	2 103	2 397
Personal care products and services	397	179	264	346	379	495	627
Reading	165	101	143	143	151	200	214
Education	460	100	403	230	367	569	1 091
Tobacco products and smoking supplies	259	119	185	184	282	314	410
Miscellaneous	749	417	649	493	733	942	976
Cash contributions	960	888	639	1 307	939	954	1 342
Personal insurance and pensions	2 957	150	2 385	462	2 474	4 689	5 187
Life and other personal insurance	398	131	176	372	392	541	677
Pensions and Social Security	2 559	19	2 208	89	2 082	4 148	4 510

Consumer Expenditures, Averages by Housing Tenure, Race, and Type of Area, 1994

Item	All consumer units	Housing tenure		Race of consumer unit		Type of area	
		Homeowner	Renter	White and other	Black	Urban	Rural
Number of consumer units (Thousands)	102 210	64 510	37 700	90 740	11 470	87 829	14 381
Income before taxes (Dollars)	36 838	44 519	23 925	38 212	25 250	37 620	31 957
Age of reference person	47.6	52.2	39.8	48.0	44.8	47.3	49.6
Average number in consumer unit							
Persons	2.5	2.7	2.3	2.5	2.8	2.5	2.6
Children under 18	0.7	0.7	0.7	0.7	1.0	0.7	0.7
Persons 65 and over	0.3	0.4	0.2	0.3	0.2	0.3	0.3
Earners	1.3	1.4	1.1	1.3	1.2	1.3	1.4
Vehicles	1.9	2.3	1.2	2.0	1.2	1.8	2.7
Percent homeowners	63	100	0	66	41	60	81
With mortgage	37	58	0	38	24	37	37
Without mortgage	26	42	0	28	17	24	44
Average annual expenditures (Dollars)	31 751	37 001	22 738	32 935	22 418	32 247	28 724
Food	4 411	4 995	3 397	4 542	3 390	4 435	4 263
Food at home	2 712	3 016	2 184	2 754	2 390	2 703	2 765
Cereals and bakery products	429	487	327	440	343	425	450
Meats, poultry, fish, and eggs	732	791	630	716	858	733	730
Dairy products	289	322	232	301	193	287	299
Fruits and vegetables	437	488	346	445	370	442	405
Other food at home	825	927	649	851	627	816	882
Food away from home	1 698	1 980	1 212	1 788	1 000	1 731	1 498
Alcoholic beverages	278	286	264	295	149	290	203
Housing	10 106	11 474	7 759	10 415	7 673	10 539	7 463
Shelter	5 686	6 061	5 044	5 866	4 261	6 039	3 535
Owned dwellings	3 492	5 502	51	3 719	1 695	3 645	2 555
Rented dwellings	1 799	37	4 815	1 718	2 443	1 975	724
Other lodging	395	522	178	429	124	418	255
Utilities, fuels, and public services	2 189	2 596	1 491	2 189	2 182	2 186	2 205
Household operations	490	612	282	518	267	527	264
Housekeeping supplies	393	486	232	409	271	394	390
Household furnishings and equipment	1 348	1 718	710	1 432	692	1 394	1 069
Apparel and services	1 644	1 880	1 236	1 651	1 592	1 716	1 207
Transportation	6 044	7 022	4 371	6 268	4 271	5 919	6 807
Vehicle purchases (Net outlay)	2 725	3 106	2 072	2 814	2 014	2 581	3 601
Gasoline and motor oil	986	1 146	712	1 020	713	946	1 232
Other vehicle expenses	1 953	2 311	1 338	2 037	1 283	1 982	1 772
Public transportation	381	458	249	396	261	410	203
Health care	1 755	2 221	957	1 860	923	1 697	2 109
Health insurance	815	1 042	427	858	476	784	1 003
Medical services	571	716	323	615	223	560	637
Drugs	286	360	158	301	168	275	353
Medical supplies	83	103	48	86	56	78	116
Entertainment	1 567	1 895	1 004	1 668	767	1 572	1 536
Personal care products and services	397	453	300	401	360	410	314
Reading	165	198	107	176	77	169	136
Education	460	506	381	485	259	487	296
Tobacco products and smoking supplies	259	254	267	266	202	247	327
Miscellaneous	749	860	557	789	428	760	677
Cash contributions	960	1 283	408	1 019	494	986	805
Personal insurance and pensions	2 957	3 675	1 729	3 099	1 833	3 019	2 579
Life and other personal insurance	398	537	159	407	321	394	418
Pensions and Social Security	2 559	3 138	1 570	2 692	1 512	2 625	2 161

Consumer Expenditures, Averages by Region of Residence, 1994

Item	All consumer units	Northeast	Midwest	South	West
Number of consumer units (Thousands)	102 210	20 473	25 983	34 374	21 380
Income before taxes (Dollars)	36 838	39 464	33 628	34 002	42 219
Age of reference person	47.6	49.4	47.5	47.5	46.4
Average number in consumer unit					
Persons	2.5	2.5	2.5	2.5	2.7
Children under 18	0.7	0.7	0.7	0.7	0.8
Persons 65 and over	0.3	0.4	0.3	0.3	0.3
Earners	1.3	1.2	1.3	1.3	1.4
Vehicles	1.9	1.5	2.1	1.8	2.2
Percent homeowners	63	60	65	66	59
With mortgage	37	33	38	37	40
Without mortgage	26	27	28	29	20
Average annual expenditures (Dollars)	31 751	32 565	30 335	30 086	35 368
Food	4 411	4 706	4 201	4 251	4 639
Food at home	2 712	2 934	2 537	2 618	2 862
Cereals and bakery products	429	481	412	402	441
Meats, poultry, fish, and eggs	732	840	647	750	705
Dairy products	289	319	269	271	313
Fruits and vegetables	437	509	401	404	463
Other food at home	825	785	809	791	940
Food away from home	1 698	1 772	1 664	1 633	1 777
Alcoholic beverages	278	313	246	262	309
Housing	10 106	11 327	9 147	9 059	11 786
Shelter	5 686	6 724	4 922	4 723	7 171
Owned dwellings	3 492	4 088	3 153	2 919	4 252
Rented dwellings	1 799	2 119	1 389	1 498	2 475
Other lodging	395	517	380	305	443
Utilities, fuels, and public services	2 189	2 336	2 104	2 269	2 022
Household operations	490	496	405	480	605
Housekeeping supplies	393	409	386	372	422
Household furnishings and equipment	1 348	1 362	1 330	1 217	1 567
Apparel and services	1 644	1 913	1 622	1 459	1 710
Transportation	6 044	5 111	6 201	6 141	6 592
Vehicle purchases (Net outlay)	2 725	1 864	3 089	2 937	2 764
Gasoline and motor oil	986	832	977	1 035	1 064
Other vehicle expenses	1 953	1 866	1 815	1 889	2 306
Public transportation	381	550	320	280	457
Health care	1 755	1 679	1 698	1 854	1 737
Health insurance	815	816	806	868	740
Medical services	571	548	507	578	661
Drugs	286	248	301	321	247
Medical supplies	83	67	85	87	89
Entertainment	1 567	1 517	1 551	1 417	1 875
Personal care products and services	397	394	384	386	430
Reading	165	191	161	136	191
Education	460	504	451	404	517
Tobacco products and smoking supplies	259	255	291	271	202
Miscellaneous	749	669	767	681	910
Cash contributions	960	1 034	897	1 004	896
Personal insurance and pensions	2 957	2 950	2 717	2 760	3 573
Life and other personal insurance	398	412	395	432	332
Pensions and Social Security	2 559	2 538	2 322	2 328	3 241

Part Seven

Occupational Injuries and Illnesses

Occupational Injuries and Illnesses

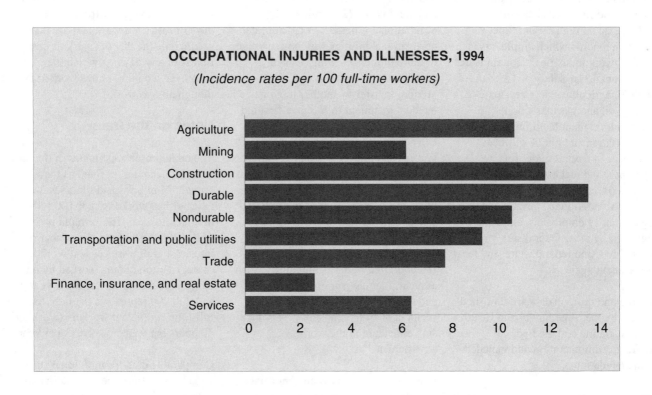

OCCUPATIONAL INJURIES AND ILLNESSES, 1994

(Incidence rates per 100 full-time workers)

This chart shows that there is a particularly high rate of occupational injuries and illnesses for durable goods manufacturing industries. This rate even exceeds that of the construction industry where a higher rate might have been expected. Conversely, the rate of occupational injuries and illnesses in the mining sector is relatively low.

NOTES

Occupational Injuries and Illnesses

Description of the Series

The Annual Survey of Occupational Injuries and Illnesses is designed to collect data on injuries and illnesses based on records which employers in the following industries maintain under the Occupational Safety and Health Act of 1970: agriculture, forestry, and fishing; oil and gas extraction; construction; manufacturing; transportation and public utilities; wholesale and retail trade; finance, insurance, and real estate; and services. Excluded from the survey are self-employed individuals, farmers with fewer than 11 employees, employers regulated by other federal safety and health laws, and federal, state, and local government agencies.

Mining and railroad data are furnished to BLS by the Mine Safety and Health Administration and the Federal Railroad Administration and included in the tabulations.

Industry data are classified according to the 1987 *Standard Industrial Classification Manual*.

Definitions

Recordable occupational injuries and illnesses are: (1) in the 1985-1991 surveys only, occupational deaths, regardless of the time between injury and death, or the length of the illness; and in all years, (2) nonfatal occupational illnesses; or (3) nonfatal occupational injuries which involve one or more of the following: loss of consciousness, restriction of work or motion, transfer to another job, or medical treatment (other than first aid). Beginning with the 1992 survey, the annual survey measures only nonfatal injuries and illnesses. To better address fatalities BLS implemented the Census of Fatal Occupational Injuries, data from which are published in the BLS, *Compensation and Working Conditions*, and other publications.

Occupational injury is any injury, such as a cut, fracture, sprain, amputation, and so forth, that results from a work accident or from exposure involving a single incident in the work environment.

Occupational illness is an abnormal condition or disorder, other than one resulting from an occupational injury, caused by exposure to environmental factors associated with employment. It includes acute and chronic illness or disease which may be caused by inhalation, absorption, ingestion, or direct contact.

Lost workday cases are cases which involve days away from work, or days of restricted work activity, or both. The number of days away from work or days of restricted work activity does not include the day of injury or onset of illness or any days on which the employee would not have worked even though able to work.

Notes on the Data

The table presents estimates in the form of incidence rates, defined as the number of injuries and illnesses or cases of lost workdays per 100 full-time employees. The formula is (N/EH) x 200,000, where N=number of injuries and illnesses or lost workday cases, EH=total hours worked by all employees during the calendar year, and 200,000 represents the base for 100 full-time equivalent workers (working 40 hours per week, 50 weeks per year).

Comparable data for individual states are available from the BLS Office of Safety, Health, and Working Conditions.

For further information, consult recent issues of the *Monthly Labor Review*.

Occupational Injury and Illness Incidence Rates by Industry, 1989-1994

(Incidence rates per 100 full-time workers)

Industry and type of case	1989	1990	1991	1992	1993	1994
PRIVATE INDUSTRY						
Total cases	8.6	8.8	8.4	8.9	8.5	8.4
Lost workday cases	4.0	4.1	3.9	3.9	3.8	3.8
Agriculture, forestry, and fishing						
Total cases	10.9	11.6	10.8	11.6	11.2	10.0
Lost workday cases	5.7	5.9	5.4	5.4	5.0	4.7
Mining						
Total cases	8.5	8.3	7.4	7.3	6.8	6.3
Lost workday cases	4.8	5.0	4.5	4.1	3.9	3.9
Construction						
Total cases	14.3	14.2	13.0	13.1	12.2	11.8
Lost workday cases	6.8	6.7	6.1	5.8	5.5	5.5
General building contractors						
Total cases	13.9	13.4	12.0	12.2	11.5	10.9
Lost workday cases	6.5	6.4	5.5	5.4	5.1	5.1
Heavy construction, except building						
Total cases	13.8	13.8	12.8	12.1	11.1	10.2
Lost workday cases	6.5	6.3	6.0	5.4	5.1	5.0
Special trade contractors						
Total cases	14.6	14.7	13.5	13.8	12.8	12.5
Lost workday cases	6.9	6.9	6.3	6.1	5.8	5.8
Manufacturing						
Total cases	13.1	13.2	12.7	12.5	12.1	12.2
Lost workday cases	5.8	5.8	5.6	5.4	5.3	5.5
Durable goods						
Total cases	14.1	14.2	13.6	13.4	13.1	13.5
Lost workday cases	6.0	6.0	5.7	5.5	5.4	5.7
Lumber and wood products						
Total cases	18.4	18.1	16.8	16.3	15.9	15.7
Lost workday cases	9.4	8.8	8.3	7.6	7.6	7.7
Furniture and fixtures						
Total cases	16.1	16.9	15.9	14.8	14.6	15.0
Lost workday cases	7.2	7.8	7.2	6.6	6.5	7.0
Stone, clay, and glass products						
Total cases	15.5	15.4	14.8	13.6	13.8	13.2
Lost workday cases	7.4	7.3	6.8	6.1	6.3	6.5
Primary metal industries						
Total cases	18.7	19.0	17.7	17.5	17.0	16.8
Lost workday cases	8.1	8.1	7.4	7.1	7.3	7.2
Fabricated metal products						
Total cases	18.5	18.7	17.4	16.8	16.2	16.4
Lost workday cases	7.9	7.9	7.1	6.6	6.7	6.7
Industrial machinery and equipment						
Total cases	12.1	12.0	11.2	11.1	11.1	11.6
Lost workday cases	4.8	4.7	4.4	4.2	4.2	4.4
Electronic and other electrical equipment						
Total cases	9.1	9.1	8.6	8.4	8.3	8.3
Lost workday cases	3.9	3.8	3.7	3.6	3.5	3.6
Transportation equipment						
Total cases	17.7	17.8	18.3	18.7	18.5	19.6
Lost workday cases	6.8	6.9	7.0	7.1	7.1	7.8
Instruments and related products						
Total cases	5.6	5.9	6.0	5.9	5.6	5.9
Lost workday cases	2.5	2.7	2.7	2.7	2.5	2.7
Miscellaneous manufacturing industries						
Total cases	11.1	11.3	11.3	10.7	10.0	9.9
Lost workday cases	5.1	5.1	5.1	5.0	4.6	4.5

Occupational Injury and Illness Incidence Rates by Industry, 1989-1994—Continued

(Incidence rates per 100 full-time workers)

Industry and type of case	1989	1990	1991	1992	1993	1994
Nondurable goods						
Total cases	11.6	11.7	11.5	11.3	10.7	10.5
Lost workday cases	5.5	5.6	5.5	5.3	5.0	5.1
Food and kindred products						
Total cases	18.5	20.0	19.5	18.8	17.6	17.1
Lost workday cases	9.3	9.9	9.9	9.5	8.9	9.2
Tobacco products						
Total cases	8.7	7.7	6.4	6.0	5.8	5.3
Lost workday cases	3.4	3.2	2.8	2.4	2.3	2.4
Textile mill products						
Total cases	10.3	9.6	10.0	9.9	9.7	8.7
Lost workday cases	4.2	4.0	4.4	4.2	4.1	4.0
Apparel and other textile products						
Total cases	8.6	8.8	9.2	9.5	9.0	8.9
Lost workday cases	3.8	3.9	4.2	4.0	3.8	3.9
Paper and allied products						
Total cases	12.7	12.1	11.2	11.0	9.9	9.6
Lost workday cases	5.8	5.5	5.0	5.0	4.6	4.5
Printing and publishing						
Total cases	6.9	6.9	6.7	7.3	6.9	6.7
Lost workday cases	3.3	3.3	3.2	3.2	3.1	3.0
Chemicals and allied products						
Total cases	7.0	6.5	6.4	6.0	5.9	5.7
Lost workday cases	3.2	3.1	3.1	2.8	2.7	2.8
Petroleum and coal products						
Total cases	6.6	6.6	6.2	5.9	5.2	4.7
Lost workday cases	3.3	3.1	2.9	2.8	2.5	2.3
Rubber and miscellaneous plastics products						
Total cases	16.2	16.2	15.1	14.5	13.9	14.0
Lost workday cases	8.0	7.8	7.2	6.8	6.5	6.7
Leather and leather products						
Total cases	13.6	12.1	12.5	12.1	12.1	12.0
Lost workday cases	6.5	5.9	5.9	5.4	5.5	5.3
Transportation and public utilities						
Total cases	9.2	9.6	9.3	9.1	9.5	9.3
Lost workday cases	5.3	5.5	5.4	5.1	5.4	5.5
Wholesale and retail trade						
Total cases	8.0	7.9	7.6	8.4	8.1	7.9
Lost workday cases	3.6	3.5	3.4	3.5	3.4	3.4
Wholesale trade						
Total cases	7.7	7.4	7.2	7.6	7.8	7.7
Lost workday cases	4.0	3.7	3.7	3.6	3.7	3.8
Retail trade						
Total cases	8.1	8.1	7.7	8.7	8.2	7.9
Lost workday cases	3.4	3.4	3.3	3.4	3.3	3.3
Finance, insurance, and real estate						
Total cases	2.0	2.4	2.4	2.9	2.9	2.7
Lost workday cases	0.9	1.1	1.1	1.2	1.2	1.1
Services						
Total cases	5.5	6.0	6.2	7.1	6.7	6.5
Lost workday cases	2.7	2.8	2.8	3.0	2.8	2.8

NOTE: Beginning with the 1992 survey, the annual survey measures only nonfatal injuries and illnesses; there is a separate Census of Fatal Occupational Injuries.

Part Eight

Work Stoppages

Work Stoppages Involving 1000 Workers or More

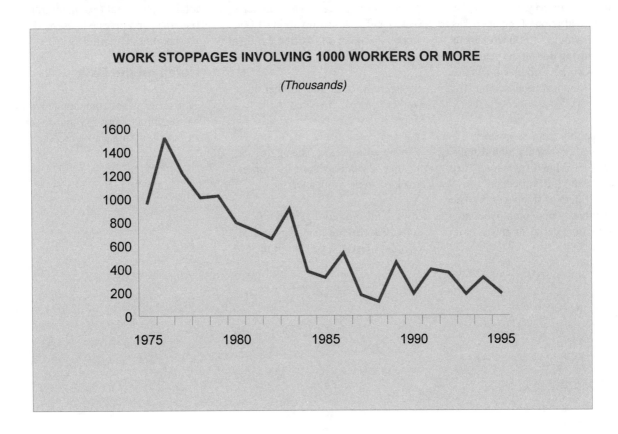

WORK STOPPAGES INVOLVING 1000 WORKERS OR MORE

(Thousands)

Workers in large plants involved in work stoppages dropped dramatically over the last twenty years as shown in the chart above. The number of stoppages and days idle also dropped.

NOTES
Work Stoppages

Description of the Series

Data on work stoppages measure the number and duration of major strikes or lockouts (involving 1,000 workers or more) occurring during the year, the number of workers involved, and the amount of time lost because of stoppage.

Data are largely from newspaper accounts and cover only establishments directly involved in a stoppage. They do not measure the indirect or secondary effect of stoppages on other establishments whose employees are idle owing to material shortages or lack of service.

Definitions

Number of stoppages. The number of strikes and lockouts involving 1,000 workers or more and lasting a full shift or longer.

Workers involved. The number of workers directly involved in the stoppage.

Number of days idle. The aggregate number of workdays lost by workers involved in the stoppages.

Days of idleness as a percent of estimated working time. Aggregate workdays lost as a percent of the aggregate number of standard workdays in the period multiplied by total employment (excluding forestry, fisheries, and private household workers) in the period.

Notes on the Data

This series is not comparable with the one terminated in 1981 that covered strikes involving six workers or more.

Work Stoppages Involving 1,000 Workers or More, 1985-1995

Year	Stoppages beginning in year[1]		Days idle during year[1]	
	Number	Workers involved (Thousands)	Number (Thousands)	Percent of estimated total working time[2]
1975	235	965	17 563	9
1976	231	1 519	23 962	12
1977	298	1 212	21 258	1
1978	219	1 006	23 774	11
1979	235	1 021	20 409	9
1980	187	795	20 844	9
1981	145	729	16 908	7
1982	96	656	9 061	4
1983	81	909	17 461	8
1984	62	376	8 499	4
1985	54	324	7 079	3
1986	69	533	11 861	5
1987	46	174	4 481	2
1988	40	118	4 381	2
1989	51	452	16 996	7
1990	44	185	5 926	2
1991	40	392	4 584	2
1992	35	364	3 989	1
1993	35	182	3 981	1
1994	45	322	5 020	2
1995	31	192	5 771	2

1. The number of stoppages and workers relate to stoppages that begin in the year. Days of idleness include all stoppages in effect. Workers are counted more than once if they are involved in more than one stoppage during the year.
2. Total working time is for all employees, except those in private households, forestry, and fisheries.

Part Nine

Foreign Labor and Price Statistics

Foreign Labor and Price Statistics

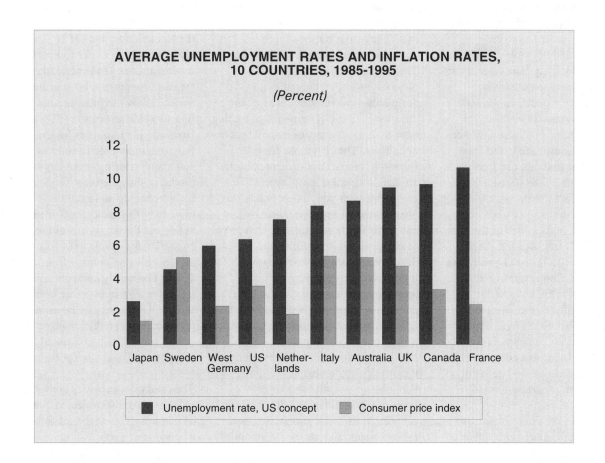

A s displayed by the bar chart, the average unemployment rate ranged from a low of 2.6 for Japan to a high of 10.6 for France. However, the range of inflation rates was much narrower—1.4 for Japan to 5.3 for Italy. There appears to be little relationship between the ranking of the unemployment rates and the ranking of inflation rates. Evidence of this exists in the United States where the country had the fourth lowest average unemployment rates but ranked closer to the middle in inflation rates.

NOTES
Foreign Labor and Price Statistics

From its inception, BLS has conducted a program of research and statistical analysis to compare labor conditions in the United States and selected foreign countries. The principal comparative measures cover the labor force, employment and unemployment, trends in labor productivity, and labor costs; hourly compensation costs for manufacturing production workers; trends in consumer prices and real compensation; and industrial disputes. All of the measures are based upon statistical data and other source materials from (a) the statistical agencies of the foreign countries studied; (b) international and supranational bodies such as the United Nations, the International Labour Organisation (ILO), the Organization for Economic Cooperation and Development (OECD), and the Statistical Office of the European Community (EUROSTAT), which attempt to obtain comparable country data; and (c) other secondary sources. The Bureau does not initiate surveys or data collection programs abroad.

International statistical comparisons should be used cautiously because statistical concepts and methods in each country are fashioned primarily to meet domestic rather than international needs. In some cases, the data are sufficiently similar in definition and concept for valid comparisons. In other cases, there are substantial conceptual differences. Wherever possible, the Bureau adjusts the data, if necessary, to improve comparability. If substantial differences remain, the Bureau attempts to describe the differences in sufficient detail so users will not draw misleading conclusions. In adjusting the data for greater comparability, the Bureau must depend on the availability of relevant information, and, in some instances, it is necessary to make estimates based on incomplete data.

The basic labor force and unemployment statistics of most foreign countries require some adjustment to bring them into closer comparability with U.S. data. This is particularly true for meaningful comparisons of unemployment rates. The statistical incomparability of national figures on unemployment is attributable to two chief causes: (1) differences in the systems for collecting data, and (2) differences in concepts or definitions. The first table provides the Bureau's comparative measures of the civilian labor force, employment, employment-to-population ratios, and unemployment approximating U.S. concepts. While adjustments have been made for all major definitional differences, it should be recognized that it is possible to achieve only approximate statistical comparability among the countries. Nevertheless, the adjusted figures provide a better basis for international comparisons than the figures regularly published by each country. It should also be recognized that intercountry differences in unemployment rates reflect substantial differences in social and institutional arrangements, as well as in economic performance.

The second table provides trend indexes of manufacturing labor productivity (output per hour), hourly compensation, unit labor costs (labor compensation per unit of output), and related measures for the United States and 11 other countries. The indexes are constructed from three basic aggregative measures: manufacturing output, total labor hours, and total compensation. The total hours measures are developed from statistics of manufacturing employment and average hours. The data on employment, hours, and compensation relate to all employed persons, including self-employed persons and unpaid family workers, in the United States, Canada, Japan, France, Germany, Norway, and Sweden, and to all employees (wage and salary earners) in Belgium, Denmark, Italy, the Netherlands, and the United Kingdom. Hours refer to hours worked in all countries. In general, the measures relate to total manufacturing as defined by the International Standard Industrial Classification (ISIC). However, the measures for France and Italy (beginning 1970) refer to mining and manufacturing less energy-related products; the measures for Denmark include mining and exclude manufacturing handicrafts from 1960 to 1966; and the measures for the Netherlands exclude petroleum refining and include coal mining from 1969 to 1976. The hourly compensation and unit labor cost indexes are computed in U.S. dollar values as well as in national currency units so that changes in costs can be related to international trade competition.

The final table provides consumer price index statistics for selected countries. The indexes reflect the market basket of goods and services purchased by the whole population or by a particular population group in each country. No adjustments for comparability are made in the total indexes except to convert them to a uniform base year (1982-1984=100).

Additional information is available in *BLS Report 909* and Supplement (September 1996).

Employment Status of the Working-age Population, Approximating U.S. Concepts, 10 Countries, 1959-1995

(Numbers in thousands; percent)

Year and category	United States	Canada	Australia	Japan	Germany¹	France	Italy	Netherlands	Sweden	United Kingdom
CIVILIAN LABOR FORCE										
1959	68 369	6 286	....	43 320	25 850	18 480	21 020	....	3 609	23 880
1960	69 628	6 462	....	44 120	25 990	18 520	20 820	....	3 669	24 130
1961	70 459	6 575	....	44 610	26 160	18 530	20 830	....	3 695	24 380
1962	70 614	6 670	....	45 040	26 210	18 720	20 680	....	3 718	24 720
1963	71 833	6 805	....	45 430	26 290	19 100	20 240	....	3 725	24 940
1964	73 091	6 994	4 559	46 040	26 270	19 430	20 220	....	3 720	25 070
1965	74 455	7 207	4 689	46 780	26 360	19 650	19 900	....	3 744	25 240
1966	75 770	7 493	4 862	47 850	26 290	19 850	19 620	....	3 795	25 320
1967	77 347	7 747	5 022	48 810	25 730	20 070	19 800	....	3 773	25 290
1968	78 737	7 951	5 140	49 690	25 690	20 190	19 780	....	3 822	25 180
1969	80 734	8 194	5 284	50 140	25 960	20 470	19 620	....	3 851	25 160
1970	82 771	8 395	5 478	50 730	26 240	20 800	19 720	....	3 909	25 110
1971	84 382	8 639	5 624	51 120	26 380	21 000	19 660	....	3 955	24 950
1972	87 034	8 897	5 752	51 320	26 470	21 150	19 450	....	3 963	25 190
1973	89 429	9 276	5 901	52 590	26 780	21 430	19 590	5 210	3 971	25 440
1974	91 949	9 639	6 053	52 440	26 660	21 660	19 900	5 290	4 036	25 470
1975	93 775	9 974	6 169	52 530	26 430	21 770	20 090	5 340	4 123	25 730
1976	96 158	10 530	6 244	53 100	26 290	22 050	20 290	5 390	4 148	25 900
1977	99 009	10 860	6 358	53 820	26 330	22 380	20 510	5 480	4 168	26 050
1978	102 251	11 265	6 443	54 610	26 520	22 540	20 570	5 540	4 203	26 260
1979	104 962	11 630	6 519	55 210	26 860	22 780	20 850	5 640	4 262	26 350
1980	106 940	11 983	6 693	55 740	27 260	22 930	21 120	5 870	4 312	26 520
1981	108 670	12 232	6 810	56 320	27 540	23 090	21 320	6 090	4 327	26 590
1982	110 204	12 398	6 910	56 980	27 710	23 320	21 410	6 150	4 350	26 560
1983	111 550	12 610	6 997	58 110	27 670	23 400	21 590	6 120	4 369	26 590
1984	113 544	12 853	7 135	58 480	27 800	23 560	21 670	6 200	4 385	27 010
1985	115 461	13 123	7 300	58 820	28 020	23 620	21 800	6 250	4 418	27 210
1986	117 834	13 378	7 588	59 410	28 240	23 760	22 290	6 380	4 443	27 380
1987	119 865	13 631	7 758	60 050	28 390	23 890	22 350	6 500	4 437	27 720
1988	121 669	13 900	7 974	60 860	28 610	23 980	22 660	6 330	4 494	28 150
1989	123 869	14 151	8 228	61 920	28 840	24 170	22 530	6 450	4 552	28 420
1990	125 840	14 329	8 444	63 050	29 410	24 300	22 670	6 660	4 597	28 540
1991	126 346	14 408	8 490	64 280	29 760	24 490	22 940	6 770	4 591	28 450
1992	128 105	14 482	8 562	65 040	30 030	24 570	22 910	6 970	4 520	28 400
1993	129 200	14 663	8 619	65 470	29 950	24 660	22 760	7 110	4 443	28 310
1994	131 056	14 832	8 776	65 780	29 820	24 790	22 640	7 180	4 418	28 310
1995	132 304	14 928	9 001	65 990	29 660	24 850	22 700	7 290	4 460	28 190
PARTICIPATION RATE										
1959	59.3	55.7	....	67.7	60.0	59.6	57.2	....	66.1	61.8
1960	59.4	56.2	....	67.9	59.8	59.5	56.1	....	66.5	61.9
1961	59.3	56.2	....	67.8	59.9	58.9	55.8	....	66.3	62.1
1962	58.8	55.9	....	66.9	59.6	57.9	54.7	....	65.9	62.1
1963	58.7	55.9	....	65.7	59.4	57.5	53.1	....	65.3	62.3
1964	58.7	56.2	59.4	64.8	59.0	57.6	52.5	....	64.5	62.2
1965	58.9	56.5	59.9	64.4	58.7	57.4	51.4	....	64.1	62.4
1966	59.2	57.3	60.6	64.6	58.2	57.3	50.0	....	64.2	62.3
1967	59.6	57.6	61.2	64.8	57.0	57.4	50.2	....	63.3	62.0
1968	59.6	57.6	61.2	64.9	56.9	57.1	49.7	....	63.8	61.6
1969	60.1	57.9	61.4	64.6	57.0	57.3	49.3	....	63.8	61.4
1970	60.4	57.8	62.1	64.5	56.9	57.5	49.0	....	64.0	61.1
1971	60.2	58.1	62.2	64.2	56.5	57.4	48.7	....	64.2	60.4
1972	60.4	58.6	62.3	63.8	56.2	57.2	47.7	....	64.1	60.8
1973	60.8	59.7	62.6	64.0	56.3	57.3	47.6	53.4	64.1	62.4
1974	61.2	60.5	63.0	63.0	55.7	57.4	47.7	53.5	64.8	62.2
1975	61.2	61.1	63.2	62.4	55.0	57.2	47.7	54.5	65.9	62.6
1976	61.6	61.5	62.7	62.4	54.6	57.5	48.0	54.1	66.0	62.7
1977	62.3	62.1	62.7	62.5	54.4	57.8	48.2	54.2	65.9	62.7
1978	63.2	63.1	61.9	62.8	54.4	57.7	47.8	54.0	66.1	62.8
1979	63.7	64.0	61.6	62.7	54.5	57.8	48.0	54.2	66.6	62.5
1980	63.8	64.6	62.1	62.6	54.7	57.5	48.2	55.4	66.9	62.5
1981	63.9	65.3	61.9	62.6	54.7	57.5	48.3	56.7	66.8	62.3
1982	64.0	64.7	61.7	62.7	54.6	57.5	47.7	56.6	66.8	61.9
1983	64.0	64.9	61.4	63.1	54.3	57.2	47.5	55.7	66.7	61.6
1984	64.4	65.3	61.5	62.7	54.4	57.2	47.3	55.7	66.6	62.1
1985	64.8	65.8	61.6	62.3	54.7	56.9	47.2	55.5	66.9	62.1
1986	65.3	66.3	62.8	62.1	54.9	56.9	47.8	56.0	67.0	62.1
1987	65.6	66.7	63.0	61.9	55.0	56.7	47.6	56.3	66.4	62.5
1988	65.9	67.2	63.3	61.9	55.1	56.4	47.4	54.3	66.9	63.2
1989	66.5	67.5	64.0	62.2	55.2	56.1	47.3	54.9	67.3	63.6
1990	66.5	67.3	64.6	62.6	55.3	55.6	47.2	56.3	67.4	63.7
1991	66.2	66.7	64.1	63.2	55.4	55.6	47.7	56.7	67.0	63.3
1992	66.4	65.9	63.9	63.4	55.1	55.8	47.5	57.9	65.7	62.9
1993	66.3	65.5	63.6	63.3	54.2	55.6	48.1	58.6	64.5	62.8
1994	66.6	65.3	63.9	63.1	53.7	55.6	47.5	58.9	63.9	62.6
1995	66.6	64.8	64.6	62.9	53.1	55.3	47.6	59.7	64.3	62.2

1. Former West Germany.

FOREIGN LABOR AND PRICE STATISTICS

Employment Status of the Working-age Population, Approximating U.S. Concepts, 10 Countries, 1959-1995—Continued

(Numbers in thousands; percent)

Year and category	United States	Canada	Australia	Japan	Germany[1]	France	Italy	Netherlands	Sweden	United Kingdom
EMPLOYMENT										
1959	64 630	5 936	....	42 340	25 340	18 190	20 020	....	3 549	23 220
1960	65 778	6 042	....	43 370	25 710	18 250	20 060	....	3 606	23 600
1961	65 746	6 136	....	43 950	26 000	18 300	20 160	....	3 640	23 900
1962	66 702	6 302	....	44 450	26 060	18 450	20 100	....	3 663	24 050
1963	67 762	6 454	....	44 840	26 170	18 800	19 760	....	3 663	24 120
1964	69 305	6 688	4 496	45 500	26 170	19 190	19 680	....	3 662	24 450
1965	71 088	6 944	4 628	46 210	26 290	19 340	19 210		3 700	24 700
1966	72 895	7 242	4 785	47 200	26 220	19 530	18 890		3 736	24 760
1967	74 372	7 451	4 928	48 180	25 390	19 650	19 130		3 693	24 470
1968	75 920	7 593	5 046	49 100	25 400	19 640	19 080		3 737	24 370
1969	77 902	7 832	5 188	49 570	25 790	19 990	18 940		3 778	24 390
1970	78 678	7 919	5 388	50 140	26 100	20 270	19 080		3 850	24 330
1971	79 367	8 104	5 517	50 480	26 220	20 420	19 020		3 854	23 970
1972	82 153	8 344	5 601	50 590	26 280	20 540	18 710		3 856	24 120
1973	85 064	8 761	5 765	51 910	26 590	20 840	18 870	5 050	3 873	24 610
1974	86 794	9 125	5 891	51 710	26 240	21 030	19 280	5 100	3 956	24 680
1975	85 846	9 284	5 866	51 530	25 540	20 860	19 400	5 070	4 056	24 560
1976	88 752	9 776	5 946	52 020	25 400	21 030	19 500	5 100	4 082	24 360
1977	92 017	9 978	6 000	52 720	25 430	21 220	19 670	5 210	4 093	24 400
1978	96 048	10 320	6 038	53 370	25 650	21 320	19 720	5 260	4 109	24 610
1979	98 824	10 761	6 111	54 040	26 080	21 390	19 930	5 350	4 174	24 940
1980	99 303	11 082	6 284	54 600	26 490	21 440	20 200	5 520	4 226	24 670
1981	100 397	11 398	6 416	55 060	26 450	21 330	20 280	5 550	4 219	23 800
1982	99 526	11 035	6 415	55 620	26 150	21 390	20 250	5 520	4 213	23 560
1983	100 834	11 106	6 300	56 550	25 770	21 380	20 320	5 420	4 218	23 450
1984	105 005	11 402	6 494	56 870	25 830	21 200	20 390	5 490	4 249	23 830
1985	107 150	11 742	6 697	57 260	26 010	21 150	20 490	5 650	4 293	24 150
1986	109 597	12 095	6 974	57 740	26 380	21 240	20 610	5 740	4 326	24 300
1987	112 440	12 422	7 129	58 320	26 590	21 320	20 590	5 850	4 340	24 860
1988	114 968	12 819	7 398	59 310	26 800	21 520	20 870	5 850	4 410	25 730
1989	117 342	13 086	7 720	60 500	27 200	21 850	20 770	5 990	4 480	26 350
1990	118 793	13 165	7 859	61 710	27 950	22 100	21 080	6 250	4 513	26 550
1991	117 718	12 916	7 676	62 920	28 480	22 140	21 360	6 370	4 447	25 930
1992	118 492	12 842	7 637	63 620	28 660	22 010	21 230	6 570	4 265	25 520
1993	120 259	13 015	7 680	63 810	28 230	21 750	20 430	6 640	4 028	25 340
1994	123 060	13 292	7 921	63 860	27 880	21 740	20 080	6 650	3 992	25 580
1995	124 900	13 506	8 235	63 890	27 720	22 000	19 970	6 760	4 056	25 710
EMPLOYMENT TO POPULATION RATIO										
1959	56.0	52.6	....	66.1	58.8	58.7	54.5	....	65.0	60.1
1960	56.1	52.6	....	66.7	59.2	58.6	54.0	....	65.4	60.6
1961	55.4	52.4	....	66.8	59.6	58.2	54.0	....	65.3	60.8
1962	55.5	52.8	....	66.0	59.3	57.1	53.2	....	64.9	60.4
1963	55.4	53.0	....	64.8	59.2	56.6	51.9	....	64.2	60.2
1964	55.7	53.7	58.6	64.1	58.8	56.9	51.1	....	63.5	60.7
1965	56.2	54.4	59.1	63.6	58.6	56.4	49.6		63.4	61.0
1966	56.9	55.4	59.6	63.7	58.0	56.4	48.1		63.2	60.9
1967	57.3	55.4	60.0	64.0	56.3	56.2	48.5		62.0	60.0
1968	57.5	55.0	60.0	64.1	56.2	55.5	47.9		62.3	59.6
1969	58.0	55.3	60.2	63.9	56.6	55.9	47.6		62.6	59.5
1970	57.4	54.5	61.1	63.8	56.6	56.0	47.4		63.1	59.2
1971	56.6	54.5	61.0	63.4	56.2	55.8	47.1		62.6	58.0
1972	57.0	54.9	60.6	62.9	55.8	55.5	45.9		62.4	58.2
1973	57.8	56.4	61.2	63.2	55.9	55.8	45.8	51.8	62.5	60.3
1974	57.8	57.3	61.3	62.2	54.8	55.7	46.2	51.6	63.6	60.2
1975	56.1	56.9	60.1	61.2	53.2	54.8	46.0	51.7	64.8	59.7
1976	56.8	57.1	59.7	61.1	52.8	54.8	46.1	51.2	64.9	59.0
1977	57.9	57.0	59.2	61.2	52.5	54.8	46.3	51.6	64.8	58.7
1978	59.3	57.9	58.0	61.3	52.6	54.6	45.9	51.3	64.6	58.8
1979	59.9	59.2	57.8	61.4	52.9	54.2	45.9	51.4	65.3	59.2
1980	59.2	59.7	58.3	61.3	53.1	53.8	46.1	52.1	65.6	58.1
1981	59.0	60.4	58.4	61.2	52.5	53.1	45.9	51.7	65.1	55.7
1982	57.8	57.5	57.3	61.2	51.6	52.7	45.2	50.8	64.7	54.9
1983	57.9	57.1	55.3	61.4	50.6	52.3	44.7	49.3	64.4	54.3
1984	59.5	57.9	56.0	61.0	50.5	51.5	44.5	49.3	64.5	54.8
1985	60.1	58.9	56.5	60.6	50.7	51.0	44.4	50.1	65.0	55.1
1986	60.7	59.9	57.7	60.4	51.3	50.8	44.2	50.3	65.2	55.1
1987	61.5	60.8	57.9	60.1	51.5	50.6	43.8	50.7	65.0	56.1
1988	62.3	62.0	58.7	60.4	51.6	50.6	43.7	50.2	65.7	57.8
1989	63.0	62.4	60.1	60.8	52.0	50.7	43.6	51.0	66.2	59.0
1990	62.8	61.9	60.1	61.3	52.6	50.5	43.9	52.8	66.1	59.2
1991	61.7	59.8	57.9	61.8	53.0	50.2	44.5	53.3	64.9	57.7
1992	61.5	58.4	57.0	62.0	52.6	50.0	44.0	54.6	62.0	56.5
1993	61.7	58.2	56.6	61.7	51.1	49.1	43.1	54.8	58.5	56.2
1994	62.5	58.5	57.7	61.3	50.2	48.7	42.1	54.6	57.7	56.5
1995	62.9	58.6	59.1	60.9	49.7	49.0	41.8	55.4	58.5	56.7

1. Former West Germany.

Employment Status of the Working-age Population, Approximating U.S. Concepts, 10 Countries, 1959-1995—Continued

(Numbers in thousands; percent)

Year and category	United States	Canada	Australia	Japan	Germany[1]	France	Italy	Nether-lands	Sweden	United Kingdom
UNEMPLOYMENT										
1959	3 740	350	....	980	510	290	1 000	....	60	660
1960	3 852	420	....	750	280	270	760	....	63	530
1961	4 714	439	....	660	160	230	670	....	55	480
1962	3 911	368	....	590	150	270	580	....	55	670
1963	4 070	351	....	590	120	300	480	....	62	830
1964	3 786	306	63	540	100	240	540	....	58	620
1965	3 366	263	61	570	70	310	690	....	44	540
1966	2 875	251	76	650	70	320	730	....	59	570
1967	2 975	296	94	630	340	420	670	....	80	830
1968	2 817	358	94	590	290	550	700	....	85	810
1969	2 832	362	96	570	170	480	680	....	73	770
1970	4 093	476	91	590	140	530	640	....	59	770
1971	5 016	535	107	640	160	580	640	....	101	980
1972	4 882	553	150	730	190	610	740	....	107	1 070
1973	4 365	515	136	680	190	590	720	160	98	820
1974	5 156	514	162	730	420	630	620	190	80	790
1975	7 929	690	302	1 000	890	910	690	270	67	1 180
1976	7 406	754	298	1 080	890	1 020	790	290	66	1 540
1977	6 991	882	358	1 100	900	1 160	840	270	75	1 660
1978	6 202	945	405	1 240	870	1 220	850	280	94	1 650
1979	6 137	870	408	1 170	780	1 390	920	290	88	1 420
1980	7 637	900	409	1 140	770	1 490	920	350	86	1 850
1981	8 273	934	394	1 260	1 090	1 760	1 040	540	108	2 790
1982	10 678	1 363	495	1 360	1 560	1 930	1 160	630	137	3 000
1983	10 717	1 504	697	1 560	1 900	2 020	1 270	700	151	3 140
1984	8 539	1 450	641	1 610	1 970	2 360	1 280	710	136	3 180
1985	8 312	1 381	603	1 560	2 010	2 470	1 310	600	125	3 060
1986	8 237	1 283	613	1 670	1 860	2 520	1 680	640	117	3 080
1987	7 425	1 208	629	1 730	1 800	2 570	1 760	650	97	2 860
1988	6 701	1 082	576	1 550	1 810	2 460	1 790	480	84	2 420
1989	6 528	1 065	508	1 420	1 640	2 320	1 760	450	72	2 070
1990	7 047	1 164	585	1 340	1 460	2 200	1 590	410	84	1 990
1991	8 628	1 492	814	1 360	1 280	2 350	1 580	400	144	2 520
1992	9 613	1 640	925	1 420	1 370	2 560	1 680	390	255	2 880
1993	8 940	1 649	939	1 660	1 720	2 910	2 330	470	415	2 970
1994	7 996	1 541	856	1 920	1 940	3 050	2 560	520	426	2 730
1995	7 404	1 422	766	2 100	1 940	2 850	2 720	530	404	2 480
UNEMPLOYMENT RATE										
1959	5.5	5.6	2.1	2.3	2.0	1.6	4.8	....	1.7	2.8
1960	5.5	6.5	1.6	1.7	1.1	1.5	3.7	....	1.7	2.2
1961	6.7	6.7	3.0	1.5	0.6	1.2	3.2	....	1.5	2.0
1962	5.5	5.5	2.9	1.3	0.6	1.4	2.8	....	1.5	2.7
1963	5.7	5.2	2.3	1.3	0.5	1.6	2.4	....	1.7	3.3
1964	5.2	4.4	1.4	1.2	0.4	1.2	2.7	....	1.6	2.5
1965	4.5	3.6	1.3	1.2	0.3	1.6	3.5	....	1.2	2.1
1966	3.8	3.4	1.6	1.4	0.3	1.6	3.7	....	1.6	2.3
1967	3.8	3.8	1.9	1.3	1.3	2.1	3.4	....	2.1	3.3
1968	3.6	4.5	1.8	1.2	1.1	2.7	3.5	....	2.2	3.2
1969	3.5	4.4	1.8	1.1	0.6	2.3	3.5	....	1.9	3.1
1970	4.9	5.7	1.6	1.2	0.5	2.5	3.2	....	1.5	3.1
1971	5.9	6.2	1.9	1.3	0.6	2.8	3.3	....	2.6	3.9
1972	5.6	6.2	2.6	1.4	0.7	2.9	3.8	....	2.7	4.2
1973	4.9	5.5	2.3	1.3	0.7	2.8	3.7	3.1	2.5	3.2
1974	5.6	5.3	2.7	1.4	1.6	2.9	3.1	3.6	2.0	3.1
1975	8.5	6.9	4.9	1.9	3.4	4.2	3.4	5.1	1.6	4.6
1976	7.7	7.2	4.8	2.0	3.4	4.6	3.9	5.4	1.6	5.9
1977	7.1	8.1	5.6	2.0	3.4	5.2	4.1	4.9	1.8	6.4
1978	6.1	8.4	6.3	2.3	3.3	5.4	4.1	5.1	2.2	6.3
1979	5.8	7.5	6.3	2.1	2.9	6.1	4.4	5.1	2.1	5.4
1980	7.1	7.5	6.1	2.0	2.8	6.5	4.4	6.0	2.0	7.0
1981	7.6	7.6	5.8	2.2	4.0	7.6	4.9	8.9	2.5	10.5
1982	9.7	11.0	7.2	2.4	5.6	8.3	5.4	10.2	3.1	11.3
1983	9.6	11.9	10.0	2.7	6.9	8.6	5.9	11.4	3.5	11.8
1984	7.5	11.3	9.0	2.8	7.1	10.0	5.9	11.5	3.1	11.8
1985	7.2	10.5	8.3	2.6	7.2	10.5	6.0	9.6	2.8	11.2
1986	7.0	9.6	8.1	2.8	6.6	10.6	7.5	10.0	2.6	11.2
1987	6.2	8.9	8.1	2.9	6.3	10.8	7.9	10.0	2.2	10.3
1988	5.5	7.8	7.2	2.5	6.3	10.3	7.9	7.6	1.9	8.6
1989	5.3	7.5	6.2	2.3	5.7	9.6	7.8	7.0	1.6	7.3
1990	5.6	8.1	6.9	2.1	5.0	9.0	7.0	6.2	1.8	7.0
1991	6.8	10.4	9.6	2.1	4.3	9.6	6.9	5.9	3.1	8.9
1992	7.5	11.3	10.8	2.2	4.6	10.4	7.3	5.6	5.6	10.1
1993	6.9	11.2	10.9	2.5	5.7	11.8	10.2	6.6	9.3	10.5
1994	6.1	10.4	9.7	2.9	6.5	12.3	11.3	7.2	9.6	9.6
1995	5.6	9.5	8.5	3.2	6.5	11.5	12.0	7.3	9.1	8.8

1. Former West Germany.

Indexes of Manufacturing Productivity and Related Measures, 12 Countries, 1970-1995

(1992=100)

Item and year	United States	Canada	Japan	Belgium	Denmark	France	Germany[1]	Italy	Nether-lands	Norway	Sweden	United Kingdom
OUTPUT PER HOUR												
1970	....	60.4	38.0	34.2	52.1	45.5	51.9	36.8	39.6	57.0	52.8	43.7
1984	81.1	91.4	71.9	84.0	95.0	80.7	85.2	77.1	86.3	87.6	85.6	69.2
1985	83.7	94.1	77.3	85.5	95.6	83.8	88.7	81.5	89.8	90.4	87.2	71.9
1986	85.9	92.6	76.9	86.7	90.0	85.2	89.3	82.6	91.2	89.5	88.6	74.7
1987	91.4	93.5	81.2	88.4	89.6	86.7	88.1	85.0	91.9	94.0	90.1	78.8
1988	93.5	93.9	84.8	91.4	92.9	92.7	91.2	86.6	93.9	93.2	90.8	83.1
1989	94.0	94.3	89.5	96.2	96.1	97.4	94.3	89.4	97.3	93.8	93.8	87.1
1990	95.7	95.8	95.4	95.6	96.0	99.1	98.2	92.8	98.6	96.8	95.0	90.1
1991	97.9	96.3	99.4	98.7	97.9	98.7	101.7	95.3	99.6	96.2	95.0	94.4
1992	100.0	100.0	100.0	100.0	100.0	100.0	100.0	100.0	100.0	100.0	100.0	100.0
1993	103.6	101.8	100.5	104.2	106.4	101.8	101.2	104.5	101.9	100.4	106.7	105.4
1994	108.1	105.6	101.2	110.1	....	110.4	108.5	106.9	109.4	102.2	115.7	109.4
1995	111.9	107.2	106.6	....	....	113.7	112.0	111.2	....	103.1	119.6	109.4
OUTPUT												
1970	....	61.0	38.8	60.3	66.8	66.9	70.9	44.8	61.8	89.2	81.6	91.2
1984	85.5	93.3	70.4	86.6	98.6	90.9	85.2	80.0	83.7	105.9	101.8	87.4
1985	87.6	98.5	76.1	88.1	101.7	91.2	88.3	82.6	86.0	109.8	104.0	89.9
1986	88.5	99.3	74.9	88.1	101.7	91.2	89.7	84.8	88.1	109.8	105.3	91.1
1987	94.9	104.1	78.4	88.4	97.6	91.1	88.0	88.5	89.3	111.9	107.7	95.3
1988	99.9	109.4	84.6	92.8	99.1	96.3	90.9	94.8	92.7	106.5	110.2	102.0
1989	100.8	110.3	90.2	98.4	100.3	101.6	94.0	98.6	96.9	100.5	111.7	106.6
1990	100.4	106.2	96.3	99.6	99.3	103.5	99.1	100.4	100.1	100.4	110.6	106.4
1991	98.5	98.7	101.4	100.0	99.2	101.7	102.8	99.7	100.6	97.0	103.5	100.6
1992	100.0	100.0	100.0	100.0	100.0	100.0	100.0	100.0	100.0	100.0	100.0	100.0
1993	105.0	104.8	96.0	97.1	100.7	96.2	92.0	96.6	97.8	102.4	101.3	101.2
1994	112.3	112.1	94.8	101.5	102.8	101.3	94.1	101.4	101.4	108.0	115.3	105.5
1995	116.2	117.2	97.8	....	106.1	104.6	94.6	107.3	....	111.1	126.1	107.6
TOTAL HOURS												
1970	104.5	100.9	102.3	176.3	128.3	147.0	136.6	121.8	156.2	156.6	154.7	208.6
1984	105.4	102.1	97.9	103.1	103.8	112.7	100.0	103.8	97.0	121.0	118.9	126.3
1985	104.7	104.8	98.4	103.0	106.5	108.9	99.6	101.4	95.8	121.5	119.3	125.1
1986	103.1	107.2	97.3	101.6	113.1	107.2	100.4	102.7	96.6	122.7	118.8	121.9
1987	103.9	111.4	96.6	100.0	109.0	105.1	99.9	104.1	97.2	119.0	119.5	120.9
1988	106.9	116.5	99.8	101.5	106.6	104.0	99.6	109.5	98.7	114.3	121.4	122.7
1989	107.3	117.0	100.8	102.3	104.3	104.4	99.7	110.2	99.6	107.1	119.0	122.3
1990	104.9	110.8	100.9	104.3	103.3	104.5	101.0	108.2	101.6	103.7	116.4	118.0
1991	100.6	102.5	102.0	101.3	101.3	103.0	101.1	104.6	101.0	100.8	109.0	106.6
1992	100.0	100.0	100.0	100.0	100.0	100.0	100.0	100.0	100.0	100.0	100.0	100.0
1993	101.4	102.9	95.6	93.2	94.7	94.5	90.9	92.4	95.9	102.1	95.0	96.0
1994	103.8	106.2	93.7	92.2	....	91.8	86.8	94.8	92.7	105.7	99.6	96.4
1995	103.9	109.3	91.7	....	....	91.9	84.5	96.4	....	107.8	105.4	98.3
COMPENSATION PER HOUR National currency basis												
1970	23.8	18.3	16.5	14.1	13.2	10.5	20.7	4.6	20.5	11.7	10.8	6.5
1984	71.4	70.9	69.7	69.8	66.9	68.1	66.2	53.5	77.9	57.3	53.2	50.9
1985	75.3	74.6	72.5	74.1	71.4	73.8	70.0	60.1	82.0	62.7	58.6	55.8
1986	78.6	77.5	76.1	77.2	72.9	76.9	73.0	62.6	85.2	68.7	63.4	60.6
1987	80.8	79.8	77.9	79.0	79.7	79.7	76.4	66.1	87.9	78.5	67.6	67.3
1988	84.0	83.3	79.2	80.6	82.5	82.8	79.3	68.7	87.6	83.3	72.0	71.7
1989	86.7	86.4	84.2	84.8	87.2	87.2	83.1	75.5	88.4	87.2	79.6	75.4
1990	90.9	91.3	90.7	89.6	92.6	91.8	89.0	84.0	90.8	92.3	87.8	83.7
1991	95.7	97.1	95.9	95.3	96.2	96.3	95.0	93.1	95.0	97.5	95.7	93.4
1992	100.0	100.0	100.0	100.0	100.0	100.0	100.0	100.0	100.0	100.0	100.0	100.0
1993	102.4	100.1	104.6	105.0	102.4	103.6	106.0	107.1	104.6	101.5	97.8	105.3
1994	105.1	102.4	106.8	108.4	....	106.2	110.5	106.4	106.1	104.8	101.8	107.4
1995	108.0	103.7	110.3	....	....	107.9	116.1	109.7	....	109.4	107.3	110.9

1. Former West Germany.

Indexes of Manufacturing Productivity and Related Measures, 12 Countries, 1970-1995—Continued

(1992=100)

Item and year	United States	Canada	Japan	Belgium	Denmark	France	Germany¹	Italy	Nether-lands	Norway	Sweden	United Kingdom
COMPENSATION PER HOUR U.S. currency basis												
1970	23.8	21.2	5.8	9.1	10.6	10.1	8.9	9.1	10.0	10.1	12.2	8.8
1984	71.4	66.1	37.2	38.8	39.0	41.3	36.3	37.5	42.7	43.7	37.5	38.6
1985	75.3	66.0	38.5	40.2	40.7	43.5	37.2	38.8	43.4	45.3	39.7	41.0
1986	78.6	67.4	57.3	55.6	54.3	58.8	52.5	51.7	61.2	57.7	51.8	50.3
1987	80.8	72.7	68.3	68.0	70.3	70.2	66.3	62.8	76.3	72.4	62.0	62.5
1988	84.0	81.8	78.4	70.4	73.9	73.5	70.5	65.0	77.9	79.3	68.3	72.3
1989	86.7	88.2	77.3	69.2	71.9	72.4	69.0	67.8	73.3	78.4	71.9	69.9
1990	90.9	94.5	79.3	86.2	90.4	89.3	86.0	86.3	87.6	91.7	86.4	84.5
1991	95.7	102.4	90.3	89.6	90.7	90.3	89.3	92.5	89.3	93.3	92.1	93.5
1992	100.0	100.0	100.0	100.0	100.0	100.0	100.0	100.0	100.0	100.0	100.0	100.0
1993	102.4	93.7	119.3	97.6	95.3	96.8	100.1	83.9	98.9	88.8	73.1	89.5
1994	105.1	90.6	132.6	104.3	....	101.4	106.4	81.4	102.6	92.3	76.8	93.1
1995	108.0	91.3	148.8	....	....	114.6	126.6	83.0	....	107.3	87.5	99.1
UNIT LABOR COST National currency basis												
1970	....	30.3	43.3	41.1	25.3	23.1	40.0	12.6	51.8	20.5	20.6	14.8
1984	88.0	77.6	96.8	83.1	70.4	84.5	77.7	69.4	90.2	65.5	62.2	73.6
1985	89.9	79.3	93.8	86.7	74.7	88.1	79.0	73.8	91.3	69.4	67.3	77.6
1986	91.6	83.6	99.0	89.0	81.0	90.3	81.7	75.8	93.4	76.8	71.5	81.1
1987	88.5	85.3	96.0	89.3	89.0	92.0	86.7	77.8	95.7	83.5	74.9	85.4
1988	89.8	88.7	93.4	88.2	88.8	89.3	86.9	79.4	93.3	89.3	79.2	86.2
1989	92.2	91.7	94.0	88.2	90.7	89.6	88.2	84.4	90.8	93.0	84.9	86.5
1990	95.0	95.2	95.0	93.7	96.5	92.7	90.6	90.5	92.1	95.4	92.5	92.8
1991	97.7	100.9	96.5	96.5	98.3	97.5	93.3	97.7	95.4	101.3	100.7	98.9
1992	100.0	100.0	100.0	100.0	100.0	100.0	100.0	100.0	100.0	100.0	100.0	100.0
1993	98.8	98.3	104.1	100.7	96.3	101.8	104.7	102.5	102.6	101.1	91.7	99.9
1994	97.2	97.0	105.6	98.5	97.8	96.2	101.8	99.5	97.0	102.6	88.0	98.1
1995	96.6	96.7	103.4	....	101.3	94.9	103.7	98.6	....	106.1	89.7	101.3
UNIT LABOR COST U.S. currency basis												
1970	....	35.1	15.3	26.6	20.4	22.1	17.1	24.7	25.2	17.8	23.1	20.0
1984	88.0	72.4	51.7	46.2	41.1	51.2	42.7	48.7	49.5	49.9	43.8	55.7
1985	89.9	70.1	49.9	47.0	42.6	51.9	41.9	47.6	48.4	50.2	45.6	57.0
1986	91.6	72.7	74.5	64.1	60.4	69.0	58.8	62.6	67.1	64.5	58.4	67.4
1987	88.5	77.8	84.2	76.9	78.4	81.0	75.3	73.9	83.0	77.0	68.8	79.2
1988	89.8	87.1	92.4	77.1	79.5	79.4	77.3	75.1	83.0	85.1	75.2	86.9
1989	92.2	93.6	86.3	72.0	74.8	74.3	73.2	75.8	75.3	83.6	76.6	80.2
1990	95.0	98.6	83.1	90.2	94.1	90.1	87.6	93.0	88.9	94.8	90.9	93.8
1991	97.7	106.4	90.9	90.7	92.7	91.4	87.8	97.0	89.6	97.0	97.0	99.0
1992	100.0	100.0	100.0	100.0	100.0	100.0	100.0	100.0	100.0	100.0	100.0	100.0
1993	98.8	92.1	118.8	93.6	89.6	95.1	98.9	80.3	97.1	88.5	68.5	85.0
1994	97.2	85.8	131.0	94.7	92.9	91.8	98.1	76.1	93.8	90.4	66.4	85.1
1995	96.6	85.1	139.5	....	109.2	100.8	113.1	74.6	....	104.0	73.2	90.6
EXCHANGE RATE INDEX												
1970	100.0	115.8	35.4	64.7	80.5	95.7	42.8	196.5	48.6	86.9	112.3	135.6
1984	100.0	93.3	53.4	55.7	58.3	60.6	54.9	70.2	54.8	76.2	70.4	75.7
1985	100.0	88.5	53.2	54.2	57.0	58.9	53.1	64.6	53.0	72.3	67.7	73.5
1986	100.0	87.0	75.3	72.0	74.6	76.4	72.0	82.6	71.8	84.0	81.7	83.1
1987	100.0	91.1	87.7	86.1	88.2	88.0	86.9	95.0	86.8	92.2	91.8	92.8
1988	100.0	98.2	98.9	87.4	89.6	88.8	88.9	94.6	88.9	95.2	94.9	100.8
1989	100.0	102.1	91.8	81.6	82.5	83.0	83.0	89.8	82.9	89.9	90.2	92.7
1990	100.0	103.6	87.4	96.2	97.5	97.2	96.6	102.8	96.6	99.4	98.4	101.0
1991	100.0	105.5	94.2	94.0	94.3	93.7	94.0	99.3	93.9	95.7	96.3	100.1
1992	100.0	100.0	100.0	100.0	100.0	100.0	100.0	100.0	100.0	100.0	100.0	100.0
1993	100.0	93.7	114.1	93.0	93.1	93.4	94.4	78.3	94.6	87.5	74.7	85.0
1994	100.0	88.4	124.1	96.2	95.0	95.4	96.3	76.5	96.7	88.1	75.5	86.7
1995	100.0	88.1	134.9	109.1	107.8	106.2	109.1	75.6	109.6	98.1	81.6	89.4

1. Former West Germany.

FOREIGN LABOR AND PRICE STATISTICS

Indexes of Consumer Prices, 16 countries, 1960-1995

(1982-1984=100)

Year	United States	Canada	Japan	Aus-tralia²	Austria	Belgium	Denmark	France²	Ger-many³	Italy	Nether-lands	Norway	Spain²	Sweden	Switzer-land	United Kingdom
1960	29.6	26.9	21.8	22.1	32.6	29.1	16.7	19.4	....	11.8	....	21.1	9.1	21.0	38.2	14.6
1961	29.9	27.1	23.0	22.7	33.8	29.3	17.4	20.0	....	12.1	....	21.6	9.2	21.5	39.0	15.1
1962	30.2	27.4	24.6	22.6	35.3	29.8	18.8	21.0	43.1	12.6	....	22.8	9.7	22.5	40.6	15.8
1963	30.6	27.9	26.4	22.4	36.2	30.4	19.8	22.0	44.4	13.6	....	23.4	10.6	23.2	42.0	16.1
1964	31.0	28.4	27.4	23.2	37.6	31.7	20.5	22.7	45.4	14.4	....	24.7	11.3	23.9	43.3	16.6
1965	31.5	29.1	29.5	24.2	39.5	32.9	21.8	23.3	46.9	15.0	....	25.7	12.8	25.1	44.8	17.4
1966	32.4	30.2	31.0	24.9	40.3	34.3	23.3	23.9	48.6	15.4	....	26.6	13.6	26.8	46.9	18.1
1967	33.4	31.3	32.3	25.7	41.9	35.3	25.0	24.6	49.4	15.9	36.2	27.8	14.5	27.9	48.8	18.5
1968	34.8	32.5	34.0	26.3	43.1	36.3	27.0	25.7	50.2	16.1	37.5	28.7	15.2	28.4	50.0	19.4
1969	36.7	34.0	35.8	27.1	44.4	37.6	27.9	27.3	51.1	16.5	40.3	29.6	15.5	29.2	51.3	20.5
1970	38.8	35.1	38.5	28.2	46.4	39.1	29.8	28.8	52.8	17.3	41.8	32.8	16.4	31.2	53.1	21.8
1971	40.5	36.2	40.9	29.9	48.5	40.8	31.5	30.3	55.6	18.2	45.0	34.8	17.7	33.6	56.6	23.8
1972	41.8	37.9	42.9	31.6	51.6	43.0	33.6	32.2	58.7	19.2	48.6	37.3	19.2	35.6	60.4	25.5
1973	44.4	40.7	47.9	34.6	55.5	46.0	36.7	34.6	62.8	21.3	52.5	40.1	21.4	38.0	65.7	27.9
1974	49.3	45.2	59.1	39.9	60.8	51.9	42.3	39.3	67.2	25.4	57.7	43.8	24.8	41.7	72.1	32.3
1975	53.8	50.1	66.0	45.9	65.9	58.5	46.4	43.9	71.2	29.7	63.4	49.0	29.0	45.8	76.9	40.1
1976	56.9	53.8	72.2	52.1	70.8	63.8	50.5	48.2	74.2	34.6	69.1	53.5	34.1	50.5	78.2	46.8
1977	60.6	58.1	78.1	58.5	74.6	68.4	56.1	52.7	77.0	41.0	73.7	58.3	42.4	56.3	79.2	54.2
1978	65.2	63.3	81.4	63.1	77.3	71.4	61.8	57.5	79.0	46.0	76.9	63.1	50.8	61.9	80.1	58.7
1979	72.6	69.1	84.4	68.8	80.2	74.6	67.7	63.6	82.3	52.8	80.3	66.1	58.8	66.4	83.0	66.6
1980	82.4	76.1	90.9	75.8	85.3	79.6	76.1	72.3	86.7	64.0	86.1	73.3	67.9	75.5	86.3	78.5
1981	90.9	85.6	95.4	83.2	91.1	85.6	85.0	82.0	92.2	75.4	91.9	83.3	77.8	84.6	91.9	87.9
1982	96.5	94.9	98.0	92.4	96.0	93.1	93.6	91.7	97.1	87.8	97.2	92.7	89.0	91.8	97.1	95.4
1983	99.6	100.4	99.8	101.8	99.2	100.3	100.0	100.5	100.3	100.7	99.8	100.5	99.9	100.1	100.0	99.8
1984	103.9	104.7	102.1	105.8	104.8	106.6	106.4	107.9	102.7	111.5	103.0	106.8	111.1	108.1	102.9	104.8
1985	107.6	108.9	104.2	112.9	108.2	111.8	111.4	114.2	104.8	121.8	105.3	112.9	120.9	116.1	106.4	111.1
1986	109.6	113.4	104.8	123.2	110.0	113.3	115.4	117.2	104.7	129.0	105.7	121.0	131.5	121.0	107.2	114.9
1987	113.6	118.4	104.9	133.6	111.6	115.0	120.0	120.9	104.9	135.1	105.5	131.6	138.5	126.0	108.8	119.7
1988	118.3	123.2	105.7	143.3	113.8	116.4	125.5	124.2	106.3	141.9	106.5	140.4	145.1	133.4	110.8	125.6
1989	124.0	129.3	108.1	154.1	116.6	120.0	131.5	128.6	109.2	150.8	107.7	146.8	155.0	142.0	114.3	135.4
1990	130.7	135.5	111.4	165.3	120.5	124.1	135.0	132.8	112.1	160.5	110.2	152.8	165.4	156.8	120.5	148.2
1991	136.2	143.1	115.1	170.7	124.5	128.3	138.2	137.2	116.0	170.6	113.6	158.0	175.2	171.5	127.5	156.9
1992	140.3	145.3	117.0	172.4	129.5	131.4	141.1	140.5	120.6	179.4	117.2	161.7	185.6	175.4	132.7	162.7
1993	144.5	147.9	118.6	175.5	134.1	135.0	142.9	143.3	125.7	187.3	120.3	165.4	194.1	183.5	137.0	165.3
1994	148.2	148.2	119.4	178.8	138.2	138.2	145.8	145.7	129.1	194.8	123.6	167.7	203.3	187.6	138.1	169.4
1995	152.4	151.4	119.3	187.1	141.2	140.2	148.9	148.3	131.3	204.9	126.0	171.8	212.9	192.3	140.6	175.1

1. All households index, except as noted.
2. Worker households index.
3. Former West Germany.

Index

Bernan Associates
Specialists in Government Information

A unique, one-stop source for U.S. Government and international agency publications

For over 40 years, Bernan Associates has been providing centralized access to a wide variety of government and intergovernmental titles from some of the largest, most prolific publishers in the world. Our vision is to be recognized as the premier source for worldwide and intergovernmental publications by supplying you with valuable product expertise and effective distribution services. We offer:

- Free Access to the Government Publications Network at www.bernan.com
- Knowledgeable Customer Relations Representatives
- Experienced Publications/Acquisitions Specialists
- Comprehensive Standing Order Services
- Trouble-free Payment Plans
- Immediate Access to the U.S. Government Publications Reference File
- Toll-free Phone and Fax Lines
- Free Catalogs and Brochures
- Complimentary Subscription to *Bernan Government Publications News*
- Timely Delivery
- Subscription Services

Visit our website at **www.bernan.com**

We distribute titles from the following publishers:

U.S. Government Publishers
- Executive Branch
- Judicial Branch
- Legislative Branch
- District of Columbia
- Smithsonian Institution Press
- Independent U.S. Government Agencies
- Boards, Committees, Commissions, Councils

U.K. Government Publisher
- The Stationery Office (formerly HMSO)

Private Publishers
- **Bernan Press** (U.S.A.)
- Editions Delta (Belgium)
- EUROPA Publications (U.K.)
- Library Association Publishing (U.K.)

Intergovernmental Publishers
- Asian Productivity Organization (APO)
- The Nordic Council of Ministers
- Office for Official Publications of the European Communities (EC)
- Organization for Economic Cooperation and Development (OECD)

United Nations & U.N. Specialized Agencies
- United Nations (UN)
- Food and Agriculture Organization (FAO)
- International Atomic Energy Agency (IAEA)
- International Labour Organisation (ILO)
- International Monetary Fund (IMF)
- United Nations Educational, Scientific, and Cultural Organization (UNESCO)
- UNESCO Bangkok
- World Bank
- World Tourism Organization (WTO)
- World Trade Organization (WTO), formerly the General Agreement on Tarrifs and Trade (GATT)

BERNAN
Associates

Available FREE
from Bernan Associates

Bernan Associates Standing Order Catalog

Our new Standing Order Catalog now features titles from the U.S. Government and international agencies. This 64-page catalog contains a comprehensive listing of our most popular Standing Order titles. Over 2,000 reference and research publications are included from some of the world's largest publishers, such as the U.S. Government Printing Office, the United Nations, UNESCO (the United Nations Educational, Scientific, and Cultural Organization), the World Bank, and the World Trade Organization — to name a few.

Standing Orders are recurring titles in a series. By placing a title on Standing Order, you are guaranteed prompt, automatic delivery of each new edition in a series as it is published. Here are just some of the services you can take advantage of when you place a title on Standing Order:

- Flexible Standing Order Policy – Simply give us notification, and you can increase or decrease Standing Order quantities to fit your needs.

- Standing Order Account Update – You can request a complete report of all titles you have on Standing Order at any time.

- Duplicate Standing Order Verification – If there is any indication that you have requested a duplicate Standing Order, we will notify you immediately.

The Internet Connection

Your Guide to Government Resources

The only newsletter exclusively devoted to finding free or low-cost information available from the U.S. Government on the Internet. **Free sample issue.**

For a complimentary copy of the *Standing Order Catalog* and/or a free sample of *The Internet Connection*, call Customer Relations at (800) 274-4447 or mail/fax the order form on the back page of this book.

Coming Soon from Bernan Press

1997 County and City Extra:
Annual Metro, City, and County Data Book
George Hall and Deirdre Gaquin, Editors

1997 County and City Extra
Annual Metro, City and County Data Book

Recognized as the definitive source for up-to-date demographic and economic information by geographic area, the *County and City Extra* contains the very latest statistics available for every state, county, metropolitan area, and congressional district, as well as every city with a population of 25,000 or more. Filled with detailed tables on: population characteristics, employment, education, income, crime, agriculture, manufacturing, trade, services, federal spending, and local government finance. Ranking tables and colored maps provide ready comparisons across jurisdictions.

"...essential purchase for any library requiring the most current statistics about states, counties, cities, and metropolitan areas."

— Library Journal

May 1997, Cloth, 1,300pp, ISBN 0-89059-071-0, $98.00 (Pre-pub price–order before May 15, 1997), $109.00 (Regular price) Standing Order No. 077.00992

Handbook of North American Industry, First Edition
Jack Cremeans, Editor

At last! A sourcebook full of detailed data on the emerging NAFTA market. Information on the Canadian and Mexican economies—with industry level detail—side by side with comparable U.S. data. Fact-filled articles on the NAFTA agreement, analysis of its effect on U.S. business, and rankings of various industries in all three NAFTA countries. Full of useful statistics on output, employment, number of establishments, and other details on Canadian and Mexican industries alongside and compared with data for the United States. **A must for everyone selling to, buying from, or interested in the very large new market created by the North American Free Trade Agreement.**

Summer 1997, Not yet priced

The Bernan Press U.S. DataBook Series™

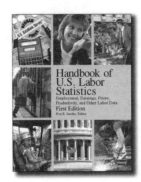
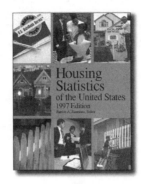

*Winner of the Choice Magazine Outstanding Academic Books Award

The **Bernan Press U.S. DataBook Series**™ is designed to provide essential, yet hard-to-find government statistics in a printed format. Our team of well-known editors has held high-ranking positions in the Department of Commerce, the Bureau of the Census, the Bureau of Labor Statistics, and other federal and national organizations.

Business Statistics of the United States: 1996 Edition *
Courtenay M. Slater, Editor

Based on the popular Business Statistics, (formerly published by the Bureau of Economic Analysis), this essential reference work presents annual and time series data on business trends through 1995. You'll find current information on: construction and housing; mining, oil, and gas; manufacturing; transportation, communications, and utilities; retail and wholesale trade; services; and government.

It also features a full statistical picture of the overall U.S. economy, including data on: gross domestic product; consumer income and spending; industrial production; money and financial markets; and more. Contains numerous charts and tables illustrating economic trends.

January 1997, Pbk, approx. 424pp, ISBN 0-89059-063-X, $59.00, Standing Order No. 077.05375

Handbook of U.S. Labor Statistics: Employment, Earnings, Prices, Productivity, and Other Labor Data: First Edition
Eva E. Jacobs, Editor

Based on the Handbook of Labor Statistics, (formerly published by the Bureau of Labor Statistics), this comprehensive research tool presents historical data on labor market trends through 1995. Topics include: population, labor force, and employment status; consumer prices; producer prices; export and import prices; consumer expenditures; and productivity.

A special feature in this edition is the recently released Bureau of Labor Statistics projections of employment by industry and occupation for 1994-2005.

March 1997, Pbk, approx. 450pp, ISBN 0-89059-062-1, $59.00, Standing Order No. 077.43472

Housing Statistics of the United States: 1997 Edition
Patrick A. Simmons, Editor

This completely new reference work is the first ever comprehensive source for current and historical information on households, housing, and housing finance. Data includes: household characteristics; prices, rents, and affordability; housing production and investment; home mortgage lending; housing stock characteristics; and federal housing programs. An ideal source for data that can be used for producing or benchmarking market reports, trend analysis, and research.

Forthcoming Summer 1997, Pbk, approx. 300pp, ISBN 0-89059-065-6, $59.00, Standing Order No. 077.43481
***

***Advanced Information

To order, contact Customer Relations at (800) 274-4447 or mail/fax the order form on the back page of this book.

Bernan Associates Order Form

4611-F Assembly Drive ■ Lanham, MD 20706 USA

If using a purchase order, please attach this form

Quantity	ISBN	Title	Begin Standing Order?		Price
	—	Standing Order Catalog	—		Free
	—	Internet Connection Newsletter (Sample)	—		Free
	0-89059-071-0	1997 County and City Extra (Pre-pub price)	Yes ☐	No ☐	$98.00
	0-89059-071-0	1997 County and City Extra (Regular price)	Yes ☐	No ☐	$109.00
	0-89059-063-X	Business Statistics of the U.S., '96 Edition	Yes ☐	No ☐	$59.00
	0-89059-062-1	Handbook of U.S. Labor Statistics, First Edition	Yes ☐	No ☐	$59.00
	0-89059-065-6	Housing Statistics of the U.S., '97 Edition	Yes ☐	No ☐	$59.00

Subtotal	
Postage & Handling*	
Tax**	
Total	

*Add Postage and Handling as follows:
U.S. 5%, minimum $4.00
Canada and Mexico 8%, minimum $5.00
Outside North America 20%, minimum $12.00
**MD and NY add applicable sales tax;
    Canada add GST

Rush Service
A Rush Service fee of $15.00 will be applied toward all rush orders.

Prices are subject to change

Terms: Net 30 days

Return Policy
All orders are on a firm-order basis. Returns are allowed ONLY if publications received are damaged/defective or titles are incorrect.

Methods of Payment

Deposit Account
Requires a minimum initial deposit of $100.00 and an ongoing balance of $50.00. Upon receipt of the check or money order, an account will be established and a special account number will be assigned. The cost of ordered publications will be deducted from the funds on deposit.

Invoice Statement Account
Send in the order on an authorized purchase order, an invoice will be included with the shipment of publications. An account number will be assigned after the first purchase. All future orders can be charged against this account number with an authorized purchase order.

Prepayment
Prepay all orders with a check or money order in U.S. dollars, drawn from a U.S. bank, payable to Bernan Associates.

MAKE RE-ORDERING EASY WITH STANDING ORDERS!

Place your publications on *Standing Order* and you are guaranteed automatic delivery of each new edition as it is published!

☐ Check here to put the Bernan Press U.S. DataBook Series™ on *Group Standing Order.*

You'll automatically receive all forthcoming titles in the U.S. DataBook Series as they are published.

077.00.111

☐ Check or Money Order enclosed
☐ Bill Me P.O.#_____ Date_____
☐ MC   ☐ Visa   Exp. Date _____
Card # _____
Signature _____

YES!
I'd like to open a Deposit Account.
Enclosed is a check for _____
                                   (minimum $100)
Account # _____
Tax Exempt # _____

Bill To

Name _____

Organization _____

Address _____

_____

Phone _____ Fax _____

Ship To

Name _____

Organization _____

Address _____

_____

Phone _____ Fax _____